Upgrading and Repairing PCs

Scott Mueller

 que® Corporation
Carmel, Indiana

Upgrading and Repairing PCs

Copyright © 1988 by Que® Corporation

Library of Congress Catalog No.: 88-62746
ISBN 0-88022-395-2

94 93 92 91   12 11 10

Interpretation of the printing code: the rightmost number in the first series of numbers is the year of the book's printing; the rightmost number in the second series of numbers is the number of the book's printing. For example, a printing code of 88-10 shows that the tenth printing of the book occurred in 1988.

Dedication

To my wife, Lynn, and daughter, Amanda, who have made this book possible by being my support team. I could not ask for better partners!

Publishing Manager

Scott N. Flanders

Product Director

Karen A. Bluestein

Senior Editor

Lloyd J. Short

Editors

Jo Anna Arnott   Jeannine Freudenberger
Sandra Blackthorn   Gregory Robertson
Kelly Currie   Richard Turner
Kelly D. Dobbs   Steven Wiggins

Technical Editor

Timothy S. Stanley

Indexed by

reVisions Plus

Book Design and Production

Dan Armstrong   Joe Ramon
Brad Chinn   Dennis Sheehan
Cheryl English   M. Louise Shinault
Lori A. Lyons   Carolyn A. Spitler
Jennifer Matthews   Peter Tocco
Cindy Phipps

Composed in Glypha and Excellent 47
by Que Corporation

Screen reproductions in this book were created by means of
the InSet program from INSET Systems Inc., Danbury, CT.

About the Author

Scott Mueller

Scott Mueller is president of Mueller Business Systems, an international personal computer consulting and training firm specializing in the design, selection, application, management, upgrade, repair, and troubleshooting of microcomputer hardware, software, and local area network systems. His experience includes work with a variety of clients ranging from small businesses to Fortune 500 corporations and the United States government. Mr. Mueller has experience with many facets of PC operations and management. He has designed and installed local area networks, created and marketed several different PC upgrade options, managed PC service and repair, and programmed in several different languages. Since 1982, Mr. Mueller has been developing and presenting seminars and training courses with the American Institute, an internationally recognized seminar company. Mr. Mueller also has written many course workbooks, and he coauthored the *IBM PS/2 Handbook*, published by Que Corporation.

Contents at a Glance

Table of Contents

I ▼ The Background and Features of Personal Computers

II ▼ IBM PC, PS/2, and Compatible Systems

III Hardware Considerations

V Troubleshooting Guides

Introduction

Welcome to *Upgrading and Repairing PCs*! This book is geared for those of you who want to upgrade, repair, maintain, and troubleshoot your own or your companies' computers. This book is designed to cover the range of hardware that is compatible with IBM's Personal Computer and Personal System/2 series of systems. Actual IBM systems are covered as well as all available IBM compatibles or clones.

What Are the Main Objectives of This Book?

Upgrading and Repairing PCs focuses on several objectives. One is to help you understand the family of computers that stems from the original IBM PC. This book examines each system in depth, outlining the differences among the models and presenting the options available for configuring each system at purchase time. And many sections give you detailed information about each of the internal components that make up a personal computer system.

Another objective is to help you understand the newer PS/2 systems from IBM. From an upgrade and repair point of view, you will examine how these systems differ from the earlier systems.

Upgrading and Repairing PCs also will help you gain an understanding of the peripheral and add-on market surrounding this incredibly popular family of systems. The IBM-based microcomputer family is rapidly moving forward in terms of power and capabilities.

1

Available storage is increasing rapidly in terms of directly addressable memory and peripheral storage such as hard disks. This book examines the options available in modern high-performance PC configurations and how to use them to your proper advantage. This book focuses on much of the hardware and software available today and relates what are the optimum configurations for achieving the maximum benefit for the time and money spent. And this book focuses on all areas of system improvement such as floppy disk, hard disk, central processor unit, math coprocessor, and power supply improvement.

The main objective of *Upgrading and Repairing PCs* is to help you learn how to maintain, upgrade, and repair your PC system. You will find discussions on proper system and component care. This book examines and indicates the most failure-prone items in the various PC systems and how to locate and identify a particular failing component. Also examined is powerful diagnostics software that enables the system to help you determine the fault and the proper procedures for repair. When you finish reading this book, you will have the required knowledge to perform repairs at circuit board and component levels.

What Is in This Book?

Upgrading and Repairing PCs is designed for individuals who really want a good understanding of how their PC systems work. Each section gives full explanations and reasons for each problem or situation that you may encounter so you will be better able to handle tough problems. You will gain a real understanding of disk configuration and interfacing, for example, that will greatly improve your diagnostics and troubleshooting skills. You will develop a real "feel" for what goes on in the system so that you can rely on your own judgment and observations and not some table of canned troubleshooting "steps." This book is really geared for people who truly are interested in these systems and just how they operate.

Upgrading and Repairing PCs is for those of you who will select, install, configure, maintain, and repair the systems that you or your companies will use. To accomplish these tasks, you will need a level of knowledge much higher than the average system user. You must know exactly which tool to use for the task at hand and how to use that tool correctly. This book can help you achieve this level of knowledge.

You receive in Chapter 1 a basic introduction to the development of the IBM PC and compatibles. Chapter 2 gives detailed information about the different types of systems you will encounter and what separates one type of system from another. Chapter 2 also explains the memory architecture of the various system types, which helps you build a foundation of knowledge essential for the remainder of the book.

Chapters 3 and 4 cover each of the IBM PC and PS/2 models, and these chapters list differences among the individual versions of each system. The technical specifications of each system also are highlighted here. This information will be especially useful for those of you who are compatible system owners so that you can determine easily where your systems differ from the IBM standard.

Chapter 5 covers compatible systems. This chapter gives detailed information on differences between compatible systems and standard IBM systems, and it also lists some important features of various compatible systems. This chapter is especially useful for those of you who are making purchasing decisions. You can use Chapter 5 as a general guideline for what features make a particular compatible good or bad.

Chapter 6 examines the proper teardown, disassembly, and inspection procedures for a system, and Chapter 7 covers each of the components that make up a typical system, from the power supply to the microprocessor.

Chapters 8 and 9 examine floppy disk drives and hard disk drives in great detail. This information will be invaluable for those of you who install drives in systems either as replacements or for upgrading a system, as well as for those of you who need to troubleshoot and repair malfunctioning drives.

Chapter 10 covers standard peripherals, such as video boards and monitors, and communications boards, such as serial and parallel ports.

Chapter 11 focuses on preventive maintenance and backup procedures. This chapter emphasizes proper system care and cleaning and examines how to maintain a system so that a minimum number of problems will occur. Backup of data also is discussed.

Chapter 12 lists specific system upgrades and examines how these upgrades may be accomplished. Adding different floppy drives (such as 3 1/2-inch drives) to any system and adding more or larger hard disk drives are covered. Other topics include speeding up a system, adding memory, and converting from one type of system to another—from an XT to an AT, for example.

Chapter 13 focuses on system diagnostics and covers the required tools you need to perform such diagnostics. The manufacturer-provided diagnostics as well as various aftermarket diagnostics utilities are discussed.

Chapters 14 and 15 cover hardware and software troubleshooting. These chapters explain the most common problems and the procedures you use to successfully discover the source of the problem.

Chapter 16 is the conclusion of the book, and an Appendix follows. In the Appendix, you will find many tables and data that will be a valuable reference. Many of you will refer to this section of the book over and over again when you're troubleshooting various system problems. Most of this information has never before appeared in one place!

I think you will find that *Upgrading and Repairing PCs* is the first book of its kind on today's market. This book covers the extreme breadth of IBM and compatible equipment but also offers a great deal of in-depth coverage of each topic. This book will be valuable as a reference tool, for understanding just how the various components of a system interact and operate, and it will be valuable as a guide to the repair and service problems you may encounter. *Upgrading and Repairing PCs* is far more than just a "repair" manual. I sincerely hope you enjoy it!

Part I

The Background and Features of Personal Computers

Includes

Personal Computer Background

System Features

Personal Computer Background

The evolutionary process leading to today's microcomputers has been extremely rapid. Although many discoveries and inventions have contributed to the machine known as the "personal computer," examining a few important landmarks can help to bring the whole picture into perspective.

The History of Personal Computing

One of the most important developments leading to the personal computer revolution was the invention of the semiconductor, or transistor, in 1948. This feat was accomplished by John Bardeen, Walter Brattain, and William Shockley, who were engineers working at Bell Laboratories. The transistor, nothing more than a solid-state electronic switch, replaced the much larger vacuum tube and consumed significantly less power in performing the tube's job. Thus, a computer system built with transistors was much smaller and more efficient.

The tube also could act as a switch but was inefficient in this role. A tube consumed a great deal of electrical power and gave off enormous heat, which was a significant problem in the earlier systems. Also, tubes were notoriously unreliable; one failed every two hours or so in the larger systems.

The switch to transistors began the trend toward miniaturization that has enabled today's small laptop PC systems, which run on batteries, to have more computing power than many earlier systems that filled rooms and consumed huge amounts of electrical power.

In 1959, engineers at Texas Instruments figured out how to put more than one transistor on the same base or substrate material and connect the transistors without wires. Thus, the integrated circuit, or IC, was born. The first IC contained only six transistors, but the Intel 80386 in many of today's systems has 280,000. Today, ICs can be built with millions of transistors on-board.

In 1969, a company called Intel made waves in the industry by introducing a 1 K-bit memory chip, which was much larger than anything else available at the time. Because of Intel's success in chip manufacturing and design, the company was approached by a Japanese calculator manufacturer called Busicomp and was asked to produce 12 chips for one of Busicomp's calculator designs. Engineers at Intel took the 12-chip design and incorporated all the desired functions and capabilities into a single "generic" multipurpose chip. This chip was different from previous designs, which were hard wired for a single purpose with "built in" instructions. The new chip read a variable set of instructions from memory, which Intel already had been producing. The concept was to design what was almost an entire computing device on a single chip. This first microprocessor was the Intel 4004, a 4-bit microprocessor, introduced in 1971. The successor to the 4004 chip was the 8008 8-bit microprocessor in 1972.

In 1973, some of the first microcomputer kits based on the 8008 chip were developed. These kits were little more than demonstration tools and could not do much except blink lights. In late 1973, Intel introduced the 8080 microprocessor, which was 10 times faster than the earlier 8008 chip and also could address a whopping 64K of memory. This breakthrough was the one the personal computer was waiting for.

With a cover story in the January 1975 issue of *Popular Electronics* magazine, a company called MITS introduced the Altair kit, which is generally considered to be the first personal computer. This kit included an 8080 processor, a power supply, a front panel with a great deal of lights, and an enormous 256 bytes (not kilobytes) of memory. The kit sold for $395 and had to be assembled. This computer included an open architecture (slots) that prompted all sorts of add-ons and peripherals from aftermarket companies. The new processor inspired other companies to write programs, including the CP/M (Control Program for Microprocessors) operating system and the first version of Microsoft BASIC.

Now things really started moving. IBM introduced its first "personal computer" in 1975. The Model 5100 had 16K of memory, a built-in BASIC language interpreter, and a built-in cartridge tape drive for storage. And the cost? Only $9,000! This price placed this system clearly out of the mainstream "personal" computer marketplace, which was dominated by experimenters (hackers) who built low-cost kits ($500 or so) as a hobby. This IBM system, needless to say, was not in competition for this market and did not sell very well. The Model 5100 was succeeded by the 5110 and 5120 before IBM introduced the IBM Personal Computer (which was called the Model 5150).

In 1976, a new company called Apple Computer introduced the Apple I for $695. This system consisted of a main circuit board screwed onto a piece of plywood. A case and power supply were not included; the buyer had to supply them. Only a handful of these computers were made, and today these collectors' items have sold for more than $20,000! The Apple I was followed in 1977 by the Apple II. The Apple II, because of its enormous success, helped to set the standards for nearly all the important microcomputers to follow, including the IBM PC.

All this activity set the stage for the introduction of the IBM Personal Computer. In 1980, the microcomputer world was dominated by two main factions of computers. One faction was the Apple II, which claimed a large following of loyal users and a gigantic software base that was growing at a fantastic rate. Also available were all the systems that had evolved from the original MITS Altair. These systems were compatible with each other and were distinguished by their use of the CP/M operating system and expansion slots that followed the S-100 (for slot with 100 pins) standard. Although built by a variety of companies and selling under various names, these systems all were able (for the most part) to use the same software and plug-in hardware.

The IBM Personal Computer

At the end of 1980, a small group called the Entry Systems Division was established at IBM. The original staff consisted of 12 engineers and designers under the direction of Don Estridge. The team's chief designer was Lewis Eggebrecht. This division was given the task of developing IBM's first real PC. (IBM considered the 5100 system developed in 1975 to be an intelligent programmable terminal rather than a genuine computer, even though it truly was a computer.)

Estridge and the design team rapidly developed the design and specifications of the new system. The team studied the marketplace, which had enormous influence in the IBM PC's design. The designers looked at the prevailing standards, learned from the success of those systems, and incorporated all the features of the popular systems—and more—into the new PC. IBM was able to produce a system that filled its niche in the market perfectly.

With the parameters for design made obvious by the market, IBM was able to bring its system from idea to delivery in one year. The company accomplished this feat by purchasing as many components as possible from outside vendors. IBM, for example, contracted out the PC's languages and operating system to a small company called Microsoft. (IBM originally contacted a company called Digital Research, which invented CP/M, but apparently Digital Research wasn't interested in the proposed deal. Microsoft was interested, and the company has become one of the largest software companies in the world.) In addition to aiding in the speedy delivery of the finished product, the use of outside vendors was an open invitation for the aftermarket to jump in and support the system. And that it did.

The debut of the IBM PC, using PC DOS, occurred on Tuesday, August 11, 1981. On that date, a new standard took its place in the microcomputer industry. Since that time, IBM has sold more than 10 million PCs, and the PC has grown into a complete family of computers and peripherals. More software is written for this family than for any other system on the market.

Chapter Summary

This chapter traced the evolution of personal computing from the development of the transistor to Intel's first memory chip. Intel's continuing development of ICs led to a succession of microprocessors, reaching a milestone in the 1973 introduction of the 8080 chip. In 1975 MITS introduced the Altair computer kit, based on the 8080 microprocessor, and the computer industry was off and running. IBM jumped into the "personal computer" market with the Model 5100 in 1975.

In 1976 Apple sold its first computers, followed in 1977 by the enormously successful Apple II. Because of its success, the Apple II played a major role in the setting of standards for all microcomputers to follow.

Finally, in 1980, IBM introduced its Personal Computer into a microcomputer world dominated by the Apple II and the somewhat Apple-compatible computers that had evolved from the Altair, both of which used the CP/M operating system. The IBM PC, designed with the needs of the market in mind and with many of its components produced by outside vendors, immediately set the new standard for the microcomputer industry.

Chapter 2 covers the technical fundamentals of IBM personal computers and their compatibles, differences between PC and AT systems, the structure and usage of memory, and how to obtain and use maintenance manuals.

2

System Features

This chapter covers the differences in system architecture of IBM and compatible systems, as well as the structure and usage of memory. This chapter also discusses how to obtain the necessary service manuals.

Types of Systems

Many types of IBM and compatible systems are on the market today, and most of these systems are similar to one another. A few important differences among the various systems should be discussed, however. These differences in system architecture are going to become more and more apparent during the next few years as the new OS/2 operating system and applications software become popular.

From a hardware and software point of view, all IBM and compatible systems can be broken down into two basic system types, with a few subcategories:

1. PC and XT types of systems

    - Industry Standard Architecture (ISA) bus

        8086 CPU (8-bit ISA)
        8088 CPU (8-bit ISA)

2. AT types of systems

- Industry Standard Architecture (ISA) bus

  80286 CPU
  80386 CPU

- PS/2 Micro Channel Architecture (MCA) bus

  80286 CPU (16-bit MCA)
  80386 CPU (32-bit MCA)

- Enhanced Industry Standard Architecture (EISA) bus

  80386 CPU

AT systems can be broken down into subcategories: those with either the standard ISA slots or the newer Micro Channel Architecture slots. Also, some AT types of systems have either 80286 or 80386 processors; the '386 systems have a few distinct capabilities with memory addressing and the possibility for 32-bit-wide access to data. The Micro Channel Architecture systems with 80386 chips have special 32-bit slots for taking advantage of the '386 capabilities.

Recently, a consortium of compatibles manufacturers have introduced a new slot system called the Enhanced Industry Standard Architecture (EISA). This system is a new type of 32-bit slot for use with '386-based systems. These manufacturers seemingly developed EISA because IBM charges excessive royalties for any competitors using the MCA slot design in IBM's systems. Because of the royalties IBM charges, the competitors developed EISA, which they can use with no royalties to IBM. Whether EISA actually becomes another standard remains to be seen because systems using this type of slot are not due until late 1989. By that time, between three and four million MCA systems will have been sold.

Table 2.1 summarizes the primary differences between a standard PC (or XT) type of system and an AT type of system. This information includes all IBM and compatible models and identifies these systems from one another.

Table 2.1
Differences between PCs (or XTs) and ATs

System Attributes	PC or XT Type	AT Type
Supported processors:	8086 or 8088	-
	V-30 or V-20 (1)	-
	80186 or 80188	-
	80286 (2)	80286
	80386 (2) or	80386 or
	80386SX (2)	80386SX
Processor modes:	Real	Real, Protected, Virtual real (3)
Expansion slot width:	8-bit ISA	16-bit ISA, MCA, or 32-bit MCA (4)
Total interrupts:	8 + NMI	16 + NMI
Total DMA channels:	4	8
Maximum RAM:	1 megabyte	16 or 4,096 megabytes (5)
Real time clock:	No	Yes
Basic configuration:	Switches/jumpers	CMOS memory
Motherboard ROM space:	F0000-FFFFF	0E0000-0FFFFF and FE0000-FFFFFF
Floppy controller:	Double density	High/double density
Boot drive:	360K or 720K	1.2M or 1.44M
Hard disk BIOS:	Controller ROM	Motherboard ROM
Hard disk tables:	Controller ROM	Motherboard ROM
Serial port UART:	8250B	16450

Supplement to Table 2.1

The following information will help you understand the material presented in table 2.1:

ISA = Industry Standard Architecture
MCA = Micro Channel Architecture
NMI = Non-Maskable Interrupt
DMA = Direct Memory Access
RAM = Random-Access Memory
ROM = Read-Only Memory
CMOS = Complementary Metal Oxide Semiconductor
BIOS = Basic Input/Output System
UART = Universal Asynchronous Receiver Transmitter

Notes:

(1) The V-30 and V-20 are NEC replacement chips for the Intel 8086 and 8088, respectively.

(2) These processors normally are on expansion cards called accelerator boards. They simply provide additional speed for the PC XT and do not give the capability to run enhanced software, such as OS/2 and Windows 386. (The exceptions are the Intel Inboard and Microsoft Mach 20 accelerator boards.)

(3) *Virtual real* mode is supported only on '386-based systems.

(4) 32-bit slots are supported on '386-based systems only.

(5) 4,096 megabytes of maximum RAM are supported on certain '386 systems only.

Table 2.1 highlights the primary differences between the PC and AT architecture. Using the information in this table, you can properly categorize virtually any system as either a PC type or an AT type. For example, a COMPAQ Deskpro is a PC type of system, and the Deskpro 286 and Deskpro 386 are AT types of systems. IBM's own XT Model 286 is actually an AT type of system. The AT&T 6300 qualifies as a PC type of system, and the 6310 is an AT type of system.

You usually can tell PC and XT types of systems by their Intel design 8088 or 8086 processors; this criterion, however, is really not the best to use because many possibilities are available. Some systems have the NEC V-20 or V-30 processors instead, but these processors are functionally identical to the Intel chips. A few PC or XT systems actually have an 80286 or 80386 processor for increased performance. These systems usually have one or more 8-bit slots of the same system bus design featured in the original IBM PC. The design of the system includes only half the total DMA and interrupts that are in an AT design, which limits severely the use of expansion slots by various adapter boards that require the use of these resources. A system of this type is capable of running most software that runs under MS-DOS but is limited from more advanced operating systems such as OS/2. A system of this type will not run OS/2 or any software designed to run under OS/2. These systems cannot have more than 1 megabyte of processor-addressable memory, of which only 640K is generally available for user programs and data.

You usually can tell AT systems by their use of the Intel 80286 or 80386 processors. Some AT systems differ in the types of slots included on the main system board. The earlier standard called for 8- and 16-bit slots that were compatible with the original IBM PC and AT. The newer standard is IBM's Micro Channel Architecture (MCA), and it consists of 16- and 32-bit slots, with the 32-bit slots present only on 80386-based systems.

Some manufacturers have integrated proprietary 32-bit slots in their non-Micro Channel AT systems, but no expansion boards are usually available to take advantage of these special 32-bit slots except memory boards produced by the system manufacturer. Because of these nonstandard implementations, several manufacturers have banded together and announced a standard 32-bit AT type of slot to compete with the Micro Channel Architecture from IBM. As mentioned earlier, this Enhanced Industry Standard Architecture (EISA) will be available in systems sometime in late 1989. The basic AT system design provides twice the number of interrupts and DMA channels for adapter boards to use, which allows for greater system expansion with fewer conflicts among adapters.

Another difference between PC and AT types of systems is the use of a real time clock; the AT architecture uses one, and the PC types of systems don't. A *real time clock* is the built-in clock implemented by a special CMOS memory chip on the motherboard that is found in any AT system. You can have a clock added on some expansion adapters of a PC system, but DOS will not recognize the clock unless some special program is run first. This CMOS memory in the AT system also stores the system's basic configuration. On any PC or

XT type of system, these basic configuration options, such as the amount of installed memory, number and types of floppy drives and hard disks, and type of video adapter, are all set through the use of switches and jumpers on the motherboard and various adapters.

PC systems decode 64K of memory for the motherboard ROM, using the last segment in the 1 megabyte of total space. The actual addresses for this memory are F0000-FFFFF in hexadecimal. An AT system decodes 128K at the end of the first megabyte as well as at the end of the last (16th) megabyte of memory. The addresses used are 0E0000-0FFFFF and FE0000-FFFFFF in hexadecimal. In the AT, each set of 128K bytes of ROM space is actually the same code—double mapped—which means that really only 128K total are available as far as the amount of actual memory, but the system has it positioned simultaneously in two different places so that the total actual memory consumed is 256K. This double mapping is required in the AT systems because of the microprocessor design.

PC systems usually have double-density floppy controllers, but AT systems must have a controller capable of both high- and double-density operation. Thus, the boot drive on any PC system must be either the double-density 5 1/4-inch 360K or 3 1/2-inch 720K drives, but the AT needs either the 5 1/4-inch 1.2M or 3 1/2-inch 1.44M drives for proper operation.

The PC types of systems use a hard disk controller with an on-board hard disk ROM BIOS. This controller ROM either will contain a set of built-in tables for supported drives or will have an "autoconfigure" option that can dynamically configure a drive by building a table entry on the spot and storing it on the drive directly. AT types of systems will have the controller BIOS embedded in the motherboard ROM, and the supported drive table also will reside in this motherboard ROM. This motherboard-resident hard disk BIOS will be designed for a particular type of controller, and any other controllers that are used must "look like" the one expected by the motherboard code.

Finally, the serial port control chip or UART is a National Semiconductor 8250B for the PC types of systems, but AT systems use the newer NS 16450.

Some of these differences, such as the expansion slots, the systems interrupts, and the DMA channel availability, are absolute. The processors are less absolute. The AT systems, however, must use the 80286 or higher, and the PC systems can use the entire Intel family of chips from the 8086 to the 80386 and even the NEC V-20 and V-30. Other parameters are less absolute, and your own system may not follow the true standard properly, especially if your system is a no-name compatible. If your system does not follow all the criteria listed for it—especially if it is an AT type of system—you can expect compatibility and operational problems in the future.

Some people may have the misconception that they always can boot from lower density floppy drives in an AT system by simply having a 360K or 720K drive in the drive A position. True, you can boot DOS that way, but an AT also can run OS/2, which is supplied only on high-density disks due to the size of the system files. Therefore, a high-density drive must be in the drive A position. Some people also may believe that the type of serial port or hard disk controller they have does not make much difference. True, under DOS you can get away with using a serial port or hard disk controller for an XT (or with an on-board BIOS), but you also cannot run any of the protected-mode operating systems, such as OS/2 or Novell Advanced Netware, on your "AT-compatible" system.

The bottom line is this: All the items listed in table 2.1 are meaningful and required for a system to follow the industry-standard definition of what an AT or PC system is.

The System Memory Map

The memory map is one of the most important areas of the system that you should understand well. This type of map shows all the memory that is possible for the system to address and how the memory is used in a particular type of system.

A PC- or XT-compatible system has 1 megabyte of processor-addressable memory workspace. This workspace is sometimes called RAM (random-access memory). The 1M of RAM is divided into several sections; some of these sections have special uses. A portion of RAM space, called *user memory*, is where conventional programs and data can reside. This space is conventionally limited to the first 640K of the total RAM. The next 128K is reserved as *video RAM* for use by video adapters. This space is where text and graphics reside when displayed on-screen.

The following 128K is reserved for ROM (read-only memory) control programs and other special memory uses for all the adapter boards plugged into the system slots. ROM is a subset of RAM that stores programs that cannot be changed. The programs are stored on special chips that have fused circuits on the chip so that the PC cannot alter them. ROM is useful for permanent programs that always must be present while the system is running. Graphics boards, hard disk controllers, communications boards, and expanded memory boards all are examples of adapter boards that may use some of this memory.

Finally, the last 128K of memory is reserved for ROM on the motherboard. This space is where the Basic Input/Output System (BIOS) resides as well as the POST (power-on self test) and bootstrap loader. These programs are the master test and control programs for the system and also enable the system to load an operating system from floppy or hard disk.

Figure 2.1 represents all the memory in an XT system and shows how the memory may be allocated. Each symbol on a line is equal to 1 kilobyte of memory. Each line or segment is 64K, and the entire map is 1,024K or 1 megabyte.

In figure 2.1, these symbols are used:

    . = Program-Accessible Memory
    v = Video RAM
    a = Adapter Board ROM and RAM
    r = Motherboard ROM BIOS
    b = IBM Cassette BASIC

Fig. 2.1.

IBM 1 megabyte memory map.

```
       : 0---1---2---3---4---5---6---7---8---9---A---B---C---D---E---F---
00000: ................................................................
10000: ................................................................
20000: ................................................................
30000: ................................................................
40000: ................................................................
50000: ................................................................
60000: ................................................................
70000: ................................................................
80000: ................................................................
90000: ................................................................
A0000: vvvvvvvvvvvvvvvvvvvvvvvvvvvvvvvvvvvvvvvvvvvvvvvvvvvvvvvvvvvvvvvvvv
B0000: vvvvvvvvvvvvvvvvvvvvvvvvvvvvvvvvvvvvvvvvvvvvvvvvvvvvvvvvvvvvvvvvvv
C0000: aaaaaaaaaaaaaaaaaaaaaaaaaaaaaaaaaaaaaaaaaaaaaaaaaaaaaaaaaaaaaaaa
D0000: aaaaaaaaaaaaaaaaaaaaaaaaaaaaaaaaaaaaaaaaaaaaaaaaaaaaaaaaaaaaaaaa
E0000: rrrrrrrrrrrrrrrrrrrrrrrrrrrrrrrrrrrrrrrrrrrrrrrrrrrrrrrrrrrrrrrr
F0000: rrrrrrrrrrrrrrrrrrrrrrrrrrbbbbbbbbbbbbbbbbbbbbbbbbbbbbbbbrrrrrrrr
```

Note that addresses A0000 to F0000 are reserved for various purposes. At least 10 segments are not reserved, each with 64K, which gives a total of 640K of memory for DOS and programs. The rest of the reserved space may be used completely in some systems and used sparsely in other systems. Not all video adapters, for example, use all 128K of the space allocated to them. Those that use less may allow DOS to use the additional memory for programs and data.

In an AT system, the memory map extends beyond the 1M boundary and continues all the way to 16 megabytes. For this reason, the industry calls any memory beyond 1 megabyte *extended memory*. A small portion of the last megabyte is reserved for a shadow or duplicate of the AT ROM BIOS, so not all of the last megabyte may be used for programs and data. This additional ROM (128K) located at the end of the last megabyte of addressable memory causes the total reserved space in an AT to be 512K, which is up from the 384K reserved in an XT system.

For an AT to be able to "see" any of the memory beyond the standard 1 megabyte of address space, the 80286 or 80386 processor must be in the processor's protected mode of operation. *Protected mode* is the native mode of these advanced processors and allows for greater access to memory, a modified instruction set, and other operational differences.

Unfortunately, these operational differences prevent the system from being compatible with the original IBM PC systems. Intel, therefore, designed an "8086/8088 mode" within the 80286 and 80386 called *real mode*, which allows for full compatibility with the earlier processors. Unfortunately, this compatibility is necessarily complete, which means that any AT running in this mode is not really an AT at all; instead, the AT is more like a "turbo" PC!

The real problem is that although the 80286 can emulate the 8086 or 8088, the 80286 cannot provide its own native features at the same time, which is the reason that you cannot merely extend DOS to take advantage of the protected-mode features of an AT. An entirely new operating system written from the ground up to run in protected mode was needed. This operating system is now known as OS/2. OS/2 does have the capability to switch rapidly from real to protected modes and back again, which seems to give it the capability to run DOS software as well as new OS/2 specific programs. But even the DOS mode under OS/2 is still limited to running within the first megabyte of the 16 total possible on an AT.

Figures 2.2 and 2.3 show the total 16M map for an AT type of system in protected mode. Figure 2.2 shows where the real-mode addressable memory ends. Figure 2.3 shows where extended memory picks up. An 80286 or 80386 system running in protected mode is required to address memory beyond the 1M boundary. In the figures, the following symbols are used:

    . = Program-Accessible Memory
    v = Video RAM
    a = Adapter Board ROM
    r = Motherboard ROM BIOS
    b = IBM Cassette BASIC

Fig. 2.2.

IBM 16 megabyte memory map to the point where real-mode addressable memory ends.

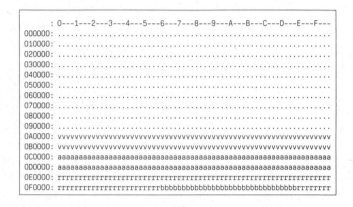

Note the "shadow" duplicate of the ROM BIOS at the end of the 16th megabyte. The memory in these last two segments is a mirror image of what is in the last two segments of the first megabyte, which is required by the 80286 and 80386 designs to provide for switching between the real and protected modes of operation.

Some systems also incorporate another type of memory called *expanded memory*. This memory really is not the same as the conventional (1 megabyte) or extended (2 to 16 megabytes) memory, which is directly addressable by the processor. Expanded memory is *not* directly addressable by the processor except through a small 64K window. Expanded memory is really a segment-switching scheme in which a memory adapter has on-board a large number of 64K segments. The system will use one available segment to map into the board, and when this 64K is filled, the board simply can "rotate" that segment out and rotate a new one in the same place as the old.

Generally, segment E000 in the first megabyte is used for all this mapping. This segment is largely unused by most adapters, so

```
          : 0---1---2---3---4---5---6---7---8---9---A---B---C---D---E---F---
100000: .......................................................................
110000: .......................................................................
120000: .......................................................................
130000: .......................................................................
140000: .......................................................................

       \
       /
       \

A large break occurs

       \
       /
       \

E80000: .......................................................................
E90000: .......................................................................
EA0000: .......................................................................
EB0000: .......................................................................
EC0000: .......................................................................
ED0000: .......................................................................
EE0000: .......................................................................
EF0000: .......................................................................
          : 0---1---2---3---4---5---6---7---8---9---A---B---C---D---E---F---
F00000: .......................................................................
F10000: .......................................................................
F20000: .......................................................................
F30000: .......................................................................
F40000: .......................................................................
F50000: .......................................................................
F60000: .......................................................................
F70000: .......................................................................
F80000: .......................................................................
F90000: .......................................................................
FA0000: .......................................................................
FB0000: .......................................................................
FC0000: .......................................................................
FD0000: .......................................................................
FE0000: rrrrrrrrrrrrrrrrrrrrrrrrrrrrrrrrrrrrrrrrrrrrrrrrrrriiiiiiiiii
FF0000: rrrrrrrrrrrrrrrrrrrrrrrrrrrbbbbbbbbbbbbbbbbbbbbbbbbbbbbbbbbrrrrrrrrr
```

Fig. 2.3.

IBM 16 megabyte memory map where extended memory picks up.

Lotus, Intel, and Microsoft (founders of the LIM specification for expanded memory called LIM EMS) decided that this segment would be used. Programs must be specially written to take advantage of this segment-swapping scheme, and then only data can be placed in this segment because it is above the area of contiguous memory that DOS can use. Also, a program cannot run while it is "swapped out" and not visible by the processor! Needless to say, this type of memory has a limited use; it is usable only by systems that don't have real extended (processor addressable) memory available to them. Chapter 10 covers expanded and extended memory usage in much more detail.

DOS Program Memory

Many people have a great deal of trouble understanding how the reserved memory affects the map as a whole. You really need to know what goes where to understand how the various hardware and software you use will work.

You always hear talk of some "DOS 640K barrier." In reality, no actual barrier is at this location, and DOS can and does work with the entire RAM address space of a PC, which is 1 megabyte. The reason that your programs cannot use all this space is that the hardware engineers of the IBM PC reserved some of the space for the system's own use. DOS can read and write to the entire megabyte but can only manage the loading of programs in contiguous memory.

DOS, therefore, can use all the memory available until it runs into some obstruction. The first obstruction in the system is the video RAM, which is the topic of the next section. This obstruction will be in different locations depending on which video adapter is installed in the system. Additionally, the different video adapters use varying amounts of RAM for their operations. In general, the higher resolution adapters use more memory than those offering lower resolution.

In a system with any standard configuration, the reserved video RAM begins at address A0000, which is at the 640K boundary. Thus, any system with a normal configuration, or especially those with EGA, MCGA, or VGA graphics, will find that the memory after 640K is reserved for use by the graphics boards, other adapters, and the motherboard ROM BIOS.

Video Memory

If you have a video adapter installed in your system, the video adapter will use some of the system's memory to hold graphic or character information for display. Some of the more advanced adapters such as the EGA or VGA adapters also have an on-board ROM that is mapped into the system's space reserved for such types of adapters. Generally, the higher the resolution and capabilities of the video adapter, the more memory the video adapter will use.

In the standard system memory map, a total of 128K is reserved for video RAM, which is where the adapter can store information currently displayed. The adapter may have additional on-board memory that is hidden or switched out, making the total memory on the card actually more than 128K. The reserved video memory is in segments A000 and B000, and space for any ROM on the video board is reserved in segment C000.

Now you will examine how standard video adapters use the system's memory. Figures 2.4 through 2.8 show where each type of standard video adapter uses memory in a system. Each symbol in these figures is equal to 1K of memory.

The following symbols are used in the figures:

    . = Reserved for Program-Accessible Memory
    a = Reserved for Adapter Board ROM and RAM
    r = Reserved for Motherboard ROM BIOS
    b = IBM Cassette BASIC

Other symbols pertain to each individual figure and are covered before the figure is presented.

Figure 2.4 shows where the Monochrome Display Adapter (MDA) uses the system's memory. This adapter uses only a small 4K portion of the reserved video RAM from B0000-B0FFF. The ROM code used to operate this adapter is actually a portion of the motherboard ROM, so no additional ROM space is used in segment C000.

In the figure, the letter M stands for Monochrome Display Adapter (MDA) video RAM.

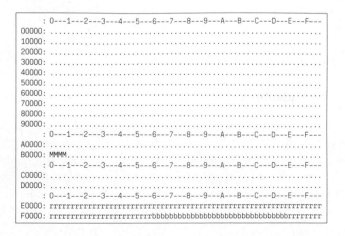

Fig. 2.4.

The Monochrome Display Adapter's memory use.

Figure 2.5 shows where the Color Graphics Adapter (CGA) uses the system's memory. It uses a 16K portion of the reserved video RAM from B8000-BBFFF. The ROM code used to operate this adapter is also a portion of the motherboard ROM, so no additional ROM space is used in segment C000.

In the figure, the letter C stands for Color Graphics Adapter (CGA) video RAM.

Fig. 2.5.

The Color Graphics Adapter's memory use.

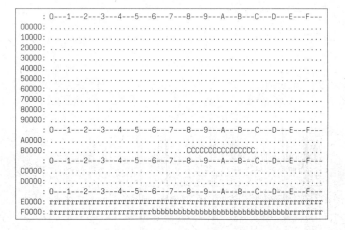

Figure 2.6 shows where the Enhanced Graphics Adapter (EGA) uses the system's memory. This adapter uses all 128K of the video RAM from A0000-BFFFF. The ROM code used to operate this adapter is on the adapter itself and consumes 16K of memory from C0000-C3FFF.

In addition to the symbols listed earlier, the following symbols are used in the figure:

E = Enhanced Graphics Adapter (CGA) Video RAM
X = EGA ROM BIOS

Figure 2.7 shows where the IBM PS/2 Display Adapter uses the system's memory. The IBM PS/2 Display Adapter is essentially a Video Graphics Array (VGA) on a board for the standard PC and AT types of systems. It uses all 128K of the video RAM from A0000-BFFFF. The ROM code used to operate this adapter is on the adapter itself and consumes 24K of memory from C0000-C3FFF.

```
         : 0---1---2---3---4---5---6---7---8---9---A---B---C---D---E---F---
   00000: ................................................................
   10000: ................................................................
   20000: ................................................................
   30000: ................................................................
   40000: ................................................................
   50000: ................................................................
   60000: ................................................................
   70000: ................................................................
   80000: ................................................................
   90000: ................................................................
         : 0---1---2---3---4---5---6---7---8---9---A---B---C---D---E---F---
   A0000: EEEEEEEEEEEEEEEEEEEEEEEEEEEEEEEEEEEEEEEEEEEEEEEEEEEEEEEEEEEEEEEEE
   B0000: EEEEEEEEEEEEEEEEEEEEEEEEEEEEEEEEEEEEEEEEEEEEEEEEEEEEEEEEEEEEEEEEE
         : 0---1---2---3---4---5---6---7---8---9---A---B---C---D---E---F---
   C0000: XXXXXXXXXXXXXXX.................................................
   D0000: ................................................................
         : 0---1---2---3---4---5---6---7---8---9---A---B---C---D---E---F---
   E0000: rrrrrrrrrrrrrrrrrrrrrrrrrrrrrrrrrrrrrrrrrrrrrrrrrrrrrrrrrrrrrrrrr
   F0000: rrrrrrrrrrrrrrrrrrrrrrrrbbbbbbbbbbbbbbbbbbbbbbbbbbbbbbbbrrrrrrrrr
```

Fig. 2.6.

The Enhanced Graphics Adapter's memory use.

In figure 2.7 these symbols are used:

V = PS/2 Display Adapter Video Graphics Array (VGA) Video RAM

X = VGA Adapter ROM BIOS

```
         : 0---1---2---3---4---5---6---7---8---9---A---B---C---D---E---F---
   00000: ................................................................
   10000: ................................................................
   20000: ................................................................
   30000: ................................................................
   40000: ,,,,,,,,,,,,,,,,,,,,,,,,,,,,,,,,,,,,,,,,,,,,,,,,,,,,,,,,,,,,,,,,,
   50000: ................................................................
   60000: ................................................................
   70000: ................................................................
   80000: ................................................................
   90000: ................................................................
         : 0---1---2---3---4---5---6---7---8---9---A---B---C---D---E---F---
   A0000: VVVVVVVVVVVVVVVVVVVVVVVVVVVVVVVVVVVVVVVVVVVVVVVVVVVVVVVVVVVVVVVVV
   B0000: VVVVVVVVVVVVVVVVVVVVVVVVVVVVVVVVVVVVVVVVVVVVVVVVVVVVVVVVVVVVVVVVV
         : 0---1---2---3---4---5---6---7---8---9---A---B---C---D---E---F---
   C0000: XXXXXXXXXXXXXXXXXXXXXXXXXX......................................
   D0000: ................................................................
         : 0---1---2---3---4---5---6---7---8---9---A---B---C---D---E---F---
   E0000: rrrrrrrrrrrrrrrrrrrrrrrrrrrrrrrrrrrrrrrrrrrrrrrrrrrrrrrrrrrrrrrrr
   F0000: rrrrrrrrrrrrrrrrrrrrrrrrrbbbbbbbbbbbbbbbbbbbbbbbbbbbbbbbbrrrrrrrrr
```

Fig. 2.7.

The IBM PS/2 Display Adapter's memory use.

For PS/2 systems with the Video Graphics Array (VGA) or Multi-Color Graphics Array (MCGA), the built-in display systems also use all 128K of the reserved video RAM space; but because these display systems are built into the motherboard, the control BIOS code is built into the motherboard ROM BIOS and, as such, needs no space in segment C000. Figure 2.8 shows where such PS/2 systems use the system memory.

In figure 2.8, the following symbol is used:

V = PS/2 Video Graphics Array (VGA) and Multi-Color Graphics
Array (MCGA) Video RAM

Fig. 2.8.

*The PS/2 VGA
and MCGA
memory use.*

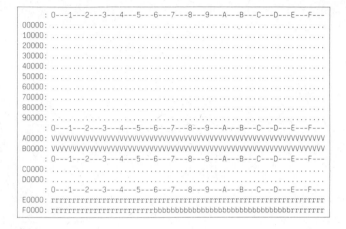

```
    : 0---1---2---3---4---5---6---7---8---9---A---B---C---D---E---F---
00000: ................................................................
10000: ................................................................
20000: ................................................................
30000: ................................................................
40000: ................................................................
50000: ................................................................
60000: ................................................................
70000: ................................................................
80000: ................................................................
90000: ................................................................
    : 0---1---2---3---4---5---6---7---8---9---A---B---C---D---E---F---
A0000: VVVVVVVVVVVVVVVVVVVVVVVVVVVVVVVVVVVVVVVVVVVVVVVVVVVVVVVVVVVVVVVVVV
B0000: VVVVVVVVVVVVVVVVVVVVVVVVVVVVVVVVVVVVVVVVVVVVVVVVVVVVVVVVVVVVVVVVVV
    : 0---1---2---3---4---5---6---7---8---9---A---B---C---D---E---F---
C0000: ................................................................
D0000: ................................................................
    : 0---1---2---3---4---5---6---7---8---9---A---B---C---D---E---F---
E0000: rrrrrrrrrrrrrrrrrrrrrrrrrrrrrrrrrrrrrrrrrrrrrrrrrrrrrrrrrrrrrrrrrr
F0000: rrrrrrrrrrrrrrrrrrrrrrrrbbbbbbbbbbbbbbbbbbbbbbbbbbbbbbbbbrrrrrrrrr
```

Each type of video adapter on the market uses two types of memory.
Video RAM is used to store the display information, and ROM code,
which controls the adapter, must exist somewhere. The nongraphics
or lower resolution adapters such as the MDA and CGA are
controlled by ROM code built into the motherboard ROM on standard
PC and AT systems. The EGA and VGA adapters for the PC and AT
systems all use the full 128K of the video RAM and also use some of
the ROM space at the beginning of segment C000. According to
IBM's technical reference manuals, the memory between C0000-
C7FFF is specifically reserved for ROM on video adapter boards.
Note that the VGA and MCGA that are built into the motherboards
of the PS/2 systems have the ROM control software built into the
motherboard ROM in segments E000 and F000, and they require no
other code space in segment C000.

The nongraphics or lower resolution adapters such as the MDA and
CGA will allow DOS access to more than 640K of system memory.
DOS can use all available memory in the first megabyte that is
contiguous, which means that all memory until the "video wall" is
hit. The location of this "wall" begins at A0000 for the EGA, MCGA,
and VGA systems, but the MDA and CGA do not use as much video
RAM, leaving some of the space usable by DOS and programs. Thus,

you can see from the figures that the MDA allows an additional 64K of memory for DOS (all of segment A000), bringing the total for DOS program space to 704K. Similarly, the CGA allows for a total of 736K. The EGA, VGA, or MCGA is limited to the normal maximum of 640K due to the large amount used by video RAM. The maximum DOS program memory workspace depends on which video adapter is installed:

Video Adapter	Maximum Memory
Monochrome Display Adapter (MDA)	704K
Color Graphics Adapter (CGA)......................	736K
Enhanced Graphics Adapter (EGA)	640K
Video Graphics Array (VGA).......................	640K
Multi-Color Graphics Array (MCGA)	640K

The actual use of this memory to 736K may or may not be possible depending on the video adapter, the types of memory boards installed, and the ROM programs on the motherboard. Later, you will learn about some ways to use this extra memory, but forgetting about the extra memory is usually best because of the lack of memory boards that can be addressed in these locations and because any video adapter upgrade disallows the use of this memory anyway!

Adapter ROM and RAM Memory

Segments C000 and D000 are reserved for use by adapter board ROM and RAM. Here are some boards that use this space:

Adapter	Memory Usage
Enhanced Graphics Adapter ROM	16K at C0000
PS/2 (VGA) Display Adapter ROM	24K at C0000
XT Hard Disk Controller ROM	8K at C8000
ESDI Fixed Disk Adapter/A	16K at C8000
Token Ring Network Adapter ROM	8K at CC000
Token Ring Network Adapter RAM	16K at D8000
LIM Expanded Memory Adapter RAM	64K at D0000

This list is just a small sample of some of the boards that use space in these segments. Note that some of the apparent usages overlap, which is not allowed in a single system. If two adapters both have ROM or RAM addresses that overlap, neither of the boards usually operates. Each board operates independently—but not together. Many adapter boards allow for the actual memory locations used to be changed with jumpers, switches, or some type of software, which may be necessary to allow two boards to coexist in a single system.

Note that the entire amount of segment D000 is used by the LIM EMS specification for expanded memory. The use of all of segment D000 by the LIM EMS can put a real crunch on the available ROM and RAM space for other adapters, and forces many of these adapters, such as the Token Ring network adapter, to be reconfigured so that their memory usage excludes this segment.

This sort of conflict can cause real problems for troubleshooters. If you simply install a Token Ring network card and an Intel Above Board (EMS board), following the factory-set default configuration with each, neither adapter card works in the same system. You are required to read the documentation for each adapter to find out what memory the adapter is using and how to change the memory it uses, to allow coexistence with another adapter. Most of the time, you can work around these problems by reconfiguring the board or changing jumpers, switch settings, or software driver parameters. In the case of the Token Ring card, changing the software driver parameters used in the CONFIG.SYS file moves the memory used by the card from D8000 to something such as C4000. This change allows these two boards to coexist and stay out of each other's way.

A good idea is to use a chart or template to mock up the memory configuration of various adapters you want to install in a system before actually installing them. This procedure helps you resolve any potential conflicts with memory addressing and ensures that you configure each board correctly the first time. After a system is configured, the template you created showing how each board in the system uses memory is important documentation when you consider any new adapter purchases. Any new adapters incorporating a ROM that must be recognized by the system will have to fit in the available workspace.

Motherboard ROM Memory

The ROM memory is part of the RAM in each system. Manufacturers permanently store this memory by fusing circuits in special chips called Programmable Read-Only Memory (PROM) chips. These chips store programs that must be activated every time the system is turned on. Because these programs must be available immediately, they cannot be loaded from a device such as a disk drive. As a matter of fact, ROM programs instruct the system during the boot-up procedure.

Segments E000 and F000 in the memory map are reserved for the motherboard ROM software. Although both segments are considered to be reserved for the motherboard ROM, only the AT systems actually reserve all the area. PC systems actually reserve only segment F000 and allow segment E000 to be used by ROM or RAM on other adapter cards. This information may be important when you're attempting to "cram" an expanded memory adapter into a system that already has a full complement of other boards using memory in segments C000 and D000.

Each system has on the motherboard a set of chips that stores the ROM BIOS. This ROM contains several routines or modules that are designed to operate the system. The main functions follow:

- Power-On Self Test. The POST is a set of routines that tests the motherboard, memory, disk controllers, video adapters, keyboard, and other primary system components. This routine will be useful when you troubleshoot system failures or problems.

- Basic Input/Output System. The BIOS is essentially the "master control program," which is the software interface to all the hardware in the system. The ROM BIOS allows a program to have easy access to features in the system by calling a ROM BIOS program module instead of talking to the device directly.

- Bootstrap Loader. This routine initiates a search for an operating system on a floppy disk or hard disk. If an operating system is found, it is loaded into memory and given control of the system.

Various systems produced by IBM and others have differing ROM BIOS software installed. Just how close in function this software is to what IBM has is a critical issue with any compatible. The compatible software needs to duplicate the functionality of an IBM ROM in order for software to run on the systems exactly as it would on an equivalent IBM system. Fortunately, this software has been relatively easy to duplicate functionally, and the modern compatibles are at no real disadvantage here.

Many different ROM interface programs are in the IBM motherboards, but the location of these programs is always fairly consistent. Figures 2.9 through 2.12 show the memory usage in segments E000 and F000.

Figure 2.9 shows the memory usage in an IBM PC and XT with a 256K motherboard. The following symbols are used:

    b = IBM ROM Cassette BASIC
    R = Motherboard ROM BIOS
    x = Decoded by Motherboard, Unavailable

Fig. 2.9.

*Memory usage in
IBM PC and XT
with 256K
motherboard.*

```
       : 0---1---2---3---4---5---6---7---8---9---A---B---C---D---E---F---
E0000: ................................................................
F0000: xxxxxxxxxxxxxxxxxxxxxxxxxxxbbbbbbbbbbbbbbbbbbbbbbbbbbbbbbbbbRRRRRRRR
```

Figure 2.10 shows the memory usage in an XT with a 640K motherboard and in the PS/2 Models 25 and 30. The following symbols are used:

    b = IBM ROM Cassette BASIC
    R = Motherboard ROM BIOS

Fig. 2.10.

*Memory usage in
IBM XT with 640K
motherboard and
in PS/2 Models 25
and 30.*

```
       : 0---1---2---3---4---5---6---7---8---9---A---B---C---D---E---F---
E0000: ................................................................
F0000: RRRRRRRRRRRRRRRRRRRRRRRRRRbbbbbbbbbbbbbbbbbbbbbbbbbbbbbbbbbRRRRRRRR
```

Figure 2.11 shows the memory usage in an XT-286, AT, and Model 30-286. The following symbols are used:

    b = IBM ROM Cassette BASIC
    R = Motherboard ROM BIOS
    x = Decoded by Motherboard, Unavailable

```
        : 0---1---2---3---4---5---6---7---8---9---A---B---C---D---E---F---
E0000: xxxxxxxxxxxxxxxxxxxxxxxxxxxxxxxxxxxxxxxxxxxxxxxxxxxxxxxxxxxxxxxxxx
F0000: RRRRRRRRRRRRRRRRRRRRRRRRRRRbbbbbbbbbbbbbbbbbbbbbbbbbbbbbbbRRRRRRRR
```

Fig. 2.11.

Memory usage in IBM XT-286, AT, and Model 30-286.

Figure 2.12 shows the memory usage in the PS/2 Models 50, 60, 70, and 80. The following symbols are used:

A = Advanced ROM BIOS (for protected-mode operation)
b = IBM ROM Cassette BASIC
R = Motherboard ROM BIOS

```
        : 0---1---2---3---4---5---6---7---8---9---A---B---C---D---E---F---
E0000: AAAAAAAAAAAAAAAAAAAAAAAAAAAAAAAAAAAAAAAAAAAAAAAAAAAAAAAAAAAAAAAA
F0000: RRRRRRRRRRRRRRRRRRRRRRRRRRRbbbbbbbbbbbbbbbbbbbbbbbbbbbbbbbRRRRRRRR
```

Fig. 2.12.

Memory usage in IBM PS/2 Models 50, 60, 70, and 80.

Note that the newer systems use more of the allocated space for their ROM BIOS. The PS/2 Models 50, 60, 70, and 80 each have an additional 64K of advanced BIOS, which is to be used when these systems are running protected-mode software. Protected mode is the mode of operation currently used by powerful operating systems such as OS/2. The earlier AT systems, which lack this advanced BIOS, still can run OS/2 but will have to load the equivalent of this advanced BIOS software from disk instead of having it in ROM.

The amount of ROM allocated from RAM in each of the IBM systems is presented in table 2.2.

Table 2.2
ROM Allocated from RAM (IBM Systems)

System	Actual ROM Size	Reserved Space
PC	40K	64K
XT (64/256 Motherboard)	40K	64K
XT (256/640 Motherboard)	64K	64K
XT-286	64K	128K
AT	64K	128K
PS/2 Model 25	64K	64K
PS/2 Model 30	64K	64K
PS/2 Model 30-286	64K	128K

Table 2.2—*continued*

System	Actual ROM Size	Reserved Space
PS/2 Model 50	128K	128K
PS/2 Model 60	128K	128K
PS/2 Model 70	128K	128K
PS/2 Model 80	128K	128K

The ROM maps of most compatibles equal the IBM system with which they are compatible. The only real exception is the Cassette BASIC portion. Cassette BASIC is a special version of Microsoft that was designed for the original IBM PC and built-in ROM to allow for diskless operation. The user of one of these systems can save and load programs and data to or from a cassette tape recorder plugged into the cassette port on the back of the original IBM PC. Because no other IBM system (and virtually no compatibles) has a cassette port, but all have the Cassette BASIC interpreter in ROM, this type of BASIC language interpreter is fairly useless.

However useless this type of BASIC language interpreter is, the disk version of BASIC from IBM uses Cassette BASIC as an overlay to save the duplication of that software code on the disk, which means that IBM's BASICA.COM will expect to find Cassette BASIC in ROM and will not work without it. No compatible system that I know of has Cassette BASIC in ROM, so none will run IBM's BASICA.COM program from the PC DOS disk.

If you have a non-IBM system, you must get an equivalent version of Microsoft BASIC called GWBASIC (Graphics Workstation BASIC) from the manufacturer of your system. This GWBASIC.EXE file will have the equivalent program code of the IBM BASICA.COM file and allow for interpreted BASIC programs to run in exactly the same way as on an IBM system.

Review of System Memory Maps

You now have learned how memory is used in any systems that are compatible with the IBM standard. Of note is the reserved memory and where it is located. Also notable is that the reserved memory cannot normally be used by any operating system, so it is deducted from what is available for programs and data.

Table 2.3 lists the maximum available memory of the different systems.

Table 2.3
Maximum Available Memory

System Type	Maximum Addressable Memory (RAM)
PC/XT (or AT real mode)	1,024K (1 megabyte)
AT (protected mode)	16,384K (16 megabytes)

System Type	Maximum Usable Memory
PC/XT (or AT real mode)	640K (0.625 megabytes)
AT (protected mode)	15,872K (15.5 megabytes)

From reviewing the table, you can see that the next "barrier" to cross is the 15.5M barrier!

Documentation

One of the biggest problems in troubleshooting, servicing, or upgrading a system is finding the proper documentation. As with the actual system units themselves, IBM has set the standard for what type of documentation a manufacturer makes available for a particular system. Some of the compatible manufacturers duplicate both the size and content of IBM's manuals for their own systems, and other manufacturers produce absolutely no documentation for their systems at all. Generally, the type of documentation provided follows in proportion to the size of the manufacturing company. Large companies can afford to produce good documentation, but the guy in his garage building "clones" cannot. Unfortunately, some of this documentation is absolutely essential for even the most basic troubleshooting and upgrading tasks. And some documentation is necessary only for software and hardware developers with special requirements.

Three main types of documents basically are available for each system. Some of the manuals cover an entire range of systems, which can help save both money and shelf space! The types of manuals you can get are the following:

- Guide to operations manuals (quick-reference manuals for the PS/2)

- Technical reference manuals

- Hardware maintenance manuals

Guide to Operations and Quick-Reference Manuals

A guide to operations manual is included with the purchase of a system. For the PS/2 systems, these manuals have been changed to quick-reference manuals. They contain basic instructions for system setup, operation, testing, relocation, and option installation. A "customer level" basic diagnostics disk (usually called the Diagnostics and Setup disk) is included.

For PC and XT types of systems, you will find listings of all the jumper and switch settings for the motherboard. These settings control the number of floppy disk drives, math chip usage, memory usage, the type of video adapter, and other items. For AT systems, the basic diagnostics disk also has the SETUP routine, which is used to set the date and time, installed memory, installed disk drives, and installed video adapters. This information is saved by the SETUP program into CMOS battery backed-up memory. For the PS/2 systems, this included disk is called the Reference disk, and it contains the special Programmable Option Selector (POS) configuration routine as well as a hidden version of the advanced diagnostics.

Technical Reference Manuals

The technical reference manuals provide system-specific hardware and software interface information for the system. The manuals are intended either for technical people who design hardware and software products to operate with these systems or for people who simply must integrate other hardware and software in a system. Three technical reference manuals are available: one is a technical reference manual for your particular system, another covers all options and adapters, and a third covers the ROM BIOS interface.

Each system has a separate technical reference manual, which should give you an idea of the specific nature of these documents. These publications provide basic interface and design information for the system units. Information is included for the system board, math coprocessor, power supply, video subsystem, keyboard, instruction sets, and other features of the system. This information is absolutely necessary for the integration and installation of aftermarket floppy and hard disk drives, memory boards, keyboards, network adapters, or virtually anything you want to plug into your system. This manual often contains schematic diagrams showing the circuit layout of the motherboard as well as pinouts for the various connectors and jumpers. The manual also includes listings of the floppy and hard disk drive tables, which show the range of installable drives for a particular system. Also in this manual are power specifications for the power supply. These figures are necessary for determining whether the system has adequate current to power a particular add-on device.

The options and adapters technical reference manual begins with a base manual that is augmented through supplements. The basic manual covers a few IBM adapter cards, and supplements are constantly issued for new adapters and options. These publications provide interface and design information for the options and adapters available for the various systems. This information includes a hardware description, programming considerations, interface specifications, and BIOS information.

The third manual is the BIOS interface technical reference manual. This publication provides Basic Input/Output System (BIOS) interface information. This is a compendium that covers all the BIOS that have been available in IBM's systems. The manual is intended for developers of hardware or software products that operate with the IBM PC and PS/2 products.

Hardware Maintenance Manuals

Each hardware maintenance library consists of two manuals: a hardware maintenance service manual and a hardware maintenance reference manual. These are real service manuals intended for service technicians, and IBM as well as the local computer retail outlet use these manuals to diagnose and service your system.

For IBM systems, two sets of these manuals are available. One set covers the PC, XT, Portable PC, AT, and PS/2 Models 25 and 30. The other manual set covers the PS/2 systems except the Models 25 and 30. Those people who are familiar with the Models 25 and 30 will not be surprised to find that these systems are treated as "old" PC or XT systems rather than "true" PS/2 systems.

The manuals are purchased in basic form and then are updated with various supplements covering new systems and options. The PS/2 Model 25 and Model 30, for example, really are covered by supplements that update the PC maintenance library, and the PS/2 Model 80 is covered by a supplement to the PS/2 maintenance library.

The basic hardware maintenance service manual for the PC or PS/2 contains all the information necessary for you to troubleshoot and diagnose a failing system. This book contains special flowcharts that IBM calls Maintenance Analysis Procedures (MAPs), which can help lead you to a proper diagnosis in a step-by-step fashion. The hardware maintenance service manual contains information on jumper positions and switch settings, a detailed parts catalog, and disks containing the advanced diagnostics. The hardware maintenance service manual is an essential part of the troubleshooter's toolkit.

As just mentioned, the Maintenance Analysis Procedures (MAPs) are flowcharts that can be extremely helpful in diagnosing system problems. Many technicians with troubleshooting experience never need to use the flowcharts, but when technicians have a tough problem, these flowcharts really help them organize a troubleshooting session. The MAPs inform you to check the switch and jumper settings before the cables, to check the cables before replacing the drive or controller, and so on. This type of information is extremely valuable and can work over a range of systems without getting too specific. I highly recommend that you obtain the IBM hardware maintenance service manual or an equivalent manual from your own manufacturer.

The basic hardware maintenance reference manual for the PC or PS/2 contains general information about the systems. It also describes the diagnostic procedures and Field Replaceable Unit (FRU) locations, system adjustments, and component removal and installation. Although valuable, this book usually is not considered a necessary item. Good information is in it, but the information is useful primarily to those with no experience in disassembling and reassembling a system or to those who would have a hard time identifying components within the system. Most people do not need this manual after the first time they take down a system for service and may consider it superfluous.

Obtaining This Documentation

I consider the technical reference manual for a system to be the most important. As a matter of fact, I will not purchase a system whose manufacturer does not make this document available. You cannot accurately troubleshoot or upgrade a system without this manual. Because of the specific nature of the information in the technical reference manual, it must be obtained from the manufacturer of the system, which means that the IBM AT Technical Reference Manual is useless to a person with a COMPAQ Deskpro 286. A person with a Deskpro 286 must get the manual from COMPAQ.

The hardware maintenance service manual is also a necessary item, although it is not available from most manufacturers. Fortunately, the manual is not nearly as system specific as the technical reference manual, so the one from IBM works quite nicely for most compatibles. Some information such as the parts catalog is specific to IBM systems and therefore does not apply to any compatible, but most of the book is general.

Many knowledgeable reviewers use the IBM advanced diagnostics (included with the hardware maintenance service manual) as a real "acid test" for compatibility. If the system is truly compatible, it should pass the tests with flying colors. Most do, which is good because many manufacturers do not have or sell a book/disk equivalent to the hardware maintenance service manual. COMPAQ, for example, has a service manual, but COMPAQ will not sell it, or any parts, to anyone who is not a COMPAQ-authorized dealer, which makes any servicing or upgrading to these systems more costly and limited by how much your particular dealer will help you. Fortunately, the IBM manual and advanced diagnostics work quite nicely on the COMPAQ systems.

To get the hardware service documentation, first contact the dealer who sold you the system and then possibly contact the manufacturer directly. I prefer the direct route myself because dealers rarely stock any of these items. You can get these items easily from IBM. To order the IBM manuals, you can call the following number toll-free:

1-800-IBM-PCTB (1-800-426-7282)

TB stands for Technical Books. The service is active Monday through Friday, from 8 a.m. to 8 p.m. Eastern time. When you call, you may request copies of the *Technical Directory*, which is a catalog listing all the part numbers and prices of the available documentation. You also can inquire about the availability of IBM PC or IBM PS/2 technical information on newly announced products that may not be listed in this directory.

For other manufacturers' manuals, the process may or may not be quite so easy. Simply contact the manufacturer directly, and the manufacturer can direct you to the correct department so you can inquire about this information.

Chapter Summary

Despite the overall similarity between IBM computers and their compatibles, important differences in system architecture do exist. The two basic types of IBM and compatible computers can be broken down into PC XT and AT categories, and this chapter discussed the differences between them.

The system memory map was examined in detail to show how the computers organize and use RAM and ROM. The differences between conventional, extended, and expanded memory also were explained. This chapter covered DOS program memory and video memory and their operation. The chapter ended with a discussion of how to obtain the various service manuals necessary for maintaining and upgrading your computer.

Part II

IBM PC, PS/2, and Compatible Systems

Includes

IBM Personal Computer Family Hardware

IBM Personal System/2 Family Hardware

IBM-Compatible (and Not-So-Compatible) Computers

3

IBM Personal Computer Family Hardware

This chapter is designed to explain and interpret all IBM Personal Computer system units and standard features. This chapter separates and identifies each of the Personal Computer systems offered by IBM, including the complete original line of PC systems that have been discontinued. Actually, because the entire original line of systems has been discontinued, much of this chapter really can be considered a history lesson! Because most of us still own and manage these types of systems, this "historical" information is quite valuable. The original line of systems are now often called Industry Standard Architecture (ISA) systems or "Classic" PCs. The PS/2 systems are examined in Chapter 4.

IBM-compatible systems are examined specifically in Chapter 5, but even compatible owners will find much interesting and useful information in this chapter. After all, the idea behind most compatible systems is to copy, clone, or emulate exactly the features of a particular IBM system. For upgrade and repair purposes, most of the compatible systems are treated as if they were particular types of IBM systems.

In Chapter 2, you learned that all systems can be broken down into two basic "types": PC or AT. AT types of systems often are broken down into several other subtypes. These are systems that use 80286 or 80386 processors and systems with Industry Standard Architecture (ISA) slots or Micro Channel Architecture (MCA) slots. A compatible owner can use this chapter to compare a compatible system with the particular IBM system after which the compatible was designed. The results of a feature-by-feature comparison with an equivalent IBM system model often are interesting because the compatibles usually offer more features and options at a lower price.

System Unit Features by Model

In the sections that follow, you learn specifically the makeup of all the various versions or models of each system, as well as technical details and specifications of each. Each system unit contains a few standard parts. The primary component is the motherboard, which contains the CPU (Central Processing Unit, or microprocessor) and other primary computer circuitry. Also included with each unit is a case with an internal power supply, a keyboard, and certain standard adapters or plug-in cards. Usually some form of disk drive also is included with each system unit.

You also receive an explanation of each system's various submodels and details about the differences and features of each model. You learn about the changes from model to model and version to version of each system, as well.

Also included for your reference is the pricing for each of the systems and options. Note that these prices are offered for comparison and reference purposes only, because all these systems have been discontinued and are no longer generally available. The listed prices are the last known retail prices for any of the systems that have been discontinued.

The IBM PC

IBM introduced the IBM Personal Computer August 11, 1981, and officially withdrew it from marketing April 2, 1987. During the nearly 6-year life of the PC, IBM made few basic changes to the system. The basic motherboard circuit design was changed in April, 1983, to allow for 64K RAM chips, and a total of three different ROM BIOS versions were used during the life of the computer; most of the other specifications, however, remained unchanged. Because the system is no longer marketed and because of the PC's relatively limited expansion capability and power, the standard PC is obsolete by most standards.

The system unit supports only floppy disk drives unless an expansion chassis is used. The system unit includes IBM configurations with either a single or dual 360K floppy disk drive. The PC was based on the 16-bit Intel 8088 microprocessor and included the BASIC language. All models have at least one 360K floppy disk drive and a keyboard. For standard memory, the PC offers 256K directly on the main board. Each system can be further expanded through customer installable options. You can add memory to the 256K by installing memory option cards.

The first bank of memory in every PC is soldered directly to the board. This feature is detrimental; it prevents you from easily repairing failing memory chips in these positions. These chips must be desoldered, and the defective chip must be replaced with a socket so that a replacement can be plugged in. If you have IBM service the defective memory, IBM will advise you to exchange the motherboard at a cost of nearly $200. A competent technician usually charges around $100 for desoldering the defective chip, soldering in a socket, and popping in a new chip. Repairing the same chip in a PC XT costs a few dollars for the chip and 10 minutes of time to replace it, because all memory in an XT is socketed.

The only disk drive available from IBM for the PC is a double-sided (320/360K) floppy disk drive. You can install a maximum of two drives in the system unit using IBM-supplied drives.

The system unit contains five slots that support expansion cards for additional devices, features, or memory. All these slots support full-length adapter cards. The PC is equipped with at least a floppy disk controller card in most configurations. A second slot is needed for a monitor adapter, leaving three slots for future expansion.

All models of the PC include a fan-cooled 63.5-watt power supply. This power supply usually does not support any further system expansion, especially power-hungry items such as a hard disk. In most cases, this low-output supply will need to be replaced with a higher output unit such as the one used in the XT.

An 83-key keyboard with an adjustable typing angle is included as standard equipment with the PC. The keyboard is attached to the system unit with a 6-foot coiled cable.

Each model of the PC system unit usually contains the following major functional components:

- Intel 8088 microprocessor
- ROM-based diagnostics (POST)
- BASIC language interpreter in ROM
- 256K of dynamic RAM
- Floppy disk interface
- One or two 360K floppy drives
- 63.5-watt power supply
- Five I/O expansion slots
- Socket for 8087 math coprocessor

PC Specifications and Highlights

This section lists the technical information for the Personal Computer system and keyboard.

The technical information for the PC system follows:

- 4.77 MHz clock speed
- 20-bit address bus
- 8-bit I/O expansion bus
- 40K of ROM
- 200-nanosecond memory access time
- 63.5-watt power supply
- Dimensions

  Length: 500 mm (20 in)
  Depth: 410 mm (16 in)
  Height: 142 mm (6 in)

- Weight of 11.3 kg (25 lbs)
- Electrical requirements of 104 V to 127 V, 50 Hz to 60 Hz
- Air Temperature

  System turned on: 60 to 90 degrees Fahrenheit
           or 15.6 to 32.2 degrees Celsius

  System turned off: 50 to 110 degrees Fahrenheit
           or 10 to 43 degrees Celsius

- Humidity

    System turned on: 8 to 80 percent RH (Relative Humidity)

    System turned off: 20 to 80 percent RH

- BTU (British Thermal Unit) output of 505 BTU per hour

And here is the technical information for the PC keyboard:

- 83 keys

- Cable length of 6 feet

- Dimensions

    Length: 20 in (500 mm)
    Depth: 8 in (200 mm)
    Height: 2.5 in (57 mm)

- Weight of 6 lbs (2.7 kg)

PC Models and Features

For most people, the power supply is the most critical. Any PC sold after March, 1983, will have the latest ROM BIOS. Those of you with earlier PC systems also will have to address the ROM problem, or you will miss out on a great deal of capability. Both of these problems are addressed in chapters 7 and 12, as well as other expansion issues related to all systems in the PC family.

Several models of the IBM PC were available during its lifetime, but the last PCs were limited to two models. These models differ only in the number of floppy drives: one or two. The models were designated as follows:

IBM PC 5150 Model 166: 256K of RAM, one 360K drive

IBM PC 5150 Model 176: 256K of RAM, two 360K drives

The PC has never been available with a hard disk, mainly because the system unit is a limited base for expansion and offers few resources to work with. Since the additional configuration of the XT with floppy disk drives only (April 2, 1985), the PC became obsolete. The primary reason is that the XT offers much more for virtually the same price, so investing in a PC was questionable.

IBM officially withdrew the PC from marketing April 2, 1987. IBM's plans for the system became obvious when the company did not announce a new model with the Enhanced Keyboard, as it did with the other IBM systems.

The original PC has limited expansion capacity, unless you invest a great deal of money in extra parts and equipment. Expansion, however, is a major issue for PC owners; after all, millions of users own plain PCs and they need some way to protect the investment.

With some creative purchasing, you actually can make a usable system of the PC. You need to add the requisite components, such as a full 640K of memory and hard and floppy drives, and you still may have a slot or two to spare. Unfortunately, carrying out this expansion may require replacing many of the boards already in the system unit with boards that can combine the same functions in less space. Only you can decide when the whole process will become too costly and when the money would be better invested in a new system.

Before you can think of expanding a PC beyond even a simple configuration, and to allow for compatibility and reliability, you usually must address two major areas:

- ROM BIOS level (version)
- Power supply

PC Costs

The PC system unit part numbers and pricing are as follows:

Description	Number	Price
PC system unit, 256K, one double-sided drive	5150166	$1,845
PC system unit, 256K, two double-sided drives	5150176	$1,995

Here are the option part numbers and pricing:

Description	Number	Price
PC Expansion Unit Model 001 with 10M fixed disk	5161001	$2,585
Double-sided diskette drive	1503810	$250
8087 math coprocessor option	1501002	$230
BIOS update kit	1501005	$35

The IBM PC Convertible

IBM introduced the IBM 5140 PC Convertible April 2, 1986, which marked IBM's entry into the laptop computer market. This system superseded the 5155 Portable PC (IBM's transportable system), which is no longer available. Many people originally believed that laptop computers were a solution in search of a problem, but the sales figures of laptop systems have quieted the detractors. The IBM 5140 system unfortunately is not one of the more successful laptop systems. Other laptops offer more disk storage, higher processor speeds, more readable screens, lower cost, and more compact cases, and they have pressured IBM to improve the Convertible. So far, the improvements have been limited to the display, meaning that this system has yet to gain respect in the marketplace.

The PC Convertible is available in several models. The Model 2 is equipped with a CMOS 80C88 microprocessor, 64K of ROM, 256K of RAM, an 80-column-by-25-line detachable liquid crystal display, two 3 1/2-inch floppy disk drives, a 78-key keyboard, an AC adapter, and a battery pack. Also included are special software programs called the Application Selector, SystemApps, Tools, Exploring the IBM PC Convertible, and Diagnostics. The Model 22 is the same as the Model 2 but with diagnostics only. You can expand both systems to 512K of RAM by using 128K RAM memory card features and may include an asynchronous modem in the system unit. With aftermarket memory expansion, the computers can reach 640K.

At the back of each system unit is an extendible bus interface. This 72-pin connector enables you to attach the following options to the base unit: a printer, a serial/parallel adapter, and a CRT display adapter. Each of these features is powered from the system unit. The CRT display adapter operates only when the system is powered from a standard AC adapter. A separate CRT display or a television set attached through the CRT display adapter requires a separate AC power source.

Each system unit includes a detachable Liquid Crystal Display (LCD). As far as LCDs go, this one is fairly good. This LCD lacks backlighting, which is present on many laptops, and its readability and resolution are poorer than the electro-luminescent or gas plasma displays used in other laptops. Apparently, the display has been selected with power consumption and battery operation in mind rather than readability or performance. When the computer is not mobile, the display can be removed for a real monitor. When latched in its closed position, the display forms the cover for the keyboard and floppy disk drives. The LCD is attached with a quick-disconnect connector, which affords easy removal if you want to place the 5140 system unit below an optional IBM 5144 PC Convertible monochrome display or IBM 5145 PC Convertible color display.

The PC Convertible system unit includes these standard features:

- Complementary Metal Oxide Semiconductor (CMOS) 80C88 microprocessor

- Two 32K CMOS ROMs containing the following:

      POST (power-on self test) of system components
      Basic Input/Output System (BIOS) support
      BASIC language interpreter

- 256K CMOS RAM (expandable to 512K)

- Two 3 1/2-inch 720K (formatted) floppy drives

- 80-column-by-25-line detachable LCD panel (graphics modes: 640-by-200 resolution and 320-by-200 resolution)

- LCD controller

- 16K RAM display buffer

- 8K LCD font RAM

- Adapter for optional printer (#4010)

- Professional keyboard (78 keys)

- AC adapter

- Battery pack

The system unit options for the 5140 follow:

- 128K memory card (#4005)

- Printer (#4010)

- Serial/parallel adapter (#4015)

- CRT display adapter (#4020)

- Internal modem (#4025)

- Printer cable (#4055)

- Battery charger (#4060)

- Automobile power adapter (#4065)

Two optional displays are available for the PC Convertible:

- IBM 5144 PC Convertible Monochrome Display Model 1
- IBM 5145 PC Convertible Color Display Model 1

PC Convertible Specifications and Highlights

The specifications of the IBM 5140 PC Convertible system are as follows:

- Dimensions

Depth:	360 mm (14.17 in) 374 mm (14.72 in) including handle
Width:	309.6 mm (12.19 in) 312 mm (12.28 in) including handle
Height:	67 mm (2.64 in) 68 mm (2.68 in) including foot pads

- Weight

Models 2 and 22 (including battery)	5.5 kg (12.17 lbs)
128K memory card	40 gr (1.41 oz)
Printer	1.6 kg (3.50 lbs)
Serial/parallel adapter	470 gr (1.04 lbs)
CRT display adapter	630 gr (1.40 lbs)
Internal modem	170 gr (6 oz)
Printer cable	227 gr (8 oz)
Battery charger	340 gr (12 oz)
Automobile power adapter	113 gr (4 oz)
5144 PC Convertible monochrome display	7.3 kg (16 lbs)
5145 PC Convertible color display	16.9 kg (37.04 lbs)

To operate the IBM 5140 PC Convertible properly, you must have PC DOS Version 3.2 or later. Previous DOS versions are not supported because they don't support the 720K floppy drive. Using the CRT display adapter and an external monitor will require that the system unit be operated by power from the AC adapter rather than the battery.

PC Convertible Models and Features

This section covers the options and special features available for the PC Convertible.

128K Memory Card

The 128K memory card expands the base memory of the system unit. Two of these cards can be added, for a system unit total of 512K.

Optional Printer

The optional printer attaches to the back of the system unit or to an optional printer attachment cable for adjacent printer operation. The printer has an intelligent, microprocessor-based, 40 cps, nonimpact dot-matrix design capable of low-power operation. The optional printer draws power and control from the system unit. Standard ASCII 96-character, upper- and lowercase character sets are printed using a high-resolution, 24-element print head. A mode for graphics capability is also provided. You can achieve near-letter-quality printing by using either a thermal transfer ribbon on smooth paper or no ribbon on heat-sensitive thermal paper.

Serial/Parallel Adapter

The serial/parallel adapter attaches to the back of the system unit, a printer, or another feature module attached to the back of the system unit. The adapter provides an RS-232C asynchronous communications interface and a parallel printer interface, which are compatible with the IBM Personal Computer asynchronous communications adapter and the IBM Personal Computer parallel printer adapter.

CRT Display Adapter

The CRT display adapter attaches to the back of either the system unit, printer, or another feature module attached to the back of the system unit. The adapter enables you to connect a separate CRT display, such as the PC Convertible monochrome display or PC Convertible color display, to the system. By using optional connectors or cables, you also can use the CRT display adapter to attach any standard CGA type of monitor. Because composite video output is available, you also can use a standard television set.

Internal Modem

With the internal modem, you can communicate with compatible computers over telephone lines. The modem runs Bell 212A (1200 baud) or Bell 103A (300 baud) protocols. The modem comes as a complete assembly, consisting of two cards connected by a cable. The entire assembly is installed in the system unit. Unfortunately, this modem is made for IBM by Novation and does not follow the Hayes standard for commands and protocols. The device, therefore, is incompatible with most communications software. Fortunately, you still can operate a regular modem through the serial port; the convenience and portability, however, are lost.

Printer Cable

The printer cable is 22 inches (0.6 meter) long with a custom 72-pin connector attached to each end. This cable provides you with the option of operating the convertible printer when physically detached from the system unit, enabling you to place the unit for ease of use and visibility.

Battery Charger

The battery charger is a 110-volt input device designed to charge the internal batteries of the system. It does not provide sufficient power output to allow system operation while the batteries are being charged.

Automobile Power Adapter

The automobile power adapter is a special adapter designed to plug into the cigarette lighter outlet in a vehicle with a 12-volt negative-ground electrical system. This device charges the Convertible's battery while allowing simultaneous use of the unit.

IBM 5144 PC Convertible Monochrome Display

The 5144 PC Convertible monochrome display is a 9-inch (measured diagonally) composite video display attached to the system unit through the CRT display adapter. Provided with the 5144 are the display stand, an AC power cord, and a signal cable that connects the 5144 to the CRT display adapter. This display does not resemble, nor is it compatible with, the IBM monochrome display for the larger PC systems. The CRT adapter puts out a signal that is the same as that supplied by the Color Graphics Adapter for a regular PC. This display is functionally equivalent to that on the IBM Portable PC.

IBM 5145 PC Convertible Color Display

The 5145 PC Convertible color display is a 13-inch color display. It is attached to the system unit through the CRT display adapter. Provided with the 5145 are the display stand, an AC power cord, and a signal cable that connects the 5145 to the CRT display adapter. This display includes a speaker for external audio output. The monitor is designed to be a low-cost unit compatible with the standard IBM CGA type of display.

The special software available for the Convertible includes these programs:

Application Selector: This program is installed as an extension to DOS and provides the user with a menu-driven interface to select and run applications software, the SystemApps, and Tools.

SystemApps: This program provides basic functions similar to many of the memory-resident programs on the market today. This application includes Notewriter, Schedule, Phone List, and Calculator. This program is equivalent in function to the popular SideKick program.

Tools: This is a menu-driven program that can be used as a front end for DOS to control and maintain the system, such as copying and erasing files, copying disks, etc. With DOS, additional functions become available, including printing, formatting, and configuring the Application Selector function keys. This program presents many DOS functions in an easy-to-use menu format.

This additional software, except system diagnostics, is *not* included with the Model 22.

PC Convertible Costs

Here are the costs of the IBM Convertible system units and optional accessories:

Item	Price
5140 PC Convertible system unit:	
Two drives/256K with system applications	$1,695
Two drives/256K without system applications	$1,675
Optional features:	
128K memory card	$160
256K memory card	$345
Printer	$295
Serial/parallel adapter	$80
CRT display adapter	$255
Internal modem	$225
Printer cable	$45
Battery charger	$25
Automobile power adapter	$25
Standard carrying case	$84
Compact carrying case	$44
5144 PC Convertible monochrome display	$180
5145 PC Convertible color display	$400

The IBM PC XT

Introduced March 8, 1983, the PC XT with a built-in 10M hard disk (originally standard, later optional) caused a revolution in personal computer configurations. XT stands for *XTended* (extended). IBM chose this name because the IBM PC XT system includes many features not available in the standard PC. The XT has eight slots, allowing increased expansion capabilities, greater power supply capacity, completely socketed memory, motherboards that support expansion to 640K without using an expansion slot, and optional hard disk drives. To allow for these advantages, the XT uses a completely different motherboard circuit design than the PC.

The system unit is available in several models, with a variety of disk drive configurations: a single 256K floppy disk drive, two 256K floppy disk drives, one floppy disk and one hard disk drive, or two floppy disk drives and one hard disk drive. The floppy disk drives are full-height drives in the earlier models and half-height drives in more recent models. Because of this arrangement, you can have two floppy drives and a hard disk in a standard IBM configuration. Hard disks available from IBM are 10M and 20M full-height hard disks. The available floppy disk drives include a double-sided (320/360K) floppy disk drive in either a full- or half-height configuration. A recent option is a 3 1/2-inch 720K floppy disk drive. The 3 1/2-inch drives are available in a normal internal configuration or as an external device. You can install a maximum of two floppy disk drives and one hard disk drive in the system unit, using IBM-supplied drives. With half-height hard disks, you can put two hard disk drives in the system unit.

The XT is based on the same 8- and 16-bit Intel 8088 microprocessor as the PC and runs at the same clock speed. Operationally, the systems are virtually identical. All models are equipped with at least one 360K floppy disk drive and a keyboard. For standard memory, the XT offers 256K or 640K directly on the main board. In addition, the hard disk models include a serial adapter.

The system unit contains eight slots that support cards for additional devices, features, or memory. Two of these slots support only short option cards due to physical interference with the disk drives. The XT is equipped with at least a diskette drive adapter card in the floppy-disk-only models and a hard disk controller card and serial adapter in the hard disk models. The result is seven or five available expansion slots (depending on the model).

All XT models include a heavy-duty fan-cooled 135-watt power supply to support the greater expansion capabilities and disk drive options. This power supply is more than double the capacity of the PC's supply.

An 83-key keyboard was standard equipment with the early XT models and is still available as an option on the newer models. This keyboard is attached to the system unit with a 6-foot coiled cable. The newer models have as standard equipment the 101-key Enhanced Keyboard and a 9-foot cable.

All models of the PC XT system unit contain the following major functional components:

- Intel 8088 microprocessor
- ROM-based diagnostics (POST)
- BASIC language interpreter in ROM
- 256K or 640K of dynamic RAM
- Floppy disk interface
- One 360K floppy drive (full- or half-height)
- 10M or 20M hard disk drive with interface (enhanced models)
- Serial interface (enhanced models)
- Heavy-duty 135-watt power supply
- Eight I/O expansion slots
- Socket for 8087 math coprocessor

XT Specifications and Highlights

The following are technical specifications for the PC XT system:

- 4.77 MHz clock speed
- 20-bit address bus
- 8-bit I/O expansion bus
- 40K of ROM
- 200-nanosecond memory access time
- 135-watt power supply

- Dimensions

    Length: 500 mm (20 in)
    Depth: 410 mm (16 in)
    Height: 142 mm (6 in)

- Weight of 14.50 kg (32 lbs)

- Electrical requirements of 90 V to 137 V, 50 Hz to 60 Hz

- Air temperature

    System turned on: 60 to 90 degrees Fahrenheit
                      or 15.6 to 32.2 degrees Celsius

    System turned off: 50 to 110 degrees Fahrenheit
                       or 10 to 43 degrees Celsius

- Humidity

    System turned on: 8 to 80 percent RH
    System turned off: 20 to 80 percent RH

- BTU Output of 717 BTU per hour

The following list is the technical data for the original PC XT keyboard:

- 83 keys

- Cable length of 6 feet

- Dimensions

    Length: 20 in (500 mm)
    Depth: 8 in (200 mm)
    Height: 2.5 in (57 mm)

- Weight of 6 lbs (2.7 kg)

The technical data for the PC XT Enhanced Keyboard follows:

- 101 keys

- Cable length of 9 feet

- Removable keycaps

- Dimensions

    Length: 19.37 in (492 mm)
    Depth: 8.27 in (210 mm)
    Height: 2.28 in (58 mm), legs extended

- Weight of 5 lbs (2.25 kg)

XT Models and Features

The XT has been available in many different model configurations during its lifetime, but originally only one model was available. This model, which included a 10M hard disk, marked the first time that a hard disk was a standard item in a personal computer and was properly supported by the operating system and peripherals. This computer helped change the industry standard for personal computers from one or two floppy disk drives to one or more hard disks.

Today, I don't even consider a PC to be usable without a hard disk. The only real drawbacks to the original XT were that it was expensive and the hard disk could not be "unbundled" or deleted from the system at purchase time for credit and added later. This fact distinguished the XT from the PC and misled many people to believe that the only difference between the two computers was the hard disk. People who recognized and wanted the greater capabilities of the XT without the standard IBM hard disk would have to wait.

The original model 087 of the XT included a 10M hard disk, 128K of RAM, and a standard serial interface. Later, IBM increased the standard memory of all PC systems to 256K, and the XT reflected the change in Model 086, which was the same as the preceding 087 except for a standard 256K of RAM

On April 2, 1985, IBM effectively rendered the original PC system obsolete by introducing new models of the XT without the standard hard disk. Designed for expansion and configuration flexibility, the new models provided a way for you to expand from a floppy disk system to a hard disk system. This design meant that the XT could be considered in configurations that previously could be filled only by the original PC. The big difference between the PC and the XT is the XT's expansion capability, provided by the larger power supply, eight slots, and better memory layout. These models cost only $300 more than equivalent PCs, rendering the PC no longer a viable option.

The extra expense of the XT is more than justified with the first power supply replacement you make with an overworked PC. The floppy disk models of the IBM PC XT follow:

  5160068 XT with one full-height 360K disk drive

  5160078 XT with two full-height 360K disk drives

Both these models have 256K of memory and use the IBM PC XT motherboard, power supply, frame, and cover. The asynchronous communications adapter is not included as a standard feature with these models.

On April 2, 1986, IBM introduced several more models of the PC XT. These recent models have some significant differences from the previous ones. The most obvious difference is the Enhanced Keyboard, which is standard with the new computers. Other differences are a 20M (rather than 10M) hard disk and high-quality, half-height floppy disk drives. The new half-height floppy disk drives allow for two drives where before only one would fit. With two drives, backing up floppy disks is painless. Also available is a new 3 1/2-inch floppy disk drive storing 720K for compatibility with the PC Convertible laptop computer. The recent XT system units are configured with a new memory layout allowing for 640K of RAM on the motherboard without the use of an expansion slot. This feature conserves power, improves reliability, and lowers the cost of the system.

Standard with the XT Models 267 and 268 are one 5 1/4-inch half-height 360K floppy disk drive and 256K of system board memory. Models 277 and 278 have a second 5 1/4-inch floppy disk drive. Models 088 and 089 are expanded PC XTs with all the standard features of the Models 267 and 268, a 20M hard disk, a 20M fixed diskette drive adapter, an asynchronous communications adapter, and an additional 256K of system board memory, for a total of 512K.

Highlights of the new models include the following:

- Enhanced Keyboard standard on Models 268, 278, and 089

    101-keys
    Recappable
    Selectric typing section
    Dedicated numeric pad
    Dedicated cursor and screen controls
    Two additional function keys
    9-foot cable

- Standard PC XT keyboard on Models 267, 277, and 088

- More disk capacity (20M)

- New features

    20M fixed disk
    20M fixed disk adapter
    5 1/4-inch half-height 360K floppy drive
    3 1/2-inch half-height 720K floppy drive

- New 3 1/2-inch 720K floppy drive for added flexibility

- Capacity for three storage devices within system unit

- Capacity to expand to 640K bytes memory on system board
  without using expansion slots

These newest models of the XT have a new, extensively changed
ROM BIOS. The new BIOS is 64K and is internally much the same as
the AT's. This ROM includes support for the new keyboard and
3 1/2-inch floppy disk drives. The POST also has been enhanced.

The new XTs are incompatible in some respects with some software
programs. All the problems so far have centered on the new
keyboard and the way the new ROM addresses the keys. The
problems are not drastic, and all the problems that I heard of were
solved almost immediately by the software companies.

Seeing how much IBM changed the computer without changing the
basic motherboard design is interesting. The ROM is different, and
the board now can hold 640K of memory without a card in a slot.
The memory trick is actually a simple one. IBM designed this feature
into the board originally and chose to unleash it with these models
of the XT.

During the last several years, I have modified many XTs to have
640K on the motherboard, using a simple technique that IBM
provided for. The new XTs achieve the greater memory capacity by
the same technique. A simple jumper and chip added to the
motherboard can alter the memory addressing of the board. The new
addressing is set up for 256K chips, which are installed in two of the
four banks. The other two banks of memory contain 64K chips, for a
total of 640K. In Chapter 12, a set of detailed instructions for
modifying any IBM XT in this way is given.

XT Costs

Here are the costs of the XT system units:

Description	Number	Price
XT system unit/PC XT keyboard, 256K:		
one double-sided drive	5160068	$2,145
one half-height double-sided drive	5160267	$2,145
two double-sided drives	5160078	$2,295
two half-height double-sided drives	5160277	$2,295
XT system unit/Enhanced Keyboard, 256K:		
one half-height double-sided drive	5160268	$1,395
two half-height double-sided drives	5160278	$1,545
XT system unit/PC XT keyboard, 256K, Async:		
one double-sided drive, one 10M fixed disk	5160086	$2,895
XT system unit/PC XT keyboard, 640K, Async:		
one half-height double-sided drive, one 20M fixed disk	5160088	$2,660
XT system unit/Enhanced Keyboard, 640K, Async:		
one half-height double-sided drive, one 20M fixed disk	5160089	$2,660

And here are the costs for the options:

Description	Number	Price
PC Expansion Unit Model 002 with 20M fixed disk	5161002	$2,090
20M fixed disk drive	6450326	$630
20M fixed disk adapter	6450327	$200
10M fixed disk drive	1602500	$695
10M fixed disk adapter	1602501	$395

Description	Number	Price
5 1/4-inch half-height double-sided disk drive	6450325	$225
Double-sided disk drive	1503810	$250
3 1/2-inch half-height 720K internal drive	6450258	$170
3 1/2-inch half-height 720K external drive	2683190	$395
8087 math coprocessor option	1501002	$230
Asynchronous serial adapter	1502074	$70

The costs of the Enhanced Keyboard accessories follow:

Description	Number	Price
Clear keycaps (60) with paper inserts	6341707	$50
Blank light keycaps	1351710	$25
Blank dark keycaps	1351728	$25
Paper inserts (300)	6341704	$30
Keycap removal tools (6)	1351717	$11

The IBM 3270 PC

On October 18, 1983, IBM announced a special version of the XT called the 3270 PC. The 3270 PC combines the functions of IBM's 3270 display system with those of the XT. This system is basically a standard XT system unit with from three to six custom adapter cards added to the slots. The keyboard and display for this system are special as well and attach to some of these special adapter cards. All this hardware is run by a program called the 3270 PC Control Program. This combination can support up to seven concurrent activities: one local PC DOS session, four remote mainframe sessions, and two local electronic notepads. With the assistance of the 3270 PC Control Program, information can be copied between windows, except that a PC DOS window may not receive information.

The 3270 PC also includes a new keyboard that addresses some of the complaints about the Personal Computer keyboard. The keyboard contains more keys in an improved layout. The Enter and Shift keys are enlarged. The cursor keys are separated from the numeric keypad and form a little group between the main alphanumeric keys and the numeric keypad. Twenty function keys are arranged in two rows of 10 at the top of the keyboard. To help clarify keystroke operations, the new keyboard is annotated. Blue legends designate PC-specific functions; black legends indicate 3270 functions. Although this keyboard is greatly improved, most of the new keys and features do not work in the PC mode. Often, special versions of programs must be obtained, or you have to disregard most of the new keys.

3270 PC Models and Features

The 3270 PC includes several specialized expansion boards that are added to an XT. These expansion boards are examined in this section.

3270 System Adapter

The 3270 system adapter supports communication between the 3270 PC and the remote 3274 controller through a coaxial cable. One physical 3274 connection can support four logical connections.

Display Adapter

The display adapter is used in place of the PC's monochrome or color/graphics display adapter and provides text-only displays in eight colors. Although the extended character graphics of the PC are available, bit-mapped graphic capabilities are not supported unless the accessory extended graphics card is added.

Extended Graphics Adapter (XGA)

The Extended Graphics Adapter (XGA) provides the storage and controls necessary for displaying local graphics in high- or medium-resolution mode. High-resolution mode is available in two colors, at 720-by-350 or 640-by-200 pixels.

Medium-resolution mode is available with a choice of two sets of four colors at 360-by-350 or 320-by-200 pixels. To run in medium-resolution mode, your system must have an available system expansion slot adjacent to the display adapter card. If a Programmed Symbols feature (discussed next) is installed next to the display adapter, the slot adjacent to the PS feature must be used. Because the aspect ratio differs for each display monitor, applications programs must control the aspect ratio parameter; a circle on the 5150/5160 PC with the Color Graphics Adapter looks slightly elliptical on the 3270 PC with the XGA unless this parameter is changed.

Programmed Symbols

The Programmed Symbols (PS) adapter provides graphics capabilities currently available on IBM 3278/3279 display stations. This card provides storage for up to six 190-symbol sets whose shapes and codes are definable. Symbol sets are loaded (and accessed for display) under program control. To accept this board, your system must have an available system expansion slot adjacent to the display adapter card. If an XGA feature is installed, you must use the slot adjacent to the XGA. The PS card is available in only Distributed Function Terminal (DFT) mode and may be used in only one of the four host sessions.

Keyboard Adapter

You use the keyboard adapter to adapt the 3270 style of keyboard to the system unit. The keyboard connects directly to this board rather than to the motherboard as it does for the PC. This board is short and must be installed in the special eighth slot of the XT system unit.

The standard XT system unit provides eight expansion slots; at least five of those slots normally are filled on delivery with the 3270 system adapter, the display adapter, the keyboard adapter, the diskette drive adapter, and the hard disk controller. If you want to add options such as the graphics adapter and a memory multifunction card, you can see that even with the XT as a base, slots are at a premium in this system. An expansion chassis is a definite consideration for the 3270.

Software

The 3270 PC runs under control of the 3270 PC Control Program in conjunction with PC DOS and supports concurrent operation of up to four remote host interactive sessions, two local notepad sessions, and one PC DOS session. The Control Program enables users to associate sessions with display screen windows and to manage those windows by a set of functions that IBM calls advanced screen management.

Windows

You can define windows that permit viewing of all (up to 2,000 characters) or part of a presentation space. In IBM's vocabulary, a *presentation space* is a logical display area presented by a single host. PC DOS presentation spaces are 2,000 characters (25 lines by 80 characters), remote host spaces are up to 3,440 characters, and notepad presentation spaces are 1,920 characters.

Up to 7 windows may appear on-screen at once. Each window is associated with a distinct presentation space. Windows may be as large as the screen or as small as 1 character and may be positioned at any point within their presentation space. Thus, a window 20 characters wide and 4 lines long may show the first 20 characters of the last 4 lines of a host session display. You can change window size and position within the presentation space at any time without affecting the content of the presentation space.

At any given moment, only one window on the 3270 PC screen is the active window. When you enter information from the keyboard, the information is directed to the session associated with the currently active window. You can switch between active windows by using keystroke commands.

You can define the foreground and background colors of host session windows not using extended data stream attributes. You also may define the background color for the 5272 screen (the color to be displayed in areas not occupied by windows).

Special Facilities

In addition to the advanced screen management functions, the Control Program offers a number of related special facilities that help you take further advantage of the 3270 environment.

Data can be copied within or between any presentation spaces except into the PC DOS screen. You accomplish this copying by marking a block of data in one window and marking a destination in some other window, much the same as a block copy in a word processor.

You can think of the notepads as local electronic scratch pads that you can use at your convenience. You can save and restore the contents of a notepad at any time by using PC DOS files as the storage medium.

You can define up to 10 screen configurations, each of which describes a set of windows configured in any way, and they can display any one configuration on command. Use PC DOS files to store the configuration information.

You can print a full copy of the display screen on a local printer. Similarly, you can print a full copy of a PC DOS presentation space on a local printer. You can print a full copy of any host presentation space on a local printer, a 3274 attached printer, or a 43xx display/ printer attached terminal printer.

The Control Program maintains a status line at the bottom of the screen, which displays current configuration information including the name of the active window. The Control Program also includes a help function, displaying active workstation functions and sessions and an on-line tutorial that explains and simulates system functions. The tutorial is a standard PC DOS program that can be run on any IBM PC.

The Control Program, with the assistance of a host-based IBM 3270 PC file transfer program, can initiate transfers of ASCII, binary, and EBCDIC files to and from remote hosts. The host-based file transfer program is host licensed and available for VM/SP and MVS/TSO.

A drawback to this software is that it is memory resident and consumes an enormous amount of space. The result is that in the PC DOS session, not many applications can run in the leftover workspace. Your only option is to reboot the computer without loading the Control Program, which is a clumsy and time-consuming procedure. Even with this tactic, the drastic differences in the display hardware and the keyboard still render this computer much less than "PC compatible." The AT version of this system offers a solution to the memory problem by allowing much of the Control Program to reside in the AT's extended memory above the 1M memory limit of the PC and XT.

Significance of the 3270

The 3270 PC is a great system to use if you are a corporate worker who deals daily with many information sources (most of which are available through an IBM mainframe SNA network). Corporate information managers greatly appreciate the concurrent access to several SNA-based databases. The 3270 PC provides the essential tools for viewing, extracting, combining, and manipulating information: multiple concurrent terminal sessions, cut and paste capability between sessions, PC productivity tools, and up- and downloading host files from PC DOS files.

For simple 3270 terminal emulation capability, however, this system is more than you need. In addition, the display and keyboard render this system partially incompatible with the rest of the PC world. Many PC applications do not run properly on this system. For those of you who depend more on PC DOS applications than on the mainframe, or for those of you to whom the multiple mainframe sessions are unimportant, using one of the simpler 3270 emulation adapters is more cost-effective.

The IBM XT 370

On October 18, 1983, IBM introduced another special version of the XT called the XT 370, consisting of a standard PC XT chassis with three special cards added. These adapters are special S/370 emulation cards, that give the computer the capability to execute the Mainframe System 370 instruction set. The boards enable you to run VM/CMS and emulate 4M of virtual memory. You can download programs and compilers from the mainframe and execute them directly on the XT. You switch between 370 mode and the standard XT by using a "hot key" sequence.

XT 370 Models and Features

The three cards that make up the XT 370 are the PC 370-P card, the PC 370-M card, and the PC 3277-EM card. These cards are examined in this section.

The P card implements an emulation of the 370 instruction set. The card contains three microprocessors. One of the processors is a heavily modified Motorola 68000 produced under license to IBM. This chip implements the general-purpose registers, the PSW, instruction fetch and decode logic, and 72 commonly used S/370 instructions. Because Motorola manufactures the chip under license to IBM, the chip probably will not appear as a Motorola product.

A second processor is a slightly modified Motorola 68000, which is listed in Motorola's catalog. This chip emulates the remaining nonfloating point instructions, manipulates the page table, handles exception conditions, and performs hardware housekeeping.

The third microprocessor is a modified Intel 8087 that executes S/370 floating point instructions. This chip is interfaced as a peripheral instead of the normal 8087 coprocessor linkage.

The M card contains 512K of parity-checked RAM. You can access this memory from the P card or from the XT's native 8088 processor. Concurrent requests are arbitrated in favor of the 8088. Although the M card lives in an XT expansion slot, the card also is connected to the P card by a special edge connector. Sixteen-bit-wide transfers between M card memory and the P card are carried out through this connector (normal XT memory transfers operate in 8-bit-wide chunks).

When operating in native PC mode, the M card's memory is addressed as contiguous memory beginning at the end of the 256K memory of the system's motherboard. In native PC mode, the XT 370 has 640K of usable RAM; some of the M card's memory is not used.

When operating in 370 mode, only the 512K RAM of the M card is usable (the memory on the motherboard is not available). The first 480K of this memory implements 480K of real S/370 space. The remaining 32K on the M card functions as a microcode control storage area for the second P card microprocessor.

Of the 480K of S/370 memory, the first 64K are consumed by VM/PC, leaving 416K of real memory for user programs. User programs larger than 416K are handled through paging.

The PC 3277-EM card attaches the XT 370 to an S/370 mainframe by a local or remote 3274 control unit (connection through coaxial cable). When VM/PC is running, the EM card uses the IBM monochrome or color display. Under VM/PC, the EM card also is used to up- and download data between a host VM system and the XT 370.

The XT 370 can run in native PC XT mode or in S/370 mode under the VM/PC Control Program. Under VM/PC, the user can alternate by a "hot key" between a local CMS session and a remote 3277 session (or, optionally, a 3101 emulation session). VM/PC does not offer a true VM-like environment. Instead, VM/PC provides an environment in which CMS applications can run. Non-CMS VM applications will not run on the XT 370.

The VM/PC system must be licensed. The system is provided on six floppy disks and includes the VM/PC Control Program, CMS, XEDIT, EXEC2, local and remote file transfer utilities, and the 370 Processor Control package.

Estimations of the XT 370 CPU's performance indicate that it is about half of a 4331 when the XT 370 is running a commercial instruction mix. When running scientific codes, you can expect twice the performance from the XT 370 as from the 4331. In general, the CPU is categorized as a 0.1 MIPS (Million Instructions Per Second) processor. This size may not sound terribly impressive when you're used to multi-MIPS, single-chip microprocessors. Remember, however, that 0.1-million S/370 instructions are likely to produce substantially more computing than 0.1-million instructions of your standard microprocessor chip.

The XT 370 running in S/370 mode can access the 512K on the M card. Of this 512K, 32K is reserved for microcode control storage and 65K is used by the VM/PC Control Program, leaving 416K for user programs. If a user program requires more memory than 416K, VM/PC uses a paging area on the XT 370's hard disk and swaps pieces of the program in and out of memory according to usage.

Swapping on the little 10M or 20M hard disks is considerably slower than on the large disks used with mainframes. Programs larger than 416K, therefore, probably will run especially slow. Field test users report long delays in loading large programs into memory, even when these programs are well under the maximum for nonpaging operation. The delays are due to the relatively slow operation of the XT 370 hard disks. Because of size and speed problems, many users of these systems would do well to consider larger and faster hard disks.

XT 370 Costs

The XT 370 is available with the use of any of the current XT configurations as a base. The cost is approximately $3,000 more than the equivalent XT alone. The three XT 370 boards also are available as an upgrade for any existing IBM PC XT. The upgrade kit contains the boards, installation instructions, and a logo kit for you to change the nameplate to read "IBM XT 370." The price of the XT upgrade is about $3,000.

The IBM Portable PC

The IBM Portable PC is a "transportable" personal computer containing a built-in 9-inch amber composite video monitor, one 5 1/4-inch half-height floppy disk drive (with space for an optional second drive), an 83-key keyboard, two adapter cards, a floppy disk controller, and Color/Graphics Monitor Adapter (CGA). The unit also has a universal voltage power supply, that allows for operation overseas on 220-volt power. The system board is the same as the original IBM XT's, with 256K of memory. Because the XT motherboard was used, 8 expansion slots are available for the connection of adapter boards, although only 2 slots could accept a full-length adapter card. The power supply is basically the same as that of an XT, with physical changes for portability and a small amount of power drawn to run the built-in monitor. From a function and performance standpoint, the Portable PC system unit has identical characteristics to an equivalently configured IBM PC XT system unit.

IBM withdrew the Portable PC from the market on April 2, 1986. This date which coincides with the introduction of the IBM Convertible laptop PC. The Portable PC is a rarity because not many were sold. This system was totally misunderstood by the trade press and user community. Most people did not understand that this system was an XT and not really a PC. Maybe IBM should have called this system the Portable XT instead. Perhaps then the system would have fared better.

The Portable PC system unit contains the following major functional components:

- Intel 8088 microprocessor

- ROM-based diagnostics (POST)

- BASIC language interpreter in ROM

- 256K of dynamic RAM

- Eight expansion slots (two long slots, one 3/4-length slot, and five short slots)

- Socket for 8087 math coprocessor

- Color/Graphics Monitor Adapter

- 9-inch amber composite video monitor

- Floppy disk interface

- One or two half-height 360K floppy drives

- 114-watt universal power supply (115 V to 230 V, 50 Hz to 60 Hz)

- Light-weight 83-key keyboard

- Enclosure with carrying handle

- Carrying bag for the system unit

Portable PC Specifications and Highlights

Here is the technical data for the Portable PC:

- 4.77 MHz clock speed

- 20-bit address bus

- 8-bit I/O expansion bus

- 40K of ROM

- 200-nanosecond memory access time

- 114-watt power supply

- Dimensions

   Length: 500 mm (20 in)
   Depth: 430 mm (17 in)
   Height: 204 mm (8 in)

- Weight of 14 kg (31 lbs)

- Electrical requirements

   United States: 100 V to 125 V, 50 Hz to 60 Hz
   European: 200 V to 240 V, 50 Hz to 60 Hz

- Air temperature

   System turned on: 60 to 90 degrees Fahrenheit
                     or 15.6 to 32.2 degrees Celsius

   System turned off: 50 to 110 degrees Fahrenheit
                      or 10 to 43 degrees Celsius

- Humidity

   System turned on: 8 to 80 percent RH
   System turned off: 20 to 80 percent RH

- BTU output of 650 BTU per hour

And here is the technical data for the Portable PC keyboard:

- 83 keys

- Dimensions

   Length: 480 mm (18.9 in)
   Depth: 190 mm (7.5 in)
   Height: 40 mm (1.6 in)

- Weight of 1.8 kg (4 lbs)

Portable PC Costs

The disk drive used in the Portable PC was a half-height drive, which was the same unit specified for use in the PC*jr*. At the time the Portable PC was introduced, PC*jr*s were the only ones IBM sold with the half-height drive. The part number and cost of this drive follow:

Description	Number	Price
Slimline 360K diskette drive for the Portable PC	6450300	$425

The IBM PC AT

IBM introduced the Personal Computer AT (for Advanced Technologies) August 14, 1984. The IBM AT system included many features previously unavailable in IBM's PC systems such as increased performance, an advanced microprocessor, high-capacity floppy disk and hard disk drives, larger memory space, and an advanced coprocessor. Despite its new design, the IBM AT retains compatibility with most existing hardware and software products for the earlier systems.

In most cases, IBM AT system performance is expected to be three to five times faster than the IBM XT for single applications running DOS on both computers. This performance increase is due to the combination of the 80286 processor, the memory accessing methodology, and the hard disk capabilities.

The system unit has been available in several models: a floppy-disk-equipped base model (068) and several hard-disk-enhanced models. Based on a high-performance 16-bit Intel 80286 microprocessor, each computer includes cassette BASIC language in ROM and a clock/calendar with battery backup. All models are equipped with a high-capacity (1.2M) floppy disk drive, a keyboard, and a lock. For standard memory, the base model offers 256K, and the enhanced models offer 512K. In addition, the enhanced models have a 20M or a 30M hard disk drive and a serial/parallel adapter. Each system can be expanded further through customer-installable options. You can add memory (to 512K) for the base model by adding chips to the system board. You can expand all models to 16M by installing memory cards.

The following disk drives are available from IBM: a 30M hard disk drive, a 20M hard disk drive, a second high-capacity (1.2M) floppy disk drive, a double-density (320/360K) floppy disk drive, and a new 3 1/2-inch 720K drive. You can install up to two floppy disk drives and one hard disk drive or one floppy disk drive and two hard disk drives in the system unit. Special floppy disks are required for you to use the high-capacity floppy disk drives properly. These disks are 5 1/4-inch, high-coercivity, double-sided, soft-sectored disks and are available from many sources. The double-sided floppy disk drive (320/360K) is available for floppy disk compatibility with the standard PC or XT systems, whereas the 3 1/2-inch drive is for compatibility with the PC Convertible laptop and the PS/2 series. You can exchange disks reliably between the 1.2M and the standard 360K drives if you use the proper method and completely understand the recording process. For those of you without access to this information or knowledge, the information is covered in this book. For complete reliability, however, you should purchase the 360K drive.

The system unit contains 8 slots that support cards for additional devices, features, or memory. Six of these slots support the advanced 16-bit or 8-bit option cards. Two of these slots support 8-bit option cards only. All system unit models, however, use one 16-bit slot for the fixed disk and diskette drive adapter. The enhanced models use an additional 8-bit slot for the serial/parallel adapter.
The result is 7 available expansion slots for the base model and 6 available expansion slots for the enhanced models.

All models include a universal power supply, a temperature-controlled variable-speed cooling fan, and a security lock with key. The power supply is user-selected for the voltage range in that country. The cooling fan significantly reduces the noise in most environments; the fan runs slower when the system unit is cool and faster when the system unit is hot. When locked, no one can remove the system unit cover, boot the system, or enter commands or data from the keyboard, thereby enhancing the system's security.

The keyboard is attached to the system unit by a 9-foot coiled cable, permitting the AT to adapt to a variety of workspace configurations. The keyboard includes key location enhancements and mode indicators for improved keyboard usability.

Each system unit for the AT models contains the following major functional components:

- Intel 80286 microprocessor
- ROM-based diagnostics (POST)
- BASIC language interpreter in ROM
- 8086 compatible real address mode
- Protected virtual address mode
- 256K of dynamic RAM (base model)

- 512K of dynamic RAM (enhanced models)
- 1.2M double-sided floppy drive
- 20M or 30M hard disk drive (enhanced models)
- Hard disk/floppy disk interface
- Serial/parallel interface (enhanced models)
- Clock/calendar and configuration with battery backup
- Keylock
- 84-key keyboard
- Enhanced 101-key 3270 style of keyboard
- Switchable worldwide power supply
- Eight I/O expansion slots (six 16-bit, two 8-bit)
- Socket for 80287 math coprocessor

AT Specifications and Highlights

The technical information for the AT system unit follows:

- 6 or 8 MHz clock speed
- 24-bit address bus
- 8-bit and 16-bit I/O expansion bus
- 64K of ROM
- Memory access time of 150 ns
- 192-watt power supply
- Variable speed fan, temperature controlled
- Dimensions

    Length: 540 mm (21.25 in)
    Depth: 439 mm (17.28 in)
    Height: 162 mm (6.38 in)

- Weight

    16.80 kg (37 lbs) base model
    19.01 kg (42 lbs) enhanced models

- Electrical requirements

    United States: 90 V to 137 V, 50 Hz to 60 Hz
    European: 180 V to 259 V, 50 Hz to 60 Hz

- Air temperature

    System turned on: 60 to 90 degrees Fahrenheit
                      or 15.6 to 32.2 degrees Celsius

    System turned off: 50 to 110 degrees Fahrenheit
                       or 10 to 43 degrees Celsius

- Humidity

    System turned on: 8 to 80 percent RH
    System turned off: 20 to 80 percent RH

- BTU output of 1,229 BTU per hour

Here is the technical data for the standard AT keyboard:

- 84 keys

- Cable length of 9 feet

- Mode indicators

    Caps Lock
    Num Lock
    Scroll Lock

- Dimensions

    Length: 18.4 in (467.5 mm)
    Depth: 8.3 in (210 mm)
    Height: 1.5 in (38 mm)

- Weight of 6 lbs (2.7 kg)

The technical data for the Enhanced Keyboard follows:

- 101 Keys

- Cable length of 9 feet

- Removable keycaps

- Mode indicators

    Caps Lock
    Num Lock
    Scroll Lock

- Dimensions

    Length: 19.37 in (492 mm)
    Depth: 8.27 in (210 mm)
    Height: 2.28 in (58 mm), legs extended

- Weight of 5 lbs (2.25 kg)

AT Models and Features

Since the introduction of the AT, several models have become available. First, IBM announced two systems: a base model (068) and an enhanced model (099). The main difference between the two systems was the standard hard disk that came with the enhanced model. IBM has introduced two new AT systems since the first systems, each offering new features.

The first generation of AT systems run a 6 MHz system clock, which dictates the processor cycle time. The cycle time is the system's smallest interval of time and represents the speed at which operations occur. Every operation in the computer takes at least one or (usually) several cycles to complete. Therefore, if two computers are the same in every way except for the clock speed, the system with the faster clock rate executes the same operations in a shorter time proportional to the difference in clock speed. Cycle time and clock speed are two different ways of describing the same thing. Discussions of clock speed are significant when considering the AT because not all models have the same clock speed.

The first two AT models were the 068 (base) model, which came with 256K on the motherboard and a single 1.2M floppy disk drive, and the model 099 (enhanced), which had a 20M hard disk drive, a serial/parallel adapter, and 512K on the motherboard. These computers came with a motherboard that IBM designates as Type 1, which is larger than the later Type 2 board and uses an unusual memory layout. The memory is configured as 4 banks of 128K chips, for a total of 512K on the board. This configuration sounds reasonable until you realize that a 128K chip does not exist. IBM created this type of memory device by stacking a 64K chip on top of another and soldering the two together. My guess is that IBM had a great deal of 64K chips to use, and the AT was available to take them.

On October 2, 1985, IBM announced a new model of the AT, called the Personal Computer AT Model 239. This system includes all the standard features of the AT Model 099, but the system has a 30M hard disk rather than a 20M hard disk. A second optional 30M hard disk drive expands the Model 239's hard disk storage to 60M. The motherboard of this unit is a second-generation design that IBM calls Type 2. It is about 25 percent smaller than the Type 1 but uses the same mounting locations for physical compatibility. All important items, such as the slots and connectors, remain in the same locations as before. Other major improvements in this board concern the memory. Gone are the 128K memory chips in favor of 256K devices. Achieving the same 512K on the board, therefore, now only takes 2 banks of chips.

The AT Model 239 includes the following highlights:

- 512K of RAM (standard)
- Type 2 motherboard with 256K memory chips
- Serial/parallel adapter (standard)
- 30M hard disk (standard)
- New ROM BIOS (dated 06/10/85)

  ROM has support for 3 1/2-inch 720K floppy drives without using external driver programs

  ROM has support for 22 hard disk types, including the supplied 30M disk

  POST fixes clock rate to 6 MHz

The Type 2 motherboard offers a much improved design over the Type 1; the Type 2 motherboard has improved internal circuit timing and layout. The improvements in the motherboard indicated that the system would be pushed to higher speeds, which is exactly what happened with the next round of introductions.

In addition to the obvious physical differences, the Model 239 includes significantly different ROM software from the previous models. This new ROM allows for support of more types of disks and has a new POST that prevents alteration of the clock rate from the standard 6 MHz models. Because support for the 30M hard disk is built directly into the new ROM, IBM also sells a 30M hard disk upgrade kit, that includes the new ROM for the original AT systems. This $1,795 kit unfortunately represents the only legal way to obtain the newer ROM.

The 30M hard disk drive upgrade kit for the Personal Computer AT Models 068 and 099 includes all the features of the 30M hard disk drive announced for the AT Model 239. The upgrade kit also contains a new Basic Input/Output Subsystem (BIOS) essential to the operation of the AT. This new ROM BIOS has support for 22 drive types (compared with the original 15 in the earlier ATs), including the new 30M drive. To support the 30M hard disk drive, a new diagnostics floppy disk and an update to the guide to operations manual are shipped with this kit.

The 30M update kit includes the following:

- A 30M hard disk drive
- Two ROM BIOS modules
- A channel keeper bar (a bracket for the fixed disk)
- A data cable for the hard disk
- A diagnostics diskette
- An insert to the *AT Guide to Operations* manual

Many people were upset initially that IBM had "fixed the microprocessor clock" to 6 MHz in the new model, thereby disallowing any possible "hot rod" modifications. Many people realized that the clock crystal was socketed on all the AT models so that the crystal could be changed easily for a faster one. More importantly, the AT circuit design is modular, so changing the clock crystal does not have repercussions throughout the rest of the system, as is the case in the PC and PC XT. For the price of a new crystal (from $1 to $30) and the time needed to plug it in, someone could easily increase an AT's speed by 30 percent and sometimes more. The Model 239's new ROM disallows these changes. Because this ROM is now retrofit into the earlier models by IBM or through the 30M hard disk upgrade, you no longer can implement a simple speedup alteration.

Many observers believed that this change was to prevent the AT from being "too fast" and therefore competing with IBM's minicomputers. This belief was untrue. Actually, the earlier motherboard was intentionally run at 6 MHz because IBM did not believe that the ROM BIOS software and critical system timing was fully operational at a higher speed. Those who increased the speed of their early computers often received error messages from DOS due to timing problems. Many companies selling speedup kits offered software to help smooth over these problems, but IBM's official solution was to improve the ROM BIOS software and motherboard circuitry and to introduce a system running at a faster speed. For those of you who want increased speed no matter what model you have, several companies sell clock crystal replacements that are frequency synthesizers instead of a fixed type of crystal. These units can wait until the POST is finished and change in midstream to an increased operating speed.

On April 2, 1986, IBM introduced the Personal Computer AT Models 319 and 339. These two similar systems are basically an enhancement of the earlier Model 239. The main difference from the Model 239 is a faster clock crystal allowing 8 MHz operation. The Model 339 offers a new keyboard, called the Enhanced Keyboard, with 101 keys rather than the usual 84. Model 319 is the same as Model 339, but it includes the original keyboard.

Highlights of the Models 319 and 339 follow:

- Faster processor speed (8 MHz)

- Type 2 motherboard with 256K chips

- 512K of RAM (standard)

- Serial/parallel adapter

- 30M hard disk (standard)

- New ROM BIOS (dated 11/15/85)

  Support for 23 types of hard disks, including the supplied 30M disk

  Support for 3 1/2-inch drives at both 720K and 1.44M capacities

  POST fixes clock rate to 8 MHz

  Support for 101-key Enhanced Personal Computer Keyboard (keyboard standard on Model 339)

  Recappable keys

  Selectric typing section

  Dedicated numeric pad

  Dedicated cursor and screen controls

  12 function keys

  Indicator lights

  9-foot cable

The most significant physical difference in these new systems is the Enhanced Keyboard on the Model 339. This keyboard is similar to a 3270 keyboard and includes 101 keys. The Enhanced Keyboard could be called the IBM ''corporate'' keyboard because it is standard on all new desktop systems. The 84-key PC keyboard, is still available with a new 8 MHz model as the Model 319.

These new 8 MHz systems are available only in an enhanced configuration with a standard 30M hard drive. This configuration affects the aftermarket because IBM is essentially taking away sales of peripherals. The customer actually does quite well, however, because IBM has decided to become a competitor in the peripherals; the drives and other peripherals actually are priced more competitively. For those of you who want hard disk drives larger than IBM's 30M, you have to live with two drives or sell the standard 30M unit. The days of the diskless PC appear to be over!

ROM support for 3 1/2-inch disk drives at both 720K and 1.44M only exists in the Models 339 and 319. This configuration is important for those of you who want to add these types of floppy disk drives as internal units to allow for media interchange with the PS/2 series. Earlier AT systems still can use the 720K and 1.44M drives, but they may need software drivers loaded from disk to allow for complete support.

AT Costs

Here are the AT system unit part numbers and pricing information:

Description	Number	Price
AT system unit/keyboard, 6 MHz, 256K:		
one 1.2M floppy drive	5170068	$3,395
AT system unit/keyboard, 6 MHz, 512K, serial/parallel:		
one 1.2M floppy drive, one 20M hard disk	5170099	$4,895
one 1.2M floppy drive, one 30M hard disk	5170239	$5,295

Description	Number	Price
AT system unit/keyboard, 8 MHz, 512K, serial/parallel:		
one 1.2M floppy drive, one 30M hard disk	5170319	$3,595
AT system unit/Enhanced Keyboard, 8 MHz, 512K, serial/parallel:		
one 1.2M floppy drive, one 30M hard disk	5170339	$3,595

A list of the options and the Enhanced Keyboard accessories follow:

Description	Number	Price
20M fixed disk drive	6450205	$1,095
30M fixed disk	6450210	$1,795
30M fixed disk drive upgrade kit	6450468	$1,795
Double-sided diskette drive (AT)	6450207	$225
High-capacity (1.2M) diskette	6450206	$275
3 1/2-inch half-height 720K external drive (AT)	2683191	$395
Serial/parallel adapter	6450215	$150
80287 math coprocessor option	6450211	$375
Floor standing enclosure	6450218	$165

Description	Number	Price
Clear keycaps (60) with paper inserts	6341707	$50
Blank light keycaps	1351710	$25
Blank dark keycaps	1351728	$25
Paper inserts (300)	6341704	$30
Keycap removal tools (6)	1351717	$11

The IBM 3270 AT

On June 18, 1985, IBM announced the AT 3270. This computer is basically the same as the original 3270 PC but configured with an AT as the base rather than an XT. IBM enhanced this system over the standard 3270 PC. New software enhancements and adapter cards allow for greater use of the DOS memory space and can place much of the Control Program into the extended memory area beyond the 1M boundary. Much of this capability is due to a card from IBM called the XMA card. Because much of the Control Program can reside in the area above 1M, DOS can find more room for applications software. This configuration doesn't eliminate the incompatibilities found in the display hardware or keyboard, but this configuration at least makes the memory needed to run an application available.

The system contains the same basic adapters as the standard 3270 PC. This system differs, however, in the capability for the Control Program to reside in the memory space over 1M, which does not exist on a standard PC or XT. IBM made several changes in the Control Program for this system and in special memory adapters such as the XMA card. These changes enhanced the compatibility of this system over the original 3270 PC.

For more information on this system, refer to the section on the 3270 PC.

The IBM AT 370

The AT/370 is basically the same system as the XT 370 except for the use of an AT as the base unit. The same three custom processor boards that convert an XT also plug into an AT. This system is at least two to three times faster than the XT version. The custom processor boards are available as an upgrade for existing ATs as well. For a more complete description of this system, refer to the section on the XT 370.

The IBM XT Model 286

On September 9, 1986, IBM introduced a new AT type of system disguised under the premise that it was IBM's fastest, most powerful PC XT. This system is the XT Model 286 and features increased memory, an Intel 80286 microprocessor, and up to three internal drives. The XT Model 286 combines the cost-effectiveness, flexibility, and appearance of an XT with the high-speed high-performance technology of the Intel 80286 microprocessor. This model may look like an XT, but under the skin, it's all AT!

The IBM XT Model 286 can operate up to three times faster than earlier models of the XT in most applications and comes standard with 640K of memory. Various memory expansion options allow users to increase memory to 16M.

Standard features of this system include a half-height, 1.2M, 5 1/4-inch, double-sided floppy disk drive; a 20M hard disk drive; a serial/parallel adapter card; and the IBM Enhanced Keyboard. You also can select an optional internal second floppy disk drive from the following list:

- A half-height 3 1/2-inch 720K floppy drive
- A half-height 3 1/2-inch 1.44M floppy drive
- A half-height 5 1/4-inch 1.2M floppy drive
- A half-height 5 1/4-inch 360K floppy drive

The performance of the IBM XT Model 286 primarily stems from the AT motherboard design with 16-bit I/O slots and an Intel 80286 microprocessor running at 6 MHz. In addition to the microprocessor, clock speed is another factor of microprocessor performance. Depending on the model, IBM ATs have a clock speed of 6 or 8 MHz with 1 wait state. The XT Model 286 processes data at 6 MHz with 0 wait states. The elimination of a wait state improves performance by increasing processing speed for system memory access. Because of the 0 wait-state design, the XT Model 286 is actually faster than the original AT models that ran at 6 MHz. Based on actual tests, the XT Model 286 is about three times faster than an XT and up to 25 percent faster than the Personal Computer AT Model 239.

Because the XT Model 286 is really an AT type of system, it has a processor that supports (at least) the Intel real and protected modes. When operating in real address mode, the 80286 is 8088 compatible; on the XT Model 286, therefore, you can use most software that runs on the standard PC types of systems. In real address mode, the system can address up to 1M of RAM. Protected virtual mode provides a number of advanced features to facilitate multitasking operations. Virtual mode provides separation and protection of programs and data in multitasking environments. In protected mode, the 80286 can address up to 16M of real memory and 1 gigabyte of virtual memory per user. In this mode, the XT Model 286 can run advanced operating systems such as OS/2 and UNIX. At the time of its introduction, the XT Model 286 was the least expensive system from IBM capable of running a multitasking operating system.

The IBM XT Model 286 comes with 640K of RAM as standard. Memory options allow the system to grow to 15.5M, which is much higher than the 640K limit of other PC XTs. If you add a multitasking operating system or DOS and a program such as IBM TopView or DOS' VDISK RAM disk, you can take advantage of the larger memory capacities that the XT Model 286 provides.

A 20M hard disk drive is a standard feature of the XT Model 286. A 5 1/4-inch, 1.2M, high-capacity floppy disk drive also is standard. A similar floppy disk drive is standard on all models of the Personal Computer AT. Floppy disks formatted using a 1.2M floppy disk drive, therefore, can be read by an AT or an XT Model 286. In addition, the 1.2M floppy disk drive can read floppy disks formatted with PC family members that use a 320/360K floppy disk drive.

The XT Model 286 features the IBM Enhanced Keyboard with indicator lights. Although many IBM personal computers use the Enhanced Keyboard, the XT Model 286 is the first PC XT to feature keyboard indicator lights. The Caps Lock, Num Lock, and Scroll Lock lights remind users of the keyboard status, helping to prevent keyboard-entry errors.

The IBM XT Model 286 contains eight I/O slots, to accommodate peripheral device adapter cards and memory expansion options. Five of the slots support the advanced 16-bit cards or 8-bit cards; three support only 8-bit cards. Two of the three 8-bit slots support only short cards.

A fixed disk and floppy drive adapter card is a standard feature of the XT Model 286. This multifunction card takes only one 16-bit slot and supports up to four disk drives (two floppy disk drives and two hard disk drives).

The serial/parallel adapter, another standard feature, is a combination card that requires only one slot (either type) and provides a serial and a parallel port. The parallel portion of the adapter has the capacity to attach devices, such as a parallel printer, that accept 8 bits of parallel data. The serial portion is fully programmable and supports asynchronous communications from

50 baud to 9600 baud. The serial portion requires an optional serial adapter cable or a serial adapter connector. When one of these options is connected to the adapter, all the signals of a standard EIA RS-232C interface are available. You can use the serial port for interfacing a modem, a remote display terminal, a mouse, or some other serial device. The XT Model 286 supports up to two serial/parallel adapters.

A standard IBM XT Model 286 offers the following features:

- Intel 80286 processor at 6 MHz with 0 wait states
- 640K of motherboard memory
- 1.2M floppy drive
- 20M hard disk
- Five 16-bit and three 8-bit expansion slots
- Fixed disk/floppy disk drive adapter (occupies one 16-bit expansion slot)
- Serial/parallel adapter (occupies one 16-bit expansion slot)
- Enhanced Keyboard with indicator lights
- Time and date clock with battery backup
- BASIC language in ROM

XT Model 286 Specifications and Highlights

This following list covers the technical information for the XT Model 286's system unit:

- 640K of memory on the motherboard
- 6 MHz Intel 80286 microprocessor with 0 wait states
- Five 16-bit and three 8-bit expansion slots
- Time and date clock with battery backup
- One 1.2M 5 1/4-inch floppy drive (half-height)
- One 20M (85 millisecond average access) hard disk
- One fixed disk and floppy drive adapter (occupies one 16-bit expansion slot)

- One serial/parallel adapter (occupies one 16-bit expansion slot)

- Enhanced Keyboard with indicator lights

- BASIC language in ROM

- 157-watt universal power supply (autosensing for line frequency and voltage)

- Dimensions

  Length: 500 mm (19.6 in)
  Depth: 410 mm (16.1 in)
  Height: 142 mm (5.5 in)

- Weight of 12.7 kg (28 lbs)

- Electrical requirements

  United States: 90 V to 137 V, 57 Hz to 63 Hz
  European: 180 V to 265 V, 47 Hz to 53 Hz

- Ambient air temperature

  System turned on: 60 to 90 degrees Fahrenheit
                    or 15.6 to 32.2 degrees Celsius

  System turned off: 50 to 110 degrees Fahrenheit
                     or 10.0 to 43 degrees Celsius

- Humidity

  System turned on: 8 to 80 percent RH
  System turned off: 20 to 80 percent RH

- BTU output of 824 BTU per hour

- Noise level: Class 3 (office environment)

- FCC class: B

- Electrical current leakage:

  The electrical current leakage of the XT Model 286 averages 350 to 450 microamps for the 230-volt range and does not exceed 225 microamps for the 115-volt range. The IBM Personal Computer XT Model 286 is specifically designed to meet current leakage requirements established by the National Fire Protection Code NFPA76B for data processing use in hospital environments.

XT Model 286 Models and Features

The XT Model 286 processor is up to 2.5 times faster internally than the prior XT family and up to 25 percent faster than the AT Model 239, depending on specific applications. The XT Model 286 is compatible with most hardware and software currently supported by the IBM Personal Computer family.

A 20M fixed disk and a 1.2M 5 1/4-inch floppy disk drive are standard on the XT Model 286. One additional floppy disk drive may be internally installed as drive B.

You can add any type of floppy drive as a second half-height floppy drive. This includes both the high- and double-density versions of the 5 1/4- and 3 1/2-inch drives.

If you need to be able to read standard 5 1/4-inch data or program floppy disks created by the XT Model 286 on other PC systems, you may want to add a 5 1/4-inch 360K floppy disk drive, which provides full read/write compatibility with those systems. If this read/write compatibility is not important, you can add a second 1.2M high-capacity floppy disk drive.

You can add any of the 3 1/2-inch drives, including the 720K and 1.44M versions. But because the 1.44M does not have any read/write compatibility problems with the 720K drives, and the 1.44M drives always can operate in the 720K mode, I suggest adding only the 1.44M 3 1/2-inch drives rather than the 720K versions. The higher density drive is only a small extra cost compared with the double-density version. Most people do not know that full ROM BIOS support for these 1.44M drives is provided in the XT Model 286.

All internal floppy disk drives use the fixed disk and floppy disk drive adapter, the standard on the XT Model 286.

For flexibility, you can opt for an external floppy disk drive. The external 3 1/2-inch floppy disk drive provides compatibility with systems with these drives.

XT Model 286 Costs

Here is a list of the XT Model 286 system unit part numbers and pricing information:

Description	Number	Price
XT Model 286 system unit, 6 MHz, 0 wait state, 640K, serial/parallel:		
one 1.2M floppy drive, one 20M hard disk	5162286	$2,495
Optional accessories:		
5 1/4-inch half-height double-sided diskette drive	6450325	$225
3 1/2-inch half-height 720K internal drive	6450258	$170
3 1/2-inch half-height 720K external drive	2683190	$395
80287 math coprocessor option	6450211	$375

Here are the Enhanced Keyboard accessories:

Description	Number	Price
Clear keycaps (60) with paper inserts	6341707	$50
Blank light keycaps	1351710	$25
Blank dark keycaps	1351728	$25
Paper inserts (300)	6341704	$30
Keycap removal tools (6)	1351717	$11

Chapter Summary

In this chapter, you examined all the systems that make up the original line of IBM Personal Computers. These systems still are used, and probably will be for years, so the information in this chapter should be useful as a reference tool.

You examined what makes up all the versions or models of each system, as well as the technical details and specifications of each. Each system unit's main components also were listed.

You were given an explanation of each system's various submodels, which should help you better understand the differences among systems that may look the same on the outside but differ internally.

Pricing information also was listed. The prices really are listed for historical and reference purposes, because IBM no longer offers any of these systems.

In the next chapter, you find the same type of analysis for the PS/2 family of systems from IBM.

4

IBM Personal System/2 Family Hardware

This chapter identifies and describes each of the IBM Personal System/2 system units and standard features. First, this chapter explains the major differences between the PC and the PS/2 systems. You will learn why the PS/2 is so similar to, yet so different from, the classic PC line.

This chapter then discusses each of the PS/2 primary models. These systems include the PS/2 Models 25, 30, and 30 286, which are based closely on the original Personal Computer line. These original systems are now sometimes called Industry Standard Architecture (ISA) systems, and they include the standard ISA type of 8-bit and 16-bit I/O expansion slots.

This chapter also examines the PS/2 Models 50, 60, 70, and 80, as well as all of their respective submodels. These systems incorporate the newer Micro Channel Architecture (MCA) slot design, which is dramatically different from the original ISA design.

Differences between the PS/2 and PC Systems

Besides the obvious physical differences between the PS/2 systems and the earlier "classic" (ISA) line of systems, the two types really are quite similar. As a matter of fact, for troubleshooting and repair, you can consider the PS/2 as simply another type of PC-compatible system. All the troubleshooting skills used on the earlier systems apply to the PS/2. To be sure, some repairs are conducted differently. For example, each of the PS/2 motherboards includes a built-in floppy disk controller. If you determine that this controller is defective (using the same troubleshooting techniques as for the earlier systems), then you must replace the entire motherboard. In contrast, with the PC systems you simply replace the floppy controller card, a much less costly operation.

After working on a PS/2 system for some time, a repair technician will discover several basic facts, both positive and negative, about the systems:

- They are much more reliable than the earlier types of systems, for several reasons. The PS/2 systems are mostly robotically assembled, eliminating most human error during assembly. Also, many of the models have no cables of any type, which eliminates one of the biggest problem areas for repairs. In addition, the systems are much better shielded than the earlier systems, which prevents them from receiving and sending stray signals.

- The systems have switchless installation, a feature that can eliminate many service calls due to operator installation errors.

- The systems can be taken apart and reassembled with either no tools or only a few tools for special operations. Stripping down a PS/2 system to the motherboard usually takes less than one minute.

- Because the motherboard includes so many features, it is likely to be replaced more often than in the earlier systems.

- Parts are more expensive than for the earlier systems, and items such as the motherboards and memory modules can be much more expensive. However, because of greatly reduced frequency of repair and the decreased labor required for each repair, maintaining a given number of PS/2 systems costs about half as much as maintaining earlier systems.

Three main areas point out the most important differences between the PS/2 and the PC systems. The following sections explain these areas.

Design and Construction

The design and construction of the typical PS/2 systems are fascinating—you can bet that they weren't designed in a day. The systems were designed with automated assembly in mind. Parts and components are modular, and you can remove and reinstall most of them without using any tools.

The no-tool disassembly concept carries over to the floppy and hard disk drives as well. You can remove the floppy disk drive simply by grabbing the front of the drive while bending a plastic tab and pulling the drive from the system unit. To replace the drive, simply slide it back into the unit until the drive snaps into place. You will amaze anyone unfamiliar with these systems when you appear on the scene, open the system, remove a drive, replace it with a new unit, and close the system, all within 30 seconds. Most people who are used to working on other types of systems, or who have never seen the inside of a PS/2, are usually quite impressed.

The small amount of labor required to service PS/2 systems will turn around the repair and service industry. With this modular construction, labor will become less expensive than parts for repair costs. Parts pricing and availability will take on an entirely new meaning when you service a PS/2.

However, the availability and price of parts can be a problem. A PS/2 system simply doesn't have very many parts; the motherboard contains many items formerly contained on expansion adapter cards. Furthermore, many of the disk drives now have integrated or built-in controllers, and items such as logic boards, which attach to the drives, are unavailable separately. This arrangement makes the systems much easier to repair, but you may end up replacing the motherboard more often than in earlier systems, where in many cases simply replacing an inexpensive adapter could solve a problem. In addition, because the custom chips are unavailable separately, the motherboards in these systems cannot be repaired. Unlike motherboards in earlier systems, the entire motherboards must be replaced (or exchanged) instead, and IBM is the only source of new or exchange motherboards.

Another design feature of the PS/2 is that several of the systems contain no cables whatsoever, which is amazing when you think of the earlier systems with their mazes of cables for carrying power and data. Eliminating cables makes items easier to install and also eliminates perhaps the largest single source of errors and problems: many of the PS/2s have no cables to mess up. The PS/2 systems are also much better shielded against stray signals because they have no (or fewer) ribbon cables, which make great antennas.

Video

The video subsystem of PS/2s differs greatly from those previously available for the standard PCs. The original systems had either a Monochrome Display Adapter (MDA), Color Graphics Adapter (CGA), or Enhanced Graphics Adapter (EGA) available as a plug-in board. The PS/2 Models 25 and 30 have a built-in video adapter on the motherboard, called the Multi-Color Graphics Array (MCGA). PS/2 Models 50 and up contain a built-in video subsystem called the Video Graphics Array (VGA), which is the higher-end system. The MCGA is a subset of the VGA and lacks color capability in the highest-resolution mode.

The VGA basically supports all video modes present in the earlier MDA, CGA, and EGA, as well as some newer VGA-specific modes. This downward compatibility is almost 100 percent, which means that only rare programs will not run on a VGA-equipped system. However, programs not written specifically for the VGA cannot take advantage of the VGA's extra resolution and color capability.

Because the VGA supersedes the EGA and all other earlier standards, IBM has stopped producing all the earlier video adapters, including the EGA. IBM now sells a VGA on a card for the earlier PC systems. This board, called the IBM PS/2 Display Adapter, plugs into an 8-bit slot in any of the earlier IBM or compatible systems. The aftermarket has already cloned this board, and many third-party vendors now have versions available. Most third-party vendors also have discontinued the EGA boards in favor of the VGA adapters.

In contrast to all the earlier graphics adapters, the VGA has analog output and requires a display that can accept this signal. The earlier graphics adapters use a digital signal, and the monitors were designed to accept this signal. Therefore, add a new monitor to your shopping list if you decide to upgrade your system to a VGA. A few monitors, such as the NEC MultiSync or the SONY Multiscan, can accept both digital and analog signals. These monitors are quite good, offering flexibility not found in IBM's monitors. However, they can be expensive.

The big push to analog displays comes for two main reasons: color and money. That is, many colors become available without a big jump in cost. The VGA system is designed to display up to 262,144 colors, which would require a digital interface design with at least 18 lines to transmit all this color information to the monitor. Using an interface with 18 digital driver circuits on the video card, running through a thick cable containing at least 18 shielded wires, to a monitor with 18 digital receiver circuits, would cost thousands of dollars. A much simpler and less costly approach is to convert the digital color information to analog information for transmission and use by the display. This approach reduces the amount of circuitry required, and the cable can be much smaller as well. The analog transmission scheme can send the same color information through many fewer wires and circuits.

Micro Channel Architecture Slots

Perhaps the most important difference between the earlier systems and the new PS/2 systems is the I/O adapter board interface bus, or slots. The PS/2 Models 50 and higher incorporate a new bus interface called the Micro Channel Architecture (MCA). The MCA is basically a new slot design that is incompatible with the PC or AT slot system but offers improvements in many areas. The first immediate consequence of this bus is that any design adapters that plug into the PC or AT 8-bit or 8/16-bit slots do not plug into the MCA. The MCA is both physically and electrically different from the earlier bus.

Although many heated discussions are raging on the performance and capabilities of the MCA, I want to avoid those debates and instead focus on some facts about the MCA that will affect the upgrade and repair of any systems so equipped. I will explain how some of the MCA's design parameters have shaped it, and what these design features will do for users.

The MCA was designed to meet the strict FCC regulations for Class B certification. These requirements are much stricter than for Class A, which covers allowable emissions in a location zoned as commercial or industrial. Class B requirements are for systems sold in residential environments and are designed to eliminate electrical interference with devices such as TV and radios. Meeting Class B requirements should give these systems a distinct advantage as clock rates (speeds) go ever higher. People in the communications and radio industry know that as the frequency of an oscillator increases, so does the problem of noise emissions. The MCA has many ground connections for shielding. As a matter of fact, there is a ground pin no further than 1/10 of an inch from any signal line in the slot.

The MCA is designed to eliminate the bane of adapter board installers: setting jumpers and switches to configure the adapters. In surveys, IBM found that as many as 60 percent of all technician service calls were "no problem" calls. They instead were switch and jumper setting sessions. And it's no wonder that these items can be a problem, considering the number of switches and jumpers on some of the memory/multifunction boards today. Setting them correctly can be terribly difficult, and nearly impossible without the board's original manual. Also, each manufacturer's board is different. Thus, if you buy new boards for several computers, you may save money if you buy whatever board is on sale that week; however, you may end up with many different adapter boards, each with a usually hard-to-read manual and a bunch of jumpers and switches to set.

IBM's answer to this problem is called Programmable Option Selection (POS), a built-in feature on all MCA equipped systems. The POS uses a special file called an Adapter Definition File (with the file extension ADF), which comes with each adapter you purchase. This file contains all the possible setting attributes for that board and is read in by the system startup disk or reference disk. The reference disk contains a special configuration routine that reads all the files and decides on nonconflicting settings for each board. The operator may also need to select particular settings when two boards are found to conflict. Once set, the settings are stored in CMOS (battery-saved memory) and are available each time the system is started. The settings also can be stored on disk for backup, in case of a battery failure or to restore a configuration to several systems quickly. The POS feature on these systems saves much labor and time, and is already beginning to affect the upgrade and repair industry. Many manufacturers have established switchless setups for their adapters to make them more "PS/2-like."

Finally, the MCA-equipped systems should be more reliable than the earlier bus interfaces, for several reasons. The rest of this section discusses the reliability of the MCA system, particularly timing considerations.

One reason the MCA-equipped systems should be more reliable than the earlier bus interfaces is that the MCA is well shielded.

Therefore, such systems are more immune to noise from radio transmissions or any electrical noise.

This reason may be minor compared with the new timing of the MCA bus. The MCA is *asynchronous*: communication between adapters and the system board doesn't depend on timing. This feature solves a problem that had become relatively common in earlier bus systems. Have you ever had problems getting a system to work, only to find that simply moving a board to a different slot or switching two boards allows the system to operate normally? (By the way, I don't think that any IBM service manual suggests that solution officially.) The problem here is one of timing. Each slot is supposed to carry the same signals as all the other slots, but that doesn't exactly happen. Effects on the bus, such as capacitance and signal propagation delays, can cause timing windows to ''appear'' differently in different slots, which affects the board's functioning in that slot. The MCA should do away with this type of problem completely. The MCA is designed so that a board can tell it to ''wait''—in effect, slowing the system by adding wait states until the board is ready.

Another timing-related problem is known to those who use some of the ''turbo'' compatible systems. In these ''hyper-systems,'' some boards cannot keep up with the system speed and refuse to work at all. Some of these boards can be made to work by slowing down the system in some way, either by adding wait states to operations or by reducing the speed of the system clock. But then you don't really have all the performance that is available. Many communications, networking, and memory adapters can be speed-limiting in this way. On the MCA, however, the bus cycles at a fixed constant speed among all the systems, no matter what the actual microprocessor clock speed. And the MCA will always wait on a board, inserting wait states until it is ready to proceed. Although this process may slow the system somewhat, the board and system will work. Therefore, the same adapter will function in the 10 MHz Model 50 or the 25 MHz Model 70, regardless of their different clock speeds.

Other MCA design parameters are for performance improvements, but these are more difficult to see. Most benchmarks have not proven any performance advantage to MCA systems over those with the standard ISA slots. However, IBM recently demonstrated the coprocessing capabilities of the MCA, and it did show excellent performance. Taking full advantage of the MCA's performance capabilities will require new adapter designs. For now, the MCA brings you increased reliability and easy setup and use. The improvements incorporated into this bus make it the standard for the future, but for now many more systems in use have the earlier bus design and the ISA type of adapter cards.

Fortunately, most of the troubleshooting techniques and methods apply equally to both the MCA and the earlier bus systems. The MCA system should suffer fewer failures, and it certainly is much easier to set up and install. But the real question is, how much are customers willing to pay for these features? Time will tell.

System Unit Features by Model

You can use the following sections in this chapter as a reference to all the PS/2 systems that IBM has produced so far. The sections include information indicating what makes up each system, as well as the technical details and specifications of each system.

The standard parts included with each system unit include

- The motherboard, which contains the CPU (Central Processing Unit, or microprocessor) and other primary computer circuitry.
- A case with internal power supply
- A keyboard
- Certain standard adapters or plug-in cards
- Usually, some form of disk drive

Each of these components is examined, and lists of technical data and specifications for each component and system unit are given.

An explanation of each of the various submodels of each system is given, with details on the differences and features of each model. These explanations include many details on changes from model to model and version to version for each system.

Also included for reference is the price for each system and option. Note that these prices are for comparison and reference only. The prices listed are the IBM recommended retail prices and may not reflect actual purchase prices in your area.

PS/2 Model 25

On August 11, 1987, IBM introduced the PS/2 Model 25, the lowest priced PS/2 family member. The Model 25 (IBM 8525) is a general-purpose system that incorporates the PC-style 8-bit slot architecture, allowing this system to accept most current adapters. The Model 25 uses the Intel 8086 processor and operates at 8 megahertz (MHz) with 0 wait states to read-only memory (ROM). This system is 40 percent smaller and more than twice as fast as the IBM Personal Computer.

The Model 25's display is integrated into the system unit, making this system appear similar to the Apple Macintosh. Two keyboards are available with the Model 25: an IBM Space-Saving Keyboard or the IBM Enhanced Keyboard, which has a numeric keypad. The Model 25 is available in both monochrome and color versions. All models come with one 3 1/2-inch (720K) floppy disk drive, 512K of random-access memory (RAM), a keyboard, and a 12-inch analog display. A second 3 1/2-inch floppy disk drive, a 20M hard disk, and an additional 128K of RAM memory are available.

The Model 25 offers the same text and graphics capabilities as the IBM PS/2 Model 30. The built-in Multi-Color Graphics Array (MCGA) can display up to 256 colors on its color monitor (from a palette of more than 256,000 colors) or 64 shades of gray on its monochrome monitor.

Two 8-bit expansion slots allow you to attach many existing personal computer feature cards. A 12-inch analog display (color or monochrome), a display adapter, an RS-232C serial adapter, a parallel adapter, and a floppy disk drive adapter are standard, increasing the base function and reducing the price.

Some PC adapters may not work in the Model 25 for various reasons. Because of the integrated functions on the motherboard of the Model 25, certain options (such as PC types of memory upgrades, floppy controllers, and graphics adapters) may conflict with what is already present but not supported. Also, because of physical constraints, adapter cards thicker than 0.8 inch may not work. The integrated MCGA does not support modes that support the 5151 Monochrome Display. The Model 25 has analog graphics output and does not support digital display devices.

Each of the models of the PS/2 Model 25 includes the following features:

- Approximately twice the speed of the IBM PC or XT

- One full-size and one 8-inch slot

- Multi-Color Graphics Array (MCGA) graphics adapter

  Displays 256 colors from 262,144 possible colors
  Displays 64 shades of gray

- 512K of RAM standard, expandable to 640K on the motherboard

- Floppy disk controller for up to two 3 1/2-inch 720K drives

- 12-inch analog display (color or monochrome)

- IBM Space-Saving Keyboard or Enhanced Keyboard

- Serial port, parallel port, mouse port, and keyboard port

- Audio earphone connector

- Socket for a math coprocessor

- Advanced technology that eliminates customer setup switches

Specifications and Highlights

The Model 25 system unit technical data is as follows:

- Dimensions

Viewing area:	207 mm by 155 mm (8.15 in by 6.1 in)
Height (top to bottom):	382 mm (15 in)
Width (side to side):	320 mm (12.6 in)
Width (footprint):	240 mm (9.5 in)
Depth (front to back):	375 mm (14.7 in)

- Weight

8525-001/G01:	14.1 kg (31 lbs)
8525-004/G04:	16.3 kg (36 lbs)

- Space-Saving Keyboard

Dimensions:	407 mm by 190 mm (16 in by 7.5 in)
Weight:	1.9 kg (4.2 lbs)

- Enhanced Keyboard

  Dimensions: 493 mm by 210 mm (19.4 in by 8.3 in)
  Weight: 2.3 kg (5 lbs)

- Air temperature with system turned on: 60 to 90 degrees Fahrenheit; 15.6 to 32.2 Celsius

- Humidity of 8 to 80 percent RH (Relative Humidity)

- Altitude of 0 to 2,133 m (0 to 7,000 ft)

- FCC Class B certification

- Acoustic levels

  Idle at one meter: 43 db average, 45 db maximum

  Operating at one meter: 44 db average, 46 db maximum

  Operating at   48 db average, 51 db
  operator position (0.6 m):   maximum

- Universal power supply of 90 to 137 VAC or 180 to 259 VAC (switch selected), 50 Hz to 60 Hz

The specifications for the PS/2 Model 25 20M Fixed Disk Drive (part number 78X8958) are as follows:

Specification	*Description*
Drive Specifications	
Formatted capacity	20M
Disk platters	2
Cylinders	610
Sectors/Track	17
Data bytes/sector	512
Encoding method	MFM
Data transfer rate	5.0 mbps (million bits per second)
Average seek time	80 ms
Physical Specifications	
Width	101.6 mm (4.00 in)
Depth	167.8 mm (6.60 in)
Height	41.3 mm (1.63 in)
Weight	0.80 kg (1.75 lbs)

The specifications for the PS/2 Model 25 20M Fixed Disk Drive with Adapter (part number 27F4130) are as follows:

Drive Specifications

Specification	Description
Formatted capacity	20M
Disk platters	2
Cylinders	400
Sectors/Track	26
Data bytes/sector	512
Encoding method	RLL
Data transfer rate	7.5 mbps
Average seek time	38 ms

Physical Specifications

Width	102.1 mm (4.02 in)
Depth	146.6 mm (5.77 in)
Height	41.4 mm (1.63 in)
Weight	0.73 kg (1.6 lbs)

Models and Features

IBM has expanded the usefulness of the Model 25 in two main ways: by offering a version for use on a Local Area Network (LAN), and by providing hard disks for data and program storage.

On June 2, 1988, IBM introduced a specially configured version of the Model 25 called the Model 25 LAN Station, or LS. This system is basically a standard Model 25 preconfigured with the IBM Token Ring Network PC Adapter for use in a LAN. The Model 25 LS is available in both monochrome (8525-L01) and color (8525-L04) versions. The Models L01 and L04 include the Enhanced Keyboard and 640K of RAM. Because the Token Ring card uses the only available full-length expansion slot, the LS models have only a single 8-inch expansion slot remaining in the system unit for other adapter boards. Both models come with one 3 1/2-inch (720K) floppy disk drive. A second 720K floppy disk drive or a 20M hard disk drive is available.

LAN software for operating on a network is not supplied with this system and must be purchased separately. Because many purchasers use LAN software from a third party such as Novell or 3Com, the fact that the software support is "unbundled" is actually beneficial. The purchaser then can choose which software to use.

For increased storage, IBM makes available two 20M hard disk drives for the Model 25. One 20M drive can be installed on a Model 25. On models with two floppy disk drives, the 20M hard disk replaces the second floppy disk drive. Both hard disk drives feature the following:

- 20M of storage

- 3 1/2-inch hard disk technology

- A keylocked bezel, which disables the keyboard

The IBM PS/2 Model 25 20M Fixed Disk Drive (78X8958) has a built-in controller that plugs into a special port on the motherboard and does not take up an expansion slot. This hard disk drive is essentially the same one that is used in the Model 30. Because of the built-in controller, this unit conserves a precious slot in the Model 25. The Model 25 has only two slots, so conserving one of them is an important advantage.

The other unit, the 20M Fixed Disk Drive with Adapter (27F4130), has a separate controller that occupies the 8-inch expansion slot. The controller uses RLL encoding and achieves higher data transmission speeds than the drive with the built-in controller. Both drives use stepper motor head actuator mechanisms. However, the second drive has a higher-speed stepper motor and also has a balanced actuator that parks the heads automatically when the power is turned off. This unit basically performs faster than the other one and provides automatic head parking as a feature. However, this drive requires a separate controller, which takes up one of the only two slots available in the Model 25. Whether the improved performance and automatic head parking are worth the loss of a slot is up to you.

Costs

The part numbers and pricing information for the system units follows:

Description	Number	Price
Mod 25 Mono, 512K, Space-Saving Kbd	8525001	$1,350
Mod 25 Mono, 512K, Enh Kbd	8525G01	$1,395
Mod 25 Color, 512K, Space-Saving Kbd	8525004	$1,695
Mod 25 Color, 512K, Enh Kbd	8525G04	$1,740
Mod 25 LS Mono, 640K, Enh Kbd, T Ring Adapter	8525L01	$2,139
Mod 25 LS Color, 640K, Enh Kbd, T Ring Adapter	8525L04	$2,484

Here is part number and pricing information for optional accessories:

Description	Number	Price
128K Memory Expansion Kit	N/A	$49
Optional 3 1/2-inch Diskette Drive	N/A	$170
Data Migration Facility	1501224	$33
20M, 3 1/2-inch Fixed Disk	78X8958	$795
20M, 3 1/2-inch Fixed Disk/Adapter	27F4130	$795

PS/2 Model 30

Announced on April 2, 1987, the IBM PS/2 Model 30 (IBM 8530) is a general-purpose system designed to offer more features and performance, especially in display graphics, than the IBM PC and XT—and at lower prices. This system includes as standard many features built into the system board, including a graphics adapter, a parallel port, a serial port, a clock calendar, 640K of RAM, and a mouse port. The Model 30 also uses many existing PC adapter cards for further expansion due to the industry standard 8-bit slot architecture.

The system is based on an 8086 microprocessor, running at 8 MHz, with 0 wait states. Performance is further enhanced through use of a 16-bit-wide data path to the motherboard memory. The result is an internal processing speed nearly comparable to a 6 MHz AT and more than twice as fast as the 8088-based PC or XT.

Major features of the Model 30 include the following:

- Many functions are integrated on the motherboard, including disk controllers, graphics, and ports
- Standard MCGA graphic displays up to 256 colors or 64 shades of gray
- Approximately twice the performance speed of 8088-based PC or XT systems
- Smaller design, with reduced power requirements
- Worldwide power supply
- Switchless installation and configuration
- 640K random-access memory (RAM)
- 16-bit access to motherboard memory
- Integrated floppy disk controller for two 720K drives
- Serial port, parallel port, mouse port, and keyboard port
- IBM Enhanced Keyboard
- Time-of-day clock with extended-life battery
- Socket for a math coprocessor
- Three expansion slots to accommodate PC or XT 8-bit adapter cards

Specifications and Highlights

The following list gives the technical specifications of the Model 30:

- Intel 8086 microprocessor operating at 8 MHz clock speed

  0 wait states
  16-bit-wide data path to motherboard memory

- 640K of RAM

- 64K read-only memory (ROM)

    Automatic POST (power-on self test) routines
    BASIC language interpreter
    IBM PC- and XT-compatible BIOS (CBIOS)

- Built-in floppy disk controller for two 720K drives

- Two disk drives available

    3 1/2-inch 720K floppy disk drives

      Two included in Model 30-002
      One included in Model 30-021

    3 1/2-inch 20M hard disk and integrated controller

      One included in Model 30-021
      80 ms average access time
      180 ms maximum access time
      512-byte-by-17-sector format
      20.8M formatted capacity

- Serial port (COM1:)

    RS-232 compatible
    25-pin, D-shell connector

- Parallel port (LPT1:)

    Centronics DIO capability
    Equivalent to printer adapter
    25-pin, D-shell connector

- Keyboard port

- Enhanced Keyboard

- Mouse port

- Integrated MCGA display adapter

    64K multiport RAM for displays
    CGA compatible (31.5 KHz double scanned)
    New modes: (31.5 KHz)

      40 by 25 by 16 colors for text (8-by-16-character box)
      80 by 25 by 16 colors for text (8-by-16-character box)
      320 by 200 by 256 colors—all points addressable
      640 by 480 by 2 colors—all points addressable

Palette of 262,144 colors
Analog drive, subminiature 15-pin, D-shell connector
70 Hz refresh rate in all but 640 by 480 mode
Not compatible with digital monitors
Loadable character font capability (512 characters)
Color summing to 64 shades of gray for monochrome
display

- Power supply of 70 watts, with internal voltage sensing for worldwide use

Low range:	100 to 125 VAC
High range:	200 to 240 VAC
Frequency:	50 to 60 Hz

- Sound

  PC-equivalent single-sound controller
  Sound transducer

- PC or XT type of 8-bit interface bus for adapters with three expansion slots available

- Time-of-day clock with extended-life lithium battery

- Dimensions

Size:	406 mm by 397 by 102 mm (16 in by 15.6 in by 4 in)
Weight:	Approximately 8 kg (17.5 lbs) (Model 30-002)

- Operating Environment

Air temperature:	60 to 90 degrees Fahrenheit or 15 to 32 degrees Celsius
Humidity:	8 to 80 percent RH
Altitude:	0 to 2,133 m (0 to 7,000 ft)

- FCC Class B certification

- Acoustic levels

Idle average at one meter:	32.7 db
Operating average at one meter:	34.6 db
Operating average at operator position (0.6 m):	37.5 db

- Security features

  Through holes for securing system

  Electromechanical lock on Model 30-021 (electronically locks keyboard and mouse, mechanically locks cover)

Models and Features

The Model 30 is available in two versions: 30-002, with two 3 1/2-inch (720K) floppy disk drives, and 30-021, with a 20M hard disk drive and a single floppy disk drive. All models have 640K RAM as a standard feature.

Multi-Color Graphics Array (MCGA), the graphics adapter function that is integrated into the motherboard, supports all existing Color Graphics Adapter (CGA) modes when an analog PS/2 display is attached. The earlier digital displays are incompatible. In addition to providing existing CGA mode support, four new expanded modes are included in the MCGA. These four modes are a subset of the new VGA processor on Models 50 and higher:

    640 by 480 by 2 colors—all points addressable
    320 by 200 by 256 colors—all points addressable
    40 by 25 by 16 colors for text (8-by-16-character box)
    80 by 25 by 16 colors for text (8-by-16-character box)

The Integrated Graphics Adapter automatically switches from color to 64 shades of gray when connected to a monochrome analog display. This feature allows those who prefer a monochrome display to execute color-based applications without compatibility problems or troublesome software reconfiguration.

Costs

The part numbers and pricing for the system units are as follows:

Description	Number	Price
Model 30, 2 720K Drives	8530002	$1,695
Model 30, 1 720K Drive, 20M Fixed Disk	8530021	$2,295

The part numbers and pricing for optional accessories are as follows:

Description	Number	Price
8 MHz 8087 Math Coprocessor	1501217	$310
Data Migration Facility	1501224	$33

PS/2 Model 30 286

On September 13, 1988, IBM introduced the IBM PS/2 Model 30 286 (8530-E21). Because this is the first PS/2 system with the full 16-bit ISA slot design found in the original AT and XT 286 systems, some said that the introduction of the Model 30 286 was the reintroduction of the AT. As far as the slot design goes, this statement is true. But don't think for a minute that this system will decrease the significance of MCA. In the eyes of IBM, this model is simply an upgraded Model 30; the company is not going "back" to the AT as the main platform for future systems. The MCA-equipped PS/2 systems are still (and will be for some time) IBM's primary platform.

The PS/2 Model 30 286 is basically a new 80286 version of the Model 30. This system shares only the shape and form of the original Model 30; the motherboard and circuitry are new. The original Model 30 is classified as a PC type of system, whereas the Model 30 286 is an AT type of system. The Model 30 286 has processor performance equal to the Model 50 and includes a 1.44M floppy disk drive and VGA graphics. The Model 30 286 uses the Intel 80286 processor and operates at 10 MHz with 1 wait state to ROM. In addition to accepting most IBM PC and XT adapter cards, the Model 30 286 also accepts most AT adapter cards. You can think of this system as equal to a Model 50, except that it uses ISA slots rather than MCA slots.

The PS/2 Model 30 286 includes the following standard features:

- Greatly improved performance over the XT, the AT, and 8086-based versions of the Model 25 and Model 30

- 10 MHz 80286 16-bit microprocessor, 1 wait state

- Optional 80287 coprocessor

- 16-bit ISA bus for adapters

- Three full-sized slots

- 512K random-access memory (RAM) standard

- Memory expansion to 4M on the system board

- 1.44M, 3 1/2-inch floppy disk drive

- Universal, automatic voltage-sensing power supply

- Keyboard port, serial/asynchronous port, parallel port, mouse port, and Video Graphics Array (VGA) port

- IBM Enhanced Keyboard

- Switchless installation and configuration

Specifications and Highlights

The following list outlines the Model 30 286 technical information:

- Intel 80286 microprocessor operating at 10 MHz

    1 wait state
    16-bit-wide data path to memory

- Random-access memory (RAM)

    512K standard, but can address a maximum of 16M of memory

    Expandable on the motherboard to 1M using the 0.5M Memory Module Kit (30F5348)

    Expandable on the motherboard to 2M or 4M by removing the 0.5M memory modules and installing one or two 2.0M Memory Module Kits (30F5360)

- 128K read-only memory (ROM)

    Automatic POST routines
    BASIC language interpreter
    IBM PC- and XT-compatible BIOS (CBIOS)
    Advanced protected-mode BIOS (ABIOS)

- Built-in floppy disk controller for two 1.44M drives

- Two disk drives available

    3 1/2-inch 1.44M floppy disk drive

    One included in each model
    Two maximum

    3 1/2-inch 20M hard disk

- Serial port (COM1:)

    RS-232 compatible
    25-pin, D-shell connector

- Parallel port (LPT1:)

    Centronics Digital Input/Output (DIO) capability
    Equivalent to printer adapter
    25-pin, D-shell connector

- Keyboard port

- IBM Enhanced Keyboard

- Mouse port

- Integrated VGA display adapter

    CGA compatible (31.5 KHz double scanned)
    New modes: (31.5 KHz)

    40 by 25 by 16 colors for text (9-by-16-character box)
    80 by 25 by 16 colors for text (9-by-16-character box)
    320 by 200 by 256 colors—all points addressable
    640 by 480 by 16 colors—all points addressable

    Palette of 262,144 colors
    Analog drive, subminiature 15-pin, D-shell connector
    70 Hz refresh rate in all but 640 by 480 mode
    Not compatible with digital monitors
    Loadable character font capability (512 characters)
    Color summing to 64 shades of gray for monochrome
        display

- Power supply of 90 watts, with internal voltage sensing for
  universal worldwide use (switch selected)

    Low range: 90 to 137 VAC
    High range: 180 to 265 VAC
    Frequency: 50 to 60 Hz

- Sound

    PC equivalent single sound controller
    Sound transducer

- Industry Standard Architecture (ISA) 16-bit I/O bus (three
  expansion slots available)

- Time-of-day clock with extended-life lithium battery

The physical specifications of the PS/2 Model 30 286 are as follows:

- Dimensions

    Width: 406 mm (16.00 in)
    Depth: 397 mm (15.60 in)
    Height: 102 mm (4.00 in)

- Weight

    8530-E21:   8.6 kg (19 lbs)
    8530-E01:   7.8 kg (17.2 lbs)

- Electrical requirements

    United States: 90 to 137 VAC, 50 to 60 Hz
    European: 180 to 265 VAC, 50 to 60 Hz

- Air temperature

    System turned on: 60 to 90 degrees Fahrenheit
                      or 16 to 32.2 degrees Celsius

    System turned off: 50 to 100 degrees Fahrenheit
                       or 10 to 43 degrees Celsius

- Humidity

    System turned on: 8 to 80 percent RH
    System turned off: 20 to 80 percent RH

- BTU (British Thermal Unit) output of 438 BTU per hour

- FCC Class B certification

The Model 30 286 includes a 1.44M, 3 1/2-inch floppy disk drive. The
specifications for this drive are listed here:

- Dimensions

  Height: 41 mm (1.6 in)
  Width: 102 mm (4.0 in)
  Depth: 150 mm (5.9 in)
  Weight: 0.68 kg (1.5 lbs)

- Capacity of 1.44M (2M unformatted) in high-density mode

- Track density of 135 tracks per inch

- 80 tracks

- Two heads

- Transfer rate of 500,000 bps (MFM) in high-density mode

- Access time

  Track to track: 6 ms
  Seek settle time: 15 ms
  Motor start time: 500 ms (maximum)
  Disk speed: 300 rpm, plus or minus 1.5 percent

The IBM PS/2 20M Fixed Disk Drive (27F4969), which is included with the 30-E21 and is optional for the 30-E01, has the following specifications:

Cylinders:	610
Number of heads:	4
Bytes per sector:	512
Sectors per track:	17
Data transfer rate:	5.0 mbps (million bits per second)
Average access time:	80 ms

Models and Features

Two models are available. The IBM PS/2 Model 30 286 (8530-E01) is a single floppy disk drive version of the Model 30 286 (without a hard disk drive). An optional 3 1/2-inch 20M hard disk drive (27F4969) is available for this model. The second model (8530-E21) includes the 20M drive as a standard feature. Otherwise, the models are identical.

The IBM PS/2 Model 30 286 is compatible with the PC, XT, and AT at the BIOS level and at most hardware interfaces. Because many items are included on the motherboard, many boards that could be used in the standard PC, XT, or AT systems will not function in the

Model 30 286, even though it has the ISA-style slots. These boards include graphics adapters, some memory adapters and other cards. Also, because of the built-in VGA, an analog display is required.

The capability to use a memory card in the PS/2 Model 30 286 depends on the flexibility of the card in establishing its starting memory address. The amount of motherboard memory installed and the required starting memory address for each memory card are given in the following list:

Motherboard Memory	Expansion Memory Starting Address
512K	512K
1M	1M + 384K
2M	2M + 384K
4M	4M + 384K

To properly operate in a system with a given amount of motherboard memory, any memory cards you use must support the listed starting address.

Costs

The part numbers and pricing information for the system units follows:

Description	Number	Price
Model 30 286, 1.44M Drive	8530E01	$1,995
Model 30 286, 1.44M Drive, 20M Fixed Disk	8530E21	$2,595

The part numbers and pricing information for optional accessories follows:

Description	Number	Price
20M Fixed Disk Drive	27F4969	$765
Data Migration Facility	1501224	$33

PS/2 Model 50

Introduced on April 2, 1987, the IBM PS/2 Model 50 is an entry-level desktop system within the IBM PS/2 family. The Model 50 includes Micro Channel Architecture (MCA).

The system unit features a 10 MHz microprocessor running with 0 or 1 wait state, depending on the model, and 1M of memory on the system board. System board memory can be expanded to 2M on Model 50 Z systems but is limited to the standard 1M on the standard model (8550-021). You can add up to 16M additional memory with memory adapter cards. The IBM Model 50 comes standard with a 1.44M, 3 1/2-inch floppy disk drive; a 20M, 30M, or 60M hard disk drive (depending on the model); a serial port; a parallel port; a mouse port; and a Video Graphics Array (VGA) port. The VGA supports new graphics and text modes but is also compatible with CGA and EGA modes.

The 80286 10 MHz 16-bit microprocessor running with 1 wait state allows the 50-021 to perform approximately 20 percent faster than either the XT 286 or AT Model 339. The Model 50 Z systems (8550-031 and 8550-061) run with 0 wait states to motherboard memory access, which translates into an additional 20 percent performance increase for most computational tasks.

The system has two levels of BIOS, which total 128K. A Compatibility BIOS (CBIOS) with memory addressability of up to 1M provides support for real-mode-based application programs. An additional version of BIOS, Advanced BIOS (ABIOS), provides support for protected-mode-based multitasking operating systems and has extended memory addressability of up to 16M.

Real mode is a mode in which the 80286 processor can emulate the earlier 8086 or 8088 processors for compatibility purposes. This is the mode under which DOS runs. *Protected mode*, a mode not found in the earlier processors, allows for specialized support of multitasking. This is the mode that more advanced multitasking operating systems such as OS/2 will run under.

Additional features of the system unit include four 16-bit I/O slots (with one slot occupied by the disk controller adapter); a 94-watt, automatic voltage-sensing, universal power supply; a time and date clock with battery backup; an additional position for a second 3 1/2-inch floppy disk drive; and the IBM Enhanced Keyboard.

The original PS/2 Model 50 (8550-021) includes the following features:

- 10 MHz 80286 16-bit microprocessor, 1 wait state

- Optional 80287 coprocessor

- MCA with a 16-bit bus

- 20M hard disk

- 1.44M, 3 1/2-inch floppy disk drive

- Universal, automatic voltage-sensing power supply

- Keyboard port, serial/asynchronous port, parallel port, mouse port, and Video Graphics Array (VGA) port

- Switchless installation and configuration

The PS/2 Model 50 Z (8550-031 and 8550-061) also includes these features:

- 10 MHz 80286 16-bit microprocessor, 0 wait states
- 1M of high-speed (85 ns) memory on the motherboard
- Maximum of 2M of memory on the motherboard
- 30M or 60M hard disk

Specifications and Highlights

The following list outlines the Model 50 technical information:

- Intel 80286 microprocessor operating at 10 MHz

    1 wait state in Model 8550-021
    0 wait states in Models 8550-031 and 8550-061
    16-bit-wide data path to memory

- 1M random-access memory (RAM)

- 128K read-only memory (ROM)
  Automatic POST routines
  BASIC language interpreter
  IBM PC- and XT-compatible BIOS (CBIOS)
  Advanced protected-mode BIOS (ABIOS)

- Built-in floppy disk controller for two 1.44M drives

- Two disk drives available

    3 1/2-inch 1.44M floppy disk drive

    One included in each model
    Two maximum

    3 1/2-inch hard disk and controller (20M, 30M, or 60M, depending on model)

- Serial port (COM1:)

    RS-232 compatible
    25-pin, D-shell connector

- Parallel port (LPT1:)

    Centronics DIO capability
    Equivalent to printer adapter
    25-pin, D-shell connector

- Keyboard port

- Enhanced Keyboard

- Mouse port

- Integrated VGA display adapter

    CGA compatible (31.5 KHz double scanned)
    New modes: (31.5 KHz)

    40 by 25 by 16 colors for text (9-by-16-character box)
    80 by 25 by 16 colors for text (9-by-16-character box)
    320 by 200 by 256 colors—all points addressable
    640 by 480 by 16 colors—all points addressable

    Palette of 262,144 colors
    Analog drive, subminiature 15-pin, D-shell connector
    70 Hz refresh rate in all but 640 by 480 mode
    Not compatible with digital monitors
    Loadable character font capability (512 characters)
    Color summing to 64 shades of gray for monochrome
      display

- Power supply of 94 watts, with internal voltage sensing for worldwide use

    Low range: 100 to 125 VAC
    High range: 200 to 240 VAC
    Frequency: 50 to 60 Hz

- Sound

    PC equivalent single sound controller
    Sound transducer

- MCA 16-bit interface bus (three expansion slots available)

- Time-of-day clock with extended-life lithium battery

The physical specifications of the PS/2 Model 50 are as follows:

- Dimensions

    Width: 360 mm (14.1 in)
    Depth: 420 mm (16.5 in)
    Height: 140 mm (5.5 in)
    Weight: 9.55 kg (21 lbs)

- Electrical requirements

    United States: 90 to 137 VAC, 50 to 60 Hz
    European: 180 to 265 VAC, 50 to 60 Hz

- Air temperature

    System turned on: 60 to 90 degrees Fahrenheit
                      or 15.6 to 32.2 degrees Celsius

    System turned off: 50 to 100 degrees Fahrenheit
                       or 10 to 43 degrees Celsius

- Humidity

    System turned on: 8 to 80 percent RH
    System turned off: 20 to 80 percent RH

- BTU output of 494 BTU per hour

- FCC Class B certification

The Model 50 includes a 1.44M, 3 1/2-inch floppy disk drive. The specifications for this drive are listed here:

- Size

    Height: 41 mm (1.6 in)
    Width: 102 mm (4.0 in)
    Depth: 150 mm (5.9 in)
    Weight: 0.68 kg (1.5 lbs)

- Capacity of 1.44M (2M unformatted) in high density mode

- Track density of 135 tracks per inch

- 80 tracks
- Two heads
- Transfer rate of 500,000 bps (MFM) in high density mode
- Access time

Track to track:	6 ms
Seek settle time:	15 ms
Motor start time:	500 ms (maximum)
Disk speed:	300 rpm, plus or minus 1.5 percent

The Model 50 also includes one of three types of hard disks. The following list summarizes the specifications of each hard disk:

Specification	20M	30M	60M
Cylinders	611	615	762
Number of heads	4	4	6
Bytes/sector	512	512	512
Sectors/track	17	25	26
Sector interleave	1 to 1	1 to 1	1 to 1
Data transfer rate	5.0 mbps	7.5 mbps	8.4 mbps
Average access time	80 ms	39 ms	27 ms

Models and Features

On June 2, 1988, IBM introduced two new models in the Model 50 series of computers. These are designated as the PS/2 Model 50 Z (8550-031 and 8550-061). These models offer improved performance and greater hard disk capacity. Higher speed (85 ns) memory provides 0-wait-state processor performance and can be upgraded to 2M on the system board. The 50 Z has a 30M or 60M hard disk drive as standard, which provides greater capacity and improved average access time over the standard 20M hard disk in the 50-021.

The standard 1.44M drive in all the Model 50 systems can format, read, and write to either 720K (double density) or 1.44M (high density) floppy disks. In double-density mode, this drive is fully compatible with the 720K (3 1/2-inch) floppy disk drive. In high-density mode, the standard drive doubles the data capability to 1.44M and the data rate to 500K bits per second.

However, because of the capabilities and design of the disk media, you should not use the 1.44M drive to format a 720K (1M unformatted) disk as 1.44M, or to format a 1.44M (2M unformatted) disk as 720K.

A 5 1/4-inch external disk drive (360K) is available to allow you to convert or operate existing 5 1/4-inch applications. To operate, this drive requires the External Diskette Drive Adapter/A. The adapter card plugs into the connector for the 3 1/2-inch drive B. When installed, the external drive becomes drive B. Unfortunately, the card then consumes one slot and the drive B position.

Responding to user complaints about the storage capacity of the original 20M Model 50, IBM offers the PS/2 60M hard disk drive as an upgrade option. You can install this drive by replacing the existing 20M or 30M hard disk in the PS/2 Model 50 (8550-021) or Model 50 Z (8550-031). No trade-in is available for the earlier drive, which the user retains. This drive is a replacement for the original hard disk drive in the 50-021 or 50-031, and provides 60M of storage and a faster access time of 27 ms. The replacement adapter card required for the 50-021 is included.

For additional memory, IBM offers the IBM PS/2 0-8M Expanded Memory Adapter/A. This card is a 16-bit, full-length circuit card sold without any installed memory. However, you can expand the card up to a maximum of 8M by using optional memory kits. You can configure the adapter memory from 0.5M to 8M by using either the 0.5M Memory Module Kit or the 2M Memory Module Kit. The 0-8M Expanded Memory Adapter/A can be installed in any open expansion slot of the Model 50 or 60. The adapter is easy to set up because it contains no jumpers or hardware switches. An additional feature is an on-board ROM that contains a POST and microcode to initialize the card.

The 0-8M Expanded Memory Adapter/A provides support for two different operating modes: expanded memory and extended memory. When used as expanded memory, the adapter is compatible with applications written to the LIM EMS Version 3.2 standard, or with the IBM 3270 Workstation Program Version 1.1. In addition, you can use the adapter as extended memory for OS/2. By installing two adapters, each filled to 8M, a user can reach the system address limit of 16M for the Models 50 and 60.

Because of the 0 wait states on the 50 Z systems, IBM offers a special motherboard memory upgrade for only these systems. This upgrade consists of one 2M, 85 ns memory kit, which you can install on the system board of the 50-031 or 50-061 by replacing the standard 1M of memory. This upgrade also brings the system board to its maximum capacity of 2M for these models.

Costs

The part number and pricing information for the system units follows:

Description	Number	Price
Model 50, 20M Fixed Disk, 1M RAM	8550021	$3,595
Model 50 Z, 0 wait, 30M Fixed Disk, 1M RAM	8550031	$3,995
Model 50 Z, 0 wait, 60M ESDI Fixed Disk, 1M RAM	8550061	$4,595

The part number and pricing information for optional accessories follows:

Description	Number	Price
2M 85 ns Motherboard Memory (50-031,50-061)	6450604	$1,395
0-8M Expanded Memory Adapter/A	1497259	$600
0.5M 120 ns Memory (1497259)	30F5348	$215
2M 120 ns Memory (1497259)	30F5360	$995
1.44M Diskette Drive	6450353	$245
Data Migration Facility	1501224	$33
60M ESDI Fixed Disk Drive upgrade	6450606	$1,695
10 MHz 80287 Coprocessor	6450356	$525
Dual Async Adapter/A	6450347	$210
Mouse	6450350	$95

PS/2 Model 60

Introduced on April 2, 1987, the IBM PS/2 Model 60 is a mid-range, desk-side system within the IBM PS/2 family. The Model 60 includes Micro Channel Architecture (MCA).

The system unit features a 10 MHz microprocessor running with 1 wait state and 1M of memory on the system board. System board memory is limited to the standard 1M, but the system can have up to 16M with memory adapter cards. The Model 60 comes standard with a 1.44M, 3 1/2-inch floppy disk drive; either a 44M or 70M hard disk drive; a disk controller; a serial port; a parallel port; a mouse port; and a Video Graphics Array (VGA) port. The VGA supports new graphics and text modes but is also compatible with CGA and EGA modes.

The 80286 10 MHz 16-bit microprocessor running with 1 wait state allows the Model 60 to perform approximately 20 percent faster than either the XT 286 or AT Model 339.

The system has two levels of BIOS, which total 128K. A Compatibility BIOS (CBIOS) with memory addressability of up to 1M provides support for real-mode-based application programs. An additional version of BIOS, Advanced BIOS (ABIOS), provides support for protected-mode-based multitasking operating systems and has extended memory addressability up to 16M.

Additional features of the system unit include eight 16-bit I/O slots (with one slot occupied by the disk controller adapter); an automatic voltage-sensing, universal power supply; a time and date clock with battery backup; an additional slot for a second 3 1/2-inch floppy disk drive; and the IBM Enhanced Keyboard.

The Model 60 includes the following features:

- 10 MHz 80286 16-bit microprocessor, 1 wait state
- Optional 80287 coprocessor
- Micro Channel Architecture with a 16-bit bus
- 1.44M, 3 1/2-inch floppy disk drive
- Large-capacity 44M or 70M drives
- Universal, automatic voltage-sensing power supply
- Keyboard port, serial/asynchronous port, parallel port, mouse port, and Video Graphics Array (VGA) port
- Switchless installation and configuration

Specifications and Highlights

The technical information for the PS/2 Model 60 is as follows:

- Intel 80286 microprocessor operating at 10 MHz

    1 wait state
    16-bit-wide data path to ROM

- 1M random-access memory (RAM) on motherboard

- 128K read-only memory (ROM)

    Automatic POST routines
    BASIC language interpreter
    IBM PC- and XT-Compatible BIOS (CBIOS)
    Advanced protected-mode BIOS (ABIOS)

- Built-in floppy disk controller for two 1.44M drives

- Two disk drives available

    3 1/2-inch 1.44M floppy disk drive

        One included in each model
        Two maximum

    5 1/4-inch hard disk and controller (44M or 70M, depending on model)

- Serial port (COM1:)

    RS-232 compatible
    25-pin, D-shell connector

- Parallel port (LPT1:)

    Centronics DIO capability
    Equivalent to printer adapter
    25-pin, D-shell connector

- Keyboard port

- Enhanced Keyboard

- Mouse port

- Integrated VGA display adapter

    CGA compatible (31.5 KHz double scanned)
    New modes: (31.5 KHz)

40 by 25 by 16 colors for text (9-by-16-character box)
80 by 25 by 16 colors for text (9-by-16-character box)
320 by 200 by 256 colors—all points addressable
640 by 480 by 16 colors—all points addressable

Palette of 262,144 colors
Analog drive, subminiature 15-pin, D-shell connector
70 Hz refresh rate in all but 640 by 480 mode
Not compatible with digital monitors
Loadable character font capability (512 characters)
Color summing to 64 shades of gray for monochrome
display

- Power supply of 207 watts, with internal voltage sensing for
  worldwide use

  Low range: 100 to 125 VAC
  High range: 200 to 240 VAC
  Frequency: 50 to 60 Hz

- Sound

  PC equivalent single sound controller
  Sound transducer

- MCA 16-bit interface bus (eight expansion slots available)

- Time-of-day clock with extended-life lithium battery

The following list gives the Model 60's physical specifications:

- Dimensions

  Width: 165 mm (6.5 in), 318 mm (12.5 in) with feet
            extended

  Depth: 483 mm (19.0 in)

  Height: 597 mm (23.5 in)

- Weight

  8560-041: 21.3 kg (47 lbs)
  8560-071: 21.3 kg (47 lbs)

- Electrical requirements

  United States: 90 to 137 VAC, 50 to 60 Hz
  European: 180 to 265 VAC, 50 to 60 Hz

- Air Temperature

  System turned on: 60 to 90 degrees Fahrenheit
  or 15.6 to 32.2 degrees Celsius

  System turned off: 50 to 110 degrees Fahrenheit
  or 10 to 43 degrees Celsius

- Humidity

  System turned on: 8 to 80 percent RH
  System turned off: 20 to 80 percent RH

- BTU output of 1240 BTU per hour

- FCC Class B certification

The following list gives the specifications for the hard disk drives available for the PS/2 Model 60:

Specification	44M	44M	70M	115M	314M
Cylinders	733	1024	583	915	1225
Number of heads	7	5	7	7	15
Bytes per sector	512	512	512	512	512
Sectors per track	17	17	36	36	34
Transfer	5 mbps	5 mbps	10 mbps	10 mbps	10 mbps
Average access	40 ms	40 ms	30 ms	28 ms	23 ms

Note: IBM uses many suppliers for hard and floppy disk drives. This is why two different sets of specifications for the 44M hard disks are listed here.

Models and Features

IBM offers two models of the Model 60. They differ only in the hard disk and controller board supplied. The 70M drive is included with the 60-071 and also can be added as a second drive in that system. The 70M drive attaches by way of the high-performance Enhanced Small Device Interface (ESDI) disk adapter provided with the system unit and does not require an additional expansion slot. The ESDI adapter (standard in the 60-071) can connect up to two drives and allows for an extremely high data transfer rate of 10 mbps as well as increased reliability.

The standard Model 60-041 includes an ST-506/412 hard disk controller, which also can connect up to two drives. The maximum transfer rate for this controller is 5 mbps, which is half that possible with the ESDI controller.

Costs

The part number and pricing information for the system units follows:

Description	Number	Price
Model 60, 44M Fixed Disk	8560041	$5,295
Model 60, 70M ESDI Fixed Disk	8560071	$5,795

The part number and pricing information for optional accessories is as follows:

Description	Number	Price
0-8M Expanded Memory Adapter/A	1497259	$600
0.5M Memory Module Kit	30F5348	$215
2M Memory Module Kit	30F5360	$995
1.44M Diskette Drive	6450353	$245
5 1/4-inch External 360K Diskette Drive	4869001	$335
5 1/4-inch External Drive Adapter/A	6450245	$60
Data Migration Facility	1501224	$33
44M Fixed Disk Drive	6450354	$1,395
70M ESDI Fixed Disk Drive	6450355	$2,395
115M ESDI Fixed Disk Drive	6450377	$3,495
10 MHz 80287 Coprocessor	6450356	$525
Dual Async Adapter/A	6450347	$210
Mouse	6450350	$95

PS/2 Model 70

The IBM PS/2 Model 70 386 was introduced on June 2, 1988. The Model 70 is a desktop, high-end system within IBM's PS/2 family. The Model 70 includes Micro Channel Architecture (MCA). The 25 MHz Model 70 system is currently the highest performance IBM PS/2 system available, even including the Model 80.

The basic system features a 16 MHz, a 20 MHz, or a 25 MHz 80386 microprocessor and 1M or 2M of high-speed memory on the motherboard. Motherboard memory is expandable to 6M or 8M depending on the model, and you can expand total memory to 16M with memory adapters. This system comes with a 1.44M, 3 1/2-inch floppy disk drive and either a 60M or 120M hard disk drive with integrated controller as standard. Also standard are a serial port, a parallel port, a mouse port, and a Video Graphics Array (VGA) port. The VGA supports new graphics and text modes but is also compatible with CGA and EGA modes.

The top-of-the-line Model 70 A21 features a 25 MHz 80386 32-bit microprocessor and an Intel 82385 memory cache controller with a high-speed 64K static memory cache. This memory cache lets the Model 70 perform approximately 150 percent faster than the 20 MHz versions of the Model 80. The Model 70 is about 250 percent faster than the Model 50.

The system has two levels of BIOS, which total 128K. A Compatibility BIOS (CBIOS) with memory addressability of up to 1M provides support for real-mode-based application programs. An additional version of BIOS, Advanced BIOS (ABIOS), provides support for protected-mode-based multitasking operating systems and has up to 16M extended memory addressability.

Additional features of the system unit include one 16-bit and two 32-bit I/O slots. Because all the hard disks available with the Model 70 have an integrated (embedded) controller, no slot is lost to a disk controller card. The Model 70 also has a 132-watt, automatic voltage-sensing, universal power supply; a time and date clock with battery backup; an additional slot for a second 3 1/2-inch floppy disk drive; and the IBM Enhanced Keyboard.

The Model 70 includes the following features:

- 16 MHz, 20 MHz, or 25 MHz 80386 32-bit microprocessor
- Intel 82385 memory cache controller with a 64K high-speed memory cache (Model 70-A21 only)
- Up to 6M or 8M of high-speed system board memory
- Optional 16 MHz, 20 MHz, or 25 MHz 80387 coprocessor
- MCA with a 16/32-bit bus
- 1.44M, 3 1/2-inch floppy disk drive
- Large-capacity 60M or 120M drives

- Hard disk with integrated controller

- Universal, automatic voltage-sensing power supply

- Keyboard port, serial/asynchronous port, parallel port, mouse port, and VGA port

- Switchless installation and configuration

- Small desktop design

Specifications and Highlights

The PS/2 Model 70 technical information is as follows:

- Intel 80386 microprocessor

  16 MHz in Model 70-E21
  20 MHz in Model 70-121
  25 MHz in Model 70-A21
  32-bit-wide data path to memory
  0-2 wait states (0 normally, 2 when paging)
  64K, 0-wait-state memory cache (70-A21)

- Standard memory

  1M in Model 70-E21
  2M in Model 70-121 and Model 70-A21

- Maximum motherboard memory

  6M in Model 70-E21 and Model 70-121
  8M in Model 70-A21

- Maximum memory

  16M maximum addressable memory, less 640K of reserved memory:

  128K reserved for video RAM
  128K reserved for adapter board ROM and RAM
  128K reserved for motherboard ROM BIOS
  128K reserved for ROM duplicate addressing
  128K reserved for high-speed ROM copy in RAM

- 128K read-only memory (ROM)

    Automatic POST routines
    BASIC language interpreter
    IBM PC- and XT-compatible BIOS (CBIOS)
    Advanced protected-mode BIOS (ABIOS)

- Built-in floppy disk controller for two 1.44M drives

- Two disk drives available

    3 1/2-inch 1.44M floppy disk drive

    One included in each model
    Two maximum

    3 1/2-inch hard disk and embedded controller (60M or 120M, depending on model)

- Serial port (COM1:)

    RS-232 compatible
    25-pin, D-shell connector

- Parallel port (LPT1:)

    Centronics DIO capability
    Equivalent to printer adapter
    25-pin, D-shell connector

- Keyboard port

- IBM Enhanced Keyboard

- Mouse port

- Integrated VGA display adapter

    CGA compatible (31.5 KHz double scanned)
    New modes: (31.5 KHz)

    40 by 25 by 16 colors for text (9-by-16-character box)
    80 by 25 by 16 colors for text (9-by-16-character box)
    320 by 200 by 256 colors—all points addressable
    640 by 480 by 16 colors—all points addressable

    Palette of 262,144 colors
    Analog drive, subminiature 15-pin, D-shell connector
    70 Hz refresh rate in all but 640 by 480 mode

Not compatible with digital monitors
Loadable character font capability (512 characters)
Color summing to 64 shades of gray for monochrome
display

- Power supply of 132 watts, with internal voltage sensing for
worldwide use

    Low range: 100 to 125 VAC
    High range: 200 to 240 VAC
    Frequency: 50 to 60 Hz

- Sound

    PC equivalent single sound controller
    Sound transducer

- MCA 16/32-bit interface with three expansion slots available:

    One 16-bit slot
    Two 32-bit slots

- Time-of-day clock with extended-life lithium battery

The following list summarizes the PS/2 Model 70's physical
specifications:

- Dimensions

    Width: 360 mm (14.2 in)
    Depth: 420 mm (16.5 in)
    Height: 140 mm (5.5 in)
    Weight: 9.5 kg (21 lbs)

- Electrical requirements

    United States: 100 to 125 VAC, 50 to 60 Hz, 4 amps
                   maximum

    European: 200 to 240 VAC, 50 to 60 Hz, 2 amps
                   maximum

- Air temperature

    System turned on: 60 to 90 degrees Fahrenheit
                      or 15.6 to 32.2 degrees Celsius

    System turned off: 50 to 110 degrees Fahrenheit
                       or 10 to 43 degrees Celsius

- Humidity

  System turned on: 8 to 80 percent RH
  System turned off: 8 to 85 percent RH

- BTU output of 751 BTU per hour

- FCC Class B certification

The following list gives the specifications for the hard disk drives available with the Model 70:

Specification	60M	120M
Cylinders	762	920
Number of heads	6	8
Bytes per sector	512	512
Sectors per track	26	32
Sector interleave	1 to 1	1 to 1
Transfer rate	8.4 mbps	10.2 mbps
Average access	27 ms	23 ms

Models and Features

Three models of the Model 70 are available: the 70-E21, the 70-121, and the 70-A21. They differ mainly in clock speed, installed hard disk storage, and memory capabilities. The following list shows the main features of each model:

Model	E61	121	A21
Microprocessor	80386	80386	80386
Clock speed	16 MHz	20 MHz	25 MHz
16/32-bit expansion slots	2/1	2/1	2/1
Standard memory	1M	2M	2M
Maximum motherboard memory	6M	6M	8M
Standard hard disk	60M	120M	120M

The 25 MHz Model 70-A21 has a few outstanding differences from the other models, which give this system a higher than expected performance level. The 70-A21 uses an Intel 82385 cache controller chip, which manages 64K of extremely high-speed static memory. This memory is accessed at 0 wait states and uses a special algorithm to ensure an exceptionally high bit ratio for cache memory access. Because of this system's speed, the computer requires extremely fast 80 ns memory, which the other models do not need.

You must keep this requirement in mind when you purchase additional memory for this system as well as when you make repairs.

The 80387 math chip selected for each system unit must match the main processor in speed, and the 80387 chips (especially the 25 MHz chip) are expensive.

Costs

The part number and pricing information for the system units follows:

Description	Number	Price
Model 70-A21, 25 MHz, 120M Disk, 2M RAM	8570A21	$11,295
Model 70-121, 20 MHz, 120M Disk, 2M RAM	8570121	$7,995
Model 70-E21, 16 MHz, 60M Disk, 1M RAM	8570E21	$5,995

The part number and pricing information for optional accessories follows:

Description	Number	Price
2M 80 ns Motherboard Memory (70-A21)	6450608	$1,495
1M 85 ns Memory (70-E21,70-121, or 6450605)	6450603	$695
2M 85 ns Memory (70-E21,70-121, or 6450605)	6450604	$1,395
2-6M 80 ns Memory Adapter with 2M	6450367	$1,595
2M 80 ns Memory for Adapter 6450367	6450372	$1,295
2-8M 85 ns Memory Adapter with 2M	6450605	$1,695
1M 85 ns Memory (70-E21,70-121, or 6450605)	6450603	$695
2M 85 ns Memory (70-E21,70-121, or 6450605)	6450604	$1,395

Description	Number	Price
1.44M Diskette Drive	6450353	$245
5 1/4-inch External 360K Diskette Drive	N/A	$335
5 1/4-inch External Drive Adapter/A	6450245	$60
Data Migration Facility	1501224	$33
25 MHz 80387 Math Coprocessor	6450607	$2,395
20 MHz 80387 Math Coprocessor	6450378	$1,195
16 MHz 80387 Math Coprocessor	6450369	$795
Dual Async Adapter/A	6450347	$210
Mouse	6450350	$95

PS/2 Model 80

IBM introduced the PS/2 Model 80 on April 2, 1987. On August 11, 1987, IBM announced the Model 80-311. The Model 80 is a floor-standing, high-end system in IBM's PS/2 family and includes Micro Channel Architecture (MCA).

The basic system features a 16 MHz or 20 MHz 80386 microprocessor and 1M or 2M of high-speed memory on the motherboard. Motherboard memory is expandable to 2M or 4M, depending on the model, and the total ROM can be expanded to 16M with memory adapters. This system comes standard with a 1.44M, 3 1/2-inch floppy disk drive and a 44M, 70M, 114M, or 314M hard disk drive and controller. Also standard are a serial port, a parallel port, a mouse port, and a Video Graphics Array (VGA) port. The VGA supports new graphics and text modes but is also compatible with CGA and EGA modes.

The 80386 32-bit microprocessor running at either 16 MHz or 20 MHz coupled with the MCA and high-speed memory allows the Model 80 to perform three to four times faster than the AT Model 339. The 80387 math coprocessor running at the same 16 MHz or 20 MHz allows the Model 80 to perform math calculations four to five times faster than an AT Model 339 with an 80287 math coprocessor.

The system has two levels of BIOS, which total 128K. A Compatibility BIOS (CBIOS) with memory addressability of up to 1M provides support for real-mode-based application programs. An additional version of BIOS, Advanced BIOS (ABIOS), provides support for protected-mode-based multitasking operating systems and has up to 16M extended memory addressability.

Additional features of the system unit include eight I/O bus slots, of which five are 16-bit slots and three are 16/32-bit slots. Each system includes a hard disk controller that occupies one 16-bit slot. This controller is an ST-506/412 controller for units with drives less than 70M, whereas models with 70M or larger hard disks include an ESDI hard disk controller. The Model 80 also has a 225-watt, automatic voltage-sensing, universal power supply with auto-restart; a time and date clock with battery backup; an additional position for a second 3 1/2-inch floppy disk drive; an additional position for a second full-height 5 1/4-inch hard disk; and the IBM Enhanced Keyboard.

The auto-restart feature on the power supply enables the computer to restart automatically when AC power returns after a power decrease or outage. This feature allows the system to be programmed for unattended restart after power outages—a useful feature on a computer in a network fileserver application.

The Model 80 includes the following features:

- 16 or 20 MHz 80386 32-bit microprocessor
- Up to 2M or 4M of high-speed system board memory
- 80 ns system board memory using 1M chips
- Optional 16 MHz or 20 MHz 80387 coprocessor
- MCA with a 16/32-bit bus
- 1.44M, 3 1/2-inch floppy disk drive
- Large-capacity 44M, 70M, 115M, or 314M hard disk
- Hard disk with integrated controller
- Automatic voltage-sensing, auto-restart power supply
- Keyboard port, serial/asynchronous port, parallel port, mouse port, and VGA port
- Switchless installation and configuration

Specifications and Highlights

The technical information for the PS/2 Model 80 is as follows:

- Intel 80386 microprocessor

  32-bit-wide data path to ROM
  16 MHz in Models 80-041 and 80-071 (1 wait state)
  20 MHz in Models 80-111 and 80-311 (0-2 wait states:
      0 normally, 2 when paging)

- Standard memory

  1M in Model 80-041
  2M in Models 80-071, 80-111, 80-311

- Maximum motherboard memory

  2M in Models 80-041 and 80-071
  4M in Models 80-111 and 80-311

- Maximum memory

  16M maximum addressable memory, less 640K of reserved
  memory:

  128K reserved for video RAM
  128K reserved for adapter board ROM and RAM
  128K reserved for motherboard ROM BIOS
  128K reserved for ROM duplicate addressing
  128K reserved for high-speed ROM copy in RAM
      (Models 80-111 and 80-311 only)

- 128K read-only memory (ROM)

  Automatic POST routines
  BASIC language interpreter
  IBM PC- and XT-compatible BIOS (CBIOS)
  Advanced protected-mode BIOS (ABIOS)

- Built-in floppy disk controller for two 1.44M drives

- Two disk drives available

  3 1/2-inch 1.44M floppy disk drive

    One included in each model
    Two maximum

  5 1/4-inch hard disk and controller (44M, 70M, 115M, or
  314M, depending on the model)

- Serial port (COM1:)

   RS-232 compatible
   25-pin, D-shell connector

- Parallel port (LPT1:)

   Centronics DIO capability
   Equivalent to printer adapter
   25-pin, D-shell connector

- Keyboard port

- IBM Enhanced Keyboard

- Mouse port

- Integrated VGA display adapter

   CGA compatible (31.5 KHz double scanned)
   New modes: (31.5 KHz)

      40 by 25 by 16 colors for text (9-by-16-character box)
      80 by 25 by 16 colors for text (9-by-16-character box)
      320 by 200 by 256 colors—all points addressable
      640 by 480 by 16 colors—all points addressable

   Palette of 262,144 colors
   Analog drive, subminiature 15-pin, D-shell connector
   70 Hz refresh rate in all but 640 by 480 mode
   Not compatible with digital monitors
   Loadable character font capability (512 characters)
   Color summing to 64 shades of gray for monochrome
      display

- Power supply of 225 watts, with internal voltage sensing for worldwide use and auto-restart

   Low range: 100 to 125 VAC
   High range: 200 to 240 VAC
   Frequency: 50 to 60 Hz

- Sound

   PC equivalent single sound controller
   Sound transducer

- MCA 16/32-bit interface (eight expansion slots available):

   Five 16-bit slot
   Three 32-bit slots

- Time-of-day clock with extended-life lithium battery

The following list gives the Model 80's physical specifications:

- Dimensions

  Width: 165 mm (6.5 in), 318 mm (12.5 in) with feet
  extended
  Depth: 483 mm (19.0 in)
  Height: 597 mm (23.5 in)
  Weight: 21.3 kg (47 lbs)

- Electrical requirements

  United States: 90 to 137 VAC, 50 to 60 Hz
  European: 180 to 265 VAC, 50 to 60 Hz

- Air temperature

  System turned on: 60 to 90 degrees Fahrenheit
  or 15.6 to 32.2 degrees Celsius

  System turned off: 50 to 110 degrees Fahrenheit
  or 10 to 43 degrees Celsius

- Humidity

  System turned on: 8 to 80 percent RH
  System turned off: 20 to 80 percent RH

- BTU output of 1245 BTU per hour

- FCC Class B certification

The specifications for the hard disk drives available for the PS/2
Model 80 are as follows:

Specification	44M	44M	70M	115M	314M
Cylinders	733	1024	583	915	1225
Number of heads	7	5	7	7	15
Bytes per sector	512	512	512	512	512
Sectors per track	17	17	36	36	34
Transfer	5 mbps	5 mbps	10 mbps	10 mbps	10 mbps
Average access	40 ms	40 ms	30 ms	28 ms	23 ms

Note: IBM uses many suppliers for hard and floppy disk drives. This
is the reason that two different sets of specifications for the 44M
hard disks are listed here.

Models and Features

Basically, four Model 80 systems are available. The units differ in the type of motherboard and in the type and capacity of the hard disk drive.

The Model 80-041 and Model 80-071 include the 16 MHz motherboard, which can accept a maximum of 2M installed memory. Any additional memory up to 16M would be installed on adapter cards in one of the slots. This system board also has a 1-wait-state memory access architecture, which makes this board slower than many others.

The Model 80-111 and Model 80-311 include a 20 MHz motherboard that can accept up to 4M of installed memory. All system board memory is accessed by a special paging scheme that allows for 0-wait-state access to all 512 bytes within a single page. When access occurs outside the available page, you must perform a page swap requiring 2 wait states. Overall, this scheme allows for faster access to memory than a non-paging, 1-wait-state system. The ROM BIOS on this system board performs a ROM to RAM copy operation on start-up that uses 128K of the total 16M of RAM. This copy is then used for all subsequent ROM operations, and because the ROM now effectively resides in 80 ns RAM, access to these routines is improved significantly.

Three of the models include an ESDI hard disk controller (the Model 80-041 includes an ST-506/412 hard disk controller). The ESDI controller supports a data transfer rate twice that of the ST-506/412 (10 mbps versus 5 mbps) and also offers much more reliable operation.

Costs

The part number and pricing information for the system units is as follows:

Description	Number	Price
Model 80-041, 16 MHz, 44M Disk, 1M RAM	8580041	$6,995
Model 80-071, 16 MHz, 70M Disk, 2M RAM	8580071	$7,995
Model 80-111, 20 MHz, 114M Disk, 2M RAM	8580111	$8,995
Model 80-311, 20 MHz, 314M Disk, 2M RAM	8580311	$11,995

The part number and pricing information for optional accessories follows:

Description	Number	Price
20 MHz 80387 Math Coprocessor	6450378	$1,195
16 MHz 80387 Math Coprocessor	6450369	$795
2M 80 ns Motherboard Memory (80-111,80-311)	6450379	$1,295
1M 80 ns Motherboard Memory (80-041)	6450375	$695
2-6M 80 ns Memory Adapter with 2M	6450367	$1,595
2M 80 ns Memory for Adapter 6450367	6450372	$1,295
2-8M 85 ns Memory Adapter with 2M	6450605	$1,695
1M 85 ns Memory for 6450605	6450603	$695
2M 85 ns Memory for 6450605	6450604	$1,395
1.44M Diskette Drive	6450353	$245
5 1/4-inch External 360K Diskette Drive	N/A	$335
5 1/4-inch External Drive Adapter/A	6450245	$60
Data Migration Facility	1501224	$33
44M Fixed Disk Drive	6450354	$1,395
70M Fixed Disk Drive	6450355	$2,395
115M Fixed Disk Drive	6450377	$3,495
314M Fixed Disk Drive	6450381	$6,495
Dual Async Adapter/A	6450347	$210
Mouse	6450350	$95

Chapter Summary

In this chapter, you looked at the PS/2 line of systems from IBM. You examined information concerning all the various PS/2 models and submodels, from the low-end to the high-end systems. The low-end PS/2 systems—the PS/2 Models 25, 30, and 30 286—are based closely on the original PC line and include the standard ISA type of expansion slots. You also examined the higher-end PS/2 Models 50, 50Z, 60, 70, and 80, as well as their respective submodels. These systems include the newer MCA slot design, which is dramatically different from the original ISA bus.

The next chapter examines the world of IBM-compatible systems, including details on the available types of compatible systems and some of the criteria you might use to justify purchasing a particular compatible system over another, or over an IBM system.

IBM-Compatible (and Not-So-Compatible) Computers

The open architecture of IBM systems has allowed a variety of non-IBM companies to introduce systems that are functionally identical to IBM's own. These systems often do more than just run the same software; many of these systems are hardware copies of IBM systems and are virtually identical in almost every respect. For this reason, many of these types of systems are called *clones*. Every time IBM makes a change in a system, compatibles or clones follow with the same kind of change.

Recent developments at IBM have dealt a strong blow to the compatibles market. The PS/2 systems with the Micro Channel Architecture are entirely new and difficult to copy. Also, IBM plans to be more strict about what it will allow as far as the "cloning" goes. For a company to protect the massive amounts of development work and money poured into a new system is only fair, and IBM is protecting the PS/2 systems with patents and license agreements. Developing a system compatible with the PS/2 systems will be possible, but the developers will have to license some of the technology for the system from IBM. The patents IBM has on the newer systems virtually guarantee that no compatible will be developed without such licensing.

Several Micro Channel-based compatibles already have been delivered, and many more are on the way. Tandy is selling a PS/2 compatible called the Model 5000, and a company called Apricot

143

became the first to deliver a Micro Channel system that is sold in Europe only. Both of these companies have secured a license agreement with IBM to legally produce these systems and pay IBM a royalty for doing so. Many more MCA systems would be on the market if not for the imposed legal issues and royalty payments, which will put a damper on the number of MCA compatibles that are eventually introduced (which is IBM's intention). Many other companies are on the verge of introducing legal compatibles with IBM licensing, but you never will find nearly the same amount of these systems as you will PC or AT compatibles.

In this chapter, you will examine compatibles from several points of view. The primary view is that of the system installer and repair person. Such a person has strict criteria for what makes a "good" compatible system. For a system even to be in the running, for example, the system must come with proper and adequate documentation. No documentation is the nemesis of any installer or repair person, and a system without documentation simply is not acceptable. From this same point of view, several other items are presented for your consideration when shopping for a compatible system. What you learn here can and should be applied to the selection of any IBM type of system. These guidelines will direct you to a system that will be compatible, serviceable, and upgradable for years to come.

Examining the Types of Compatibles

Although many brands, makes, and models of IBM and IBM-compatible systems exist, all the systems can be broken down into several types. Any IBM or compatible system can be classified into one of two primary categories: PC XT compatible or AT compatible. Any system that runs IBM software can be put into one of these categories. A COMPAQ Deskpro 386/25, for example, is really just another AT compatible (although when it's compared to the original IBM AT, the COMPAQ Deskpro 386/25 offers a great deal more performance). Even IBM's own systems can be classified as compatibles; the PS/2 Model 30, for example, is really a PC XT compatible (although when it's compared to the original PC or XT, the Model 30 offers a great deal more performance).

The distinction between the two types of systems comes primarily from the architectural differences of the microprocessors making up the systems. Intel processors have two basic modes of operation: real and protected modes. Systems that can run only in *real mode* are considered PC XT compatible systems, and they never will make the jump to the next level of systems software called OS/2. Systems that also can run in *protected mode* will run OS/2 and can be classified as AT-compatible systems.

AT compatibles that run the Micro Channel interface have different types of expansion adapters available and are very different from the viewpoint of the system installer, upgrader, or repair person. These systems basically are much easier to work on, have fewer components, are more reliable, and offer greater potential for performance. AT compatibles with 80386 processors have access to an additional mode called *virtual 8086 mode*, which allows multiple real-mode simulations to coexist simultaneously in a true multitasking environment. These systems also offer an improved method for switching from real to protected modes, which OS/2 will do quite frequently when running older DOS programs. The 80386-based AT compatibles also offer improved memory-switching capabilities.

Learning the Levels of Compatibility

When developing a compatible computer, you can achieve a few basic levels of similarity to IBM systems. In order of increasing desirability, these levels of similarity follow:

1. Operating system level

2. ROM BIOS level

3. Hardware level

    A. Motherboard and CPU

    B. Peripherals and I/O controllers

Operating System Level Compatibility

For the most part, compatibles at only the first level (operating system level) are the least desirable and are shunned generally by the industry. Operating systems compatibles use licensed, customized versions of Microsoft's MS-DOS. These systems also have a ROM BIOS that is not quite like any from IBM. Because of these differences, these systems will not run the IBM version of MS-DOS, called the IBM Personal Computer DOS (PC DOS). PC DOS will not run for the following reason: any DOS makes calls to the ROM BIOS for specific functions; if the particular ROM is not identical to IBM's, compatibility at that level is not achieved. As long as a version of MS-DOS is customized for the nonstandard ROM, any software will run if it runs on top of DOS and makes no calls to the ROM BIOS or directly to the hardware. This type of software is sometimes called "well behaved" software. Unfortunately, however, most popular software *does* make calls to ROM, and such hardware and software are "ill behaved." Thus, most popular software cannot run or special versions of the programs are required for the particular system in question.

Many systems have been developed that are compatible only at this level. A few examples are the DEC Rainbow 100, Texas Instruments Professional, and Tandy 2000. To be compatible only at this level is definitely not fashionable today. Most people would be well advised to stay away from any system that is compatible only at the DOS level. One interesting tidbit of information is that the development of OS/2 encourages the emergence of new systems that are compatible at this level, largely because OS/2 totally isolates any software running under it from the hardware. Because no software can have access to the hardware, OS/2 itself will be able to mask any differences between various manufacturers' hardware systems. ROM-level compatibility also is unimportant because OS/2 can (and on most systems does) load the ROM from disk, and what used to be called the ROM BIOS code is effectively now part of the OS/2 system itself. For all of this to actually take place, you will be required to get your OS/2 from the same company that manufactured your hardware.

ROM BIOS Level Compatibility

A large number of systems are compatible at the ROM level. These systems have a ROM BIOS interface that appears to software to be exactly like the ROM BIOS of a particular IBM system. Thus, the same software (generally) that runs on a particular IBM system can run on this system.

The actual BIOS code differs from IBM's but only in the area of the actual interface to the hardware. This difference is necessary because compatibles operating at this level will have hardware that differs from any particular IBM system. This feature doesn't generally cause any problems unless you attempt to run actual BIOS code from an IBM system in a compatible of this type. Rarely does anyone try to run actual BIOS code in this type of compatible, though. And at the chip level, doing so is illegal. Thus, making a copy of IBM's ROM BIOS chips and placing them in the motherboard of a compatible system would not be legal. This procedure wouldn't work anyway unless that system truly was hardware compatible with the particular IBM system from which the ROM was copied. Systems that are compatible at this level usually run actual IBM PC DOS unless something is very different about the actual hardware. Any software that runs on top of DOS also remains unaffected unless, again, some special dependence on a hardware feature that is different exists.

With OS/2, compatibility at only this level is a problem. As indicated earlier, when OS/2 is loaded, it actually loads a copy of a ROM BIOS from disk. This copy is called the *protected mode ROM BIOS* or *Advanced BIOS* (ABIOS). A system that is compatible only at this level will not run IBM OS/2, which may or may not be a problem. If your particular system manufacturer does not offer a specially customized version of OS/2 containing new ABIOS code that was designed specifically for your system, a real problem occurs. If your manufacturer does not offer something like that, you may never be able to run OS/2 because the IBM version will run only on true hardware-compatible systems. Unlike DOS, no "generic" versions of OS/2 are available because of the amount of customization necessary for particular hardware systems. Usually, compatibility at the BIOS level becomes a real problem only to the owners of AT compatibles because PC XT compatibles will never run OS/2 anyway.

In some instances, compatibility at only this level will lock the PC XT system owner out of some upgrades. For example, the top speedup boards on the market, such as Orchid Tiny Turbo 286, Twin Turbo, or the Intel Inboard 386/PC, will run only on those systems that are truly hardware compatible with IBM's PC and XT. These boards (which are among the best speedup boards on today's market) will *not* run on a COMPAQ Deskpro, AT&T 6300, Leading Edge Model M, any "Turbo" XTs, or even the IBM PS/2 Models 25 and 30. These systems are BIOS compatible but have not reached the third level of compatibility—the hardware level.

Hardware Level Compatibility

To be a true hardware-level compatible, a system must match a particular IBM system at the basic motherboard hardware level. In other words, the system must use the same Hardware Interrupt Request (IRQ) channels, Direct Memory Access (DMA) channels, and I/O port addresses for the same purposes that IBM does, and the system must offer the same slot or bus interface (at the same clock rate) that IBM does. The majority of today's systems seem to offer this level of compatibility, which means that an adapter board that works in a particular IBM system unit also will work in a unit of the compatible. ROM code should be much the same as IBM's. And you may be able to run IBM's own ROMs in a system like this. For AT types of systems, actual IBM OS/2 should boot and run. A customized version from the system Original Equipment Manufacturer (OEM) may exist, but that would not preclude the use of the IBM OS/2.

Some differences in the hardware may make the system marginally compatible. Clock rate and the number of wait states inserted by the system during bus cycles, for example, can have a big effect on which peripherals will or will not work. The AST Premium 286 offers a jumper-selectable wait-state setting of 0 or 1. Running 0 wait states, the system picks up about 20 to 30 percent speed over running 1 wait state. Many boards do not care, but some do. Certain memory boards, network boards, and other communications adapters will not work at the 0-wait-state setting. The symptoms are that the particular board in question is defective. Resetting the AST motherboard to 1 wait state slows down the system but allows the boards in question to run without problems.

COMPAQ takes a good approach with its systems. The COMPAQ Deskpro 286 and 386 systems run at clock rates between 12 MHz and 25 MHz. Few conventional AT types of adapter boards will run at these speeds, but the COMPAQ uses a unique dual bus and clock system that runs the standard AT bus at 8 MHz with 1 wait state. This keeps all the adapter cards just as happy as if they were in an actual IBM AT. To improve memory access performance, you must purchase from COMPAQ a separate board for memory that will work at the desired clock rate and number of wait states.

Peripherals and I/O controllers are an aspect of hardware compatibility that is usually glossed over. Differences exist in these devices between the PC XT and AT types of systems. For example, in PC XT systems, IBM used a serial (RS-232C) port, which incorporates a National Semiconductor 8250 UART (Universal Asynchronous Receiver Transmitter) device. In the AT, IBM used a newer chip by National Semiconductor: the 16450 UART. Mixing serial ports with these respective UARTs was never a problem under DOS, but under OS/2, you need to have the 16450 version in your AT. If, instead, you have the PC XT type of serial port with the 8250, no serial communications of any kind will operate under OS/2.

Similar problems exist with the hard disk controllers on AT systems. For the AT, IBM used a Western Digital 1002-WA2 or the later model 1003-WA2. These controllers have no on-board ROM BIOS and, instead, run off of the BIOS interface built into the motherboard ROM. To successfully run OS/2 on your AT-compatible system, you need to follow that standard. In other words, any hard disk controller with an on-board ROM BIOS or that isn't hardware compatible with the Western Digital controllers also will not work for any protected-mode environments such as OS/2 or Novell Netware.

Finally, the graphics adapter can be a sensitive issue in a protected-mode environment. The reason is that every graphics adapter beyond the standard Color Graphics Adapter (CGA) has an on-board ROM BIOS interface. This on-board BIOS will not operate in protected mode, so any protected-mode operating system must load the correct drivers to run the graphics board. Many users already have found that their particular EGA or, especially, VGA adapters will not operate under OS/2. For standard types of adapters, such as serial ports, disk controllers, and graphics boards, the solution to this problem is to get boards that are truly hardware compatible with those IBM has used. Some of those boards have been listed already. For other nonstandard types of peripherals that must work under OS/2, you must get special OS/2 drivers from the OEM of the particular board.

The bottom line here is that most users will desire a compatible that is truly hardware compatible with one of IBM's systems. Sometimes, you cannot easily tell. One thing to remember is that this level of compatibility is much more important for AT types of systems than for PC or XT types. The reason is due to OS/2 and the dependence OS/2 has on the hardware. The best way around this problem is to purchase AT types of systems from an OEM who also has the proper customized version of OS/2 to go along with the system. PC or XT system owners will not have to worry about this problem, but do note that most of the best "accelerator" products for these systems on the market are very hardware dependent.

Knowing What To Look For (Selection Criteria)

As a consultant, I am called often to make a recommendation for a system purchase. Making these types of recommendations is one of the most frequent tasks a consultant will perform. Many consultants charge a large fee for this advice. Unfortunately, most "consultants" don't really have any rhyme or reason to their selections and instead base their choices on magazine reviews or, even worse, on some personal bias. To help eliminate this haphazard selection process, I developed a simple checklist that will help you select a system. This list takes into consideration several important system aspects that are overlooked by most. The goal is to ensure that the selected system is truly compatible and is one with a long life of service and upgrades ahead.

Compatible Selection Checklist

I have found that thinking like an engineer when performing this selection helps. Consider every aspect and detail of the systems in question. Consider all future uses and upgrades. Technical support at a professional (as opposed to user) level is extremely important. As part of your initial purchase decision, and for the type of support mentioned to be provided, make sure that extensive documentation is available. Evaluate nonstandard parts and make sure that a spare-parts program from the OEM is present to allow you to purchase these parts when a system needs service. Standard parts and their sources must be identified so that you can establish avenues for purchase other than the OEM and substitute parts where desired or needed. Interfaces present at all connectors must be known and identified so products that can plug into these connectors can be located.

Here is the questionnaire/checklist for you to use in evaluating *any* IBM-compatible system:

1. Is a technical reference manual available?

   Is a service manual available?
   Are advanced diagnostics available?

2. Is there an OEM version of

   MS-DOS?
   OS/2 (especially for ATs)?

3. Is the ROM BIOS a known OEM compatible? Examples include

   IBM
   COMPAQ
   Zenith
   AT&T

   Or is the ROM supplied by one of the known-quantity ROM development software houses? Examples include

   Phoenix Software
   Award Software

4. Is the system design conservative? In particular,

   Is motherboard memory (RAM and ROM) socketed?
   Is the CPU socketed?
   Are parts rated for operating speed?
   Do the expansion slots run at 8 MHz with 1 wait state?
   Is the power supply adequate for upgrades?
   Does the system run cool?

5. Does the system adhere to established standards? In particular,

   Does the IRQ and DMA usage match IBM?
   Does the I/O port usage match IBM?

   And especially for AT systems,

   Does the CMOS memory and clock work like IBM's does?

6. Is support available? In particular,

> Are parts available (especially unique components)?
> Is technical support direct from the OEM?

If you can answer yes to all these questions, the system is definitely worth purchasing! You may not need to meet *every* one of these criteria, but if you miss more than a few of these checks, you may want to stay away from that system. The items at the top of the list are the most important, and the items at the bottom are perhaps of lesser importance to some. (I think each item is important!) Some systems, due to unique constraints, may not be able to pass every check in the list. COMPAQ, for example, will not make a system service manual available to the purchaser; only dealers get this information. Also, you must obtain any technical support or spare parts through the dealer because COMPAQ does not deal directly with the purchaser of the system.

Items 1 and 2 as well as parts of item 4 definitely eliminate from consideration the typical no-name systems that are built in some garage. Systems such as the "Joe's Computer Shack Super-Turbo-American-Generic-Limited-Plus AT" will *not* meet this criteria. When you call Joe and ask him whether you can buy the technical reference manual, he will not even have one. Because Joe doesn't have one, you are put at his mercy whenever you have a technical question that needs an answer. And more than likely, Joe will not have answers to any but the simplest questions. Not a workable alternative to the manual! And remember that you also received a "generic" version of MS-DOS with your system. That version is fine for DOS, but are you aware that no plans exist for a generic version of OS/2? The OS/2 operating system is too hardware specific for a generic version to be developed. What do you think Joe will have to say when all his Turbo AT customers call and ask why the $325 IBM OS/2 package Joe told them to buy doesn't run on his system?

Note that these selection criteria fully qualify many systems on the market. For example, Zenith, COMPAQ (with minor exceptions), NEC, Toshiba, AST, and Dell Computer systems, as well as the newer Tandy and AT&T systems, all are qualified by these criteria. Note that all these systems are from bigger-name companies, and these systems may cost a bit more than the "generic" systems referred to earlier.

The rest of this chapter discusses in detail the criteria in this checklist.

Documentation

As mentioned earlier, extensive documentation is an important factor to consider when you're planning to buy a system. This section examines four forms of documentation: system documentation, technical reference manuals, hardware maintenance and service manuals, and advanced diagnostics software.

System Documentation

One of the most important things you can have for your system is good system documentation. Repairing, upgrading, or troubleshooting a system is nearly impossible without it. Many people are intimidated by the volume, technical nature, and cost of some of the documentation available for a particular system, but consider the purchase a necessary evil. This area separates the true manufacturers from the guy in his garage slapping together motherboards and cases. Good documentation also keeps you from trying these two horrible approaches when you have a question or problem:

Trial and error
The dealer

Of these approaches, many consider trial and error to be much more productive than calling the dealer. Some dealers, of course, can support the typical end user properly. But very few dealers want to become intimately involved with your upgrade project, and no dealer will repair your system for free. Unless you want to waste innumerable hours with unresponsive technical-support departments or simply play a guessing game when troubleshooting or upgrading your system, demand that certain technical reference documents be made available to you for your system. Do expect to have to seek and locate these documents and pay for them when the documents are found. Reference documents rarely (if ever) are included with the system purchase price and in some cases can be difficult to obtain.

Technical Reference Manuals

The technical reference manual is the most important of all the manuals available for a particular system. I absolutely refuse to purchase any system that does not have an appropriate technical reference manual. Actually, I usually buy this manual long before the system itself, because the information contained within the manual is necessary for me to conduct a proper review of the system.

In Chapter 2, information was given on the contents of these manuals as produced by IBM. IBM excels in this area. The system documentation sets a standard that is difficult for other manufacturers to follow. Having documentation as good as IBM's is not really necessary, but having a basic technical reference manual with detailed information *is* necessary. You will need this information later to know the details for installing particular floppy drives, hard drives, memory adapters and chips, communications adapters, and practically anything else. Expect to pay between $25 and $150 for a good technical reference manual. To obtain this document for your system, contact the Original Equipment Manufacturer (OEM). Chapter 2 has more information on obtaining this documentation for IBM systems.

Hardware Maintenance and Service Manuals

The service manuals are desirable for anyone who will have to troubleshoot the system. This type of manual is not an absolute necessity, and, in fact, several manufacturers will have no documentation of this sort. Other manufacturers (such as COMPAQ) may have this type of documentation but refuse to make it available to users, which is generally OK because the actual IBM documentation in this case will be satisfactory—even for a compatible.

The hardware maintenance and service manuals from IBM contain several items:

- Jumper and switch settings for IBM systems
- A parts catalog for IBM systems
- Detailed diagnostic flowcharts
- Advanced diagnostics disks

The first two items will not do the compatible owner any good, but the last two items will be valuable in almost all cases for actual IBM systems or compatibles. The diagnostic flowcharts are called Maintenance Analysis Procedures (MAPs) by IBM and are quite useful. These flowcharts are a list of step-by-step instructions for troubleshooting a failure down to the smallest plug-in part in the system. "Down to the smallest plug-in part" generally means down to the board level, but items such as memory are troubleshooted down to the actual failed component. These MAPs are written so that you follow a logical progression. You check and test a cable before scrapping a controller card, for example, or you test a controller card before tossing a disk drive, or you check switch and jumper settings before even touching any hardware. Although a person with experience in troubleshooting and diagnosis may not use these flowcharts often, the flowcharts can be handy when all your own tried-and-true procedures have failed. The flowcharts are especially handy when the pressure is on and you're not thinking clearly.

The advanced diagnostics are included with the hardware maintenance and service manual. The manual for the PC, XT, portable, and AT comes with two diagnostics disks. One disk is for PC types of systems, and the other is for AT types of systems. Supplements (updates) are available for newer systems such as the PS/2 Models 25 and 30, which provide a new disk, and the XT-286, which comes with a disk that replaces and supersedes the AT disk.

The hardware maintenance and service manual for the PS/2 comes with the same "reference disk" that you got when you bought the system. You may not have realized that you had the advanced diagnostics for the PS/2 Models 50, 60, 70, and 80 all along. The advanced diagnostics are hidden on the disk and may be accessed only through a special "back door" that activates them. This door becomes known to anyone who pays for the hardware maintenance and service manual because the door is fully documented within. The idea here is to prevent the average user from knowing about and subsequently wandering about the advanced diagnostics. Many of the disk tests destroy data and should not be run by inexperienced personnel.

What is the command to activate the advanced diagnostics for the PS/2? Simply boot the reference disk, go to the main menu, and press Ctrl-A (for Advanced). The menu is replaced with a new one: the Advanced Diagnostics menu. That's it. Even though you already have the diagnostics, you still may want to consider getting a copy of the manual; valuable information is in it.

Advanced Diagnostics Software

The *advanced diagnostics software* is a powerful set of routines that can inspect and test all major areas of the system—and quite a few minor ones. Additionally, any peripherals that are fully compatible with IBM's own can be tested by these diagnostics. The advanced diagnostics will run on any system compatible at the hardware level with any IBM system. The advanced diagnostics software becomes a sort of acid test for compatibility. Remember how people used to use things like Microsoft's Flight Simulator or Lotus 1-2-3 for testing compatibility? I always used the IBM advanced diagnostics instead. I got a much better evaluation of the system's performance and compatibility then and still can today.

This diagnostics software also can test most add-on devices that are similar to those from IBM. For example, you can test the hard disk and controller as long as the interface is compatible with what IBM used. Graphics boards can be tested as if they were the particular IBM board that they replaced; examples of the IBM boards are the Color Graphics Adapter (CGA), Enhanced Graphics Adapter (EGA), and so on. I usually find that any hardware-compatible system will pass at least the motherboard tests (they work even without an actual IBM ROM), memory tests, floppy controller and disk tests, and usually the hard disk controller and drive tests. Non-IBM graphics boards usually fail the IBM tests, and most non-IBM communications boards such as terminal emulators and network adapters are not even recognized. This is the case even if they are in an IBM system unit.

In a later chapter, you will look at some aftermarket (non-OEM) replacements for the advanced diagnostics that may or may not be available from your system's manufacturer. Several of these replacements have been adjusted to work on compatible systems perhaps better than the diagnostics from IBM. In many cases, these replacements also have more powerful test and diagnostic routines than those in the IBM version.

Systems Software

The operating systems software for your system is extremely important. This software is an essential part of the system because nothing can be done without it. The operating systems software really should be considered equal in importance to the ROM BIOS code that runs the system because, in fact, the operating system is an extension or replacement for the ROM BIOS. You may ask, "Why didn't they just put the entire DOS in ROM? And then when I turn on the system, it will be ready to go." The answer is that an operating system is complicated and often is changed. Would you want to take your system in for service every time a new DOS came out? Also, would you want to be restricted to using only one type of DOS? Of course not, so the system designers put as little of an operating system as possible into the system in the form of ROM chips or firmware. The term *firmware* indicates a program that is burned into a ROM chip. Software that is "hard" is called firmware.

The importance of system software is easy to understand. Now where do you get this software? Hopefully, you can get it from the company that makes your system. The Original Equipment Manufacturer (OEM) of the system must supply this software because it is highly customized to the particular hardware design. Unfortunately, many lower cost compatibles do not have OEM versions of any operating systems. And having a system with no real operating system can cause problems. Where will you get one? Where will you get upgrades to new versions? Will new versions be produced for other systems but not yours? These are tough questions and are examined in this section.

OEM-Licensed DOS (from Microsoft)

When asked what operating system they use, many people respond, "MS-DOS." Others may say they use PC DOS or COMPAQ DOS. Those who say they use MS-DOS, however, may not be entirely correct. Just what is MS-DOS? And what, for instance, is the difference between MS-DOS and PC DOS?

MS-DOS stands for the Microsoft Disk Operating System, a collection of programs designed and produced by Microsoft and IBM by virtue of a special joint development agreement. The programs are specifically designed to run on IBM (and compatible) systems. Microsoft owns the source code and sells licenses to various system OEMs who then adapt the code to run on their systems. These OEMs then produce the documentation and provide all support for their specific version of DOS. Microsoft has not, does not, and will not sell DOS as a stand-alone retail product. In other words, no such thing as "pure" MS-DOS exists. You will find only specific "flavors" or implementations of MS-DOS that are given names by the OEMs who produce them—names such as IBM PC DOS, COMPAQ DOS, AT&T DOS, AST DOS, and so on.

Here is an analogy from the automotive world. General Motors often produces a variety of different makes and models of automobiles based on the exact same chassis. Suppose that I drive a 1988 Pontiac Firebird. If you ask me what type of car I drive, I could answer, "I drive a GM F-body automobile." That answer is correct, but not detailed enough. True, the Firebird is an F-body (GM corporate designation), but so is the Chevrolet Camaro. You cannot really buy a pure "F-body" car from General Motors; you must have either a Firebird or Camaro. GM does not sell raw F-bodies to the public. GM instead sells the bodies to the Pontiac and Chevrolet motor divisions, and they customize the autos to produce the final result. This F-body assembly plant is in Van Nuys, California, and in this plant, Firebirds and Camaros are manufactured side by side, by the same workers, and on the same assembly line. The engines, transmissions, brakes, frames, suspensions, and virtually all mechanical items are exactly the same between the two cars. The cars differ only in exterior appearance items.

DOS is sold the same way. It is licensed to a particular computer system manufacturer who then takes the raw source code and adapts this code to run properly on his or her particular system.

This analogy helps to answer the other question: What is the difference between MS-DOS and PC DOS? Now you can see that, as stated, this question is not answerable in definite terms. PC DOS is a real product that can be dissected and analyzed, and MS-DOS is a general term that applies to all the specific types of DOS produced from the same "assembly line" beginnings. That question is the same as this question: "What is the difference between a GM F-body automobile and a Pontiac Firebird?" How do you answer that? The Firebird *is* an F-body automobile, but so is the Camaro. Likewise, PC DOS *is* MS-DOS, but so is COMPAQ DOS, AT&T DOS, Zenith DOS, AST DOS, Toshiba DOS, NEC DOS, and so on.

Now you come to a problem. Remember Joe from Joe's Computer Shack? Joe wanted to sell an implementation of MS-DOS for his systems, and so he called Microsoft. Microsoft spoke to Joe about licensing MS-DOS and told him that he could get a binary adaptation kit that would help him customize the piles of source code that he would receive. Joe also found out that he would have to write and print all the documentation and produce all the packaging for his product, which he could call JOE's DOS. Then he was told about the licensing fees, which run into tens and even hundreds of thousands of dollars! Because Joe only sells about five systems a week and runs a small store, he could hardly justify the costs and does not have the programming staff required to do the adaptation. So Joe told his customers to get PC DOS; after all, his systems are 100 percent compatible with IBM's, right?

Wrong. Joe's customers began calling. "Why can't I run any interpreted BASIC programs? Why don't some of the earlier systems you sold me recognize the date and time during boot? Why am I having so many problems with overwriting floppy data in drive A when switching disks? Why on some systems does the hard disk have constant errors?" Joe then told his customers to get COMPAQ DOS because in the COMPAQ version, the entire BASIC interpreter is provided and the BASICA program file does not rely on the Cassette BASIC, which is found only in the ROM of true IBM systems. This solution may not have solved the other problems. In fact, new calls came in. "Why does the MODE command no longer operate properly, Joe?"

Today, lots of "Joe's" are selling low-cost generic compatibles, and Microsoft has finally recognized this fact. As of DOS 3.2, Microsoft now has a special version just for the generic compatibles: the Microsoft MS-DOS Packaged Product. A dealer like Joe can get this version from Microsoft on a small-quantity basis but must sign an agreement stating that he will perform all the testing to verify that this version works correctly on his systems, provide all support to end users who purchase the product, and sell it only *with a computer*. You cannot buy this generic MS-DOS without a computer system. Any upgrades and bug fixes are handled by Joe or possibly by Microsoft directly. This generic version is not "tweaked" to run better on any particular system but is instead designed to run on IBM or 100-percent compatible systems. Any systems not fully compatible with IBM still must use a specially customized version of DOS licensed from Microsoft and produced by the OEM. If for any reason the generic version does not work in some way on a particular system, Microsoft probably will not fix the problem.

The bottom line is this: to ensure that your system really is fully compatible with current and later releases of DOS, you must buy your system from an OEM who has a direct license from Microsoft for DOS and who produces his own DOS product. You could buy an AST Premium 286, for example, because AST has a license from

Microsoft and produces its own DOS product (called AST DOS) specifically for the system. In all honesty, you rarely will have problems with various compatibles running the prepackaged Microsoft DOS. In fact, most will run IBM PC DOS quite nicely, but not the BASIC interpreter. I really don't consider mandatory this criteria of having an OEM-produced DOS for PC XT types of systems, but this type of DOS will be valuable insurance for the future.

OEM-Licensed OS/2 (from Microsoft)

When examining OS/2 in the same manner as DOS, you will find that the issues are more straightforward: no generic version of OS/2 will come from Microsoft. Such a version will be available only as a licensed product to OEMs, who must adapt it to their systems. If you have purchased an AT system whose manufacturer does not produce an implementation of OS/2, you may be in trouble. (Joe's customers will be in trouble when they find out that Joe will never have any OS/2 for them and that they must take their chances with the IBM version.) As a professional consultant, I cannot have my clients left out in the cold like this, so in order for me to recommend an AT type of system for purchase, an OEM version of OS/2 must be designed specifically for that system.

Any system that is 100-percent hardware compatible with IBM obviously will run the IBM version. Many compatibles so far actually run the IBM version—and maybe most compatibles will. But for now, I will not purchase a system on a "hope" that may turn out to be just a "dream."

Understand, also, that even if your motherboard is fully compatible with IBM's AT systems and would run OS/2, you also must be compatible at the adapter-card hardware level. By adding nonstandard adapter cards to an IBM AT, you can render it unable to run OS/2. For example, IBM OS/2 currently comes with drivers for the Western Digital type of hard disk controllers. Because IBM used the 1002-WA2 and 1003-WA2, these drivers will work fine. Western Digital also has a new faster version called the 1006, and it also will work with OS/2. But if your AT system has a hard disk controller with a built-in ROM used to run the card, uses an 8-bit interface to the system board, uses proprietary compression and caching systems, or does not incorporate the ST-506/412 interface, you will need a special OS/2 driver program for that controller to work. These drivers must be supplied by the OEM of the particular board you use. Be prepared to wait. I am using an SCSI host adapter in my AT system, for example, that provides the system with an incredibly fast and powerful interface to hard disks and other devices. If this system remains in my system, however, I cannot boot OS/2 because the company that produces the device will not have drivers ready for several months. Be prepared for similar experiences with each and every type of adapter card that deviates from established standards.

All these problems will be solved with time and effort. Most (if not all) of the early Video Graphics Array (VGA) adapters, for example, definitely will not work with OS/2, but most of the current versions will work with OS/2. Any purchasers of the earlier boards must upgrade or exchange their board for one that really works.

Here is the bottom line: don't buy an AT system from an OEM who does not have a complete system available, with a customized version of OS/2 to accompany it.

ROM BIOS

The issue of ROM BIOS compatibility is important. If the BIOS is not compatible, any number of problems can arise. Several reputable companies who produce compatibles have developed their own proprietary ROM BIOS that works just like IBM's. These companies also update their ROM code frequently, to keep in step with the latest changes IBM has incorporated into its own ROMs. Because IBM generally does not sell ROM upgrades or provide them to its systems unless the upgrade is absolutely necessary (IBM decides what is necessary), keeping current with an actual IBM system is more difficult than with most of the compatible systems on the market. Also, many of the compatibles' OEMs have designed ROMs that work specifically with additional features in their systems while effectively masking the effects of these improvements from any software.

OEM

Many OEMs have developed their own compatible ROMs independently. Companies such as COMPAQ, Zenith, and AT&T have developed their own BIOS, which have proven compatible with IBM's. These companies also offer upgrades to newer versions that often can offer more features and improvements. If you use a system with a proprietary ROM, make sure that it is from a larger company with a track record and one that will provide updates and fixes as necessary.

The Phoenix and Award Software Companies

Two software companies specialize specifically in the development of a compatible ROM BIOS product. These companies are Phoenix and Award. Each company will license its ROM BIOS to a motherboard manufacturer so that the manufacturer can worry about the hardware rather than the software. To get one of these ROMs for a motherboard, the OEM must answer a multipage questionnaire about the design of the system so that the proper BIOS can be selected. The combining of a ROM BIOS and the motherboard is not a haphazardly performed task. No single generic compatible ROM exists, either. Phoenix and Award ship many variations to different manufacturers; each one is custom-tailored to that particular system, much like DOS.

Although Phoenix will customize the ROM code for a particular system, it will not sell this ROM's source code to the OEM. The OEM must obtain each new release from Phoenix as the new release becomes available. Many OEMs will not need every new version, so they may skip several version changes before licensing another new one from Phoenix. Award takes the slightly different tact of making available the ROM's source code that is licensed to the OEM. The OEM can customize the product further and, in a sense, take all future ROM development in-house. Many OEMs now prefer this arrangement, which gives them more absolute control over what code is in the ROM. Some OEMs who appear to have developed their own ROM code actually started with a base of source code that was licensed to them by Award.

The bottom line is this: unless the ROM BIOS is a truly compatible custom OEM version such as that of COMPAQ, Zenith, or AT&T, you may want the ROM BIOS of one of the known quantities, such as Phoenix or Award, installed in the system. Phoenix and Award have established themselves as ROM BIOS standards in the industry, and their frequent updates and customization ensure that the system containing these ROMs will have a long life of upgrades and service ahead.

Conservative Design

For systems that I recommend for business use, a principle of conservative design is important. I usually stay away from systems that are advertised to perform "impossible" feats of speed and performance or that have features and prices that are simply too good to be true. Many of these systems use substandard components and often run at higher speeds than the components were designed for. These systems will have limited testing and debugging and can have frustrating lockups, incompatibilities, and servicing problems.

If the expansion bus is running too fast or with inaccurate timing, many adapter cards will not run or will not run properly in the system. If the system improperly runs a form of RLL encoding with drives and cabling that were never designed for the additional bandwidth, serious problems in data integrity will result. If a cheap power supply is used and runs at (or past) its limit, the system will experience a number of problems and failures. These issues all deal with the original design of the system. I believe in conservatism and a little overkill with these matters, which is part of the reason that my own systems, and those I recommend for others, run so well for so long!

Use of Correct Speed-Rated Parts

I have seen a great deal of substandard parts used in some systems. A system, for example, is sold as a 14 MHz AT system, but when you look under the hood, you find a CPU rated for only 12 MHz. You call the dealer who says the company "burns in" its systems to ensure that the parts do run at the speed that they say. If the companies that manufacture chips could put a stamp on the chip that said it was a truly reliable 14 MHz part, they would! After all, these companies could sell the chip for more money if it really would be OK. Unfortunately, it wouldn't be OK. Don't purchase any system if the speed of the system exceeds the design of the respective parts.

You usually find this sort of activity in some of the compatibles that are running very fast and that also have unusually good prices. Ask before you buy. Are the parts really manufacturer rated for the system speed?

Table 5.1 provides a speed decoding chart for the CPU chips that you will see in IBM-compatible systems.

Table 5.1
Speed Decoding Chart

CPU Chip	Math Chip	Suffix	Max. Speed
8088 or 8086	8087	no marks	5 MHz
		-3	6 MHz
		-2	8 MHz
		-1	10 MHz
80286	80287	-6	6 MHz
		-8	8 MHz
		-10	10 MHz
		-12	12 MHz
		-16	16 MHz
		-20	20 MHz
80386	80387	-16	16 MHz
		-20	20 MHz
		-25	25 MHz

Slot Speed

For true compatibility and board exchangeability, you need to know how fast a particular system will run the slots. Most high-speed compatibles employ a dual clock that ensures that the system slots for both PC XT or AT systems do not run the bus at a rate faster than 8 MHz or with less than 1 wait state. If the system can allow faster operation than this, you are free to try it. But if the system bus cannot be slowed to this level, you will find that many adapter cards will not work in that particular system. Many memory cards are sensitive, especially the expanded-memory types of boards. Also, most of the network adapters or other highly specialized communications adapters are speed sensitive.

Power Supply Output

I make sure that adequate power output is available to run various expansion devices. The power supply also should supply enough airflow to cool the system adequately. A system lid or case may feel warm but should never feel hot to the touch. Most of the time, the power output specification is stamped on the power supply of the system or is found in the technical reference manuals for the system. Consult the technical manuals for each disk drive you purchase as well as for each adapter you intend to plug in, to see if enough power is available to run all these devices reliably. In a later chapter, you will examine the consequences of overstressing the power supply.

Adherence to Standards

Look to see that certain standards are followed. IBM has declared specific uses for certain Interrupt Request lines (IRQ), Direct Memory Access (DMA) channels, and I/O ports. Also be certain that the CMOS memory and real time clock are set up like they are set up in the IBM units (make sure that data is organized the same way and the port locations are the same). Make sure that your system follows the IBM standards. You can find this information in the technical reference manual for the system. In the Appendix, several charts are provided that describe these items and how they are allocated in an IBM system unit.

Support

Support from the system manufacturer is important. Some manufacturers rely solely on their vendors (dealers) to provide support, which is not always a good idea because dealers rarely can provide real technical support. Besides simply being able to ask technical questions, the source of support should also include a spare-parts program and be able to exchange major components for rebuilt replacements. Most of the larger companies, such as IBM, Tandy, AT&T, Toshiba, NEC, and Dell, support their own products directly, as well as through the dealer. Others, such as COMPAQ, don't support their products directly; any support you seek must be handled through your dealer.

Spare-Parts Program

In any system, look for the availability of a spare-parts program. In other words, can you obtain any of the unique parts that make up a system? These parts can include motherboards, power supplies, proprietary adapter cards, special memory boards and chips, unique hardware, and cosmetic parts such as cases, front panels, etc. I like how *Popular Mechanics* magazine reviews an automobile. At the end of the review, a list is presented that gives the cost of most of the commonly replaced items on the car, such as brakes, front and rear body parts, alternators, etc. This list can give you a great deal of insight when comparing a low-cost foreign model (that has exorbitant parts and maintenance prices) with a domestic model (that has cheaper, more commonly available parts).

Because of the number of systems sold, many suppliers are available for these types of items for any of IBM's systems. You can pick up a power supply or any type of drive or adapter at a low cost because of the competition. Other vendors prefer to lock you in to high-cost custom parts, which you cannot find at a discount. Every COMPAQ item, for example, that *can* be physically different from an IBM item *is* different. You must get your power supplies, your motherboards, and often your disk drives from COMPAQ. And COMPAQ will not sell any parts directly; you must go through dealers.

In the end, purchasing a system that has an ample supply of parts available and that will be supported by the aftermarket pays off. The PS/2 systems are currently in parts shortage, and most of the parts for these systems must be purchased from IBM. Currently, few aftermarket power supplies are available, but you already can find disk drives that fit the unique interiors of these systems. Little concern exists over any lack of aftermarket support for the PS/2; plenty of support will be there. Some people may hold off on a PS/2 purchase until IBM can supply repair parts more readily and until more aftermarket solutions are available to problems.

Exchange of Major Components

Most of the larger manufacturers offer a board exchange policy. For expensive components, such as the motherboard, you can trade in a defective component for a good one for much less money than an outright purchase. You may want to consider this information when you look at other vendors' systems.

Chapter Summary

In this chapter, you examined the compatible marketplace from the point of view of a system installer or troubleshooter, and you kept in mind that you plan to upgrade the system later. You were given a quick guide and checklist for what to look for in a compatible system that will meet the needs of a business user, be serviceable for years to come, and have plenty of upgrade options.

The next chapter gives you detailed information on how to tear down and inspect your system.

Part III

Hardware Considerations

Includes

System Teardown and Inspection

Primary System Components

Floppy Disk Drives

Hard Disk Drives

Peripherals

6

System Teardown
and Inspection

In this chapter, you will examine the procedures for tearing down
and inspecting a system. You will learn about the types of tools
required, the procedure for disassembling the system, and the
various components that make up the system. A special section
discusses some of the test equipment you can use, and another
section covers some problems you might encounter with the actual
hardware (screws, nuts, bolts, and so on).

Using the Proper Tools

In order to troubleshoot and repair PC systems properly, you need
the following basic tools:

- Simple hand tools for basic disassembly and reassembly
  procedures

- Wrap plugs for diagnosing port problems

- Meters that allow accurate measurement of voltage and
  resistance

In addition, you might need soldering and desoldering tools for
problems that require these operations. The next section discusses
these basic tools in more detail.

Hand Tools

What becomes apparent immediately when you work with PC systems is that the tools required for nearly all service operations are simple and inexpensive. You can carry most of the required tools in a small pouch. Even a top of the line ''master mechanic's'' set will fit inside a briefcase. The cost of these toolkits ranges from about $20 for the small-service kit to $500 for a briefcase-sized kit. This cost range is different from the automotive world. Most automotive technicians spend $5,000 or more for the tools they use.

In this section, you will learn about the tools required to make up a set that is capable of basic board-level service on PC systems. One of the best ways to start such a set of tools is with a small kit sold especially for servicing PCs.

Here is a list of the basic tools you can find in any of the small ''PC toolkits'' sold for about $30:

- 3/16-inch nut driver
- 1/4-inch nut driver
- Small Phillips screwdriver
- Small flat blade screwdriver
- Medium Phillips screwdriver
- Medium flat blade screwdriver
- Chip extractor
- Chip inserter
- Tweezers
- Claw-type parts grabber
- T10 TORX driver
- T15 TORX driver

You use the nut drivers to remove the screws that secure the system unit covers, adapter boards, disk drives, power supplies, and speakers in the earlier PC, XT, and AT types of systems. Some manufacturers have substituted slotted or Phillips types of screws for the more standard hexagonal head screws, so the other screwdrivers will work for these systems. You use the chip extractor and insertion tools to install or remove memory chips (or other smaller chips) without bending any pins on the chip. Usually, you will pry out larger chips such as microprocessors or ROMs with the small screwdriver. The tweezers and parts grabber can be used to hold any small screws or jumper blocks that are difficult for you to hold in your hand. The parts grabber is especially useful when a small part is dropped into the interior of a system; you usually can remove the part without completely disassembling the system. Finally, the TORX driver is a special star-shaped driver that matches the screws found in most COMPAQ systems and in some other systems as well.

Although this basic set is useful, some other small hand tools should be purchased:

- Needlenose pliers
- Wire cutter/stripper
- Vise
- File

The pliers are useful for straightening pins on chips, applying or removing jumpers, crimping cables, or grabbing small parts. The wire cutter/stripper has obvious uses in making or repairing cables or wiring. You can use a vise for installing connectors on cables and crimping cables to a desired shape. You can use a file for smoothing rough metal edges on cases and chassis as well as for trimming the faceplates on disk drives for a perfect fit.

With a simple set of hand tools, you will be equipped for nearly every PC repair or installation situation. The total cost for these tools should be less than $100, making this set of tools economical as well.

Soldering and Desoldering Tools

For certain situations, such as repairing a broken wire, reattaching a component to a circuit board, removing and installing chips that are not in a socket, or adding jumper wires or pins to a board, you will need to use a *soldering iron* to make the repair. Even those of you who do only board-level service will find that you need a soldering iron in some situations.

You will need a low-wattage iron—usually about 25 watts. More than 30 watts will generate too much heat and possibly damage the components on the board. Even with a low-wattage unit, you must limit the amount of heat to which you subject the board or components on the board. You can limit the amount of heat with quick and efficient use of the soldering iron and with the use of heat-sinking devices that are clipped to the leads of the device being soldered. A *heat sink* is something designed to absorb heat before the heat reaches the component that the heat sink is protecting.

To remove components that were originally soldered into place from a printed circuit board, you can use a soldering iron with a solder sucker. A *solder sucker* is a small tube with an air chamber and a plunger and spring arrangement. (Do not try to use the "bulb" type of solder sucker.) The unit is "cocked" when you press the spring-loaded plunger into the air chamber. When a device is to be removed from a board, the point at which one of the component leads joins the circuit board is heated from the underside of the board with the soldering iron until the solder melts. As soon as melting occurs, you move the solder-sucker nozzle into position and press an actuator. This procedure allows the plunger to retract, creating a momentary suction that inhales the liquid solder from the connection and leaves the component lead dry in the hole. The heating and sucking is always done from the underside of a board, not from the component side. You repeat this action for each component lead joined to the circuit board. When you master this technique, you can remove a small chip such as a 16-pin memory chip in a minute or two, with only a small likelihood of damage to the board or other components. Larger chips with many pins can be difficult to remove and resolder without damaging other components or the circuit board itself.

If you really intend to add soldering and desoldering skills to your arsenal of abilities, you will need practice. Take a useless circuit board and practice removing various components from the board; then reinstall the components. During removal of the components, try to get the component off the board by using the least amount of heat possible. Also perform the solder melting operations as quickly as possible, limiting the time that the iron is actually applied to the joint. Before installing any components, clean out the holes through which the leads must project and mount the component into place. Then apply the solder from the underside of the board, using as little heat and solder as possible. Attempt to produce joints as clean as the joints that the board manufacturer performed by machine.

Soldered joints that do not look "clean" may keep the component from making good connection with the rest of the circuit. This is called a "cold solder joint" and is normally created by not using enough heat. Remember that the wrong place to practice your soldering skills is the motherboard of a system you are attempting to repair. Don't attempt to work on real boards until you are sure of your skills.

Wrap Plugs

For diagnosing serial and parallel port problems, you will need *wrap plugs*, which are used to circulate or "wrap" signals. These plugs allow the serial or parallel port to send data to itself for diagnostic purposes. Several types of wrap plugs are available. You will need one for the 25-pin serial port, 9-pin serial port, and 25-pin parallel port. IBM sells these plugs separately as well as a special version that includes all three types in one plug:

Description	Part Number
Parallel wrap plug	8529228
Serial wrap plug, 25-pin	8529280
Serial wrap plug, 9-pin (AT)	8286126
Tri-connector wrap plug	72X8546

Meters

Many troubleshooting procedures require that you measure voltages and resistances. You accomplish this task by using a Volt-Ohm Meter (VOM). These meters are analog devices (using an actual meter) or digital readout devices that you can hold in your hand. The devices have a pair of wires, called *test leads* or *probes*, that are used to make the connections so readings can be taken. Depending on the meter's setting, the probes will measure electrical resistance, Direct Current Voltage (DCV), or Alternating Current Voltage (ACV).

Each of the measurement types usually has several ranges of operation. The DC voltage, for example, can be read in several scales to a maximum of 200 mv (millivolts), 2 V, 20 V, 200 V, and 1,000 V. Because computers use both +5 and +12 volts for various operations, you would use the 20 V maximum scale for making your measurements. Making these measurements in the 200 mv or 2 V scales would "peg the meter" and possibly damage it because the voltage would be much higher than expected. Using the 200 V or 1,000 V scales would work, but your readings at 5 V and 12 V would be proportionately so small compared to the maximum that accuracy would be low. If you are making a measurement and are unsure of the actual voltage, start at the highest scale and work your way down. Some of the higher cost meters have an *autoranging* capability; the meter actually selects the best range for any measurement automatically.

Some prefer one of the small digital meters. You can buy these meters for as little as $40, and they are extremely accurate. And some of these meters are not much bigger than a cassette tape! If cost is not a problem, you can purchase a small digital meter with autoranging for about $250. These meters are the most accurate and easiest to use.

Now that you have examined the tools needed to tear down and inspect your system, you can examine the procedures for disassembling your system.

Learning the Disassembly Procedures

The process of physically disassembling and reassembling systems is not difficult. Because of marketplace standardization, only a couple different types and sizes of screws are used to hold the systems together, and the physical arrangement of the major components is similar even among systems from different manufacturers. Also, not very many individual components are in each of the systems. This section breaks down the disassembly and reassembly procedure into the following sections:

- Case or cover assembly
- Adapter boards
- Disk drives
- Power supply
- Motherboard

And this section discusses how to remove and install these components for each of the primary system types: PC, XT, AT, and PS/2.

PC and XT Types of Systems

The procedure for disassembling the PC or XT types of systems offered by IBM and other manufacturers is simple. Only two tools are required: a 1/4-inch nut driver for the external screws holding the cover in place and a 3/16-inch nut driver for all the other screws.

The Cover

To remove the system unit cover, follow these steps:

1. Turn off the system and unplug the power cord from the system unit.

2. Turn the system unit around so that you are facing the rear of the unit and locate the screws that hold the system unit cover in place (see fig. 6.1).

3. Remove the cover screws by using the 1/4-inch nut driver.

4. Slide the cover toward the front of the system unit until it stops; then lift up the front of the cover and remove it from the chassis.

Adapter Boards

To remove all the adapter boards from the system unit, first remove the system unit cover as described previously and then do the following for each adapter:

1. Note which slots all the adapters are in. If possible, make a diagram or drawing.

2. Use the 3/16-inch nut driver to remove the screw holding the adapter in place (see fig. 6.2).

3. If any cables are plugged into the adapter, note their position and remove them. The odd-colored stripe on one side of the ribbon cable always denotes pin number 1 in a correctly wired

Fig. 6.1.

The screws holding the PC and XT system unit cover in place.

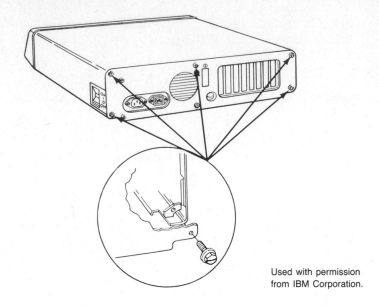

Used with permission from IBM Corporation.

system. The power connector is shaped so that it can be inserted only the correct way.

4. Remove the adapter by lifting with even force at both ends.

5. If any jumpers or switches are on the adapter, note their positions.

When removing adapters, *always* note the positions of jumpers and switches, especially when documentation for the adapter is not available. Even when documentation is available, undocumented jumpers and switches are used often by the manufacturer for special purposes such as testing or unique configurations. ***Note:*** Jumpers and switches normally are named on the circuit board; for example, SW1 and SW2 are used for switch 1 and switch 2, and J1 and J2 are used for jumper 1 and jumper 2. If these jumpers or switches are ever disturbed later, you always can return to the original configuration if it was noted when the adapter was first removed. Making a diagram that shows these features of a particular card is usually the best procedure.

Disk Drives

Removing drives for PC and XT systems is fairly easy. The procedures are similar for both floppy and hard disk drives. Always

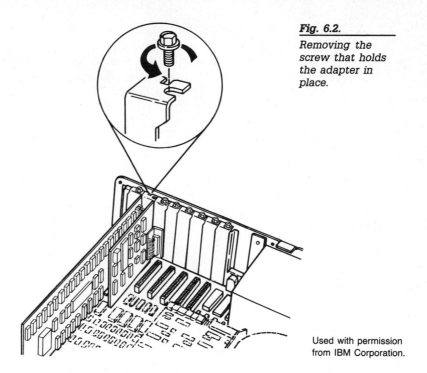

Fig. 6.2.
Removing the screw that holds the adapter in place.

Used with permission from IBM Corporation.

back up your hard disks completely and park the heads before removal from the system. The possibility always exists that data will be lost or the drive will be damaged from rough handling. Hard disks are discussed in more detail in a later chapter.

When removing the drives from a PC or XT type of system, first remove the cover and all adapters as previously described and then follow these steps:

1. Lift up the front of the chassis so that the unit is standing with the rear of the chassis down and the disk drive facing straight up. Locate any drive retaining screws in the bottom of the chassis and remove them. On IBM equipment, you will find these screws in XT systems with hard disks or half-height floppy drives (see fig. 6.3). Note that these screws may be shorter than others used in the system. And you must remember to reinstall a screw of the same length in this location later; you can damage the drive by using a screw that is too long.

2. Set the chassis flat on the table, locate the drive retaining screws on the outboard sides of the drive, and remove them (see figs. 6.4 and 6.5).

3. Slide the disk drive forward about two inches and disconnect the power and signal cables from the drive (see figs. 6.6 and 6.7). The odd-colored stripe on one side of the ribbon cable always denotes pin number 1 in a correctly wired system. The power connector is shaped so that it can be inserted only the correct way.

4. Slide the drive completely out of the unit.

Fig. 6.3.

Removing drive retaining screws on the bottom of the chassis.

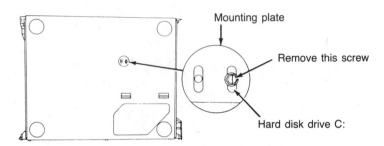

Mounting plate

Remove this screw

Hard disk drive C:

Used with permission from IBM Corporation.

Fig. 6.4.

Removing the retaining screws on the outboard sides of a floppy disk drive.

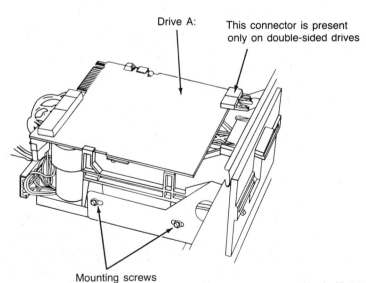

Drive A:

This connector is present only on double-sided drives

Mounting screws

Used with permission from IBM Corporation.

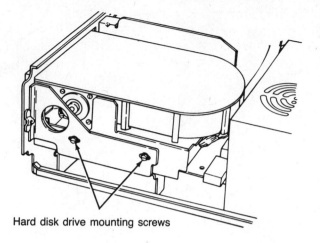

Fig. 6.5.

Removing the retaining screws on the outboard sides of the hard disk drive.

Hard disk drive mounting screws

Used with permission from IBM Corporation.

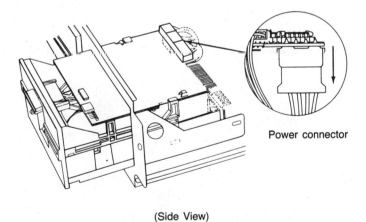

Fig. 6.6.

The power connector on a floppy disk drive.

Power connector

(Side View)

Used with permission from IBM Corporation.

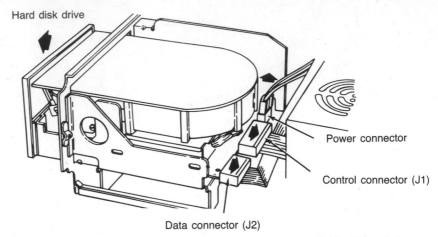

Fig. 6.7.

Disconnecting the power and signal cables from the hard disk drive.

Hard disk drive

Power connector

Control connector (J1)

Data connector (J2)

Used with permission from IBM Corporation.

Power Supply

In PC and XT types of systems, the power supply is mounted in the system unit with four screws in the rear and two interlocking tabs on the bottom. Removing the power supply is simple, but the procedure usually requires that you remove the disk drives before getting the power supply out. You will at least have to loosen the drives to slide them forward for clearance when removing the supply.

To remove the power supply, first remove the cover, all adapter boards, and the disk drives as previously described. If sufficient clearance exists, you may not have to remove the adapter boards and disk drives. Then proceed as follows:

1. Remove the four power-supply retaining screws from the rear of the system unit chassis (see fig. 6.8).

2. Disconnect the cables from the power supply to the motherboard. Disconnect the power cables from the power supply to the disk drives. Always grasp the connectors themselves; never pull on the wires (see fig. 6.9).

3. Slide the power supply forward about a half-inch to disengage the interlocking tabs on the bottom of the unit. Then lift the power supply out of the unit (see fig. 6.10).

Power supply mounting screws

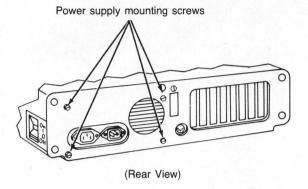

(Rear View)

Used with permission
from IBM Corporation.

Fig. 6.8.

*Removing the
power-supply
retaining screws
from the rear of
the chassis.*

System/expansion board power connectors   Power supply

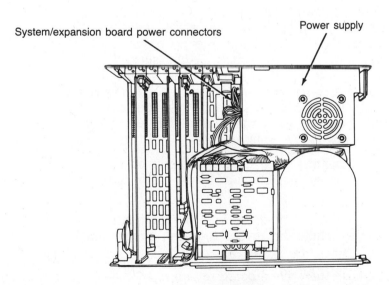

System unit

(Top View)

Used with permission
from IBM Corporation.

Fig. 6.9.

*Disconnecting the
cables from the
power supply to
the motherboard.*

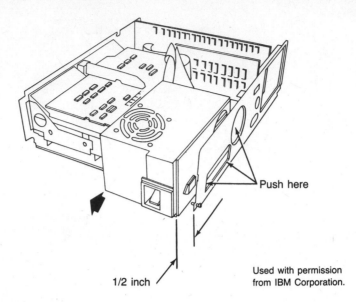

Fig. 6.10.

Sliding the power supply forward to disengage the interlocking tabs on the unit's bottom.

Push here

1/2 inch

Used with permission from IBM Corporation.

Motherboard

After all the adapter cards are removed from the unit, you can remove the motherboard itself. The system board in the PC and XT type of system is held in with only two screws and several plastic standoffs. The purpose of the standoffs is to elevate the board from the metal chassis so that it does not touch the chassis and cause a short. The standoffs slide into slots in the chassis. When reinstalling the motherboard, always make sure that these standoffs are located properly in their slots. If one or more standoffs have not properly engaged the chassis, you may crack the motherboard when you tighten the screws or install any adapter cards.

To remove the system board, first remove all adapter boards from the system unit as previously described and then proceed as follows:

1. Disconnect all electrical connectors from the motherboard; these connectors include the keyboard, power supply, and speaker.

2. Locate and remove the system-board retaining screws.

3. Slide the motherboard away from the power supply about a half-inch until the standoffs have disengaged from their mounting slots (see fig. 6.11).

4. Lift the motherboard up and out of the chassis.

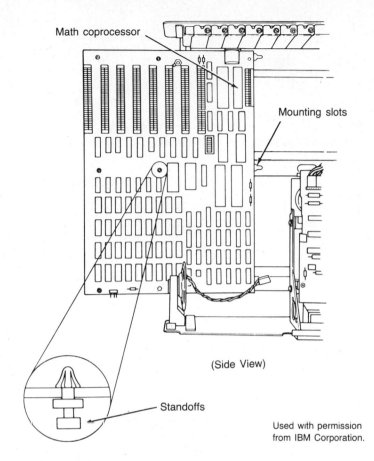

Math coprocessor

Mounting slots

Fig. 6.11.

Sliding the motherboard away from the power supply until standoffs disengage from mounting slots.

(Side View)

Standoffs

Used with permission from IBM Corporation.

AT Types of Systems

Disassembling any of the AT types of systems offered by IBM and other manufacturers is simple. Only two tools are required: a 1/4-inch nut driver for the external screws holding the cover in place and a 3/16-inch nut driver for all the other screws.

Most of the procedures are exactly like those for the PC and XT systems. One difference, however, is that IBM used a different method for mounting the disk drives in the AT. Plastic or fiberglass rails are attached to the drives, and the drives slide into the system unit chassis on these rails. The chassis has guide tracks for the rails to fit into, which allows you to remove the drive from the front of the unit without having to access the side to remove any mounting screws.

The Cover

To remove the system unit cover, follow these steps:

1. Turn off the system and unplug the power cord from the system unit.

2. Turn the system unit around so that you are facing the rear of the unit and locate the five screws that hold the system unit cover in place (see fig. 6.12).

3. Remove the cover screws by using the 1/4-inch nut driver.

4. Slide the cover toward the front of the system unit until it stops; then lift up the front of the cover and remove it from the chassis.

Fig. 6.12.

The screws holding the AT system unit cover in place.

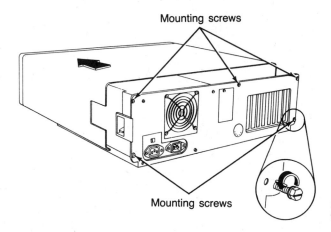

Mounting screws

Mounting screws

Used with permission from IBM Corporation.

Adapter Boards

To remove all the adapter boards from the system unit, first remove the system unit cover as described previously and then do the following for each adapter:

1. Note which slots all the adapters are in. If possible, make a diagram or drawing.

2. Use the 3/16-inch nut driver to remove the screw holding the adapter in place (refer back to fig. 6.2).

3. If any cables are plugged into the adapter, note their positions and remove them. The odd-colored stripe on one side of the ribbon cable always denotes pin number 1 in a correctly wired system. The power connector is shaped so that it can be inserted only the correct way.

4. Remove the adapter by lifting with even force at both ends.

5. If any jumpers or switches are on the adapter, note their positions.

When you remove adapters, be sure to note the positions of jumpers and switches, especially when documentation for the adapter is not available. Even when documentation is available, undocumented jumpers and switches are used often by the manufacturer for special purposes such as testing or unique configurations. If these jumpers or switches are ever disturbed later, you always can return to the original configuration if it was noted when the adapter was first removed. As mentioned earlier, jumpers and switches normally are named on the circuit board (SW1 for switch 1, J1 for jumper 1, and so on). Make a diagram that shows these features of a particular card.

Disk Drives

Removing drives from AT systems is easy. The procedures are similar for both floppy and hard disk drives. Always back up hard disks completely and park the heads before removal from the system. The possibility always exists that data will be lost or the drive will be damaged from rough handling.

To remove the drives from an AT type of system, first remove the cover as previously described; then follow these steps:

1. Depending on whether the drive is a hard disk or a floppy disk drive, it will be retained by a metal keeper bar with two screws or two small L-shaped metal tabs held in by a single screw each. Locate these screws and remove them, along with the tabs or keeper bar (see figs. 6.13 and 6.14).

2. Slide the disk drive forward about two inches and disconnect the power cables, signal and data cables, and ground wire from the drives (see figs. 6.15 and 6.16). The odd-colored stripe on one side of the ribbon cable always denotes pin number 1

in a correctly wired system. The power connector is shaped so that it can be inserted only the correct way.

3. Slide the drive completely out of the unit.

Fig. 6.13.

Removing mounting tabs and the keeper bar on a hard disk drive.

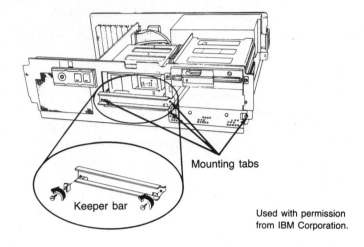

Mounting tabs

Keeper bar

Used with permission from IBM Corporation.

Fig. 6.14.

Removing the metal tabs on a floppy disk drive.

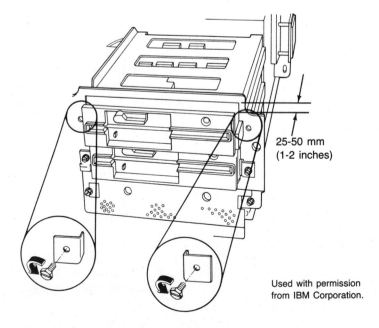

25-50 mm (1-2 inches)

Used with permission from IBM Corporation.

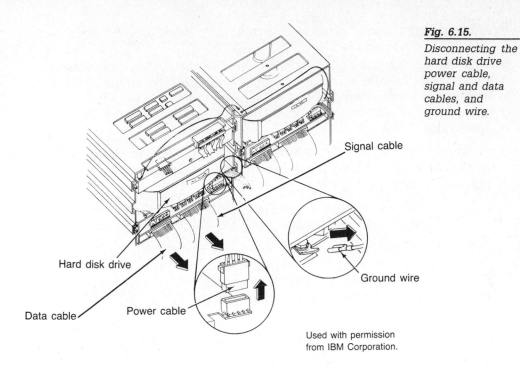

Fig. 6.15.

Disconnecting the hard disk drive power cable, signal and data cables, and ground wire.

Signal cable

Ground wire

Hard disk drive

Data cable

Power cable

Used with permission from IBM Corporation.

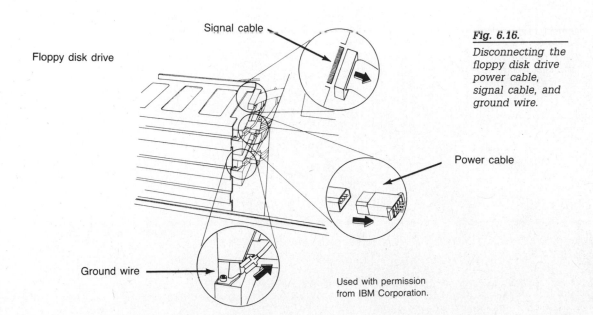

Signal cable

Floppy disk drive

Fig. 6.16.

Disconnecting the floppy disk drive power cable, signal cable, and ground wire.

Power cable

Ground wire

Used with permission from IBM Corporation.

Power Supply

In AT systems, the power supply is mounted in the system unit with four screws in the rear and two interlocking tabs on the bottom. Removing the power supply is simple, but the procedure usually requires that you slide the disk drives forward for clearance when removing the supply.

To remove the power supply, first remove the cover, loosen the disk drive mounting screws, and move the disk drive forward two inches as previously described. Then do the following:

1. Remove the four power-supply retaining screws from the rear of the system unit chassis (see fig. 6.17).

2. Disconnect the cables from the power supply to the motherboard. Disconnect the power cables from the power supply to the disk drive. Always grasp the connectors themselves; never pull on the wires (see fig. 6.18).

3. Slide the power supply forward about a half-inch to disengage the interlocking tabs on the bottom of the unit. Then lift the power supply out of the unit.

Fig. 6.17.

Removing the power-supply retaining screws from the rear of the chassis.

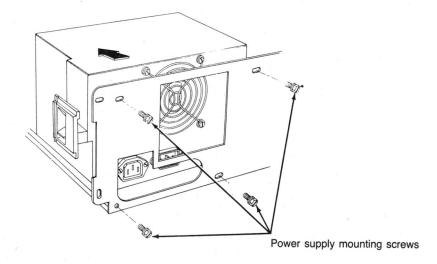

Power supply mounting screws

Used with permission
from IBM Corporation.

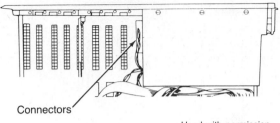

Fig. 6.18.

Disconnecting the cables from the power supply to the motherboard.

Connectors

Used with permission
from IBM Corporation.

Motherboard

After all the adapter cards are removed from the unit, you can remove the motherboard itself. The system board in the AT type of system is held in with only two screws and several plastic standoffs. The purpose of the standoffs is to elevate the board from the metal chassis so that it does not touch the chassis and cause a short. The standoffs slide into slots in the chassis. When reinstalling the motherboard, always make sure that these standoffs are located properly in their slots. If one or more standoffs have not engaged the chassis properly, you may crack the motherboard when you tighten the screws or install any adapter cards.

To remove the system board, first remove all adapter boards from the system unit as previously described; then follow these steps:

1. Disconnect all electrical connectors from the motherboard; these connectors include the following:

    Keyboard
    Power supply
    Speaker
    Battery
    Keylock

2. Locate and remove the system-board retaining screws.

3. Slide the motherboard away from the power supply about a half-inch until the standoffs have disengaged from their mounting slots (see fig. 6.19).

4. Lift the motherboard up and out of the chassis.

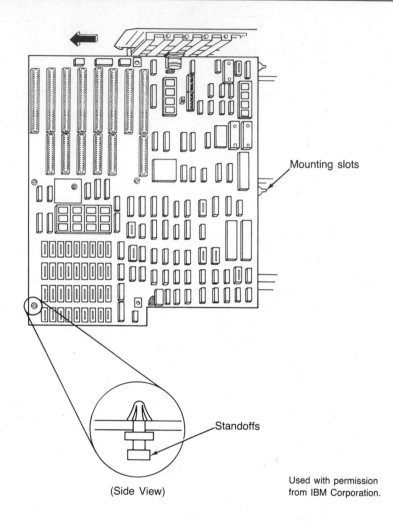

Fig. 6.19.

Disengaging standoffs from their mounting slots.

Mounting slots

Standoffs

(Side View)

Used with permission from IBM Corporation.

PS/2 Systems

The disassembly of IBM's PS/2 systems is incredibly easy. In fact, the easy disassembly and reassembly is one of the greatest features of the new systems. They were designed to be assembled primarily by robots and automated machinery. This type of machinery does not deal well with conventional fasteners such as screws, nuts, and bolts. Most of the PS/2 systems, therefore, are assembled with what amounts to "snap together" technology. This approach to construction makes them easier to assemble by machine, as well as much easier for people to do it.

From a physical construction standpoint, three basic types of PS/2 systems are available. The Models 30 and 30-286 share a common chassis and mechanical design, although their circuit boards are very different. The Model 25 also can be grouped with these systems, although the Model 25 has some physical differences with the other two systems—namely, a built-in monitor. The Models 50 and 70 represent the "ultimate" in ease of disassembly and reassembly. These units do not have a single cable in their default configuration and are almost entirely snapped together all the way down to the motherboard and all disk drives. The Models 50 and 70 share many physical components and are difficult to tell apart from the outside. Finally, IBM has the Models 60 and 80, which are the full-size, floor-standing systems. These two systems are virtually identical from a physical standpoint and share most of the physical components, even though the motherboards are different.

The next section discusses the easy disassembly and reassembly procedures for the PS/2 systems. Each of the three main system types is covered in its own section. Each section describes the procedures in a step-by-step fashion.

Models 30 and 30-286

This section describes the disassembly procedures for the PS/2 Model 30 and Model 30-286. These systems are modular in nature, and most of the procedures are simple.

Cover

Before you remove the cover from the system unit, make sure that the following conditions are met:

- The hard disk is parked.

- The system is off.

- The power cord is unplugged from the socket.

- All external options are disconnected.

- If the key lock option is installed, make sure that the lock is in the unlocked position and the key is removed.

- The cover on the Model 30 is removed. Loosen all four screws located at the bottom corners on the sides of the system and then slide the cover back and lift it up and off.

- The rear cover that covers the system's back panel is removed. You remove this cover by loosening the screw on each corner of the rear cover on the back of the system. Then pull the rear cover back and away from the system unit (see fig. 6.20).

Fig. 6.20.

Removing the rear cover (Models 30 and 30-286).

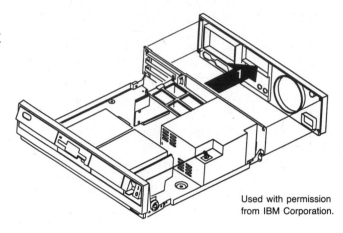

Used with permission
from IBM Corporation.

3 1/2-Inch Floppy Disk Drive

The procedure for removing the floppy drive is simple. First, prepare the heads for removal by inserting a disk or cardboard head protector in the drive. Then follow these steps:

1. Remove the front cover (bezel) from the drive by pushing down on the two plastic tabs on the top of the bezel.

2. Pull the bezel away from and off of the front of the system.

3. Disconnect the disk cabling by gently pulling the cable away from the drive.

4. Remove the plastic nails from each side of the drive bracket.

5. Press up on the plastic tab under the front of the drive.

6. Pull the drive forward out of the system (see fig. 6.21).

Fixed Disk Drive

Before removing the fixed disk, make sure that the heads have been parked. You can use the diagnostics disk to perform this task. The

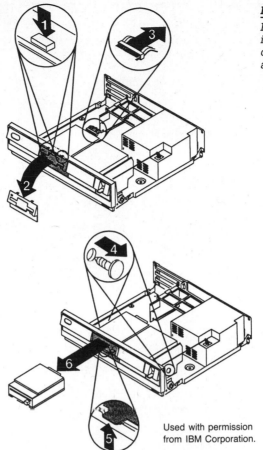

Fig. 6.21.
Removing a 3 1/2-inch floppy disk drive (Models 30 and 30-286).

Used with permission
from IBM Corporation.

drive then may be removed. Note that these procedures are the same as for the floppy drive. Follow these steps:

1. Remove the front bezel from the drive by pushing down on the two plastic tabs on the top of the bezel and pulling it away from and off of the front of the system.

2. Disconnect the disk cabling by gently pulling the cable away from the drive.

3. Remove the plastic nails from each side of the drive bracket.

4. Press upward on the plastic tab under the front of the drive and pull the drive forward out of the system.

Adapters

To remove any adapter cards from the system, follow these procedures.

1. Remove the screw from the bracket retaining the card.

2. Slide the adapter sideways out of the system unit (see fig. 6.22).

Fig. 6.22.

Removing adapter cards (Models 30 and 30-286).

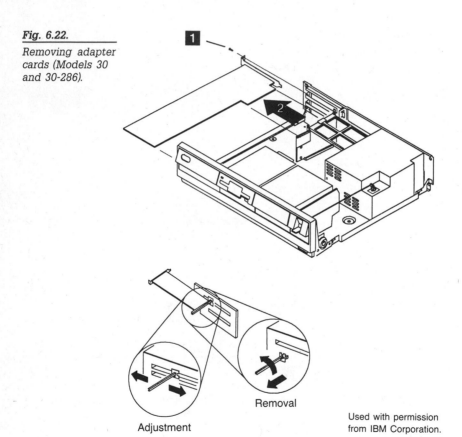

Adjustment

Removal

Used with permission from IBM Corporation.

Note that if you add new options, their installation may require that you remove the plastic insert on the rear panel. Also, if you add a 3/4-length adapter, you must adjust the sliding support bracket to support the adapter properly.

Bus Adapter

These systems have a bus adapter card that actually contains the slots. This adapter plugs into the motherboard. To remove this device, follow these instructions:

1. Push in on the two tabs on top of the bus adapter support.

2. Gently rotate the end of the support upward and disengage the tabs in the power supply.

3. Lift up the bus adapter to remove (see fig. 6.23).

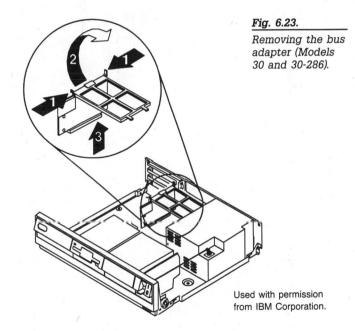

Fig. 6.23.

Removing the bus adapter (Models 30 and 30-286).

Used with permission
from IBM Corporation.

Power Supply

Follow these steps to remove the power supply:

1. After removing the rear cover and the bus adapter support (see preceding instructions), disconnect the power connector from the power supply to the motherboard by pulling the connector straight up.

2. Disengage the power switch link from the power supply.

3. Remove from the back of the power supply the three screws that secure the power supply to the system frame.

4. Gently slide the power supply toward the front of the system in order to disengage the power supply from the base of the frame.

5. Lift the power supply up and away from the unit (see fig. 6.24).

Fig. 6.24.

Removing the power supply (Models 30 and 30-286).

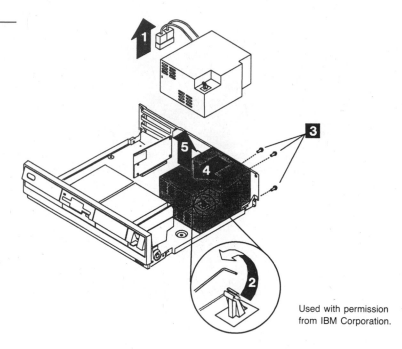

Used with permission from IBM Corporation.

Single Inline Memory Modules (SIMMs)

One of the benefits of using Single Inline Memory Modules (SIMMs) is that they are so easy to remove or install. When removing memory modules, remember that because of physical interference, you must remove the memory module package closest to the disk drive bus adapter slot before removing the package closest to the edge of the system board. To remove a SIMM properly, follow these procedures:

1. Gently pull outward the tabs on each side of the SIMM socket.

2. Rotate or pull the SIMM up and out of the socket (see fig. 6.25). Be careful not to damage the connector, because if you damage the motherboard SIMM connector, you could be looking at an expensive repair. Never force the SIMM; it should come out easily or you are doing something wrong.

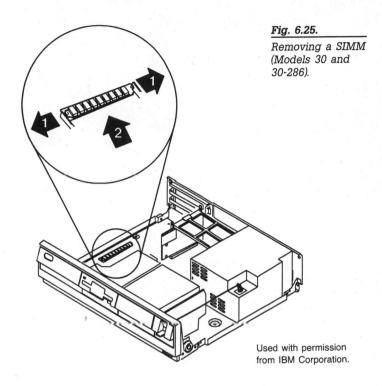

Fig. 6.25.

Removing a SIMM (Models 30 and 30-286).

Used with permission from IBM Corporation.

System Board

The motherboard is held in place with eight screws, all of which must be taken out. Follow these steps:

1. Remove all eight screws.

2. Carefully slide the system board to the left.

3. Lift the system board out of the system unit (see fig. 6.26).

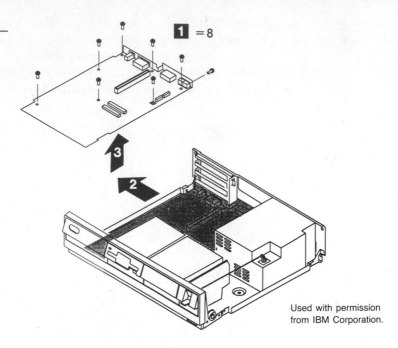

Fig. 6.26.

*Removing the
system board
(Models 30 and
30-286).*

Models 50 and 70

This section describes the disassembly procedures for the PS/2
Models 50, 50Z, and 70. These systems are modular in nature, and
most of the procedures are simple.

Cover

Before you remove the cover from the system unit, make sure that
the following conditions are met:

- The hard disk is parked.
- The system is off.
- The power cord is unplugged from the socket.
- All external options are disconnected.

To remove the cover of these systems, follow this simple procedure:

1. Unlock the cover lock.
2. Loosen the two cover thumbscrews on the back of the system.
3. Slide the cover toward you and lift the cover off (see fig. 6.27).

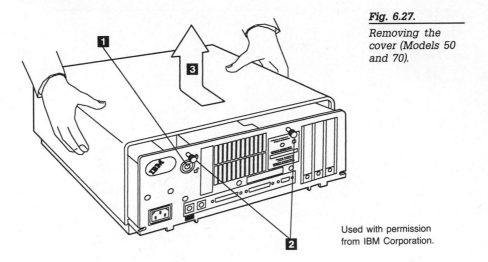

Fig. 6.27.

Removing the cover (Models 50 and 70).

Battery and Speaker Assembly

The battery and speaker are contained in a single assembly. To avoid accidentally discharging the battery, remove the battery before removing the battery and speaker assembly. Install this assembly before replacing the battery. To perform this operation, follow these steps:

1. Romovo tho battery by bending the tabs on the holder toward the rear and pulling the battery straight up.

2. Push the tab on the bottom of the speaker unit in order to disengage the speaker assembly from the support structure.

3. Lift the entire battery and speaker assembly up and out of the system (see fig. 6.28).

Fan Assembly

The fan assembly can be removed easily from these systems. Follow these procedures to remove the fan:

1. Disengage the two plastic push button tabs on either side of the fan assembly by prying them upward. If necessary, use the small pry tool located at the front right corner of the system.

2. Pull the entire assembly up and out of the system (see fig. 6.29).

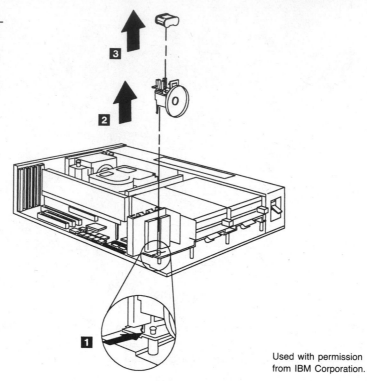

Used with permission
from IBM Corporation.

Fig. 6.28.

*Removing the
battery and
speaker assembly
(Models 50
and 70).*

Adapters

Removing adapter boards also is a simple procedure with these
systems. An important part of the procedure is to make a diagram of
the adapter and cable locations. A good practice is to put all
adapters back into the same slot from which they were removed,
because otherwise the CMOS memory configuration must be run.
You then can remove the adapters by following this procedure:

1. Make sure that all cables are disconnected. Loosen the
   retaining thumbscrew at the base of the card bracket.

2. Grasp the option adapter and gently pull the adapter up and
   out of the system unit (see fig. 6.30).

3 1/2-Inch Floppy Disk Drive

Removing floppy drives from these systems is one of the simplest
operations of all. Just push up on the tab underneath the floppy
drive and slide the drive out toward you.

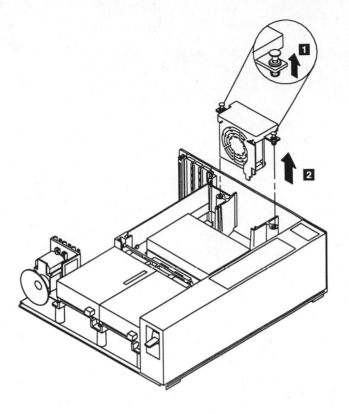

Fig. 6.29.

Removing the fan assembly (Models 50 and 70).

Used with permission from IBM Corporation.

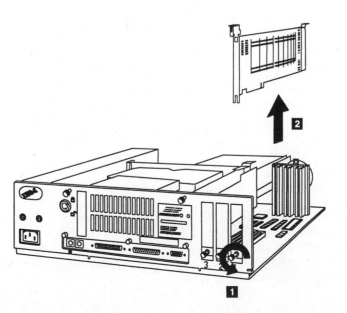

Fig. 6.30.

Removing an adapter (Models 50 and 70).

Used with permission from IBM Corporation.

Fixed Disk Drive and Adapter

Removing the hard disk is almost as easy as removing the floppy drives. Before removing the hard disk, make sure that you have backed up all the information on the fixed disk and that the heads have been parked.

1. On the side where the power supply is located, press down the two plastic tabs.

2. Slide the fixed disk drive toward the power supply and up.

3. Grasp the adapter at each end and gently pull the adapter up (see fig 6.31).

Fig. 6.31.

Removing the fixed disk drive (Models 50 and 70).

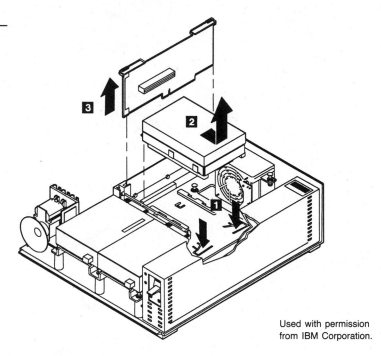

Used with permission from IBM Corporation.

Drive Support Structure

In order to remove the support structure from the system unit, you must remove the following components:

- Cover
- Battery and speaker assembly

- Fan assembly
- Option adapters
- Disk drives
- Fixed disk drives

Once these items have been removed, pull up all six white plastic push button lock tabs and lift the assembly up (see fig. 6.32). If necessary, you can use the small pry tool located at the front right side of the system to pry up the lock tabs.

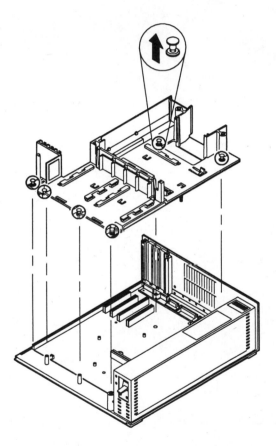

Fig. 6.32.

Removing the drive support structure (Models 50 and 70).

Used with permission from IBM Corporation.

Power Supply

To remove the power supply, follow these procedures:

1. Unscrew the screw on the front left side on the system.

2. Unscrew the two screws on the back of the power supply.

3. Slide the power supply to the right and remove from the system unit (see fig. 6.33).

Fig. 6.33.

Removing the power supply (Models 50 and 70).

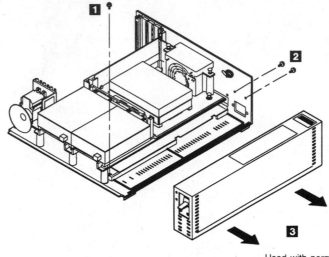

Used with permission from IBM Corporation.

System Board

In order to remove the motherboard from the system unit, you must first remove the following components:

- Cover
- Battery and speaker assembly
- Fan assembly
- Option adapters
- Disk drives
- Fixed disk drives
- Disk support structure
- Power supply

With all these components removed from the system unit, the removal of the motherboard itself is a simple procedure:

1. Remove all six retaining screws (three on the back of the system unit and three on the system board).

2. Gently lift the system board up and out of the system (see fig. 6.34).

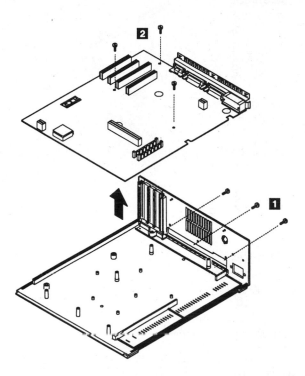

Used with permission from IBM Corporation.

Fig. 6.34.

Removing the system board (Models 50 and 70).

Single Inline Memory Modules (SIMMs)

One of the benefits of using Single Inline Memory Modules (SIMMs) is that they are so easy to remove or install. When removing memory modules, remember that, because of physical interference, you must remove the memory module package closest to the disk drive bus adapter slot before removing the package closest to the edge of the system board. To remove a SIMM properly, follow these procedures:

1. Gently pull the tabs on each side of the SIMM socket outward.

2. Rotate or pull the SIMM up and out of the socket (see fig. 6.35). Be careful not to damage the connector, because if you damage the motherboard SIMM connector, you could be looking at an expensive repair. Never force the SIMM; it should come out easily or you are doing something wrong.

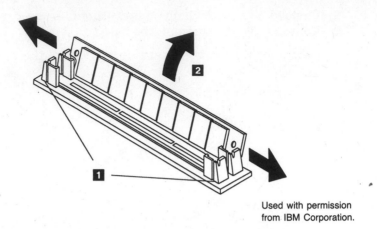

Used with permission from IBM Corporation.

Fig. 6.35.

Removing a SIMM (Models 50 and 70).

Models 60 and 80

This section describes the disassembly procedures for the PS/2 Models 60 and 80. These models are the floor-standing PS/2 systems. They are not quite as easy to work on or as modular as the desktop systems, but they still are easy to service compared with the earlier PC and AT types of systems. Most of the repair procedures do not involve the use of any tools at all.

Cover

Before you remove the cover from the system unit, make sure that the following conditions are met:

- The hard disk is parked.
- The system is off.
- The power cord is unplugged from the socket.
- All external options are disconnected.

To remove the cover of these systems, follow this simple procedure:

1. Unlock the cover lock.
2. Loosen the two cover screws on the side of the system.
3. Tilt the cover toward you.
4. Lift the cover up (see fig. 6.36).

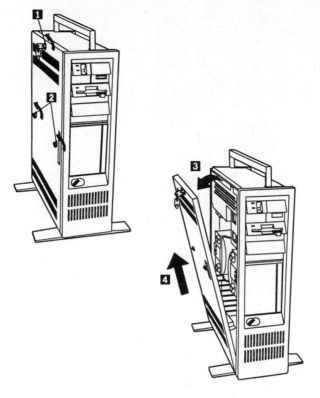

Fig. 6.36.
Removing the cover (Models 60 and 80).

Used with permission
from IBM Corporation.

Adapters

Removing adapter boards is a simple procedure in these systems. An important part of the procedure is to make a diagram of the adapter and cable locations. A good practice is to put all adapters back into the same slot from which they were removed, because otherwise the CMOS memory configuration must be run. You then can remove the adapters by following this procedure:

1. Make sure that all cables are disconnected. Loosen the retaining thumbscrew at the base of the card bracket.

2. Grasp the option adapter and gently pull the adapter up and out of the system unit (see fig. 6.37).

Battery and Speaker Assembly

The battery and speaker are contained in a single assembly. To avoid accidentally discharging the battery, remove the battery first

Fig. 6.37.

Removing an adapter (Models 60 and 80).

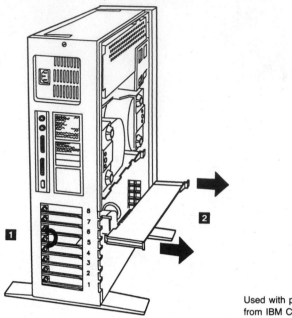

Used with permission from IBM Corporation.

before removing the battery and speaker assembly. Install this assembly before replacing the battery. To perform this operation, follow these steps:

1. Remove the battery by bending the tabs on the holder to the rear and pulling the battery straight up.

2. Disconnect the battery and speaker cable.

3. Push the tab on the bottom of the speaker unit in order to disengage the speaker assembly from the support structure (see fig. 6.38).

4. Lift the entire battery and speaker assembly up and out of the system.

Front Bezel

The Models 60 and 80 have a large front panel or bezel that you must remove to gain access to the floppy disk drives. This panel easily snaps off if you follow these instructions: grasp the bottom, near the feet of the unit, and pull out (see fig. 6.39). The bezel should snap off freely.

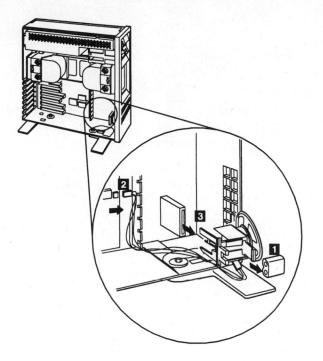

Fig. 6.38.

Removing the battery and speaker assembly (Models 60 and 80).

Used with permission from IBM Corporation.

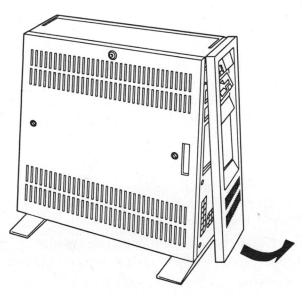

Fig. 6.39.

Removing the front bezel (Models 60 and 80).

Used with permission from IBM Corporation.

Power Supply

In order to remove the power supply, you first must remove the cover and front bezel. Then you can remove the power supply by following these instructions:

1. Disconnect all cables from the power supply. Remove the three screws that retain the power supply (one is near the power switch and the other two are located near the back of the supply).

2. Lift the power supply out the side of the unit (see fig. 6.40).

Fig. 6.40.

Removing the power supply (Models 60 and 80).

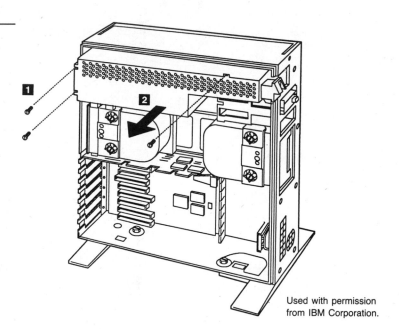

Used with permission from IBM Corporation.

Disk Drive

Removing floppy drives from these systems is one of the simplest operations of all. The floppy drives are located next to the power supply. Follow these instructions to remove them:

1. Push the tab underneath the floppy drive up and simultaneously press a tab on the rear of the drive sideways.

2. Slide the drive out the front of the unit (see fig. 6.41).

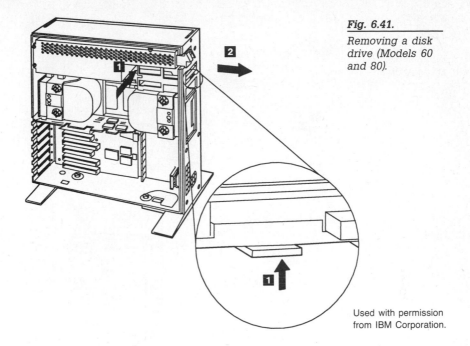

Fig. 6.41.

Removing a disk drive (Models 60 and 80).

Used with permission from IBM Corporation.

Disk Drive Cable Retainer

These systems use a retainer to hold the cables in place when the floppy drives are plugged in. To remove this cable retainer, follow these instructions:

1. Press the tabs located on the side of the cable retainer.

2. Rotate the retainer out toward the back of the system unit.

3. Pull the retainer off (see fig. 6.42).

Fixed Disk Drive D

Removing the hard disk is a simple operation. Make sure that you have a backup of the information on the drive before removing the disk. After the backup is made, you can remove the drive by following a simple procedure. Note that drive D must be removed before drive C because of physical interference. The front bezel also must be removed before you can remove the drive. Follow these steps:

Fig. 6.42.

Removing the disk drive cable retainer (Models 60 and 80).

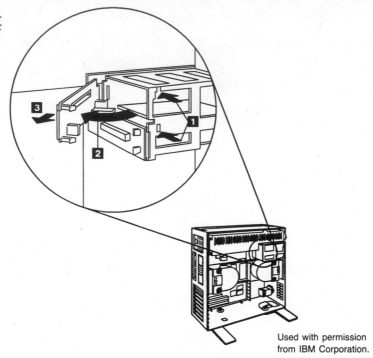

Used with permission from IBM Corporation.

1. Disconnect the ground wire and all cables from the fixed disk drive. Turn both thumbscrews counterclockwise.

2. Slide the fixed disk drive out the front of the system unit (see fig. 6.43).

Fixed Disk Drive C

Removing the hard disks is a simple operation. Remember, before removing the disk, make sure that you have a backup of the information on the drive. After the backup is made, you can remove the drive by following a simple procedure. Note that drive D must be removed before drive C because of physical interference. The front bezel also must be removed before you can remove the drive.

1. Disconnect the ground wire and all cables from the fixed disk drive. Turn both thumbscrews counterclockwise.

2. Slide the drive a little toward the front and lift the fixed disk drive sideways out of the system (see fig. 6.44).

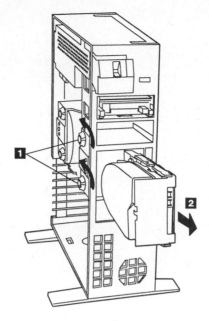

Fig. 6.43.

Removing fixed disk drive D (Models 60 and 80).

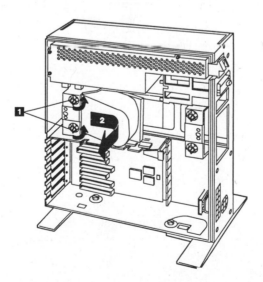

Fig. 6.44.

Removing fixed disk drive C (Models 60 and 80).

Fixed Disk Drive Support Structure

A large metal hard disk drive support structure is used to clamp the hard disks in place. You must remove this structure must be removed in order to remove the motherboard. This structure can be be removed easily with the following procedure:

1. Remove the four screws located on the front portion of the structure.

2. Slide the structure forward and lift it up and sideways out of the system (see fig. 6.45).

Fig. 6.45.

Removing the fixed disk drive support structure (Models 60 and 80).

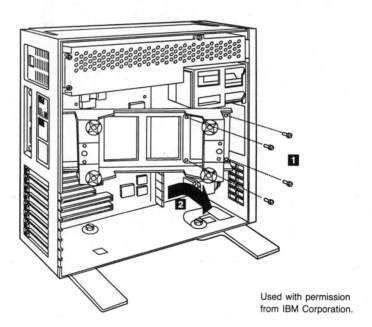

Used with permission from IBM Corporation.

System Board

In order to remove the motherboard from the system unit, you first must remove the following components:

- Cover
- Option adapters
- Fixed disk drives
- Fixed disk support structure

With all these components removed from the system unit, the removal of the motherboard itself is a simple procedure. Follow these steps:

1. Disconnect all cables from the system board. Remove all eight retaining screws.

2. Gently lift the system board up and out of the system (see fig. 6.46).

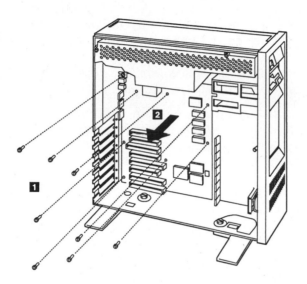

Fig. 6.46.

Removing the system board (Models 60 and 80).

Used with permission from IBM Corporation.

Now that you have examined the procedures for disassembling a system, you will examine the various components that make up a system.

Recognizing System Components

The most important single part of each system is the motherboard or system board. These boards are different for each type of system available. Sometimes, a manufacturer even changes the system board for a given system to add features or improve the design. IBM has made such changes for several of its systems. In some cases, the changes from one type to another are subtle; higher density memory chips, for example, are used in the PC Type 2 motherboard.

That change is difficult to detect at a glance. At other times, changes are more complete, as in the AT Type 2 motherboard. This board is completely different from the Type 1 design in both layout and size. The mounting and connector positions are the only unchanged items.

Non-IBM systems have yet different system-board designs. Some manufacturers have even gone to a *backplane* type of design, which means that the only real components on the "motherboard" are the slot connectors. All circuitry including the main CPU is contained on adapter boards. When a system is designed in this fashion, the motherboard is called a backplane. Zenith, for example, favors this design in many of its desktop systems. Upgrading a system built like this can be easy. To change from an 80286-based system to a 80386-based system, for example, all you do is change one card.

The IBM PS/2 systems have gone the opposite route from backplane design. These systems incorporate as much circuitry as possible on the motherboard. Disk controllers, video circuits, serial and parallel ports, and mice ports, for example, are included on the motherboard. This design allows fewer total system parts, a more standard base configuration to build on, and easy diagnosis and servicing. Unfortunately, when any one of the on board components fails, the entire motherboard must be replaced, which is much more expensive than if the component was on a plug-in board.

Tables 6.1 and 6.2 show the changes between the different system boards used in a particular PC or PS/2 system.

Table 6.1
Motherboards Used in Standard PC Systems

PC

Type 1   Used 16K RAM chips in four banks for a total of 64K. Had Version 1 or 2 of the ROM BIOS, which is now obsolete.

Type 2   Used 64K RAM chips in four banks for a total of 256K. Had Version 10/27/82 of the ROM BIOS, which was the last version offered.

XT

Type 1   Used 64K RAM chips for a total of 256K. ROM BIOS Version 11/08/82 was used.

Table 6.1—*continued*

XT

Type 2	Used 256K RAM chips in two banks and 64K RAM chips in two banks, for a total of 640K. ROM BIOS Versions 01/10/86 or 05/09/86 were supplied.

AT

Type 1	Used 128K stacked RAM chips. Runs 6 MHz and used BIOS Version 01/10/84 or 6/10/85.
Type 2	Physically smaller than Type 1. Used 256K RAM chips. Supplied with ROM BIOS Versions 6/10/85 (6 MHz) or 11/15/85 (8 MHz).

Table 6.2
Motherboards Used in PS/2 Systems

Model 50

Type 1 (-021)	Has 1 wait state design. Board holds 1M of memory.
Type 2 (-031 -061)	Physically much smaller than Type 1 and has components mounted on both sides of the board. Has 0 wait state design. Board holds 2M of memory.

Model 70

Type 1 (-E61 -121)	Runs 16 MHz or 20 MHz with 0-2 wait states using a memory paging scheme. Maximum of 6M of memory on board.
Type 2 (-A21)	Runs 25 MHz with a 64K 0 wait state memory cache system. Maximum of 8M of memory on board.

Model 80

Type 1 (-041 -071)	Runs at 16 MHz with 1 wait state. Maximum of 2M of memory on board.
Type 2 (-111 -311)	Runs at 20 MHz with 0-2 wait states using a memory paging scheme. Maximum of 4M of memory on board.

The next section discusses some problems you may encounter with the actual hardware.

Managing Hardware

One of the biggest aggravations you will encounter when dealing with various systems on today's market is the different types and designs for the hardware that holds the units together. Most types use screws that can be driven with 1/4-inch or 3/16-inch hexagonal drivers. IBM uses these types of screws in all the original PC, XT, and AT systems. Other manufacturers may use different hardware. COMPAQ, for example, uses TORX screws in most of its systems. A TORX screw is a screw with a star-shaped hole driven by the correct-sized TORX driver. These drivers carry size designations such as T-8, T-9, T-10, T-15, T-20, T-25, T-30, T-40, etc. Another variation on the TORX screw is the tamper-proof TORX screw. You will find these screws in IBM's power supplies and in power supplies and other assemblies from other manufacturers. These screws are just like the regular TORX screws except a pin sticks up directly in the middle of the star-shaped hole in the screw. This pin prevents the standard TORX driver from entering the hole to grip the screw. A special tamper-proof driver that has a corresponding hole for the pin is required. Another alternative is to use a small chisel to knock out the pin in the screw. Usually, any device that is sealed with these types of screws is considered a complete replaceable unit and rarely, if ever, needs to be opened up.

The more standard slotted or Phillips types of screws are used by many manufacturers, also. These screws are relatively easy to deal with from a tool standpoint, but these fasteners lack grip and are more easily rounded off than the other types mentioned. The cheaper versions also tend to lose bits of metal as they are turned with a driver, which isn't good if those metal bits fall onto the motherboard. You may want to stay away from cheap fasteners wherever possible; the headaches you receive from dealing with stripped screws are just not worth it.

Another area of aggravation in dealing with hardware is that two types of thread systems are available: English and metric. IBM used mostly English threaded fasteners in the original line of systems, but many other manufacturers used metric threaded fasteners in their systems.

With disk drives, the difference really becomes apparent. The American manufactured drives use English fasteners, and drives made in Japan or Taiwan use metric fasteners. Any time you replace a floppy drive in an earlier model IBM unit, you will run into this problem. All American floppy drive manufacturers either have gone out of business or have ceased making floppy drives. IBM used Tandon and Control Data Corp. (CDC) as suppliers for the original line of systems, but these companies no longer make floppy drives. Their drives used English fasteners. Floppy drive makers today, such as Mitsubishi, Sony, Teac, Panasonic, and others, all are using metric fasteners. Try to get the correct screws and any other hardware, such as brackets with the drive, because these things may be difficult to find at the local hardware store. The drive OEM manual will have the correct data as to where any holes are located in a particular drive and what the thread size is.

Most hard disks today still are made by American manufacturers, so most hard disks also use English fasteners. Any of the Japanese drives will use the metric fasteners, of course.

Here is one final note of caution: Some of the screws in a system may be length critical, especially screws used to retain disk drives. You can destroy some hard disks by using a screw that is too long. By tightening the screw, you can puncture or dent the sealed disk chamber. When installing a new type of drive into a system, always make a trial fit of the hardware and see how far the screws can run into the drive before interfering with any components on the drive itself.

Chapter Summary

This chapter discussed the initial teardown and inspection of a system and looked at the types of tools that are required, from simple hand tools to meters for measuring voltage and resistance. You learned about the physical disassembly procedure itself and how to recognize the various components that make up the system. The last section mentioned some of the problems you might encounter with the actual hardware (screws, nuts, bolts, and so on) in a system.

Primary System Components

This chapter studies the primary components that make up a typical system's base configuration. These components include the following:

- Motherboards
- Microprocessors
- Memory
- Slots
- Standard adapters
- Power supply
- Keyboards

Most systems come with a *system unit* and a *keyboard*. The system unit includes a motherboard, which contains a microprocessor, usually some memory, and slots for expansion of the system. Many systems include one or more standard adapter boards in these slots. Examples are disk controllers or serial and parallel ports. At least one floppy disk drive is typically included also. (For more on floppy disk drives, refer to Chapter 8.) A system unit also houses a power supply, which provides the correct voltage and current to run the system. The keyboard is an external device attached to the system unit with a cable. Knowing how all these components operate can help you when you're trying to track down problems or repair systems.

Note that these components comprise only the *base* configuration. You need additional devices to complete the typical system. Most systems, for example, don't include a display adapter, the display itself, or ports for the connection of printers or modems. Often, systems include only a minimum of memory, which you must expand before you can do any serious computing. And the base configuration of most systems doesn't include a hard disk. (Of course the IBM PS/2 systems confuse this issue because they do come with everything you need, except the display.) For more information on the peripherals used in a typical system, see Chapter 10.

The Motherboard

Easily the most important component in any PC system is the main or "mother" board. Sometimes the terminology can be confusing, because IBM refers to a *system board* or *planar*. The terms motherboard, system board, and planar are interchangeable. Each of the motherboards in the PC family contains functionally the same components as the motherboards in the PS/2 family.

One important thing to note is that not all systems have a motherboard in the true sense of the word. Some systems have the components that are normally found on a motherboard located instead on an expansion adapter card plugged into a slot. In these systems, the board with the slots is called not a motherboard but a *backplane*. Systems using this type of construction are called backplane systems.

Each system design, the motherboard and the backplane, has advantages and disadvantages. Most of the original personal computers were designed as backplanes in the late 1970s. Apple and IBM shifted the market to the now traditional motherboard with a slots-type of design because this type of system is generally cheaper to mass produce than one with the backplane design. The advantage of a backplane system, however, is that you can easily upgrade it to a new processor and new level of performance by changing a single card. For example, you can upgrade a system with an 80286-based processor card to an 80386-based card by simply changing the one card. A motherboard-design system requires the motherboard itself to be changed, which is a more formidable task.

Market realities have confused the distinction between the upgrades of these two system designs. Intel, for example, now sells a board for the AT, called the Inboard 386/AT, which contains an 80386 processor and memory. You could justifiably call this board a "mothercard," because it replaces many functions of the motherboard into which it is plugged. The original motherboard is now acting much like a backplane. Zenith and Kaypro are currently known for producing systems in the backplane design, but most other manufacturers have followed IBM in producing a typical motherboard-based system.

Any particular system usually has a motherboard specifically designed for that system. The motherboard in IBM's original AT system, for example, was a new design produced especially for that system. Once produced, however, a motherboard sometimes goes through revisions during the life of a system. Beginning with systems sold during October 1985, for example, the AT motherboard design was changed in order to increase reliability and reduce manufacturing cost. The new design was called "Type 2" and was also found on the -319 and -339 versions of the AT, which increased the clock speed of the system to 8 MHz. (For more on speed, see the section on "Speed Ratings of Microprocessors.")

You need to be aware, then, that two apparently identical systems may in fact have different physical motherboard designs or revisions, often depending on when the system was manufactured. Sometimes the revisions are minor, as in the IBM XT, but they can be major, as in the AT example cited in the preceding paragraph. (Chapter 2 discusses the changes IBM made in motherboards between the different model systems.)

Sometimes IBM uses a motherboard from one system in another system. The Portable PC is one example. The IBM Portable PC contains an XT Type 1 motherboard. Usually, however, all the various models of a particular system use the same motherboard design. The differences among the models are primarily in configurations and optional accessories.

IBM has manufactured only a few different types of motherboards for all the PC and PS/2 types of systems. Here's a summary of these motherboards:

For PC Family Systems	*For PS/2 Family Systems*
PC Type 1 (16/64K)	Model 25
PC Type 2 (64/256K)	Model 30
IBM PC Convertible	Model 50
XT Type 1 (64/256K)	Model 50Z (zero wait state)
XT Type 2 (256/640K)	Model 60
AT Type 1 (6 MHz, 128K RAM chips)	Model 70 (16 MHz)
	Model 70 (20 MHz)
AT Type 2 (6 MHz or 8 MHz, 256K RAM chips)	Model 70 (25 MHz with 64K cache)
	Model 80 (16 MHz)
XT 286 (''baby'' AT type)	Model 80 (20 MHz)

IBM has used all these motherboards in the various IBM PC and PS/2 family systems. Note that the entire earlier PC family (not including the PC*jr*) comprises only 8 different motherboards. The PS/2 family of systems already has 10 different motherboard designs, and many more will probably follow. This multiplicity of design is the result of increased automation in the assembly of these systems. Implementing a design change for the new motherboards is now an easy task.

If you know exactly what model of system unit you have, you can determine what motherboard was original to that unit. Table 7.1 shows the relationship of motherboards to IBM system unit models.

Table 7.1
Motherboards Used by IBM System Models

Motherboard	*Systems Using that Motherboard*
PC Type 1 (16/64K):	IBM PC Models 5150
	-001 -824
	-014 -X14
	-064 -X64
	-074 -X74
	-813
PC Type 2 (64/256K):	IBM PC Models 5150
	-104 -166
	-114 -176
	-164 -X66
	-174 -X76
IBM PC Convertible:	IBM PC Convertible Models 5140
	-002 -022

Motherboard	Systems Using that Motherboard
XT Type 1 (64/256K):	IBM XT Models 5160 -068 -087 -078 -470 -086 IBM Portable PC Models 5155 -068 -076 IBM Industrial Computer Models 5531 -001 -021 -011 IBM 3270 PC Models 5271 -002 -024 -004 -026 -006 IBM 3270 PC G or GX Models 5371 -012 -016 -014 IBM XT 370 Models 5160 -568 -589 -588
XT Type 2 (256/640K):	IBM XT Models 5160 -267 -278 -268 -088 -277 -089 IBM 3270 PC Models 5271 -030 -051 -P30 -P51 -031 -070 -P31 -P70 -050 -071 -P50 -P71
AT Type 1:	IBM PC AT Models 5170 -068 -099 IBM Industrial Computer Model 7531 -041

Table 7.1—*continued*

Motherboard	Systems Using that Motherboard
	IBM Industrial Computer Model 7532 -041
	IBM 3270 PC AT Model 5273 -020
	IBM 3270 PC AT G or GX Models 5373 -160 -A61 -A60 -162 -161 -A62
	IBM PC AT 370 Model 5170 -599
	IBM Series/1 5170 Model -495
AT Type 2:	IBM PC AT Models 5170 -239 -339 -319
	IBM 3270 PC AT Models 5273 -070 -071 -P70 -P71
	IBM 3270 PC AT G or GX Models 5373 -A29 -E29 -A39 -E39
	IBM PC AT 370 Models 5170 -739 -939 -919
	IBM PC AT 5171T (TEMPEST) Models -168 -339
	IBM Series/1 5170 Model -496
XT 286 (AT type):	IBM XT 286 Model 5162 -286

Motherboard	Systems Using that Motherboard
PS/2 Model 25:	IBM PS/2 Model 25 Models 8525 -001 -G04 -G01 -L01 -004 -L04
PS/2 Model 30:	IBM PS/2 Model 30 Models 8530 -002 -021
PS/2 Model 50:	IBM PS/2 Model 50 Model 8550 -021
PS/2 Model 50Z (zero wait state):	IBM PS/2 Model 50Z Models 8550 -031 -061
PS/2 Model 60:	IBM PS/2 Model 60 Models 8560 -041 -071
PS/2 Model 70 (16 MHz):	IBM PS/2 Model 70 Model 8570 -E21
PS/2 Model 70 (20 MHz):	IBM PS/2 Model 70 Model 8570 -121
PS/2 Model 70 (25 MHz with 64K cache):	IBM PS/2 Model 70 Model 8570 -A21
PS/2 Model 80 (16 MHz):	IBM PS/2 Model 80 Models 8580 -041 -071
PS/2 Model 80 (20 MHz):	IBM PS/2 Model 80 Models 8580 -111 -311

Knowing what motherboards are part of the original equipment for the various models can be helpful when the time comes to service the system. This information can be especially useful when you have access to many systems, for example, in a large organization. In this situation, you want to know the "inventory" of different motherboards among all your systems. This kind of information can help you locate the new part you need or the earlier system unit you can strip for parts.

The Microprocessor

The *microprocessor* or Central Processing Unit (CPU) is the "brain" of the PC and performs all the system's calculating and processing. All the IBM PC and PS/2 units and compatibles use microprocessors from the Intel family of chips.

The Data Bus and the Address Bus

One of the most common ways to describe a microprocessor is the size of the processor's *data bus* and *address bus*. A bus is simply a series of connections designed to carry common signals. Imagine running a pair of wires from one end of a building to another. If you connect a 110-volt AC power generator to the two wires at any point and place outlets at convenient locations along the wires, you have constructed a "power bus." No matter which outlet you plug into, you have access to the same "signal," which in this example is 110-volt AC power.

Any transmission media with more than one outlet at each end can be called a bus. A typical computer system has several buses, and a typical microprocessor has two important buses for carrying data and memory-addressing information: the data bus and the address bus.

The microprocessor bus discussed most often is the *data bus*, which is the bundle of wires (or pins) used to send and receive data. The more signals that can be sent at one time, the more data can be transmitted in a given interval, and the faster the bus.

Data in a computer is sent as digital information, consisting of a time interval in which a single wire carries 5 volts to signal a "1" data bit or 0 volts to signal a "0" data bit. Therefore, the more wires you have, the more individual bits you can send in the same time interval. A chip such as the 80286 that has 16 wires for the transmission and reception of such data is said to have a 16-bit data bus. A 32-bit chip such as the 80386 has twice as many wires dedicated to simultaneous data transmission and can send twice as much information in the same time interval as a 16-bit chip.

A good way to understand this flow of information is to consider an automobile highway and the traffic it carries. If a highway has only one lane in each direction of travel, only one car can pass in a direction at a time. If you need to have more traffic flow, you can add another lane and then have twice as many cars pass in a given time. You can think of an 8-bit chip as the single-lane highway because with this chip 1 byte flows at a time. (One byte equals 8 individual bits.) The 16-bit chip, with 2 bytes flowing at a time, is like a two-lane highway. If you need to move a large amount of automobiles, as you do in larger cities, you might have 4 lanes (in each direction), which corresponds to a 32-bit data bus and the capability to move 4 bytes of information at a time.

Just as you can describe a highway by its width, you can describe a chip by the "width" of its data bus. When you read an advertisement describing a computer system as a 16-bit or 32-bit system, the ad is usually referring directly to the data bus of the CPU. This number gives a rough idea of the chip's (and therefore the system's) performance potential.

Here are the data bus sizes for the Intel family of microprocessors used in IBM and compatible PCs:

Microprocessor	Data Bus Size
8086	16-bit
8088	8-bit
80186	16-bit
80188	8-bit
80286	16-bit
80386	32-bit
80386SX	16-bit

Sometimes confusing the data bus issue is the fact that not all the chips are "pure." Some of the processors have an internal data bus (made up of data paths and storage units called registers) that is different from the external data bus. The 8088, 80188, and 80386SX are examples of this structure. Each of these chips has an internal data bus that is twice the width of the external bus. These are sometimes called *hybrid designs* and are usually low-cost versions of a "pure" chip. The 80386SX, for example, can pass data around internally with a full 32-bit slot, but for communications to the outside world, the chip is restricted to a 16-bit-wide data path. The purpose of this design is to allow a systems designer to build a lower cost motherboard with only a 16-bit bus design and still maintain full compatibility with the full 32-bit 80386.

Completely different from the data bus, the *address bus* is the set of wires carrying the addressing information used to describe the memory location to which the data is being sent or from which the data is being retrieved. As with the data bus, each wire in an address bus carries a single bit of information. This single bit is a single digit in the address. The more wires (digits) used in calculating these addresses, the greater the total number of address locations. The size (or width) of the address bus indicates the maximum amount of random-access memory (RAM) that a chip can address.

The highway analogy can be used for you to see how the address bus fits in. If the data bus is the highway itself, and the size of the data bus is equivalent to the width of the highway, then the address bus relates to the house number or street address number. The size of the address bus is equivalent to the number of digits in the house address. If you live on a street where the address is limited to a two-digit number, then no more than 100 (00 to 99) distinct addresses can exist for that street. Add another digit, and the total number of available addresses increases to 1,000 (000 to 999).

Remember that a computer works in the binary numbering system, so a two-digit number gives only four unique addresses (00, 01, 10, and 11), and a three-digit number provides only eight addresses (000 to 111). Examples are the 8086 and 8088 processors, which each use a 20-bit address bus giving a maximum of 1,048,576 (1 megabyte) address locations.

Table 7.2 describes the memory-addressing capabilities of the Intel microprocessors.

Table 7.2
Address Bus Sizes

Microprocessor	Address Bus Size (digits)	Bytes	Kilobytes	Megabytes
8086/8088	20	1048576	1024	1
80286	24	16777216	16384	16
80386	32	4294967296	4194304	4096
80386SX	24	16777216	16384	16

The data bus and address bus are independent of one another, and chip designers can use whatever size they want for each bus.

Usually, however, chips with larger data buses have larger address buses. The sizes of these buses can give you important information about a chip's relative power, measured in two important aspects. The size of the data bus gives you an indication of the information-moving capability of the chip, and the size of the address bus tells you directly just how much memory a particular chip can handle.

Using a Coprocessor Chip

Each of the central processors can use a *coprocessor chip* as an option. The coprocessors provide hardware for arithmetic functions that would place an excessive drain on the main CPU. Here's a summary of the coprocessors available for the Intel family of microprocessors:

Microprocessor	Math Coprocessor
8086	8087
8088	8087
80186	8087
80188	8087
80286	80287
80386	80387 (or 80287)
80386SX	80387SX

The math chips (as the coprocessors are sometimes called) can perform certain mathematical operations at 10 to 100 times the speed of the corresponding main processor. Math chips are also much more accurate in these calculations than the primary CPU is.

One drawback to using a coprocessor, however, is that the instruction set is different from that of the CPU. A program must specifically detect the existence of the coprocessor and then execute the correct instructions explicitly for the coprocessor before it is used. Otherwise, the chip simply draws power and does nothing else. Fortunately, most of the modern programs that can benefit from the use of the coprocessor can correctly detect and use the chip if it is present in a system. These programs are usually math-intensive programs such as spreadsheets, statistical programs, or graphics programs. A word processor doesn't benefit at all from the math chip and for this reason doesn't use it.

For those programs that do utilize the chip, the increase in performance for a given application can be quite dramatic—usually a multifold increase in speed. If the primary applications you run will take advantage of a math coprocessor, you should upgrade your system to include one.

Currently most PCs are socketed for the math coprocessor as an option, but almost no systems include the processor as standard equipment. A few systems on the market don't even have a socket for the math coprocessor due to cost and size considerations. Usually these are the portable systems such as the IBM Convertible or low-end systems such as the PC*jr*. For more specific information on the math coprocessors, see the discussions of the particular chips—8087, 80287, and 80387—in the next section.

Types of Microprocessors

IBM and compatible vendors have used all the Intel chips in various PC systems over the years. To understand fully the capabilities of a particular system, as well as to perform any type of servicing, you must at least know what type of processor runs under the hood. Here's a summary of which microprocessors operate with most IBM systems:

Microprocessor	System Units
8086	PS/2 Models 25, 30
8088	PC, XT, Convertible, Portable, PC*jr*
80286	AT, XT 286, PS/2 Models 50, 50Z, 60
80386	PS/2 Models 70, 80

The other processors in the family—the 80186, 80188, and 80386SX—haven't been used by IBM in any systems. Several compatible vendors, however, have produced systems that use these chips. IBM undoubtedly will follow suit by using the 80386SX in the future because it offers more power than the 286 at nearly the same price. Actually, with use of the 386SX, the 286 systems will drop in price, giving more power for less money. Because of the demand for speed and memory, the 186 and 188 will not be used. These chips were simply glorified 86 and 88 chips. Intel also is working on a new chip called the 80486, which is expected to be quite a powerhouse. This chip probably will be formally introduced some time in 1989, with systems that use the chip on the market by 1990 or 1991. The 486 will be much faster and will offer new, more powerful modes of operation.

In the sections that follow, you will examine these various microprocessors in more detail.

The 8086 and 8088

Intel first introduced the 8086 microprocessor in 1976. This microprocessor was one of the first 16-bit chips on the market and had at the time one of the largest memory address spaces (20 bits, or 1M) available. The only problem with the design was that it was costly. Both the chip itself and a motherboard designed around the chip were expensive. The cost was high because the system included the 16-bit data bus, which is simply more expensive to design than a system using an 8-bit bus. The generally price-sensitive marketplace was slow to accept the 8086. Although having 16 bits was desirable, the mainstream systems at the time were all 8-bit systems. Users apparently weren't willing to pay for the extra performance found in the full 16-bit design. This situation led Intel to introduce the 8088 chip in 1978.

The 8088 is basically just a lower cost version of the 8086. The 8088 is identical to the 8086, with the exception of the external communications circuits, which are modified (restricted) to conform to an 8-bit design. With this hybrid chip, a systems designer can offer a system that can run 16-bit software (using the 16-bit internal registers), have access to 1M of memory (because of the 20-bit address bus), but still keep in line with the cost of the then current 8-bit designs. The 8088 is referred to as a 16-bit processor (even though the external data bus is only 8 bits wide) because of the internal 16-bit-wide registers and data paths.

The 8088 is the microprocessor at the heart of all of IBM's PC- and XT-based computers. IBM originally selected this chip because of the cost issue. The 8088 allowed the original design team to put together the original IBM PC 5150-001 and sell it for $1,355. (This price was for a 16K system unit with no drives! A similarly configured Apple II system at that time cost around $1,600.)

The IBM PC and XT motherboards run the 8088 processor chip at a clock speed of 4.77 MHz. Contrast this speed to that of many clones currently on the market, which run their chips at sometimes more than double this rate by using faster versions of the 8086/88. The speed at which the processor operates has a direct effect on the speed of program execution. (For more on speed, see this chapter's section on "Speed Ratings of Microprocessors.")

The PS/2 Models 25 and 30 use the 8086, which IBM had previously ignored. Many compatible systems, such as the COMPAQ Deskpro and the AT&T 6300, had been using the 8086 for some time. The improved communications capability of the 8086 gives it about a 20 percent improvement in throughput over an identical-speed (in MHz) 8088. This improvement is one reason that IBM can claim that the 8 MHz 8086-based Model 30 is 2.5 times faster than the 4.77 MHz 8088-based PC or XT, even though 8 MHz is not more than twice the clock speed.

The 80186 and 80188

The 80186 and 80188 share the same relationship to each other that the 8086 and 8088 do. The 80186 is a full 16-bit design, and the 80188 is the hybrid chip that compromises the 16-bit design with an 8-bit external communications interface.

As a matter of fact, the similarities of this pair of microprocessors to the earlier 8086 and 8088 don't stop there. The 80186 is just a slightly modified version of the 8086, with a few improvements and many built-in support functions that would normally require external chips. If compared CPU to CPU, the 80186 is almost exactly the same as the 8086. But the 8018X chips have many CPU support functions built in. The chips in the 8018X series effectively combine 15 to 20 of the most common 808X series system components into a single chip. This design can greatly reduce the total number of components in a computer design while offering the same levels of performance.

Although the 8018X chips help the systems designer who wants to reduce the component count in a system design, the chips place design restrictions on the final product. Using one of these chips to construct a system that is extremely compatible with the IBM PC seems to be difficult. The 186 and 188 incorporate some new instructions and capabilities—but not many when compared with the 286 and 386 chips. These slight differences seem to cause problems with the 186 and 188 when they are supposed to emulate the 86 and 88 chips. A few systems—and even a "turbo" board or two for the IBM PC and XT systems—have been built using these chips. Overall, however, systems designers in the IBM-compatible realm have overlooked the 80186 and 80188.

Aside from the compatibility problem, the chips just didn't offer a great deal of performance over the earlier 8086 and 8088, and the 80286 was a much more desirable component to use. Also, the costs of the individual components that the 8018X series was designed to replace had become inexpensive, which made the 8018X chips less attractive. In spite of these limitations, the 8018X chips have found a following among board designers for highly intelligent peripheral adapter cards, such as local area network adapters. The reason is that because of the decrease in chips needed, these processors can fit easily on an adapter that plugs into one of the slots of the motherboard.

The 8087

The 8087 chip is often referred to as the NDP (Numeric Data Processor), or math chip. It is a coprocessor designed to perform math operations at many times the speed and accuracy of the main processor. The primary advantage of using this chip is the increased execution speed of a number-crunching program, such as a spreadsheet. Using the 8087 has several disadvantages, including software support, cost, power consumption, and heat production.

The primary disadvantage of installing this chip in a PC is that only with programs that were written to use this coprocessor will you notice any speedup, and then not for all operations. Only math-intensive programs—spreadsheets, statistical programs, CAD software, and engineering software—support the chip. But even then the effects are variable from application to application, and support is limited to specific areas. Lotus 1-2-3 Release 2.01, for example, which does support the math coprocessors, still will not use a coprocessor for addition, subtraction, multiplication, and division! The applications that will *not* use the 8087 include word processing programs, communications software, database programs, presentation-types of graphics programs, and many more.

As a test, I developed two spreadsheets, each with 8,000 cells. The first spreadsheet had addition, subtraction, multiplication, and division tasks split evenly among the 8,000 cells. The second spreadsheet had 8,000 cells with formulas using SQRT, SIN, COS, and TAN calculations split among the cells. The results are surprising. Here are the recalculation times:

	XT without 8087	XT with 8087
Sheet #1 (standard math)	21 seconds	21 seconds
Sheet #2 (high-level math)	195 seconds	21 seconds

This chart shows that the addition of an 8087 to a standard IBM XT did nothing for the first spreadsheet but calculated the second sheet in almost 1/10 of the time. Thus, if your spreadsheets consist of nothing but addition, subtraction, multiplication, and division calculations, save your money. You can derive no benefit from the math chip. For a spreadsheet consisting of engineering types of calculations or business math in which high-level functions are used, however, the addition of the math chip may speed up your recalculations by as much as 10 times. The instruction set and design of the chip were intended specifically for math calculations. This uneven effect of the math coprocessors is customary for most applications. You must decide whether the performance benefits are worthwhile.

The 8087 chip can be fairly expensive, ranging from about $100 to $300, depending on the maximum speed rating. Although that may sound like a great deal of money for a single chip, the benefits can be quite valuable. Just remember to purchase the chip with the correct maximum speed rating: one that is greater than or equal to the actual speed at which your system will run the chip.

To find the actual speed at which your system will run the chip, look for the information in your technical reference manual. I cannot stress enough how important good documentation is.

The 8087 and 80387 always will run at the same rate of speed as the main processor, whatever that speed is. The reason is that the main CPU and the math coprocessor must run in synchronization with each other. In an IBM XT, for example, the 8088 runs at 4.77 MHz, and so does the 8087. You must purchase an 8087 that is designed to run at this speed (4.77 MHz) or faster, or the chip will fail. In the PS/2 Model 80-111, the main 80386 CPU runs at 20 MHz, and you must purchase an 80387 that is rated at 20 MHz or faster or the chip will fail. So to add a math chip to any system that uses an 8087, or 80387 math coprocessor, you simply purchase one that runs at equal to or better than the same speed of your system's CPU. To find the speed of the system's CPU, you can look at the technical specifications listed in Chapters 3 and 4, or you can look up the information in the system's technical reference manual, which you should have.

Systems that use the 80286 do not run the CPU and math chip in synchronization. They are *asynchronous*, which means that the chips can run at different speeds. The 80287 math chip usually will run at two-thirds of that speed (as it does in the IBM AT), but that may not always be the case. Some systems may run them at the same speed. The PS/2 50 and 60, for example, run the 80287 at 10 MHz, which is exactly the same speed as the 80286 CPU.

The math chips are quite power hungry because of the number of transistors included. A typical 8088 has only about 29,000 transistors on board, but the 8087 has about 75,000. (Nearly all the 75,000 transistors are dedicated to math functions, which is the reason that the 8087 can perform math so well.) This figure translates to nearly three times the calculating horsepower, as well as three times the electrical power drain. In a heavily loaded PC, the 8087 could be the straw that breaks the camel's back, meaning that the power supply may be insufficient to operate under the increased load. The chip draws nearly 0.5 amps of current.

Another problem is the amount of heat generated—a healthy 3 watts of energy. This heat can raise the temperature of the chip to more than 150 degrees Fahrenheit (158 degrees is the approved maximum temperature for most 8087s). For this reason, these chips are ceramic in construction. The power and heat are not a problem in the XT or Portable, because these systems are built to take it. But the PC usually requires a higher wattage power supply to handle the load.

In spite of some of the drawbacks, most of the newer programs are being written to support the chip, and the prices are definitely coming down. For various design reasons, this chip has a far greater effect on the speed of the PC and XT than the 80287 has on the AT. Installing an 8087 can extend the useful life of the PC or XT because the chip closes some of the performance gap between the PC- or XT-based computers and the AT-based computers. In short, the chip is definitely an asset whenever the software supports it.

The 80286

The 80286 microprocessor is the CPU behind the IBM AT. This chip, manufactured by Intel and introduced in 1981, is in the same family as the 8088, which is used by the PC and the XT. When developing the AT, IBM naturally selected the 80286 as the basis for the new system because this chip allowed for a great deal of compatibility with the earlier systems. The 80286 is upward compatible with the 8086 and 8088, which means that software written for those chips should run on the 80286.

The 80286 has two modes of operation: *real address mode* and *protected virtual address mode.* These two modes are distinct enough from one another to make the 80286 like two different chips in one. In real mode, an 80286 acts essentially as an 8086 chip would and is fully object code compatible with the 8086 (or 8088). *Object code compatibility* means that the processor can run already compiled programs just as they are, executing every system instruction in the same manner as the 8086/88 would.

An 80286 chip in real mode is limited, however, in the sense that the chip cannot perform any of the additional operations or use any of the extra features that have been designed into the chip. This mode is the one in which the AT is run most of the time. PC DOS is currently limited to support for the real mode only. Unfortunately, the power of the system is thus restricted a great deal. In real mode, the processor can address only 1M, the same amount of memory as the 8088. Essentially because of this restriction, an AT running PC DOS is little more than an extremely fast PC. Although that may sound good enough, that is not the destiny of the AT. The real mode was provided so that much of the 8086- and 8088-based software could run with little or no modification until new software could be written to use the chip in protected mode.

In the protected mode of operation, the 80286 chip is truly something new. In this mode, the processor automatically maps 1 gigabyte (1,024M) of memory into a physical address space of 16M. The 80286 also supports multitasking operation in the form of memory protection to isolate the operating system and ensure the safety of each task's programs and data. Programs are allowed to run in protected areas of memory so that if one of the programs on a multiple-program system simultaneously locks up or fails, the entire system doesn't need a reset or cold boot. What happens in one area of memory cannot affect the programs running in other areas.

In protected mode, any program believes that it actually has access to 1 gigabyte of memory. The chip, however, can address only 16 megabytes of physical memory. When a program calls for more memory than physically exists, the CPU swaps some of the currently running code to disk and allows the program to use the now free space. The program does not know that this swapping is going on. The software simply believes that 1 gigabyte of actual memory exists. This swapping technique is completely controlled by the operating system and built-in hardware on the chip and is called *virtual memory*. Because of virtual memory, the size of programs under OS/2 or UNIX can grow to be extremely large, even though you never actually have more than 16 megabytes available. Programs that do require a great deal of swapping and virtual memory management run very slowly, however, so most programmers still list that a certain amount of free memory is needed to run their programs effectively.

Another side effect is that the more physical memory you can install, the faster systems running OS/2 or UNIX will run. In particular, 80386-based systems actually can address 4 gigabytes of memory and still completely emulate the 80286 way of doing things. An 80386 system with an actual 1 gigabyte of physical memory would be able to run OS/2 by simulating the virtual memory with actual memory beyond 16 megabytes. This would make the system extremely fast when compared with an 80286 system because now the "swapping" actually would be happening in physical memory as managed by the 80386, not on the disk as in the case of the 80286. Unfortunately, 1 gigabyte of high-speed memory costs nearly half a million dollars today, and even 16 megabytes cost close to $10,000! These are more "real" limitations!

The 80286 can address 16M of real hardware memory, but it can also address 1 gigabyte of virtual memory. Virtual memory is a chip-based simulation of real memory, using secondary storage such as disks. A running program believes that it has up to 1 gigabyte, while the processor is handling the swapping of programs and data from real memory to disk when the need arises. All of this swapping is transparent to the program and the user.

Although all the features of the 80286 in protected mode are attractive, they are generally unavailable at the current time because PC DOS runs only in real mode. You might ask, "Why doesn't IBM or Microsoft rewrite DOS so that it runs in both real and protected modes?" IBM has. The result is called OS/2.

OS/2 can run most old DOS programs just as they ran before, in real mode, and also can run a new breed of software in protected mode. The drawback to this sort of operation is that while in real mode, all the protection provided by protected mode is no longer in effect.

Also, OS/2 will not multitask in real mode nor allow access to any memory beyond 1M. These limitations are due to the hardware and not the software.

In protected mode, OS/2 allows multitasking and access to the entire 1 gigabyte of virtual or 16M physical address space provided by the 80286. Other operating systems, such as UNIX or XENIX, also support the AT in protected mode. OS/2 is not yet as popular as DOS has been, and not as many applications have been developed for OS/2 as are available under DOS. But for most of us, the switch to OS/2 is inevitable, for it is required to unleash the true power of the 80286 (and 80386) architecture.

The 80287

The 80287 is the numeric data processor that works with the 80286 in the AT. This chip is much the same as the 8087 chip in a PC or XT. But some different considerations and circumstances should be noted. The AT has a healthy power supply and generous thermostatically controlled fan cooling, for example, so the heat and power problems generally don't apply in this case.

The 80287 contains basically the same internal processing capabilities as the 8087, but the interface is modified to work with the 80286. The interface between the 80286 and 80287 is different from the 8086 and 8087 relationship. The 80286 and 80287 don't run in sync like the other chips. The interface is asynchronous and is less efficient than the 8087 interface. Also, the internal circuitry to the 80286 divides the system clock by 2 for the processor clock, and the 80287 divides the system clock frequency by 3. For this reason, most AT types of computers run the 80287 at one-third the system clock rate. For most systems, the 80287 usually runs at two-thirds of the speed of the 80286 due to the designs of each chip. First, these chips do not run in synchronization, so they *can* run at different speeds. In the design of the 80286, Intel provides a pin on the chip through which the system clock signal is input. This fundamental timing signal then is divided by 2 inside the chip to generate the processor clock. The 80287 has two clock input modes. If the 80287 is running off of the same clock signal as the 80286 processor, the internal circuitry inside the 80287 divides the system clock by 3. If a higher performance 80287 is desired, the motherboard designer can use a separate 8284 or 82284 clock driver chip and an appropriate crystal to drive the 80287 at any speed desired. But unless the board is specifically designed this way, the 80287 will run at two-thirds of the speed of the 80286.

In an 8 MHz IBM AT Model 339, for example, you have a 16 MHz crystal driving a 16 MHz system clock. The 80286 takes that signal and divides the frequency by 2 to get 8 MHz, which is now used as the processor clock. The 80287 takes the system clock and divides the frequency by 3 to get 5.33 MHz, which now becomes the clock signal for the 80287. Thus, the 80286 will run at 8 MHz, and the 80287 will run at 5.33 MHz. This is the procedure that most AT compatibles use, also.

Other systems may be different. In my XT Model 286 (AT type of system), for example, the system clock is 12 MHz, which is taken by the 80286 processor and divided by 2 to get the processor clock, which becomes 6 MHz. For the 80287, IBM takes a different route from the standard AT and uses the Video Oscillator crystal, which is 14.31818 MHz, in combination with a separate 8284 clock generator chip, to feed the 14.31818 MHz signal to the 80287. This clock signal is then taken by the 80287 and divided by 3 to get the 287 clock, which becomes 4.77 MHz. So, for my XT Model 286, the system clock is 12 MHz, the 286 clock is 6 MHz, and the 287 clock is 4.77 MHz. In a "normal" AT system with a 12 MHz system clock, the 287 clock would have been only 4.00 MHz, which is one of the reasons that the XT Model 286 is slightly faster than a "normal" AT.

For the PS/2 Models 50, 50Z, and 60, IBM uses different circuitry. The result is that the 286 and 287 clocks both are the same 10 MHz. As you can see, Intel and the system designer really decide how all of this will be, and if you want to know specific information about your system, look in the technical reference manual.

The following chart shows the 80286 and 80287 clock speeds (in MHz) for AT types of systems:

System Clock	80286 Clock	80287 Clock
12.00	6.00	4.00
16.00	8.00	5.33
20.00	10.00	6.67
24.00	12.00	8.00
32.00	16.00	10.67

Most AT types of systems run the 80287 slower than they run the main processor. As a matter of fact, in the stock IBM AT Models 068 or 099, the math chip runs at a slower clock rate than an IBM PC or XT.

Imagine this scenario: Two competitive users from a company each have a computer. The first user has an IBM XT, and the second user has an AT (6 MHz). They both use 1-2-3 as their primary application. The AT user delights in being able to out-calculate the XT user by a factor of 3 times. The XT user wants to get the faster AT system but instead purchases an 8087 math chip for $100 and installs it. The XT user then finds that the XT calculates many of the spreadsheets 10 times faster than before, or more than 3 times faster than the AT. This feat frustrates the AT user, who thought that the AT was a faster system. The AT user therefore purchases an 80287 for $200 and discovers that the AT is now equal in speed to the XT for many of the sheet recalculations. In a few situations, however, the XT still outruns the AT.

The AT user now wants to know why the 80287 chip, which costs twice as much as the equivalent chip for the XT, did not make the AT "superior" to the XT by any significant margin for spreadsheet recalculations. (For any other "normal" processing—processing that does not involve or use the math functions—the AT still holds its superiority in speed.)

The answer can be found in the 80287 chip. It has the same "math unit" internally as the 8087 chip, so at equal clock rates they should perform the same. The 80287 is not "better" than the 8087 in any real way, unlike the superiority of the 80286 to the 8086 or 8088. Finally, the 80287 in the 6 MHz AT runs at only 4 MHz, and the interface between the 80286 and 80287 is asynchronous, not in sync like the 8088- or 8086-to-8087 interface. All these elements add up to the fact that the performance gain in most AT systems from adding the math coprocessor is much less substantial overall than the same type of upgrade for any of the PC or XT types of systems.

How can this differential in performance gain be improved? Because the 80286 and the 80287 do run asynchronously, the clock signal that drives the 287 may come from another source, which may run the chip at any speed. In the IBM XT-286, for example, the video clock (14.31818 MHz) is used to derive a 4.77 MHz 287 clock speed rather than the 4.00 MHz that results from using the 12 MHz system clock. The PS/2 systems have circuitry that allows both processors in the Models 50, 50Z, and 60 to run at 10 MHz.

Some companies that now sell math coprocessor chips have designed a simple circuit that includes a crystal and an 8284 clock generator chip all mounted on a special socket. This special socket is plugged into your 287 socket, and then the 287 is plugged in on top of the special socket. Sometimes, these small circuit boards (which may not be much bigger than a single socket) are called daughter boards. Because the crystal and clock generator are now separate from the motherboard circuitry, this daughter board now can run the 80287 at any speed desired, up to the maximum rating of the chip itself.

You could, for example, add an 80287-10 to your old 6 MHz AT and actually run the 287 at 10 MHz with one of these daughter boards; without the daughter board, the chip would run at only 4 MHz. These boards are available from nearly any of the 287 chip vendors such as MicroWay or Hauppauge. I highly recommend their use if you run math-intensive programs because these chip vendors usually bundle the board in "free" if you buy any of the higher speed (more expensive) 80287 chips. Remember that this type of speedup cannot apply to systems that use 8087 or 80387 chips because these systems run those chips in complete and perfect synchronization with the main processor. In those systems, the math coprocessor always must run at exactly the same speed as the main CPU.

The only way to know for sure at what speeds your 287 processor will run is to consult your system's technical reference manual. To take advantage of this asynchronous clocking between the 286 and 287, many vendors of the math chips have designed small daughter boards that fit in between the 287 chip and socket and supply a new clock signal for the chip to use. With this sort of mechanism, you can basically decide what speed the math chip should run, without affecting the rest of the system in any way. You can run the math chip at speeds of up to 8, 10, 12 MHz, or more.

An important item to note about the 80287 is the relative cost of the chip. Although the 8087 usually costs about $100, you will spend two to three times that amount, or from $200 to $300, for the 80287. The high-speed versions can cost even more.

If after considering all these issues, you decide to invest in an 80287 chip, remember that the rated speed of the chip you purchase should be equal to or greater than the speed at which you actually run it. Adding the 80287 to an AT is a good idea if the software will support the chip, but only if you're using one of the faster chips on its own, faster-clocking circuit board. Otherwise, the benefits may not be enough to justify the cost.

The 80386 and 80386SX

The Intel 80386 is a full 32-bit processor optimized for high-speed operation and multitasking operating systems. The 80386 has been causing quite a stir in the PC industry because of the performance levels this chip brings to a desktop system. Intel introduced the chip in 1985, but it didn't appear in commercial PC types of systems until late 1986 and 1987. The chip debuted in the COMPAQ Deskpro 386 and several other IBM AT clones and finally appeared in an IBM system, the PS/2 Model 80. Since then, IBM has introduced the Model 70, which also uses the 386 chip. Compared with the current 8088 and 80286 systems, the 80386 chip offers staggering performance in almost all areas of operations. But performance is not the only issue here. This chip has other capabilities that should get your attention.

It can execute the same instructions as an 80286 and an 8086/8088 in fewer clock cycles. The 80386 also can switch to and from protected mode (the 80286 cannot switch *from*) under software control, without resetting the system, which saves an enormous amount of time. The 80386 can address 4 gigabytes of physical memory and have software believe that 64 terabytes of memory exists through the built-in virtual memory manager. The 80386 has a new mode called virtual real mode, which can enable several real-mode sessions to run simultaneously under a manager.

Probably the most exciting feature of this chip (besides speed) is its available modes of operation:

- Real mode
- Protected virtual mode
- Virtual real mode

Real mode is an "8086 compatible" mode just like that of the 80286 chip. The 80386 running in real mode can run unmodified 8086 type of software. An 80386 system running in this mode is acting as a "Turbo PC." PC DOS and any software written to run under DOS needs this mode to run. OS/2 allows DOS programs to run in this mode, but only one program at a time. Any program running in this mode has access to a maximum of 1M of memory.

Protected mode is fully compatible with the 80286 chip's protected mode. Many people call this mode of operation the chip's "native mode," because it is where an advanced operating system such as

OS/2 runs the chip. In the 80386 protected mode, Intel extended the memory-addressing capabilities by a new Memory Management Unit (MMU) that allows highly sophisticated memory-paging and program-switching capabilities. Because these features are added as true extensions to the 80286 type of MMU, the 80386 remains fully compatible with the 286 at a system code level.

Virtual real mode is something entirely new. In this mode, the processor can run with hardware memory protection while simulating the real-mode operation of an 8086. Therefore, multiple copies of PC DOS and other operating systems can run simultaneously on this processor, each in a protected area of memory and each oblivious to the others. If the programs in one segment should crash, the rest of the system is protected, and software commands can "reboot" the blown partition. Thus, any PC with an 80386 has the capability to "become" multiple PCs under software control.

These capabilities are becoming realities under the control of virtual machine manager programs such as Windows/386. Under Windows/386, an 80386-based system can run a copy of PC DOS with an application in each window. Each window allows access to 1M of memory and acts as if it were a window on a stand-alone PC. Each window's applications will also run simultaneously or truly multitask, which means that all the programs run simultaneously and no task switching is done with software (all the multitasking capability is in the hardware instead). These capabilities are not possible with lesser processors such as the 80286.

Because the 80386 is a full 32-bit processor, the chip has 32-bit internal registers, a 32-bit internal data bus, and a 32-bit external data bus. The chip has an on-board Memory Management Unit (MMU) that allows for a (32-bit) 4-gigabyte physical address space and a (46-bit) 64-terabyte virtual memory space. The 80386 sports 280,000 transistors in a Very Large Scale Integrated (VLSI) circuit. The device comes in a 132-pin package and draws approximately 400 milliamperes (ma), which is less power than even the 8086! This characteristic is due to the chip's construction in Complementary Metal Oxide Semiconductor (CMOS) materials. CMOS design allows devices to consume extremely low levels of power.

A new version of the 386, called the 80386SX, has recently surfaced. This chip was code-named the "P9" chip during its development and received much press during that time. The SX version of the chip bears the same relationship to the standard 386 as the 8088 does to the 8086. That is, the 386SX is restricted in communications to using only a 16-bit external interface, even though all the internals are the same as the standard 386. The 80386SX was designed as a low-cost alternative for systems designers looking for 386 capabilities with 286 system pricing.

In addition to the 16-bit external interface, another area of restriction is that the 386SX uses only a 24-bit memory-addressing scheme rather than the full 32-bit scheme that is implemented in the standard 386. The SX can therefore address only a maximum of 16M of physical memory rather than the 4 gigabytes of physical memory that the 386 can normally address. This limit isn't a problem for most current systems, because they cannot really utilize memory beyond 16M. Most system architectures don't allow Direct Memory Access (DMA) transfers to or from memory beyond the 16M boundary even if the system could accept the memory.

One often-heard fallacy about the 80386SX is that you can plug one into a 286 system and give the system 386 capabilities. Not true. The new SX chip is not pin-compatible with the 286 and will not plug into the same socket. Although an upgrade product could be designed to adapt the chip into an 80286 system, much of the performance gain from changing from 286 to 386 architecture would be lost because of the restricted 16-bit interface to memory and peripherals. The bottom line is that a 16 MHz 386SX is no faster than a 16 MHz 286. The 80386SX chip will make its mark in new systems design, signaling the death knell for the 286 because of the superior memory management unit and the extra virtual 8086 mode, which the 286 does not have.

The 80387

The 80387 numeric coprocessor is a high-performance math unit designed specifically to work with the 80386. Although you can use the earlier 287 in 80386 system design, the levels of performance associated with that union left much to be desired. The 387 chip runs in sync with the 80386 and therefore at the same clock rate.

The only problem with this chip is the current high price. At the higher clock rates, the price of the 387 chip can run more than $2,000. The standard 16 MHz chips cost about $500. You need to take this cost into consideration when investigating the 80387. If the software supports the math chip, the performance gains are quite impressive, especially at the higher clock rates.

The 80486 and Beyond

Intel is reportedly in the final stages of designing the 80486 processor. Little is known about the chip's final form, except for what has leaked out here and there as rumors and scattered pieces of information. The 486 will apparently be quite a performer, with about two to four times the throughput of a standard 386. The chip is reported to contain more than one million transistors and will be fully compatible with the 80386, and it will be adding new functions. Intel is supposedly going to introduce the 80486 some time in 1989. Desktop PC compatible systems will undoubtedly begin using this chip one to two years after the introduction date.

Speed Ratings of Microprocessors

One common area of misunderstanding about microprocessors is their speed ratings. This section first covers speed in general and then moves to some specifics about the various processors in the Intel family.

A computer system's *clock speed* is measured as a frequency, usually expressed as a number of cycles per second. Technically, a crystal oscillator is what controls the actual clock speeds. This oscillator uses a small sliver of quartz in a small tin container. As a voltage is applied to the quartz, it begins to vibrate (oscillate) at a harmonic rate dictated by the shape and size of the actual crystal (sliver). These oscillations emanate from the crystal in the form of a current that alternates at the harmonic rate of the crystal itself. This alternating current is the clock signal. Because a typical computer system runs millions of these cycles per second, the abbreviation megahertz (MHz) is used to measure speed. One Hertz is equal to one cycle per second. One megahertz is 1,000,000 Hertz. The term Hertz was named for the German physicist Heinrich Rudolph Hertz, who in 1885 confirmed through experimentation the electromagnetic theory, which stated that light was a form of electromagnetic radiation and propagated as waves.

A single cycle is the smallest element of time for the microprocessor, but not much can occur within a single cycle. Every action requires at least one cycle and usually multiple cycles. To transfer data to and from memory, for example, an 8086 chip needs 4 cycles plus wait states. (A *wait state* is a clock tick in which nothing happens to make sure that the microprocessor is not getting ahead of the rest of the computer.) An 80286 needs only 2 cycles plus wait states for the same transfer. As for executing instructions, most processor instructions take anywhere from 2 to 100 or more cycles to execute. One reason that the 80386 is so fast is that it has an average instruction execution time of 4.4 clock cycles. If two processors have the same cycling time, the processor that can execute instructions in fewer cycles is faster. For example, a 6 MHz 8086-based system is about half as fast as a 6 MHz 80286-based system, even though the clock rates are the same.

How can two different processors that run at exactly the same clock rate perform differently, with one running "faster" than the other? The answer is simple: efficiency. Here is an analogy. Suppose that you are comparing two engines. An engine has a cycle, called a revolution of the crankshaft. This cycling time is measured in revolutions per minute (rpm). Now, if you have two engines that both can run the same maximum rpm, the engines should run the car at the same speed, right?

Wrong! Suppose that you are shopping for a car, and you want a fast sports car. You first stop at the Volkswagen dealer, and the dealer shows you the new Rabbit GTI sports model. You ask, "What is the redline on the engine?" The dealer tells you that the Rabbit GTI has a 4-cylinder engine that redlines at 7,500 rpm. You are impressed, record the information, and go to the next dealer. Your next stop is with the Chevrolet dealer, who steers you toward the new Corvette model. You ask the same question, and the dealer tells you that the Corvette has a V-8 engine that redlines at 5,500 rpm. This sounds bad! You figure that if the engine in the VW turns 7,500 rpm, it will propel the car much faster than the 'Vette, whose engine only turns 5,500 rpm. Of course the Corvette is the much faster car—and by a big margin.

Using engine rpm to compare how fast two cars will go is like using MHz to compare how "fast" two computers will go! Too many other variables are involved for this simplistic comparison to be made. The big V-8 engine in the Corvette will do more "work" in each revolution of the engine, and by the same analogy, the 80286 also will do more "work" in a single CPU cycle. It is more efficient! The 386 is about four times more efficient than the 8088 in instruction execution; although an 8088 requires nearly 20 cycles for the average processor instruction to execute, the same average instruction takes only 4 cycles on a 386 chip. Combine that with a higher clock rate and you have the reason that a 16 MHz 386 system is about 10 times faster than a 4.77 MHz 8088-based system.

Clock speed is a function of the system's design and is usually controlled by an oscillator, which in turn is controlled by a quartz crystal. Typically, the crystal oscillation frequency is divided by some amount to get the actual processor frequency. The divisor amount is determined by the original design of the processor (Intel) and related support chips, and also by how the system board was designed to use these chips together as a system. For example, in IBM's PC and XT systems, the main crystal frequency is 14.31818 MHz, which is divided by 3 to achieve a processor clock speed of 4.77 MHz. In an IBM AT system, the crystal speeds are either 12.00 or 16.00 MHz, which is divided by 2 to result in a 6.00 or 8.00 MHz processor clock.

If all other variables, such as the type of processor, number of wait states (empty cycles) added to memory accesses, width of the data bus, and so on, are equal, then you can compare two systems by their respective clock rates. But be careful with this type of comparison, because unknown variables (such as the number of wait states) often can influence the speed of a particular system, causing the unit with the lower clock rate to run faster than you expect, or likewise causing a system with a numerically higher clock rate to run slower than it "should." In particular, the construction and design of the memory subsystem can have an enormous impact on the final execution speed of a system.

When building a processor, the manufacturer tests it for operation at various speeds, temperatures, and pressures. After it's tested, the processor receives a stamp indicating the maximum safe speed at which the unit will operate under the wide variation of temperatures and pressures encountered in normal operation. The rating system is usually quite simple. For example, if you remove the lid of an IBM PS/2 Model 50, you can see markings on the processor that look like this:

```
80286-10
```

The number indicates that the chip is an 80286 that runs at a maximum operating speed of 10 MHz. This chip is acceptable for any application in which the chip runs at 10 MHz *or less*. If you have a system such as the AT Model 339 or Model 319, which uses an 80286-8, and the processor fails, you can replace that processor with any 80286 rated at 8 MHz or higher. The 80286-6, which is rated at only 6 MHz, would not be suitable for this replacement, because its maximum speed rating is less than the 8 MHz at which the AT runs the chip.

Sometimes the markings don't indicate the actual speed. In the 8086, for example, a "-3" translates to 6 MHz operation. Table 7.3 lists the available microprocessors and coprocessors and the manufacturers' markings and corresponding clock rates.

Table 7.3
Microprocessor Clock Rates

Main CPU	Coprocessor	Chip Suffix	Maximum Speed
8086 or 8088	8087	(none)	5 MHz
		-3	6 MHz
		-2	8 MHz
		-1	10 MHz
80286	80287	-6	6 MHz
		-8	8 MHz
		-10	10 MHz
		-12	12 MHz
		-16	16 MHz
		-20	20 MHz
80386 or 80386SX	80387 or 80387SX	-16	16 MHz
		-20	20 MHz
		-25	25 MHz
		-33	33 MHz

Note: The 386SX and 387SX have only one version that runs at 16 MHz. No plans exists for faster versions at the moment. The 33 MHz 80386 and 80387 have not yet been announced. Intel has indicated that this probably will be the next speed level available.

A disturbing practice that currently seems to be prevalent is the sale of systems with substandard speed-rated components, especially microprocessors. The microprocessor is probably the single most expensive part in a system, and the lower speed components often cost much less than their higher speed counterparts. As a matter of fact, the price can sometimes double when you go from one speed designation to another. Some manufacturers use the lower rated part in order to save a substantial amount of money in the system manufacturing process.

You may be wondering how a chip can even run at a greater speed without failing. But in fact most chips can run at a higher speed than they are rated. For example, 80386-16 chips probably can run at 20 MHz in a normal environment. When checking that part, Intel tested at many extremes in temperature and pressure, as well as for an amount of time that allowed the manufacturer to know with confidence that the particular component will always perform to the rated specification. The part is *guaranteed* to run at the rated speed. To offer such a guarantee means that the manufacturer must have some "cushion" in the design, a cushion that is lost when the part is run beyond the rated speed.

Here's a sample scenario: While thumbing through the back of one of the popular PC magazines, you spy an ad from Joe's Computer Shack. Joe is selling the "Super Turbo American Generic Premium Limited Extra 386 Plus," which is advertised to run at 28 MHz. (An immediate tip-off here is that Intel doesn't make an 80386-28!) You purchase this system because you cannot believe the price for such a fast system. Even COMPAQ and IBM don't have systems running this fast.

When your new system arrives in the mail, you open up the system to look at the 386 chip. You discover that the 386 chip is covered with a heat sink, a metal device that draws heat away from an electronic device. (This discovery provides another clue, because Intel designs the chips to run at rated speed without heat sinking.) You pry away the heat sink, which is either glued on with heat sink compound or attached with a special clamping mechanism. You discover an 80386-20 or 80386-25 under the heat sink. (Sometimes the markings will even have been rubbed off or overwritten.)

When you call Joe, his explanation for the deception is that he "tests all the chips by running the systems with a diagnostics program." If they pass Joe's test, then he certifies them as acceptable. According to Joe, "After all, Intel always makes their parts to run beyond the ratings."

Intel would not agree with Joe's methodology and, as a matter of fact, would no longer warrant the chip. If the chip had passed Intel's strict testing procedures for the higher speed (which involve much more than running the chip for a few minutes in a PC), Intel would have given the chip a different stamping and sold it for more money!

You would be surprised at just how many "Joes" are out there selling cheap PC clone systems in this manner. You will never find a name-brand system such as IBM, COMPAQ, Zenith, Tandy, and so on, built with that sort of "garage engineering." If the CPU is underrated, probably so are many other components on the motherboard. Such a system will probably behave strangely, especially at higher operating temperatures.

Testing Microprocessors

Although the manufacturer of a particular microprocessor has specialized equipment designed to test its own processor, you will have to settle for a little less. Usually the best microprocessor test device that you have access to is a known functional system. You can then use the diagnostics available from IBM and other systems manufacturers to test the motherboard and processor functions. Most all systems today have processors that are mounted in a socket for easy replacement, because the processor is easily the single most expensive chip in the system.

A company called Supersoft offers specialized diagnostics software, called Service Diagnostics, which is written to test various microprocessors. Special versions are available for each processor in the Intel family. If you don't want to purchase this kind of software, you can perform a "quick and dirty" evaluation of your microprocessor by using the normal diagnostics program that is supplied with your system. Most systems don't function at all with a defective microprocessor, because it is the brain of the system. If you encounter a system that appears to have a dead motherboard, try replacing the microprocessor with a microprocessor from another motherboard that is known to function properly. You may be surprised to find that the processor in the original board is the culprit. If the system continues to "play dead," however, then obviously the problem lies elsewhere.

Known Processor Defects

As much as we would like to believe that our systems are perfect and bug free, sometimes even the brains of our systems can have problems. And sometimes these problems are built in from the factory in the form of actual bugs or defects in the design. These types of defects are rare, but some examples exist, and *knowing* when you run into one of these defects pays off. Otherwise, strange problems can occur that may cause you to replace or repair other areas of the system that are not really bad at all. This section gives details on some of the known defects in the processors in many of our systems.

Early 8088s

Some early 8088 microprocessors had a bug that allowed interrupts to occur after a program changed the stack segment register. Normally, an interrupt is not allowed until the instruction after the one that changes the stack segment register. This bug is a subtle one that may be causing problems if your system is an older one. Most programmers have adopted coding procedures that work around the bug, but you have no guarantee that all software includes these "work arounds" or fixes. Another problem is that this bug may affect operation of the chip with an 8087 math coprocessor. Approximately 200,000 IBM PC units were manufactured with the defective chip, all of which were early units sold during 1981 and 1982.

Originally, when the 8087 math coprocessor chip was sold, IBM always included in the package an 8088 to be installed with the math chip. This practice led to rumors that these parts were somehow "matched." Not true. IBM had merely found an easy way to make sure that anybody using IBM's 8087 chips didn't have the defective 8088. The company included a bug-free 8088 because the actual cost to IBM for this chip was negligible and including it eliminated many potential service problems.

If you're unsure about the 8088 chip in a particular system, you can either use diagnostics software to diagnose the problem or identify a good or bad chip directly from appearance. If you can open the unit to view the 8088 chip, the manufacturer and copyright date printed on the chip are the clues to which version you have. Any 8088 chips made by manufacturers other than Intel are bug free, because Intel licensed the chip mask to other manufacturers so that they could produce the chips. Intel began this licensing program after the bug had already been fixed. If the chip was manufactured by Intel, then the older, defective parts have a copyright date of 1978 alone, and the newer, good parts have copyright dates of 1978 *and* 1981 or some later year.

The following marking on Intel 8088 chips indicates a chip with the interrupt bug:

```
8088

(c) INTEL 1978
```

The following markings on Intel 8088 chips indicate chips that have the bug corrected:

```
8088

(c) INTEL '78 '81
```

```
8088

(c) INTEL '78 '83
```

Although many diagnostics programs can identify the chip, you can do it yourself with DEBUG from DOS Versions 2.0 and later. Simply load DEBUG and enter the command

    A 100

to assemble some instructions. Next enter the following three instructions and follow each with a carriage return to exit the assemble mode and return to the DEBUG prompt:

    MOV ES,AX
    INC AX
    NOP

Then type *T* to execute a T, or Trace, command, which is supposed to execute the next single instruction, display the contents of the 8088's registers, and stop.

The Trace normally executes only one instruction. When that instruction is a MOV to a segment register, however, as is in this case, the Trace command executes the second instruction before interrupting the program. The third instruction is a dummy no-operation instruction.

Now look at the value shown by the *T* command for the register AX. If AX = 0000, you have found a bugged microprocessor. If AX = 0001, the second instruction was executed properly, and you have a good chip. If the second instruction is indeed executed, then it increments the value of the AX register by 1. A screen dump of the DEBUG session should look like the following example, where the "XXXX" is the segment address, which varies from system to system:

```
-A 100
XXXX:0100 MOV ES,AX
XXXX:0102 INC AX
XXXX:0103 NOP
XXXX:0104
-T

AX=0001  BX=0000  CX=0000  DX=0000  SP=FFEE  BP=0000  SI=0000  DI=0000
DS=XXXX  ES=0000  SS=XXXX  CS=XXXX  IP=0103    NV UP EI PL NZ NA PO NC
XXXX:0103 90              NOP
-Q
```

In this session, AX equals 0001, which indicates a good chip. You can purchase a replacement 8088 for $10 or so from most chip houses. If your chip is definitely bad, or you suspect it for any reason, a replacement is cheap insurance against this problem.

Early 80386s

Some of the earliest Intel 80386 processors had a small bug that you may encounter when troubleshooting what seems like a software problem. This bug was apparently in the chip's 32-bit multiply routine. The bug manifests itself only when you're running true 32-bit code, which means a program such as UNIX/386 or Windows/386. Some of the specialized 80386 memory management software systems also may invoke this subtle bug. The 16-bit operating systems such as DOS and OS/2 probably will not encounter this bug.

The bug usually causes the system to lock up and therefore may be difficult to diagnose because this problem generally is an intermittent software-related problem. Unfortunately, this bug is difficult to test for, and only Intel, with proper test equipment, can actually determine whether your chip is really bugged. Some programs can diagnose this problem, but although they identify a defective chip, they cannot identify all defective chips. If the program does indicate that the chip is bad, you definitely have one of the defective ones; but if the program passes the chip, you still may have a defective one.

Intel asked its 80386 customers to return any possibly defective chips for screening, but many vendors did not return all the questionable chips. Intel tested the chips and replaced any defective chips. The known defective chips were later sold to bargain liquidators or systems houses that wanted a chip that would not run 32-bit code. These "known defective" chips were stamped with a logo that reads "16-bit SW Only," which means that the chip is authorized to run 16-bit software only.

The chips that were tested and found to be good, and all subsequent chips that have been produced as bug free, were marked with a double sigma ($\Sigma\Sigma$) code, which indicates a good chip. Any 80386 chips not marked with either the "16-bit SW Only" or the "$\Sigma\Sigma$" designation have not been tested by Intel and may be defective. Return these chips to the system manufacturer, who will then send the chip back to Intel for a free replacement.

Here is what the chips look like:

```
80386-16
```

The preceding marking indicates that a chip has not yet been screened for the defect; it may be either good or bad.

```
80386-16
16-bit SW Only
```

The preceding marking indicates that a chip has been tested and found to have the 32-bit multiply bug. This chip works with 16-bit software, such as DOS, but not with 32-bit "386 specific" software such as Windows/386.

```
80386-16

ΣΣ
```

This mark indicates a chip that has been tested and found to be defect free. This chip is the one you want because it fulfills all the capabilities promised for the 80386.

Memory

The architecture of the CPU (the microprocessor) has the final word on a computer's memory capacity. The 8088, with its 20 address lines, can keep track of and directly reference up to 1,024K, or 1M, of memory. The hardware design of the PC reserves the top 384K of that memory for special purposes, so you have access to 640K for your programs and data. The 80286 CPU in the AT has 24 address lines, so it can keep track of up to 16M of memory. The 80386 CPU, used in the PS/2 Models 70 and 80 and many compatibles, has a full set of 32 address lines, which allow a staggering 4 gigabytes of memory.

The 80286 and 80386 each emulate the 8086 by implementing a hardware mode of operation called real mode. Under real mode, all Intel processors—even the mighty 80386—are restricted to using only 1M, and 384K of that is still reserved by the motherboard design. Only under the protected mode of operation can the 80286 and 80386 use their maximum potential for memory addressing.

A limitation particular to 80386-based systems is that the current motherboard designs don't make full use of the memory beyond 16M. Some motherboards will not address that memory at all. You can identify these systems by their lack of a special 32-bit slot of some kind. Even those systems with a 32-bit slot don't allow for Direct Memory Access (DMA) transfers between devices and any memory after 16M, which severely limits the usefulness of any memory in that region. Also, operating systems specifically written for the 80286 chip, such as OS/2, will not manage memory beyond the 16M boundary, which further establishes 16M as the next barrier to overcome.

Today you basically have to deal with two primary types of memory architectures: the PC type and the AT type. The PC type of system has a 1M boundary with 384K reserved by the hardware, and the AT type of system has a 16M (16,384K) boundary with 0.5M (512K) reserved by the hardware. The 1M and 16M figures amount to walls in memory capacity. The current motherboard and operating system structure prevents you from using more memory even if the system is capable of it (as with the 80386, for example).

Much activity has arisen concerning the removal of these memory boundaries. The market currently offers several types of "fixes" for the problem, but most of these are limited in what they can do. Some involve software such as a new or different operating system. Other solutions involve specialized hardware, such as expanded memory adapters, or special memory control and management programs that take advantage of unique 80386 capabilities. On the PC and XT side of things, some hardware design activity has produced a couple of techniques for tricking the system into using vast amounts of memory without the microprocessor ever realizing it. These expanded memory boards are examined in more detail in Chapter 10.

The following sections discuss the different types of motherboard memory, how memory is organized in the system, the system ROM, memory speed ratings, and ways to test your memory.

Motherboard Memory

A system usually has some type of primary circuit board. As mentioned previously, most systems, such as those from IBM and compatibles, use a motherboard, which contains slots for expansion adapters. Other systems have adopted the backplane design in which the primary circuit board is a card plugged into one of the slots. In each case, this primary circuit contains the system's processor and some amount of installed memory.

The advantage of memory installed directly on the motherboard is that, for many systems, access to this memory is faster than any memory accessed through an expansion slot. And even if you don't have any advantage in speed, you do have an advantage in the savings of slots. The more memory you can get on the motherboard, the fewer memory expansion adapters you need.

Most of the faster 80386-based systems on the market have a special 32-bit slot for adding memory to the system. Those systems that do not include this slot, however, face a large penalty in speed for any memory addressed through a standard 16-bit slot. Some systems, such as the IBM Model 70, have a special caching system on the motherboard that controls memory access at an extremely high rate of speed. These caching systems contain high-speed memory that serves as a buffer between the microprocessor and memory. The cache acts as an intelligent buffer, which can often ensure that nearly all memory locations desired by the processor are found in the cache and presented to the processor at high speed. Any values needed by the processor that are not in the cache must be read at a slower rate.

Physical Storage and Organization

Motherboard memory may be physically installed in several forms. The conventional use is standard Dual Inline Pin (DIP) memory chips.

Memory Chips

Several types of memory chips have been used in PC system motherboards. Most of these are the single-bit-wide chips, which are available in several capacities:

16K by 1 bit   These devices were used in the original IBM PC with a Type 1 motherboard and are quite small in capacity compared with the current standard. You will not find much call for these chips except for in original IBM PC systems.

64K by 1 bit   These chips were used in the standard IBM PC Type 2 motherboard and in the XT Type 1 and 2 motherboards. Many memory adapters, such as the popular vintage AST 6-pack boards, also use these chips.

128K by 1 bit   These chips were used in the IBM AT Type 1 motherboard and often were a strange physical combination of two 64K chips stacked on top of one another and soldered together. True single-chip versions were also used for storing the parity bits in the IBM XT 286.

256K by 1 bit   These chips have enjoyed popularity in the current majority of motherboards and memory cards. The IBM XT Type 2 and IBM AT Type 2 motherboards, as well as most compatible systems, use these chips.

1,024K by 1 bit   These 1-megabit chips have been gaining in popularity lately and are starting to be used in many compatible motherboards and memory cards. IBM has not used these chips in raw chip form but has been using special 1-megabit chips in the Single Inline Memory Modules (SIMMs) found in the PS/2 motherboards. (See the next section for more information on SIMMs.)

DIP memory chips are allocated on the motherboard (and on memory cards) in *banks*. The banks usually correspond to the data bus capacity of the system's microprocessor. In 8088-based systems, for example, the banks are 8 bits plus 1 parity bit (usually 9 chips) wide; and in 8086- and 80286-based systems, the banks are 16 bits plus 2 parity bits (usually 18 chips) wide.

The IBM PC Type 2 and XT Type 1 motherboard contains 4 banks of memory labeled as Bank 0, 1, 2, and 3. Each of these banks uses 9 64K-by-1-bit chips. The total number of chips present is 4 times 9, or 36 chips. They are organized as shown in figure 7.1.

Fig. 7.1.

The organization of the memory banks for an IBM XT Type 1 motherboard.

Bank 0 | [P] [0] [1] [2] [3] [4] [5] [6] [7]

Bank 1 | [P] [0] [1] [2] [3] [4] [5] [6] [7]

Bank 2 | [P] [0] [1] [2] [3] [4] [5] [6] [7]

Bank 3 | [P] [0] [1] [2] [3] [4] [5] [6] [7]

Front

P = Parity bit
0-7 = Bits 0 through 7

In an AT type of system, the memory is organized into banks of 18 chips. The organization of the IBM AT Type 2 motherboard is shown in figure 7.2.

Fig. 7.2.

*The organization
of the memory
banks for an IBM
AT Type 2
motherboard.*

```
[ 7]  [15]
[ 6]  [14]
[ 5]  [13]
[ 4]  [12]
[ 3]  [11]
[ 2]  [10]
[ 1]  [ 9]
[ 0]  [ 8]
[ P]  [ P]
```

Bank 0

Note that in this particular application, the chips are organized in a
vertical column rather than in rows. This design is totally arbitrary
and up to the designers of the board.

One-bit wide chips used to be almost a universal standard among
PC systems, but today many systems use 2-bit- or 4-bit-wide chips.
Because the "wider" chips are more dense, they allow you to
assemble banks of memory with fewer chips. To construct a 16-bit
bank of 128K bytes with 128K-by-1-bit chips, for example, you need
18 chips. But you could construct a similar 16-bit bank of 128K bytes,
using 8 128K-by-2-bit chips and 2 additional 128K-by-1-bit chips for
the parity bits.

As an alternative to individual memory chips, many modern systems
have adopted the Single Inline Memory Module (SIMM) for memory
storage.

The Single Inline Memory Module (SIMM)

A SIMM is basically a tiny board with memory chips soldered onto
it. This little "boardlet" plugs into a tiny "slotlet" that may be on
the motherboard or memory card in a conventional slot. Chips are
always soldered onto the SIMM, so removing and replacing the
individual memory chips themselves becomes unfeasible. Instead,
you need to replace the entire SIMM if it fails in any way. The SIMM
is treated as if it were one large "memory chip."

Each SIMM is roughly the size of one or two fingers and is
extremely compact, considering the amount of memory it contains.
SIMMs are available in several capacities, including the following:

256K
512K
1,024K
2,048K

SIMMs were designed to eliminate the problem of "chip creep," which plagues any system that has memory chips installed in sockets. *Chip creep* occurs when a chip works its way out of its socket because of the normal thermal cycling that a system goes through when it is powered on and off. Eventually, chip creep leads to poor contact between the chip leads and the socket, causing memory errors and problems.

The original solution to this creeping problem was to solder all the memory chips directly onto the printed circuit board. Unfortunately, however, this approach made the chips difficult to replace. And because memory chips fail more frequently than most other types of chips, soldering the chips to the board made the unit troublesome to service.

The SIMM is the best of both worlds. The chips are always soldered to the SIMM, but you can replace the SIMM itself if necessary. Although this solution is a good one, it can greatly increase the parts cost of repair. Instead of replacing just one defective chip, you end up replacing what amounts to an entire bank. The PS/2 Model 50Z, for example, comes with a single SIMM that contains 1M. If a single bit in this megabyte fails, the SIMM must be replaced at a cost of $500, which is much more than the cost of a single 1-megabit chip.

SIMMs are found in most newer systems on the market today, including nearly all of IBM's PS/2 systems, the XT-286, many compatibles, and even the Apple Macintosh systems. A SIMM isn't a proprietary memory system but an industry standard device. You therefore should be able to purchase SIMMs at most of the same places you purchase a normal memory chip. A SIMM is a much better alternative than fully soldered memory and definitely more desirable than a system manufacturer's own proprietary memory device.

Knowing the memory's organization is necessary when you need to diagnose defective memory chips. You should consult your technical reference manual to determine the physical organization of memory for your particular system.

Parity Checking

One standard that IBM has set for the industry is that each 8 bits is accompanied by a single *parity* bit. The parity bit allows the system to have a built-in cross-check for the integrity of each byte in the system. The system uses the extra parity bits to perform parity checking for each byte of data stored. IBM uses *even parity* as a standard for its systems, meaning that as the 8 individual bits are stored, the motherboard circuitry evaluates the 8 bits by counting the number of 1s. The parity bit is then stored as a 1 or a 0— whichever number causes the total number of 1s to be an even number. Here are some examples:

```
                 Data Bits
Bit:     Parity 0 1 2 3 4 5 6 7
Value:     1     1 0 1 1 0 0 1 1
```

In this example, the total number of data bits with a value of 1 is an odd number (5), which dictates that the parity bit must have a value of 1 to force an even sum for all 9 bits.

```
                 Data Bits
Bit:     Parity 0 1 2 3 4 5 6 7
Value:     0     0 0 1 1 0 0 1 1
```

In this example, the total number of data bits with a value of 1 is an even number (4), which dictates that the parity bit must have a value of 0 to force an even sum for all 9 bits.

When reading memory back from storage, the system checks this parity information. If a particular byte has an odd number of bits with a value of 1, then that byte must have an error. What you don't know is in fact which bit has changed, or if even a single bit has changed. If three bits changed, for example, that byte would still flag a parity-check error; but if two bits changed, the byte would pass unnoticed. When a parity-check error is detected, the motherboard parity-checking circuits generate a Non-Maskable Interrupt (NMI), which halts processing and diverts the system's attention to the error at hand. This NMI causes a routine in the ROM to be executed. The routine clears the screen and then displays a message in the upper left corner of the screen. The exact message differs depending on the type of computer system. Here are examples of parity-check messages for three types of systems:

For the IBM PC: PARITY CHECK X

For the IBM XT: PARITY CHECK X
                         YYYYY (Z)

For the IBM AT and late   PARITY CHECK X
model XT: YYYYY

where

X = 1 or 2:
1 = Error occurred on the motherboard
2 = Error occurred in an expansion slot

YYYYY = 00000 through FFFFF, which indicates in hexadecimal
notation the byte in which the error has occurred

(Z) = (S) or (E):
(S) = Error occurred in the system unit
(E) = Error occurred in the expansion chassis

The third (and final) step is that the ROM parity-check routine halts
the CPU. The system locks up and you must perform a hardware
reset or power off/on cycle to restart the system. All unsaved work
is lost in the process.

In Chapter 14, the hardware troubleshooting guide, you see how to
use these numbers to help locate the defective component.

How Memory Is Organized

Systems designers have reserved for internal uses a certain portion
of the maximum amount of memory in each system. This *reserved
memory* is used for things such as graphics and ROM programs. The
remaining memory is called *user memory* and is the portion of
memory in which an operating system loads itself and any
applications programs. Table 7.4 lists the amount of memory
available on various systems.

Table 7.4
Memory Allocation

System Type	PC	AT
Maximum Addressable Memory (RAM)	1,024K	16,384K
Reserved Memory:		
Video Memory	128K	128K
Adapter Board ROM and RAM	192K	128K
Motherboard ROM	64K	128K
Duplicate of Motherboard ROM	n/a	128K
Remaining RAM	640K	15,872K

Figure 7.3 shows how the real- and protected-mode memory space is allocated. The first memory allocation graph shows memory used by real mode or the first megabyte of protected-mode memory. The second memory allocation graph shows the last megabyte of protected-mode memory.

Use the following guidelines when referring to figure 7.3:

    . = user memory
    v = video RAM
    a = adapter board ROM and RAM
    r = motherboard ROM BIOS
    b = IBM Cassette BASIC

Video memory is a 128K portion of memory reserved for the storage of graphics and text material for display. This memory is located from memory address A0000 to BFFFF. The lower resolution adapters may use only a portion of this video memory, but the higher resolution EGA and VGA adapters use it all.

Adapter board ROM and RAM space is allocated for various adapter cards that need a place for their on-board control software. Some network boards use this space for RAM in order to transfer data to and from the system. Expanded memory adapters that conform to the Lotus Intel Microsoft Expanded Memory Standard (LIM EMS) use 64K of this space for a bank switching scheme to access the rest of the memory on the particular EMS adapter board.

Motherboard ROM space is just that: space for the motherboard control program that is sometimes called the Basic Input/Output System (BIOS). On IBM systems only, the requisite Cassette BASIC

Fig. 7.3.

*The memory
allocation of real
and protected
modes.*

```
          : 0---1---2---3---4---5---6---7---8---9---A---B---C---D---E---F---
000000: ................................................................
010000: ................................................................
020000: ................................................................
030000: ................................................................
040000: ................................................................
050000: ................................................................
060000: ................................................................
070000: ................................................................
080000: ................................................................
090000: ................................................................
0A0000: vvvvvvvvvvvvvvvvvvvvvvvvvvvvvvvvvvvvvvvvvvvvvvvvvvvvvvvvvvvvvvvvvv
0B0000: vvvvvvvvvvvvvvvvvvvvvvvvvvvvvvvvvvvvvvvvvvvvvvvvvvvvvvvvvvvvvvvvvv
0C0000: aaaaaaaaaaaaaaaaaaaaaaaaaaaaaaaaaaaaaaaaaaaaaaaaaaaaaaaaaaaaaaaa
0D0000: aaaaaaaaaaaaaaaaaaaaaaaaaaaaaaaaaaaaaaaaaaaaaaaaaaaaaaaaaaaaaaaa
0E0000: rrrrrrrrrrrrrrrrrrrrrrrrrrrrrrrrrrrrrrrrrrrrrrrrrrrrrrrrrrrrrrrr
0F0000: rrrrrrrrrrrrrrrrrrrrrrrrbbbbbbbbbbbbbbbbbbbbbbbbbbbbbbbbrrrrrrrr
      \
      /
      \
      /
          : 0---1---2---3---4---5---6---7---8---9---A---B---C---D---E---F---
F00000: ................................................................
F10000: ................................................................
F20000: ................................................................
F30000: ................................................................
F40000: ................................................................
F50000: ................................................................
F60000: ................................................................
F70000: ................................................................
F80000: ................................................................
F90000: ................................................................
FA0000: ................................................................
FB0000: ................................................................
FC0000: ................................................................
FD0000: ................................................................
FE0000: rrrrrrrrrrrrrrrrrrrrrrrrrrrrrrrrrrrrrrrrrrrrrrrrrrrrrrrrrrrrrrrr
FF0000: rrrrrrrrrrrrrrrrrrrrrrrrbbbbbbbbbbbbbbbbbbbbbbbbbbbbbbbbrrrrrrrr
```

interpreter is also located in this space. Note that this memory is duplicated at the end of the protected-mode space. This duplication is due to the way switching is accomplished from real to protected modes, and the idiosyncrasies of the 80286 and 80386 processors.

System ROM

The system ROM for each of the IBM computers contains three primary programs: the POST (power-on self test), the Basic Input/Output System (BIOS), and Cassette BASIC. Compatibles have the first two but lack the Cassette BASIC. The idea behind placing a small essential set of software in ROM is to allow the computer to bootstrap itself automatically and to retain flexibility for easy changes in the future.

Over the years, the ROM in the various PC models has undergone some changes, which have almost always been associated with either a completely new system or a new motherboard design for an existing system. Several definite reasons exist for these changes. The introduction of the XT, for example, gave IBM a good opportunity to fix a few things in the ROM and also add necessary new features, such as automatic support for a hard disk. IBM retrofitted many of the same changes into the PC's ROM at the same time.

An in-depth knowledge of the various kinds of ROM is something that a programmer might find useful, so IBM makes the necessary information available in the technical reference manuals that are sold for each system. A new ROM BIOS technical reference manual covers all IBM systems in one book. Complete ROM listings (with comments) accompanied the earlier technical reference manuals, but that specific information is not supplied in the later ones.

Certain things about ROM, however, are important for *everyone* to know. IBM has had more than 20 specifically different ROM BIOS programs for the PC and PS/2 families. Each one is different in some respects from all the others. Sometimes a single system has had different versions of ROM over the course of that system's availability. For example, at least three versions of the ROM existed for the PC, XT, and AT systems. A couple of extremely important changes have been made in the ROM software (sometimes called firmware), so knowing which ROM is in your system can be useful.

The particular version of ROM that you have is indicated by the date encoded in the chip. The ROM also contains an identification byte (the second to last byte) indicating the system type and a part number for reference. The value of the byte at location FFFFE (hexadecimal) directly corresponds to the system type, as shown in table 7.5.

If you want to determine which BIOS module is installed in your system, you can display the date the BIOS module design was completed. Simply key in the following four-statement BASIC program:

```
10 DEF SEG = &HF000
20 For X = &HFFF5 to &HFFFF
30  Print  Chr$(Peek(X));
40 Next
```

Table 7.5
IBM ROM Versions

ID Byte	Submodel Byte	System	Date	Revision
FF	00	PC	04/24/81	-
FF	00	PC	10/19/81	-
FF	00	PC	10/27/82	-
FE	00	PC XT	11/08/82	-
FD	00	PCjr	06/01/83	-
FC	00	PC AT	01/10/84	-
FC	00	PC AT	06/10/85	Rev. 1
FC	01	PC AT	11/15/85	Rev. 0
FC	02	PC XT 286	04/21/86	Rev. 0
FC	04	PS/2 Model 50	02/13/87	Rev. 0
FC	04	PS/2 Model 50Z	04/18/88	Rev. 3
FC	05	PS/2 Model 60	02/13/87	Rev. 0
FB	00	PC XT	01/10/86	Rev. 1
FB	00	PC XT	05/09/86	Rev. 2
FA	00	PS/2 Model 30	09/02/86	Rev. 0
FA	00	PS/2 Model 30	12/12/86	Rev. 1
F9	00	PC-Convertible	09/13/85	Rev. 1
F8	00	PS/2 Model 80/16	03/30/87	Rev. 0
F8	01	PS/2 Model 80/20	10/07/87	Rev. 0

You can identify your ROM version by running this small program, which will show you a date. When the date appears on-screen, look in table 7.5 for an exact match. For example, I currently have an XT that shows a date of 11/08/82. This date clearly indicates the first XT ROM version, as shown on the chart, and I also can see that two versions are later than mine. In addition, I have an XT 286 with a ROM date of 04/21/86. According to the chart, that ROM is the only one that IBM ever put into that system, so I know that I have the latest (and only) version of that ROM in my system. Also note that this ROM has the same ID byte as the AT but differs in the submodel byte. This difference means that IBM considers the XT 286 to be an AT; and software that looks at the ID byte to determine the type of system it is running on (such as DOS and OS/2) comes to the conclusion that it is running on an AT. As far as any software and hardware is concerned, then, the XT Model 286 is an AT.

The date is important; it has the same relative meaning as a version number does for software. IBM later began to code an official revision number, which is what the last column represents. Now versions can be identified by this number as well. The ID is the most significant piece of information, followed by the submodel byte and, within a submodel, the revision numbers.

For example, the PS/2 50Z has a revision number of 3, which means that it is the fourth version that has been developed for this submodel (the Model 50 and 50Z are the same submodel). The original Model 50 has the first ROM (revision 0), and the revision 1 and 2 ROMs have never surfaced in a system, although IBM must have gone through these revisions in-house. This situation is analogous to having a program go from Version 1.0 to Version 1.3. What happened to Versions 1.1 and 1.2? Only the author knows for sure.

Entering the RUN command (typing *run* and pressing Enter) causes the date to be printed out. If you have a PC, a date later than or equal to 10/27/82 indicates that you don't need a BIOS update. A date of 10/19/81 or earlier in a PC indicates that you must install a BIOS update. This update allows the system to recognize the full 640K memory space and to use an adapter with extended BIOS, such as a Fixed Disk controller, Enhanced Graphics Adapter, PC Network Adapter, Expansion Unit, or IBM Personal Computer Cluster Adapter.

Only IBM Personal Computer Models 1, 13, 14, 64, and 74 require updating of BIOS. These units were all sold before March 1983. Any computers sold after March 1983 had the ROM mentioned. Models that have had an Expansion Unit Model 1 attached don't need further updating, because the new BIOS was included with this option. Later models (including 104, 114, 164, 166, 174, and 176) were built with the new functions included in their respective BIOS. The serial numbers of PCs originally manufactured with the early BIOS modules have a serial number of 0300960 or lower. PCs with the newest ROM have the letter "B" inside of a circle stamped on the back of the system chassis in white ink.

For those of you interested in a PC ROM upgrade, IBM introduced on April 6, 1984, a BIOS Update Kit (Part Number: 1501005). (This number isn't the part number in the chip but rather the number for the upgrade kit that your dealer can obtain.) The BIOS Update Kit, which costs $35, is a replacement-parts kit that updates earlier models of the Personal Computer System Board (which use 16K memory modules) with a new BIOS module. Although getting this newer chip is a good idea, the BIOS upgrade chip has become unavailable from IBM. It is discontinued and no longer in stock. If an alternative is not discovered, you might as well place a glass dome over the PC and donate it to the Smithsonian. The PC would have more value as a museum piece than as a computer!

Several liquidators have purchased large quantities of these original 10/27/82 ROM chips from IBM. These chips are exact NOS (New Old Stock) originals and are not copies or illegal duplicates. They can be purchased for about $25 and no exchange is required. The company I recommend is the following:

> Mentor Electronics, Inc.
> 7560 Tyler Blvd. #E
> Mentor, OH 44060
> 216-951-1884   216-951-9924

> Costs:

> | | |
> |---|---|
> | 1 chip | $25 |
> | 1 tube (16 ea) | $280 |
> | 6 tubes (96 ea) | $1,500 |

You also can contact Phoenix Software, which manufactures compatible ROM BIOS chips for compatible motherboard manufacturers. This company sells a chip for about $50 that is specifically customized for an IBM PC motherboard.

The XT has had three ROMs to date. The first ROM is found in the majority of XT systems and in the Portable PC. The two newer ROMs are totally different from the preceding one and even have a different ID byte. These new XT ROMs are structured much like that of an AT. The new ROMs are 64K in total size instead of the 40K size of the older ROMs.

Much of the new ROM deals with a greatly revised and enhanced POST, as well as interfacing to the new Enhanced Keyboard. I also see support in the new ROM for things such as the AT 1.2M drive and the 3 1/2-inch 720K drives in the PS/2 systems. The changes were significant for the newer XTs, enough for IBM to assign the system an entirely new ID byte. This change means that the term *IBM compatible* is again redefined. Of all these new features, the only real apparent difference is support for the new keyboard and floppy disk drives.

As for the AT ROM, some interesting things are going on. The newer ATs with the IBM 30M hard disk have been supplied with a new controversial ROM that is significantly different from previous versions. One change has been an alteration of the drive tables encoded in the chip to support more hard disk parameter tables, including the new 30M drive. The ROM dated 6/10/85 directly supports 23 different types of hard disks and the 3 1/2-inch floppy disk drives at the 720K capacity.

Another (and a somewhat controversial) change has been an alteration in the POST to cause the system to fail POST diagnostics if you have altered the clock rate of the system to be faster than the normal 6 MHz. This feature effectively prevents anyone from using some of the commonly available ''speedup kits,'' which run the system at a faster clock rate through the installation of a faster clock crystal. You probably have this version of ROM if you have an IBM 30M drive or an AT that uses 256K RAM chips on the motherboard. Find the date in the ROM and refer to table 7.5 to be sure.

This ''speed fixing'' may sound like a bad move on IBM's part, but it was intended to eliminate some potential problems with floppy disk timing that many users experience with a speedup. The aftermarket has already stepped in with hardware devices to take care of the speed problem for the newer chips. You can purchase the 06/10/85 ROM from IBM only as part of the 30M hard disk upgrade kit ($1,795). The chip is not available separately.

The newest ROM for the AT is found in the units running at 8 MHz in stock form. This ROM appears much like the preceding one, with additional timing and POST changes to handle the increased speed properly, but also includes a couple of significant changes. The hard disk tables have one new entry, for a total of 24 drives directly supported by the ROM. The floppy drive tables have been updated to support the 3 1/2-inch floppy disk drives at the full 1.44M capacity found in the PS/2 systems. Also, this ROM fully supports the newer Enhanced Keyboard. This ROM is not available for the earlier models (pre-8 MHz ATs).

This type of ROM information should be particularly useful to those of you who have a mixture of PC equipment in your company, with perhaps some of it dating back several years. Knowing the exact configuration of all your equipment can help when you're dealing with different systems. Subtle differences hidden in your systems can often be the cause of some strange problems.

Memory Speed Ratings

Memory chip speed is reported in elements of time called *nanoseconds*. One nanosecond is the time that light takes to travel 11.72 inches. PC system memory speeds vary from about 200 to about 20 nanoseconds.

Different systems require memory chips that perform at different levels of performance. The speed of memory required depends on many things, but probably the most important is the system clock speed. Dividing the system clock frequency into 1 second gives the *cycle time* for a particular system. Cycle time is the amount of time for 1 cycle. If your system runs at 8 MHz, it performs 8 million cycles per second. You simply divide 1 second by 8 million, and you arrive at the time it takes for 1 cycle, which in this case is 125 nanoseconds or 0.000000125 seconds. For example, here are the cycle times for ATs and XTs:

AT System Timing		XT System Timing	
Clock rate (MHz)	*Cycle time (ns)*	*Clock rate (MHz)*	*Cycle time (ns)*
6	167	4.77	210
8	125	5	200
10	100	6	167
12	83	7	143
16	63	8	125
20	50	9	111
25	40	10	100

These times don't reflect the required speed for memory chips, which is up to the system designer. Usually, at least two cycles are required for memory access because of the way the microprocessors work. A system designer also can add *wait states*, which are "do-nothing" cycles, to memory access that slow the system down enough to work with slower speed memory chips. As you can see, the 25 MHz systems can use some fast memory. For that reason, these systems typically employ some sort of caching scheme. Having as many megabytes as the processor can handle would be far too costly, so a smaller cache or ''intelligent buffer'' of ultrahigh-speed memory is used to supply the processor's demands. The cache itself is supplied by the rest of the RAM system, which consists of chips with much slower rates.

When replacing a failed memory module, you must pay attention to the speed requirements for that module. Otherwise, the replacement will not work. You can substitute a different speed chip only if the speed of the replacement chip is equal to or faster than that of the failed unit. Substituting faster memory usually provides nothing in the way of improved performance, because the system still operates that memory at the same speed as before. In some cases, however, in systems that haven't been engineered with a great deal of ''forgiveness'' in the timing between the memory and the system, the substitution of faster memory chips may improve reliability.

Whether your memory has failed or is simply not fast enough, you will notice the same common symptoms. The usual effect is that the system performs parity checks constantly. Or it may not operate at all. The POST may also report errors if the memory is not up to snuff.

Some people believe that you must have all the chips in a single bank rated at the exact same speed. Other users carry this ''memory superstition'' to even greater lengths, believing that all the chips must be from the same manufacturer or even the same lot. These suppositions are simply not true.

As long as your chip is the correct type and meets all the specifications (pinouts, width, depth, and refresh timing), the so-called access time is something that always can be less (faster) than the application requires. These faster chips always can replace a slower chip of the same ''type.''

A discussion of just how memory chips work is beyond the scope of this book, but knowledge of this area tells you that faster access chips always can replace slower ones, even in the same bank. If you use chips that are slower than required or chips with incorrect pinouts, width, depth, or RAS versus CAS sequencing, you will have many parity checks and problems.

If you are unsure about what chips you should buy for your system, contact the system manufacturer or a reputable chip supplier.

To check the rating of a particular chip, simply examine the chip. For example, here's what a typical 256K-by-1-bit 100-nanosecond chip looks like:

```
41256-10

8804
```

The *41256* is the manufacturer's part number. Some sort of pictorial logo is usually included on the chip to indicate the manufacturer. The *256* portion of the part number identifies this chip as a 256K chip. Following the part number is a suffix, in this case a *-10*. This figure indicates 100 nanoseconds. Other speeds are indicated in this same manner, with some differences. Here are suffixes you may see, and the speeds they represent:

Suffix	Speed (in nanoseconds)
-20	200
-15	150
-12	120
-10	100
-85	85
-80	80

The number on the lower part of the chip, in this case *8804*, indicates that this chip was manufactured during the fourth week of 1988. Sometimes the date code appears in Julian format. The normal form of a Julian format date code is the number of days after 1/1/1900. For example, the date 1/1/1990 equals 32,874 days after the first of the century. This type of number may be used to indicate the date of chip manufacture.

Testing Memory

The best way to test memory is to install and use it, with your PC system acting as the testing tool. Although dedicated systems designed to test chips are available, these systems are usually extremely expensive or limited in capability. For example, one commercially available unit for testing chips sells for $200 but can test only 64K or 256K chips, and the unit cannot even tell you if the speed of the chip doesn't meet specifications.

What you *do* need in addition to your otherwise functioning system is a memory test program. Many of these programs are available, usually included in a diagnostics program. The POST, which is in the ROM, can be an effective test for problem memory, but usually a larger and more sophisticated disk-based program does a better job. The diagnostics program that accompanies a system is usually adequate, but even better programs are available. In Chapter 13, these types of programs are covered in detail.

Slots

As discussed earlier in this chapter, several different motherboard designs have been included in the various IBM computers. One of the major criteria setting one motherboard apart from another is the type and number of slots that are available for expansion. Knowing the major differences and similarities of these slots is important because these slots serve as the platform on which all future expansion of the system will be built. In the following sections, you will examine each of the different types and slot designs of the various system models.

Types of Slots

Two basic types of slot designs are found in IBM and compatible systems today. These types are the Industry Standard Architecture (ISA) slots and the Micro Channel Architecture (MCA) slots. Each main slot or bus design has a primary connector and an extension connector, which adds capabilities for certain systems. The MCA also adds a special video extension connector on one of the slots. In summary, these types of slots are the following:

Industry Standard Architecture (ISA)
8-bit connector
16-bit extension connector

Micro Channel Architecture (MCA)
16-bit connector
16-bit connector with video extension connector
32-bit extension connector

Examining the System Differences in Slot Designs

The basic IBM PC established the original slot design. Today this design is known as the *PC family 8-bit slot*. This type of slot is designed to transfer data 8 bits at a time and has 20 addressing lines to allow the handling of 1M of memory. All configurations of the PC motherboards have had 5 expansion slots. The XT introduced later had 8 slots. Because of the greater number, the slots had to be positioned closer together. The slots are about 1 inch apart in the PC and only about 0.75 inch apart in the XT. Because of this design, some of the extremely thick, or double-stacked, expansion cards that fit fine in a PC will require 2 adjacent slots in an XT.

Most board manufacturers today realize that many of their boards will be installed in XTs, so boards are usually designed to fit those systems. The only modern cards that seem to cause problems in XT systems are some of the "hard disks on a card." (The Hardcard from Plus Development Corporation, however, is an example of a hard card that doesn't have the problem of taking the space of two slots when it only should take the space of one slot.)

In the XT or Portable PC, the eighth slot, the one closest to the power supply, is a special slot. Only certain cards can be installed there. Any card installed in this eighth slot must supply a special "card selected" signal to the motherboard on pin B8, which few cards have been designed to do. (The IBM Asynchronous Adapter Card and the Keyboard/Timer Card from a 3270 PC are two examples of cards that fit in that slot.) Additionally, the timing requirements for the eighth slot are stricter.

The reasoning for this strange slot in the XT is that IBM developed the system to support a special configuration called the 3270-PC, which is an XT with from three to six special adapter boards installed. The eighth slot was specifically designed to accept the keyboard/timer adapter from the 3270 PC. This board needed special access to the motherboard because it replaced the motherboard keyboard circuitry. Special timing and the "card selected" signal made this access possible. (Contrary to what many users have believed, the eighth slot has nothing to do with the IBM expansion chassis.) By the way, the IBM expansion chassis was a box developed by IBM that looked like another system unit. Because the IBM XT had eight slots, one full-height floppy drive, and one full-height hard drive, the expansion gave room for more expansion slots and additional floppy and hard drives.

Like the XT, the AT has eight slots. Because of the greater addressing capability of the 80286 microprocessor, however, some of these slots are equipped to handle many more signals than the PC or XT in order to tap the power and speed that the processor is capable of providing. IBM took the safe route, keeping the slot design the same for the most part but adding an extension connector to six of the slots to carry the extra wires. Thus, any standard PC or XT expansion card can plug directly into the AT with no changes.

The slot extension connector does interfere with those cards that have what is known as a *skirt*, which drops down toward the motherboard just after the connector. To handle these cards, IBM omitted the expansion connector from two of the slots so that they could physically handle any PC or XT expansion card. (Note, however, that some of the earlier XT types of cards don't work in the AT even though they can plug in.) Rather than use earlier PC or XT boards, you will most often purchase expansion cards that are designed specifically for the AT. Boards designed for the AT take advantage of the extension slot; you get a 16-bit transfer rather than an 8-bit transfer and, thus, greater speed. Most of the dedicated AT cards take advantage of the fact that the AT is a larger box and therefore cram a large amount of circuitry on a board.

Note that two heights are available for cards commonly found in AT systems: those that use the full 4.8 inches of available space and those that are only 4.2 inches tall. The shorter cards became an issue when IBM introduced the XT Model 286. Because this model has an AT motherboard in an XT case, it needs AT types of boards with the 4.2-inch maximum height. Most board makers simply trimmed down their boards some so that now many are making only 4.2-inch tall boards, which will go in either the standard AT or the XT Model 286. The precise dimensional limits for XT and AT expansion boards are the following:

XT Card Maximum Dimensions
    4.2 inches (106.68 mm) high
    13.2 inches (335.28 mm) long
    0.5 inches (12.7 mm) wide

AT Card Maximum Dimensions
   4.8 inches (121.92 mm) high
   13.2 inches (335.28 mm) long
   0.5 inches (12.7 mm) wide

Some XT types of cards do not work in the AT even though they physically plug in, because of Interrupt, DMA Channel, ROM address, and other problems.

Micro Channel Architecture is the name of the all-new bus design, which is found in all IBM PS/2 50 and higher models. This slot design is superior in every way to the older ISA bus. Because the new design also is totally different, no boards that plug into an ISA bus system will plug into an MCA system or vice versa. The number of pins, their signals, and even physical dimensions of the new bus connectors are totally different from the old ISA bus design.

Basically three types of slots are involved in MCA design. Every slot has a 16-bit connector; it is the basis of the MCA. This connector is the primary one, and it is found in all MCA systems.

MCA systems that are based on the 80386 processor chip have several slots with a 32-bit extension connector, which is designed to allow for higher transfer rates and performance by taking advantage of the processors' increased communications and memory addressing capabilities. An important thing to note about this 32-bit extension connector is that even though it is an extension to the original connector, as the 16-bit extension connector was in the ISA design, the difference here is that this 32-bit extension was designed at the same time as the rest of the MCA. Systems with this extension connector made their debut at the same time as the MCA itself, which means that this was not something that was "added on" at a later date but is instead something that was designed in from the start.

The third type of MCA slot is a standard 16-bit MCA connector with a special video extension connector added. This special slot appears in every MCA system, and only one slot in each system has this design. This slot is designed to allow a high-resolution video card to have special access to the motherboard VGA circuitry so that the new card does not have to duplicate unnecessarily this circuitry for compatibility. This design means that no matter what new type of video board you decide to add to an MCA system, all your programs will run because you never lose the built-in VGA circuits. The built-in VGA circuits do not have to be disabled. Instead, your new card will coexist with the VGA circuits and can even "borrow" some things, such as the digital-to-analog converter, which can make these add-on video boards less expensive because they can use circuitry on the motherboard rather than build in duplicates of that circuitry.

The MCA allows systems to achieve a new level in the "ease of use" category, as anyone who has set up one of these systems can tell you. An MCA system has no jumpers and switches—not on the motherboard or on any expansion adapter. You don't need an electrical engineering degree to be able to plug a card into a PC.

The new MCA bus has many other advantages. These advantages and the general implementation of the bus are listed in Chapter 4.

Diagnosing Problems

Have you ever "fixed" a problem with two boards or a system unit by shuffling the locations of some board from one slot to another? All the slots in a particular system are supposed to be identical from one to the next. The only exceptions are the strange eighth slot in the XT and the 8-bit slots in the AT, which are the same as the other slots minus the extension connector. Although each slot is supposed to be "generic" as far as which board goes where, a timing problem sometimes can crop up.

Note that the MCA runs asynchronously with the main processor, and IBM has published strict timing requirements for any boards that plug into an MCA slot, so these "slot swapping" sessions should become a thing of the past. And the MCA is much more reliable from a timing point of view (and about any other points of view as well).

Placing Boards in the Slots

Here are some simple recommendations concerning the placement of boards in slots in any system. Electrically, there is no reason that any particular board must go into a particular slot. (The XT's eighth slot is the only exception.) The timing and signals in the AT's slots are all the same, for example, with the only difference being that two of them are missing the 16-bit extension connectors. And because the signals for the absent connectors are still present on the motherboard, an enterprising individual with a soldering iron could in fact put the missing extension connectors back in place. So what *is* a good rule for board placement?

Here's one: Think about air circulation as you add boards and cables to a system. If you place the longest boards in the outboard slots, and the shorter boards in the inboard slots, you promote the cross-ventilation airflow that is essential for system cooling. Remember also to route cables so that they don't restrict airflow or try to limit that restriction to as little as possible.

Here is another handy tip: If you have a board that expands your system memory, place this board in a slot as near to the power supply as possible. This places the board closer to the motherboard circuitry and may avoid parity-check errors. Being closer to the system board circuitry cuts down on memory access times. Often, parity-check errors are derived because of a timing problem.

Standard Adapters for Each System

With all the various configurations available for each system, you may have difficulty knowing what you're supposed to be getting—and also what you need to add—to end up with a system that does what you want it to do. This section attempts to shed some light on the adapters (cards or circuit boards that plug into an expansion connector or bus slot) that are automatically included with each system.

The IBM PC almost always came with at least a floppy controller. Although "diskless" versions of the PC were available, these were few and far between. You usually could not find a dealer who wanted to order one of these PCs. The standard floppy controller can address a total of four drives. These drives must be double-density drives, because the PC and XT floppy controllers only support the low data rate of 250 KHz, and the AT floppy controllers support the higher data rates of 300 KHz and 500 KHz. Part of what defines an AT is that it has a floppy controller that can do this.

The PC/XT controller has both an internal and an external connector, each of which supports a daisy chain of two drives. A *daisy chain* is a single cable that runs from the controller and "stops" at each of the two (maximum) drives. IBM and compatibles always use a daisy chain arrangement. The daisy chain arrangement differs from the radial structure. A radial structure is equivalent to a star arrangement: each disk drive has a separate cable that radiates from the centrally located controller.

The base models of the XT were configured exactly the same way as the PC—that is, with the floppy disk controller. The XT and the PC used the same controller. The enhanced XT models that featured a hard disk also included a separate hard disk controller. As a bonus, IBM added a serial port card in the "funny" eighth slot in these systems.

The hard disk controller that IBM used for the XT was the Xebec Model 1210, made by Xebec Corporation. Although IBM wrote a custom ROM for the controller, Xebec shipped a compatible version of ROM when you bought the 1210 controller directly from Xebec. IBM supplied two different versions of ROM for the hard disk controller: one version for the 10M hard disk systems and a newer ROM with the 20M hard disk systems. The controller itself also had at least two different revisions. The versions were identical in performance and operation, even though the newer units had fewer components.

The AT comes with a single disk controller card at minimum. In the AT, this card is a dual-function controller because it handles both the diskette drive interface and the fixed disk interface. Although the card is capable of connecting to two of each type of drive simultaneously, the AT cannot hold four drives, at least not without some "creative metal working" or other modifications.

These disk controllers were made for IBM by Western Digital. IBM used two different versions of the Western Digital family of controllers in the AT and XT 286. The original unit was the Western Digital WD 1002-WA2, and the later AT systems and the XT 286 came with the WD 1003A-WA2. This latter controller was reduced in height to fit inside the shorter XT 286 chassis. The enhanced model of the AT includes the IBM Serial/Parallel adapter card, which allows the attachment of printers, modems, or both.

Note that all these systems as they are configured, without options, are not functional systems. All of them need some sort of video board in order to operate at all. Additional memory is almost an absolute requirement for most of the systems. The PC and XT systems need a printer port and a clock calendar to be "normally" configured by today's standards. Also, those units that don't have a hard disk must add either just the disk (the AT) or both a disk and controller (the PC or XT).

Contrast this to the PS/2 systems, which include the following items on the motherboard:

- A video interface in the form of a Multi-Color Graphics Array (MCGA) or Video Graphics Array (VGA) subsystem

- At least 640K of memory (some include as much as 2M)

- A serial, parallel, and mouse port

- A built-in floppy controller

Also, all but the lower end Models 25 and 30 include at least a 20M hard disk. Literally all that you need to add for the PS/2 configurations is a monitor! This system is a far cry from the original PC, which was like buying a car and having to remember that you needed wheels, seats, headlights, and so on.

Of course, drawbacks exist to this new trend of "bundling" everything with the system. For one thing, the initial price seems higher. You cannot save money by shopping around and getting the best prices for each individual component, as you could with the earlier systems. Also, when any component in the PS/2 system fails, the part usually is built into the motherboard, which you then must replace. Replacing the motherboard is quite expensive when the system is out of warranty. And, finally, you cannot be as creative with "individualizing" the configuration to your own specific needs, as was possible with the earlier piecemeal systems.

The Power Supply

One of the most failure-prone components in PC systems is the power supply. You thus should investigate this subject in some depth. You need to know just what a power supply does, what the limitations of a supply are, and what potential problems and solutions exist.

First, here's a quick overview of what the supply is supposed to do in these systems. The power supply in a PC is designed to convert the 120-volt 60 Hz AC current into something that the computer can use, which is specifically both 5- and 12-volt DC current. Usually, the digital electronic components and circuits of the system (motherboard, adapter cards, and disk drive logic boards) use the 5-volt power, and the motors (disk drive motors and the fan) use the 12-volt power. You need to be sure that the system has a good, steady supply of both types of current so that the system can operate properly.

One thing that the power supply does to ensure that the system doesn't run without proper power levels is to prevent the computer from starting up until all the correct power levels are present. Each power supply completes internal checks and tests before allowing the PC to start up. The power supply sends to the motherboard a special signal, called "power good." If this signal is absent, the computer will not run. The effect of this setup is that when the AC voltage dips and the power supply becomes overstressed or overheated, the power good signal goes down, forcing a system reset or complete shutdown. If you have ever seen your system appear dead when the power switch is on and the fan and hard disks are running, you know the effects of losing the power good signal. IBM used this conservative design with the view that if the power goes low, or the supply is overheated or overstressed, causing output power to falter, then the computer shouldn't be allowed to operate. You can even use this "power good" feature as a method of designing and implementing a reset switch for the PC. When you cause this signal to go low (ground), you can force the computer to restart.

The power good line is wired to the 8284 or 82284 clock generator chips, which control the clock and reset lines to the microprocessor. When you ground the power good line with a switch, this chip and related circuitry stop the processor by killing the clock signal and then reset the processor when the power good signal appears after you release the switch. The total effect is a full hardware reset of the system.

On the other hand, the AT shines in the power department. The AT has a 192-watt capacity supply with a variable-speed, thermostatically controlled cooling fan to take care of any high-heat situations. Other than the normal failures, supply difficulties don't exist for the AT. A normal failure is one that is not specifically caused by overloading, power surges, or any other torture, but is instead just a failure of the power supply because of normal defects or thermal expansion or contraction.

The PS/2 systems have been built with proper power supplies as well. As a matter of fact, most modern systems have an adequate power supply from inception. Most of the manufacturers have learned the hard way that doing a little overengineering in this area pays off.

Dealing with Power Supply Problems

A weak or inadequate supply can put a damper on your ideas for system expansion. Some systems were designed with beefy power supplies, as if to anticipate a great deal of add-in or expansion components being added to the system. The XT and AT systems were built in this manner. Some systems have inadequate power supplies right from the start, however, and cannot accept the number and types of power-hungry options you may want to add.

In particular, the PC's 63.5-watt supply is inadequate for all but the most basic system. Add a graphics board, hard disk, 8087 chip, and 640K of memory, and you will kill the system in no time at all. The total power draw of all the items in the system determines the adequacy of the power supply.

Another problem with underengineered power supplies is that they run hot and force the system to do so as well. The repeated heating and cooling of solid-state components causes any computer system to fail eventually, and engineering principles dictate that the hotter the temperature of a PC, the shorter its life. Many people recommend replacing the PC supply with the 130-watt supply from an XT, which solves that problem once and for all. You can bolt in the XT supply, using the same mounting and physical configuration of the original PC supply. The only problem with this recommendation is the price. IBM's XT power supply, part number 8529247, sells for $290. (Here's an interesting note: The PC supply costs $344.)

An alternative to the XT and PC power supplies is a 200-watt unit from PC Cooling Systems, which sells for about $169. With almost four times the output capabilities of the PC supply and nearly twice that of the XT, this unit is built like a tank. To help reduce the temperature of the system even further, the supply has four disk drive power connectors and two cooling fans. The PC Cooling Systems unit is a bolt-in swap that uses the same mounting screws and connectors as the originals.

Here's another special heat-related tip for PC users. If you seal the ventilation holes on the bottom of the chassis from where the disk drive bays begin all the way to the right side of the PC, you drop the interior temperature some 10 to 20 degrees Fahrenheit—not a bad feat for two cents worth of electrical tape! IBM "factory applies" this tape for every XT. The result is greatly improved interior aerodynamics and airflow over the heat-generating components.

A question that arises often and directly relates to the discussion on temperature concerns whether to turn the system off when you're not using it. The answer is no. You should not repeatedly turn the system on and off. The reasoning is simple. Many users believe that flipping the system on and off frequently is harmful because it "shocks" the system. But the real culprit is temperature. In other words, it's not so much electrical "shock" but thermal shock that destroys a system.

Regardless of whether you turn the system on or off ten times or a thousand times a day, if you allow the unit to heat and cool frequently, you're asking for problems. Here's why. When you heat and cool metal, you harden it and make it—and the solder in your system—brittle. The constant expansion and contraction then eventually causes the work-hardened metal to crack, which is what causes the failure. Also, socketed devices tend to work their way out of the sockets, and the movement enables corrosion to work into any sockets and connector joints. Many "blown" power supplies amount to nothing more than a cracked or broken solder joint or a failed transistor that died when it became separated from its heat sink. (The heat sink glue fails after repeated heating and cooling.)

Although repairing these faults is simple, the process is cumulative, and the problem will someday return. Keeping the unit at a constant temperature seems to be the most important item contributing to longevity.

Studying Power Supply Ratings

IBM provides charts indicating the technical specifications of each of IBM's system unit power supplies. You can find these charts in the technical reference manual for each system or often taped right on the power supply as a sticker.

Table 7.6 includes several reference charts that list the specifications of the power supplies of each of IBM's units. The input specifications are reported in volts, and the output specifications are reported in amps at several voltage levels. The "Specified Output Wattage" is the figure that IBM reports as the output wattage level. You can convert the amperage figures to output wattage by using this simple formula:

Wattage = Voltage * Amperage

Table 7.6
Power Supply Specifications

For PC Family Systems:

	PC	PPC	XT	XT 286	AT
Input Voltage					
Minimum Voltage	104	90	90	90	90
Maximum Voltage	127	137	137	137	137
Universal (220 V)	no	yes	no	yes	yes
Switch or Auto*	-	switch	-	auto	switch
Output Amperage					
+ 5	7	11.2	15	20	19.8
− 5	0.3	0.3	0.3	0.3	0.3
+12	2	4.4	4.2	4.2	7.3
−12	0.25	0.25	0.25	0.25	0.3
Calculated Output Wattage	63.5	113.3	129.9	154.9	191.7
Specified Output Wattage	63.5	114	130	157	192

For PS/2 Family Systems:

Model:	30	50	60	70	80
Input Voltage					
Minimum Voltage	90	100	100	100	100
Maximum Voltage	137	125	125	125	125
Universal (220 V)	yes	yes	yes	yes	yes

Input Voltage

Switch or Auto*	auto	auto	auto	auto	auto
Specified Output Wattage	70	94	207	132	225

*Switch and Auto refer to the method of voltage selection. "Switch" indicates the need for manually flipping a switch, and "Auto" is an automatic switching system.

My XT Model 286, for example, will run on both 110- and 220-volt power, and all I have to do is plug it in; the system will automatically recognize the incoming voltage and switch circuits accordingly. This is different from my Portable PC, which will run on both levels of power but requires me to flip a switch manually to select the proper circuits.

Note that most of the power supplies are considered to be "universal," meaning that they will run on 220-volt 50-cycle current, which is used in Europe and many other parts of the world. Of the power supplies that can switch to 220-volt input, most are automatic, but a few require you to set a switch on the back of the power supply to indicate which type of power you will be accessing. (The automatic units sense the current and switch automatically.)

Calculating Power Usage

One way to see whether your system is capable of any expansion is to calculate the levels of power drain of the various system components and then deduct that total from the maximum power that is supplied. This calculation may help you also to decide when to upgrade the power supply to a more capable unit. Suppose, for example, that you're using an IBM PC system unit and you examine some typical power consumption figures for various components of that unit.

The PC comes with a 63.5-watt power supply. The levels of power to be concerned about are the 5- and 12-volt levels. The PC power supply can provide 7.0 amps of 5-volt power and 2.0 amps of 12-volt power. Here's the situation when you subtract the amount of power necessary to run the various system components:

5-volt power	7.0 amps
Less:	
Motherboard (full memory, 8087)	4.0
Video adapter	1.0
Two full-height floppy drives	1.2 (0.6 each)
Multifunction (6-pack type) board	1.0
Remaining power	**−0.2**
12-volt power	2.0 amps
Less:	
Two full-height floppy drives	0.9 (0.9 each)
Cooling fan	0.25
Remaining power	**0.85**

As you can see from these figures, you're in some trouble. On the 5-volt side, you're in an overload situation with this configuration, and you have only three slots full and no hard disk. A typical full-height hard disk consumes 1.5 amps of 5-volt power, and a half-height drive draws 0.8 amps. Needless to say, you don't have enough power left to drive anything at all.

As for the 12-volt power, you're at least not overloaded in the basic configuration. But suppose that you want to add a hard disk. The full-height drives draw around 4.0 amps of power for the first 15 to 30 seconds and then drop to a continuous draw of about 2.0 amps. A typical half-height drive draws about 2.2 amps of power during the first 15 to 30 seconds and then tapers off to about 0.9 amps of continuous draw. In this example, you may have enough 12-volt power for a small half-height hard disk. Some of the newer 3 1/2-inch hard disks don't draw much power. The power draw of a disk drive is almost directly related to the drive's physical size. Some of the hardcard units can draw low power also. For a typical PC system, however, even these units are too much to handle unless you're willing to replace the power supply with one having more capacity.

In this sample situation, you need an upgraded power supply, which you can purchase from many sources, including IBM and the aftermarket. Most users choose at least a 130-watt or better supply. The PC Cooling Systems unit referred to earlier has 20.0 amps of 5-volt output and 8.0 amps of 12-volt output, which is nearly four times what is available in a PC. Using this supply in a PC ensures that the system has enough power to drive nearly anything that you could add to the unit.

Many people wait until an existing unit fails before they replace it with an upgraded version. This view is the "don't fix it unless it's broken" attitude, which can be good to have if you're on a budget. But power supplies often do not simply fail but can become intermittent or allow fluctuating power levels to reach the system, which results in "flaky" operation. You may be blaming the system lockups that you're having on buggy software, when in fact the culprit may have been the overloaded power supply.

Some of you may be thinking, "I have all that stuff, including a hard disk, in my PC, and it is still running fine with the original supply." Although you may occasionally encounter a healthy 90-year-old who has smoked three packs of cigarettes a day for many years, you know that the odds are against it. The same applies for the PC's power supply. If you have been running with your original power supply for a long time, you're treading on thin ice and can and should expect some problems.

One thing to consider is that the figures most manufacturers report for maximum power output are full duty cycle figures, which means that these levels of power can be supplied continuously. You can usually expect that a unit that supplies some level of power continuously can supply *more* power for some noncontinuous amount of time. A supply can usually offer 50 percent greater output than the continuous figure indicates for as long as one minute of time. This cushion is often used to supply the necessary power to start a hard disk spinning. After the drive has spun to full speed, the power draw drops to some value within the system's continuous supply capabilities. Drawing anything over the rated continuous figure for any great length of time causes the power supply to run hot and fail early and can prompt several nasty symptoms of "flakiness" in the system.

You should make the following types of calculations for your system. The first figures you need are the specifications for the output levels of your particular power supply. You can find these specifications in the technical reference manual for your system. (The figures for IBM's systems are included in table 7.6.) Then you need the power consumption figures for each type of component in the system. Most boards draw less than 1 amp, but some boards, such as network adapters or internal modems, can draw even more. Disk drives are also quite power hungry, drawing both 5- and 12-volt power. You can obtain the figures for consumption of these types of products from the product manufacturers. IBM has an options and adapters technical reference manual for the IBM boards and disk drives. The Original Equipment Manufacturers (OEM) manuals for your disk drives and adapter boards usually contain this type of information.

In Chapter 14, you learn about the symptoms you can expect from a blown or failing power supply and the necessary steps to correct the problem. The chapter also tells you how to test the supply for correct operation.

Replacing the Power Supply

As mentioned earlier, replacement power supplies are available from many manufacturers. One thing to consider is the shape or so-called "form factor" of the power supply. For example, the power supply used in the IBM AT differs physically from the one used in the PC or XT. Therefore, the AT and PC supplies are not interchangeable. The difference is in the actual size, shape, screw hole positions, connector type, number of connectors, and switch position. The XT power supply does have the same form factor as the PC supply, however, and would be a bolt-in swap. The two power supplies differ in power output capabilities only.

IBM has used only two different form factor supplies for the earlier line of systems:

1. PC Type, used in the PC, XT, and XT 286. The most powerful version of this supply (electrically) was the one used in the XT 286. All are physically interchangeable.

2. AT Type, used in all models of the IBM AT systems.

As far as the PS/2 systems are concerned, only the power supplies from the Model 60 and Model 80 use the same form factor and are interchangeable. All the other models have supplies unique to the particular model. To date, no aftermarket supplies are available for the PS/2 systems because the IBM factory-supplied units are quite beefy for each application.

One risk you run with some of the compatibles is that they may not use one of the two original PC family form factor supplies. If a system does use the PC Type or AT Type form factor power supply, replacement units are available from hundreds of vendors. You often have a smorgasbord of supplies from which to choose—everything from heavy duty units at various levels of capability to units that are available at different levels of quietness.

The unfortunate user of a system with a nonstandard form factor supply doesn't have this kind of choice and will have to get a replacement from the original manufacturer of the system—and usually pay through the nose for the unit as well. Although you can find PC and AT form factor units for as little as $50, the proprietary units from some manufacturers run as much as $400. When *Popular Mechanics* magazine does an automobile review, it always lists the replacement costs of the most failure-prone and replacement-prone components from front bumpers to alternators to taillights. This type of information is often overlooked by a PC buyer, who finds out too late the consequences of having nonstandard components in the system.

An example of compatible systems with proprietary power supply designs are those from COMPAQ. None of COMPAQ's systems use the same form factor supply as the IBM systems, which means that usually the only place you can get a replacement is from COMPAQ itself. If the power supply in your COMPAQ Deskpro system goes south, you can expect to pay $395 for a replacement, and the replacement unit from COMPAQ will be no better or quieter than the one that you are replacing. You do not have much choice in the matter, because almost nobody offers COMPAQ form factor power supplies except COMPAQ. One exception is that PC Cooling Systems now offers replacement power supplies for the earlier COMPAQ Portable systems and may also offer supplies for the Deskpro series. The replacement portable power supply has more than three times the output power of the original supply from COMPAQ and costs less money.

Keyboards

In this section, you will examine the keyboards that are available for IBM and compatible systems. IBM has had three different keyboard designs over the last few years:

- 83-key PC and XT keyboard
- 84-key AT keyboard
- 101-key Enhanced Keyboard

The Enhanced Keyboard has appeared in three different versions, but all three are exactly the same electrically and can be interchanged. The different models are the following:

- Enhanced Keyboard without LED panel (lock indicators)
- Enhanced Keyboard with LED panel (lock indicators)
- Enhanced Keyboard (PS/2 logo)

The first two are cosmetically the same, but the second unit was designed for systems that support the full bidirectional capability needed to operate the LED panel that shows the status of the Caps Lock, Num Lock, and Scroll Lock keys. The third version is the same as the second, with the exception of having a logo on the top that matches the PS/2 system logo. Electrically, all these keyboards are exactly the same, but the first is missing a small add-on circuit board to control the lights. Note that any PC or XT types of systems cannot operate these lights because they do not have the bidirectional interface necessary for light operation. If you use an XT and the IBM Enhanced Keyboard with the LED panel, the lights remain dark.

Any of the IBM keyboards can be ordered separately as a spare part. The newer Enhanced Keyboards come with an externally detachable keyboard that plugs into the keyboard with a special connector much like a telephone connector. The other end of the cable is one of two types. The earlier systems use a 5-pin DIN type of connector, and the PS/2 systems use a new miniature 6-pin DIN connector. Because of the interchangeability of the newer Enhanced Keyboards, I can actually plug a 101-key unit from an XT into a PS/2 simply by switching the cables. Of course, I also can plug the PS/2 style 101-key unit into any XT or AT system simply by switching cables. The PS/2 style cable is available in two different lengths. Because of the superior "feel" of the IBM units, I often have equipped compatible systems with these keyboards. The part numbers of all the IBM keyboards and cables follow:

P/N	Description
8529297	83-key U.S. keyboard assembly with cable
8286165	84-key U.S. keyboard assembly with cable
1390290	101-key U.S. keyboard without LED panel
6447033	101-key U.S. keyboard with LED panel
1392090	101-key U.S. keyboard (PS/2 logo)
6447051	Enhanced Keyboard cable with DIN connector
61x8898	Enhanced Keyboard cable with mini-DIN connector (3 feet long)
72x8537	Enhanced Keyboard cable with mini-DIN connector (10 feet long)

Note that the original type of keyboards are sold with a cable having the larger 5-pin DIN connector already attached. The Enhanced Keyboards are sold without a cable. You must order the proper cable as a separate item.

The PC and AT keyboards are completely different from each other. In addition to having different key layouts, the internal electronics are different. The 83-key keyboard uses an 8042 microprocessor, and the other keyboards use a 6805 microprocessor.

The 101-key keyboard was designed as a replacement for both the 83-key and the 84-key units, and theoretically works as a complete replacement for the earlier keyboards for any system. One problem, however, is that the individual system ROM BIOS may not be able to operate the 101-key keyboard correctly. If this is the case, the 101-key keyboard does not work at all (as with all three ROM versions of the IBM PC), or only the new added keys do not work (F11 and F12 function keys). You can tell if your system has complete ROM BIOS support for the 101-key unit, because when this keyboard is plugged in and the system unit is turned on, the Num Lock light automatically comes on and the numeric keypad is enabled. Most users are not aware that this is a built-in function and are irritated that this happens, because all the earlier keyboards do not cause this to happen. Remember that this is not really a function of the keyboard at all but is instead a function of the motherboard ROM BIOS, which is identifying an enhanced 101-key unit and turning on the Num Lock as a "favor."

Because of the processor in each one, these keyboards really are intelligent devices; they are computers in their own right. They have their own built-in memory and run a self-test when they are turned on.

The Standard (Personal Computer) Keyboard

The IBM keyboard has been one of the most criticized components of the system. The cause for all the bad press IBM received concerning the keyboard is its awkward layout. The Shift keys are too small, and even in the wrong place on the left side, and the Enter key is also too small. This oversight is considered a crime especially because IBM is the company who brought us the Selectric typewriter, which has always been perceived as some sort of standard of quality.

Although the poor layout opened the doors for quite a few companies to produce replacement keyboards for the PC, most people still use the IBM board. The reason is probably not related to the cost of purchasing a new board but rather that the IBM keyboard is simply the highest quality keyboard on the market. Nothing else comes close to the feel and action of the IBM keyboard.

The Enhanced Keyboard

IBM silenced all the criticism with the introduction of first the AT keyboard and then the "corporate" Enhanced Keyboard for the RT-PC and the newer models of the XT and AT. I use the word "corporate" because this unit is now supplied for every type of system and terminal that IBM sells. It is a universal keyboard with a much improved layout, full-size Shift and Enter keys, and indicator lights to show the status of the lock keys on the board.

Figures 7.4 through 7.6 show the various keyboards.

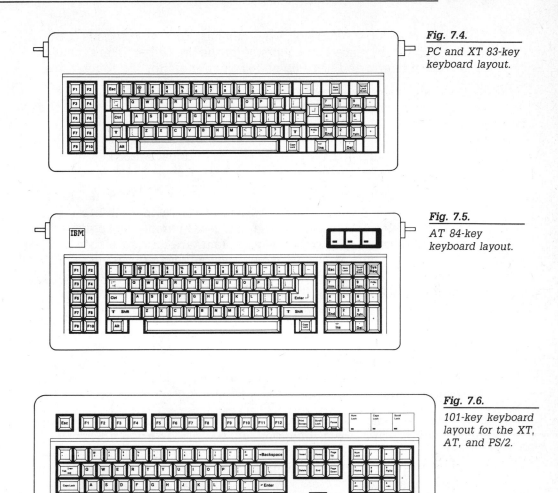

Fig. 7.4.

PC and XT 83-key
keyboard layout.

Fig. 7.5.

AT 84-key
keyboard layout.

Fig. 7.6.

101-key keyboard
layout for the XT,
AT, and PS/2.

The keyboard layout can be divided into four sections:

1. Typing area
2. Numeric pad
3. Cursor/screen controls
4. Function keys

The 101-key arrangement is similar to the Selectric keyboard layout.
The Tab, Caps Lock, Shift, Enter, and Backspace keys have a larger

striking area and are located in the familiar Selectric locations. Ctrl and Alt keys are placed on each side of the space bar. The typing area and numeric pad have home-row identifiers for the touch typist.

The cursor and screen control keys have been separated from the numeric pad, which reserves the numeric pad for numeric input. (As with the other Personal Computer keyboards, you can use the numeric pad for cursor and screen control when you're not in Num Lock mode.) A division sign key and an additional Enter key have been added to the numeric pad.

The cursor control keys are arranged in the inverted *T* format. Ins, Del, Home, End, PgUp, and PgDn keys are separated from the numeric pad and located above the dedicated cursor control keys. The function keys, spaced in groups of four, are located across the top of the keyboard. Two additional function keys are provided (F11 and F12). The Esc key is isolated at the upper left of the keyboard. Dedicated Prt Sc/Sys Req, Scroll Lock, and Pause/Break keys are provided for commonly used functions.

One of the Enhanced Keyboard's many useful features is removable keycaps. With clear keycaps and paper inserts, you can customize the keyboard. Keyboard templates are available to provide specific operator instructions. IBM provides a 9-foot cable for attaching the keyboard to the system unit.

This new keyboard will probably appear on any desktop system that IBM introduces for some time to come. For those of you who want all systems to change completely to the new keyboard, however, the prognosis is not good. IBM has changed the ROM on the new systems to support the new keyboard properly but has not offered any ROM upgrade to allow this support for earlier systems.

I conducted a somewhat informal test, plugging the new keyboard into an earlier XT. The keyboard worked fine. Of course none of the keys that didn't exist previously, such as F11 and F12, were operable, but the new arrow keys and the numeric keypad worked well. The Enhanced Keyboard also seems to work on the AT systems but cannot function on any PC systems. Because these were short-term tests, you should test a keyboard yourself before you purchase one. But for the numeric keypad functions alone, you may want to investigate the purchase of the new keyboard for an earlier system. You can buy the keyboard as a separate item for $275 from any IBM dealer. Other manufacturers also offer the Enhanced Keyboards that work on XTs and greater as well.

Cleaning the Keyboard

One of the best ways to maintain a keyboard in top condition is periodic cleaning. As preventive maintenance, you should vacuum the keyboard weekly. Or you can use the canned compressed air available at electronics supply houses. Before you dust off the keyboard with the compressed air, turn the keyboard upside down so that particles of dirt and dust that have collected inside fall out rather than simply become rearranged.

On all the keyboards, each individual keycap is removable, which can be handy if one of the keys is sticking or acting erratically. For example, a common problem is a key that doesn't work every time you press it. This problem is usually the result of dirt collecting under the key itself. Simply pull off the keycap with your fingers, a bent paper clip, or the special tool that IBM sells for this purpose. You can order six keycap removal tools from IBM for $11, and they work quite well. After removing the cap, spray the compressed air into the space under the cap to dislodge the dirt. Then replace the cap, and check the action of the key.

When removing the keycaps, be careful not to remove the space bar on the original 83-key PC and 84-key AT types of keyboards. This bar is difficult to reinstall. The newer 101-key units use a different arrangement that you can remove and reinstall quite easily.

Spills can also be a problem. If you tip a soft drink or cup of coffee into the keyboard, all may not be lost. You should immediately purchase several gallons of purified distilled water. Partially disassemble the keyboard, and use the water to wash the components. (See the next section on "Repairing the Keyboard" for disassembly instructions.) If the spilled liquid has dried, let the keyboard soak in some of the water for a while. Then, when you're sure that the keyboard is clean, pour another gallon over it to wash off any residual dirty water. After the unit completely dries, it should be perfectly functional. You may be surprised to hear that you can drench your keyboard, but in fact all circuit boards are washed during the manufacturing process. Just make sure that the keyboard is dry before you attempt to operate it, or the components may short out, because water is a conductor of electricity.

Repairing the Keyboard

Repairing and cleaning the keyboard often require that you take it apart. An important thing to know about this job is when to stop. Any IBM keyboard generally has these four major parts:

- Cable
- Case
- Keypad assembly
- Keycaps

You can easily break down a keyboard to these major components and replace any one of them. But do not disassemble the keypad assembly, or you will be inundated with a shower of tiny springs, clips, and keycaps. Finding all these parts (several hundred of them) and piecing the unit back together is not a fun way to spend time. And the keyboard may not be assembled as well as it was before coming apart.

Another problem is that you cannot purchase separately the smaller parts, such as the contact clips and springs. The only way to obtain these parts is from another keyboard. If you ever have a keyboard that is beyond repair, keep it around for these parts. They may come in handy some day.

Most repair operations are usually limited to changing the cable or cleaning some component of the keyboard from the cable contact ends to the key contact points. The cable for a keyboard takes quite a bit of abuse and therefore can easily fail. The ends are stretched, tugged, pulled, and generally handled roughly. The cable uses strain reliefs, but you still may have problems with the connectors making proper contact at each end, or even with wires that have broken inside the cable itself. You may want to carry a spare cable for each type of keyboard you have. Extra cables provide inexpensive insurance.

All keyboard cables plug into the keyboard and PC with connectors, so you can easily change the cables without splicing wires or soldering any connections. With the earlier 83-key PC and 84-key AT keyboards, you have to open the case to access the connector where the cable attaches. On the newer 101-key Enhanced Keyboards, the cable plugs into the keyboard from the outside of the case, using a modular jack and plug similar to a telephone jack. This design, one of the best features of this new keyboard, also makes the keyboard universally usable on nearly any system except the original PC.

The only difference, for example, between the Enhanced Keyboards for an AT and for a PS/2 system is the attached cable. The PS/2 systems use a cable that is tan in color and has a smaller plug at the computer side. The AT cable is black and has the larger DIN type of plug at the computer side. You can interchange any of the Enhanced Keyboards as long as you use the correct cable for the system.

If you do plug an Enhanced Keyboard into a system that didn't originally support the LEDs for indicating Caps Lock, Scroll Lock, or Num Lock, these lights remain inactive when plugged into that system. If the system did originally support the lights but doesn't have ROM support for the Enhanced Keyboard, the Num Lock light does not come on during the system boot. If the system fully supports the Enhanced Keyboard in ROM, the Num Lock light comes on during boot so that the numeric keypad functions in numeric mode. You are expected to use the separate arrow keys on the keyboard or turn off the numeric lock manually. If you don't like this "improvement," you can include in your AUTOEXEC.BAT file a program that turns off the numeric lock.

Cleaning the individual keyswitch assemblies, the entire keypad, or the cable contact ends, as well as completely replacing the cable, are the only ways feasible to "repair" a keyboard. The individual spring and keyswitch assemblies are not available as a separate part, and disassembly of the unit to that level is inadvisable due to the difficulty of reassembly. Besides cleaning, the only things that can be done are to replace the entire keypad assembly (virtually the entire keyboard) or the cable itself.

Chapter 14 covers the steps in troubleshooting keyboard problems and discusses in what sequence you should proceed.

Chapter Summary

This chapter has taken you on a thorough tour of the various system units of the IBM personal computers and their assorted components: the motherboard, the microprocessor, memory, slots, standard adapters, the power supply, and keyboards. The information that you have gained in this chapter can help you understand why many items in the PC and PS/2 systems operate as they do. Understanding the way the system truly operates gives you valuable insight into many of the problems that can occur with these systems and can turn you into an expert troubleshooter: someone who, rather than just recites a problem solution from memory, uses creativity to solve problems. In-depth troubleshooting of these system components is discussed in Chapter 14.

8

Floppy Disk Drives

This chapter examines floppy disk drives and disks in great detail. You will explore how floppy disk drives and disks function, how DOS uses a disk, what types of disk drives and disks are available, and how to install and service these drives and disks properly. You will learn about all the types of drives available for today's personal computer systems; these drives include both the 5 1/4-inch and 3 1/2-inch drives in both high- and double-density versions. You may find of special interest the addition of the 3 1/2-inch drives to the early PC family systems, which allows them to be compatible with the new PS/2 systems.

Examining Disk Drive Theory and Operation

In this section, you will examine the components that make up a typical drive. Then you will examine how these components operate together to read and write data—the physical operation of the drive. Finally, you will examine the logical operation of the drive, which shows how the drive is perceived by DOS and the system and how data is written to a typical disk.

Drive Components

A floppy drive, regardless of its type, consists of several basic common components. To properly install and service a disk drive, you must be able to identify these components and understand what their function is (see fig. 8.1).

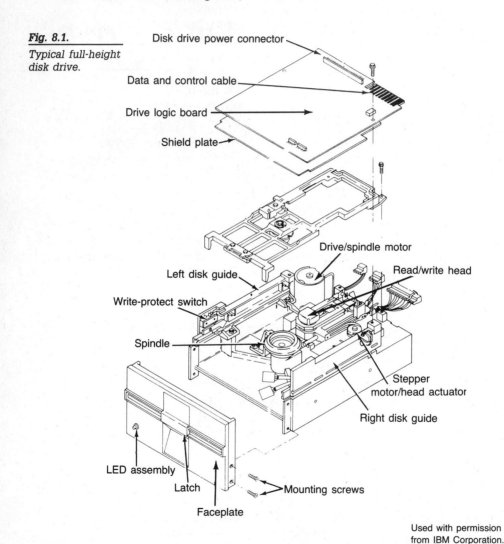

Fig. 8.1.

Typical full-height disk drive.

Disk drive power connector

Data and control cable

Drive logic board

Shield plate

Drive/spindle motor

Left disk guide

Read/write head

Write-protect switch

Spindle

Stepper motor/head actuator

Right disk guide

LED assembly

Latch

Mounting screws

Faceplate

Used with permission from IBM Corporation.

Read/Write Heads

Any disk drive today has two read/write heads, making the modern floppy disk drive a double-sided drive. A head exists for each side of the disk, and both heads are used for recording and reading on their respective disk sides. At one time, single-sided drives were available for PC systems (the original PC had such drives), but today single-sided drives are a fading memory. The head mechanism is moved by a motor called a *head actuator*. The heads can move in and out over the surface of the disk in a straight line to position themselves over various tracks. The heads move in and out tangentially to the tracks that they record on the disk. The heads are mounted on the same rack or mechanism, so they move in unison and cannot move independently of each other. The heads are made of soft ferrous (iron) compounds with electromagnetic coils. Each head is actually a composite design, with a record head centered within two erase heads in the same physical device (see fig. 8.2).

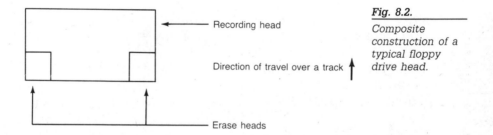

Fig. 8.2.

Composite construction of a typical floppy drive head.

The recording method is called *tunnel erasure*; as the track is laid down, the trailing erase heads erase the outer bands of the track, trimming it cleanly on the disk. The heads thereby force the data to be present only within a specified narrow "tunnel" on each track. This process prevents the signal of one track from being confused with the signals of adjacent tracks. If the signal was allowed to "taper off" to each side, problems would occur. The forcibly trimmed track prevents these problems.

Alignment is the placement of the heads with respect to the tracks they must read and write. Head alignment can be checked only against some sort of reference standard disk recorded by a perfectly aligned machine. These types of disks are available, and you can use one to check your drive's alignment.

The two heads are spring loaded and actually grip the disk with a small amount of pressure. Floppy disk drives spin at 300 or 360 rpm, which doesn't present an excessive friction problem. Some newer disks are specially coated with teflon or other compounds to further reduce this friction and allow the disk to slide more easily under the heads. Because of the contact between the heads and the actual disk, a buildup of the oxide material from the disk forms on the heads over time. This buildup can be cleaned off of the heads periodically as part of a preventive-maintenance or normal service program.

Head Actuator

The *head actuator* is a mechanical motor device that actually causes the heads to move in and out over the surface of a disk. These mechanisms for floppy disk drives universally use a special kind of motor, a *stepper motor*, which moves in both directions some amount equal to or less than a single revolution. This type of motor does not spin around and around; rather, the motor can complete only a partial revolution in each direction. Stepper motors move in fixed increments, or *detents*, and must stop at a particular detent position. Stepper motors are not infinitely variable in their positioning. Each increment of motion, or some multiple thereof, defines each track on the disk. The motor can be commanded to position itself to any relative increment within the range of its travel. To position the heads at track 25, the motor is commanded to go to the 25th detent position.

The stepper motor usually is linked to the head rack with a coiled split steel band. This band winds and unwinds around the spindle of the stepper motor, translating the rotary motion into linear motion. A stepper motor usually has a full travel time of about 1/5 of a second—about 200 milliseconds. On average, a 1/2 stroke would be 100 milliseconds, and a 1/3 stroke would be 66 milliseconds. The timing of a 1/2 or 1/3 stroke of the head actuator mechanism often is used to determine the reported average access time for a disk drive. This *average access time* is the normal amount of time the heads spend moving from one track to another at random.

Spindle Motor

The *spindle motor* is used to spin the disk around. The normal speed of rotation is 300 or 360 rpm, depending on the type of drive. Most earlier drives used a mechanism where the spindle motor actually turned the disk spindle with a belt, but all modern drives use a direct-drive system with no belts. The direct-drive systems are more reliable and less expensive to manufacture, as well as smaller in size. The earlier belt-driven systems do have more rotational torque available to turn a sticky disk, which is due to the torque multiplication factor of the belt system. Most newer direct-drive systems now employ an automatic torque-compensation capability that automatically sets the disk rotation speed to a fixed 300 or 360 rpm and that compensates with additional torque for sticky disks or less torque for slippery ones. This type of drive also eliminates the need to ever adjust the rotational speed of the drive.

Most of today's direct-drive systems employ this automatic speed feature, but many of the earlier ones may require that you adjust the speed periodically. Looking at the spindle provides you with one clue to the type of drive you have. If the spindle contains strobe marks for 50 Hz and 60 Hz strobe lights (fluorescent lights), that drive probably has an adjustment for speed somewhere on the drive. Drives without the strobe marks almost always include an automatic tachometer control circuit that prevents the need for adjustment. The technique for setting the speed involves operating the drive under fluorescent lighting and adjusting the rotational speed until the strobe marks appear motionless, much like the "wagon wheel effect" you see while watching old western movies. The procedure is described in the section called "Speed Adjustment."

To locate the spindle speed adjustment, you must consult the Original Equipment Manufacturers (OEM) manual for the drive. IBM provides the information for its drives in the *Technical Reference Options and Adapters* manual as well as in the hardware maintenance reference manuals. Even if IBM sells the drives, the drives are most likely manufactured by another company, such as Control Data Corporation (CDC), Tandon, YE-Data (C. Itoh), Alps Electric, or Mitsubishi. I recommend contacting these manufacturers for the original manuals for the drives you have.

Circuit Boards

A disk drive always incorporates one or more circuit boards called *logic boards*. These boards contain the circuitry used to control the head actuator, read/write heads, spindle motor, disk sensors, and any other components on the drive. The logic board also represents the drive's interface to the controller board in the system unit.

The standard interface used by all PC types of floppy disk drives is the Shugart Associates SA-450 interface. This interface was invented by Shugart in the 1970s and has been the basis of most floppy disk interfacing. The selection of this industry-standard interface is the reason that you can purchase "off the shelf" drives (raw or bare drives) that can plug directly into your controller. (Thanks, IBM, for deciding to stick with industry-standard interfacing; it has been the basis of the entire PC upgrade and repair industry!) Other companies, especially Apple, have stayed away from industry standards, which can make tasks such as drive integration a nightmare unless, of course, you buy everything from these companies. IBM always stayed with standards wherever possible, which is the reason that the architecture of the PC and PS/2 system is so open.

Logic boards can fail and be difficult to obtain for a particular drive. The price of one of these boards often is more than the price of replacing the drive itself. I usually recommend keeping failed drives that can be used for the remaining good parts—such as logic boards.

Faceplate

The faceplate or *bezel* is the plastic piece that is the front of the drive. These pieces usually are removable and can come in different colors and configurations.

Most drives use a bezel that is slightly wider than the drive itself. These types of drives must be installed from the front of a system, because the faceplate is slightly wider than the hole in the system unit case. Other drives have faceplates that are the same width as the chassis of the drive; these drives can be installed from the rear, which can be an advantage in many cases. In the later version XT systems, for example, IBM uses this design in its drives so that two half-height drives can be bolted together as a unit and then can be slid in from the rear, to clear all the mounting bracket and screw hardware. On many occasions, I have filed the edges of a drive faceplate in order to install the drive from the rear of a system—which must be done in some cases.

Connectors

All disk drives have at least two connectors—one for power to run the drive and the other to carry the control and data signals to and from the drive. These connectors are fairly standardized in the industry; a 4 in-line connector is used for power, and a 34-pin edge connector is used for the data and control signals. Some of the smaller 3 1/2-inch drives now use a tiny version of the power connector, and some drives may have the other connector modified as well. But the manufacturers make these drives for special applications where the different style of connectors may be required.

In the PS/2 systems, for example, IBM uses a special version of a Mitsubishi 3 1/2-inch drive called the MF-355W-99, but for a standard PC or AT type of system, you will want the MF-355B-82 (black faceplate) or MF-355B-88 (beige faceplate). These latter drives offer an adapter that allows the standard power connector and disk-drive control and data connector to be used. These drives are ideal for upgrading an earlier system.

Drive Configuration Devices

Several items must be located on any drive that is to be installed in a system. These items control the configuration and operation of the drive and must be set correctly depending on which system is being used and where in the system the drive is being installed.

Here are the items that need your attention in an installation situation:

- Drive-select jumper
- Terminating resistor
- Diskette changeline/ready jumper
- Media-sensor jumper

You will learn how to actually configure these items later in the chapter. Here, you will learn just what these devices are used for.

Drive-Select Jumpers

The *drive-select jumper* is set to indicate to the drive and controller the number that a particular drive should be. Each drive in a controller and drive subsystem must have a unique drive number. This jumper basically indicates whether the particular drive is to respond as A: or B:. Some idiosyncrasies can occur when you're setting this jumper in various systems due to strange cable configurations, etc. The drive usually allows four settings, labeled DS1, DS2, DS3, and DS4. Some drives start with 0, and the settings are labeled DS0, DS1, DS2, and DS3. On many drives, these jumpers are not labeled at all, and you have three resources to consult for information on how to set the drive. You can consult the OEM manual, use your experience with previous drives from the same manufacturer, or simply make an educated guess. I recommend going for the manual every time, with a dash of experience thrown in for good measure.

In most cases, the first drive-select position corresponds to A:, the second position corresponds to B:, and so on. In many systems, however, this configuration may be wrong because of some creative rewiring of the cable. IBM, for example, crosses six wires (the drive-select and motor-enable lines) in the floppy interface cable between drives B and A to allow both drives to be jumpered the same way, as if they both were drive B. This setup allows the dealers and installers to buy the drives prejumpered by IBM and to install them with a minimum of hassle. Sometimes this setup confuses people who attempt to install drives properly without knowing about this twisted cabling system. If you install a drive and find that it either does not respond at all or responds in unison with the other drive in the system, you probably have the drive-select jumper set incorrectly for your particular application. If you have two drives and both respond in unison, the drive intended to be B: has been set as A:. If neither drive responds, the one intended as A: has been set as B:. Setting the drive-select jumper is discussed in the section called "Drive Configuration."

Terminating Resistors

The terminating resistor must be set or placed on the last drive on the end of the cable from the controller to the drives. In most systems, this drive should be the lowest lettered drive (A:). The drive plugged into the connector in the center of the cable must have the terminating resistor (or terminator) removed or disabled for proper operation.

The *terminating resistor* is designed to absorb any signals that reach the end of a cabling system so that no reflection of the signals goes back down the line. A terminating resistor is installed in the controller to terminate the cable at that end; you must worry only about terminating the drive end properly. Sometimes a system operates with incorrect terminator installation, but the system may give erratic disk errors. Additionally, with the wrong signal load on the controller, you run the risk of burning it out by causing excessive power consumption.

The terminating resistor usually looks like a memory chip—a 16-pin Dual Inline Package (DIP) device. Actually, this device is a group of eight resistors wired physically in parallel with each other to terminate separately each of the eight data lines in the interface subsystem. Not all drives use the same type of terminating resistor, however, and it may be found in different places for each manufacturer's drive models. This situation is another where the OEM manual for the drive comes in handy because the manual contains complete documentation on the location, physical appearance, enabling and disabling instructions, and even the precise value required for the resistors themselves. Do not lose the terminator if it is removed from a drive. You may need to reinstall it later if you relocate the drive to a different position in a system or even to a different system altogether.

A recent trend is that some drives now have a permanently installed terminating resistor that is enabled or disabled with a simple jumper. This type of terminating resistor is preferable to one that you might remove and then accidentally lose. Finally, many of the newer 3 1/2-inch drives use a technique for termination called *distributed termination*, which means that each drive has a lower value terminating resistor and therefore carries a part of the termination load. These terminating resistors are permanently fixed to the drive and never need to be removed. This feature makes configuration of these drives one step simpler.

Terminating resistors are discussed in more detail in the section called "Drive Configuration."

Diskette Changeline/Ready Jumper

In an XT type of system, pin 34 of the disk drive interface is not used at all, but in an AT system, this pin is used to carry a signal called Diskette Changeline or DC. Although the XT does not use pin 34, most drives that don't support the DC signal do use the pin to carry a signal called Standard Ready or SR.

The Diskette Changeline signal is used by the AT to determine whether the disk has been changed. A value of 1 indicates that the disk has been changed, and a value of 0 indicates that the disk has not been changed. The DC signal has a value of 1 unless a disk is present in the drive and a step pulse has been received by the drive to move the heads, in which case the signal is set to 0. The signal remains set to 0 until the door is opened. When you move the door lever on a high-capacity drive, the DC signal is reset to 1. After the disk has been accessed and until the door is opened again, the signal is set to 0.

The AT uses this signal to increase significantly the speed of the floppy interface. Because the AT now can know whether you have changed the disk, the AT can keep a copy of the disk's directory and file allocation table information in RAM buffers. On every subsequent disk access, the operations will run much faster because this information does not have to be reread off of the disk on each individual access. If the DC signal has been reset (has a value of 1), the AT knows that the disk has been changed and appropriately rereads this information off of the disk.

You can observe the effects of the DC signal by trying a simple experiment. Boot DOS on an AT and place a floppy disk with data on it into drive A. Drive A must be a high-capacity drive, although the disk may be a double-density 360K disk. Now type this command:

DIR A:

The disk lights up and the directory is displayed. Note the amount of time that the disk is actually read before the directory is displayed on-screen. Now, without touching the drive, retype *dir a:* and keep an eye on the drive access light. Note again the amount of time before the actual directory is displayed. You will notice that the directory of A: is displayed the second time almost instantly; no time was spent reading the disk. The directory information simply was read back from RAM buffers instead of being read again from the disk. Now open and close the drive door while keeping the disk in the drive. Type *dir a:* again. This time, the disk again spends some time reading the directory before anything is displayed, because the AT now believes that you have changed the disk.

The PC and XT controllers (and systems) do not care at all about the status of this signal. These systems don't care what value the drive presents to pin 34. The PC and XT operate under the assumption that the disk always has been changed, and these systems reread the disk directory and file allocation table on each access. This is one reason that these systems are slower in using the floppy disk drives.

A real problem can occur when some drives are installed in an AT system. As mentioned previously, some drives use pin 34 for a Standard Ready signal. The SR signal is a value of 1 when the drive has a disk installed and is rotating. If you install a drive that has pin 34 set to SR, the AT thinks that it always is receiving a Diskette Changeline value of 1 while the drive is operating or 0 while the drive isn't operating, which can cause the system to believe that the same disk is in the drive. Even if you change the disk, the AT still believes that the first disk is in the drive and holds that first disk's directory and file allocation table information in RAM. This information is automatically written to any subsequent disks that are written to in that drive.

If you ever have seen an AT disk drive that shows "phantom directories" of disks not even installed or that, after you change a disk, still shows the directory of the first disk and refuses to read the second one, you have experienced this problem firsthand. The unfortunate side effect is that any disks are in extreme danger in this system. You likely will be overwriting the directories and file allocation tables of many disks with the wrong information. Data recovery from such a catastrophe will require some work with a program such as DEBUG or the Norton Utilities. This problem can be caused by an incorrectly configured drive, as well as by a drive where the door switch mechanism no longer operates correctly. A temporary solution to the problem is to remember to press the Ctrl-Break or Ctrl-C combination every time you change a floppy disk in the drive. These commands cause DOS to flush the RAM buffers and reread the directory and file allocation table on the next disk access.

To recap, PC and XT systems do not care at all about pin 34, but AT systems need pin 34 set to Diskette Changeline (DC). If the drive does not support the DC signal and you want to install it in an AT, pin 34 must be open but not set to Standard Ready (SR). No IBM type of system uses the SR signal at pin 34.

Media-Sensor Jumper

A jumper selection exists that is only on the 1.44M 3 1/2-inch drives. This jumper selection is called the Media-Sensor (MS) jumper, and it must be set to enable a special media sensor in the disk drive, which senses a special hole found only in the 1.44M high-capacity disks.

This setup is how the drive can determine what level of recording strength to use, and it is required for these drives because of the design of the Western Digital hard disk and floppy controllers used by IBM in the AT systems. These high-density 3 1/2-inch drives simply will not operate properly in the lower density mode unless the drive has control over the write current. The only type of 1.44M drive usable for upgrading earlier systems is one with this sensor, and with this sensor enabled. Strangely, the PS/2 systems from IBM do not use drives with this sensor because the special floppy controller built into the motherboard can manipulate the drive correctly in both modes.

Physical Operation

The physical operation of a disk is fairly simple to describe. The disk itself rotates at either 300 or 360 rpm; the faster mode is reserved for the high-density controllers and drives. With the disk spinning, the heads can move in and out approximately the distance of 1 inch, writing either 40 or 80 tracks. These tracks are written on both sides of the disk and, therefore, are sometimes called cylinders. A single cylinder comprises the tracks on the top and bottom of the disk. The heads record by using a tunnel erase procedure where a track is written to a specified width, and then the edges of the track are erased to prevent interference with any adjacent tracks.

The tracks are recorded at different widths for different drives. Here are the track widths in millimeters for each of the four types of floppy drives supported in PC systems:

Drive Type	No. of Tracks	Track Width
5 1/4-inch 360K	40 per side	0.330 mm
5 1/4-inch 1.2M	80 per side	0.160 mm
3 1/2-inch 720K	80 per side	0.115 mm
3 1/2-inch 1.44M	80 per side	0.115 mm

The differences in recorded track width can result in problems with data exchange between various drives. The 5 1/4-inch drives are affected because the double-density drives record a track width of more than twice that of the high-density drives. Thus, a real problem occurs if a high-density drive is used to update a double-density disk with previously recorded data on it.

The high-density drive, even in 360K mode, cannot completely overwrite the track left by the 40-track drive, which presents a problem when the disk is returned to the person with the 360K drive; that drive will see the new data as "embedded" within the remains of the previously written track. The drive will not be able to distinguish either signal, and an Abort, Retry, Ignore type of error message results. This problem will not occur if a *new* disk (one that never has had data recorded on it) is first formatted in a 1.2M drive with the /4 option, which formats the disk as a 360K disk. The 1.2M drive then can be used to fill the disk to its 360K capacity, and every file will be readable on the 40-track 360K drive.

I use this trick all the time to exchange data disks between AT systems that have only the 1.2M drive and XT or PC systems that have only the 360K drives. The key is to start with a disk that is new or has been magnetically wiped clean by a bulk eraser. Simply reformatting the disk will not work because formatting actually is writing data to the disk.

Another subtle problem with the way a disk drive physically works is that the recording volume varies depending on what type of format you are trying to apply to a disk. The high-density formats use special disks that require a much higher volume level for the recording than the double-density disks do. I always stump my classes with this question: Which type of disk is *more* sensitive—a 1.2M disk or a 360K disk? If you say that the 1.2M disk is more sensitive, you are wrong! The high-density disks actually are approximately *half* as sensitive to magnetic recording as are the double-density disks.

The high-density disks are known as *high coercivity* disks because they require a magnetic field strength that is much higher than the double-density disks require. Magnetic field strength is measured in oersteds. The 360K disks require a field strength of only 300 oersteds, and the high-density disks require a field strength of 600 oersteds. The high-density disks require double the strength of recording, which is the reason that you cannot (and should not) format a 1.2M high-density disk as if it were a 360K disk, or a 360K disk as if it were a high-density disk.

In particular, the latter seems to appeal to people looking for an easy way to save some money. These people buy inexpensive 360K disks and format them in a 1.2M drive at the full 1.2M capacity. Most of the time, this format actually seems to work, with maybe a large amount of bad sectors; otherwise, most of the disk seems usable. But you should not actually store any important data on this incorrectly formatted disk because the data is recorded at twice the recommended strength and density. Over time, the adjacent magnetic domains on the disk begin to affect each other, causing migration of the domains due to the magnetic attraction and repulsion effects. This process is illustrated later in this chapter, in the section called "Coercivity." Over time, the disk seems to erase itself. The process may take a day, a week, a month, or more, but the result is pretty much inevitable.

Another problem results from this type of improper formatting. You ruin the 360K disk! The high-density format has placed a recording on the disk at twice the strength it should have been. How do you remove it and correct the problem? If you attempt to reformat the disk in a 360K drive, the drive writes in a reduced write current mode and cannot overwrite the high-volume recording that you mistakenly placed on the disk. If you attempt to reformat the disk in the high-density drive with the /4 parameter, which indicates 360K mode, the high-density drive also goes into reduced write current mode and again cannot overwrite the recording.

Two ways are available, however, for you to correct the problem. One way is to throw away the disk and write it off as a learning experience! Or you can use a bulk eraser, a device that can remove all the magnetism from the disk and essentially return it to factory-new condition. You can purchase bulk erasers at electronic supply stores for about $25.

The opposite problem is also very real. You cannot use one of the good high-density disks formatted at the 360K capacity. If you do attempt to use one, the drive goes into low write current mode and does not create a magnetic field strong enough to record on the "insensitive" 1.2M disk. The result is an immediate `Invalid media` or `Track 0 bad - disk unusable` message from DOS. Fortunately, the system usually will not allow this mistake to be made!

The 3 1/2-inch drives don't have the same problems as the 5 1/4-inch drives—at least for data interchange. Because the high- and double-density drives both write the same number of tracks and are the same width, no problem occurs when one type of drive is used to overwrite data written by another type of drive. IBM, therefore, doesn't need to offer a double-density version of the 3 1/2-inch drives for the PS/2 50, 60, 70, and 80. These systems include the high-density drive only, which is completely capable of imitating perfectly the 720K drives found in the Models 25 and 30. These high-density drives, however, can be trouble for inexperienced users. Again, you must be sure to use the 1.44M high-density disks only at the 1.44M format and the 720K only at the 720K format. You will have serious problems if you simply place a 720K disk into a drive in a PS/2 Model 50, 60, 70, or 80 and enter *format a:*. You again will need the services of a bulk eraser. And if you really do decide to use the resulting disk, you will have massive data loss over a period of time.

This last problem could have been averted if IBM had decided to use disk drives in the PS/2 systems that included the disk media sensor, the special switch that senses the unique hole found only on the right side of the high-density disks. Drives that use this hole to control the status of reduced write current never will be able to format a disk incorrectly. Here, the hardware saves you and causes the FORMAT command to end in failure with an appropriate error message if you attempt to format the disk incorrectly. If you are purchasing any 1.44M drives for upgrading earlier systems, the 1.44M drives must have this sensor to control operation of the drive.

The bottom line is this: By knowing just how a drive works physically, you can eliminate most of these "Pilot Error" problems that many users are having and can distinguish this kind of easily solvable problem from a more serious hardware problem. You can be a much better user of a system if you truly understand just how it works.

Logical Operation

In this section, you will examine how DOS sees a drive. You will learn definitions of the drives according to DOS. Each type of drive can create disks with different numbers of sectors and tracks. Also, you will examine the definitions for cylinders and clusters.

How DOS Uses the Disk

Although a technical understanding of the way DOS maintains information on your disks is not necessary, you will be a more informed user if you understand the general principles.

From the DOS point of view, data on your PC disks is organized in tracks and sectors. *Tracks* are narrow concentric circles that go around the disk. *Sectors* are pie-shaped slices of the disk. DOS 1.0 and 1.1 read and write 40 tracks (numbered 0 through 39) and 8 sectors (numbered 1 through 8) per track. DOS 2.0 and higher automatically formats 9 sectors for greater capacity on the same disk. On an AT with a 1.2M disk drive, DOS 3.0 supports high-density drives that format 15 sectors per track at 80 tracks, DOS 3.2 supports the 3 1/2-inch disks that format 9 sectors per track at 80 tracks, and DOS 3.3 supports the 3 1/2-inch disks that format 18 sectors at 80 tracks. The distance between tracks and, therefore, the number of tracks on a disk is a built-in mechanical and electronic function of the drive. Table 8.1 gives a summary of the types of formats available from DOS 3.3 and higher.

Table 8.1
Floppy Disk Drive Formats

5 1/4-Inch	Double Density	High Density
Bytes per sector	512	512
Sectors per track	9	15
Tracks per side	40	80
Sides	2	2
Capacity (K)	360	1,200

3 1/2-Inch	Double Density	High Density
Bytes per sector	512	512
Sectors per track	9	18
Tracks per side	80	80
Sides	2	2
Capacity (K)	720	1,440

The capacity differences between different formats mainly come from the different numbers of tracks and sectors per track.

When you buy new disks, they are like blank sheets of paper, containing no information at all. Formatting the disk is like adding lines to the paper so you will be able to write straight. Formatting puts onto the disk the information DOS needs to maintain a directory and files. And using the /S option after the FORMAT command is like making that paper a title page. You put onto the disk certain parts of DOS.

The track nearest the outside edge of a disk (track 0) almost entirely is reserved by DOS for its purposes. Track 0, Sector 1, contains the "boot record" or boot sector that the system needs to begin operation. The next few sectors contain the file allocation table, which is the disk "reservation clerk," keeping records of which portions of the disk have information and which portions have empty space. Finally, the next few sectors contain the directory (information about the files); you see part of this portion when you use the DIR command.

In computer jargon, this process is "transparent to the user," meaning that you don't have to (and generally cannot) decide where information will go on your disks. But because this process is "transparent" doesn't necessarily mean that you shouldn't be aware of the decisions DOS makes for you.

DOS always attempts to use the earliest free available sectors on a disk when it writes data, which quickly allows files to become fragmented as they are written to fill a hole on the disk created by the deletion of some smaller file. The larger file completely fills the hole; then DOS continues to look across the disk from the outermost tracks to the innermost tracks for more free space. The rest of the file is deposited in the next available free space. This procedure goes on and on until eventually all the files on your disk are hopelessly intertwined. This situation is not really a problem for DOS because it was designed to manage files this way. The real problem is a physical one. Retrieving a file that is in 50 or 100 places across the disk takes much longer than if that file was in one piece. Also, if the files were in one piece, recovering data in the case of a disaster would be much easier. I would undo the fragmentation on a disk for the latter reason alone but, in the process, also would enjoy a disk that feels much faster in file access.

What can be done? You can copy all the files one by one to an empty disk. Or, in the case of a hard disk, you can back up, format, and restore. These operations on the hard disk are fairly drastic and definitely time-consuming. I recommend that you do this procedure twice a year with a hard disk system. The operation can be tricky, especially with the notoriously unreliable BACKUP command. If you have a decent backup system, such as a tape drive, the operation is simplified. Many new utility programs also are available, and they can compress, pack, unfragment, or otherwise tune up a hard disk or restore file contiguity without the need for the reformat and restore operations. Be warned that these programs do not eliminate the need for a backup and are inherently dangerous. Before using any of these programs, make sure that a backup is performed. What shape do you think your disk would be in if the power failed during one of these unfragmenting sessions (not to mention that some of the programs have had bugs in them or have been incompatible with new releases of DOS)?

Cylinders

"Cylinder" is the term usually used today in place of the term "track." A *cylinder* is actually all the tracks that are under read/write heads on a drive at one time. For floppy drives, a disk cannot have more than two sides, and the drive has two heads, which gives two tracks per cylinder. As you will learn later, hard disks can have many disk platters, each with two heads, for many more tracks per single cylinder.

Clusters

A *cluster* is now called an *allocation unit* in DOS 4.0. The term is appropriate because a single cluster is the smallest unit of the disk that DOS can deal with when writing or reading a file. A cluster is one or more sectors—usually more than one. Having more than one sector per cluster reduces the size of the file allocation table and allows DOS to run faster by having fewer individual units of the disk to worry about. The tradeoff is in wasted disk space. Because DOS can manage space only in the cluster unit, every file consumes space on the disk in increments of one cluster. Table 8.2 lists the default cluster sizes used by DOS for the various disk formats.

Table 8.2
Default Cluster Sizes Used by DOS

Drive Type	Default Cluster Size
5 1/4-inch 360K	2 sectors or 1,024 bytes
5 1/4-inch 1.2M	1 sector or 512 bytes
3 1/2-inch 720K	2 sectors or 1,024 bytes
3 1/2-inch 1.44M	1 sector or 512 bytes

The high-density disks have smaller cluster sizes, which seems strange because these disks have many more individual sectors than double-density disks. The reason is that these high-density disks are faster than the double-density counterparts, so IBM and Microsoft thought the decrease in cluster size and speed would be welcome. You will learn later that for hard disks, the cluster size can vary more greatly between different versions of DOS and different disk sizes.

Examining the Types of Floppy Drives

In this section, you will examine all the various types of floppy disk drives available for your PC system. You will learn about 5 1/4-inch and 3 1/2-inch drives and examine the high- and double-density versions of each. You also will learn about the various physical combinations that may be available, such as full-height and half-height versions or 3 1/2-inch drives mounted in 5 1/4-inch frames.

5 1/4-Inch Drives

A variety of 5 1/4-inch drives have been used in PC systems over the years. Some very early (vintage 1981-82) systems had single-sided drives installed in them. Today, the minimum is a 360K double-sided drive, and the largest capacity 5 1/4-inch drive commonly installed in PC systems is the 1.2M high-density drive. This section covers these drives.

Single-Sided Drive

A single-sided drive, as the name explains, uses only one side of the disk on which to record data. When the IBM PC was first introduced, it had only single-sided drives. Depending on the DOS version, a single-sided drive allows for the storage of either 160K or 180K per disk. These drives really are quite out of date. You never should consider installing these drives in your systems, and if you have any single-sided drives now, get rid of them!

A single-sided drive makes an excellent bookend or paperweight but is not something you will want in your systems. Cost is the reason for eliminating these drives. You can purchase double-sided half-height drives today for less than $100, so using single-sided drives simply does not pay. Because of the "lowest common denominator" principle, you still will see a few software companies supplying programs on disks formatted as single-sided disks. The reason is so that anybody can use the software, even those with earlier PCs. I haven't seen a single-sided disk drive in several years, and most software these days expects double-sided drives.

360K Double-Sided Drives

Most PC system users have double-sided drives in their systems. The capacity of these drives is up to 360K for any DOS Version 1.1 or later. As the name explains, both sides of the disk are used for recording, and this process is totally transparent to the user. You do not flip the disks over to record the other side; actually, the drive records both sides simultaneously, and you see the disk as one large continuous area of storage. These drives are made by a variety of manufacturers. IBM primarily uses Tandon. CDC full-height drives are in the earlier systems, and YE-Data (C. Itoh) and Alps Electric half-height drives are in the newer systems. CDC and Tandon no longer manufacture floppy disk drives, so getting any of the earlier full-height drives is now a problem. Actually, this is not really a problem but a good reason for replacing any failing full-height drives with half-height versions.

1.2M High-Capacity Drives

The 1.2M disk drives for the AT are made by a company called YE-Data, a division of C. Itoh Electronics, and also Alps Electric. These disk drives often are called high-capacity, high-coercivity, or high-density drives, which refers to the media that is required for proper operation. The drives are designed for 80-track double-sided operation and handle the 15 sectors per track that DOS formats.

These drives spin at 360 rpm in the high-density mode and can transfer data with the AT controller at twice the rate of a standard 360K drive. Because of the higher rotational speed and data transfer requirements for this drive, a controller that supports a data rate of 500 KHz is required, which excludes the standard controllers found in the IBM PC and XT systems. These double-density controllers only support a 250 KHz data rate. The AT controllers support the proper data rate for these drives, and aftermarket controllers are available from a variety of sources, which adds the capability to use these drives in a PC or XT type of system.

Because of the physical design of the drive and heads (namely the recorded track width), anything recorded in these drives—even in the correct 360K format—may not read accurately in a standard 360K disk drive. For this reason, IBM offers as an option a second drive for the AT that is a regular double-sided 360K drive. You can ensure data exchange, however, by making sure that any 360K format recording is done on a disk that never has been written on by an actual 360K drive. This procedure ensures that an actual 360K drive can read this disk later. The 1.2M drives have absolutely no trouble reading any 5 1/4-inch disk that was recorded by any other IBM PC system, even if the disk was recorded with DOS 1.0.

To use these drives properly, make sure that the media is up to snuff. Don't use the low-coercivity disks in the high-density (1.2M) mode. If you understand how these drives record in that mode, you know how foolish this procedure is! For high-density recording, you must specify the high-capacity styles of disks with an 80-track density and a coercivity rating of at least 600 oersteds. As mentioned earlier, coercivity is a measure of the magnetic retention and density capabilities of the media. These disks usually have a cobalt-compound coating rather than the iron-oxide coating on regular disks.

3 1/2-Inch Drives

All 3 1/2-inch drives are available only in a half-height configuration. Essentially two types of 3 1/2-inch drives are available: a high-density and double-density version. The high-density drive can read and write 1.44 megabytes to a disk, and the double-density version reads and writes 720K to a disk. This section discusses these drives in detail.

720K Drives

When IBM introduced the PC Convertible laptop system along with DOS 3.2 in April, 1986, it started adopting the 3 1/2-inch disk as the new standard. Now, every system that IBM sells, and that many other manufacturers sell as well, comes standard with these drives. This 3 1/2-inch drive has 720K of storage capacity. This type of unit is available as an internal or external option for the PC, XT, or AT.

These drives can use the existing drive controller with no changes. DOS Version 3.2 or higher is required for support of the drive. These drives spin at 300 rpm and work much like the larger 5 1/4-inch drives; they simply are smaller and use 80 tracks per side rather than 40. This is the reason that these drives can store 720K of data, which is double the amount of double-density 5 1/4-inch disks.

1.44M High-Capacity Drives

The 1.44M 3 1/2-inch drive was formally introduced by IBM with the PS/2 introduction in April, 1987. This drive is the new standard floppy disk drive for all the PS/2 systems and can be retrofitted to the earlier systems as well. This type of drive operates in an AT with the existing controller card but works only at the lower capacity 720K capability in a PC or XT. The PC or XT disk controller does not support the higher 500 KHz data rate required for high-density operation. Aftermarket suppliers have controllers for those systems that allow the high-density drives to work to full capacity.

These drives achieve their capacity by using the high-density (high-coercivity) media, which takes 80 cylinders with 18 sectors per track. This is a higher linear track density than many hard disks that store only 17 sectors per track. These disks are only 3 1/2 inches in diameter; many hard disks are still 5 1/4 inches in size. Using these disks is a real pleasure after being limited to the 360K 5 1/4-inch disks for so long.

Here's an interesting piece of information. The last version of the AT motherboard ROMs has support for this type of drive and can take one as a simple bolt-in operation. This ROM carries the date of November 15, 1985, so you can see just how far ahead IBM was thinking on this subject. These drives are available from many manufacturers, but so far IBM has been using primarily Mitsubishi drives.

Half-Height versus Full-Height Drives

IBM officially endorsed half-height drives with the introduction of the Portable PC and the PC*jr*. The introduction of these drives coincided with the introduction of DOS 2.1, which was the first to support these drives. Most half-height drives are just a little slower than the full-height drives, and a couple of timing parameters had to be adjusted in DOS to compensate for this fact. All subsequent versions of DOS do support the half-height drives with no problems. Now all IBM systems except the original PC use half-height drives (see figs. 8.3 and 8.4).

The half-height drives offer primarily space savings over the full-height drives. For example, I can equip an XT with two half-height drives in the left bay while placing a full-height hard disk in the right. With two floppy drives, I am able to perform disk copying and backups with greater ease than if I had only one. If you are going to purchase a new system or replace drives in an earlier one, I recommend that you use half-height drives.

You will find a few drawbacks when using these drives. One drawback is that they can be somewhat difficult to mount in the system. Because the standard PCs and XTs were designed to have the full-height drives, you will need custom-made brackets and a

Fig. 8.3.

Half-height disk drive.

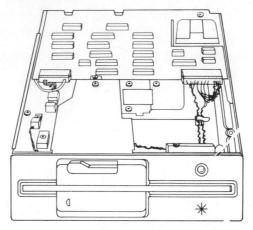

Used with permission from IBM Corporation.

Fig. 8.4.

Full-height disk drive.

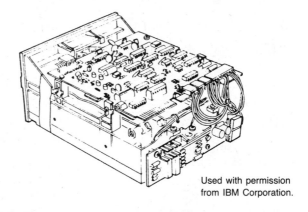

Used with permission from IBM Corporation.

power cable splitter to install two half-height drives in place of one full-height drive. Also, because most of the half-height drives use a direct-drive motor assembly rather than the belt-driven assembly that full-height drives use, the half-height drives produce less rotational torque and may have a hard time with certain brands of disks or with a disk that has been compacted or pressed flat. These drives have less capability than full-height drives to overcome internal friction in a disk. On occasion, I have found disks that I could not read in my half-height drives that read perfectly in the full-height drives. These conditions are rare, however; with the proper mounting supplied by whoever sells you the drives, half-height drives truly are the way to go.

IBM used Qume drives for the PC*jr* and Portable PC but used either YE-Data or Alps Electric drives in the AT and XT systems. These drives are from Japanese manufacturers and are quite good. Not a single American company manufactures floppy drives anymore.

Different Densities

This section describes how the different density capabilities of the high- and double-density drives sometimes can cause problems with formatting disks. You always must ensure that a disk is initially formatted to the density in which it was supposed to be run. In some cases, you will want to have a high-density drive format a double-density disk. You can do this procedure by using the correct FORMAT commands. In this section, you will learn how to use DOS correctly so that your disks are formatted properly.

How To Make 1.2M Drives Read and Write 360K

The procedure for making 1.2M drives read or write any 360K disk is simple. Just place any previously formatted 360K disk in the drive and use it as you normally would. In other words, pretend that the drive is really a 360K drive because nothing special needs to be done. You actually will be able to read or write on the disk with absolutely no problems—yet.

A problem does occur if you decide to take this disk back to an actual 360K drive and attempt to read it. Remember that the recorded track width of the 1.2M drive is half that of the 360K drive, so if any tracks have been recorded previously by an actual 360K drive, these tracks are twice as wide as the tracks that will be recorded by the 1.2M drive. If you actually write to the disk with the 1.2M drive, you will not actually be overwriting the entire track width but only the center portion of it. When this disk is returned to an actual 360K drive, the wider head system in the 360K drive now sees two signals on any overwritten tracks; the new data will be nestled within the image of the old data, which could not be completely overlaid by the 1.2M drive. An immediate Abort, Retry, Ignore error message from DOS usually occurs for any of the updated portions of the disks.

If you need to record data in an AT 1.2M drive and later read it properly in a 360K drive, the easy solution is to make sure that any recording in the 1.2M drive is done on new disks. A new disk has no magnetic information on it, which allows the smaller recorded track width to be written on the 1.2M drive and read properly in the 360K drive because now the more narrow track will be written in "clean space." The 360K drive, therefore, will no longer be confused by any "ghost images" of previously recorded wider tracks.

Other than starting with a new disk, the only other way to accomplish your task is to use a disk that is erased by a bulk eraser. You cannot reformat a disk that has been used already in order to erase it. Formatting actually records on the disk and causes the track width problem. The new or bulk-erased disk must be formatted by the 1.2M drive. Remember this simple rule: Any track recorded by a 360K drive cannot be overwritten by a 1.2M drive—even in the 360K format.

How do you format a 360K type of disk in an actual 1.2M drive? If you simply execute the FORMAT command without any parameters, DOS attempts to format the disk to its maximum capacity. Because the 1.2M drives do not have any media-sensing capability, DOS assumes that the disk capability is equal to the maximum capability of the drive itself and attempts to create a 1.2M format on the disk. The write current also is increased during any recording in this format, which is incompatible with the actual 360K media. To format this 360K disk properly, then, you can choose from several alternative commands:

For DOS 4.0, 3.3, 3.2, 3.1, and 3.0, type

> FORMAT A: /4

For DOS 4.0 and 3.3, type

> FORMAT A: /N:9 /T:40

For DOS 4.0 only, type

> FORMAT A: /F:360

Each of these commands accomplishes the same function, which is to place a 40-track, 9-sector format using reduced write current mode on a 360K disk.

How To Make 1.44M Drives
Read and Write 720K

You do not have quite the same problems with 1.44M drives and 720K drives that you have with the 5 1/4-inch drives. The reason is that the 3 1/2-inch drives all have the same recorded track width so the 1.44M drives have absolutely no problems recording 720K types of disks. The only time that problems can occur is with the initial disk formatting; as I already described, if a user attempts to format a disk at a capacity the disk isn't designed for, problems can occur. (If you purchase 3 1/2-inch drives with media sensing, you even are prevented from messing up this procedure!) For these reasons and more, I applaud the industry move to the 3 1/2-inch drives. The sooner all existing 5 1/4-inch disk drives are discarded, the better!

Any drive with a media sensor can use the mechanism built into each disk that informs the drive of precisely which disk type is being used. The write current is then controlled, and improper disk formatting is prevented.

If a standard FORMAT command is entered with no parameters, DOS always attempts to format the disk to the maximum capacity of the drive. If you place a 720K disk into a 1.44M drive and simply enter the FORMAT command with no parameters, DOS attempts to create a 1.44M format on the disk. If the drive has no media sensor (PS/2 systems, for example), the drive shifts into high write current mode and begins creating an 18-sector, 80-track format on the disk. Now this disk is ruined and must be either thrown out or treated by a bulk eraser. If the drive does have a media sensor, the FORMAT command aborts with an error message. Note that the media sensor really does not communicate to DOS the correct information to format the disk; the media sensor simply prevents incorrect formatting. You still have to know the right commands. Here are the correct FORMAT commands and parameters to use to format a 720K type of disk in a 1.44M drive:

For DOS 4.0 or 3.3, type

    FORMAT A: /N:9 /T:80

For DOS 4.0 only, type

    FORMAT A: /F:720

Note that versions of DOS earlier than 3.3 do not support the 1.44M drive at all.

Examining Floppy Disks

In this section, you will examine floppy disks in detail. This section covers the physical construction of a disk and explains the terms used to describe the parts of a disk. You also will examine the different types of disks available, including high- and double-density disks, and will learn about the proper care for a disk. This section dispels some myths about disk handling as well.

Disk Construction

The 5 1/4-inch and 3 1/2-inch disks each have a unique construction and physical format (see fig. 8.5). Differences and similarities exist between these two different-sized disks. In this section, you will take a look at the physical properties and construction of these disk types.

When you look at a typical 5 1/4-inch floppy disk, you can see several things. Most prominent is the large round hole in the center. When you close the disk drive's "door," a cone-shaped clamp grabs and centers the disk through this center hole. Many disks come with "hub-ring reinforcements," thin plastic rings like those used to reinforce three-ring notebook paper, which are intended to help the disk withstand the mechanical forces of the clamping mechanism. You usually will find that the high-density disks lack these reinforcements because placing them accurately on the disk is difficult and they cause alignment problems.

On the right side, just below the center of the hub hole, is a smaller round hole called the "index hole." Carefully turn the disk within its protective jacket to see the small hole in the disk itself. This index hole is used by the drive as the starting point for all the sectors on the disk. This hole is like the "Prime Meridian" for the disk sectors. A disk with a single index hole is called a *soft-sectored* disk; the software (operating system) decides the actual number of sectors on the disk. Some earlier equipment (such as Wang word processors) use *hard-sectored* disks. These disks have an index hole to demarcate each individual sector. Hard-sectored disks should not be used in a PC.

Below the hub hole is a slot shaped much like a long race track; through this slot, you can see the disk surface itself. This slot is the

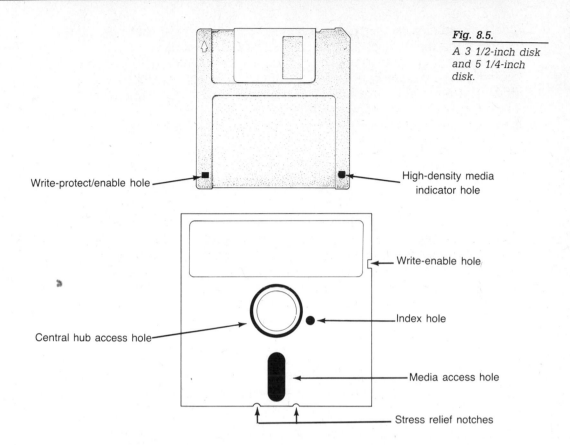

Fig. 8.5.

A 3 1/2-inch disk and 5 1/4-inch disk.

media-access hole. The disk drive heads read and write information to the disk surface through this slot.

At the right side, about one inch from the top, is a rectangular punch from the side of the disk cover. This punch is the *write-enable notch*. If this notch is present, writing to the disk has been enabled. Disks without this notch (or with the notch taped over) are known as *write-protected* disks. This notch may not be present on all disks, particularly on those you have purchased with programs on them.

On the rear of the disk jacket are two small oval notches at the bottom of the disk, flanking the head slot. These notches relieve stress on the disk and help prevent it from warping. The drive also may use these notches to assist in keeping the disk in the proper position in the drive.

The 3 1/2-inch disks use a much more rigid plastic case that helps stabilize the disk, which is how these disks can record at track and data densities greater than the 5 1/4-inch disks. A metal shutter protects the media-access hole. This shutter is manipulated by the drive and remains closed whenever the disk is out of a drive, which helps to insulate the media itself from the environment and your fingers. This shutter also eliminates the need for a disk jacket.

Instead of using an index hole, the 3 1/2-inch disks use a metal center hub with an alignment hole. This metal hub is grasped by the drive, and the hole in the hub allows the drive to position the disk properly.

On the lower left part of the disk is a hole with a plastic slider—the *write protect/enable hole*. When the slider is positioned so that the hole is visible, the drive is prevented from recording on the disk. When the slider is positioned to cover the hole, writing is enabled and you can record on the disk. More permanent write protection is available; some commercial software programs come on disks with the slider removed, which means that you cannot easily enable recording on that disk.

On the other side of the disk from the write-protect hole, you may find another hole in the jacket of the disk. This hole is the *media density selector hole*. If this hole is present, the disk is constructed of high-coercivity media and is therefore a high-density disk. The absence of this hole means that the disk is a double-density (low-coercivity) disk. Many modern 3 1/2-inch drives have a media sensor that controls recording capability based on the existence or absence of this hole.

Both the 3 1/2-inch and 5 1/4-inch disks actually are constructed of the same materials. Both types of disks use a plastic base (usually mylar) coated with a magnetic compound. The compound usually is an iron-oxide based compound for the standard density versions (standard density being single- or double-density); a cobalt compound usually is used in the high-coercivity (high-density) disks. The rigid jacket material of the 3 1/2-inch disks often causes people to believe incorrectly that these disks are some sort of "hard disk"—not really a floppy disk. But the actual disks themselves are just as floppy as the 5 1/4-inch variety.

Types and Specifications

In this section, you will examine all the types of disks you can purchase for your system. Of special interest are the technical specifications that can separate one type of disk from another. This section defines all the specifications used to describe a typical disk.

Soft- and Hard-Sectored Disks

Disks either are soft sectored or hard sectored. For the PC, soft-sectored disks have only one index hole on the disk surface. Once per revolution, this hole is visible through the hole in the protective jacket, and the drive, controller, and DOS use this hole to establish the location of the first sector on any track. Hard-sectored disks have a hole for each sector, and thus each hole marks the beginning of a new sector. If you try to use a hard-sectored disk in a PC, the system will get confused. Sometimes, hard-sectored disks are not specifically labeled as such, but they do specify 10 sectors or 16 sectors. Don't buy them.

Single- or Double-Sided Disks

Whether a disk is single sided or double sided is really an issue only for *lower density disks*. No single-sided high-density drives have ever been made, so no need has ever developed for disks to match those drives. The original IBM PC did have single-sided drives, but they were discontinued in 1982.

A single-sided disk is constructed of the same material as a double-sided disk. The only difference seems to be that the single-sided disks are "certified" only on one side, and the double-sided disks are certified on both sides. When disks are *certified*, the manufacturer states that some sort of test was performed on the disk to validate it and to ensure that the disk works as advertised. Unfortunately, this statement does not mean that your specific disk was tested—only a statistical sample of a large batch of disks. In my opinion, therefore, "certified" merely is a sales and marketing term rather than a term that has actual meaning for a single disk. Maybe another word for "certified" is "guaranteed" because a manufacturer who uses this label may not have tested your disk, but he or she probably will replace it if you say that the disk is bad.

Because the single-sided disks are less expensive than the double-sided versions, many PC users have determined that they can save money by using single-sided disks even in double-sided drives. And this procedure does work. Making some disks with recording surfaces on one side and other disks with recording surfaces on both sides is economically impractical for manufacturers, so today's "single-sided" disks look and usually behave exactly the same as double-sided disks. Therefore, depending on the brand of disks you buy, you generally can format and use successfully single-sided disks in double-sided drives—at substantial savings in disk costs.

Fortunately, this practice involves no real danger. The reason is that you must format each and every disk you use. When you format a disk, DOS determines whether bad sectors (sectors that cannot reliably hold information) are on it. If DOS finds any bad sectors, it tells you how many bytes are in bad sectors and seals off these places against any future attempts to put data there. Formatting really is your own "certification" of the disk. If a floppy disk that I format comes back with any bad sectors, I usually throw the disk away. For the cost, using a problem disk is not worth the risk to me. Because you have to certify your own disks anyway, why pay the disk manufacturers to do it as well?

Saving money by using single-sided disks is possible only with the lower density disks. High-density single-sided disks don't exist, and mixing densities and formats is absolutely not recommended. IBM never used the single-sided versions of the 3 1/2-inch drives, but Apple and other manufacturers did. Using the single-sided 3 1/2-inch disks in place of double-sided disks also is possible.

Density

Density, in simple terms, is a measure of the amount of information that can be packed reliably into a given area of a recording surface. The key word here is "reliably."

With disks, two types of "densities" exist: longitudinal density and linear density. *Longitudinal density* is indicated by how many tracks can be recorded on the disk. This type of density often is expressed as a number of tracks per inch (TPI). *Linear density* is the capability of an individual track to store data and often is indicated as a number of bits per inch (BPI). Unfortunately, both types of densities often are interchanged incorrectly when users discuss various disks and drives. Table 8.3 lists each of the disk types available.

Table 8.3
Disk Types

Media Types	Tracks per Inch (TPI)	Bits per Inch (BPI)	Coercivity (Oersteds)
5 1/4-inch			
Double density	48	5,876	300
Quad density	96	5,876	300
High density	96	9,646	600
3 1/2-inch			
Double density	135	8,717	300
High density	135	17,434	600

Note that the general name given to a particular media often does not indicate the true nature of the density. For example, the change from double density to quad density in the 5 1/4-inch disks really is a change in track density only, and the difference between quad density and high density is in the linear density of each track.

Note also that IBM completely skipped over the quad-density disk type. No IBM personal computer of any type ever has used a quad-density drive or required quad-density disks. You don't need to purchase such a disk unless you simply want a better quality double-density disk. A quad-density disk simply is a better double-density disk. Both the quad- and double-density disks store the same linear data on each track. Both types of disks use the same formula for the magnetic coating on the disk, but the quad-density versions represent a more tested, higher quality disk.

The high-density disks are entirely different. For the disk to store the increased linear density, an entirely different magnetic coating is required. High-coercivity coatings are used. In both the 5 1/4-inch and 3 1/2-inch high-density disks, this high-coercivity coating is used to allow the tremendous bit density for each track. A high-density disk never can be substituted for a double- or quad-density disk because the write current must be different for these different media formulations.

Coercivity

The coercivity specification of a disk refers to the magnetic field strength required to make a proper recording on the disk. Coercivity is measured in oersteds and is a value indicating magnetic strength. A disk with a higher coercivity rating requires a stronger magnetic field to make a recording on that disk. Lower ratings mean that the disk can be recorded with a weaker magnetic field. In other words, the lower the coercivity rating, the more sensitive the disk.

As mentioned earlier, when I ask people whether the high-density disks are more or less sensitive than the double-density disks, the answer almost always is *more* sensitive. But you now can see that this answer is not true. The high-density disks are half as sensitive as the double-density disks. A high-density drive can record with a much higher volume level at the heads than the standard double-density drive can. For these high-density drives to record properly on a double-density disk, the drive must be able to use a reduced write current mode and enable this whenever the lower density disks are installed.

Most AT system users cringe when they see the price of the high-density disks that their systems require. The same is true for the PS/2 system users and the high-density 3 1/2-inch disks. The temptation is simply to use the lower density disks as a substitute in an attempt to save money. Formatting a "regular" disk at the high-density capacity is foolish. This procedure is facilitated by DOS, which always attempts to format a disk to the maximum capacity of the drive unless you specifically order otherwise by using the proper parameters in the FORMAT command. If you use no parameters and simply type *format a:*, the disk is formatted as if it were a high-density disk. Many users think that this practice is somehow equivalent to the practice of using single-sided disks in place of double-sided disks, but they are wrong. Do not use double-density disks in place of high-density disks, or you will experience severe problems and data loss. Coercivity and write current are the reasons.

The reasons for using the high-coercivity disks are simple. When designing the high-density drives, engineers found that the density of magnetic flux reversals became such that the adjacent flux reversals began to affect each other. They started to cancel each other out or, through attraction and repulsion, caused each other to migrate on the disk. Any data written at these high densities simply began to erase itself over time!

An analogy can be constructed here. Suppose that you have a wooden track on which you place magnetic marbles evenly spaced at four inches apart. At this distance, the magnetic forces from each marble are too weak to affect the adjacent marbles. But suppose that the marbles are placed only two inches apart. The magnetic forces now may start to work on the adjacent marbles so that the marbles begin to move by themselves, possibly clumping together. Figure 8.6 illustrates this process.

Fig. 8.6.

The effect that adjacent magnetic domains can have on each other if magnets are too strong and too easily moved.

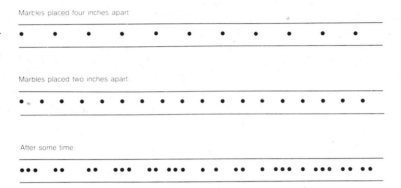

You can eliminate this migration and clumping if you simply make the marbles weaker. If the marbles are made half as strong as before, you can put the marbles twice as close together without any interaction between them. This concept is the whole idea behind the high-coercivity disks. They are weaker magnetically, which is the reason they need twice the recording strength for an image to be stored.

Try this simple experiment to verify this principle. Attempt to format a high-density disk with a double-density format. You will find that DOS comes back with an `Invalid media` or `Track 0 bad - disk unusable` message. This disk apparently will not take a recording in double-density mode because the double-density recording also is low volume. The disk cannot make a recording on the disk, so the message is displayed.

The opposite attempt appears to work, which is unfortunate for users, as you will learn shortly. You can format a standard double-density disk as if it were a high-density disk, and DOS does not seem to protest. You may notice a high number of bad sectors, but DOS allows the format to proceed to completion in any case.

This situation is unfortunate for two reasons. First, you are recording on this low-coercivity disk with a density that requires weak magnetic domains to eliminate interaction between the adjacent domains. A low-coercivity disk stores magnetic domains that are twice as strong as they should be, and over time, these domains will interact. You will experience mysterious data losses over the next few days, weeks, or months. Second, you're placing a recording on this disk at twice the signal strength it normally should be. This "industrial strength" recording may not be removable by any disk drive. The disk basically is destroyed. You will never be able to reformat the disk correctly as a double-density disk because any double-density reformat will be accomplished with reduced write current. The reduced write current may not be able to overwrite the high write current signal that was recorded incorrectly. The only possible way to remove this "burned in" recording is to use a bulk eraser, which renews the disk by removing all magnetic information. Or you can toss the disk into the trash.

Do not use the wrong media for the format you are attempting to perform. You must use the correct type of disk. You will not be able to get away with mixing densities like you could interchange single- and double-sided disks. Note that the 3 1/2-inch disks have a perfect mechanism for foiling the naive user—the media sensor. Make sure that all your high-density 3 1/2-inch drives contain this sensor and that it is set to function (through the use of a jumper or switch). This type of drive will set the write current and operating mode by the actual disk that is inserted; for example, you are prevented from attempting to cram 1.44M on a 720K disk. Remember that IBM does not use this sensor, so incorrectly formatting a disk is possible on the PS/2 systems.

Care and Feeding

You probably have been advised before that you can damage or destroy disks easily by doing the following:

- Touching the recording surface with your fingers or anything else

- Writing on a disk label with a ballpoint pen or pencil

- Bending the disk

- Spilling coffee, etc., on the disk

- Overheating a disk (by leaving it in the hot sun in your car, for example)

- Exposing your disk to stray magnetic fields

Actually, disks are hardy storage devices, and I honestly can say that I never have destroyed a disk by writing on it with a pen. And touching a disk does not ruin it but, instead, gets the disk and your drive head dirty with oil and dust. The real danger to your disks comes from magnetic fields, which can be found in places you never dreamed of.

For example, many color monitors (and all color television sets) have a degaussing coil around the face of the tube. This coil is used to demagnetize the shadow mask inside when the monitor is turned on. The coil is connected directly to the AC line and is controlled by a thermistor, which passes a gigantic surge of juice and then tapers off to nothing as it warms up.

For a demonstration, put the color monitor right next to your monochrome display. When you turn on the monitor, the monochrome display makes a ''boing'' sound and then steadies down.

If you keep your disks anywhere near (within a foot of) the front of the color monitor, your disks are exposed to a shot of AC magnetic field every time you turn on the monitor. This exposure isn't a good idea, because the field is designed to demagnetize things. The effect is cumulative and, unfortunately, irreversible.

Another major offender is the telephone. The ringer in a typical phone uses a powerful electromagnet to move the striker into the bell. The ringer circuit is about 90 volts, and sufficient power is in these electromagnetic fields to degauss any disks laying on the desk next to or partially underneath the phone. Keep the disks away from your telephone.

Popular Myths

Myths always seem to be associated with things people cannot see, and you certainly cannot see data as it is stored on a disk. This section dispels a couple of myths associated with disks.

X-ray Machines

One of my favorite myths to dispel is the one about how airport X-ray machines will damage your disks. I have a great deal of experience in this area because I have traveled around the country for the past six years with disks and portable computers in hand. I currently fly about 150,000 miles per year, and my equipment and disks have been through X-ray machines more than 100 times each year. I find that most people commit a fatal mistake when approaching the X-ray machines in an airport with disks or computers. People don't pass the disks and computers through.

An X ray is only a form of light, and your disks and computers will not be affected by this light. What damages your materials is the metal detector! I have seen this scenario time and time again: A person with magnetic media or a portable computer approaches the security check. The person becomes tense and then says, "Oh, no, I have disks and a computer! They must be hand inspected." Then the person refuses to place the disks and computer on the X-ray belt and either foolishly walks through the metal detector, disks and computer in hand, or passes the items to the security guard, handing them over in close proximity to the metal detector. Metal detectors make excellent degaussing coils! The X-ray machine is the *safest* place for you to pass your disks or computer.

Some of you may worry about the effect of X-ray radiation on the EPROM (Erasable Programmable Read-Only Memory) in your systems. Don't worry. EPROMs are erased by direct exposure to intense ultraviolet light. Specifically, an EPROM requires exposure to a 12,000 μw/cm^2 ultraviolet light source at a wavelength of 2,537 Angstroms for a time period of 15 to 20 minutes and at a distance of 1 inch. The airport X-ray machine is off by a factor of 1 to 10 thousand in wavelength and is nowhere near the strength, duration, or distance required for erasure. Be aware that virtually every manufacturer of circuit boards will x-ray those boards (with components installed) during inspection and to ensure quality control.

I have conducted unscientific tests. I had one disk that I used as my boot disk (before hard disk) and passed the same disk through the X-ray machines in various airports for two years, averaging two to three passes a week. The same disk still boots any system and has never been reformatted. I have several portables with hard disks installed, and one has been through the X-ray machine every week for more than two years. I prefer to pass the machinery through the X-ray machine because it offers the best shielding from the magnetic fields produced by the metal detector. Besides, if you place your computer system on the belt and walk through fast enough, you can peek at the screen as your system comes through and see what the inside really looks like.

Static Electricity

Static electricity is blamed for a wide variety of computer ills. I do know that static can be a real problem, particularly in the dry western states, but the personal computer is a fairly hardy device. And I do not find that static causes *all* the problems it is blamed for. However, I am certainly more aware of controlling static discharge while working on the inside of a system or especially while working on boards or components that are removed from the system. Before handling the interior of the system, for example, a good idea is to equalize your body's electrical potential to that of the PC by touching the power supply first.

Installing Floppy Disk Drives

The actual procedure for installing floppy drives is simple. You install the drive in two basic phases. The first phase is to configure the drive for the installation, and the second phase is to actually perform the physical installation. Of these two steps, the first one usually is the most difficult to perform, depending on your knowledge of disk interfacing and access to the correct OEM manuals.

Drive Configuration

Configuring a floppy drive consists of setting the various jumpers and switches mounted on the drive to match the system in which the drive is to be installed, as well as tailoring the function of the drive to that desired by the installer. Each drive has a stable of these jumpers and switches, and many drives are different from each other. You will find no standards for just what these jumpers and switches should be called, where they should be located, or how they should be implemented. To set up a specific drive correctly, you must have information from the manufacturer of the drive to know all the options. This information can be found in an Original Equipment Manufacturers (OEM) manual. I think that this manual is a "must have" item when purchasing any disk drive.

Although additional options may be available, most drives have certain configuration features that must be set for any installation. Here are the standard options that typically need attention during an installation procedure:

- Drive-select jumper

- Terminating resistor

- Diskette changeline/ready jumper

- Media-sensor jumper

Floppy drives are connected by a cabling system called a *daisy chain*. The name is descriptive because the cable strings from controller to drive to drive in a chain. All drives have a drive-select (sometimes called DS) jumper that must be set to indicate the physical drive number a particular drive will be. Where the drive is connected on the cable does not matter; the DS jumper indicates how the drive is to respond. Most drives allow four settings, but the controllers used in all PC systems support only two on a single cable. The PC and XT floppy controllers, for example, support four drives but only on two separate cables—each a daisy chain with two drives maximum.

Each drive on a particular cable must be set to have unique drive-select settings. A normal configuration is to set to the first drive-select position the drive you want to respond as the first drive (A:). Set to the second drive-select position the drive you want to be B:. On some drives, the DS jumper positions are labeled 0, 1, 2, and 3, and other drives use the numbers 1, 2, 3, and 4 to indicate the same positions. For some drives, then, a setting of DS0 is drive A; but for others, DS1 indicates drive A. Likewise, some drives use a setting of DS1 for drive B, but others use a setting of DS2 to indicate drive B. On many drives, the actual jumpers on the drive circuit board are completely unlabeled. You must consult the drive's manual to find out which jumpers are for which settings.

A typical daisy-chain drive cable is connected as shown in figure 8.7.

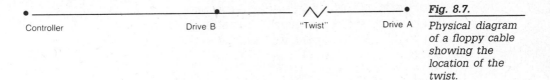

Controller   Drive B   "Twist"   Drive A

Fig. 8.7.

Physical diagram of a floppy cable showing the location of the twist.

Make sure that the DS settings for each drive on a single cable are different, or you will have both drives responding to the same signals. If you have incorrect DS settings, both drives will respond simultaneously or neither drive will respond at all.

One item that can confuse the drive-select configuration is the type of cable you use. IBM puts a special twist in its cables that forces the appearance that both drives have the same DS settings. An IBM floppy cable is a 34-pin cable with lines 10 through 16 sliced out and cross-wired (twisted). This twisting basically cross-wires the first and second drive-select and motor-enable signals, causing the DS setting of the drive following the twist to be inverted. IBM does this procedure so that all the drives in an IBM system, whether A: or B:, are jumpered the same way, which simplifies installation and configuration because both floppies can be preset by IBM so that your attention to this matter isn't necessary.

If you buy drives from the aftermarket (which is definitely recommended), however, you must know about this special twist. Drives installed on this cable will be set to the second drive-select position, which is DS1 or DS2 on most drives. Many compatibles have duplicated IBM in this respect, so watch for the twisted cables when installing drives in any system. All IBM systems use the cable twist to modify the DS settings of the first drive. The twist always appears between the two drives in the daisy chain cable—never between the controller and drive.

A terminating resistor must be placed (or activated) in the drive plugged into the cable that is the farthest away from the controller. The function of this resistor is to prevent electrical echo on the signal cable. All drives come with this resistor installed. The terminating resistor must be disabled for any drives that are not the farthest away from the controller.

In a typical cabling arrangement for two floppies, for example, drive A (which is actually at the end of the cable) has the terminating resistor installed, and all other floppy drives on the same cable (namely B:) have this resistor removed. Which letter the drive responds to really is not important; what *is* important is that the drive at the end of the cable has this resistor installed and functioning and that all other drives on the same cable have this resistor removed.

The terminating resistor usually looks like a memory chip; but it may be white, blue, black, gray, or some other color, and memory chips usually are just black. IBM always labels this device with a sticker that says "T-RES" so the resistor can be identified easily. On some systems, the resistor is a built-in device that is enabled or disabled with a jumper. If you have the removable type, be sure to store the resistor in a safe place because you may need it later.

Table 8.4 explains how a drive should be configured with the drive-select jumper and terminating resistor. You can use this table as a universal drive-select and terminating-resistor configuration chart. It applies to all types of drives, including floppy disk drives and hard disks.

Table 8.4
Configuring Drive-Select Jumpers and Terminating Resistors

Drive	Twisted Cable	Straight Cable
Drive A or C (end of cable)	DS = 2nd TR installed	DS = 1st TR installed
Drive B or D (center of cable)	DS = 2nd TR removed	DS = 2nd TR removed

DS stands for drive-select jumper; TR stands for terminating resistor.

The assumption in table 8.4 is that you always plug drive B into the center connector on the cable and always plug drive A into the end connector. This arrangement may seem strange at first, but it really is required if you ever put together a single-drive system. The lowest physical drive must be the end or last drive on the cable. The twist in the cable always will be between the two drive connectors on a cable and not between the controller and a drive.

Two other options may be available for you to set: the status of pin 34 of the drive's connector and the function of a media-sensor feature. The guidelines for setting these options follow.

If the drive is a 360K drive, set the status of pin 34 to open regardless of the type of system in which the drive is being installed. If the drive is not a 360K drive and is going into an AT, set pin 34 to act as a Diskette Changeline signal. For all PC and XT types of systems, set all drives to the open condition on pin 34. The Standard Ready setting is never correct for pin 34; always use an Open or a Diskette Changeline setting.

Only 1.44M drives have the media sensor. Set these drives so that the sensor controls the drive's density mode and, therefore, the drive's write current as well.

Physical Installation

Physically *installing* a drive is actually plugging in the drive. This procedure is explained in Chapter 6, "System Teardown and Inspection." Here, the concerns are using the correct brackets and screws for the system and the correct drive that is being installed.

A special bracket usually is required whenever you're installing a half-height drive in place of an earlier full-height unit. These brackets present a set of holes for the top drive to plug into; the lower set of holes are for the bottom drive. Remember, also, that nearly all floppy drives today use metric hardware, but all the early American-manufactured drives used the standard English threads.

Make sure that the power cable is installed properly. This cable is keyed so that it cannot be plugged in backward. Also install the data and control cable. If no key is in this cable that allows only a correct orientation, use the odd-colored wire in the cable as a guide to the position of pin 1. This position mates with the drive correctly when you plug in the cable so that the odd-colored wire is plugged into the connector toward the notch in the board.

Repairing Floppy Drives

Attitudes about repairing floppy drives have changed over the years. The major reason is the decreasing costs of drives themselves. When drives were more expensive, people often considered repairing them rather than replacing the entire drive. But with the cost of drives decreasing each year, certain repair procedures that are labor or parts intensive actually have become almost as expensive as replacing the drive with a new one.

Because of the cost considerations, repairing floppy drives usually is limited to cleaning the drive and heads and lubricating any of the mechanical mechanisms. On drives that have a speed adjustment, adjusting the speed to be within the proper operating range is also common. Note that most of the newer half-height drives do not have any adjustment for speed. These drives use a circuit that automatically sets the speed at the required level and compensates for variations with a feedback loop. If such an autotaching drive is off in speed, the reason usually is that this circuit failed. Replacement of the drive usually is necessary.

Cleaning

Cleaning a drive is simple. You can proceed in two ways. One method is to use one of the simple head-cleaning disks that are available at any computer supply store. These devices are simple to operate and don't require that the system unit be opened for access to the drive itself. The other method is the manual method; you use a cleaning swab with a liquid such as pure alcohol or freon. This method requires that you open the system unit to expose the drive and, in many cases (especially with the earlier full-height drives), also requires that you remove and partially disassemble the drive itself. The manual method can result in a better job, but often the work required is not worth the difference.

The cleaning disks come in two basic styles: those using a liquid that is squirted onto the disk as the cleaning agent and others that are totally dry and rely on the abrasive material on the cleaning disk. I recommend that you never use the dry cleaning-disk systems. Always use a wet system with which the alcohol or freon solutions are applied to the cleaning disk. The dry disks actually can damage the heads if used improperly or too often, but the wet systems are safe to use.

The manual method requires that you gain access to the heads themselves, to swab them off manually with a lint-free foam swab soaked in the alcohol or freon solution. This method requires some level of expertise from the person doing the cleaning, because simply jabbing at the heads incorrectly with a cleaning stick may knock the drive heads out of alignment. You must carefully use an in-and-out motion, lightly swabbing off the heads. No side-to-side motion (relative to the way the heads travel) should be used; this motion can snag a head and knock it out of alignment. The manual method does make easier the process of properly cleaning the other areas of dirt collection inside the drive, which results perhaps in a more thorough job than the cleaning disk can accomplish.

For most users, though, I do recommend the wet cleaning-disk method because it is the easiest and safest method to use.

How often should you clean a disk drive? Only you can really answer that question. What type of environment is the system in? Does heavy cigarette smoking occur around the system? If so, cleaning will be required more often. Usually, a safe rule of thumb is to clean drives about once a year in clean office environments where no smoke or other particulate matter is in the air. In a heavy-smoking environment, cleaning may need to be stepped up to every six months or perhaps even sooner. In really dirty industrial environments, cleaning may have to be done every month or so. Your own experience will have to be your guide in this matter. If the system is experiencing drive errors reported by DOS with the familiar Abort, Retry, Ignore prompts, you should clean your drive to see whether that solves the problem. If cleaning does solve your problem, you probably should step up the interval for preventive-maintenance cleaning of the drives.

In some cases, you may want to place a small amount (a *very* small amount) of lubricant on the door mechanism or other mechanical contact points inside the drive. Do not use oil! Use a pure silicone lubricant. Oil collects dust quite rapidly after it is applied and usually causes the oiled mechanism to gum up later. Silicone does not attract dust in the same manner and can be used safely. Use very small amounts of silicone; do not drip or spray silicone inside the drive. Basically, you must ensure that the lubricant goes only on the part that needs it. If you get the lubricant all over the inside of the drive, the lubricant may be difficult to remove later.

Speed Adjustment

Most earlier disk drives, especially the full-height drives, have a small variable resistor that is used to adjust the rotational speed of the drive. In particular, the Tandon and CDC full-height drives used by IBM in the PC and XT systems have this adjustment. The location of the variable resistor is described in the hardware maintenance reference manuals that IBM sells for these systems.

If you have the Tandon drive, the adjustment is made through a small brass screw on a variable resistor that is mounted on the motor control board, which is attached to the rear of the drive (see fig. 8.8). This resistor is usually blue, and the screw itself is brass. To gauge the speed, you can use a program such as the IBM advanced diagnostics, which is supplied with the hardware maintenance and service manual; the DYSAN disk Interrogator; or a purely mechanical method, which relies on a fluorescent light to act as a strobe.

Fig. 8.8.

Drive speed adjustment for Tandon TM-100 series drive.

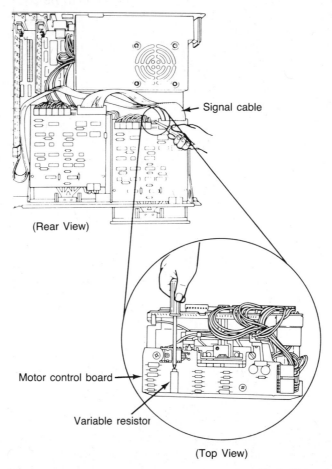

(Rear View)

Signal cable

Motor control board

Variable resistor

(Top View)

Used with permission from IBM Corporation.

The software methods use a disk to evaluate the running speed of the drive. Usually, you turn the screw until the speed reads correctly according to the program you use. This speed would be 300 rpm. The mechanical method requires that you remove the drive from the system and place it upside down on a bench. Sometimes, the drive is set sideways on the power supply so that the case of the drive is grounded. Then the underside of the drive is illuminated with a standard fluorescent light. These lights act as a strobe that flashes 60 times per second due to the cycling speed of the AC line current. On the bottom of the drive spindle are strobe marks for 50 Hz and 60 Hz (see fig. 8.9). In the United States, 60 Hz power is used, so those marks should be used. The 50 Hz marks are for European power, which is 50 cycle. While the drive is running, you turn the small screw until the strobe marks appear to be stationary, much like the "wagon wheel effect" you see in old western movies. When these marks are completely stationary as viewed under the light, the speed of the drive's rotation is correct.

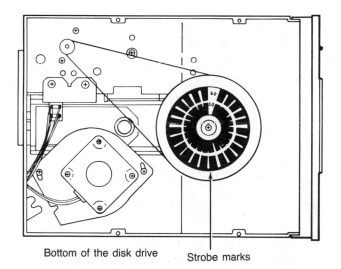

Bottom of the disk drive   Strobe marks

Fig. 8.9.

Bottom view of disk drive showing speed adjustment strobe marks.

Used with permission from IBM Corporation.

With CDC drives, the adjustment resistor is mounted on the logic board, which is on top of the drive. The small brass screw to the left of this board is the one you want. Other drives may have an adjustment also. The best way to tell whether a drive has an adjustment for speed is to look for the telltale strobe marks on the spindle of the drive. If the marks are there, the drive probably has an adjustment; if the marks are not there, the drive probably has an automatic speed circuit and requires no adjustment. The OEM manual for the drive will have the information for any of these adjustments and for where they will be made, if at all.

Alignment

Aligning disk drives is usually no longer done because of the high relative cost. To align a drive properly requires access to an oscilloscope ($500), a special Analog Alignment disk ($75), and the OEM service manual for the drive, as well as about a half hour to an hour of time. Needless to say, with the price of most types of floppy drives hovering at or below the $100 mark, aligning drives is not always a cost-justifiable alternative to replacement. One exception exists. In a high-volume situation, doing drive alignments may pay off. Another alternative is to investigate local organizations that perform drive alignments as a service. These organizations usually charge $25 to $50 for an alignment. Weigh this cost against the replacement costs and age of the drive. I actually have purchased new 360K floppy drives for $30, but I usually pay $75. At these prices, I no longer consider alignment a viable option.

Chapter Summary

In this chapter, you examined floppy drives and floppy media (disks) in great detail. One of the most important things for you to do when you're installing a drive into any system is to ensure that the drive is configured correctly. This chapter covered drive configuration in detail. With this information, the process of installing drives correctly should now be easy!

You also examined many of the problems that confound floppy drive users, such as the problems in reading and writing double-density disks with high-density drives. This chapter gave a thorough discussion of the differences between high- and double-density drives and disks, and the consequences of using the wrong type of disk in the wrong drive were mentioned. Simple drive servicing such as cleaning and speed adjustment were explained so that these operations can be performed in-house. After reading this chapter, you now know a great deal about floppy drives. The next chapter discusses hard disk drives in great detail.

9

Hard Disk Drives

To most users, the hard disk drive is the most important yet most mysterious part of the computer system. A *hard disk drive* is a sealed unit that holds all the data in a system. When the hard disk fails, the results are almost never inconsequential. To maintain, service, and expand your system properly, you must fully understand the hard disk unit. Knowing exactly how your hard disk functions is important because you will gain knowledge about maintaining your system, purchasing new units or replacement units, and repairing failing units.

In my seminars, I have found that computer users have an amazing interest in these units, and they want to know what to do when a problem occurs. Very little has been published on this subject that a PC manager or user can rely on. Most so-called "hard disk" books really are thinly disguised DOS books. And nowhere—until now—could users find a "nuts and bolts" book on the subject that really spells out just what kinds of drives are available, how they are installed, how the interfaces work, how the drive is set up to be recognized by the system, and what to do when problems occur. This chapter changes the situation. I have collected a wealth of information and experience on the subject, and I give this information and experience to you in this chapter.

You will take a thorough look at the hard disk, from the drives themselves to the cables and controllers that run them. In particular, you will look in detail at the construction and operation of a hard disk drive as well as at some of the various types of units that are available. You will learn about the various disk interfaces that you can select and the faults and merits of working with each one. And the procedures for configuring, setting up, and installing various drives are discussed. You will see just how a drive can be integrated into a system with some basic procedures.

Examining the Background of the Hard Disk

One advantage of working with IBM personal computer systems and compatibles is that IBM always has relied on industry-standard devices for PC and PS/2 peripherals. The compatibles, of course, have copied this wise plan. Therefore, you can take virtually any disk drive "off the shelf," plug it in, and go. This "plug and play" capability is exactly the reason that you can find affordable hard disk storage and a wide variety of options in capacities and speed for the IBM types of systems. If IBM had designed and used a proprietary disk interface, the market would be different today. Apple Computer, Inc., does not use standards, so the disk drives and peripherals for Apple systems always outprice the IBM systems, which is perhaps the primary reason that business users largely stay away from Apple systems. With IBM systems, you can use "raw" drives and interface them to the system by using commonly available tools and software. This capability gives you the flexibility in systems configurations that you enjoy today.

The term *hard disk* comes from the way these disks are constructed: from rigid platters of metal—usually aluminum. Unlike those in floppy disk drives, these platters cannot bend or flex at all. In most drives, these platters cannot be removed, and IBM calls these platters "fixed disk drives" for this reason. Removable platter hard disk drives actually have been available, but these drives were largely unreliable, expensive, and nonstandard.

One term associated with hard disks is "Winchester." Hard drives often are called Winchester drives. This term dates back to the 1960s. During that time, IBM developed a high-speed hard disk drive with 30 megabytes of fixed platter storage and 30 megabytes of removable platter storage. The drive had platters that spun at high speed and heads that were designed to float over the platters while they were spinning. This drive became known as the 30-30 drive and soon gained the nickname "Winchester" after the famous Winchester 30-30 rifle. After that time, all drives using a high-speed spinning platter with a floating head also became known as Winchester drives. The term has no real technological or actual meaning and is now used simply as a direct synonym for *hard disk*.

Examining Hard Disk Construction and Operation

Now you will examine the physical construction and components that make up the commercially available hard disk drives on today's market. Then you will examine just how these units operate and function.

Drive Components

A hard disk drive is made up of several physical components (see fig. 9.1). All drives share certain components, which makes this discussion applicable to just about every drive on the market. Some differences do exist in the actual implementations of these components, as well as in the quality of materials used. All hard disk drives share the following components:

- Disk platters
- Read/write head
- Head actuator
- Spindle motor
- Logic board
- Configuration items
- Connector
- Bezel

Fig. 9.1.

Drive components.

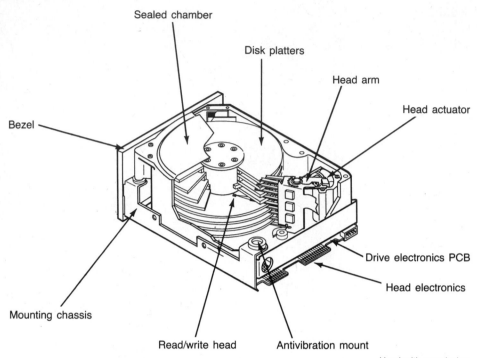

Sealed chamber

Disk platters

Head arm

Head actuator

Bezel

Drive electronics PCB

Head electronics

Mounting chassis

Read/write head

Antivibration mount

Used with permission
from IBM Corporation.

The platters, spindle motor, heads, and head actuator mechanisms usually are contained in a sealed chamber called the Head Disk Assembly (HDA). The HDA usually is treated as a single component because it is rarely opened. The other parts, which are external to the drive, can be disassembled from the drive itself; these parts include the logic boards, bezel, and any other configuration or mounting hardware.

Disk Platters

A typical hard disk has one or more platters or disks that usually are found in two diameters, much like floppy drives. The most common types of disks are those with 5 1/4-inch or 3 1/2-inch platters. Drives with 8-inch or even 14-inch platters are available, but these expensive high-capacity drives typically have not been associated with PC systems. Also, drive formats that are physically smaller than 3 1/2 inches have been developed, but these platters are not yet popular with manufacturers.

When you're considering a hard disk, remember that disk size is rarely as important a factor as it is when you're considering a floppy drive. Hard disk platters usually are "fixed," or nonremovable, so interchanging platters among different drives is out of the question. What matters physically are the dimensions of the drive's exterior including any chassis or mounting components. Most of the 3 1/2-inch drives are even available in a 5 1/4-inch type of chassis so that you easily can install the drives in a system originally designed to support 5 1/4-inch drives. The most important physical information about a particular drive, then, is not necessarily the size of the internal platters but the external form factor. Three sizes of drives basically are available for PC types of systems:

- 5 1/4-inch full-height

- 5 1/4-inch half-height

- 3 1/2-inch half-height

Most of the 5 1/4-inch drives do use the 5 1/4-inch platters, but some are repackaged 3 1/2-inch drives in a larger frame. All the 3 1/2-inch form-factor drives must have 3 1/2-inch or smaller platters. An important part of the form-factor issue is that the exterior dimensions of the 5 1/4-inch full-height, 5 1/4-inch half-height, and 3 1/2-inch half-height drives are exactly the same as the dimensions for the floppy drives of those physical sizes, which allows system builders to offer flexible configurations with different numbers of floppy or hard disks depending on the user requirements.

As mentioned previously, each platter is made of a rigid metal— usually aluminum for light weight. Both the 5 1/4-inch and 3 1/2-inch platters are usually 1/8-inch thick. The platters are coated with a magnetically retentive substance or *media*, which is actually responsible for storing information. Two popular media are used for hard disk platters: oxide media and thin film media.

Most earlier drives use oxide media on the drive platters. Oxide media is popular because it is inexpensive and easy to apply. Oxide media has a long history and is a mature technology. The procedure for creating storage media has been used since 1955. Many drive vendors still use oxide media for many of their drives, and oxide still is used in some fairly high-end drives.

Oxide media is made of various compounds containing iron oxide as the "active" ingredient. A magnetic layer is created by a process where the aluminum platter is coated with a paste containing iron oxide particles. Spinning the platters at a high speed evenly spreads this media across the disk. The material flows from the center of the platter to the outside because of centrifugal force, which allows an even coating of material to be placed on the drive, with few imperfections. The surface is then cured and polished. Then a protective layer is added and burnished smooth. Normally, this media is about 30 millionths of an inch thick. If you could peer into a drive with oxide-media-coated platters, you would see that they are brown or amber.

As drive densities increase, the media needs to be thinner and more perfectly formed. The capabilities of oxide coatings have been exceeded by the newest generations of high-capacity drives. Developing these newer drives required a new media that is very thin and well formed to allow for lower head recording height, which allows the increases in density to be possible. In most high-end drive systems, you will find plated media rather than the oxide coatings of the past.

Thin film media is aptly named because the thickness of the media is much less than can be achieved by the normal coating method. Thin film media also is known as "plated" or "sputtered" media. These names reflect the processes of getting this thin film of media on the platters.

Plated media is manufactured by a process of placing the media material on the disk with an electroplating mechanism, much like chrome plating on the bumper of your car. The aluminum substrates (platters) are immersed in a series of chemical baths that coat the substrate with layers of metallic film. The final layer is about 3 millionths of an inch of a cobalt alloy that is the actual media itself.

Sputtering is the name of a special procedure in which magnetic media is deposited on the platters in a near vacuum. Thin film sputtered disks are created by a process of first coating the aluminum platters with a layer of nickel phosphorus and then applying the cobalt alloy magnetic material by a continuous vacuum deposition process called sputtering. During this process, magnetic layers as thin as 2 millionths of an inch are deposited on the disk similar to the way wafers are coated with metallic films in the semiconductor industry. The sputtering technique is then used to lay down an extremely hard 1-microinch protective carbon coating. The platters usually are electrically charged to attract the media particles as they are vaporized. This process is the most expensive because the requirements of a near perfect vacuum are difficult to meet.

The surfaces of sputtered platters contain magnetic layers as thin as 2 millionths of an inch. The surface is also very smooth, thus allowing the head to fly close to the disk surface. With the head closer, the density of the magnetic field can be increased to provide greater storage capacity. The head can fly over the surface as closely as 6 to 8 millionths of an inch. Additionally, the increased intensity of the magnetic field provides the higher signal amplitudes needed for good signal-to-noise performance.

Both the sputtering and plating processes result in a thin, hard film of media on the platters. One benefit of the plated media is that because it is so hard, the likelihood of surviving contact with the heads at high speed is increased. The older oxide coatings are scratched more easily. Because the thin film media can handle much greater densities with accuracy, you will find this media on most larger capacity drives as well as on many of the newer 3 1/2-inch platter drives. If you could open a drive to peek at the platters, the thin film platters would look like the surface of a mirror: chrome plated and highly polished.

Sputtering results in the most perfect, thinnest, and hardest disk surface that can be commercially obtained today. It is now used in the majority of thin film media equipped drives. This translates into increased storage capacity in a smaller area, fewer head crashes, and a drive that will give you many years of trouble-free use.

Most hard drives have several platters, although some of the smaller half-height drives have only one. How many platters the drive has is limited by the drive's physical size. So far, the maximum number of platters for the 5 1/4-inch full-height drives is 8, and the half-height 5 1/4-inch and 3 1/2-inch drives have a maximum of 5 platters.

Read/Write Heads

A hard disk drive usually has one read/write head for each platter side, which gives a usual range of 2 to 16 heads for any drives. The multiple heads are all connected or "ganged" together on a single movement mechanism. All the heads, therefore, move in unison across the platters (see fig. 9.2).

The mechanical aspects of the heads are quite simple. Each head is on an arm that is spring-loaded to force the heads into the platters.

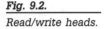

Fig. 9.2.

Read/write heads.

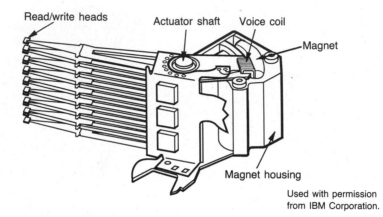

Used with permission from IBM Corporation.

Each platter is "squeezed" by the two heads above and below it. If you could open a drive and pick up the head with your finger, the head would snap back into the platter when released.

At rest, the heads sit on the platter, but when the drive is spinning at full speed, air pressure develops underneath the head and lifts it up off of the platter's surface. The gap between the heads and the platter on a drive that is spinning fully is between 10 and 20 millionths of an inch! The small size of this gap is the reason that you must never open the disk drive's Head Disk Assembly (HDA). Any particle of dust or dirt that gets into this mechanism can cause the heads to read improperly or, worse, cause the heads to oscillate and strike the platters while at full speed. This occurrence is called a head crash and may damage (scratch) the platter and possibly the head as well.

So that the interior of the drive will be clean, the HDA is assembled in a class-100 or better clean room, meaning that a cubic foot of air cannot contain more than 100 0.5-micron particles. One person breathing while standing motionless breathes out 500 such particles in a single minute. These rooms contain special air filtration systems that continuously evacuate and refresh the air. A drive's HDA must not be opened unless it is inside such a room. Because these environments are excessively expensive, few companies (except those who manufacture the drives) are prepared to service hard disk drives.

Two types of heads are used in the modern hard disk drive:

- Composite ferrite heads
- Thin film heads

The composite ferrite heads are the traditional type of magnetic head design. This type of head uses an iron oxide core with electromagnetic coils wrapping it. A magnetic field is produced when the coils are energized, and a field also is induced when a magnetic field is passed near the coils. This gives the heads full read and write capability. These heads are larger and heavier than the thin film heads and must use a larger flying height to record on the disk. These heads are relatively inexpensive to produce and are plentiful.

The thin film heads actually are a specially produced semiconductor chip. These heads are really a complex circuit in and of themselves. They are produced by the same procedure as any semiconductor chip, with one exception: the shape here is critical. The heads must have a U-shaped groove in the bottom to allow air pressure buildup. These heads are lightweight and can fly at a much lower height than the composite types of heads. Flying height has been reduced to as little as 6 millionths of an inch in some designs. This reduced height allows for a much stronger signal to be picked up and transmitted between the head and platters, which increases the signal-to-noise ratio, which improves accuracy. At the high track and linear densities in some drives, a standard composite head cannot pick out the data signal from the background noise. Most of the highest capacity drives today use the thin film heads to achieve their tremendous densities.

Air Filters

Hard disk drives do have air filters, but they are not changeable. The reason is that the filters really never get dirty. A hard disk is a permanently sealed unit and as such is not comparable to many mainframe hard disk drives. These mainframe drives circulate air from outside the drive through a filter that must be changed periodically.

A PC type of hard disk does not circulate any air; the filter inside the unit is designed only to filter the small particles of media that are scraped off the platters during head takeoff and landing or any metal flakes or small particles that may dislodge inside the drive itself. Because hard disk drives are permanently sealed and do not circulate any outside air, they can run in extremely dirty environments. Airborne particulates such as cigarette smoke do not affect a hard disk drive. However, many other components in the system, such as floppy drives, keyboards, and any connectors or sockets in the system, will sustain damage from cigarette smoke.

The only way that air does get into or out of a hard disk is from a change in atmospheric pressure. All drives have a pressure-equalization system with a filtered port to bleed air into or out of the HDA as necessary (see fig. 9.3). Little air moves across this barrier, and the filter is a submicron type of permanent filter that cannot be changed.

Head Actuators

Perhaps much more important than the heads themselves is the mechanical system that moves the heads—the *head actuator*. This mechanism moves the heads across the disk and positions them accurately over the desired cylinder. Many variations of head actuator mechanisms are used today, but they all are categorized as two different types:

- Stepper Motor Actuators
- Voice Coil Actuators

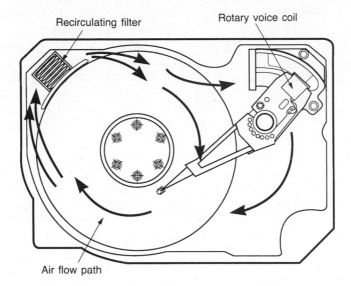

Recirculating filter

Rotary voice coil

Air flow path

Used with permission
from IBM Corporation.

Fig. 9.3.

*Pressure
equalization
system.*

The use of one or the other type of positioner has profound effects
on the drive's performance. The effect is not limited to speed; it
includes accuracy, sensitivity to temperature, position, vibration, and
overall reliability. Any drive equipped with a stepper motor actuator
is much less reliable (by a factor of 5 to 10 or more) than any voice
coil actuator drive. And because the failure of a drive to read and
write data reliably directly affects you, you need to know more about
this subject.

The head actuator simply is the most important single specification
in the drive. Knowing which head actuator mechanism is in a drive
tells you all about the drive's performance and reliability
characteristics.

Here is a chart that shows the two types of hard disk drive head
actuators and the performance parameters affected:

Performance Parameter	Stepper Motor	Voice Coil
Relative speed	Slow	Fast
Temperature sensitive	Yes (Very)	No
Positionally sensitive	Yes	No
Automatic head parking	No	Yes
Preventive maintenance	Periodic	None required
Reliability	Poor	Excellent
Relative cost	Inexpensive	Expensive

All floppy disk drives position their heads by using a stepper motor actuator. The accuracy of the stepper mechanism is suited to a floppy drive where the track densities usually are nowhere near that of a hard disk. However, all the cheaper, low-capacity hard disks also use a stepper motor system. All hard disks with a capacity of more than 100M are voice coil; no stepper motor drives are in that capacity range. But for hard disk drives with less than a 100M capacity, usually both stepper motor and voice coil drives are available for a given capacity and physical form factor. The cost differential between equal-capacity voice coil drives and stepper motor drives is only about 30 percent to 50 percent, which means that if you can purchase a 40M stepper motor hard disk for $400, a 40M voice coil unit will cost $500 to $600. This 30- to 50-percent rule usually holds true, but not always. For example, I have found new 80M voice coil drives available for the same price as new 40M steppers. Where you shop makes a difference.

The industry seems to have classified the stepper motor units as XT types of hard disks, and the voice coil units have been called AT types of units. This classification is totally arbitrary and has no actual meaning other than perhaps a reference to the drives' speed and cost. The owner of an AT seemingly will pay more for a drive that is faster because the faster drive will more closely match the potential of the faster system. You can, however, put any type of drive into any type of system; "AT types" or "XT types" of drives don't really exist.

Stepper Motor Actuators

A *stepper motor* is an electrical motor that can "step" or move from position to position with mechanical detents. These motors feel like they're clicking or buzzing if you grip the spindle of one and spin it by hand. The feel is much like that of many volume controls on stereo systems. A stepper motor cannot position itself between step positions; instead, it must stop at one of the predetermined detent positions. These motors are physically small—about 1 to 3 inches—and can be square, round cylindrical, or even round like a flat pancake. These motors usually are outside the sealed HDA, although the spindle of the motor penetrates the HDA through a sealed hole. You can find stepper motors in one of the four corners of a hard disk drive that uses them, and the motors usually are easily visible from the exterior of the drive.

The stepper motor is mechanically linked to the head rack by either a split steel band coiled around the motor spindle or a rack and pinion gear mechanism. As the motor steps, each detent or click stop position translates to the movement of one track through the mechanical linkage. Some systems may use several motor steps for each track. So in positioning the heads, the drive is commanded to move to track 400, and the motor begins the stepping motion and proceeds to the 400th detent position and stop. The heads then are over the desired cylinder.

Stepper motor mechanisms are affected by a variety of problems. The biggest problem is one of temperature. As the drive platters heat and cool, they expand and contract, which causes the tracks to move in relation to some predetermined track position. The stepper mechanism cannot move in increments of less than a single track to correct for these temperature-induced errors. What happens is that the drive blindly positions the heads to a particular cylinder according to a predetermined number of steps from the stepper motor. When the drive is low-level formatted, the initial track and sector marks are placed on the platters at whatever positions the heads are at as commanded by the stepper motor. If all subsequent reading and writing occur at the same temperature as the initial format, the heads always record precisely within the track and sector boundaries.

But at different temperatures, the actual head position does not match the track position. When the platters are cold, the heads miss the track location, because the platters actually have shrunk and the tracks have moved inward toward the center of the disk. When the platters are warmer than the formatted temperature, the platters grow larger and the actual track positions are located outward from where the heads end up being located. Gradually, as the drive is used over time, the data is written inside, on top of, and outside the actual track and sector marks. Eventually, the drive fails to read one of these locations where the effect has built up to excessive amounts of mistracking. This situation usually is manifested in a DOS Abort, Retry, Ignore? error message.

The temperature sensitivity of stepper motor drives also is manifested by drives that have the "Monday morning blues." When you power up the system cold (on Monday morning, for example), a 1701 or 1790 POST (power-on self test) error occurs. If you leave the system on for about 15 minutes to allow the drive to come up to operating temperature, the system boots normally. This problem sometimes occur in reverse—when you allow the drive to get particularly warm, for example (when a system is in direct sunlight or during the afternoon when room temperature is highest). In these cases, a DOS type of error message appears with the familiar Abort, Retry, Ignore? prompt.

The most widely used stepper motor actuator systems employ a split metal band to transmit the rotary stepping motion to the in and out motion of the head rack. The band is made of special alloys to limit thermal expansion and contraction as well as stretch. One end of the band is coiled around the spindle of the stepper motor, and the other is connected directly to the head rack. The band itself is found inside the sealed HDA and is not visible from the outside of the drive.

Some companies (notably Miniscribe) have used a rack and pinion gear mechanism to link the stepper motor to the head rack. This procedure involves a small pinion gear on the spindle of the stepper motor that moves a rack gear in and out. This rack gear is connected to the head rack, causing it to move. The rack and pinion mechanism is more durable than the band mechanism and provides slightly greater physical and thermal stability. One additional problem is the amount of play in the gears (called *backlash*). This play in the gears increases over time as the gears wear and eventually renders the mechanism useless. The rack and pinion gears and mechanism always are found inside the sealed HDA and are not visible from the exterior.

Voice Coil Actuators

The *voice coil actuator* is on all high-quality, superior hard disk drives as well as on all disks with 100M capacity or more. This actuator is much different from the standard stepper motor actuator.

A voice coil actuator works by pure electromagnetic force. The actual construction of this mechanism is much like that of a typical audio speaker, which uses a stationary magnet surrounded by a "voice coil" that is connected to the speaker's paper cone. Energizing the coil causes the coil to move, which produces sound from the speaker cone. In a typical hard disk voice coil system, an electromagnetic coil moves on a track through a stationary magnet. No contact occurs between the coil and the magnet other than magnetic interaction. The coil mechanism is connected directly to the head rack. As the electromagnetic coils are energized, they attract or repulse the magnet and cause the head rack to move. Such systems are quick and efficient, and most of these systems are much quieter than a system that is stepper motor driven.

Because this system has no "click stops" or detent positions, as does a stepper motor, it must have some unique design features. The first of these features is the "dedicated surface." To understand what "dedicated surface" means, consider how the system works. The system can slide the heads in and out smoothly, like a trombone mechanism, so a way needs to be available to stop the head rack over a particular cylinder. When the drive is manufactured, one of the sides of one platter is "deducted" from normal read/write usage, and a special set of index marks that indicate proper track positions are recorded. The head that sits above this surface has no recording capability, so these marks can never be erased. As the drive is commanded to move the heads to a particular track—track 400, for example—the internal drive electronics use the signals received by this special head to indicate the position of the heads. As the heads are moved, the track counters are read from the index surface (398... 399... 400 STOP). When the correct track is "seen" to be under the head rack, the heads are commanded to stop moving. The electronics then "fine tune" the position so that before writing is allowed, the heads are positioned exactly over the track where the strongest signals are received by the index head.

Actually, the complete name of this mechanism is "dedicated surface, closed loop, servo controlled" mechanism. "Dedicated surface" refers to the platter surface that is lost in order to store the special index tracks. Because of the dedicated surface, most voice coil drives have an odd number of heads. That is usually a giveaway clue, indicating a voice coil actuator. "Closed loop" indicates that the index (or servo) head is wired to the positioning electronics in a closed loop system. This also is called a feedback loop. The feedback from this index head is used to position the other heads accurately. The feedback acts as a guide head to the rest of the rack. "Servo controlled" refers to this index or servo head itself, which is used to dictate or control head-positioning accuracy.

Note that this type of mechanism is not affected by temperature changes. When the temperature is cold and the platters have shrunk, the voice coil system compensates because it never positions to predetermined track positions; instead, the voice coil system hunts down the particular track and, through the use of the servo head, positions precisely over that track at the track's current position, regardless of the formatted temperature. Likewise, when the temperature is hot, the voice coil system automatically compensates and track positioning is precise.

A special advantage of using a voice coil positioner is automatic head parking. When a hard disk drive is powered off, the heads are pulled back into the platters to "land" by the spring tension in each head arm. You usually will want to ensure that this landing occurs where no data exists, although the drive is designed to sustain thousands of takeoffs and landings. But some amount of abrasion always occurs during the landing and takeoff process, and the abrasion removes just a "micropuff" of the media. If the drive is jarred during the landing or takeoff process, the results can be worse. In a voice coil drive, the heads are positioned and held by magnetic force. When power is removed from the drive, the magnetic field holding the heads stationary over a particular cylinder dissipates. The head rack is then allowed to skitter loose back and forth over the drive surface, causing potential damage. As part of the voice coil design, therefore, a weak spring must be attached to the head rack at one end, and a head stop must be attached at the other end. This spring normally is overcome by the magnetic force of the positioner, but when the drive is powered off, the spring gently drags the head rack into a park-and-lock position before the drive slows down and the heads land. This process is *automatic head parking* and is a standard function of any voice coil positioner. You activate the parking mechanism by simply turning off the system. You never need to run any sort of park program, and the heads even park themselves automatically during a power outage. The drives automatically unpark when powered on.

Two main types of voice coil positioners are available: linear voice coil actuators and rotary voice coil actuators. They differ only in the physical arrangement of the magnets and coils themselves.

The *linear* actuators move the heads in and out over the platters in a straight line, much like the so-called "tangential tracking" turntables sold today. In these systems, the coil moves in and out on a track surrounded by the stationary magnets.

The *rotary* voice coil systems employ the same magnets and coil, but now the coil is spun around a spindle and is surrounded by the stationary magnets. This rotary motion is transmitted directly to the heads because the head arms are mounted to the coils. The physical movement of this type of system is exactly like a conventional record player or turntable. The head arms swing in and out over the surface of the platters like the record tonearm, and the voice coil mechanism itself is at the arm pivot location.

I have no data to suggest which actuator is better, but I have observed that all the highest end drives from the best manufacturers are rotary actuator systems.

Spindle Motors

The motor that actually spins the platters is called the *spindle motor* because it is connected to the spindle around which all the platters revolve. These motors always are directly connected; no belts or gears are used. The motors must be noise free, or they transmit "rumble" to the platters and disrupt reading and writing operations. The motors must be precisely controlled for speed. The platters on nearly all hard disks revolve at exactly 3,600 rpm, and the motor must have a control circuit with a feedback loop to monitor and control this speed precisely. Because this speed control must be automatic, the drives do not have a speed adjustment, and nothing can be done if the speed is off.

On most drives, this spindle motor is on the bottom of the drive just outside the sealed HDA. Some companies build the motor directly into the HDA—actually mounting the motor in the center of the platters themselves. Maxtor is one company that builds motors this way, and Maxtor can place 8 platters into a normal 5 1/4-inch full-height form-factor drive. Having that many platters would be impossible if the motor was outside the platters; the drive would be too tall.

Note that these motors, particularly on the larger form-factor drives, can consume a great deal of 12-volt power. Most of the drives require 2 to 3 times the normal operating power when the motor is first spinning the platters up. This heavy draw lasts about 15 seconds, until the drive platters have reached a stable 3,600 rpm.

Spindle Ground Strap

Most drives have a special grounding strap attached to a ground on the drive and resting on the center spindle of the platter spindle motor. This device is the single most likely cause of excessive drive noise.

This grounding strap usually is made of copper and often has a carbon or graphite button that actually contacts the motor spindle. This device is designed to dissipate static that is generated by the spindle motor. If the platters and motor generate static due to friction, and no place exists for this electrical potential to bleed off, static discharge through the heads may result. Static also can discharge through the internal bearings in the motor, which burns the lubricants inside the sealed bearings. The grounding strap is designed to bleed off this static buildup so that no damage is done to the rest of the drive.

The carbon button often wears, and a "divot" results from where the spindle of the motor contacts the button spinning at 3,600 rpm. This divot causes the strap to vibrate and "sing" with a high-pitched squealing noise. The noise also may be a whining sound and may come and go depending on temperature and humidity. Sometimes, banging the side of the machine can jar the strap so that the noise changes or goes away completely. Most people mistake this noise for something much more serious, like a total drive motor failure or bearing failure. These latter problems rarely occur, and the noise more than likely is from the ground strap.

You can remedy the situation in several ways:

- Tear off the strap.
- Lubricate the contact point.
- Dampen the strap with rubber.

Of these "fixes," the first one is the least desirable. Tearing off the strap does eliminate the noise, but think about other possible ramifications. Although the drives do still work (silently), the device was put there for a reason. I doubt that the engineer who placed the strap on the drive thought that it was unnecessary. Otherwise, why did the drive manufacturer spend money to put it there?

Lubrication usually is a good solution. You will want some sort of conducting lube such as a graphite compound. Do not use standard oil or grease. I have used the graphited "lock lube" lubricants. You can find these lubricants at auto parts stores for frozen car locks. Any lubricant will work as long as it is conductive to static electricity. Simply dab a small amount onto the end of a wooden stick or toothpick and place a small drop directly onto the point of contact. With some drives, this strap is in an easily accessible position; with other drives, you have to partially disassemble the drive to get to the strap. You may have to remove the drive logic board or other external items to get to the strap.

The last way to fix this problem is to take some rubber and fix or glue it to the strap. This procedure changes the harmonics of the strap and usually dampens out any vibrations. An easy way for you to do this is to use some of the silicone bathtub caulk available at hardware stores. Dab a small amount onto the copper strap (do not interfere with the contact location), and the problem should be solved permanently. Some manufacturers already use this technique after recognizing this noise problem.

Logic Boards

Any disk drive, including hard disk drives, have one or more *logic boards* mounted on the drive. These boards contain the electronics that control the drive's spindle and head actuator systems, as well as present data to the controller in some agreed upon form. With some drives, the controller is even built in directly on the drive, which can save on the total chip count in a system. You will find these types of drives in the smaller portable systems.

You can remove or replace logic boards because they simply plug into the drive. Logic boards usually are mounted with standard screw hardware. If a drive is failing and you have a spare, you may be able to verify a logic board failure by taking the board off of the known good drive and mounting it on the bad one. If your suspicions are confirmed, you can order a new logic board from the manufacturer of the drive. Be prepared for sticker shock, though, because parts such as this often cost more than when you simply replace the entire drive with a new or refurbished unit. The drive manufacturer will have details on these costs, the availability of a refurbished unit, and taking yours as a trade in.

Configuration Items

A couple of items must be set to configure a hard disk drive for installation in a particular system. These configuration items usually are mounted on the disk drive logic board, which usually is on the bottom of the drive. You don't have to worry about as many items on a hard disk drive as you do on a typical floppy drive, which makes a hard disk quite easy to install from the physical point of view.

The items that must be set or configured are similar to those on a floppy drive:

- The drive-select jumper
- The terminating resistor

These items perform the exact same functions as they do on a floppy drive.

Drive-Select Jumpers

The *drive-select jumper* selects the "channel" to which the drive is supposed to respond. The drive controller sends control signals on two channels—one for each drive. Each drive in a system must be set to respond to a different channel, which limits the number of drives per controller to two. If a system has only one drive, that drive must be set to channel 1. Systems with two drives must have the lowest letter drive (usually C:) set to the first channel and the other drive (usually D:) set to the second channel.

As in the floppy drives, IBM uses a cable in its systems that twists the drive-select and motor-enable lines to switch the channels for the last drive on the cable. This procedure is done so that all drives installed in such a system have the same jumper- or drive-select settings, which makes the installation of a hard disk easier because IBM preconfigures all its drives to use the second channel or drive-select position. Both drives connected to such a cable appear to have the same drive-select setting, which is the second one. Thus, both drives look as if they are set to be drive D. The drive at the end of the cable is plugged into a connector that has the lines twisted so that the drive's setting is switched; the D: setting is changed automatically to C:.

If you are using a cable with the IBM type of twist, both hard disks on a single controller must be set to the second drive-select position. If you are using a straight-through cable, both drives must carry different drive-select settings; the drive set to the first drive-select position must respond as C:, and the other must respond as D:. Note that the typical hard disk cabling system employs three cables for two drives. One cable is a single 34-pin control cable, which is daisy chained to both drives. This cable has the optional twist. The cable appears much like the 34-pin cable for floppy drives, but if it is twisted, the cables are not interchangeable because different lines will be twisted. The other two cables are smaller 20-pin data cables; one is available for each drive and is plugged into a single connector for each on the controller. These data cables never are twisted and are not daisy chained.

Terminating Resistors

Finally, a hard disk always contains a terminating resistor when shipped from the factory. You must ensure that the terminator is removed from any drive that is not at the end of the control cable—drive D in most systems. The drive at the end of the control cable (C:) must have the terminator installed.

The functions of the terminating resistor for hard disks are exactly the same as for floppy drives. The idea is to provide electrical signal termination so that the control signals to and from the drive and controller are not reflected and echo along the cable. Using the terminating resistor is necessary to achieve the proper signal-to-noise ratio and to provide the proper electrical load for the controller. Improper drive termination results in drives that do not read or write at all or that do so with excessive problems. The controller also can be damaged through improper termination due to excessive electrical loads with no terminators in place.

Cables and Connectors

The standard drives that interface through the ST-506/412 or ESDI interfaces (interfaces are discussed later in this chapter) always have four connectors (see fig. 9.4):

- Interface control connector
- Interface data connector
- Power connector
- Ground connector (tab)

The interface connectors are the most important; they carry the drive's instructions and also carry data to and from the drive. The control connector is a larger 34-pin connector that can be daisy chained between two drives and a single controller. This cable and connector system is used to pass instructions from the controller to the drive to cause head movements and other operations. The drive can acknowledge these actions to the controller through this cable. The daisy-chain arrangement is much like that used for floppy drives. The drive responds to two usable channels (out of a maximum of four), labeled drive selects 1, 2, 3, and 4. Only the first two channels are usable on PC controllers.

Fig. 9.4.

Rear view of typical hard disk showing connector locations.

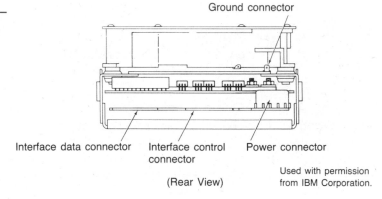

Ground connector

Interface data connector   Interface control connector   Power connector

(Rear View)

Used with permission from IBM Corporation.

The data cable is a smaller 20-pin cable that runs from the controller to each drive separately. This cable is not daisy chained. Therefore, a two-drive system has one control cable from the controller to each of two drives and two separate data cables, one for each drive. The controllers have three connectors to support the two-drive maximum limit. The data cable does what its name suggests: carries data to and from the drive.

The power connector usually is the same as that of a floppy, and the same power supply connector plugs into it. The drives use both 5- and 12-volt power; the 12-volt power is used to run the drive's motors and head actuator. Make sure that your power supply can adequately supply power for the hard disk drives that are installed. Many of the drives draw much more power than any floppy drive ever can.

The power required for a typical hard disk is concentrated on the 12-volt side of the power supply output because the motors in the disks require 12-volt power. Many full- and half-height hard disks can draw up to 4.0 amps of 12-volt power on start-up for the first 15 seconds. This tapers off to a nominal draw of 1.5 amps and a seeking draw of 2.5 amps. You must be sure that your power supply can supply that amount of power for the drive. In the IBM XT Model 089, for example, IBM uses a 10M full-height hard disk that draws this amount of power. The rating of the XT power supply indicates that 4.2 amps of 12-volt power are available constantly, which allows for starting the hard disk and the cooling fan, which takes an additional 0.2 amps. After the system is powered up, the hard disk needs 2.5 amps during seek operations, which also must run concurrently with the floppy drive operation. The floppy drive uses 0.9 amps of 12-volt power while spinning, so while you're copying files from a floppy to a hard disk, the power demands on the supply are the following:

Hard disk =	2.5 amps
Floppy disk =	0.9 amps
Cooling fan =	0.2 amps
Total =	3.6 amps

These power demands fit in with the specification of the IBM XT supply, which has 4.2 amps available at all times. The IBM PC supply would be inadequate because it only has 2.0 amps of 12-volt power available! See Chapter 7 for a more detailed look at these calculations.

Note that physically smaller hard disks, such as some of the half-height 5 1/4-inch and particularly the 3 1/2-inch platter drives, can draw less power than this due to the use of smaller, less powerful motors and electronics. You should consult the disk drive OEM manual for the exact power-draw data for your particular drives.

A grounding tab is on most drives and can be used to provide a positive ground connection between the drive and the chassis of the system. In a PC or XT system, the hard disk is mounted with screws, which hold the drive directly to the chassis of the PC, so the ground wire is unnecessary. But on the AT systems from IBM and others, the drives are installed on plastic or fiberglass rails, which do not provide a proper ground path. These systems must provide a grounding wire that is plugged into the drive through this grounding tab. Failure to ground the drive may result in improper operation, intermittent failure, or general read and write errors.

Bezel

Most hard disk drives offer as an option a front faceplate or *bezel* (see fig. 9.5). A bezel is not usually supplied as a standard item but as an option for the drive.

Fig. 9.5.

Removable faceplate.

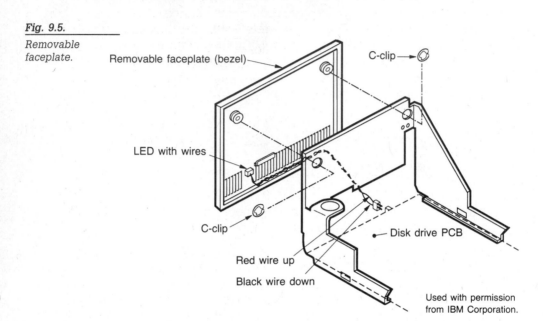

Used with permission from IBM Corporation.

The bezels are available in several sizes and colors to match various systems on the market today. For the standard full-height 5 1/4-inch form-factor drives, only one choice of bezel is available, but for the half-height drives, you can get the bezel in either half- or full-height forms. Using a full-height bezel on a half-height drive allows a single drive to be installed in the bay of a PC or XT without leaving a huge hole in the front of the system. To add a second half-height drive, you may want to order the half-height bezels so that both drives can be stacked one on top of another. The 3 1/2-inch form-factor drives are available in many configurations, including both 3 1/2-inch bezels and 5 1/4-inch form-factor bezels. You often have a choice of three colors: black, cream, or white.

Some bezels have a Light Emitting Diode (LED) that flickers when your hard disk is in use. This LED is mounted in the bezel with a wire hanging off the back that plugs into the drive. Some drives have the LED mounted on the drive itself. In this case, the bezel has a clear or colored see-through window so you can see the light flicker on the drive.

The hard disk in AT systems is completely hidden by the cover of the unit, so a bezel isn't needed. In fact, using the bezel may prevent the cover from sitting properly on the chassis. Another problem occurs with the AT installation: if the drive has a LED, the LED remains on as if it were a ''power on'' light rather than an access light. The reason is that the controller used in the AT has a direct connection for the LED on the controller itself, and the drive LED function will be altered.

Physical Operation

In many ways, the physical operation of a hard disk is similar to that of a floppy disk. A hard drive uses spinning disks with heads that move over the disks and store data in *tracks* and *sectors*, just like a floppy disk. A few differences exist, however.

Hard disks usually have multiple platters, each with two sides on which to store data. Most drives have two or three platters, meaning four or six sides. The same tracks on each side of each platter together make up a *cylinder*. You will find one head per platter side, and all the heads are mounted on a common carrier device or rack. The heads are moved in and out across the disk in unison and cannot move independently.

Hard disks are much faster than floppy drives. Hard disks spin approximately 10 times faster—usually at 3,600 rpm. This spinning speed combined with a fast head-positioning mechanism makes the hard disk much faster than a floppy drive.

The heads in a hard disk do not (and should not) touch the platters during normal operation. When the system is powered off, the heads actually do land on the platter. While the drive is on, a cushion of air keeps the head suspended a short distance above the platter. If this cushion is disturbed by a particle of dust or shock of some kind, the head may come into contact with the platter spinning at 3,600 rpm. This occurrence is called a head crash and may mean anything from a few lost bytes to a totally trashed disk. Most disks have special lubricants and hardened coatings to withstand much of this type of abuse.

Because the drives are sealed from the environment and contamination, they can have high track densities. Many drives have 900 or more tracks per inch of media. Because the drives must be assembled in clean rooms under absolutely sanitary conditions, few companies are capable of repairing a drive. Your only safety, then, is some form of backup device, because every hard disk eventually will fail someday.

Examining the Many Types of Hard Disks

You can choose from many types of hard disks when you add a drive to your system. Differences exist in physical size or form factor, interfaces, quality, and price.

Interfaces

Several different electrical interfaces are available in today's hard disk market. You basically have three popular interfaces to consider when purchasing or upgrading a hard disk:

- ST-506/412
- ESDI
- SCSI

The procedure for selecting the type of drive you want may be academic. Suppose that you want to add a second drive to an AT system, for example; IBM used an ST-506/412 controller, so any drive you select must have that interface. The particular interface you use is not always that important, but the drive and controller interfaces must match. Usually, no way is available to take a given drive and change the interface used. More than 90 percent of all hard disks today use the ST-506/412 interface, but the ESDI and SCSI are becoming more popular, especially on the higher end system. Interfaces are explained in more detail later in this chapter.

Form Factor

You can choose from several physical form factors when selecting a drive. The *form factor* is the drive's physical platter and exterior dimensions. Figure 9.6 shows a typical full-height 5 1/4-inch hard disk. You have other choices, however. The choices follow:

- 5 1/4-inch full-height
- 5 1/4-inch half-height
- 3 1/2-inch half-height

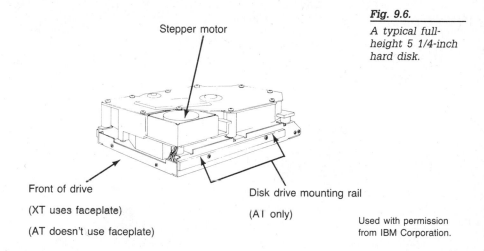

Stepper motor

Front of drive

(XT uses faceplate)

(AT doesn't use faceplate)

Disk drive mounting rail

(AT only)

Fig. 9.6.

A typical full-height 5 1/4-inch hard disk.

Used with permission from IBM Corporation.

These dimensions usually refer to the drive's physical external size and mounting requirements. Sometimes, for example, a company can provide a 3 1/2-inch drive mounted in a 5 1/4-inch half-height chassis to adapt the drive to fit a larger opening in the system. Two half-height drives can fit over and under one another in the same space as a full-height drive. The data storage capacities vary, but at the time of this writing, the largest drives actually available in each category are the following:

- 5 1/4-inch full-height: Maxtor XT 8760 with 651M
- 5 1/4-inch half-height: CDC Wren V with 190M
- 3 1/2-inch half-height: CDC Swift with 172M

These drives are the largest commercially available drives for the form factors, and this information changes all the time. I have observed that the maximum capacities of hard disk drives double every two years. By 1990, you will see single drives well into the gigabyte range, and even portable systems could have 250 megabytes or more.

Other than capacity differences due to the maximum numbers of platters that can be fit inside the HDA, the only real difference between typical full- or half-height hard disks is the physical size and mounting. Make sure that you get the correct hardware and brackets, etc., for whatever drive you select. Until recently, most half-height drives used stepper motor actuators, which placed the half-height drives at a reliability and performance disadvantage. Today, however, the market is mixed. You can buy inexpensive stepper-motor half-height drives or quality voice coil drives as your requirements and budget permit.

Head Actuator Mechanisms

The most important item to consider when you choose a particular drive is the type of head actuator used in the drive. A big difference exists between drives with the stepper motor or voice coil actuators.

Use stepper motor drives when cost far outweighs all other considerations. Stepper motor drives should not be used in the following circumstances: where reliability is important or the environment is harsh; in portable systems or systems that must operate under extremes of temperature, noise, or vibration; where preventive maintenance cannot be provided, because they require periodic reformats to maintain data integrity; and under any demanding situations such as a network file server. Stepper motor drives are acceptable in low-volume usage, where preventive maintenance can be provided at least annually or semiannually. Stepper motor drives almost always are used in low-cost systems or home-use systems. As long as the environment can be controlled and the drive is reasonably cared for, these drives will perform adequately.

Use voice coil drives in all other situations, especially where extreme demands are put on the drive. Voice coil drives are ideal for portable systems or systems that suffer extremes of temperature, noise, or vibration. These drives are ideal where a fast drive must be used, such as a network file server. A voice coil drive requires little or no preventive maintenance, so the first low-level format is usually the only one ever done. Thus, this type of drive can be used in high-volume situations where a single support person must support many machines. Voice coil drives are more expensive, but you receive very real payoffs in reliability and performance and maintenance, which more than offset the initial cost.

Examining Hard Disk Features

To make the best decision when purchasing a hard disk for your system or to understand what differentiates one brand of hard disk from another, you must consider many features other than the types of platters and actuator mechanisms. Some drives automatically park the heads over a nondata area at power down, and others require that you execute a program prior to power down to achieve the same result. Reliability is important, and although the type of actuator mechanism has the most to do with this specification, other items can affect reliability as well.

Speed and performance are desirable for many applications. You need to know how to evaluate a drive's performance in relation to another drive. Most drives have a type of mounting using rubber isolators or dampeners to ensure that the drive's head disk assembly is attached to the chassis of the drive. This shock mounting generally makes these drives more rugged than those with no such isolation from the chassis. This next section examines all the issues that you should consider when evaluating drives.

Head Parking

Head parking is a big issue with hard disks, and it often is misunderstood.

When any hard disk comes to a stop, the heads do land onto the media. But the process happens as the drive slows down, so when the head does land, the drive is not turning very fast. Usually, the story ends right here; the heads land on whatever cylinder they were positioned over last—usually over areas of the disk that contain data.

Any drive with a voice coil actuator offers a feature known as automatic head parking. These systems have a spring attached to the head; while the drive is operational, an electric coil overcomes the spring tension and moves the head around the disk. In this setup, when power is lost, the spring can automatically pull the head rack away from data areas of the disk to a special landing zone.

Although all voice coil drives do in fact park the drive heads automatically, almost no stepper motor drives do. If you want to find out whether your drive autoparks, simply determine whether the drive has a voice coil or stepper motor positioner. Some exceptions to this rule may exist. Some stepper drives may incorporate a parking mechanism. Out of the hundreds of brands, makes, and models on the market, however, I have found only a single exception: the Seagate ST-251. This drive is a stepper drive that autoparks through the use of a weight on the end of the head arm. If you can imagine a record player tonearm with the antiskating weight on the end of the arm, you know how this weight works. When the drive is powered off, the weight causes the head arm to swing into the inner cylinders of the drive. This drive must be run flat and right side up for this mechanism to work properly.

All the stepper-motor-actuated drives that lack this automatic parking feature can be parked through software. Before you shut down the system, run a park program that secures the heads. The drawback is that if the power goes down unexpectedly, you cannot park the heads. The head parking program is on the diagnostics disk supplied in the guide to operations manual. The same parking program also is supplied on the advanced diagnostics disk supplied with the hardware maintenance service manual. Simply boot these disks and select menu item number 3, PREPARE SYSTEM FOR MOVING. The heads of any attached disks will be parked. Then shut down the system. This procedure invokes a program on the disk called SHIPDISK.COM. Different SHIPDISK.COM files are available for XT and AT systems.

Several years ago, IBM issued a warning to its dealers recommending against running SHIPDISK.COM from the DOS prompt. IBM said a slight chance exists that you can lose data because the program can wipe out track 0 of the disk. The memo indicated that SHIPDISK.COM should be run only from the menu.

SHIPDISK.COM parks the disks and then executes a software interrupt to return to the diagnostics disk menu. The interrupt used is set only by the special diagnostics DOS found on the diagnostics disk and is not set by standard DOS. If you run this program at the DOS prompt, when the SHIPDISK.COM program attempts to return to the diagnostics DOS menu through the "untamed" interrupt, random code is run in the system. An untamed interrupt means that no pointer is established properly that indicates the location of the program routine to run when the interrupt is invoked. The system goes to a random location and executes whatever is there, which usually locks up the system immediately. This lockup is mistaken to be intentional when in fact it is not. In some situations, the random code does not simply lock up the system but causes random data to be written to the drive. If this happens at track 0, the partition table is wiped out and all access to the drive is made impossible. So the bottom line is this: Do not run SHIPDISK.COM from the DOS prompt. Run it from the diagnostics menu.

For AT systems, IBM supplies a separate program, SHUTDOWN.EXE, that can be run from the DOS prompt. This program is on the AT diagnostics and advanced diagnostics disks. You can copy this program to the hard disk and enter the command *shutdown* at the DOS prompt. You will see a picture of a switch, which turns off as the heads are parked. The program then halts the system, requiring a complete power down. This program will not work on a non-AT type of system.

Note: Do not run a hard disk parking program for your system that is not designed for the system. I have several types of systems and disks in my lab, and I have tried all the right and wrong programs on all of them (I have used the AT SHUTDOWN.EXE program on a PC or XT and the PC or XT SHIPDISK.COM on an AT). I never lost anything or physically hurt a disk, but I saw instances where some parking programs damaged data. A parking program *cannot* physically hurt a drive. You may hear some strange noises because drives can make different sounds when resetting the heads to track 0 or when forced into a parking mode by a seek to a high enough cylinder. I have heard of instances where a defective parking program caused track 0 to be overwritten, which destroyed the partition table on the drive. You can gain access to the drive again if you repartition the drive by using FDISK to exactly the same specifications as before. This procedure rewrites the partition information only, allowing access to the data again. If a parking program is written to park a disk of a specific number of cylinders, it may not function properly on other drives.

You should get a parking program with your system. If your system is from IBM, refer to my previous discussion of where to find these programs. If you have a compatible, contact the system vendor for such a program. The Htest/Hformat utility from Paul Mace Software is a hard disk technician's tool that contains a universal parking program. Additionally, programs are available in the public domain that will park a stepper motor hard disk.

Should you park the heads every time you shut down the drive? Some people think so, but IBM says that you don't have to park the heads on a drive unless it is to be moved. My own experiences are in line with IBM's recommendations. But a more fail-safe approach is to park the heads at every shutdown. If you are using voice coil drives, this point is moot because these drives automatically do this every time. For stepper motor drives, I usually recommend that you park the heads at every shutdown. The procedure is simple and really cannot hurt.

Reliability

When you're shopping for a drive, notice one of the "features" described in the brochures: the Mean Time Between Failures, or MTBF. These MTBF figures usually start at 20,000 hours, and some drives report MTBF figures as high as 50,000 hours or more. I recommend that you ignore these figures, because no measurable difference in actual reliability exists between drives based on these figures. These figures are simply statistical values that are theoretical and not actual. Most drives that boast these figures have not even been manufactured for that length of time. One year of 5-day work weeks with 8-hour days is equal to 2,080 hours of operation. Assuming that you never turn off the system for 365 days and run the full 24-hours per day, you operate your system 8,760 hours each year.

For these figures to have any real weight, you must take a sample of drives and measure the failure rate for at least twice the rated figure, which means that you should watch the test drives for 40,000 to 100,000 hours to measure how many fail in that time. To be accurate, you must wait until all the drives fail, recording the operating hours at each failure. Then after they all fail, you can average the running time for all the test samples together, which should give you the average life expectancy of the drive. If the MTBF is reported as 30,000 hours (most common today), the test sample should be run for 30,000 to 60,000 hours to be accurate at all, which translates to 3.4 to 6.8 years of testing. Note that the drive carries this specification on the day it is introduced, which points out that the figure is a fantasy number.

I also have seen vendors "play" with these numbers. CDC rates, for example, its Wren II half-height drive at 20,000 hours MTBF (this drive is one of the most reliable in the world), and I have seen a vendor who sells this drive rate the very same unit at 50,000 hours. That figure is bogus. The final word is that these figures do not translate to reliability in the field. I have seen the worst drives boast high MTBF figures, and the best drives have lower ones.

Speed

When you're selecting a hard disk for your computer, one of the first features you should examine is the speed of the drive. Although all hard disks seem to be an order of magnitude faster than floppies, hard disks come in a wide range of speeds. The best indicator of the drive's speed usually is its price. An old saying from the automotive world is appropriate here: "Speed is money. How fast do you want to go?"

Speed means several things when you're talking about hard disk drives. You can measure the speed of a disk drive in two ways:

- Average access time
- Transfer rate

The *average access time* is the amount of time on average taken to move the heads from one cylinder to the next. Although many ways are available to measure this specification, running many random track seek operations and dividing the timed results by the number of seeks results in the average time for a single seek. Some manufacturers indicate that this is measured as the time for a seek across one-third of the total number of cylinders. This rate depends on the drive only; the interface or controllers used have little effect on this specification. In some instances, the setup of the controller to the drive can have some effect on seek times; this information is explained later.

The *transfer rate* is the rate of speed that the drive and controller can send data to the motherboard. Transfer rate depends on the interface used as well as the disk controller and system throughput. The drive itself is rarely the limiting factor controlling this figure. This rate is limited to a maximum value by the particular interface used. The theoretical maximum throughput of the ST-506/412 interface is 5 megabits per second, for example, but the ESDI interface is limited to 24 megabits per second. These rates are the absolute limits, and actual transfer rate depends on the controller and drive itself. The actual setup and installation of a drive and controller system can have a big effect on the observed throughput. A system that is set up improperly will not take advantage of the performance that the components are capable of. You will learn about the proper setup of a drive and controller later in this chapter.

Of these two performance specifications, the transfer rate is the most important to overall system performance. You can double or triple the transfer rate on many systems without changing the drive itself but just changing the controller. The only pure drive-only speed measurement is the average access time. This specification is a gauge of the capabilities of the head actuator.

The speed at which the heads can move usually is rated in average access time, which is measured in milliseconds. The original IBM XT comes equipped with drives that have an average access time of around 85 ms to 115 ms, and the AT comes equipped with drives in the 35 ms to 40 ms range. That difference is as big as it looks. Anything better than 40 ms is considered fast, and some of the fastest drives clock in at around 15 ms. These drives cost several thousands of dollars. Any drive in the range greater than 40 ms is really slow, but these drives cost only hundreds of dollars. You will find a big difference in price and performance for hard disk drives.

Shock Mounting

Most hard disks manufactured today have a "shock mounted" HDA, which means that some sort of rubber cushion is between the actual disk drive body and mounting chassis. Some drives do use more rubber than others, but for the most part, it is all the same thing. Although most hard disks do have these shock mounts, some exceptions do exist—especially the very low-cost drives. These low-cost units (such as the Seagate ST-225) completely lack any rubber-isolation mounts for the HDA. Do not use drives that aren't shock mounted in any portable systems or where the environmental conditions are less than what you will find in a comfortable office. I never recommend a drive that is not shock mounted in some form or another.

Cost

The cost of today's hard disk drives varies from the $200 Seagate ST-225 20M drive at the low end to the $5,000+ Maxtor XT 8760 650M drive at the high end. If you are buying a drive, you will pay something between these figures. The biggest influences on cost are capacity and the head actuator mechanism. As capacities rise, so does (not surprisingly) the cost. Also, any drive with a voice coil actuator costs about 30 percent to 50 percent more than an equal-capacity drive with a stepper motor.

Selecting Drives

When you're selecting a drive for your system, consider how the drive will be supported. Just how will the system know what type of drive is connected? IBM typically has the drive setup or type information stored in a ROM somewhere in the system. In the XT, IBM uses a controller with a ROM that contains the hard disk controller BIOS (Basic Input/Output System) and a list or table of four drive types indicating the supported drives. You set jumpers or switches to indicate which of the four drives in the table you are installing. In the AT systems, the 15-, 22-, or 23-entry drive table is contained in the motherboard ROM. The type is selected and stored by the SETUP program that comes with the system.

The Drive Parameter Table

Perhaps the easiest way to deal with the drive-table problem is to use or purchase only drives that are supported by the existing table in a system. Because IBM places the drive table for the XT on the hard disk controller itself, many aftermarket controllers are developed that have different drive tables. When you purchase a particular controller and drive combination, the vendor ensures that the tables in that particular controller match the drive. To alter the tables for an existing controller means downloading the contents of the controller's ROM to disk, where it can be edited and the correct table values can be inserted. Then that data is used to burn a new ROM that is inserted back into the controller to support the desired drive.

IBM's XT hard disk controllers have used two different ROMs over the years, but they each have only four entry tables, which means that room is available for only four different drives to be supported by a single ROM. Thus, virtually every time you want to add a different type of hard disk to an XT, you have to reburn this ROM with the correct values for the new drive. You can try to anticipate any future upgrades and burn in the values for these drives as well, but with a limit of only four entries, you can anticipate only up to three other types of drives.

A new generation of controllers for the PC and XT has been developed to alleviate the problem with the XT disk controller. These new controllers have the capacity to "ask" you what type of drive is being connected and store this information in a specially reserved track on the drive. Then every time the system is booted, this information is read from that location. And the system now has the correct drive type indicated, which essentially allows for a drive table with an infinite number of entries. No matter what the parameters are for your particular drive, the system can support it because this "autoconfigure ROM" is built into the controller. I recommend that no matter what type of disk drive you select, make sure that your controller is an autoconfigure type. This type of controller supports any drive that matches the interface specification and eliminates problems with table entries that do not match your drives. These controllers are discussed again later, and some specific recommendations are made.

Table 9.1 lists the drive parameters in all IBM XT hard disk controllers.

Table 9.1

Drive Parameters in IBM XT Hard Disk Controllers

IBM 10M fixed disk controller (Xebec 1210):

Table Entry	Disk Type	Cyl	Heads	Write Precomp	Landing Zone	Capacity Megabytes
0	-	306	2	0	-	5
1	-	375	8	0	-	26
2	-	306	6	256	-	15
3	-	306	4	0	-	10

IBM 20M fixed disk controller (Xebec 1210):

Table Entry	Disk Type	Cyl	Heads	Write Precomp	Landing Zone	Capacity Megabytes
0	1	306	4	0	305	10
1	16	612	4	0	663	21
2	2	615	4	300	615	21
3	13	306	8	128	319	21

In the AT systems, IBM goes a different route. Instead of using a ROM on the controller card to support the card and drive tables, IBM incorporates the hard disk ROM BIOS as part of the main system ROM that resides in 2 (sometimes 4) chips on the motherboard. This ROM also contains a hard disk table with at least 15 entries. The later AT ROMs have tables with 22 and 23 entries. The XT 286 (really a late model AT) has a table with 24 entries. And the PS/2 systems currently have up to 33 entries in some models. In each of these tables, the 15th entry is not usable, and the tables are downward compatible in the newer systems. For example, the PS/2 Model 80-111 has 32 table entries in its ROM, and any of the entries that are present in the earlier systems match exactly on the specifications. Drive Type 9, for example, will be the same in all these systems from the earliest AT to the newest PS/2 systems.

Because the hard disk ROM BIOS of the AT is built into the motherboard ROMs, you cannot easily change the type of controller. Any new controller must be exactly like the original controller, or the ROM BIOS on the motherboard will not operate the new controller correctly. If the new controller has a ROM on board, it will conflict with the system board ROM. To disable the motherboard ROM support of the hard disk controller, you can run the standard SETUP program and simply tell the system that no hard disk drives are installed, which disables the hard disk BIOS on the motherboard and allows the controller's own BIOS to be recognized and used. In this case, an autoconfigure type of controller with dynamically variable drive tables can be used. You must replace the controller with another that has an on board ROM BIOS.

An unfortunate problem is that any drive not supported directly by the CMOS memory setup routine is not recognized by any operating system that runs in protected mode, including OS/2, XENIX (UNIX), and Novell Advanced Netware. The rule of thumb here is this: If the AT controller you are purchasing has any on board ROM, you must ask about special drivers for OS/2, XENIX, or Netware. The reason is that most ROMs do not function in protected mode, and the drivers must be loaded from disk instead.

Another solution is to modify the drive-table entries somehow so that a desired drive is supported. You can accomplish this task by downloading, patching, and reburning the original motherboard ROM chips. Unfortunately, this practice is not legal according to IBM. Another alternative is to replace your motherboard ROM with a compatible ROM such as one from Phoenix or Award. Each company sells a set of AT ROMs for about $50. These ROMs usually have a full 47 entries in their drive tables, and some may contain up to 255 entries. One of these entries more likely will match your drive than the 15, 22, or 23 entries (depending on the version) in IBM's own ROMs.

Another alternative is available. Several companies such as Golden Bow and Geneva Enterprises have released "ROM dubbing" boards that can patch themselves into the motherboard ROM, which allows for replacing one of the existing types with one of your own. You can keep the standard controller, run under protected mode, and support virtually any type of drive. These dubbing kits sell for about $100.

Table 9.2 lists the entries in the IBM AT type of fixed disk parameter table that includes all system ROM BIOS introduced up to the April 18, 1988, PS/2 Model 50Z.

Table 9.2
Fixed Disk Parameter Table
IBM AT Type

Type	Cyl	Hd	WPC	Ctrl	LZ	S/T	Meg	Mb	Notes
1	306	4	128	00h	305	17	10.16	10.65	
2	615	4	300	00h	615	17	20.42	21.41	
3	615	6	300	00h	615	17	30.63	32.12	
4	940	8	512	00h	940	17	62.42	65.45	
5	940	6	512	00h	940	17	46.82	49.09	
6	615	4	65535	00h	615	17	20.42	21.41	
7	462	8	256	00h	511	17	30.68	32.17	
8	733	5	65535	00h	733	17	30.42	31.90	
9	900	15	65535	08h	901	17	112.06	117.50	More than 8 heads
10	820	3	65535	00h	820	17	20.42	21.41	
11	855	5	65535	00h	855	17	35.49	37.21	
12	855	7	65535	00h	855	17	49.68	52.09	
13	306	8	128	00h	319	17	20.32	21.31	
14	733	7	65535	00h	733	17	42.59	44.66	
15	0	0	0	00h	0	0	0	0	Reserved (do not use)
									End table 01/10/84 AT
16	612	4	0	00h	663	17	20.32	21.31	
17	977	5	300	00h	977	17	40.55	42.52	
18	977	7	65535	00h	977	17	56.77	59.53	
19	1024	7	512	00h	1023	17	59.50	62.39	
20	733	5	300	00h	732	17	30.42	31.90	
21	733	7	300	00h	732	17	42.59	44.66	
22	733	5	300	00h	733	17	30.42	31.90	
									End table 06/10/85 AT
23	306	4	0	00h	336	17	10.16	10.65	
									End table 11/15/85 AT
24	612	4	305	00h	663	17	20.32	21.31	
									End table 04/21/86 XT 286
25	306	4	65535	00h	340	17	10.16	10.65	
26	612	4	65535	00h	670	17	20.32	21.31	
									End table 12/12/86 PS/2 30

Table 9.2—*continued*

Type	Cyl	Hd	WPC	Ctrl	LZ	S/T	Meg	Mb	Notes
27	698	7	300	20h	732	17	40.56	42.53	Defect map (Cyl + 1)
28	976	5	488	20h	977	17	40.51	42.48	Defect map (Cyl + 1)
29	306	4	0	00h	340	17	10.16	10.65	
30	611	4	306	20h	663	17	20.29	21.27	Defect map (Cyl + 1)
31	732	7	300	20h	732	17	42.53	44.60	Defect map (Cyl + 1)
32	1023	5	65535	20h	1023	17	42.46	44.52	Defect map (Cyl + 1) End table 10/07/87 PS/2 80
33	614	4	65535	20h	663	25	29.98	31.44	Defect map (Cyl + 1) End table 04/18/88 PS/2 50Z
34	0	0	0	00h	0	0	0	0	Unused (Reserved)
35	0	0	0	00h	0	0	0	0	Unused (Reserved)
36	0	0	0	00h	0	0	0	0	Unused (Reserved)
37	0	0	0	00h	0	0	0	0	Unused (Reserved)
38	0	0	0	00h	0	0	0	0	Unused (Reserved)
39	0	0	0	00h	0	0	0	0	Unused (Reserved)
40	0	0	0	00h	0	0	0	0	Unused (Reserved)
41	0	0	0	00h	0	0	0	0	Unused (Reserved)

Type	Cyl	Hd	WPC	Ctrl	LZ	S/T	Meg	Mb	Notes
42	0	0	0	00h	0	0	0	0	Unused (Reserved)
43	0	0	0	00h	0	0	0	0	Unused (Reserved)
44	0	0	0	00h	0	0	0	0	Unused (Reserved)
45	0	0	0	00h	0	0	0	0	Unused (Reserved)
46	0	0	0	00h	0	0	0	0	Unused (Reserved)
47	0	0	0	00h	0	0	0	0	Unused (Reserved)

Explanations of Abbreviations Used in Table 9.2

Type: The drive type by number for table selection

Cyl: Total number of cylinders (or vertically aligned tracks)

Hd: Total number of heads (or tracks per cylinder)

WPC: Write precompensation starting cylinder

Ctrl: Control byte, which has values according to the following:

        Bit 0: Not used
        Bit 1: Not used
        Bit 2: Not used
        Bit 3: More than 8 heads
        Bit 4: Not used
        Bit 5: OEM defect map present at max. cyl. + 1
        Bit 6: Disable retries
        Bit 7: Disable retries

LZ: Landing zone cylinder for head parking

S/T: Number of sectors per track

Meg: Drive capacity in *megabytes*

Mb: Actual drive capacity in *millions of bytes*

Note: Megabytes (Meg) and millions of bytes (Mb) are sometimes used interchangeably, which is not exactly correct because they are not exactly the same figure. One megabyte is equal to 1 kilobyte times 1 kilobyte, where 1 kilobyte is equal to 1,024 bytes and 1 byte is equal to 8 bits. Therefore, 1 megabyte is equal to 1,048,576 bytes or 8,388,608 bits.

Four figures commonly are used when drive capacity is advertised:

Unformatted capacity in millions of bytes (Mb)
Unformatted capacity in megabytes (Meg)
Formatted capacity in millions of bytes (Mb)
Formatted capacity in megabytes (Meg)

In table 9.2, I calculated the formatted capacities of each of the drives and reported the figures in millions of bytes (Mb) and megabytes (Meg). I include both figures because advertisements for drives or discussions of drives may include either figure, and both are correct.

As an example, I currently am running a Control Data Corporation (Imprimis) Wren III half-height SCSI drive in my Portable PC. In formatted capacity, this drive has

512 bytes per sector

35 sectors per track

1,022 tracks per head

5 heads

for a total of 91,571,200 bytes. That 91.5 million bytes is equal to only 87.33 megabytes of capacity. If you were in the marketing department for a drive vendor (dealer) and were selling these drives, which number would you use in the advertisement? I would use the larger one and would say that the drive is a 91.5 Mb drive rather than an 87.33 Meg drive. Both numbers are entirely correct. Actually, if I wrote the advertisement, I would use the drive's unformatted capacity, which in this case is 106 Mb (or 101 Meg). The figures that can be used for my CDC Wren III half-height SCSI drive follow:

Unformatted capacity: 106 Mb
                                   101 Meg

Formatted capacity: 91.5 Mb
                                   87.33 Meg

To sum up, my drive has four figures to use, and each of the figures is as technically correct and accurate as the other.

The PS/2 ESDI systems read the drive type directly off of the drive through a special ESDI command, which completely eliminates the use of any drive tables whatsoever. Therefore, you will not find any table entries for the ESDI drives in any of the PS/2 systems. This feature is one of the advanced ESDI interface features.

Specific Brands and Recommendations

In this section, I give some recommendations for purchasing drives and some recommendations of manufacturers.

I recommend *only* voice coil drives because they are much more reliable and durable in the long run. The benefits far outweigh the small additional cost. Generally, the use of thin film (sputtered or plated) media is also a bonus, although many high-quality drives still use oxide-coated media. For any high-performance considerations, look into drives and controllers with the ESDI or SCSI interface. These interfaces offer much greater reliability and performance than the ST-506/412 interface can.

I recommend the manufacturers listed in the remainder of this section. This list cannot cover all manufacturers because many new companies and drives are being introduced all the time.

For premium drives, where reliability and performance are paramount, the following companies make some of the highest quality drives in the industry:

Control Data Corporation (now called Imprimis)
Maxtor
Priam (also known as Vertex)
Micropolis

Note that these companies produce only voice coil drives.

For a good value in drives, where cost is more important, you can find many manufacturers of midrange drives that use voice coil actuators but are available at a lower cost. The Seagate ST-4000 series is an example. Because this drive is sold in such high volumes (Seagate is the largest disk drive company), it is available at very competitive prices. Many other companies also offer reasonably priced voice coil drives. Some of the best bargains today are from the following:

Seagate (ST-4000 series only)
Miniscribe (6000 and 8000 voice coil only)
Microscience (voice coil only)

Note: Although these drives are the voice coil type, the companies that make these drives also make stepper motor drives, which I do not recommend.

I recommend that you stay away from the following companies' products that are still available, because of problems with the drives. Note that these companies are out of business and made only stepper motor drives:

Computer Memories Inc. (CMI)
Tulin
LaPine

CMI drives were the drives originally selected by IBM for the 20M drive in the AT, and these drives were responsible for most of the AT drive problems in that system's beginnings. After IBM recognized that the drives were failing constantly, the company changed suppliers to Seagate for the 20M and, later, 30M AT drives. Fortunately, these CMI drives have all but self-exterminated. Be aware that plenty of liquidators with many of these units in stock are waiting to unload the units on unsuspecting customers.

Selecting Hard Disk Controllers and Interfaces

You must consider many options when evaluating and selecting a hard disk interface and controller for your system. One of your primary considerations is to use something compatible with what you already have. Another consideration is the speed of the controller. Many systems today come with hard disks and controllers already installed. Using devices that are interface compatible with the existing controllers and drives is much simpler and less expensive than forcing a change to some new standard. In many cases, you simply can change the controller from one brand to another, keeping the actual interface specification the same, and gain as much as a three-fold increase in speed with the same drives as before! If you are willing to begin from scratch and select a controller and disk together without requiring that they work with any of your other drives or controllers, then you have much more leeway in choosing a subsystem.

This next section examines the standard controllers in most systems and how you can work with these controllers, as well as replace them with much faster units. Also discussed are the different types of drive interfaces available today: ST-506/412, ESDI, and SCSI. Choosing among these interfaces is important because the choice also affects any of your disk drive purchases as well as the ultimate speed of the controllers that you can use.

The primary job of the hard disk controller is to transmit and receive data and control signals to and from the drive. All hard disks can transmit and receive data just as fast as they spin, which means that as the drive is turning, raw data pulses are simply transmitted to the controller, which then must send these signals to the motherboard of the system.

Interleave Specification

The information stored on a floppy or hard disk is arranged in a series of concentric circular rings called tracks. When examining disk drives, especially hard disks, you should watch the drive's reported average access time, the time taken (on average) for the heads to be positioned from one track to another. Because moving across all the tracks on the disk takes longer than moving only one track, the average access time often is calculated by a process of making hundreds or thousands of individual random seeks across the disk, observing the total time taken, and dividing that time by the number of actual random seeks completed. The result is the average amount of time for each seek. Unfortunately, the importance of this specification is often overstated, especially in relation to a specification known as the data transfer rate.

The actual transfer rate of data between the drive and the motherboard is more important than access time because most drives spend more time reading and writing information than simply moving the heads around on the disk. The speed with which a program or data file is loaded or read is most affected by this data transfer rate. A faster seeking disk drive helps with the sorting of large files, where a great deal of "random access" to individual records of the file occurs and therefore many seek operations occur. But the majority of normal file load and save operations are affected most by the rate at which data can be read and written to and from the drive. This transfer rate is a factor that depends on the disk controller and not the drive itself.

The disk controller is the device that controls the data transfer of information to and from the drive. Each track on a disk is divided into sectors, shaped much like slices of a pie. The actual number of sectors on a disk can vary, depending on the density of the disk and the encoding scheme used. Disks currently are available with 17, 25, 26, 32, 34, 35, and 36 sectors per track. Other numbers of sectors per track are possible, but the numbers listed are the ones I have found on any drives available for PC systems.

Two things do not change: the rotational speed of the drive, which is 3,600 rpm, and the number of bytes in each sector, which is 512. A particular disk's maximum transfer rate is dictated, therefore, entirely by the number of sectors per track because all the other factors such as rotational speed and the amount of data in each sector is fixed. Any drive with 17 sectors per track, for example, will have the same transfer rate as any other drive with 17 sectors per track. The problem is that not all controllers can accept and transfer data at the rate possible by the drive. Also, not all motherboards are fast enough to accept data at the full rate possible by the drive even if the controller could manage it.

As an example, suppose that you have a disk with 17 sectors on each track. For this example, you are going to number the sectors on each track consecutively:

1, 2, 3, 4, 5, 6, 7, 8, 9, 10, 11, 12, 13, 14, 15, 16, 17

Now suppose that the controller was just commanded to position the heads to a particular track and read all 17 sectors from that track. The heads move and arrive at the desired track. After an average of one-half of a disk revolution, the sector numbered 1 arrives under the heads. As the disk is spinning at 3,600 rpm (60 revolutions per second), the data is read from sector 1, and as it is being transferred to the system board, the disk continues to spin. Finally, the data is moved into the motherboard, and the controller is now ready for sector 2.

A problem exists, however. Because the disk continued to spin at such a high rate of speed, several sectors passed under the head as the controller was doing its work, and the heads are now coming up on sector 5. Because you now want to read sector 2, the controller must wait as the disk spins until sector 2 comes under the heads. After some time, sector 2 is under the heads and is read. While the controller is again transferring the data to the motherboard, sectors 3, 4, and 5 move under the heads. When the controller is finally ready to read sector 3, the heads are coming up on sector 6.

As you can see, this procedure just isn't working out! The controller again must wait until sector 3 comes under the heads before it can be read. At this pace, 17 full revolutions of the disk will be needed to read all these sectors. Each revolution takes 1/60 of 1 second. So 17/60 of 1 second will be needed to read this track—nearly 1/3 of 1 second, which is quite a long time by computer standards.

Can this performance be improved? In examining how the controller was operating, you see that after the controller reads a particular sector from the disk, the controller seems to take some time to transfer the 512 bytes to the motherboard. The next sector that the controller is capable of catching is the fourth from the first one. The controller can catch every fourth sector, which in our original sector numbering scheme looks like this:

1, 2, 3, 4, 5, 6, 7, 8, 9, 10, 11, 12, 13, 14, 15, 16, 17

These sectors can be read in one revolution.

You do not want to read or write the sectors out of order, which would be too confusing for the controller, not to mention DOS, so why don't you simply *number* the sectors out of order! The new numbering scheme can take into account just how fast this controller can work, and the sectors can be numbered so that each time the controller is ready for the next sector, the one coming under the heads will be the next sector. This sector numbering scheme is shown in table 9.3.

Table 9.3
Renumbering Sectors on the Disk (Interleaving)

1, 14, 10, 6, 2, 15, 11, 7, 3, 16, 12, 8, 4, 17, 13, 9, 5

These sectors would be read in the first revolution.

1, 14, 10, 6, 2, 15, 11, 7, 3, 16, 12, 8, 4, 17, 13, 9, 5

These sectors would be read in the second revolution.

1, 14, 10, 6, 2, 15, 11, 7, 3, 16, 12, 8, 4, 17, 13, 9, 5

These sectors would be read in the third revolution.

1, 14, 10, 6, 2, 15, 11, 7, 3, 16, 12, 8, 4, 17, 13, 9, 5

These sectors would be read in the fourth revolution.

After 4 complete revolutions, you will read all the 17 sectors on the disk. Renumbering sectors on the disk is called *interleaving*, and the interleave ratio used in this example is 4 to 1, which means that the next numbered sector is physically 4 sectors away from the preceding one. The result is that 4 complete revolutions read an entire track, which saves some time because only 4/60 of 1 second is taken instead of 17/60 of 1 second at the 1 to 1 interleave.

From this information, you can reason that if you reorganized the disk so that the interleave was 3 to 1, only 3 revolutions would be needed to read a single track, which would be 3/30 of 1 second and thus faster than a 4 to 1 interleave. The problem here is with the controller and, to a much lesser extent, the system that the controller is plugged into. The way that I described this controller, it would have passed the beginning of the desired next sector if the interleave on the disk actually was 3 to 1. By missing each and every "next sector," you now will take a full 17 revolutions to read the track. In this case, a 3 to 1 interleave would be a disaster, as would a 2 to 1 or 1 to 1 interleave. The correct interleave for any system depends primarily on the controller and then on the speed of the system that the controller is plugged into.

A controller and system that can handle a consecutive sector or 1 to 1 interleave must be able to transfer data as fast as the disk can present it, which is quite a feat. Table 9.4 lists the theoretical transfer rates for various sectored disks at a 1 to 1 interleave to a 6 to 1 interleave.

Table 9.4
Data Transfer Rates in Kilobytes per Second

		Interleaves					
Interface	Sectors	1:1	2:1	3:1	4:1	5:1	6:1
ST-506/412 MFM	17	510	255	170	128	102	85
ST-506/412 RLL	25	750	375	250	188	150	125
ST-506/412 RLL	26	780	390	260	195	156	130
ESDI or SCSI	32	960	480	320	240	192	160
ESDI or SCSI	34	1,020	510	340	255	204	170
ESDI or SCSI	35	1,050	525	350	263	210	175
ESDI or SCSI	36	1,080	540	360	270	216	180

The disk controller in this example can handle 128K per second from the drive. The 1 to 1 interleave may seem unattainable, but in actuality, advances in controllers have made a 1 to 1 interleave possible and affordable. All AT and PS/2 systems are capable of this transfer rate. The only system units that really cannot use a 1 to 1 interleave, regardless of how good the controller is, are the original 4.77 MHz PC and XT types of systems. These systems have a maximum throughput to the slots of just under 400K per second, which is not quite fast enough for a 1 to 1 interleave. All the IBM PS/2 systems including the Models 50 and higher have default (standard) 1 to 1 interleaves! IBM is actually among the first personal computer manufacturers to sell systems with data transfer rates this fast.

Also note that a 1 to 1 interleave with a 17-sector disk is one thing, but with the ESDI interface on the Models 60, 70, and 80, IBM is using disks with 32, 34, 35, and 36 sectors per track, which results in more than 1 megabyte of data transfer each second! Later in this chapter, I recommend controllers that will allow any AT or AT-compatible system also to run a 1 to 1 interleave, and I recommend controllers that will allow as low as a 2 to 1 interleave for even the early and slow PC and XT systems.

If you have a standard IBM XT or AT system with a hard disk, the standard interleave used in these systems was 6 to 1 for the XT and 3 to 1 for the AT. After thorough examination of these systems and controllers, I have found that the best interleave possible for these systems is actually one lower in each case. The best interleave for the Xebec 1210 controller in a 4.77 MHz PC or XT is 5 to 1, and the best interleave for the Western Digital 1002 and 1003 controllers in a 6 MHz or 8 MHz AT system is 2 to 1. IBM picked the higher values resulting in lower performance, but IBM is known for conservatism, and this follows along with a conservative philosophy. If you simply reformat these systems to the lower interleave number, you will gain about 20 to 30 percent in data transfer performance, at no real cost!

Note that the interleave factor can be either too "loose" or too "tight" (a high number is loose, and a low number is tight). Operating with an interleave factor that is too loose results in lower performance than normally should be achieved. Operating with an interleave factor that is too tight is more serious; the controller will miss the next sector every time, which slows down the disk to pathetic rates of speed. Note also that no matter what the interleave is, whether too loose, right on, or too tight, the disk still functions with no errors, which is the reason that so many systems are incorrectly interleaved. The only way to know whether your system is incorrectly interleaved is to make some performance tests that can show you just what the performance of your system is at different interleaves and compare these test results with performance figures from your disk as it is now. One of the tested interleave values will result in the best transfer rate, which hopefully is the interleave your system is set to. The only way to change an interleave is through a low-level format of the disk.

Standard Controllers

IBM supplies certain standard controllers in the systems it sells. These controllers usually are made for IBM by some outside third party. Knowing who IBM buys from pays off, because you often can purchase the same part directly from the original manufacturer and save the markup that IBM charges to put its name on the product.

If you go to IBM to purchase either the XT Fixed Disk Controller or the AT Fixed Disk Controller, for example, the cost will set you back about $400 to $500 each. For about $100 to $150, I can buy the exact same controllers that IBM uses! The only difference is that my controllers will not have a sticker stating they were manufactured for IBM Corporation. By the way, this example applies to virtually every component in the earlier systems and even many components in the PS/2 systems. I always attempt to eliminate the middle man and buy closer to the actual source of manufacture. I save a great deal of money in parts costs, and I am assured the same or better quality—and full compatibility with the original IBM parts.

IBM has used the following controllers in its XT and AT systems:

XT with 10M and 20M disks:

- Xebec Model 1210 Hard Disk Controller

AT with 20M and 30M disks:

- Western Digital WD1002-WA2
- Western Digital WD1003A-WA2

PC and XT

The hard disk controller used in the original 10M-equipped XT is manufactured by Xebec Corporation. The specific model is the Xebec 1210 controller. The Xebec 1210 is an ST-506/412 controller that uses Modified Frequency Modulation (MFM) encoding to record data on a drive. This controller does have a ROM produced by IBM that contains the hard disk BIOS. If you purchase this controller from Xebec, you get a slightly different but completely compatible ROM. Xebec allows system integrators to copy their ROM in order to modify the built-in drive tables for a specific drive.

The later version of the IBM controller is supplied with the IBM XT with a 20M hard disk. This controller actually is the same Xebec 1210 but with a new ROM that contains different drive tables. Xebec never did sell an autoconfigure version of this controller, which would have made integrating different drives much easier.

This controller is one of the slowest controllers on the market. The controller supports at best 5 to 1 interleave on a stock PC or XT system. Note that if you use the IBM advanced diagnostics for the PC or XT, the low-level formatter produces a standard 6 to 1 interleave, which results in a paltry 85K-per-second data transfer rate. By changing the interleave to 5 to 1, you can wring 102K per second out of this controller.

One benefit of using this controller is that Xebec makes a Model 1220 that combines the function of the floppy controller for two floppy drives. This controller is hardware compatible with the 1210 and even takes the IBM or standard Xebec ROM. The floppy controller then is removed from the system, and the 1220 ends up saving a slot.

I recommend replacing this controller with an autoconfigure controller whenever you get the chance. Most other controllers also are significantly faster than the Xebec.

AT

For the AT, IBM uses two specific controllers made by Western Digital: the WD 1002-WA2 and the WD 1003A-WA2.

The original 1002 is used in the AT as a combination hard disk and floppy disk controller. Both of these controllers are standard ST-506/412 controllers that supply MFM encoding to the drive. Neither of these controllers contains a ROM BIOS that is left to the motherboard ROM. The latter 1003 version is shorter in height to fit in the XT 286. IBM also uses this controller in the newer AT systems, because it fits in these systems as well. The 1003 basically is an upgraded 1002 with a much lower chip count.

Both of these controllers support a 2 to 1 interleave even on a standard 6 MHz original AT system. The IBM advanced diagnostics' low-level formatter can put down a 2 to 1 interleave if it is selected properly, but the default is for 3 to 1 unless it is changed. Most users can realize a performance gain if they reformat to the lower interleave.

Model 30

The Model 30 uses a special interface built into the motherboard to run the hard drive. This interface appears as a modified ST-506/412. Normal drives do not plug into this modified interface without some sort of adapter cables. Most aftermarket hard disk installations for the Model 30 involve a regular PC or XT type of controller, but these end up wasting a precious slot that the built-in controller conserves.

The built-in controller normally is set to put down a 3 to 1 interleave, resulting in a disk transfer rate comparable to an untweaked AT system.

Models 50, 60, 70, and 80

The Models 50, 60, 70, and 80 in the PS/2 line use two different interfaces: the ST-506/412 or the ESDI interface. Each interface incorporates a controller running a 1 to 1 interleave, which results in data transfer rates from about 500K per second to 1,000K per second. The latter rates are for the ESDI interface drives and controllers that IBM uses in all the PS/2 systems equipped with drives of 70M or larger.

IBM makes these ST-506/412 and ESDI controllers. Some of the newer drives even have these controllers built right into the drive's logic board, which reduces the chip and circuit count, which lowers cost and improves reliability. And in the desktop Models 50, 50Z, and 70 systems, the drives are interfaced to the system without any cables at all. Either the drive and controller directly mate together, or the drive with an integrated controller plugs directly into a Micro Channel slot through the use of an "interposer" card. This further increases reliability and makes the installation literally a "snap." The other compatible system vendors have some catching up to do in this area.

Aftermarket Controllers

I can recommend several aftermarket controllers for the XT and AT types of systems.

For a standard ST-506/412 MFM encoded controller in an XT type of system, I recommend these controllers:

    Scientific Micro Systems (SMS) Omti 5520A-10
    Western Digital WDXT-GEN

If your drive is rated for RLL encoding and meets the demanding requirements to support this encoding (such as having a voice coil actuator), you may use these RLL encoded versions of the preceding controllers:

    Scientific Micro Systems (SMS) Omti 5527A-10
    Western Digital WD1002A-27X

In each case, the SMS controllers listed allow a 2 to 1 interleave in a stock 4.77 MHz PC or XT, which results in an incredible 255K-per-second transfer rate in these systems. Many "turbo" compatibles with 8 MHz clocks can run the SMS Omti controller at a full 1 to 1 interleave. Simply replacing the stock IBM (Xebec 1210) XT controller with one of these controllers triples the throughput over the stock XT. IBM runs a slow 6 to 1 interleave on the Xebec controller. At a list price of less than $99, the Omti is the cheapest "turbo" board on the market for the PC or XT.

The Western Digital controllers only allow a 4 to 1 interleave in a stock PC or XT, which makes them at least twice as slow as the SMS Omti controllers. All these controllers have autoconfigure ROMs that allow dynamic configuration of the drive and freedom from drive-table limitations.

If you need an ST-506/412 MFM encoded controller for the AT, consider the following:

> Western Digital WD1006V-SM2
> Western Digital WD1003S-WA4

Each controller is a combination hard disk and floppy controller. These controllers are a direct bolt in replacing the original 1002 or 1003 that IBM uses in the AT systems. The 1006 controller is capable of supporting a 1 to 1 consecutive sector interleave, which results in a transfer rate of 510K per second. This controller will put the AT back in competition with the PS/2 systems as far as performance goes. This controller is three times faster than the one on a standard AT as delivered from IBM. The 1003 version listed here only supports the 2 to 1 interleave but has the unique feature of combining a serial and parallel interface on the board as well. Because these boards are fully supported by the AT BIOS, they run OS/2 or any other protected-mode operating system in which a replacement BIOS is loaded from disk. Other manufacturers make controllers for the AT, but all the others have to be "Western Digital compatible" because that is what the ROM BIOS and OS/2 drivers expect to see. Until Western Digital came out with the 1006 models, no real 1 to 1 interleave AT controllers were available that would boot unmodified IBM OS/2.

If you want an ST-506/412 RLL encoded controller for the AT, and your drives and cables are up to par, consider using this controller:

> Western Digital 1006V-SR2

This controller is much like the other 1006; it supports a full 1 to 1 interleave. But this controller uses RLL encoding, which increases track density to 26 sectors and increases the transfer rate to 780K per second. This controller also has an on board BIOS that can autoconfigure the drives. The drawback is that this controller may not be supported in the autoconfigure mode under OS/2 without a special driver. If your drive tables can be modified to match the drive, you can disable the on board BIOS and simply run with the direct support of the system CMOS configuration. Because this controller is becoming popular and is made by Western Digital, I assume that other drivers will be available to support full autoconfigure mode under OS/2.

If you decide to venture into the ESDI world and really see what a hard disk can do today, several controllers are available that you might want to look at. For an ESDI controller that works in the 8-bit PC or XT bus, I recommend the following:

Scientific Micro Systems (SMS) Omti 6510

For an AT 16-bit ESDI interface controller, I recommend the following:

Western Digital WD1007A-WAH
Scientific Micro Systems (SMS) Omti 8640

The Western Digital model contains only the hard disk interface and does not support the floppy drives. To replace the lost floppy function when substituting this card for the standard Western Digital 1002 or 1003, you can use the Western Digital WD1002A-FOX floppy controller, which supports up to four drives with an optional external connector. The SMS Omti controller is unique in that it has ST-506/412, ESDI, and a floppy interface built in.

If you want to use the SCSI interface, I can recommend several adapters. For either the 8-bit or 16-bit XT or AT bus, you can use the following:

Future Domain TMC-830 DNK
Future Domain TMC-871 DNK

Both of these adapters are SCSI host adapters, but the 871 model includes a high-density floppy controller. With these kits comes complete software, including setup and driver software for DOS, XENIX, and Novell Netware. OS/2 drivers are due shortly.

For an SCSI and floppy controller with a full 16-bit interface, consider the following:

Western Digital 7000-FASST2

This, like the future domain adapter, includes a full set of driver and installation software for DOS, XENIX, and Netware. Again, OS/2 drivers are on the way.

For any of the Micro Channel-equipped IBM PS/2 systems, the included controllers are quite good. All of IBM's Micro Channel controllers support full 1 to 1 interleaving and are available in either ST-506/412 MFM or ESDI versions. IBM currently supports ST-506/412 RLL encoding only with drives that have embedded controllers, which follows along with IBM's desire for reliability with these systems (as you will see when you learn the MFM versus RLL encoding later in this chapter).

Western Digital currently makes several controllers for the PS/2 systems that may be used in lieu of IBM's own controllers. For an ST-506/412 MFM encoded controller, consider the following:

Western Digital WD1006V-MC1

For the same ST-506/412 interface, but with RLL encoding, try the following:

Western Digital WD1006V-MCR

If you need an ESDI controller for the Micro Channel, use the following:

Western Digital WD1007V-MC1

And, finally, if your tastes run to SCSI and you need a version for the Micro Channel, I recommend these controllers:

Future Domain SCSI Micro Channel Adapter
Western Digital 7000-MSC

No matter what types of hard disks you intend to plug into your system, you will find an adapter to meet your needs. This list does not include every type of adapter on the market; each controller here has been selected for various reasons, including actual experimentation, comparison, and evaluation. These controllers work in accordance with accepted standards for the actual interface and supplied software. Many of these controllers stand out for various reasons; some are compatible with the existing controllers in the systems, and some improve speed and reliability.

Interface Specifications

Three popular interfaces are available for PC types of hard disk drives:

ST-506/412
ESDI
SCSI

ST-506/412

The ST-506/412 interface was developed originally by Seagate Technologies around 1980. The interface was designed specifically for a drive that Seagate manufactured; the drive is called the ST-506 drive. This drive is a 6M unformatted (5M formatted) drive in a full-height 5 1/4-inch form factor. Needless to say, by today's standards this drive is a tank! In 1981, Seagate introduced the ST-412 drive, which added a feature to the interface called buffered seek. The ST-412 is noted for being one of the drives IBM selected originally for the XT. This drive is a 10M (12M unformatted) drive and also qualifies as a tank today.

Most other drive manufacturers who wanted to introduce a hard disk for PC systems decided to adopt the Seagate-developed standard rather than reinvent the wheel. Thus, this interface became as popular as it is today. One nice thing about this interface is that it is a "plug and play" design. Because the interface was developed by one company and left alone by all the other companies that later adopted it, the interface has remained constant. Thus, you can grab virtually any drive off the shelf, plug it into an ST-506/412 controller, and make it work. No custom cables or special modifications are needed for any drives. The only item to customize is the drive-table support in the system.

The only problem with this interface is that it is growing a little gray around the edges and is not quite up to snuff in this "386" world. After all, this interface was designed originally for a 5M drive. Also, the drive capacity is limited; you will not find any manufacturers of drives larger than 140M using this interface. All the larger drives on the market use ESDI or SCSI.

The ST-506/412 interface specifies that the data separator or encoder/decoder is located on the controller. This encoder/decoder converts the digital signal into a series of magnetic flux transitions for storage on the drive itself. The particular method used for the conversion of digital information into the analog flux change signals is called the *encoding scheme*. Several different coding schemes are used for disk drives, but two are popular in PC applications:

> Modified Frequency Modulation (MFM)
> Run Length Limited (RLL 2,7)

The primary difference between the two encoding schemes is the density that they achieve. The standard ST-506/412 format defines that the drive will contain 17 sectors per track, with each sector containing 512 bytes of data. With an RLL encoding scheme, the number of sectors per track is raised to 25 or 26, which results in about 50 percent more data on each track and, at the same interleave value, a 50 percent greater transfer rate.

Data Encoding Schemes

Two types of encoding schemes are discussed in this section: the MFM and the RLL.

MFM stands for Modified Frequency Modulation, which is a type of encoding scheme for converting digital information into magnetic flux changes that are stored on a disk drive. Encoding schemes are used in telecommunications for converting digital data bits into various tones for transmission over the telephone line. For disk drives, the digital bits are converted into a pattern of magnetic impulses or "flux reversals" that actually are stored on the disk. The item that does the conversion to and from the encoded data is called a modulator/demodulator when you are referring to telephone system encoding. You know this device as a *modem* for short. For the disk interface, the device that accomplishes the conversion to flux reversals and the reconversion back to digital data is called an encoder/decoder or *endec*.

MFM is a fixed-length scheme, where a set pattern of bits always will consume the same linear space on the disk. The encoding scheme determines the efficiency of the recording on the disk. The MFM encoding scheme was devised originally as a way to build in clocking information with data pulses. With this particular method, flux reversals on the disk always will be evenly spaced in time so that the beginnings of one bit can be separated from another. This type of scheme allows even single bit errors to be detected easily and corrected by the controller electronics.

Under the ST-506/412 interface, the number of sectors per track will be 17 if the data is encoded with MFM. Floppy disk drives including all the 5 1/4-inch and 3 1/2-inch formats also currently use MFM encoding for data storage.

The RLL encoding scheme stands for Run Length Limited. The RLL usually is followed by two numbers. An example is RLL 2,7. The first number indicates the minimum run of zero bits between two ones, and the second number indicates the maximum number of zeros between two ones—or the limit. RLL encoding has far less regular intervals between flux changes and is more prone to errors than MFM encoding. Essentially, each MFM bit cell is now broken down into three RLL bit cells, each of which may have a flux reversal. This places far greater demands on the timing of the controller and drive electronics because these flux reversals now may arrive at highly irregular intervals. Virtually no clocking information exists, so accurately reading the timing of the flux changes is now paramount. Also, because this code is not a fixed-length code, a single bit error cannot be detected and may corrupt as many as five total bits, which means that the controller must have a much more sophisticated error detection and correction routine.

The great benefit of RLL is the increased density and, consequently, the increased transfer rate as well. The nominal increase in density and transfer rate over MFM encoding is 50 percent, which allows a drive that did store 20M under MFM encoding to store 30M. Note that the actual density of the flux reversals per inch of track will not change, so the magnetic density is not changed—just the data density.

An analogy can be made with the secret codes that you may have used as a child. Many children devise their own secret code so that they can send messages to each other that only they can read. Imagine a code where each letter of the alphabet is converted to the letter at the opposite end of the alphabet. The letter A is converted to Z, the letter B is converted to Y, and so on. This encoding scheme can be used to encode a message in writing. Note that this encoding scheme is no more "dense" than the original message was. If the original message was 500 letters long, the encoded message also will be 500 letters long.

Now suppose that a new code is developed, where certain words are given a unique letter or symbol to represent them. Now a message that was originally 500 letters may be coded as a 50-symbol message, where each single symbol represents an entire word in the original message. This new encoding scheme is 10 times more efficient than the preceding one. The problem, though, is that this scheme may be more difficult to interpret quickly; any error in the new scheme results in the loss of an entire word rather than a single letter (which easily can be corrected in context), and many symbols must be memorized if every possible word is to be encoded.

This denser encoding scheme is exactly how RLL works; with approximately the same "flux density," the drive now can appear to store 50 percent more information. The problems are mainly ones of reliability and data integrity.

Because of the way the ST-506/412 interface is designed, the MFM endec or RLL endec resides on the controller card in the PC, which is where the actual encoding and decoding take place. Thus, unfortunately, the endec is placed a long way from the actual data transmitting and receiving source. Taking an existing system that has a controller with an MFM endec and changing to a controller with an RLL endec is analogous to changing a modem from a 2400-baud unit to a 9600-baud unit in order to "increase the density" of the signal transmitted over the phone line. If this procedure is done with local calling in mind, few problems should result. But if you intend to use one of the newer 9600-baud modems over a dial-up MCI long-distance line between Chicago and Honolulu, you are in trouble. Because of the number of switches, lines, and distance that the signal must travel, an excess of noise and time-delay disturbances results, and these disturbances interrupt communication at this speed and render it virtually unusable. A data-quality line is probably required for long-distance communications at these speeds. At lesser speeds, the effects of noise and propagation delay are not as pronounced, and communications at 1200 baud probably would be completely successful without data-quality lines.

The endec's placement in the ST-506/412 interface is, for RLL-encoded systems, an engineering disaster. Unfortunately, you often will see an advertisement in some computer magazine that states, "Try the new Super Turbo Controller that will increase your disk capacity and speed by 50 percent!" What the ad isn't telling you is that you may be in for a real hassle with continuous read/write errors, constant reformatting, and constant data loss.

To allow for accurate RLL encoding and decoding, many more demands are placed on the drive and controller. In particular, the sensitivity to timing means that the drive must be a high-quality unit with a voice coil positioner at the least. A stepper motor drive has too many tracking and temperature errors to allow accurate RLL encoding and decoding to occur. Most drive manufacturers "RLL certify" ST-506/412 drives that also have plated (sputtered) thin film media. This media has a higher signal-to-noise ratio and bandwidth in general than the standard oxide-coated media does.

Try to stay away from RLL encoding controllers for the ST-506/412 interface; however, if you don't take this suggestion, follow these precautions and you will have success with no measurable loss in data integrity:

- If possible, use a drive with the controller built-in, which places the endec on the drive.

- Only use voice coil drives.

- Use drives with thin film (sputtered, plated) media.

- Ensure that the low-level format is done properly and at operating temperature and position.

- Make the cables short and use gold-plated connectors.

- Route the cables away from noise sources (fans, network cards, etc.) in the system unit.

In short, if you optimize all the other considerations, you can set up a workable, reliable, high-capacity, high-speed ST-506/412 interface using RLL encoding. If you use the cheapest stepper motor, oxide-media drives, use cheap cables that are too long and simply stuffed into the system unit, and fail to do a proper low-level format, you simply are asking for trouble. Unfortunately, I see these occurrences all the time, which is giving RLL encoding an undeservedly bad name.

Notice that I always mention ST-506/412 when discussing RLL encoding. The reason is that in the ESDI and SCSI interface, the data separator or endec is actually part of the drive itself and cannot be changed with a different controller. All the controllers simply send pure digital information to the drive, which does all the encoding and decoding internally. This procedure amounts to a local telephone call. For this primary reason, these interfaces are much more reliable than the older ST-506/412 interface and share none of the problems with RLL encoding. Actually, most ESDI and SCSI drives now use RLL encoding, and you really have no choice in the matter because this capability is built into the drive itself and has nothing to do with the controller. Absolutely nothing is wrong with RLL as long as it is done correctly.

ESDI

ESDI stands for Enhanced Small Device Interface and is a specialized hard disk and tape drive interface established as a standard in 1983 by Maxtor Corporation. Maxtor led a consortium of drive manufacturers to adopt its proposed interface as a new high-performance standard. Provisions for increased reliability also were made; the encoder/decoder or endec was built into the drive itself, for example. ESDI is a high-speed interface and is currently capable of 24 megabits per second in transfer rate as a specified top end limit. Most drives running ESDI are limited to a maximum of 10 or 15 megabits per second at this time.

An important feature of the ESDI is that it has been adopted throughout the industry without each individual manufacturer making changes. The ESDI is another "plug and play" type of interface—more so than the older ST-506/412 interface because the ESDI has enhanced commands so that the controller can read the drive's capacity parameters directly off the drive as well as control defect mapping. This enhanced communications protocol is how the drive-table problem is completely avoided by IBM in its high-end ESDI systems. COMPAQ also adopted ESDI in the higher end Deskpro 386 systems.

Currently, not many ESDI interface controllers are available for the PC or XT systems; they really cannot handle the greater throughput anyway. Western Digital has a controller called the WD1007A-WAH that is an ESDI controller supporting two hard drives and no floppies. If you replace your standard controller with one of these controllers in an AT system, you also must purchase a separate AT type of floppy controller. I think that Western Digital eventually will introduce a combination hard/floppy version of this ESDI controller.

Most ESDI implementations have drives that are formatted to 34 sectors per track, which is twice the standard ST-506/412 implementation of 17 sectors per track and results in about twice the data transfer rate assuming that the interleave is 1 to 1. Almost without exception, any ESDI controller supports a 1 to 1 interleave, which allows for a 1,020K-per-second transfer rate.

In the PC world as controlled by IBM, the ESDI interface is rapidly becoming the new standard, replacing the older ST-506/412 interface. IBM now uses ESDI interfacing on all PS/2 systems that incorporate 70M or greater drives. For example, the PS/2 Model 80-041 comes with a 44M ST-506/412 drive that runs a 1 to 1 interleave at 17 sectors per track using MFM encoding, and the PS/2 Model 80-071 comes with a 70M ESDI drive that runs a 1 to 1 interleave at 36 sectors per track using RLL encoding. This information means that at 1 to 1 interleaving, the 44M drive can transfer all 17 sectors of data to the system in a single revolution of the disk, and with 60 revolutions per second, the result is a maximum transfer rate of 510K per second; the ESDI drive running 1 to 1 interleaving can transfer all 36 sectors in a single revolution, and with 60 revolutions per second, the result is a maximum transfer rate of 1,080K per second. The 70M drive has more than twice the data transfer rate of the 44M drive because of the use of the ESDI interface. COMPAQ and other high-end compatible systems manufacturers now also supply 1 to 1 interleave ESDI systems on all of their higher end systems as well.

SCSI

SCSI stands for Small Computer Systems Interface. This interface has its roots in the SASI (Shugart Associates System Interface), which preceded it. SCSI is sometimes called "scuzzy" by the computer community. This interface actually is not a disk interface at all but is really a systems-level interface, which means that SCSI is not really a type of "controller." Instead, you can plug up to eight "controllers" into a single SCSI system, and they all can talk to one another. One of these controllers is called a "host adapter." It is plugged into a slot in the PC and acts as the gateway for the SCSI bus and the system. Therefore, SCSI doesn't really work directly with a hard disk, and the disk drive still needs a controller to talk to SCSI.

You can, for example, use both ST-506/412 and ESDI drives and their respective controllers, which plug into the SCSI interface. An SCSI host adapter in your system allows it to talk to all of the attached devices much like a small Local Area Network (LAN). A single SCSI bus supports as many as eight so-called "logical units" or ports. One of these ports is the adapter card in your PC, so the other seven ports can be various other items. A serial port controller can be plugged into one of the ports, a floppy controller in another port, an

ST-506/412 hard disk controller with two drives in another port, an ESDI controller with two drives in another port, a graphics scanner in another port, and so on. You get the idea!

A single SCSI host adapter in your system can add expandability to the system because of the number of other items that can be connected. Apple originally rallied around the SCSI interface as an inexpensive way out of the bind the company put itself in with the Macintosh. When Apple realized its mistake in making the Macintosh a closed system (no slots), the company realized that the easiest way to gain expandability was to build in an SCSI port. External peripherals now can be added in this way to the slotless Macs. Because the PC systems always have been expandable, you didn't see the same push toward SCSI as in the Apple world. With eight slots supporting different devices and controllers in the PCs, SCSI wasn't needed.

Now SCSI is starting to become popular for even the IBM-based world because of the great expandability and the number of devices that are coming out with built-in SCSI interfaces. If you don't have a drive with a built-in drive controller and SCSI port adapter, you must follow this complicated procedure for installing a hard disk on the SCSI bus: first you must decide which type of hard disk you want and what interface it will be—either ST-506/412 or ESDI. If you choose ESDI, you get an SCSI to ESDI adapter, which has both an SCSI port and an ESDI controller built in. This adapter runs two hard disks and allows them to talk through the SCSI bus. In the PC system unit, you install an SCSI host adapter, which allows your system unit to talk to the ESDI controller, with the SCSI bus as the medium. You also need to rewrite your systems software because the controller no longer can be accessed directly but has to be spoken to through the protocols defined by SCSI.

This procedure obviously is overly complicated. You are adding unnecessary circuitry that would not be needed if you simply could plug the ESDI controller directly into the PC slots. Also, the software that talks to the controller would not have to be rewritten. This reasoning is why SCSI generally has been avoided by the PC community. Note, however, that the SCSI system just mentioned can have as many as 7 of these ESDI to SCSI controllers with each running two drives, which means a maximum of 14 total ESDI drives with the possibility that each one can be a Maxtor 650M unit. That's 9,100 megabytes or 8.8 gigabytes of storage!

Many drive manufacturers now are simply building a complete drive controller and SCSI port adapter directly into the drive itself. This scheme really simplifies things. You now will have a single SCSI host adapter in your system to which you can connect up to seven additional drives with "embedded" SCSI adapters. Knowing just what type of controller (ESDI, ST-506/412, etc.) actually is inside the drive is not even important because you cannot get to it. You can talk only to the drive with the SCSI protocols, which significantly reduces the total number of circuits in a system, and the chip count as well, and adds a great deal of flexibility and expandability into the system. Because of devices with embedded controllers and SCSI ports, you probably will see a great number of SCSI-based peripherals in the future. Remember that these peripherals are not limited only to disk drives but also may include tape drive, printers, plotters, scanners, and virtually anything else.

The lack of a real standard is stalling the acceptance of SCSI in the PC marketplace. SCSI is a "standard" in much the same way that RS-232 is a standard, probably because the SCSI standard has been designed primarily by a committee and no single manufacturer has led the way. A little too much flexibility is available, and each manufacturer has his or her own idea of just how SCSI should be implemented. What you have are various "flavors" of SCSI in the marketplace. Software is the glue that allows these different implementations of SCSI to work together, which unfortunately complicates things. SCSI is not "plug and play" because of these problems. Apple loves SCSI and does have its own flavor. IBM so far has rejected SCSI due to its nonstandard nature. Right now, the ANSI committee that controls SCSI is working on a new version called SCSI II, which will be more well defined than the current standard. Rumors also are circulating that IBM will introduce a "standard" SCSI adapter for PC systems, with complete operating systems support. If the SCSI bus continues to gain acceptance in the PC world, it may become the standard peripheral interface in the future.

I have done some experimentation with SCSI interfacing in the PC world and have met with a great deal of success after the required software and ROM-based drivers are in place. If you consider implementing the SCSI interface in your systems, you will find that companies such as Future Domain, Western Digital, and Adaptec have much to offer in the way of XT, AT, and PS/2 Micro Channel adapters, as well as software drivers and ROMs that allow the interface to work.

Installing Hard Disks

In this section, you will look at the installation of a typical hard disk and how it is integrated into a particular system. The installation procedure requires several steps, and each one has a particular order of progression to the next. The drive has to be configured correctly, physically installed, formatted, configured to receive an operating system, and have the systems software installed.

Here is an outline of the major steps to follow in the installation of a hard disk for any PC, XT, AT, or PS/2 system:

    I. Drive configuration
       A. Drive-select jumpers
       B. Terminating resistors
    II. Physical installation
    III. Machine to disk configuration
    IV. Formatting and software installation
       A. Low-level format
          1. Defect mapping
          2. Interleave selection
       B. Partitioning
       C. High-level format

These steps are discussed in this section. They are simple to follow and, if done properly, result in the successful installation of a bootable hard disk. Extra care is taken to ensure that certain considerations for reliability and data integrity are followed—that this installation will last a long time and give few problems, for example.

Drive Configuration

Configuring a hard disk drive is similar to configuring a floppy drive, but it actually is much less complicated. Only two things need to be set: the drive-select jumper and a terminating resistor.

In this book, I will use as my example the installation of a standard ST-506/412 type of drive into XT and AT systems. An ESDI installation is essentially similar in most respects, but SCSI installations can be different because of the lack of real SCSI standards for IBM types of PC systems. In this case, follow the installation instructions that come with the drive and host adapter, and I recommend that you purchase everything from one company.

Drive-Select Jumper Setting

Before a hard disk can be installed, it must be configured properly. The first item to be configured is the drive-select jumper setting. The drive-select jumper is set so that the drive and controller can communicate properly on the same "channel." Separate channels are available for up to four drives in the ST-506/412 and ESDI controller specifications, and SCSI systems allow up to seven controllers with possibly up to four drives on each controller. The more standard, embedded SCSI systems have a single controller built in or embedded in the drive, which reduces the total to seven possible drive addresses, called *logical units*.

Setting the drive-select jumpers for a hard disk is almost exactly the same as setting these jumpers for floppy disk drives. Both drives must be drive selected depending on the type of cable being used.

Cable Types

Two cables run from the controller to a hard disk drive. These cables consist of a larger 34-pin *control* cable and a smaller 20-pin *data* cable. The control cable is run in a daisy-chain arrangement to either one or two hard disks. This cable may be wired as a straight-through design, or it may have a twist in some of the wires before the last physical connector on the cable (the drive C connector). The data cable is wired straight through. Two data-cable connector positions are on the controller—one for each of two drives. These cables are not daisy chained but run from the controller to each drive separately.

IBM always uses a twist in the fixed disk control cable to "fool" the first drive. In this case, wires 25 through 29 are twisted. Note that you must not use a floppy drive cable as a hard disk control cable if the floppy cable also is twisted. IBM twists wires 10 through 16 on the floppy disk cable, which are not the same as for the hard disk. I always prefer to use a straight cable because it eliminates this confusion and makes the cable usable for either floppy drives or hard disks.

The drive-select setting is simple if you have the twisted cable. The drive at the last physical connector on the end of the cable after the twist is drive C, and it is set as the second drive-select position (DS1 or DS2). As with floppy drives, the setting of DS1 or DS2 for the second drive depends on whether the first drive setting is labeled DS0 or DS1. The drive plugged into the control-cable center connector between the other drive and the controller card is drive D, and it also is set to the second drive-select position (DS1 or DS2).

If the cable is not twisted, drive C is set to the first drive-select position (DS0 or DS1), and drive D is set to the second drive-select position (DS1 or DS2).

As the drive is installed, make sure that the cables are connected properly, with the odd-colored wire in the cable aligned toward the notches in the drive circuit boards. Also be sure that a spare power connector exists to plug into the hard disk. The IBM PC and XT types of power supplies have only two drive power connectors. IBM and other companies sell a power "Y" splitter cable, which can be used to adapt one cable from the power supply to power two drives. Make sure that your power supply can handle the load of the additional drive(s) or purchase an aftermarket unit that can. Most of the better aftermarket supplies have four drive power connectors, eliminating the need for the "Y" splitter cables.

Terminating Resistors

A terminating resistor must be installed on the drive that is physically the farthest from the controller—in other words, the last one on the daisy chain. In any IBM system, the terminating resistor is installed in drive C. The other drive plugged into the middle of the cable (drive D) must not have a terminating resistor installed. See the OEM drive manual to locate the terminating resistor.

Physical Installation

The physical installation of a hard disk is much the same as for a floppy drive. You must ensure that you have the correct hardware such as screws and brackets for half-height drives before you can install the drive. Also, different faceplate or bezel options are available; make sure that you have the right bezel for your application. The AT, for example, will not need any sort of faceplate at all, and if one is on the drive, the faceplate probably should be removed.

AT systems require plastic rails that are secured to the sides of the drives so they can be slid into the proper place in the system. COMPAQ does not use the same type of rails that work in an AT. When you purchase a drive, the vendor usually includes the AT rails free of charge, but you have to go to COMPAQ to purchase its special rails. PC and XT types of systems do not need these rails but may need a bracket to allow double stacking of half-height drives. Also available from various drive vendors are blank half-height bezels that you can use to fill the hole above a half-height drive installed in a full-height bay. Alternatively, many half-height drives can be ordered with a full-height bezel so that no hole is created.

System to Disk Configuration

With the drive physically installed, you can begin the configuration of the *system* to the *drive*. You have to inform the system about this drive so the system can boot from that drive when powered on. This information can be set and stored in several ways, depending on the type of system you have.

In order to begin the setup procedure, you need to know several specific items about your hard disk drive, controllers, and the system ROM BIOS. To continue properly, you must have the OEM manuals for these devices to continue properly. Make sure that when you purchase any disk or controller products, the vendor includes these manuals. Many vendors do not include the manuals unless you specifically ask. If the vendor doesn't know what you're talking about, buy from a vendor who does. For IBM-supplied disks and controllers, you can get the original manufacturer's (usually not IBM) documentation or use the IBM documentation. The controller cards and drives are all documented in the *Technical Reference Options and Adapters* manual. Note that you also may need to purchase updates to these books to cover your particular system. The motherboards with ROM BIOS documentation are in the standard technical reference manuals for each system.

You need to know these facts about your particular drive:

    Number of cylinders
    Number of heads
    Starting cylinder for write precompensation
    Range of acceptable head step pulse timing
    Locations of all defects by cylinder and head

All this information, with the exception of the defect list, is in the drive manual. The defect list usually is on a sticker on the top or front of the drive—or possibly on a piece of paper attached to the drive. You must copy and record this defect information because it is required later for a proper low-level format.

You need to know various facts about your particular controller. If the controller is one of the recommended autoconfigure XT types, you need to know the following:

What Interrupt Request Channel (IRQ) is used?
What DMA channel (DRQ) is used?
What ROM memory locations are used?
What is the start location for the autoconfigure routine?
What I/O ports are used?
What head step pulse rates are possible?
What is the best interleave possible?

If the controller is not an autoconfigure type, you need to know the following:

What are the built-in drive-table values?
How are drive types selected?

If the controller is an AT type, the list is much simpler:

What Interrupt Request Channel (IRQ) is used?
What I/O ports are used?
What head step pulse rates are possible?
What is the best interleave possible?

The AT controllers do not have (or should not have) any on board ROM or autoconfigure routine. If these controllers do, you are on your own with items such as OS/2, XENIX, and Network software. AT controllers also don't use DMA channels for data transfer; instead, they use the high-speed I/O ports in the AT. For most of these controllers, like those used by IBM, the head step pulse rate is fixed by the motherboard ROM BIOS at 35 μsec. The motherboard ROM also contains the available drive types, and the SETUP program is used to select the desired type.

If the system is an AT type, you need the following information about the ROM BIOS:

What are the supported drive-type values?
What is the selected head step pulse rate?

For IBM systems, this documentation is provided in the technical reference manuals. The Appendix includes a list of the supported drive types, and the head step rate selected is 35 μsec. For other non-IBM systems, you need your system technical reference manual to locate this information.

Once you have amassed this information, you can continue with the installation of your drive.

Tell the System What Is Connected

Next, you will want to inform the system of the kind of drive that is attached so the system eventually will boot off of the drive. I am going to demonstrate the installation of a drive in both an XT and AT type of system. In both cases, I will use the same drive. With knowledge of drive interfacing, you can install just about any drive in any system.

The example drive that will be installed is a drive I actually have in one of my systems: a Maxtor XT 1140, which is an ST-506/412 drive designed for MFM encoding. This drive is a full-height 5 1/4-inch platter drive that will fit easily in an XT or AT system. The drive is a 140M unformatted, 119M formatted, drive. You can use the drive in any system where you have an ST-506/412 interface controller. It is a fairly high-performance drive with an advertised 27 ms seek time (across 119M) and has 8 platters with 15 read/write heads plus 1 servo head.

In this example, the first thing you need to do is read the drive manual and locate the required information discussed in the preceding section.

The information you need follows:

```
918 cylinders
15 heads
No write precompensation required
2 to 3100 μsec head step pulse timing acceptable
2 to 13 μsec head step pulse timing optimum
7 defects total:
    Cyl 188 Hd 7
    Cyl 217 Hd 5
    Cyl 218 Hd 5
    Cyl 219 Hd 5
```

Cyl 601 Hd 13
Cyl 798 Hd 10
Cyl 835 Hd 5

At this point, you physically install the drive. You set the drive-select jumper correctly depending on the type of cable being used. And you also ensure that the last physical drive on the control cable has the terminating resistor in place and that the other drive (if one exists) has the terminating resistor removed.

Now that the drive is physically installed and the necessary information is secured, you need to undertake the system configuration and software installation of this drive.

Autoconfigure Controllers for a PC and XT

In my example, to install such a drive into an XT, I could use the original XT controller (Xebec 1210); but the built-in tables in that controller don't match my drive. I would have to download the ROM to disk and patch it to contain the correct drive-table values, which is costly.

If you can wield the DOS DEBUG program and have access to an EPROM burner, this controller can have the correct table ''patched'' in to one of the existing four table positions. If that procedure is done, this controller will operate correctly with the drive.

I used this procedure on my original vintage 1983 XT controller. The result? My system works fine but still only runs a best interleave of 5 to 1. With faster autoconfigure ROM controllers available at an inexpensive price, I would be a fool to do this today. Instead, I will purchase a Scientific Micro Systems Omti 5520A-10 controller, which has complete autoconfigure capability (no ROM burning) and supports a 2 to 1 interleave in the slow XT. This controller can be installed with no hassle, and it runs a full three times faster than the old Xebec and costs only $75. (Times sure have changed. My original Xebec 1210 cost me $795 in 1983!)

The next step is to read the manual to gather the required information before proceeding with the installation:

Interrupt Request Channel (IRQ) = 5
DMA Channel (DRQ) = 3
ROM locations used = C8000 to C9FFF
Autoconfigure start location = C8006

I/O ports = 320 to 32F
Step pulse rates = 10, 25, 50, 70, 200, and 3000 μsec
Best interleave = 2 to 1 (4.77 MHz XT)

You need some of this information simply to ensure that this card is uniquely configured compared with other cards in the system. You cannot have any other cards using the same IRQ, DMA, ROM, or I/O ports as this card. Write down this information for future reference and cross-check for conflicts any time other cards are added to the system. The autoconfigure start location, step pulse rates, and interleave information is necessary for you to complete the setup.

You need to activate the controller's built-in autoconfigure routine. This type of controller then prompts you for the information about the drive (normally found in ROM tables) and then proceeds to actually record this information directly onto the drive in a cylinder reserved for this purpose by the controller. The advantage here is that any time you change drives, this controller always can adapt. You never will have to patch any ROM-based tables, because this drive stores them dynamically on the drive. After this routine is completed, every time the system is powered up, the controller reads this information and "knows" how to boot from this drive.

To run this autoconfigure routine, follow these steps:

1. Boot DOS 3.3 or higher.

2. Run the DOS DEBUG program

3. At the DEBUG prompt, enter *G=C800:6*.

That last instruction tells DEBUG to move the system instruction pointer to the autoconfigure ROM start location. You must find this information in the controller manual because different manufacturers' autoconfigure controllers have different starting locations. Here are the locations for several popular brands:

Manufacturer	Actual Location	Segment:Offset Form
SMS OMTI	C8006	C800:0006 or C800:6
Western Digital	C8005	C800:0005 or C800:5
Adaptec	C8CCC	C800:0CCC or C800:CCC

If you are using DEBUG, note that the memory locations cannot be entered as the actual location but must instead be entered in the *Segment:Offset* form shown in the preceding list.

After that last DEBUG instruction is entered, the autoconfigure routine should announce its presence. You are asked several questions that require some of the information you gathered about the drive and controller. You are asked how many heads and cylinders the drive has, what the starting write precompensation cylinder is, and how fast the step pulses should be sent. Using the information on the drive and controller that you gathered, you simply will answer these questions.

For the step pulse rate in my example, I will indicate that the controller should pulse the drive with step pulses spaced 10 μsec apart. I made this decision by looking at the range of spacing the drive will accept, comparing it to what the controller can send, and selecting the fastest rate that both can agree on. This procedure is not unlike configuring a serial printer and serial port for 9600 baud transmission. Why not go as fast as the hardware will allow? The data from this particular drive's manual also states that drive seek performance degrades if step pulses are sent at a spacing greater than 13 μsec. This specification can really "tweak" a drive's seek performance!

You also are asked the desired interleave. I have determined an interleave of 2 to 1 as the best value for this controller in a 4.77 MHz PC or XT system. I determined this information with a simple trial and error testing session where I formatted the disk at various interleaves, from 6 to 1 (the IBM XT default) down to 1 to 1, with this controller in the same type of system. The transfer rate basically improved with each lower interleave until I tried 1 to 1; at this time, the transfer rate slowed by more than 800 percent. At 1 to 1, this controller cannot keep up with the rate at which the next sector will come under the heads, and 17 full revolutions of the disk are required to read a track, compared with 2 revolutions to read a track at a 2 to 1 interleave.

Finally, you are asked whether the drive has any defects and, if so, to enter them. This drive has seven defects, which are printed on a sticker on top of the drive as well as included on a printed sheet in the box from the manufacturer. Entering this information causes the low-level format program to specially mark these tracks with invalid checksum figures, which ensures that nothing ever will be able to read or write these locations. Later, when DOS is used to high-level format the disk, the DOS format program will be unable to read these locations and will mark the file allocation table with information so that the locations never will be utilized. Failing to enter these locations properly at this time may allow these defective tracks to be used by data and program files, which will cause any files that ''land'' in these locations to be candidates for corruption. Always mark these locations.

With this type of controller, the actual low-level format is part of the autoconfigure routine. After you answer all these questions, the drive is low-level formatted, the defects are marked, and a scan is made for any defects that were marked improperly or that became bad after the manufacturer's original tests. And, finally, the autoconfigure information is written to a specially reserved track on the disk. When this process is completed, the drive is ready for DOS installation.

AT SETUP Program and Drive Types

To install this drive into an AT in my example, I will use the original AT controller (Western Digital WD1003A-WA2). This controller does not have any on board ROM to worry about and therefore is not an autoconfigure type. For AT types of systems, you set the drive type by looking up your particular drive information in the table of types located in the system ROM. In my case, I will have to match the parameters of my drive to one of the table entries in the system ROM.

The required information about this controller follows:

    Interrupt Request Channel (IRQ) = 14
    I/O ports = 1F0 to 1F7
    Step pulse rate = 35 μsec (selected by BIOS)
    Best interleave = 2 to 1 (6 MHz to 8 MHz AT)

Because this controller is really two controllers on one piece of real estate, with a floppy controller as the second, some additional information specific to the floppy controller is needed:

    Interrupt Request Channel (IRQ) = 6
    DMA channel (DRQ) = 2
    I/O ports = 3F0 to 3F7

You need some of this information simply to ensure that this card is uniquely configured compared with other cards in the system. You cannot have any other cards using the same IRQ, DMA, ROM, or I/O ports as this card. Write down this information for future reference and cross-check for conflicts any time any other cards are added to the system. The step pulse rates and interleave information are all that is really necessary for you to complete the setup.

The data from this particular drive's manual states that drive-seek performance degrades if step pulses are sent at a spacing greater than 13 μsec. This is unfortunate because this controller can run either 16 μsec or 35 μsec, but the choice of settings is made by a value in the AT motherboard ROM BIOS. The AT ROM "hard codes" this to the 35 μsec setting for step pulse rate, and it cannot be changed unless you can make the controller run independent of the ROM setting. This controller cannot be made to run independent of the ROM setting; some others, however, can. My experience has been that the drive actually runs 25 ms seeks with the proper step pulse rate, but in the AT, the slower step pulse rate causes the drive to run an average access of 29 ms, which is 4 ms slower than it should be. If I want to bother with patching the AT ROM BIOS, I can change the step pulse rate figure for the controller to 16 μsec, which probably would pick up a couple milliseconds of average seek time. I am not sure that the result would be worth the hassle, but I will put it on my list of things to do in case I find myself with some extra time.

After you have the proper information from the drive and controller, you need to match the drive's parameters to the motherboard ROM drive-table entries. You will find this table in the Appendix. The information is from the various system technical reference manuals and is accurate only for IBM's systems. Notice that how far the table extends depends on which ROM you have in your system. In my example system, I have the "Princess Model" AT Model 339, which has an 11/15/85 ROM with 23 entries in the drive tables. If you have a COMPAQ, Zenith, AT&T, Tandy, or Dell, for example, you will need the technical reference manual for that system to locate your tables. The values for table entries 1 to 14 generally will be the same as IBM, but any values from 16 on definitely will be different. "Type 19" probably will be different in any system with a different ROM BIOS. Without this information, you will have to get out DEBUG and go hunting. (Now you know why I refuse to purchase systems without technical reference manuals! I simply have better things to do than "hack" around a system looking for information that should be provided in a book.)

With the drive tables and actual drive information in hand, you need to find a table entry that matches on heads, cylinders, and the write precompensation starting cylinder. You may not find an exact match on any of these values, which is OK. You can use any type that has fewer actual cylinders and heads indicated than your drive really has, but you cannot use any type that has more.

My drive has 918 cylinders and 15 heads, for example, so Type 9 looks like the best match. Type 9 indicates 900 cylinders and 15 heads, which is OK because these values are less than or equal to the actual number the drive has. If you select a type that indicates more cylinders or heads than the drive has, you quickly will become familiar with the 1790 or 1791 POST error codes. These error codes indicate a "fixed disk 0 (or disk 1) error," which means "you must try again."

This drive requires no write precompensation; this specification also matches Type 9 because Type 9 indicates a precompensation start cylinder of 65535, which is simply the largest number that can be stored with 16 bits. No matter how big the drive is, write precompensation will never begin. For any tables with a value of 0 for this figure, write precompensation should be done for all cylinders.

The "landing cylinder" designation is totally unnecessary because this drive automatically parks and locks its heads when the system is powered down.

To select Type 9, you simply boot the Setup or Diagnostics disk that comes with the guide to operations manual and run the SETUP program. Here is where you normally set the date and time, memory, type of video board, and so on. Proceed to the section where you specify the hard disk type and enter *9*. Then simply reboot the system. You are done with this procedure.

Sometimes you will find drives that don't match the table entries very well at all. With the Type 9 drive, you will not get to use the last 18 cylinders of the drive, which is not a catastrophe but does cost almost 2M of room on the disk. You will get to use only 117M rather than the actual 119M on the disk.

One way around the table-match problem is to purchase drives that match your tables. That solution is too obvious or simple for some people and can limit you, especially in the earlier ROM-equipped systems. Note that most compatible systems have table entries all the way to number 47, but IBM AT systems stop much earlier than that. Another way around the drive-table limitation is to patch the correct entries in for the desired drive and simply reburn your own ROMs. This solution is illegal from a commercial point of view and is limited to "hacker" status, which means that I can do this procedure to my own system but cannot sell patched IBM ROMs legally. Another way around the limits is to purchase and install a set of clone ROM BIOS chips to replace the IBM chips. For example, you can purchase a Phoenix AT ROM BIOS set for about $50. A final solution to the problem, which lets you keep your original ROMs, is to purchase and install one of the ''ROM dubbing'' kits that can effectively patch in whatever table entries you want—legally and with no hassle. This last solution seems to be one of the best.

ROM Dubbing Kits for AT Drive-Type Tables

''ROM Dubbing'' kits are available from several companies. You can purchase these kits as a set of two plug-in ROM chips that are added to the AT motherboard in the two empty ROM sockets (as a plug-in card for the early ATs that have all four sockets filled with ROM chips already). The card also can be used for the XT 286, which only has two ROM sockets that are filled already.

The kits that I recommend are available from these companies:

Geneva Enterprises (Second Nature ROMs)
Golden Bow (Dub-14)

These kits conveniently get you around the ROM drive-table limitations in any AT type of system. With these kits, you can use any drive to its full capacity.

Formatting and Software Installation

Now you will learn about the formatting and software setup of the drive. You follow basically three steps to complete this process. The outline of these steps follows:

1. Low-level format
   A. Defect mapping
   B. Interleave selection
2. Partitioning
3. High-level format

Low-Level Format

The low-level format includes drive defect mapping and interleave selection. You will need information about the drive and controller.

A low-level format is a *real format*, which means that here is where the actual tracks and sectors of the disk are outlined and written. You should do this procedure to any newly purchased or acquired disk drives. A proper low-level format is one of the most important things you can do to ensure that the drive has a long and trouble-free life. An improper low-level format causes the drive to lose data and have many read/write failures. The low-level format procedure is also the primary "repair" procedure for dealing with hard disk drives.

Defect Mapping

Defect mapping always is done properly during the low-level format. As mentioned earlier, the drive in my example has seven defects, which were printed on a sticker on top of the drive as well as included on a printed sheet in the box from the manufacturer. Entering this information causes the low-level format program to specially mark these tracks with invalid checksum figures, which ensures that nothing ever will read or write these locations. Later, when DOS is used to high-level format the disk, the DOS format program will be unable to read these locations and will mark the file allocation table with information so that these locations never are utilized. Failing to enter these locations properly at this time may allow these defective tracks to be used by data and program files, which will cause any files that "land" in these locations to be candidates for corruption. Always mark these locations.

Interleave Selection

Interleave selection always is done by a low-level format routine. You should know the best value for your particular controller and system combination.

Software Tools

Several types of low-level format programs are available. The ones that I recommend follow:

- A controller's autoconfigure ROM
- Htest/Hformat by Paul Mace Software
- IBM's advanced diagnostics

If the controller has an autoconfigure ROM, you usually must use the format routing built into the controller's autoconfigure system. This is the only way that the special information the controller will look for can be written to the disk.

For AT systems or other systems with controllers that do not have an autoconfigure routine, I recommend the Htest/Hformat program from Paul Mace Software. This program is simply the finest hard disk technician's tool available on today's market.

This program has many capabilities that make it a desirable addition to your toolbox. Some of the features are discussed next.

Htest/Hformat includes an interleave testing program called Hoptimum, which tests your disk at different interleave values and makes the determination of which offers the best performance. After making this determination, the program actually can redo the entire disk at the new interleave by performing a low-level format of one cylinder at a time, backing up and restoring each cylinder as it goes. The result is that the program can calculate the best interleave, reset the disk to that interleave, and retain all the data on the drive—all while running unattended! You must, of course, make sure that you do a backup of the disk before this process is started because, otherwise, if any power interruptions or problems occur, you might find a corrupted disk when you get back. Never trust any program such as this one with data that is not backed up.

Htest/Hformat also performs perhaps the best surface analysis or surface scan of any program available. This program is the one to have if you suspect defects that are additional to the ones the manufacturer indicated on the defect list. This program also is essential if you actually have lost the original defect list and need to be sure that any improper areas of the disk are marked.

Htest/Hformat also works independently of any operating systems, so it is compatible with DOS, OS/2, XENIX, Novell Netware, or any other software. Htest/Hformat has a host of other minor functions, such as controller and drive test programs and a program that prints out the currently marked defects on the drive so you can be sure that your predecessor marked these locations properly. This program costs $89 and is an essential part of my "toolkit."

The standard low-level format program for IBM systems is the advanced diagnostics program that comes with the hardware maintenance and service manuals. The diagnostics program is a comprehensive system test, and the hard disk formatter for AT systems is only one part of the program.

This program is fine for formatting and testing hard disks, and it has numerous features. A couple of problems exist, however. The AT version does not allow an interleave selection of 1 to 1, which may not be a problem for most but will render this program useless if you upgrade to a controller that can handle a 1 to 1 interleave. The XT version simply does not allow any interleave selection other than 6 to 1, which renders this routine useless on PC or XT systems. Also, the PC or XT version does not allow the entry of the manufacturer's defect list—an unforgivable oversight.

Despite some problems, the AT version of this format program is quite useful if you don't have a controller that can handle a 1 to 1 interleave. The PC or XT version is unusable, which fortunately isn't a big problem because most PC or XT system users will use an autoconfigure type of controller that has the proper built-in formatter anyway.

Partitioning

Partitioning means preparing the boot sector of the disk so that the DOS FORMAT program can operate correctly. Partitioning was first made necessary to allow several different operating systems to coexist on a single hard disk.

DOS FDISK

The DOS FDISK program is the accepted standard for partitioning hard disks. The FDISK program can create up to four partitions on a disk, and two of these partitions can be used for DOS.

As far as DOS is concerned, two total DOS partitions can exist—the primary and extended partitions. Here you find some version differences. DOS 3.3 allows the primary partition to be only as big as 32M, but the extended partition can be as big as the rest of the disk. This secondary partition must be split into logical DOS volumes (drive letters) of 32M or less. Therefore, the total organization of the disk is this: the primary partition usually is assigned drive letter C, and the extended partition can contain drives D through Z. Each drive letter can be associated with only as much as 32M of disk space. My larger Maxtor disk will have to be split into the two partitions, with a 32M primary partition as C: and the rest of the disk assigned to an extended partition with the logical DOS drive letters D, E, and F. The D: and E: volumes also will be 32M, but the F: volume will be the remainder of the disk—about 16M in this case.

The DOS 32M Limitation

This limitation is finally broken with DOS 4.0. The new DOS allows partition sizes (drive letters) to be associated with as much as 2 gigabyte partitions. Apparently, you will not be running into this limitation in the near future. The partitioning scheme also is compatible with earlier DOS 3.3 if you stick with sub-32M partitions like the previous DOS would accept. Until I can upgrade all my software utilities and tools to understand the larger partitions, I will keep my disk split as sub-32M volumes.

Aftermarket Partitioning Utilities

With the advent of DOS 3.3 and 4.0, most of the aftermarket partitioning utilities are not really needed except for special cases. I recommend that you stay away from these types of utilities and instead upgrade to a newer version of DOS. Many problems are associated with using these partitioning programs that DOS simply doesn't have because the support of the larger partitions is "built in."

High-Level Format

The final step is to complete the DOS high-level format, which will write a blank file allocation table and create a blank root directory on the disk. This procedure usually is done with the standard DOS FORMAT program. Follow this syntax:

```
FORMAT C: /S /V
```

This command high-level formats drive C (or Volume C if it is a multivolume drive) and places the hidden operating system files on the first part of this partition, as well as prompts for the entry of a volume label to be stored on the disk at completion.

Repairing Hard Disk Drives

Repairing hard drives is usually something you cannot do if the problem is really a true "hard" problem. The majority of hard disk problems are of the "soft" type, where a new low-level format and defect mapping session will take care of the problem. These "soft" problems are characterized by a drive that sounds normal but gives various read/write errors. "Hard" problems are those that are mechanical in nature, such as when the drive sounds as though loose marbles are inside the sealed HDA, or you can hear loose parts inside the drive. Scraping and grinding noises constantly emanating from the drive—with absolutely no reading or writing capability at all—also qualify as a "hard" error. A low-level format probably will not put those types of drives back into service. In those cases, you will do best to send the drive back to the manufacturer where the drive can be opened in a clean room environment and repaired properly. Several third-party repair depots also are available that specialize in hard disk drives and have the requisite clean room facilities. See the vendor list in the Appendix for a list of drive manufacturers and companies that specialize in hard disk drive repair.

Be prepared to discover that the cost of repair may be more than half the cost of a completely new drive, so you may have to decide whether to repair or simply replace the drive in question. Almost always, trying to have any of the cheaper 20M or 30M stepper motor drives repaired is foolish. If these units fail, discard them and purchase something better in their place. The larger voice coil drives are economical to have repaired because the replacement costs are much higher.

Chapter Summary

In this chapter, you have examined hard disks and controllers in great detail. The physical and logical operation of the disk was covered as well as the installation and configuration of hard disks and controllers. You can use much of this information to select and configure a hard disk system properly. When a hard disk system is properly designed and installed, you will experience a much lower incidence of problems compared with systems that are haphazardly installed. Because most problems are ones of software, installation, or formatting, you can use this information to restore many failing drives to normal operation.

The next chapter continues your tour through the system and focuses on other peripherals such as video subsystems, memory boards, and communications adapters.

10

Peripherals

When you equip an IBM or compatible computer, you have a wide variety of options and accessories to choose from. Numerous choices can be made with the display options, memory adapter types, and communications boards when you're setting up or installing an IBM or compatible computer. In this chapter, you will examine the choices and learn about the features and drawbacks of each of the available systems. All the standard video systems will be discussed and examined, including the new MCGA and VGA standards that are part of the PS/2 systems from IBM. Memory adapters will be discussed, including conventional, extended, and expanded memory boards, and communications adapters such as serial and parallel ports will be examined.

Video Display Hardware

During the early years of the IBM PC and compatibles' development cycle, the video system choice was an extremely simple one. Did you want color or not? The Monochrome Display Adapter and Display was available for those who did not desire color, and the Color Graphics Adapter and Display was available for those who wanted color. Since then, a multitude of adapters and display options have hit the market, giving you many additional choices. The PS/2 has a new type of video standard that makes many of the early standards obsolete.

In the area of video adapters and displays, abiding by industry standards is extremely important. Many video systems are not supported by every program and system peripheral. In this book, I avoid any proprietary standards, because they have little to offer the typical system user other than headaches caused by incompatibility problems. So far only IBM has had the muscle needed to define these standards, and even IBM has produced a few video display products that failed to become industry standards. Here are the IBM display systems that are verifiable standards in today's industry:

Monochrome Display Adapter
Color Graphics Adapter
Enhanced Graphics Adapter
Video Graphics Array (PS/2 Display Adapter)

These adapters and video standards are supported by every program that runs on IBM or compatible equipment.

Adapters and Displays

Various display adapters usually require different displays because they use different horizontal and vertical scanning frequencies. Table 10.1 lists the horizontal and vertical scan rates produced by the various IBM adapters.

Table 10.1
Scan Rates Produced by IBM Adapters

Adapter	Horizontal	Vertical
MDA	18.432 KHz	50 Hz
CGA	15.750 KHz	60 Hz
EGA	18.432 KHz	50 Hz (MDA mode)
EGA	15.750 KHz	60 Hz (CGA mode)
EGA	22.000 KHz	60 Hz (EGA mode)
PGA	30.480 KHz	60 Hz
MCGA	31.500 KHz	70 Hz (all modes except 640 × 480)
MCGA	31.500 KHz	60 Hz (640 × 480 mode)
VGA	31.500 KHz	70 Hz (all modes except 640 × 480)

Adapter	Horizontal	Vertical
VGA	31.500 KHz	60 Hz (640 × 480 mode)
8514	31.500 KHz	70 Hz (all modes except 640 × 480 and 1,024 × 768)
8514	31.500 KHz	60 Hz (640 × 480 mode)
8514	31.500 KHz	43.5 Hz (1,024 × 768 mode)

The vertical scan rate indicates how often the screen flashes per second. Less "flicker" is seen in displays with high vertical scan rates. For a display to work with a particular adapter, the display must match these scan frequencies. A monitor can be destroyed if an inappropriate adapter is used. Some of the newer monitors, multiscan or multisync, support multiple scanning frequencies. The NEC Multisync is one of the most popular, but my favorite is the Sony 1302A Multiscan.

When switching modes on some of these multiscanning monitors, the image may not occupy the full screen. The image may appear shrunken in the display's center. Some of the images may be off-center and require additional monitor adjustment. Be sure that you see how a display operates with your particular adapter before committing yourself to the purchase.

Monochrome Display and Adapter

The original and simplest display combination you can choose is the IBM Monochrome Display and Printer Adapter card and the IBM Monochrome Display. A character-only combination, the display has no inherent graphics capabilities. This combination was originally a top-selling option because the combination is fairly cost effective. As a bonus, this combination also provides a printer interface that does not consume an extra slot. The display is known for clarity and high resolution, making this combination ideal for businesses, especially businesses that use word processing or spreadsheets.

Because the monochrome display is a character-only display, you do not have the capability to run software requiring graphics. Originally, the only drawback seemed to be that you couldn't play games on a monochrome display, but today even the most serious business software uses graphics and color to great advantage. With the 9-by-14 dots character box (matrix), the IBM monochrome monitor displays attractive characters.

Color Graphics Display and Adapter

If a generic display for a non-PS/2 existed, the Color Graphics Adapter would be that display. With the introduction of programs that use dot-addressable graphics, the Color Graphics Adapter became popular because many IBM monochrome owners wanted more than simple character graphics.

This adapter has two basic modes of operation: Alphanumeric (A/N) or All Points Addressable (APA). In alphanumeric mode, the card operates in a 40-column-by-25-line mode or an 80-column-by-25-line mode with 16 colors. In both modes, the character set is formed with a resolution of 8 pixels by 8 pixels. In APA mode, two resolutions are available: a medium-resolution color mode (320 by 200) and a two-color high-resolution mode (640 by 200). In the medium-resolution mode, four colors are available. With the Color Graphics Adapter, you can choose from a number of monitors because the horizontal scanning rate of the c/g board is the industry standard of 15.75 KHz. You can purchase an amber monitor for $125 and upgrade to an RGB monitor later. The choices you are faced with at the time of the RGB purchase are overwhelming when you consider brands and features.

Dot pitch indicates the distance between the dots making up the display. The smaller the pitch is, the sharper the image is. The IBM PC color monitor has a pitch of 0.43 mm, but because the monitor uses a black-matrix tube, a good-looking picture with vivid colors is produced.

Most of the color monitors sold for the IBM PC are RGBs, not composite monitors. The color signal of a composite monitor contains a mixture of colors that must be decoded or separated. RGB monitors receive red, green, and blue separately and combine the colors in different proportions to generate other colors. RGB monitors offer better resolution than composite monitors and do a much better job of displaying 80 columns.

If low cost is the biggest concern, this monitor and adapter combination should prove to be a worthwhile purchase. The resolution, however, is not as good as IBM's other offerings. For most applications, I recommend using a VGA-compatible adapter and display, because most new software is being written to use this standard. The CGA card is becoming outdated.

Enhanced Color Display and Adapter

The IBM Enhanced Graphics System, discontinued when the PS/2 systems were introduced, consisted of a graphics board, a graphics memory expansion board, a graphics memory module kit, and a high-resolution color monitor. The whole package cost about $1,800. The aftermarket gave IBM a great deal of competition in this area, and you could put together a similar system from non-IBM vendors for about $700.

One nice thing about the EGA was that you could proceed in modular steps. Because the card worked with any of the monitors IBM had out at the time, you could use the card with the IBM Monochrome Display, the earlier IBM Color Display, or the new IBM Enhanced Color Display. With the EGA, the IBM Color Monitor displays 16 colors in 320-by-200 or 640-by-200 mode. With the EGA, the IBM Monochrome Monitor shows a resolution of 640 by 350 with a 9-by-14 character box (text mode).

With the EGA, the IBM Enhanced Color Display is capable of 640 by 350 with 16 colors. The character box for text is 8 by 14 compared to 8 by 8 for the earlier CGA board and monitor. The 8-by-8 character box can be used, however, to display 43 lines of text. Through software, the character box can be manipulated up to the size of 8 by 32. The 16 colors can be selected from a palette of 64.

You can enlarge a RAM-resident 256-member character set to 512 characters by using the IBM Memory Expansion Card. A 1,024 character set is added with the IBM Graphics Memory Module Kit. These character sets are loaded from programs.

You may be wondering where all this memory is going to fit into the PC's memory map. The memory fits in the unused space between the end of RAM user memory and the current display adapter memory. The Enhanced Graphics Color Adapter has a maximum 128K of memory that maps into the RAM space just above the 640K boundary. If you have installed more than 640K, you probably will lose the extra memory after installing the EGA. The Graphics Memory Expansion Card adds 64K to the standard 64K for a total of 128K. The IBM Graphics Memory Module Kit adds another 128K for a total of 256K. This second 128K of memory is only on the card and does not consume any of the PC's memory space. Note that almost every aftermarket EGA card came configured with the full 256K of memory without having to add expansion options.

The PS/2 VGA system supersedes the EGA and is much better in many respects. The EGA had problems emulating the earlier CGA or MDA adapters, and some software that worked with the earlier cards would not run on the EGA until the authors modified the program. More than two years passed before a substantial amount of software was available that supported the EGA display system. The VGA system had the benefit of being installed in more than two million systems during the first year, creating a great deal of software support in a very short time. For these reasons, I do not recommend further purchases of EGA display systems. The VGA systems have much more to offer and are sometimes less expensive.

Professional Color Display and Adapter

The Professional Graphics Display System is a video display product that IBM introduced in 1984. The system, which cost $4,290, was too expensive to become a mainstream product. The system is composed of a Professional Graphics Monitor and a Professional Graphics Card Set. When fully expanded, this card set uses three slots in an XT or AT system, which is a high price to pay. The features, however, are impressive. The PGA offers three-dimensional rotation and clipping as a built-in hardware function. The adapter can run 60 frames per second of animation, because the Professional Graphics Adapter uses a built-in dedicated microcomputer. The PGA has an 8088 microprocessor, 320K of RAM, and 64K of ROM. The resolution of this system is 640-by-480 pixels. Note that the VGA system built into the PS/2 motherboards also has this resolution capability.

The expense and complexity of this system limits the system to supporting only specialized applications. The PGA system was designed for applications such as Computer Aided Design (CAD). The capabilities of an AT with this board and monitor set combined with software such as AutoCAD resulted in a system with the power and functionality of CAD systems costing up to $50,000 or more at the time. The Professional Graphics card and monitor were targeted toward the engineering and scientific areas rather than financial or business applications. This system was discontinued when the PS/2 was introduced and has been replaced by the VGA and 8514 graphics standards for these newer systems.

Personal System/2 Displays and Adapters

Personal System/2 adapters support a new family of displays: the Personal System/2 Monochrome Display 8503, the Personal System/2 Color Display 8512, the Personal System/2 Color Display 8513, and the Personal System/2 Color Display 8514.

Digital versus Analog

One of the most striking differences between the new PS/2 video standards and the earlier standards is that the new system is an *analog* system (and the earlier displays were *digital*). Why are the PS/2 displays going from digital to analog, when virtually everything else you come into contact with is going to digital? For example, I have dumped my record collection and turntable (analog) for a new compact disk player (digital). The newer VCRs have digital picture storage for smooth slow motion and freeze-frame capability. Also available are digital televisions that enable you to watch several channels on a single screen by splitting the screen or placing a picture within another picture. The PBX systems in most companies are digital. The entire telephone network is going digital. With everything else going digital, why did IBM decide to change the video of the PS/2 systems to analog? The answer is *color*.

Most personal computer displays introduced before the PS/2 were digital. This type of display generates different colors by firing the red, green, and blue (RGB) electron beams in an on or off mode. You can display up to 8 colors (2 to the third power). In the IBM displays and adapters, another signal, *intensity*, doubles the number of color combinations from 8 to 16 by displaying each color at one of two intensity levels. This digital display is easy to manufacture and offers simplicity with consistent color combinations from system to system. The real drawback of the digital display system is the limited number of possible colors.

In the PS/2 systems, IBM went to an analog display circuit. Analog displays work like the digital displays that use the RGB electron beams to construct various colors. The big difference is that each color in the analog display system can be displayed at 64 levels of intensity. This versatility provides a total of 262,144 possible colors (64 to the third power). When making computer graphics appear realistic, color is more important than high resolution, because the human eye perceives a picture with more colors as more realistic. IBM has moved graphics into an analog form to take advantage of the color capability.

Video Graphics Array

PS/2 systems contain the primary display adapter circuits on the motherboard. The circuits are called the Video Graphics Array and are implemented by a single custom VLSI chip designed and manufactured by IBM. This is a completely new standard and originally was found only in the PS/2. To adapt this new graphics standard to the earlier systems, IBM introduced the PS/2 Display Adapter. Called a VGA card, this adapter contains the complete VGA circuit on a full-length adapter board with an 8-bit interface, giving earlier systems and compatibles the capability to have VGA graphics.

The VGA BIOS (Basic Input/Output System) is the control software residing in the system ROM for controlling VGA circuits. With the BIOS, software can initiate commands and functions without having to manipulate the VGA directly. Programs become somewhat hardware independent and can call a consistent set of commands and functions built into the system's ROM control software. Future implementations of the VGA will be different in hardware but will respond to the same BIOS calls and functions. New features will be added as a superset of the existing functions. The VGA, therefore, will be compatible with the earlier graphics and text BIOS functions that were built into the PC systems from the beginning. The VGA can run almost any software that was written originally for the MDA, CGA, or EGA.

In a perfect world, software programmers would write to the BIOS interface instead of directly to the hardware, promoting software interchanges between different types of hardware. More frequently, however, the programmer wants the software to perform better and writes the program to control the hardware directly. The programmer achieves a higher performance application dependent on the hardware it is first written to. You have to make sure that your hardware is 100-percent compatible with the standard so that software written to a standard piece of hardware runs on your system. Note that just because a manufacturer claims this register level of compatibility does not mean that the product is 100-percent compatible or that all software runs as it would on a true IBM VGA. Right now, the only manufacturer of a truly compatible VGA adapter is IBM.

The VGA displays up to 256 colors on-screen, from a palette of 262,144 (256K) colors. Because the VGA outputs an analog signal, a monitor that accepts an analog input is required. The 200 line modes produced by the new MCGA and VGA are double-scanned; each of the lines is repeated twice before a new set is scanned. The 200 line modes, therefore, really consist of 400 lines, but the lines can be controlled only in pairs.

Color summing to 64 gray shades is done in the ROM BIOS for monochrome displays. The summing routine is initiated if the BIOS detects the monochrome display when the system is booted. This routine uses a formula that takes the desired color and rewrites the formula to involve all three color guns, producing varying intensities of gray. The color that would be displayed, for example, is converted into 30 percent red plus 59 percent green plus 11 percent blue to achieve the desired gray.

The VGA uses up to 64 shades of gray when converting color modes of operations for display on the IBM Monochrome Display 8503. Users who prefer a monochrome display, therefore, can execute color-based applications.

Table 10.2 lists the VGA display modes.

Table 10.2
VGA Display Modes

Type	Colors	Chars × Lines	Char Box	Picture Elements
A/N	16/256K	40 × 25	8 × 8	320 × 200
A/N	16/256K	80 × 25	8 × 8	640 × 200
A/N	16/256K	40 × 25	8 × 14	320 × 350
A/N	16/256K	80 × 25	8 × 14	640 × 350
A/N	16/256K	40 × 25	9 × 16	360 × 400
A/N	16/256K	80 × 25	9 × 16	720 × 400

Table 10.2—*continued*

Type	Colors	Chars × Lines	Char Box	Picture Elements
APA	4/256K	40 × 25	8 × 8	320 × 200
APA	2/256K	80 × 25	8 × 8	640 × 200
A/N	MONO	80 × 25	9 × 14	720 × 350
A/N	MONO	80 × 25	9 × 16	720 × 400
APA	16/256K	40 × 25	8 × 8	320 × 200
APA	16/256K	80 × 25	8 × 8	640 × 200
APA	4/256K	80 × 25	8 × 14	640 × 350
APA	16/256K	80 × 25	8 × 14	640 × 350
APA	2/256K	80 × 30	8 × 16	640 × 480
APA	16/256K	80 × 30	8 × 16	640 × 480
APA	256/256K	40 × 25	8 × 8	320 × 200

A/N = Alphanumeric
APA = All Points Addressable

8514 Display Adapter

The PS/2 Display Adapter 8514/A offers higher resolution and more colors than the standard VGA. This adapter is designed to use the PS/2 Color Display 8514 and plugs into a Micro Channel slot in any PS/2 model so equipped. All operation modes of the built-in VGA continue to be available. An IBM Personal System/2 8514 Memory Expansion Kit is available for the IBM Display Adapter 8514/A. This kit gives increased color and gray scale support.

The IBM Display Adapter 8514/A has the following advantages:

- Hardware assistance for advanced text, image, and graphics functions

- New high-content display modes

- Increased color and monochrome capability

- Support for the new family of IBM displays

- MDA, CGA, EGA, and VGA modes available

- 256/256K colors and 64/64 gray scales with Memory Expansion Kit

In order to take full advantage of this adapter, the 8514 Display should be used. This display is matched to the capabilities of the adapter.

Multi-Color Graphics Array

The Multi-Color Graphics Array (MCGA) is a graphics adapter that has been integrated into the motherboard of the Models 25 and 30. The MCGA supports all Color Graphics Adapter (CGA) modes when an IBM analog display is attached. Any previous IBM display is not compatible. In addition to providing existing CGA mode support, the MCGA includes four new expanded modes.

The MCGA uses up to 64 shades of gray when converting color modes of operations for display on the IBM Monochrome Display 8503. Those who prefer a monochrome display can execute color-based applications.

Technical specifications of the MCGA are as follows:

- CGA compatible (31.5 KHz double-scanned)
- Not compatible with digital monitors
- 64K multiport RAM for displays
- Palette of 262,144 colors
- Analog drive, subminiature 15-pin, D-shell connector
- 70 Hz refresh rate in all but 640-by-480 mode
- Loadable character font capability (512 characters)
- Color summing to 64 gray shades in BIOS for monochrome display

Table 10.3 lists the new MCGA display modes.

Table 10.3
New MCGA Display Modes

Type	Colors	Chars × Lines	Char Box	Picture Elements
A/N	16/256K	40 × 25	8 × 16	
A/N	16/256K	80 × 25	8 × 16	
APA	2/256K	80 × 30	8 × 16	640 × 480
APA	256/256K	40 × 25	8 × 8	320 × 200

A/N = Alphanumeric
APA = All Points Addressable

IBM Analog Monitors

When IBM introduced the analog VGA, the company had to introduce new monitors that were compatible with the new graphics standard. The following monitors were introduced:

PS/2 Monochrome Display 8503
PS/2 Color Display 8512
PS/2 Color Display 8513
PS/2 Color Display 8514

The IBM PS/2 Monochrome Display 8503 may be used with any of the newer IBM PS/2 system units or display adapters. The monochrome display is the lowest cost IBM display for Personal System/2 and is the natural choice for users who have little interest in color. In text applications, the monochrome display produces sharper characters than color displays. Graphics are supported with different shades of gray. This monochrome display is ideal for applications that are entirely text-based, because of the high resolution. Another ideal application is as the display for a network file server system. This display is all that is necessary for the occasional monitoring of server activity and performance. The 8503 display is the least expensive display available.

The IBM Color Display 8512 takes maximum advantage of the capabilities of the PS/2 MCGA at a low cost. The 8512 is particularly effective when the primary application is the presentation of color images, including video projections or developing images to use as slides.

Some users may select the 8512 display as the output device for VGA-equipped systems such as the PS/2 Model 50 or 60. The IBM Color Display 8513, however, is better suited to that environment. The 8513's visual characteristics surpass the 8512's in clarity and sharpness, primarily because of the fine spacing between the dots used to create characters and images on-screen.

The 8513 is the color display that should be directed toward users whose text and graphics applications involve long hours of usage. Applications in which word processing or spreadsheets are used benefit greatly from this monitor's increased resolution in text mode. The smaller the screen is, the finer the resolution appears. The best of both worlds is an extremely high-resolution, large-screen display that reduces eyestrain.

The IBM PS/2 Color Display 8514 is positioned as the top IBM PS/2 display offering. With the 1,024-by-768-by-256 color capability, you can create strikingly realistic images. This display may be used with any combination of the new IBM PS/2 Model 30, 50, 60, or 80 system units or adapters. An IBM PS/2 Display Adapter 8514/A is required to exploit the 8514 display's full capabilities. The 8514 is intended for applications that require advanced functions, high resolution, and high performance. When configured with an IBM PS/2 Display Adapter 8514/A, the 8514 display is well suited for specialized graphics, image workstation, scientific and engineering, and host-interactive environments. Host-interactive graphics are graphics applications that run in the mainframe (or host) environment, with the PC acting as a highly intelligent graphics terminal operating interactively with the mainframe. The larger screen size and the capability to display 146 columns and 51 rows offer additional advantages for applications such as spreadsheets and word processing.

The 8514 stands out in desktop publishing and CAD environments, in which the increased resolution is combined with the 8514 display adapter to take advantage of the display's capabilities. Rumors from IBM indicate that the VGA eventually will include all the capabilities of the 8514 adapter—the next step in the evolution of PC graphics standards.

Troubleshooting and Servicing

The servicing of most graphics adapters and monitors is simple, even though servicing often is left undone. Whether an adapter or display is found to be defective or dysfunctional, it usually is replaced as a single unit. Most of today's cards cost much more to service than to replace, and the documentation required to service the adapters properly is not available. You cannot get schematic diagrams, parts lists, wiring diagrams, and so on, for most adapters. Many adapters now are constructed with surface-mount technology that requires an investment in a $5,000 rework station before you can remove and replace these components by hand. You cannot use a $25 pencil type of soldering iron on these boards.

Servicing displays is slightly different. Although a display often is replaced as a whole unit, many displays are too expensive to replace. Your best bet is to contact the company from whom the display was purchased. Often the manufacturer is the only one who can repair the monitor. If your NEC Multisync XL display goes out, for example, a swap with another monitor can confirm that the display is the problem. After the problem is narrowed down to the display, a call to NEC provides you with the location of the nearest factory repair depot.

You cannot repair this display yourself or even have standard repair shop personnel, such as TV service people, work on the unit. First, opening the case of a color display exposes you to as high as 35,000 volts of electricity. Touching the wrong item can be fatal. The display circuits can sometimes hold these high voltages for hours, days, or even weeks after the power is shut off. A qualified service person needs to discharge the tube and any power capacitors before proceeding. Second, the required documentation is not available for repairing any of the modern displays. These displays do not have schematic diagrams, board layouts, parts lists, or any of the items necessary for you to properly diagnose the display.

For most displays, you are limited to making simple adjustments, and for color displays, the adjustments can be quite formidable if you do not have experience in this area. Even factory service technicians often lack proper documentation and service information for newer models. They usually exchange your unit for another and repair the defective one later. Never buy a display that does not have a local factory repair depot.

Memory Boards

When discussing memory and memory adapter boards, you should consider the following three types of memory:

- Conventional Memory
- Extended Memory
- Expanded Memory

Memory differs in several ways, from where the memory is located to what processors can address what types of memory. Figure 10.1 shows the relative "locations" of the different types of memory in relation to the system logical memory map.

The map in figure 10.1 was constructed with an 80286-based system as a model. The 80386 system map is the same, but the total amount of extended and conventional memory adds up to 4 gigabytes. The 80286 processor has a total of 16 megabytes of memory including conventional and extended memories. This 16 megabytes is all the

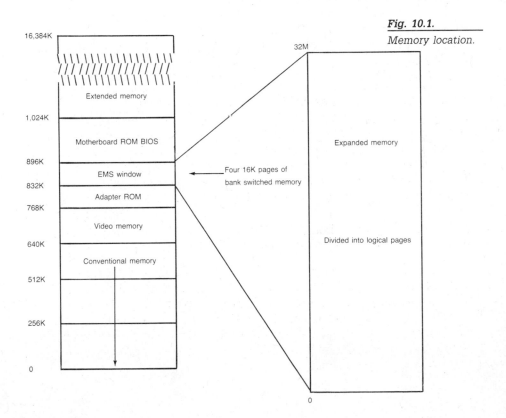

Fig. 10.1.

Memory location.

memory addressable by the processor. Expanded memory lies completely out of the processor-addressable portion, except for the 64K window through which expanded memory is accessed. Expanded memory cannot be used for running applications programs, which explains why expanded memory is slower than conventional and extended memory.

The memory layout in PS/2 systems is almost the same as the memory structure in classic PC systems. Models 25 and 30 are nearly identical to the PC and XT. Models 50 and 60 are the same as the XT-286 and AT. Model 80 is the only system with a new memory architecture, but even Model 80 is not dramatically different.

Any system using an 8088 or 8086 processor, such as the original PC and XT or PS/2 Models 25 and 30, controls memory access through a 20-bit-wide address bus. An address bus is the numbering scheme used to uniquely identify all locations in random-access memory (RAM). The address bus width has an effect on how much RAM a system can address. With the 20-digit binary number used for addressing, these systems generate a total of 1 megabyte of memory locations. Any system using an 80286 processor, such as the XT-286, AT, PS/2 Model 30-286, PS/2 Model 50, and PS/2 Model 60, uses a memory addressing system with 24 lines or digits. With this addressing system, a maximum of 16 megabytes of RAM is available. Any 80386-based system, such as the PS/2 Model 70 and PS/2 Model 80, uses a 32-bit memory addressing system that allows for a total of 4 gigabytes of RAM. This amount of processor-addressable memory equals the IBM 3090 Model 600 Sierra mainframe system that costs $10 million. Not bad for a system that sits on or beside a desk.

The memory-addressing capabilities of the various processors in native (protected) modes are listed in table 10.4.

Table 10.4
Memory-Addressing Capabilities

	8088/8086	80286	80386
Number of address digits	20	24	32
Bytes	1,048,576	16,777,216	4,294,967,296
Kilobytes (1,024 bytes)	1,024	16,384	4,194,304

	8088/8086	80286	80386
Megabytes (1,024 kilobytes)	1	16	4,096
Gigabytes (1,024 megabytes)	0.0009765625	0.015625	4

These figures reflect only what is technically possible, not what is practical or immediately available. For example, because the Model 80 has only three 32-bit slots, you need individual memory cards with more than 1.3 gigabytes per card. At a cost of $500 per megabyte, 4 gigabytes of memory would cost more than $2 million.

Microprocessor Operating Modes

Real mode is the mode of operation defined by the characteristics of Intel's 8086 and 8088 microprocessors. When Intel designed the 80286 and 80386 microprocessors, the company wanted to add new features and retain compatibility with the large base of software that existed for the 8086 and 8088. Intel incorporated an 8086/8088 mode within the newer 286 and 386 processors. This combination is called real mode or 8086/8088 compatibility mode. When the newer processors are in real mode, the emulation of the earlier 8086 is complete, including any limitations that apply to the earlier chip.

Protected mode is the native mode of the 286 and 386. Protected mode enables the 286 and 386 to perform as designed, with access to full memory-addressing capabilities. This mode is incompatible with software written for real mode. If you want to run in protected mode any software written for real mode, the software has to be rewritten. OS/2 can run DOS-based software by temporarily switching the processor to real mode. While this switch is in effect, all processing (multitasking) under OS/2 is suspended until protected mode is reactivated.

When Intel designed the 80286, the company included a method of instructing the chip to go from real mode into protected mode. Intel did not include a method for getting the chip back into real mode. The reasoning was that the whole idea of protection is to prevent rampant software from crashing the system. What good would a gate be if everybody had the key? Now an application for a protected to real mode switch has arisen—OS/2. Switching between real and protected mode is how the compatibility box in OS/2 can run DOS and DOS applications software. By switching the processor back into real mode, you can run a DOS application in an environment devoid of protection. The only documented way to switch from protected to real mode is to reset the chip by placing a high signal on the processor's reset pin.

When the chip is reset, the system reinitiates the boot process. Rebooting normally performs a power on test of all memory and loads DOS from the first found disk drive. Rebooting wipes out anything running under OS/2 as if the operator used the Ctrl-Alt-Del combination. Before performing the reset, OS/2 places a special flag value in the CMOS battery backed-up memory present in every AT. This value is checked at boot time to see whether you are performing a real boot or a switch from protected mode. If a switch is indicated, normal booting procedures are skipped and the system is sent to a start-up code location.

While this reset operation is in progress, the system does not listen to hardware interrupts. Information coming in over a network adapter, communications port, keyboard, or other interrupt-driven device is lost. This operation is like having to turn off the engine to shift your car from third to fourth gear. While the engine is off, you have no power steering or brakes, so hope that no sudden curves are ahead. Like data coming in over a communications port, the curves would be missed.

The compatibility box allows DOS programs to run under OS/2. The compatibility box should not be used while communications programs are operating, including network software. You also should not use the compatibility box while the system is performing a real time operation such as monitoring a laboratory instrument with a data acquisition adapter.

The 80386 does have an instruction to switch modes. With this instruction, the system saves and switches much faster than the 80286.

Virtual 8086 mode is unique to the 80386 and 80386SX chips and enables the user to run several protected real mode sessions as one or more subtasks by the 80386. This mode emulates an entire 8086 system within the 80386 chip. Multiple DOS programs can run as though they were running on a single-processor DOS system. Each *virtual machine* requires one megabyte of space for the simulation. Only Windows '386 supports this kind of arrangement. You cannot run Windows '386 with OS/2 or UNIX. Eventually, a '386 specific version of OS/2 that runs multiple DOS sessions in a multitasking environment may be developed.

Conventional Memory

Conventional memory exists between 0 kilobytes and 1 megabyte (with 384K reserved and 640K usable) on any IBM or compatible system. Conventional memory is used by 8088, 8086, 80286, or 80386 in real mode. Note that the full 1 megabyte of conventional memory cannot be used by any operating system because the hardware uses 384K for video RAM, adapter ROM and RAM, and the motherboard ROM BIOS. A usable portion of 640K of conventional memory is left.

The maximum addressable memory for the IBM PC is 1 megabyte, not 640K. When IBM introduced the PC in 1981, the company indicated that the unit could have only 256K because that was all the memory you can access with IBM memory boards installed. By 1983, IBM indicated that the maximum amount of usable memory could be 640K.

The problem with addressing any memory above 640K is that the remaining 384K is reserved for system operations. How much memory DOS has access to depends on how your system uses that reserved space and how the memory adapters are installed. The limitations you face with DOS are the following:

- DOS cannot address memory beyond 1,024K because DOS runs in real mode with a maximum of only 1,024K of addressable memory.

- DOS manages its own code and program code in contiguous memory, starting with the first byte in the system at address 00000h. The first obstruction (such as the video RAM) is the cap that prevents further memory from being managed. A program running under DOS, however, can store data in any addressable memory, including memory beyond the DOS range.

The result of these limitations is that DOS handles programs that fit in the 1-megabyte workspace, less any reserved memory after the video RAM. Table 10.5 shows the maximum usable DOS memory available in systems equipped with different video adapters.

Table 10.5
Maximum Usable DOS Memory

DOS Memory	Video Adapter
736K	Color Graphics Adapter (CGA)
704K	Monochrome Display Adapter (MDA)
640K	Enhanced Graphics Adapter (EGA)
640K	Video Graphics Array (VGA)

The 8086/8088 addresses 1 megabyte of memory. From this memory, BIOS, the adapter board, and video memory are subtracted, leaving from 640K to 736K free for DOS and DOS-based applications. If you have a CGA or MDA video board and want to use this extra memory, you have to find a card that supports 640K as a *starting address*. One card that comes to mind is the discontinued Hicard. Other cards may support 640K as a starting address, but you probably can get only 704K, not 736K, because most memory boards use designs that allow expansion in 64K increments. I do not know of any board (except Hicard) that allows the system to fill the remaining 32K, without overlaying the CGA video memory.

Extended Memory

To allow for even more memory expansion, you have two options. One is to install the more advanced 80286 and 80386 that support 16 megabytes and 4 gigabytes, respectively. The portion of memory past the first megabyte is *extended memory*.

Extended memory is the area most important for future operating systems such as the IBM Operating System/2 that runs in the protected mode of the '286 and '386 processors. This operating system takes full advantage of up to 16 megabytes of memory.

Real-mode operation, which is required for DOS, does not support access to extended memory. If users need to transfer data to and from extended memory, they must switch the system from real to protected mode. Hardships encountered when using extended memory led to the development of *expanded memory*.

Expanded Memory

Expanded memory is not in the processors' direct address space and is accessed by *bank switching*. This technique (memory paging) provides small windows of memory (physical pages) through which blocks of expanded memory are traded with your base memory. A program places data elements in expanded memory as a type of cold storage until the data is needed. One problem with this method is that for every piece of data a program places in expanded memory, a database must be created to keep track of the information. When the data is required, this database is consulted to recall the correct memory page through the window.

The Expanded Memory Specification (EMS) describes a method in which four contiguous physical pages of 16K each (forming a block of 64K) can access up to 32M of expanded memory space through the Expanded Memory Manager (EMM). The page frame is located above 640K. Only video adapters, network cards, and similar devices are normally between 640K and 1,024K.

When large programs seemed to be running out of memory in the 640K workspace, several manufacturers sought ways to make more memory available to their customers. Lotus Development Corporation was the original designer of expanded memory, because most 1-2-3 users eventually ran out of memory when developing huge spreadsheets. (The Lotus program keeps all active data in memory.) Lotus, Intel, and Microsoft collaborated to devise the LIM Expanded Memory Standard (EMS).

Many Lotus users bought these boards sight unseen, expecting them to deliver on the claims. (Users expected to have actually 2 megabytes or more of usable memory. The advertisements led you to believe that expanded memory is just the same as conventional memory, and the more you have, the bigger the program and data files you can load.) These consumers were in for a shock. Little did users know that if they bought LIM EMS boards with 2M of memory, they probably could use less than 512K. Users also did not realize how limited and how slow the use of this memory was.

Problems with the LIM EMS are caused by several things. First, because expanded memory is not actual memory to the processor, nothing important can be placed there. Second, the memory window sits above the video RAM area, where DOS cannot manage programs and where storing actual program code is forbidden. Third, Lotus could not place spreadsheet numeric values in expanded memory because every time the user pressed the Recalc button, every value had to be recalled from the EMS. This process would slow down the program, and Lotus has a reputation for having fast recalculation times. Data stored in EMS memory is limited to items such as labels.

You can observe how much paging in and out can happen by trying a simple experiment. Create a simple text database in Lotus that uses most of the conventional memory and a good portion of expanded memory. Then execute a SORT operation and take a long break. You can leave the program working for hours.

Because of the program's need to keep a database of what was placed in expanded memory, you still can run out of conventional memory long before the expanded memory is even half gone. Using all the expanded memory is impossible. The industry has a temporary solution to a memory problem that really will be solved when the new Lotus Release 3, which will support OS/2, is released sometime in 1989. This version uses up to 15.5M of memory, with no limitations or slowdowns.

Several subtypes of expanded memory are available, which makes the decision about what product to buy extremely difficult. These different implementations are not fully compatible with each other. They are

AST Enhanced Expanded Memory Standard (EEMS)
IBM Expanded Memory Adapter (XMA)

The new version of the LIM EMS, Version 4.0, combines the features of all three standards into a unified standard. Not all boards, however, fully support the EMS 4.0 specification. The newest boards from Intel, the AST boards, and the earlier AST boards support the new EMS 4.0 specification. The AST and subsequent LIM 4.0 improvements included increased page size and the capability to position page windows anywhere in the memory map.

Despite some of the drawbacks mentioned, investing in an EMS board may be worthwhile. With the new specification, a breed of memory management programs has appeared with the capacity to manage multiple programs in the conventional memory workspace. Aided by the improved paging in the new specification, these programs can move programs and datasets in and out of expanded memory. DESQview is one of the more popular programs with this capability and has a strong following. Expanded memory boards also can function as conventional or extended memory boards. When you convert a system to run OS/2, for example, you can reconfigure expanded memory boards to operate as extended memory boards. Remember that expanded memory is obsolete with OS/2 and not needed in any protected-mode system.

Systems with an 80386 processor never need an expanded memory board because the 80386 chip has advanced memory management capabilities that enable you to use the 4 gigabytes of possible extended memory space as simulated expanded memory. This simulation is fast, because the capability is built into the processor. Having an 80386-based system makes memory purchasing decisions simple; the only type of memory you want is conventional and extended. The drivers that perform the simulation of extended to expanded memory usually are supplied with the 80386 systems. COMPAQ, for example, supplies users with a disk containing the COMPAQ Expanded Memory Manager (CEMM). This type of driver is now part of the IBM DOS 4.0 package under the name XMAEM.SYS. (These emulators are for 80386-based systems only.)

Types of Memory Devices

When examining memory from a hardware point of view, you can break it down to the smallest removable component. Two forms are available in which memory is supplied for a system today: the chip and the SIMM (Single Inline Memory Module). In this section, you will look at how to identify different memory chips and what effect the newer SIMMs have on the memory in your system. You will find that most newer systems are installing memory in the SIMM format, which makes troubleshooting and diagnosing problems in memory much easier, as well as reduces labor in replacing these failed components. The real drawback to the SIMM is the cost.

Chips

At one time or another, you should take a memory board out of a system and examine it. You should be able to identify the board's capacity by counting the installed chips. When repairing a memory board, you need this information to help locate the physical position of a defective memory chip, especially when you are given only an error's logical location.

Memory on a board usually is organized into banks of chips. Systems with an 8-bit architecture have banks that are 8 usable bits wide. Systems with a 16-bit architecture have banks that are 16 usable bits wide. Because of IBM's use of *parity checked memory* in the PC and subsequent systems, an additional bit exists for each 8 bits. A bank that is 8 bits wide really contains 9 bits because of the extra parity bit. Because most chips supply a single bit for a given byte, these banks, therefore, contain 9 physical chips. Any true 16-bit system, therefore, has banks containing 18 chips, because of the two parity chips in those banks.

You should be able to identify how the banks are placed on the board. Usually, some writing on the board labels them as "Bank 0," "Bank 1," and so on. Each of the banks has 8 bits numbered 0 through 7, and an extra parity bit.

Examine a chip in one of the banks and look at the writing on the top. A typical memory chip resembles figure 10.2.

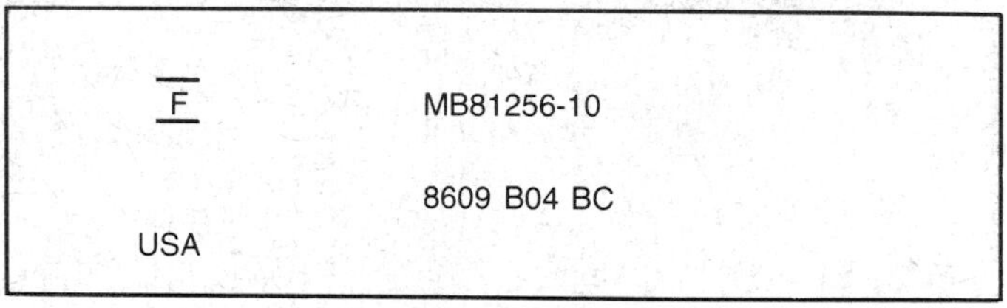

Fig. 10.2.

A typical memory chip.

```
        F          MB81256-10

                   8609 B04 BC

   USA
```

Each item on the chip means something. As mentioned in Chapter 7, the -10 corresponds to the speed of the chip in nanoseconds (a 100 nanosecond rating). The number MB81256 is the chip's part number. In the part number, you usually can find a clue about the chip's capacity. The key digits are 1256. The 256 indicates the *depth* of the chip in k bits; the chip is a 256k bit chip. The 1 indicates the *width* of the chip in single bits; this chip is a single bit wide. In order to make a full byte with parity, 9 of these single-bit-wide chips are required. Single-bit-wide chips are the most common. For example, a chip with a part number KM4164B-10 indicates a 64K-by-1-bit chip at a speed of 100 nanoseconds. The key digits in the part number for size determination are 164.

The following is a list of some common types of chips, designated by the last digits in their part numbers:

```
 164 = 64K by 1 bit
 264 = 64K by 2 bits
 464 = 64K by 4 bits
1128 = 128K by 1 bit
2128 = 128K by 2 bits
4128 = 128K by 4 bits
1256 = 256K by 1 bit
2256 = 256K by 2 bits
4256 = 256K by 4 bits
```

Chips wider than 1 bit are used to construct banks of less than 9 or 18 chips—9 in the case of an 8-bit arch (PC, XT) and 18 in the case of a 16-bit arch (286, 386). For example, in the IBM XT-286, an AT type of 16-bit system, the last 128K bytes of memory on the motherboard consist of a bank with only 6 chips, 4 that are 64K by 4 bits wide and 2 that are 1 bit wide, storing 18 bits.

In figure 10.2, the symbol centered between the two lines is the manufacturer's logo. The F symbol indicates Fujitsu Microelectronics. A cross-reference showing which symbols indicate which manufacturers is in the Appendix. The 8609 designation indicates the date of manufacture. In this example, the chip was made during the ninth week of 1986. Sometimes a manufacturer uses a Julian date code that looks different. To decode the chip further, contact the manufacturer for a catalog.

If you can distinguish the size of the chip in depth and width and the speed rating, you have all the information needed to order a replacement. Knowing other items can help in some cases. For example, you can identify a bad batch of chips by noting that many with the same date code are failing.

SIMMs

Single Inline Memory Modules (SIMMs) are more reliable than the standard memory chips in most systems. They also are easier to replace compared with individual chips. Because each SIMM contains entire bytes of memory rather than individual bits, determination of the physical fault domain in troubleshooting problems is simpler. You no longer have to narrow the problem to a particular failed bit within a byte. With a SIMM, figuring out the failed byte is enough to determine the physical fault domain. The higher memory densities achieved by SIMMs contribute to their use in smaller systems. They also can be used to place more memory on a single adapter card. The smaller MCA boards contribute to the use of SIMMs for any PS/2 MCA applications. The reason is that the new MCA boards offer much less real estate to work with than the original PC and AT adapter boards, so manufacturers must investigate new ways of stuffing more memory and features on these smaller boards. A great deal of SIMM memory will occupy a much smaller space than an equivalent amount of memory installed as regular chips. PS/2 system boards are now available with 8 megabytes or more on a single adapter board. That density could only be achieved with SIMMs. The SIMM will replace the individual memory module within the next few years, at least for newer systems.

SIMMs usually are constructed with 256k bit or 1 megabit chips. Several of these chips are used to make up individual bytes of memory. SIMMs are available in different widths and depths. Make sure that you can identify the parts in your system so that you can order proper replacements. Many of today's high memory content boards are packed with SIMMs. You can purchase a single memory board today with up to 16 full megabytes. This purchase is the only memory board you need for many systems and brings most systems up to full-expansion capacity. Of course, the 16-megabyte memory card for the faster systems may cost $8,000, which may be more expensive than the system.

Communication Ports

The basic communications ports in any PC system are the serial and parallel ports. The serial ports are primarily used for devices that must communicate bidirectionally with the system; such devices include modems, mice, scanners, digitizers, or any other device that "talks" as well as receives information from the PC. The parallel ports are used primarily for printers and operate as one-way communications ports. Printers usually do not have much to say! The parallel ports in the PS/2 systems are redesigned and are bidirectional. These ports can be used to receive data. In fact, the Data Migration Facility, which can be used to copy disks from earlier systems to the PS/2 systems (to overcome 5 1/4-inch to 3 1/2-inch physical incompatibility), does use the parallel port for high-speed input on the PS/2, but the earlier systems can only transmit data through their parallel ports. This section examines these serial and parallel ports in more detail.

Serial Ports

The asynchronous serial interface is the primary system-to-system communications device. *Asynchronous* means that no synchronization or clocking signal is present. Characters may be sent with any arbitrary time spacing. The intervals between characters may be completely irregular, as when a typist is providing the data.

Each individual character is framed by a standard start and stop signal. A single 0 bit called the start bit precedes each character to tell the receiving system that the next 8 bits constitute a byte of data. One or 2 stop bits follow the character to signal that the character has been sent. At the receiving end of the communication, characters are recognized by the start and stop signals instead of being recognized by the timing of their arrival. The asynchronous interface is character oriented and has about 20 percent overhead for the extra information needed to identify each character.

Serial refers to data sent over one wire with each bit lining up in a series as they are sent in order. This type of communication is used over the phone system because this system provides one wire for data in each direction. Serial ports for the PC are available from many manufacturers. You usually can find them on one of the available multifunction boards or on a board with at least a parallel port. IBM made single cards with only a serial or a parallel port, but these were not very popular. All IBM AT models that included a hard disk also came with an IBM serial/parallel port board, and all XT models with IBM hard disks came with a single serial port card in slot 8.

Many people incorrectly think that "a serial port is a serial port." Under DOS, for example, you can use the XT serial port card in an AT but cannot use the AT serial port card in an XT without some problems. Under OS/2, you cannot even use the XT serial port card in an AT. The differences are not caused by the interface, because all these cards use the 8-bit interface. The control program for the port is the real problem. The control program is in the ROM BIOS on the system's motherboard. Under OS/2, the standard AT ROM BIOS does not function because the BIOS was not designed to run under protected mode. The serial port control programs must be loaded from disk when OS/2 is booted. This software does not run on ports designed for PC or XT systems. Many users with less expensive AT clones are running PC or XT serial port cards because they are less expensive than the right card. These users are in for a surprise when they run OS/2 and discover that the serial ports do not work.

Serial ports may connect a variety of devices such as modems, plotters, printers, other computers, bar code readers, scales, device control circuits, and so on. Basically, anything that needs a two-way connection to the PC uses the industry-standard Reference Standard number 232 revision c (RS-232c) serial port. This device enables data transfer between otherwise incompatible devices. The most common uses for serial ports are to connect modems and printers.

The PC BIOS and operating system handles only two serial communications links: COM1: and COM2:. These ports can be in high demand within a system. You also must ensure that two serial ports within one system do not conflict. Every board is set up as COM1: from the factory, and the second one you add must be reconfigured to COM2:. Reconfiguring usually is done by setting switches on the card.

Because each board on the market today is different, you always should consult the OEM manual for that particular card if you need to know how the card should or can be configured. IBM includes this information with each card's documentation. IBM also offers technical reference options and adapters manuals as well as hardware maintenance and service manuals, which also cover in detail all the jumper and switch settings for IBM adapter cards. Other manufacturers simply include a manual with the card that describes the card and includes the configuration information.

Parallel Ports

A parallel port has eight lines for sending all the bits for one byte of data simultaneously across eight wires. This interface is fast and usually is reserved for printers rather than computer-to-computer communications. The only problem with parallel ports is that cables cannot be extended for any great length without amplification or introducing errors into the signal.

The parallel port of the PC, XT, and AT is unidirectional. Data will travel only one way from the computer to the port, to the parallel device. The parallel port on the PS/2, however, is bidirectional. Data can travel to or from the port.

The bidirectional capability of the PS/2 parallel ports is not used in most applications. The only application that uses the bidirectional capability is IBM's Data Migration Facility for exchanging data between systems with 5 1/4-inch disks and PS/2 systems with 3 1/2-inch disks. The printer port is used on earlier systems to send data to PS/2 systems that use the port as a receiving device. Data transfer with this method is faster than with the serial port because the parallel port sends data 8 bits at a time. This bidirectional capability, however, might create a new use for the parallel port as a gateway for input from high-speed data transfer devices that talk, such as scanners, bar code readers, and video cameras.

Diagnosing Problems

To diagnose problems with serial and parallel ports, you need diagnostics software and a wrap plug for each type of port. The diagnostics software works with the wrap plugs to send signals through the port. The plug wraps around the port so that the same port receives the information it sent. This information is verified to ensure that the port works properly. For further information, see Chapter 14, "Hardware Troubleshooting Guide."

Many problems stem from using the wrong serial port card in a system. Most clone manufacturers are guilty of this practice in AT systems, because using the right card costs more money. The big difference in serial ports is in the Universal Asynchronous Receiver Transmitter (UART) chip. UARTs are the primary port circuits. Several different versions exist, and they have different applications. Some of them should be used only in certain systems, because the system ROM BIOS is designed specifically to support certain chips. OS/2, which replaces the ROM BIOS when it runs, also is designed for a specific UART. Using a port with the wrong UART results in problems such as the port hanging, incompatibilities with software, lost characters, or total functional failure.

All UART chips used by IBM are made by National Semiconductor. You identify the chips by looking for the largest chip on the serial port card and reading the numbers off that chip. Usually the chips are socketed, and replacing only the chip may be possible. Table 10.6 lists UART chips in PC or AT systems.

Table 10.6
UART Chips in PC or AT Systems

Chip	Description
8250	This original chip was used by IBM in the PC serial port card. This chip has several known bugs, but none of them have proven to be serious. The PC and XT ROM BIOS are written to expect at least one of the bugs. This chip was later replaced by the 8250B.
8250A	The second version of 8250 should not be used in any system. This chip fixes several bugs from the preceding version, but because one of the bugs is expected by the PC and XT ROM BIOS, this chip does not work properly with those systems. The 8250A should work in an AT system that does not expect the bug but does not work adequately at 9600 baud.
8250B	The last version of the 8250 fixes bugs from the previous two versions. The bug in the original 8250 that is expected by the PC and XT ROM BIOS software has been put back into this chip, making the 8250B the most desirable chip for any non-AT serial port application.
16450	The higher speed version of the 8250 was selected for the AT by IBM. This chip has fixed the 8250 bugs so that the 16450 does not operate properly in any PC or XT systems expecting a certain bug to be present. OS/2 requires this chip, and the serial port does not function properly under OS/2 without the 16450. The 8250 chips work in an AT under DOS but do not run properly at 9600 baud.
16550	The new UART has a larger I/O buffer than the 16450. This chip may not work properly with all software and generally should not be used.

Note: The bug referred to in the table is a spurious interrupt that is generated by the 8250 at the end of an access. The ROM BIOS code in the PC and XT has been written to work around this bug. If a chip without the bug is installed, random lockups may occur. The AT 16450 chip does not have the bug; however, the AT ROM BIOS was written with this in mind.

Chapter Summary

This chapter discussed and examined several main peripherals that work with your systems. Descriptions were given of the various types of available video adapters and monitors, along with some recommendations. This chapter also examined memory adapters and the available memory configurations. Finally, the chapter looked at the serial and parallel communications ports on a system.

Part IV

System Maintenance, Backups, Upgrades, and Diagnostics

Includes

Preventive Maintenance and Backups

System Upgrades and Improvements

System Diagnostics

11

Preventive Maintenance
and Backups

In this chapter, you will learn about the steps you can take to ensure proper operation of your system. Preventive maintenance can be the key to having a system that gives years of trouble-free service. A properly administered preventive-maintenance program pays for itself many times over by reducing problem behavior, data loss, and component failure and by giving your system a long life. And preventive maintenance increases your system's resale value. In some cases, I have found that an ailing system was "repaired" by nothing more than a preventive-maintenance session. In this chapter, you will learn about the various procedures involved in preventive maintenance, as well as how often to perform these procedures.

You also will learn about a variety of backup options. To be prepared when things do go wrong, you need to be concerned about backup. A sad reality in the computer repair and servicing world is that hardware always can be fixed, but data is another story. For example, most hard disk service routines require that a low-level format be done. This low-level format wipes any remaining data off of the disk.

In Chapter 15, "Software Troubleshooting Guide," you will learn some techniques for recovering data from a damaged disk or disk drive, but these procedures are not fail-safe. Depending entirely on the location of the damage, the amount of damage, and the type of hardware and software involved, you may be able to recover some things from the disk. In many cases, however, the task may be hopeless or require too much work. Some recovery operations, for example, may require the rebuilding of an entire file allocation table—byte by byte.

Because disk data recovery is such an inexact science and depends a great deal on the type and severity of damage, as well as the expertise of the recovery specialist, data-recovery services are expensive. I charge a minimum of $100 per hour for these services, and you get no guarantees. Backing up is the only "guarantee" you have to ensure that you will see your data again.

Most of the backup discussion in this chapter is limited to professional backup solutions. "Professional solutions" here means that you are going to have to spend some money on hardware and software designed for backups. Floppy disk drives and the DOS BACKUP and RESTORE commands just don't do the job.

Developing a Preventive-Maintenance Program

Developing a preventive-maintenance program is important to everyone who uses or manages personal computer systems. There are really two types of preventive maintenance: active and passive. Active preventive maintenance includes the various procedures that, when applied to a system, promote a longer trouble-free life. Passive preventive maintenance includes all the things you can do to protect a system from the environment, such as using power-protection devices, ensuring a clean temperature-controlled environment, and keeping the system from excessive vibration. In other words, basic passive preventive maintenance is treating your system well. Active preventive maintenance primarily involves cleaning the system and all the system components.

This section describes active preventive maintenance, beginning with how to clean and lubricate all the major components in a system.

Another active preventive-maintenance technique is to reformat the hard disks. By reformat, I mean low-level format. Reformatting restores the track and sector marks to their proper locations and forces you to back up and restore all the data on the drive. Not all drives may need this sort of procedure, but if you are using stepper-motor-actuator drives, reformatting is definitely recommended.

How often should you implement active preventive maintenance procedures? The answer is (of course!) it depends. The answer really depends on the environment of the system and the quality of the components of the system. If your system is in an extremely dirty environment, such as a machine-shop floor or the service area of a gas station, you may need to implement the cleaning part of active preventive maintenance every three months or so. For most clean office environments, cleaning should be done every year to two years. You really have to decide by your own experiences with your particular equipment and environment. If you open up the system after one year and find tumbleweeds rolling around inside, maybe you need to shorten the interval.

As for hard disk reformatting, again you have to let your own equipment and environment be your guide. If you have super inexpensive, stepper-motor-actuator, nonshock-mounted hard disks that are running in an environment where the ambient temperature varies, you will probably have to reformat the drive every six months or so. Normal stepper motor drive reformatting is done every year to every two years. Most voice coil drives will run indefinitely in a "nice" environment but may need periodic reformats if the environment is exceptionally harsh. You will have to let your own systems be your guide. If, about one year after the last low-level format, your drives start exhibiting the infamous Abort, Retry, Ignore error messages, then maybe you need to reformat the drive at some interval shorter than a year; maybe six months works for you. Only experience with many systems over time can give you these answers; I can provide only some guidelines.

Cleaning the System

One of the most important operations in a good preventive-maintenance program is regular and thorough cleaning of the system. All IBM and compatible systems use a forced air cooling system; a fan is mounted in, on, or near the power supply and exhausts air to the outside. Because this fan is an exhaust fan, outside air is drawn into every opening in the system chassis and cover. This draw-through system is the most efficient system that can be designed without an air filter. This draw-through system also allows for even cooling inside the system.

Some "industrial" computers from IBM and other companies do use a forced air system that uses the fan to pressurize the case, which means that air exhausts out of any holes in the chassis or lid. The key to the pressurization system is that the fan also contains an air filter that must be cleaned and changed. Because these industrial models are designed for extremely harsh environments, the use of an air filter is almost mandatory. Most systems that you have contact with, however, are depressurization systems. Mounting any sort of air filter on these types of systems is impossible because too many places exist where air comes into the system.

In any system in which no filtration of the incoming cooling air occurs, dust builds up. Any cigarette smoke or other particulate or chemical matter that is in the environment also is drawn into the system and collects on everything. This dust and garbage buildup can cause severe problems in a system if allowed to go unchecked. The dust layer acts as an insulator to heat, which prevents proper cooling of the system and may cause a system to overheat and damage components. The dust may contain other chemicals such as those in cigarette smoke. These chemicals can conduct electricity, causing minor current shorts and electrical signal paths where they should not be. The chemicals also rapidly accelerate corrosion on any of the components in the system that are installed in sockets or where boards plug into slots. Cable connectors also can be affected by this corrosion.

Hard disk drives do not have the same problems with dust and dirt that floppy drives do, because the Head Disk Assembly (HDA) in a hard disk is a completely sealed unit, and no dust or dirt can enter. Cleaning a hard disk means simply blowing off the dust and dirt from the outside of the drive. No internal cleaning can be performed.

Floppy disk drives are another story, however. Because these drives are directly in an incoming air path, they accumulate an amazing amount of garbage in a short time. Floppy drives are, after all, the source of a large "hole" in the system through which air is directly drawn in. As a simple experiment, try holding a lit cigarette in front of a floppy disk drive with the system powered on. You will find that the system inhales the smoke, which is the reason I would enforce a company policy that bans cigarette smoking anywhere near computer equipment of any type.

Obtaining the Required Tools and Accessories

To properly clean the system and all the boards inside, you need several items and tools. To properly clean your system, you usually must first disassemble most of it. Some people go as far as removing the motherboard. Removing the motherboard does result in the best possible job, but in the interest of saving time, just make sure that you take the system apart at least to the point where the motherboard is completely visible. All the plug-in adapter cards must be removed, and usually the disk drives must be removed as well. Although you can clean the heads of a floppy drive with a cleaning disk and without even opening up the system unit's cover, you want to do a more thorough cleaning. In addition to the heads, you also want to clean and lubricate the door mechanism and clean any logic boards and connectors on the drive. This procedure usually requires that you remove the floppy drive. You want to do the same procedure with a hard disk: clean the logic boards and connectors, as well as lubricate the grounding strap. To do so, you must remove your hard disk.

Besides the tools that are required for you to disassemble the unit (see Chapter 6), you will need the following:

- Liquid cleaning solution
- Canned air
- A small brush
- Lint-free foam cleaning swabs

Optionally, you also may want to add the following:

- Conductive lubricant
- Silicone lubricant
- Room Temperature Vulcanizing (RTV) sealer
- Computer vacuum cleaner
- Antistatic wrist grounding strap

Make sure that the liquid cleaning solution is designed for computer cleaning. The solution should contain Freon, isopropyl alcohol, or some mixture of the two. Pure Freon is probably the best, but it is expensive. The material must be moisture free and residue free. I prefer the solution to be in liquid form—not a spray. The sprays are far too wasteful, and I never spray this solution directly onto any components anyway.

I use a solution called Magnetic Head/Disk Cleaner from a company named Chemtronics. This cleaner is a mixture of Freon TF and isopropyl alcohol in a pure liquid form. You will find it in any good electronic parts store. This solution serves a variety of cleaning purposes, from cleaning disk drive heads to contacts and components anywhere in the system. This solution is safe for all plastics and is a fairly light solvent. In summary, this cleaner doesn't eat paint or melt plastic, and it is safe for use on practically everything in the system.

Canned air is basically just what its name suggests. This air must be "computer grade" air, however, so it is more expensive than just "regular" air. Seriously, canned air must be completely moisture and residue free and for computer use. Canned air must not contain Freon TF as the propellant. The use of Freon TF is not approved because it generates an extremely high static charge due to friction as the Freon TF leaves the nozzle of the can. I like Chemtronics' 70 PSI, which refers to the pressure of the air in the can. This product uses dichlorodifluoromethane, which is actually Freon R12, the same chemical in your car's air conditioning system. And 70 PSI does not generate static as it is sprayed.

The makeup of any of the chemical sprays referred to in this section will be changed in the near future. The reason is that the chemicals used as propellants are environmentally unsafe and are destroying the ozone layer. These chemicals are on the verge of being banned and will no longer be marketed. The companies that make these chemicals now are looking for environmentally safe replacement chemicals to use in the future. I don't know what these chemicals will be, but I do know that the cost of the new chemicals will be much higher than the cost of those currently available.

Some people prefer to use a vacuum cleaner rather than canned air, but the canned air is better for cleaning in smaller locations. The vacuum cleaner is more useful in situations where you do not want to remove the motherboard completely from a system. You can use the vacuum cleaner to suck out the dust and debris, without simply blowing it all over the place with the canned air. For outbound servicing (when you are going to the location of the equipment instead of the equipment coming to you), the canned air is much easier than the vacuum cleaner for you to carry in a toolkit.

The small brush that you need can be a makeup brush or photography type of brush. You use this brush to loosen accumulated dirt and dust before blowing off this dirt with the canned air or vacuuming with the vacuum cleaner.

The cleaning swabs should be of the foam type, which do not leave any lint or dust residue of their own. Don't use any cotton swabs. Cotton swabs leave cotton fibers all over everything that you touch them to. The cotton fibers make a mess and may become conductive depending on what they touch. Unfortunately, foam cleaning swabs can be expensive—10 to 20 cents each.

For the lubrication and dampening of hard disk grounding straps, I recommend a conductive lubricant such as the graphited lubricants designed for automobile door locks. I use a solution made by AGS called Lock Ease, which you can purchase at most automotive parts supply stores. This solution contains finely ground graphite suspended in a carrier solution. Once the solution evaporates, a graphite film remains where the solution has been applied. This film can stop the squealing noise that many hard disks make due to the grounding strap. The graphite solution ensures that the grounding function still operates because graphite conducts electricity.

You can purchase the RTV sealer from an automotive supply house also. You apply this sealer to the grounding strap. The sealer acts as a rubber dampener, dampening the vibrations that produce the annoying squeal.

You use the pure silicone lubricant to lubricate the door mechanism on floppy disk drives. This lubricant also can be used to lubricate the head slider rails or printer head slider rails, allowing smooth operation. Using silicone rather than conventional oils is important because the silicone does not gum up and collect dust and other debris. Always use the silicone sparingly; do not simply spray it anywhere near the equipment. Instead, apply a small amount to a toothpick and use it to dab the silicone onto the disk drive components where needed. You may soak a lint-free cleaning stick to lubricate the metal print head rails in a printer.

You may want to use the grounding strap in cases where the static levels are high, to ensure that you do not zap any boards as you work with them. Some of the cleaning operations may generate a static charge.

With all these items on hand, you now are equipped for most preventive-maintenance operations.

Reseating Socketed Chips

One of the primary preventive-maintenance functions is to undo the effects of "chip creep." As your system heats and cools, it also expands and contracts. This physical expansion and contraction causes any components plugged into sockets to gradually work their way out of those sockets. For this reason, you need to find all the socketed components in the system and make sure that these components are properly reseated.

Memory chips are prime candidates for this operation. In most systems, all the memory chips are socketed. Most of the other logic components are soldered in. Also expect to find in sockets the ROM chips in the system, the main processor or CPU, and the math coprocessor. In most systems, these items are the only components that are socketed; everything else is soldered in. But exceptions may exist. A component in sockets in one system may not be in sockets in another system (even from the same manufacturer). Sometimes, this is a function of a parts-availability problem at the time the boards are manufactured. Instead of holding up the assembly line, the manufacturer adds a socket rather than the component. When the component finally becomes available, it is plugged in and the board is finished.

The idea is to make sure that all these socketed components are fully seated in their sockets. I do this procedure by placing my hand on the underside of the board and then applying downward pressure with my thumb from the top side directly on the chip to be seated. For any larger chips, seat the chip in two operations: press separately on each end of the chip with your thumb to be sure that the chip is fully seated. The processor and math coprocessor chips usually are seated in this manner. Sometimes, the force required can be quite high, but in most cases, you hear a crunching sound as the chip makes its way back into the socket. You may be surprised to know that even if you fully seat each chip, you can open up your system in a year and seat the chips again. In a year or less, the creep usually is noticeable.

Because of the high forces required for you to press the chips down, this operation is difficult if you do not remove the board. For motherboards, this operation can be quite dangerous if you don't support the board directly from the underside with your hand. Enough pressure on the board causes it to bow or bend in the chassis, and the pressure can crack it before the chip seating takes place. The plastic standoffs that separate and hold up the board from the metal chassis are spaced too far apart to properly support the board with this kind of pressure. Only attempt this operation if you can remove the board and support it adequately from underneath.

Cleaning the Boards

The next step is to clean the boards and all connectors in the system. In this example, the cleaning solution described earlier and the lint-free swabs are the cleaning tools used.

The first thing to do is clean the dust and debris off of the board itself and then clean any connectors on the board. To clean the boards, first use the brush to gently wipe the boards, loosening and removing any dust and debris. You use the brush because simply blasting the board with compressed air does not remove all the dirt and dust. After you loosen the debris with the brush, you can blow off the debris or vacuum it up with ease. ***Caution:*** Be careful with static. I recommend that you do not attempt this operation in the dead of winter in an extremely dry, high-static environment. Make sure that the humidity is such that static is prevented. I also recommend that you keep a finger or thumb on the ground of the motherboard or card as you wipe it off. You may want to use one of the static grounding wrist straps, which should be connected to the ground of the card or board that you are wiping. This strap ensures that no electrical discharge occurs between you and the board.

Cleaning Connectors and Contacts

On a motherboard, items you will want to clean include the slot connectors, power supply connectors, keyboard connector, speaker connector, and anything else you can find. For most plug-in cards, items you will want to clean include the edge connectors on the cards that plug into slots on the motherboard as well as any other connectors, such as external connectors mounted on the card bracket.

Simply submerge the lint-free swabs into the liquid cleaning solution. If you have the spray, hold the swab away from the system and spray a small amount directly onto the foam end, until the solution starts to drip off. Then use the soaked foam swab to wipe down the connectors on the boards. On the motherboard, pay special attention to the slot connectors. Be liberal with the liquid; resoak the foam swap repeatedly and really "wash" the connectors. Don't be afraid if some of the liquid drips onto the surface of the motherboard; this solution is entirely safe for the whole board, and you actually can submerge the whole board in a bathtub of the stuff without any ill effects. Allow the solution to wash the dirt off of the gold contacts in the slot connectors. Then continue by dousing any other connectors on the board. Clean the keyboard connector, any grounding positions where screws will ground the board to the system chassis, power supply connectors, speaker connectors, battery connectors, and so on.

If you are cleaning a plug-in board, pay special attention to the edge connector that mates with the slot connector on the motherboard. When people handle plug-in cards, they often don't pay attention and actually touch the gold contacts on these connectors. Touching the gold contacts coats them with oils and debris, which prevents proper contact with the slot connector when the board is installed. Make sure that all finger oils and residue are wiped off of these gold contacts.

Many people use the common pink eraser to rub clean these edge connectors. I do not recommend this procedure for two reasons. The first reason is that the eraser also takes off some of the gold with the eraser. If you rub too vigorously or clean the board too many times, you eventually rub off the gold; when the gold is gone, the tin solder or copper underneath is exposed, which tarnishes rapidly. You now have a contact that will corrode quite rapidly and give you problems in the future. Then you may have to clean it very often. The second reason for you to avoid using the eraser is that the rubbing action actually can generate a static charge that you will send through the board. This charge may harm any of the components on the board. Instead of using an eraser, use the liquid solution and swab method described previously.

You also will want to use the swab and solution to clean the ends of any ribbon cables or other types of cables or connectors in the system. Clean the floppy drive cables and connectors, the hard disk cables and connectors, and any others that you find. Don't forget to clean off the edge connectors that are directly on the disk drive logic boards as well as the power connectors to the drives.

Cleaning Drives

The procedure for cleaning floppy drives was explained in Chapter 8, so the information is not repeated here. But do pay attention to this detail: use the brush and canned air to dust off the interior of the drive and use the silicone lubricant on whatever items need lubrication.

For hard disks, take this opportunity to lubricate and/or dampen the grounding strap. This procedure was discussed in Chapter 9. If you lubricate this point only, the squeal may come back in a year or so. The rubber dampening usually is a more permanent fix for this sort of problem, so I apply it whenever possible.

Reformatting Hard Disks

Reformatting the hard disk is an operation that many users don't think about as part of their preventive-maintenance program. This operation is for stepper motor drives only; voice coil drives, unlike the stepper motor drives, don't have the tracking problems that build up over time.

For this operation, you lay down the track and sector ID marks and boundaries, remark the manufacturer's defects and any other defects that were originally marked, and perform a surface scan for any new bad sectors that may have developed since the last format. Temperature variations, case flexing, physical positioning, and other problems can add up to an eventual "soft failure" of a stepper-motor-actuated hard disk. This soft failure sometimes appears as a gradual number of read and write problems. You also may have problems booting the disk for the first time each day or booting the disk if the system has been shut off for some time (like over the weekend). The problem is a mistracking between where the data is written to the drive and where the track and sector ID marks are. Also, if the drive is used in a wide variety of temperatures and environmental conditions, the data will be written at various offsets from the actual desired track locations.

The reformatting procedure for hard disks is the equivalent of aligning a floppy drive. For hard disks, however, the concern isn't for the actual locations of each track. The drive must position accurately to the same track location repeatedly. Because of the inherent problems in tracking with stepper motor drives, and the lack of a track following system, mistracking errors will accumulate and eventually add up to a failure to read or write a particular location. To correct this problem, you need to lay down a new set of track and sector ID marks that correspond as closely as possible to the position from which the heads actually read and write data. With stepper motor drives, then, you need to perform a low-level format.

For this new format to effectively promote accurate reading and writing, the format must be done at the drive's full operating temperature and in the final mounted position. The drives should be in the correct physical attitude when the reformat is performed. If when installed, the drive will run on its side, the format must be done in that position.

For any of the inexpensive drives that lack any form of shock mounting system (such as the Seagate ST-225, -238, -251, or any -2XX drive), make sure that the drive is completely installed before low-level formatting. When you run the mounting screws into these drives, you actually are screwing directly into the Head Disk Assembly (HDA), which will cause it to warp slightly depending on how tightly you make the screws. Make sure that the screws are just a little more than finger tight. Don't "crank" on them, or your drive may fail if the screws are loosened at all! Screws that are too tight also can cause read and write problems due to stress in the HDA. Having this type of drive completely installed places the HDA under the same physical distortion stress that it is read and written at, which makes the format accurate.

To accomplish the reformat, you can use several tools. I recommend either the IBM advanced diagnostics (because you should have this program anyway) or the Htest/Hformat program from Paul Mace Software. If your controller has an autoconfigure type of ROM, you probably will have to use the format routine built into the controller or the special data that the controller saves to the drive to "know" the drive's physical parameters will not be written. The advantage of using a program like Htest/Hformat is that it actually can perform the format "in place," by formatting one track at a time and saving and restoring the data from each track as the program proceeds. Using this program saves a great deal of time because a restore operation will not have to be done. Note that although the restore will not have to be done, you must do a backup! If you don't perform the backup before attempting any of these "in place" types of low-level formats or disk interleave changes, and the power fails during the process or a parity-check error occurs, you can tell your data good-bye. If all goes as intended and the program works without flaw and your system doesn't lose power during the process, your data will be intact and the restore operation will not be needed.

How often should you do this reformat? The answer depends mostly on the types of drives that you have. If the drives are really inexpensive—drives such as the Seagate ST-2XX series—and you have them formatted under ST-506/412 with RLL encoding, you probably will have to do the reformat more than once a year. People who have to support large installations set up like this example become known as "hard disk reformatting specialists." A joke in the industry is that some of these drives actually require winter and summer formats because of temperature sensitivity! This "joke" is actually the truth in some cases.

If you have the ST-2XX series with MFM, you will have to reformat anywhere from every six months to once every two years. Usually every year is a rule of thumb if you don't leave the system running continuously. If the system runs continuously, you can reformat every two years or more.

If you have one of the better stepper motor drives with a rubber isolated HDA that is not running RLL under ST-506/412, you may have to reformat only every two years. The best way to tell is to note how often, on average, you have to reformat a disk to repair a read/write problem and head the problem off by performing the format before data loss occurs.

Note that this discussion does not apply to voice coil drives because they do not have the problems with hysteresis over time that the stepper motor drives do. *Hysteresis* is a measurement of the repeat positional accuracy of a drive. In other words, you measure hysteresis by commanding a drive to position to a particular cylinder and then, at some later time and different temperature, by again commanding the drive to position to the same cylinder. The voice coil drive always positions to the same position relative to the disk platter due to the track following servo guide head, but the stepper motor drive is "fooled" by temperature and any other environmental or physical stress changes because it is essentially a "blind" positioning system.

Examining the Operating Environment

Oddly enough, one of the most overlooked aspects of microcomputer preventive maintenance is protecting the sizable investment in hardware from environmental abuse. Computers are relatively forgiving, and they are generally safe in an environment that is comfortable for people. Computers, however, are often treated with no more respect than desktop calculators, and the results of this type of abuse are many system failures. Before you acquire a system, you should prepare a proper location for that system.

The proper location is one that is away from airborne contaminants such as smoke or other pollution. The system should not be exposed to any direct sunlight, such as light from a window. And because of temperature variations near a window, staying entirely away from windows is a good idea. The system should have an environmental temperature that is as constant as possible. Power should be provided through properly grounded outlets. This power should be stable and free from electrical noise and interference. And the system should be kept away from radio transmitters or any other sources of radio frequency energy.

Heating and Cooling

You must ensure that the system operates in an ambient temperature that is within the system's specified functional range. Most manufacturers provide data as to the correct operating temperature range for their systems. Two temperature specifications may be available: one indicating allowable temperatures for when the system is running and another indicating allowable temperatures for when the system is off.

IBM, for example, indicates the following temperature ranges as acceptable for the AT:

    AT system turned on: 60 to 90 degrees Fahrenheit
    AT system turned off: 50 to 110 degrees Fahrenheit

Some systems may encounter variations in temperature, which presents real problems. You should try to run a system at a constant ambient temperature, or several problems can occur. You may encounter excessive chip creep. If the variations are extreme and occur over a short period of time, signal traces on circuit boards can crack and separate, solder joints can break, and accelerated corrosion of contacts in the system can occur, as well as a host of other problems. Try to keep the environmental conditions around the system unit as constant as possible to reduce these types of problems.

Hard disk drives can be affected by temperature variations. Writing to a disk at very different ambient temperatures can (on some drives) cause data to be written at different locations relative to the actual track centers, which accelerates read and write problems later. For the health of the disk and the data it contains, avoid rapid changes in ambient temperatures. If rapid temperature changes do occur (for example, when a new drive is shipped to a location during the winter and then is brought indoors), you should allow the drive to acclimate to room temperature before operating it. In extreme cases, condensation will form on the platters inside the drive Head Disk Assembly. This condensation will be disastrous for the drive if it is powered on before the condensation is allowed to evaporate. Most drive manufacturers specify a timetable based on beginning and ending temperatures that you should use as a guide to acclimate a drive to room temperature before operation. Several hours to a day usually will be needed for a drive to be ready to operate after it has been shipped or stored in a cold environment.

The bottom line here is that temperature changes do affect a system due to the physical stress from thermal expansion and contraction. This stress can break circuit traces, crack solder joints, damage solid state components such as chips, and play havoc with hard disk drives. Although most office environments will not provide any problems, some specialized cases may exist where this type of problem may appear. So do give some consideration to the placement of your equipment.

Power Cycling (On/Off)

As you have just learned, the temperature variations a system encounters cause a great deal of stress to the physical components making up the system. But the largest temperature variations a system usually encounters are those that occur during system warm-up from an initial power on. Powering on a cold system subjects it to the greatest internal temperature variations possible. For these reasons, limiting the number of cold power-on cycles a system is exposed to greatly improves the system's life and reliability.

If you want a system to have the longest, most trouble-free life possible, you should take any steps possible to limit the temperature variations that the system will encounter. Two simple ways are available to limit the extreme temperature cycling that occurs during a cold start-up. You can leave the system off all the time or leave it on all the time. Of these two possibilities, of course, you will want to choose the latter option. Leaving the power on is the best way I know to promote system reliability. I recommend that you keep the system unit powered on continuously.

Think about the way light bulbs fail, and you will understand that thermal cycling can be dangerous. When do light bulbs burn out the most? When you first turn them on. The reason is that the filament must endure incredible thermal stresses when changing temperature from ambient to several thousands of degrees in less than one second. Some people argue that you should leave the system on because of the electrical shock from the inrush of power when the system is started. But solid state components really are not affected by this because the amount of power they consume is relatively small for each component.

The problems that can occur at immediate power on are in the power supply. The start-up current draw for the system and for any motors in the system is quite high compared to the normal operating current draw. Because all this current must come from the power supply, it has an extremely demanding load for the first few seconds of operation, especially if several disk drives are to be started. Motors are nasty with power-on current draw. This demand often overloads a marginal circuit or component in the supply and causes it to burn or break with a "snap." I have witnessed the death of several power supplies right at power-on time. Keep the temperature of solid state components constant and limit the number of start-ups that you put the power supply through. The only way to do this is to leave on your system. I run all my systems 24 hours a day, 7 days a week, all year.

Because of realities such as systems that are unattended during night or weekend hours, security problems, power consumption issues, and so on, you may not be able to leave your systems on 24 hours a day, 7 days a week. A compromise is in order. Power on the system only once a day. Take this good advice and don't power the system on and off several times each day. I often see this situation when systems are shared by several users. Each user powers on the system to perform some work on the PC and then powers off the system when done. The next user comes into the office later, after the system has been cooling for some time, and repeats the cycle. These systems tend to have many more problems with component failures.

If you are concerned about running your hard disk continuously, let me dispel any fears. Running your hard disk continuously may be the best thing you can do for your drive. By leaving the drive powered on, you have the best method for reducing the temperature-change-induced read and write failures that many drives experience. If you are using extremely inexpensive drives with stepper motor actuators, leaving the drive running constantly improves reliability several times over and increases the time between low-level formats due to mistracking. The bearings and motors in a drive also function longer if the power-on temperature cycling is reduced. If you ever have had a disk that wouldn't boot after the drive was turned off for a prolonged period (over the weekend, for example) and fixed the problem by a subsequent low-level format, you most likely wouldn't have had the problem if your drive had remained powered on.

If you are in a building with an automatic thermostat, you have another reason to be concerned about temperatures and disk drives. Some buildings have thermostats that turn off the heat overnight or over the weekend. These thermostats are programmed to bring up the temperature rapidly right before business hours each day. In Chicago, for example, the outside temperatures in the winter can dip to 20 degrees below zero (not including the wind-chill factor). An office building interior temperature can drop as low as 50 degrees during the weekend. When you arrive Monday morning, the heat has been cranking for an hour. But the hard disk platters have not yet reached even 60 degrees when you turn on the system unit. During the first 20 minutes of operation, the disk platters rapidly rise in temperature to 100 degrees or more. If you have an inexpensive stepper motor hard disk and actually begin writing to the disk at these low temperatures, you are in for trouble. Again, many systems with these "cheap" drives don't even boot properly under these circumstances and must be warmed up before they even boot DOS.

Here is some good advice: If you will not leave on the system permanently, at least allow the system to warm up for 15 minutes or more before writing to the hard disk. Power up the system and go for a cup of coffee, read the paper, or do whatever you need to do; but wait 15 minutes before using the system. This practice will do wonders for the reliability of the data on your disk!

One problem can occur if you leave on your system all the time. The problem involves your monitor or display. Leaving on your display *is* just as good as leaving on the rest of the system, but you should make sure that the screen is blank so that nothing shows on-screen. The phosphor on the picture tube can burn if an image is left on the screen continuously. The higher persistence phosphor monochrome screens are most susceptible, and the color displays with low-persistence phosphors are the least susceptible. If you ever have seen a monochrome display with the image of 1-2-3 permanently burned in—even while the display is off—you know what I am talking about. The monitors that display flight information at the airport also show these phosphor burn effects.

Several ways are available for you to eliminate information from the screen, or blank it, while leaving the monitor powered on. One way is to turn the brightness and contrast levels all the way down. This technique is quite effective, but it is a manual method; the operator must remember to do the job. To have the screen blank without operator intervention, you can purchase one of the commonly available programs that accomplish this task. These programs usually run as Terminate and Stay Resident (TSR) programs. The program watches the clock and the keyboard simultaneously; if the program sees several minutes go by with nothing being typed at the keyboard, it shuts off all signals to the display, blanking the screen.

These programs have their own quirks, such as incompatibilities with some software, but they generally are one of the best solutions in a larger company. You can, of course, just turn off the display but leave on the system unit. That procedure saves the phosphor in the display and allows the system unit to have the benefits of reducing temperature variation.

Static Electricity

Static electricity can cause numerous problems with a system. These problems usually appear during the winter months, when humidity is low, or in extremely dry climates, where the year-round humidity is low. In these cases, you may need to take special precautions to ensure that the systems can function properly.

Static discharges outside the system unit chassis are rarely a source of permanent problems in the system. The usual symptom is in the form of a parity-check (memory) error or a totally locked up system. Because of static problems of this sort, I have seen systems lock up if an operator simply walks by. Any time the system unit is opened or you are handling circuits outside the system unit, however, you must be more careful with static. You can damage a component with static discharges if these charges are not routed to a ground. I usually recommend that you handle boards and adapters by a grounding point first, to minimize the potential for any static damage. But most static problems experienced by functional systems are caused by improper grounding.

One of the easiest ways to prevent static problems is with a solid stable ground, which is extremely important for computer equipment. A poorly designed grounding system is one of the largest causes of a poor computer design. A good way to solve static problems is to prevent the static signal from getting into the computer in the first place. The chassis ground in a properly designed system serves as a static guard for the computer to redirect the static charge safely to the ground, which means that the system must be plugged into a properly grounded three-wire outlet.

If the problem is extreme, you can resort to other measures. One is to use a properly grounded static mat underneath the computer. Touch this mat first before touching the computer itself. This procedure ensures that any static discharges are routed to the ground, away from the system unit internals. If problems still persist, you may want to check out the electrical building ground. I have seen installations where three-wire outlets exist, but they are not properly grounded. You can test the outlets with an inexpensive outlet tester, which you can purchase at most hardware stores.

Power Line Noise

A system needs a steady supply of clean power to run properly. In some installations, the power line that the computer is connected to also serves heavy equipment, and the voltage variations resulting from the cycling of this equipment can cause problems with the computer system. Certain types of equipment on the same line also can cause voltage "spikes," short transients of sometimes 1,000 volts or more, which actually can cause physical damage to the computer.

Although rare, these spikes obviously can be crippling. In addition, the quality of the power varies, even on a dedicated circuit.

Noise in digital circuitry is a classic problem, but with a well-designed system, noise should not have to be your concern.

You should keep a few factors in mind during the site-preparation phase of system installation:

- If at all possible, the computer system should be on its own circuit, with its own breaker. This setup doesn't guarantee freedom from interference, but it helps.

- The circuit should be checked for a good, low-resistance ground, proper line voltage, freedom from interference, and "brownout" or voltage spikes from nearby equipment.

- A three-wire circuit is a must, but some people willingly use "grounding plug adapters" to adapt a grounded plug to a two-wire socket. This setup is not a good idea; the ground is there for a reason.

- Characteristically with power wires, noise problems increase with resistance, which is a function of wire size and length. For this reason, avoid extension cords unless they are absolutely necessary and are heavy-duty extension cords.

- Inevitably, you are going to want to plug in some other equipment. Plan ahead so you can avoid temptations to use too many items on a single outlet. If possible, provide a separate power circuit for noncomputer-related accessories.

Here are some of the worst power corrupters of a PC system:

- Air conditioners
- Coffee makers
- Copy machines
- Laser printers (same as copy machines)
- Space heaters
- Vacuum cleaners
- Power tools

Any of these items can draw an excessive amount of current and play havoc with any PC systems on the same electrical circuit. I know of some offices in which all the computers crash daily at 9:05, when all the coffee makers are turned on! Also watch the copy machines and laser printers; these components should not share a circuit with any computer equipment. Another big problem in larger companies involves the interconnecting office dividers or carrels. Many of these dividers contain their own electrical circuit that is used to power everything in the "office." They interconnect and plug into each other, so I pity the person at the end of the electrical chain.

I have seen cases of a personal computer with a repeating parity-check problem, and all efforts to repair the system seemed in vain. The problem occurred again and again. The reported error locations from the parity-check message also were inconsistent, which is my clue that the problem is with power. The problem could have been the power supply in the system unit itself or the external power supply from the wall outlet. This problem was solved one day when I was standing back watching the system and observed the parity-check message occur just as the person two dividers down turned on a copy machine. Placing the computers on a separate line solved the problem.

By following the guidelines indicated here, you will be creating the proper power environment for your systems, which will allow trouble-free operation.

Radio Frequency Interference (RFI)

An item that can be overlooked at times is Radio Frequency Interference (RFI). This problem is caused by any source of radio transmissions that may be near the computer systems. Living next door to a 50,000-watt radio station is one sure way to have problems, but less powerful transmitters cause problems too. Portable radio telephones can cause problems; sporadic keystrokes appear as if an invisible entity is typing on your system. At other times, the system locks up completely because of this problem.

The solutions here are more difficult to state; each case probably will need to be handled differently. Sometimes, merely reorienting the system unit eliminates the problems because radio signals can be directional in nature. At other times, you will have to invest in specially shielded cables for any wires that run outside of the system, including the keyboard cable. The best way to eliminate the problem is to correct it at the source. Filters sometimes can be added to a radio transmitter that will suppress spurious emissions that can cause problems. And the problems sometimes will persist until the transmitter is switched off. RFI problems obviously can be difficult to track down and solve!

By the way, remember that your own systems also can be a source of RFI. Computer equipment must meet one of two classifications to be certified and salable according to the FCC: either Class A or Class B.

Class A is a specification for computing devices that are sold for use in commercial, business, and industrial environments but must not be used in residential environments. *Class B* indicates that the equipment has passed more stringent tests that allow the equipment to be used in residential environments as well as any environments allowed under Class A. IBM ensures that all the systems it sells meet the more strict Class B designations. In fact, one of the main reasons for the Micro Channel Architecture design was to exceed these FCC classifications by a wide margin. IBM knew that as computing clock speeds go up, so do the radio emissions. You are going to see clock rates of 33 MHz and 40 MHz in the near future, and IBM will have a distinct advantage over any manufacturers still using the by then antique AT bus designs. Those vendors using the old bus design will have to invest in expensive chassis and case shielding to combat the problem, which will put IBM at a real manufacturing cost advantage.

Dust and Pollutants

Dirt, smoke, dust, and any other pollutants are not good for your system. The power supply fan will ensure that anything airborne will be carried through your system and collect inside. If the system is to be used in an extremely harsh environment, you may want to investigate some of the industrial model systems on the market for these types of conditions. IBM used to sell an industrial model of the XT and AT systems, but these models were discontinued when the PS/2 was introduced. So far, no industrial model PS/2 systems are available.

Compatible vendors, however, have filled this niche; many companies make special "hardened" versions of their systems for harsh environments. These systems usually use a different cooling system than the normal PC. A large cooling fan is used to pressurize the case rather than depressurize it like most systems do. The air that is pumped into the case passes through a filter unit that must be cleaned and changed periodically. The system is pressurized so that no contaminated air can flow into the system. Air only flows outward. The only way for air to enter is through the fan and filter system.

These systems also may have special keyboards that are impervious to liquids and dirt. Some of them are flat membrane types of keyboards, which are difficult to type on but are extremely rugged, and others resemble the standard types of keyboards but have a thin plastic membrane that covers all the keys. This membrane also can be added to the normal types of keyboards to seal them from the environment.

Cigarette smoke causes problems with the floppy disk drives in most systems because these drives are a direct entry point for incoming air. And the contaminants in cigarette smoke accelerate corrosion on the internal connectors and sockets in the system, which renders the system unreliable. You will be forced into more frequent cleaning sessions if smoking is permitted near the computers.

A new breed of humidifier also causes problems. This new type of humidifier uses ultrasonics to generate a mist of water that is sprayed into the air. Although the extra humidity will be beneficial for curing any problems with static electricity resulting from a dry climate, the contaminants in the water can cause many problems! If you do use one of these systems, you usually will begin to notice a white ashy sort of deposit forming everywhere. This deposit is the result of minerals that are suspended in the water. These minerals are abrasive, not to mention corrosive. If this deposit collects on the disk drive heads, it ruins the heads and scratches any disks that are inserted. The only safe way to run one of these ultrasonic humidifiers is with pure distilled water. The costs of doing so will soon make you consider other options, like disconnecting the unit permanently.

You should use the standard type of water bath humidifier and place it in a different room than the computer system if possible. This type will eliminate most of the lime and mineral deposits that can form because they will not be carried aloft by this type of unit like they are with ultrasonic units.

Do your best to keep the environment clean, and you will find that your system will run better. And you will not have to open your unit nearly as often for a complete preventive-maintenance cleaning.

Using Power-Protection Systems

Power-protection equipment can come in many varieties and is quite confusing to most people who are not acquainted with what is available. In this section, you will learn about the types of systems that are available. Note, however, that under normal conditions in a typical office environment, no such special equipment is necessary. Under some special instances, though, special steps should be taken in the form of a power-protection device.

Before considering any further levels of power protection, you may be interested to know that the power supply in your system (provided that it is a good one) already affords you a substantial amount of protection. The power supplies in IBM equipment are designed to provide over-voltage protection, over-current protection, and power conditioning. The power supplies will protect your PC from many power problems that normally would be considered harmful.

An independent laboratory subjected several PC power supplies to various 6,000-volt spikes and surges. All the power supplies protected the actual equipment from damage; the worst thing that happened was that some of the systems rebooted if the surge was more than 4,000 volts, and others shut down when the voltage spike was more than 2,000 volts. Each system sustained no damage and was restarted when the power switch simply was toggled.

I do not use any form of power protection on my systems and have had some incredible power surges at my location. I personally witnessed my systems survive near-direct lightning strikes and powerful surges, and the worst that happened was that the systems shut down. I recently lost a modem to such a surge, but all the system units (four running at the time) survived with absolutely no damage. They merely shut themselves down.

This shutdown is a built-in function of the supply, and you can reset the supply by flipping the switch from on to off and back again. The power supply in the PS/2 Model 80 is an autorestart supply. This power supply acts the same as the others in an over-voltage situation—by shutting everything down—but the difference is that after normal power resumes, this supply resets itself and powers the system back up. This feature is desirable for any system that is functioning as a network file server or for any system in a remote location because no manual resetting is required.

The first time I witnessed a large surge with an immediate shutdown of all the systems, I was extremely surprised. All the systems became silent, but the monitor and modem lights were on. I thought that everything was blown, but a simple toggle of each system unit power switch reset the power supplies, and the units powered up without further incident.

Since that first time, this shutdown has happened several more times, always without further incident. If your system has a reasonably well-made power supply, as all the IBM systems do, you already have a high level of protection built into the system. Some of the very inexpensive aftermarket power supplies probably do not have this sort of protection, so be careful if you have an inexpensive clone system. In those cases, further protecting your system may be wise.

Four main types of power-protection devices are available:

- Surge suppressers
- Line conditioners
- Standby Power Supplies (SPS)
- Uninterruptible Power Supplies (UPS)

Surge Protectors

The simplest form of power protection is any one of the commercially available *surge protectors*, devices that are inserted between the system and the power line. These devices cost between $20 and $200. These units can absorb the high-voltage transients produced by nearby lightning strikes, power equipment, and so on. Surge protectors can be effective; but some of the protectors do very little, and others actually work as advertised.

These surge protectors use various devices, usually Metal Oxide Varistors (MOVs), which can clamp and shunt away all voltages above a certain level. These devices are designed to accept voltages as high as 6,000 volts and divert any power above 200 volts to ground. These devices take care of normal surges, but surges such as a direct lightening strike blow right through them. These devices also can lose their effectiveness with successive surges.

I find that these types of devices provide little protection beyond what the power supply in the PC already does, and I usually do not recommend them. From another perspective, however, these devices probably cannot do any harm to the system, so why not use one? Note that any of the better units cost around $100, and most of the inexpensive $25 units are not really worth much. I call these inexpensive units "placebos" because they do not give your system any advantage but may give you some psychological comfort.

If you do decide that a surge protector is what you need, I can recommend a few of them. In a comprehensive test done by *PC Magazine* in May, 1986, several surge protectors were subjected to 6,000-volt surges. The testers then measured the voltages that were allowed through the units. The protectors made by PTI Industries and Dynatech Computer Power came out on top.

You will find a list of all recommended vendors in the Appendix.

Line Conditioners

Besides over-voltage or over-current conditions, other problems can occur with incoming power. The voltage may dip below the level needed to run the system, which is called a *brownout*. Other forms of electrical noise may be on the power line, such as radio frequency interference or electrical noise caused by motors or other inductive loads.

Remember two things when wiring together digital devices (such as computers and their peripherals). Any wire is an antenna and will have a voltage induced in it by nearby electromagnetic fields, which can come from other wires, telephones, CRTs, motors, fluorescent fixtures, static discharge, and, of course, radio transmitters. Also, digital circuitry responds with surprising efficiency to noise of even a volt or two, making those induced voltages particularly troublesome.

The *line conditioner* is designed for a wide variety of problems; it filters the power, bridges brownouts, suppresses over-voltage and over-current conditions, and generally acts as a buffer between the power line and the system. The line conditioner is a real "surge suppresser," and it does much more. The line conditioner is an active device as opposed to a passive, cheaper surge-protector device. Line conditioners provide true power conditioning and can take care of myriad problems. They contain transformers and other circuitry that can bridge a brownout or low-voltage situation temporarily. These units cost several hundreds of dollars, depending on the capacity of the unit.

Backup Power

At the next level, you enter the world of backup power-protection devices. Two types are available. One is the Standby Power Supply (SPS), and the other is the Uninterruptible Power Supply (UPS). These units can provide power in the case of a complete blackout, which provides the time needed for an orderly shutdown of the system. The UPS is a special device because it does much more than simply provide backup power. The UPS is also the best kind of line conditioner that you can purchase.

Standby Power Supplies (SPS)

The SPS is a system that uses a special circuit that can sense the AC line current. If the sensor detects a loss of power on the line, the system quickly switches over to a standby battery and power inverter. The power inverter converts the battery power to 110-volt AC power, which is then supplied to the system.

These systems do work, but sometimes a problem occurs with the switch to battery power. If the switch is not fast enough, the system unit shuts down or reboots anyway, which defeats the purpose of the backup power supply in the first place. These units also may or may not have any internal line conditioning of their own; many units simply place you directly on the regular power line under normal circumstances and offer no conditioning at all. Such a system still may require the use of a line conditioner for full protection. These SPS systems usually cost from $200 to several thousand dollars, depending on the output capacity.

Uninterruptible Power Supplies (UPS)

The best overall solution to any power problems is to provide a power source that is completely uninterruptible. These systems are known as true UPS systems and are constructed much the same as the SPS systems, with the exception of the switching circuit.

In a true UPS, you are running off of the battery and inverter all the time. You essentially have your own private power system that generates its own power completely independent of the AC line. A battery charger is connected to the line or wall current. It must keep the battery charged at a rate equal to or greater than the rate at which power is consumed. When power is disconnected, the true UPS continues on, because the battery charger is all that is lost. Because you always are running off of the battery, no switch takes place and no system disruption is possible. The battery now begins discharging at a rate dictated by the amount of load your system places on the unit, which gives you plenty of time to execute an orderly shutdown of the system. Based on an appropriately scaled storage battery, the UPS functions continuously, generating power and preventing unpleasant surprises.

UPS cost is a direct function of the length of time it can continue to provide a given amount of power. Therefore, purchasing one that allows you just enough time to close files and provide an orderly shutdown may be sufficient. In most "micro" applications, this solution is the most cost-effective. The UPS systems cost from $1,000 to tens of thousands of dollars, depending on capacity.

Many SPS systems are masquerading as true UPS systems. In the power-protection industry, many companies advertise UPS systems that are not the real thing. The dead giveaway is the unit's "switch time." If any specification for switch time exists, the unit cannot be a true UPS because they *never* switch.

Because of total isolation from the line current, the UPS is also unmatched as a line conditioner and surge suppresser. The UPS is simply the best and most desirable form of protection. The only issue is cost, which can be quite high. A real UPS costs from $1 to $2 per watt of power supplied. To find out just how much power your system requires, simply take a look at the UL sticker on the back of the unit. This sticker lists the maximum power draw in watts, or sometimes just volts and amperes. If only voltage and amperage are listed, simply multiply the two together to obtain a wattage figure.

As an example, the back of an IBM PC AT Model 339 indicates that the system can require as much as 110 volts at a maximum current draw of 5 amps. The most power that this AT ever can draw is about 550 watts. This wattage is for a system with every slot full, two hard disks, and one floppy—the maximum level of expansion possible, in other words. The system cannot draw any more power than that. If it does, a 5-ampere fuse in the power supply will blow. On average, the system probably will draw only 300 watts; but to be safe when making calculations for UPS capacity, use the 550-watt figure. To run two fully loaded AT systems, you need an 1100-watt UPS. And don't forget two monitors, each drawing 100 watts, so the total is 1300 watts. A UPS of at least that capacity or greater is required, to provide for some "headroom." Don't run a UPS beyond its capacity because the battery may not be able to keep up with the load.

Besides the total available output wattage, several other factors can differentiate one UPS from another. The best units produce a true sine wave output, and the cheaper ones generate a square wave. Each unit has a specification for just how long it can sustain output at the rated level. If your systems draw less than the rated level, you will have some additional time. But be careful. Most UPS systems are not designed for you to sit and compute for hours through an electrical blackout. These systems really are designed to provide power to whatever is needed, to remain running long enough to allow for an orderly shutdown. You will pay quite a sum for any units that provide power for more than 15 minutes or so.

Finally, remember that the system units should be well grounded— and not just for human safety. A good ground system acts as an electromagnetic shield, which in the process alleviates some of the dangerous effects of static. Also note that the built-in power protection of most systems is adequate for normal situations. And for the extreme cases, a UPS is your best bet for power protection as well as backup power in the case of a total blackout.

Using Data Backup Systems

When I am done repairing a system that has suffered a disk crash of some kind, I can guarantee that the disk subsystem will be completely functional. What I cannot guarantee is that any of the original files will be on the disks. In fact, generally, I can guarantee that the disk will be wiped clean! The system user will have to reinstall all the lost data from backup. If no backup was done, no more data will exist!

Nothing will destroy a person's faith in technology faster than telling that person that the last year or more of work (in the form of disk files) is no longer there! "Have you backed up your disk today?" would be a catchy phrase for a bumper sticker. Be sure that your data is intact in the form of one or more backups, because if your system goes down, you may never see the data again. Never let a backup interval go longer than what you are willing to lose to a catastrophe. You can always reload or even repurchase copies of software programs that may have been lost, but you cannot buy back your own data.

Many users' definition of "fixing" a system is to have everything as it was, including the files on the disks. They do not understand that although the hardware always can be "fixed" (even if it means replacing everything), the data may or may not still be available. Data recovery is almost an art and can be very difficult, time-consuming, or even impossible in many situations. I cannot over-stress the need for complete and up-to-date backups.

Backup Policies

All users and managers of computer systems should construct a plan for regular backups of the disks. Someone in the office should have responsibility for performing these backups so that the job is not left undone. A backup interval should be selected based on the amount of activity on the system. Some users will find that daily backups are required, and others will find that a weekly arrangement is more suitable. Backups rarely will need to be scheduled at more than weekly intervals. Some users will settle on a mixed plan: weekly complete backups with daily backups of only the changed files.

The procedures for backing up and for dealing with copy protection are explained in the following sections.

Backup Procedures

Backups should be performed to removable media. Backup is not proper when performed on nonremovable media such as another hard disk. Because of the low cost of hard disks today, some users actually install two hard disks and back up one to the other. Even worse, some users split a single disk into two partitions and back up one partition to the other. These backups are *false* backups because they are not really safe. What if the system is subjected to a massive electrical surge or failure? The contents of both drives may be lost.

What if the system is stolen in the middle of the night? Again, both backups will be lost. What about physical damage such as a fire? Or suppose that the table holding your system collapses? Again, all data will be lost. You cannot justify any backup that is not done to removable media, which can be taken out of the system and stored in a safe place.

Perform your backups to removable media on a rotating basis. A good arrangement is to use a tape backup system with three tapes per drive. Each week, the data is backed up to a single tape. The second week, a second tape is employed. That way, if restoring is necessary and this second tape has been damaged, you always can use the preceding week's backup. The third week, you should use another tape again, and you should place the first tape in a different physical location as insurance against fire, flood, theft, or other disaster. The fourth week, each of the tapes are rotated so that the off-site tape now is used again for backup, and the second tape is moved off-site. This system always has two progressively older backups on-site, with the third backup off-site as a form of disaster insurance. Only removable media can provide this type of flexibility, and tape is one of the best forms of removable media for backup.

To provide for proper backup of your systems, try to think of every possible contingency and design your backup plan to counteract any foreseeable problem. Make your users aware of the need for backup and aware that nothing can be considered safe without it.

Copy Protection

Standing in the way of proper backup of your software is copy protection. Software makers would like for you to have to use your original master copies of programs on a day-to-day basis, and they would like to require that disks be available for you to place in a floppy drive for validation even though the system may contain an expensive hard disk! Needless to say, I am totally opposed to any form of copy protection and think that it has no place in a business environment.

Any experienced computer user knows that you should never use any original disks when installing or configuring software. My first action when purchasing a program is to make a copy of the program and store the original away. In fact, I use the the original disk solely for making additional copies. This way, I am protected if I make a mistake in the installation or use of the software.

My personal response to copy protection is to boycott any software company engaged in this ridiculous practice whenever possible. Unprotected alternatives always are available for whatever program you desire. You even may discover that the unprotected alternative is actually a better program. With rare exceptions, I never purchase copy-protected software. For those of you who don't make the software purchasing decisions in your organization, however, this advice really cannot be followed.

For those cases where you must use a piece of protected software, I can recommend special programs such as CopyWrite by Quaid Software Ltd. and Copy II PC by Central Point Software. With these programs, you can back up and even remove the protection from most copy-protected programs on the market. These programs cost around $50 and are an absolute necessity when you're forced to deal with copy-protection schemes. In effect, these programs completely nullify the protection and duplicate any software, and they even remove the protection from many programs.

Remember that you have a legal right to back up your software; this right is guaranteed under the U.S. copyright law. Do not allow some software license agreement to bamboozle you into thinking otherwise.

The best way to fight copy protection, however, is with your wallet. I don't use, purchase, or recommend any copy-protected software. Most companies will respond to this economic pressure; many of them respond by removing the protection from their programs. Fortunately, because of this economic pressure, the scourge of copy protection has almost been completely eliminated from the business-software marketplace.

Backup Software

When considering your backup equipment, you will find a two-sided world. Hardware is available and software is available. As you will learn in the next two sections, the default software is poor, but some aftermarket software is the simplest to change.

The BACKUP Command

The BACKUP and RESTORE commands have been notoriously bad ever since they appeared with DOS 2.0. These commands, in fact, have had bugs and problems that prevent proper use in several versions of DOS, including all versions up to 3.3. Because of these problems and poor performance, your best bet is not to rely on these programs. DOS BACKUP and RESTORE can be used with any lower capacity systems or when no other alternatives are available (such as when you're stranded on a desert island). Otherwise, you will be wise to consider alternatives.

Aftermarket Software

Investigate some of the aftermarket software designed to accomplish the task of backing up. I recommend these two programs:

- FASTBACK by 5th Generation Systems
- DS Backup by Design Software

Even with these programs, backing up a hard disk larger than 20M to floppy disks generally is not acceptable. The system that I currently use has a 91M disk drive, which would take 247 360K floppy disks to back up. Have you ever tried to manage 247 floppy disks? Because this drive is full, I am changing to a 190M disk, which will require more than 500 floppy disks to back up. Regardless of how good these software floppy backup programs are, they still require the use of the floppy disk drive, which is terrible for backup purposes. For any disk system larger than 20 megabytes, you need to purchase a dedicated backup system, preferably using a form of removable tape.

Backup Hardware

As mentioned earlier, when considering backup equipment, you have a choice of software and hardware. In this part, you will learn about the default hardware (floppy drives). You also will learn that for a real professional solution to the backup problem, you need to investigate some alternative hardware designed for the task.

Floppy Disk Drives

You already have a floppy drive, and that is about the only advantage to using one for backups—it's "free." But, remember, the disks aren't free.

As I mentioned earlier, I currently need about 250 floppy disks to back up my system (91M). I run a system of three backups on a rotating basis, as described in an earlier section. Therefore, I need 750 floppy disks to back up the system properly. I want good disks for my backup, which cost about $1 each, so I need to spend about $750 for floppy disks alone. And for the software, I could use the DOS BACKUP and RESTORE commands, but they are exceedingly slow and buggy. Using one of the faster aftermarket programs speeds things up. Many of these programs even compress the data and conserve on the number of disks used. They cost about $150.

Now I need to sit down and feed 250 floppy disks into the drive, one after another, while the program fills them up. I need to label and number the disks so that they are not misplaced or used out of order. This process is time-consuming. Assume that I can handle each disk in 30 seconds total time. The process will take 125 minutes or just more than two hours! When I upgrade the capacity of my disk to 190M, this process will take four hours and require 1,500 disks. Now for the clincher. I currently have five systems, with an average capacity of 60 megabytes each. I will need nearly 2,300 disks to back up properly by using the rotating method. That backup procedure costs $2,300, not including the cost of my time.

I would be a fool even to dream about using the floppy drive to back up my system. Instead, I use a single tape drive and tapes that hold 60 megabytes each. The drive costs $1,200, and the tapes are $20 each. I need only $300 worth of tapes to achieve my triple backups of each system, and the tape unit currently backs up all of them. I have installed adapter cards in several of the systems, which allows me to plug in directly and back up, or I can back up over the Token Ring network that links the systems together. The system I use achieves an actual rate of 5 megabytes per minute during backups, which means that the average 60M system is completely backed up in 12 minutes front to back. I can set this system to perform the backup in the middle of the night, totally unattended, so none of my time is used.

For a total of about $1,500, I have achieved a reliable, proper, complete, high-speed, and simple backup of every system that I own. That is real economy. If you have more than 20 megabytes to back up—or more than one system—a tape backup product is the only way to go. Tape backup products are discussed next.

Tape Backup Systems

A good, reliable backup is important when you're using a large storage device such as a hard disk. With "all your eggs in one basket," you need this form of insurance. With any large disk of 20 megabytes or greater, you should have some form of hardware backup device instead of just the floppy drive. Tape backup is available in configurations easily supporting 60 megabytes and more. This type of backup is fast and accurate. Remember that your data is probably worth much more than the physical hardware itself and often is simply irreplaceable. A tape system makes the backup convenient, and therefore the backup probably will get done. If you make backup a difficult, time-consuming operation, you simply will forget to do it in the long run.

Here are some parameters that describe the basic functionality of the tape system:

1. Type of media
    A. DC-600
    B. DC-2000

2. Hardware interface
    A. QIC-02
    B. SCSI
    C. SA-450 (floppy)

3. Software
    A. Proprietary
    B. SyTOS (Sytron Tape Operating System)

These parameters are explained in the sections that follow.

Types of Media

I like to stay with systems that use industry-standard media. *Media* refers to the type of tape format actually used. Although many different types of systems use many different types of media, I am concerned only with a handful of standard media types. Two primary standards are the 3M Data Cartridge 600 (or DC 600) and DC-2000 media. The type of media that you select will dictate the capacity of the tape unit storage. The DC-600 is the one that I really recommend, and it currently represents the best and most cost-effective media type of all the standards.

DC-600 drives currently store 60M, 125M, 150M, or 320M, depending on the actual format and quality of tape used. The DC-2000 media only stores 40M per tape and may be suitable for low-end (such as home) use. Make sure that the system is capable of handling your largest drive either directly or through the use of multiple tapes. The unit will allow you to change tapes in the middle of a backup session to achieve greater capacities, but the backup is more inconvenient this way and requires the presence of an operator, eliminating the possibility of unattended overnight backups. For the professional business environment or where top-performing and reliable backup is needed, you should select DC-600 rather than the DC-2000 media.

I recommend only tape systems that use these media because they offer the greatest value per dollar, are the most reliable, and hold a large amount of storage. I recommend that you stay away from devices that use the 3M DC-1000 tapes, Phillips audio types of tapes, or VCR tape systems. These systems are slow, prone to error, and inconvenient to use; some do not handle larger capacities, and they are just not standard. Two possibilities for future standard use are the Digital Audio Tape (DAT) format and the IBM 3480 type of tape format. These tape systems are newer and have not yet achieved a great deal of popularity in the PC world.

Hardware Interface

Of the three hardware interface standards, either the QIC-02 (for Quarter Inch Committee 02) or SCSI (for Small Systems Computer Interface) is used by all professional backup systems. The lower end home-use systems use the Shugart Associates 450 (SA-450) interface, which is the standard floppy controller. The particular interface that you select basically controls the speed of backup, whether an adapter card and slot are required, and the reliability and capacity of the unit.

In the PC and XT systems with their 4-drive floppy controllers, you have an extra connector on the back of the floppy controller that can be used for tape backup units. This connector saves the use of a slot in these systems. Unfortunately, the AT systems require some sort of multiplexer card to allow the sharing of one of the internal floppy ports to allow these systems to work.

I don't recommend these floppy interface systems in general because they are slow, and the floppy controller lacks any form of error detection and correction capability, which can make the backups unreliable. A system using the SA-450 interface achieves a maximum data rate of 2M per minute, which is less than half the QIC-02 or SCSI interfaces. These floppy interface systems are suitable for the home computer user on a tight budget but should not be used in business or professional environments. Another problem is that the interface limits the capacity to 40 megabytes, and the tapes may need to be formatted prior to use.

The QIC-02 interface is specifically designed for tape backup products and represents a real industry standard. Most companies offer products that use this interface. The QIC-02 is capable of achieving a backup rate of 5M per minute in actual use. The interface itself is usually a short adapter card that requires a free slot in the system. You can purchase these adapters separately, allowing many systems to use the same externally mounted drive. Unfortunately, a free slot is required, which may not be possible in a regular PC.

Perhaps the best hardware interface is the Small Systems Computer Interface (SCSI), which allows high data rates to be achieved. The current norm is 5M per minute as limited by the actual tape drives themselves. When faster media and drives are available, SCSI can take advantage of the greater speed.

This interface comes in the physical form of an SCSI host adapter card that plugs into the system unit and can connect to the tape drive. Although this SCSI adapter does require a slot, it also can connect to other devices such as hard disk drives with embedded SCSI interfaces. The use of the single host adapter for as many as six hard disk drives and one tape unit is a strong case in favor of SCSI as a general disk and tape interface. The use of SCSI in the PC world, however, is still not as popular as the other dedicated interfaces. The reason is that SCSI is not as standardized as most manufacturers would like.

I could recommend that you stay with the "safe" QIC-02 for tape and ST-506/412 or ESDI for hard drives, or I could recommend that you use SCSI for all the drives and tape units. The choice is yours. As long as you get all the necessary operating systems drivers, you cannot go wrong with SCSI. I definitely think that this interface will become more popular in the future, and it already is overtaking the other interfaces in system use.

Software

Now you need to consider the software that is to run the tape system. Most manufacturers have written their own software, which is proprietary and used only by that particular manufacturer. In other words, even though you may be using a tape unit with the exact same media and interface, if the software is different, you will not be able to interchange data between the units. One type of software will not recognize the data formats of another proprietary software system. A light is at the end of the tunnel, though, in the form of a software system that is becoming an industry standard. The software is called SyTOS (Sytron Tape Operating System).

SyTOS was developed by a company called Sytron and has been selected by IBM as the standard software for its units. Because of this IBM selection, SyTOS is now becoming a standard. Because of market pressures to be compatible with IBM, other tape drive vendors now are offering SyTOS with their systems. Two systems that use the same media, interface, and software will read and write each other's data formats. This is the advent of true data interchangeability among different tape manufacturers. I recommend that you consider using a system that runs SyTOS software for those reasons. Of course, the proprietary software is generally just as good, if not better, but you will be able to exchange data tapes only with other users of the same systems.

Any software should be able to do certain basic operations. Make sure that the software will do what you need and only consider software that has the following features:

- The software can back up an entire DOS partition (image backup).

- The software can back up any or all files individually (file-by-file backup).

- The software allows a selective file-by-file restore from an image backup as well as a file-by-file backup.

- The software can combine several backups on a single tape.

- The software can be run as commands from DOS BATCH files.

- The software will work under a network.
- Backups can span multiple tapes.
- Backups can be completely verified.

If the software you are considering does not have any of these features, look for another system. These basic features are essential.

Physical Location: Internal or External

Physical location is a simple factor that often is not considered in detail. I almost never recommend any tape backup unit that is mounted internally in the system unit. I always recommend that you purchase a tape unit that is externally mounted in its own chassis and that connects to the system unit through a cable and connectors.

Tape units are fairly expensive, and I would never tie up a backup unit for only one system. The amount of time that one system actually will use the unit makes this proposition wasteful. With an external unit, I can share the backup unit with many systems. All I have to do is equip each system unit with the required interface. These extra interface cards are available for about $100 each, which is the total cost of adding each subsequent system to full backup capability. I already share my system among five computers and will continue adding systems to the backup pool. In some companies, the backup unit will be mounted on a wheeled cart so that it can be moved easily from computer to computer.

Those of you with only one system may have a legitimate argument for using an internal system. But you will wish that you had an external system on the day a new system arrives. Every computer user I know has eventually added a second system or upgraded to a more powerful unit.

A perfect example can be made with the PS/2 systems. Suppose that you have an internal unit in your AT and decide to upgrade to a PS/2 Model 50, 60, 70, or 80. You will not be able to use that same backup unit for the PS/2 system. But if you purchase an external tape system, you simply can purchase the Micro Channel interface board for your unit, plug it in, and back up both the earlier AT and the PS/2 system. External backup will not become obsolete when new systems are purchased. And external backup puts much less strain on your system because the external unit has its own power supply and will not consume power from your system unit. The external devices simply win all the way around.

Tape Backup Recommendations

I recommend units from any manufacturer that meets the following requirements:

Type of media:	DC-600
Hardware interface:	QIC-02 or SCSI
Software:	SyTOS or good proprietary software

Many manufacturers meet these requirements. Here are my favorites:

Cipher Data Products (makes IBM's DC-600 units)
Tecmar
Mountain

I usually do not like to recommend against any manufacturer, but I want to stress that you should evaluate carefully any units from a company called Tallgrass. Tallgrass units use a nonstandard recording format that makes them some of the slowest systems in their class, and these units have had numerous reliability problems due to a total disregard of any industry-standard interfaces or formats. Also carefully compare to other systems any DC-1000 units from any company for these same reasons. I would simply avoid DC-1000 media units. Before selecting any of these units, make sure that you compare them to other more industry-standard devices. Any unit that meets the specifications I mentioned previously is sure to be a great product.

Examining Warranty and Service Contracts

Warranties are a fairly recent trend in the industry. IBM now offers a one-year warranty on all its systems, which sets a new standard for others to live up to. In the past, when IBM offered only a 90-day warranty, many other manufacturers followed IBM's lead and did the same. Much the same as in the auto industry, when one of the big players starts to ''up'' the warranty period as a major selling feature of the system, other manufacturers in competition follow suit. The standard warranty is now a full year, and some companies even offer two-year warranties.

IBM has a unique option for the warranties on PS/2 systems; you can upgrade the warranty to a full on-site service contract for $25! I personally think this option is amazing. If I exercise this option for $25, any time my system has a problem during the first year, I can call IBM and the company will have to send someone to my location to repair the unit on my site as a free warranty repair! One car ride to a service center costs me more than $25 in wasted gasoline and time, so this option is worthwhile, to say the least. I would pay the $25 just for the pleasure of having the service people come to me for an entire year. Because of this IBM ''feature,'' other companies also are offering inexpensive warranty upgrades and service contracts.

My own personal philosophy is that service contracts are not worth the price in most cases. I have working experience in the retail computer environment, and I know what a service contract really is all about. A service contract usually is a way for the dealer or vendor to have a monthly paycheck coming in with little or no effort. Most service contracts are about 10 to 15 percent of the cost of the system each year. A service contract for a $5,000 system, for example, costs $500 to $750 per year!

As an example, the standard IBM Customer Carry-in Repair (CCR) service contract for the AT Model 339 is about $550 per year, which works out to be the price of the 30M hard disk and controller each year. IBM's exchange price on the motherboard is also about that price. You have to bring the system to IBM, and this contract does not cover any extra accessories that you have added. Only the original equipment is covered. Knowing the real-world reliability of these systems, the dealers make a bundle by charging these figures.

These prices may affect the type of service you get. Many people with a service contract believe that the high cost is justified. Often, when a user has a problem, a service person pays a visit and tells this user that the entire motherboard is bad or the hard disk needs to be removed, and the service person replaces it. The trend in outbound service is to *replace* everything until the system works and take the old parts back to the shop where they can be diagnosed and repaired properly. But, remember, most hard disks are ''repaired'' with a low-level format. The service person replaces your disk with the spare that he or she brings along, because replacing the disk is faster, and leaves the impression that your expensive service contract is really worth the price; you get a "new" hard disk because yours was "defective." In reality, though, the "defective" drive is taken back to the shop and low-level formatted. And, eventually, it will end up in somebody else's system in the same manner.

The motherboards often are handled the same way. Instead of properly diagnosing a memory problem down to the chip or component level in the field, the service person simply tells you that the board is bad and replaces it with the spare one he or she brought. The "bad" board is then taken back to the shop, properly diagnosed and repaired, and ends up in somebody else's system. Again, you believe that this service contract is justified because your whole motherboard was "bad" and you got a "new" one. You would be much less impressed with your expensive service contract if the service people paid you a visit, did a simple troubleshooting procedure, and then simply replaced a single $10 memory chip or spent 15 minutes reformatting the hard disk.

My point is that with some basic troubleshooting skills, some simple tools, and a few spare parts, you can completely eliminate the need for most of these expensive service contracts. Unfortunately, some companies practice deceptive servicing procedures to justify the expensive service contracts they offer, which leaves the computer user with an overall bad impression of computers in general. Users are made to believe that these types of component failures are the norm, and they have a mistaken impression about the overall reliability of today's systems.

You may indeed find a case where such a contract can be justified and beneficial, however. For a system that must function at all times and is so expensive that a complete spare system cannot be purchased, or for a system in a remote location far away from your centralized service operation, you may be wise to invest in a good service contract that provides timely repairs when you cannot. In some cases, using a service contract is worthwhile when the system is an exotic one, unlike any others that you may have. Most PC systems used today have become commodity items, but some systems have not yet achieved this commodity status. For these systems, a service contract may be a valid consideration.

Sometimes you may need to make other considerations. The PS/2 systems from IBM, for example, contain few overall components. Many of these parts are manufactured by IBM alone and have not yet achieved commodity status. For the first year after the PS/2 introduction, for example, few replacement components for the system have been available from third-party companies. The biggest reason is that until at least one year has elapsed, each PS/2 system is under the factory warranty, and people just don't pay for replacement parts that they can get free from IBM. And if users upgrade for $25 to the on-site warranty, IBM even brings the part to you and installs it at no charge.

Now, however, many of these systems are coming off of their warranties, and service is becoming a major consideration. Because the systems have so few components, the relative price of each part is quite high. The Model 50Z, for example, comes standard with 1M of memory on the motherboard, which is installed as a single SIMM (Single Inline Memory Module). A SIMM is a small board that has all the memory soldered onto it. If any memory fails at all in this system, the diagnosis part is simple because only one memory ''chip'' exists—the one SIMM. The only real problem is that this 85-nanosecond 1M SIMM costs about $500. That is one expensive chip!

Now if that unit fails, it is not repairable and must be replaced. The service contract pricing for the PS/2 systems from IBM is about one-third of what IBM charged for its original systems. The service contract price for this Model 50Z is under $200, which caused me to take notice. Although I certainly can repair these systems, the parts can be extremely expensive. If I have several of these systems, I can justify carrying a spare-parts inventory, which negates the need for the contract. I can purchase a Model 50Z for about $3,000; if I am tending to at least 15 to 20 of these systems, I certainly can justify the purchase of an entire unit as a spare and perhaps forego the service contract. Protecting yourself with redundant equipment generally becomes practical if you have more than 10 computers of the same brand. For extremely time-sensitive applications, however, you may be wise to buy a second system right along with the primary unit—such as in a network file server application. Only you can decide where service contracts or spare systems are needed and make the appropriate cost-justification analysis.

Remember that service contracts can be a viable option in certain cases. Before contacting for service, you should consider your options carefully. You basically have three sources for service contracts:

- Manufacturer supplied (or authorized)

- Dealer or vendor supplied (or authorized)

- Third-party supplied

Although most users usually take the manufacturer or dealer service, sometimes the third party goes further to close the deal; the third party, for example, sometimes includes all the equipment installed, even "strange" or aftermarket items that the dealers or manufacturers don't touch. In other cases, the manufacturer may not have his or her own service organization but, instead, has a deal with a major third-party nationwide service company to provide authorized service.

Once a particular organization has been selected, several levels of service often are available. Starting with the most expensive, these levels of service typically include the following:

- Four-hour on-site response

- Next-day on-site response

- Courier service (A service company picks up the unit and returns it when it's repaired.)

- Carry-in or "depot" service

For the PS/2 systems, for example, IBM offers only a full 24 hours a day, 7 days a week, on-site service contract. IBM claims that a technician is dispatched usually within four hours of your call. For the earlier systems, but not the PS/2, IBM also offers a courier service contract. No other types of contracts are available from IBM. Warranty work is normally a customer carry-in depot arrangement but can be upgraded to the full on-site contract for only $25. After the first-year $25-contract expires, you can continue the full on-site service contract for various rates (see table 11.1).

If you ever have purchased a service contract in the past, you will be quite surprised by these prices. With the PS/2 systems, IBM has rewritten the rules completely for PC servicing. The same type of on-site annual contract for one of the earlier 20M AT systems, for example, costs $507 annually compared with the $180 for the PS/2 Model 50! The third-party service companies are having a hard time competing with these newer prices. IBM claims that the PS/2 systems are five times more reliable than the earlier systems, and the service-contract pricing is about one-third of what the earlier systems cost. If the claims of additional reliability are true, IBM is making out quite good even with the lower pricing. If the claims are not true (which is doubtful), IBM is losing money.

Table 11.1
PS/2 Service Contract Fees after Warranty

PS/2 Model	Annual Service Contract
Model 25 -001, -G01	$80
Model 25 -004, -L04	$90
Model 30 -002	$115
Model 30 -021	$160
Model 50 -021, 50Z	$180
Model 60 -041	$190
Model 60 -071	$200
Model 80 -041	$210
Model 80 -071	$220
Model 80 -111	$305
Model 80 -311	$350

The third-party service companies almost cannot compete with this pricing because IBM also controls the parts supply to these companies. Although the standard systems contain many parts that have become commodities, the PS/2 systems have not had quite the same aftermarket parts supply. A service company that is truly serious about service can get new parts or repair all existing internal parts with only one exception: the motherboard. Motherboards must be obtained from IBM, and IBM does not sell any of the proprietary chips on these boards so that they could be repaired. Motherboards use mostly surface-mount components anyway, so repair would be extremely difficult even if parts could be found. Because the motherboards now contain several items on-board (floppy controller, video, memory, serial, parallel, mouse, etc.), the motherboards may need to be replaced more often than in the earlier systems. The outright purchase or exchange prices on these boards are much more than the cost of an annual contract.

The bottom line is this: For most standard types of systems, any service contracts beyond the original warranty are probably a waste of money. For other systems that have not yet achieved commodity status, or for those systems that must be up and running at all times, you may want to investigate a service contract option, even though you may be fully qualified and capable of servicing the system yourself.

The PS/2 systems are a special case; they have low-priced on-site warranty upgrade and inexpensive service contracts, which can be tempting. But, remember, many of the components such as disk drives can be purchased from non-IBM sources, and items such as the power supplies can be repaired by third-party companies who specialize in these items. The motherboard is the only item that cannot be repaired easily or exchanged inexpensively. Also, physically working on the PS/2 systems is easy; these systems have a snap-together no-tool design. Only you can make the decision of how your systems should be serviced after carefully weighing all the options and costs involved.

Chapter Summary

In this chapter, I have discussed the steps you can take to ensure proper operation of your system. You have examined both active and passive preventive maintenance. Preventive maintenance can be the key to a system that gives many years of trouble-free service. You have learned about the various procedures involved in preventive maintenance and the frequencies with which these procedures should be done.

Backup is discussed as a way to be prepared when things do go wrong. The only "guarantee" that you will ever see your data again is to back it up. In this chapter, you also looked at a variety of backup options.

Finally, I discussed the commonly available warranty and service contracts provided by the manufacturers. Sometimes these contracts can save you worry about tough-to-service systems or systems whose parts are largely unavailable on short notice.

12

System Upgrades and Improvements

IBM and compatible systems are the easiest systems to upgrade and improve because of the support received from the aftermarket and IBM. Numerous options are available for extending a system in virtually any targeted area. You can extend the life of earlier systems by adding functions and features that match the newest systems on the market.

Keep an eye on the cost of upgrades because you can reach a point where changes become so major or expensive that purchasing a new system may be a better choice. You can accumulate an upgrade bill that exceeds the purchase price of a newer system with equal or better features.

You also face the danger that you will create a Frankenstein system with strange quirks and eccentric operation. In business, you have no room for a marginally functional system. Many of the possible upgrades are classified under *hacker* status. These upgrades are fine for a personal system or an experimental system, but should not be executed when the PC is used in a business environment.

Upgrading by Expanding Memory

Adding memory to a system is one of the more useful upgrades that you can perform. You can add three types of memory: conventional, extended, and expanded. Chapter 10 defines these three types of memory and describes their functions.

All systems should have 640K of conventional memory. After filling conventional memory capabilities, you may expand memory further in a PC or XT type of system. PC or XT systems cannot use extended memory; however, expanded memory can greatly enhance the abilities, though not the speed, of your computer. IBM has given expanded memory its blessing by adding expanded memory support with DOS 4.0. When adding expanded memory, ensure that the memory is Expanded Memory Specification 4.0 (EMS 4.0) or the Enhanced Expanded Memory Specification (EEMS), which have greater capabilities over the earlier EMS 3.2.

With the AT, you get the immediate functionality of expanded memory and the future functionality of extended memory under OS/2. You can take advantage of up to nearly 16M. You should not install expanded memory in a system running OS/2. Fortunately, any AT type of expanded memory board can be switched easily from expanded to extended memory.

The cost of a couple of megabytes of expanded memory for an early PC may be much more than the entire system is worth. You may wish to use the money to purchase faster equipment with greater expansion capabilities, such as an 80286 or 80386 computer.

If you decide to upgrade to a different, more powerful computer system, remember that you cannot salvage the memory from PC or XT systems. The 8-bit memory boards are useless in AT or Micro Channel systems, and the memory chips and their speed are probably inadequate for newer systems. Many of the newest systems exclusively use high-speed SIMM modules instead of chips. Having a pile of 150 nanosecond 64K or 256K chips is useless if your next system is a PS/2 Model 80 or another high-speed system that uses SIMMs or memory devices faster than 150 nanoseconds. Be sure to weigh carefully your future needs, including any increases in computing speed and the need for a multitasking operating system such as OS/2, with the amount of money you will spend to upgrade current equipment.

Upgrading Motherboard Memory

This section discusses *motherboard memory*, the memory installed directly on the motherboard—not the memory residing on adapter boards. Recommendations are made for selecting and installing chips. The last part of this section contains instructions for an interesting modification for the IBM XT Type 1 motherboard. This modification enables a full 640K of memory to be placed on the motherboard, eliminating the need for memory expansion boards. IBM's later XT Type 2 motherboards already include this modification.

Selecting and Installing Chips

If you are upgrading a system board with memory, follow the manufacturer's guidelines about which memory chips or SIMMs to purchase. The manufacturer also indicates how fast and expensive these components are. For example, IBM specifies different speed memory for different motherboards. Table 12.1 lists the installed memory speed found in the various IBM motherboards.

The listed memory access times are for the memory found on the motherboards of the various systems. Usually, for standard PC systems, the time shown also indicates the speed for memory installed via the expansion slots, because the slots run in synchronization with the main processor. Using slower memory than specified results in various memory error messages and a system that may not operate.

Because of the higher level of controls and capabilities of the Micro Channel interface, however, PS/2 systems' memory adapters may be able to run slower than main memory. The asynchronous design of the MCA enables adapters to remain independent of the speed of the processor. The MCA inserts wait states as required to accommodate any slower adapters. For example, all of the memory adapters that IBM offers for the PS/2 50 and 60 use 120 nanosecond memory chips. These adapters also are specified for the Model 50Z that runs with no wait states and uses 85-nanosecond memory on the motherboard. These slower 120-nanosecond memory adapters cause the MCA in the 50Z to insert a wait state when the adapters are accessed, so that only the motherboard memory runs with 0 wait states. Several third-party board manufacturers offer special 0-wait-state boards for the 50Z.

The bottom line for motherboard memory speed is to use the speed indicated by the manufacturer. Using faster memory on the motherboard creates no performance benefit, but does work. The

Table 12.1
IBM Motherboard Memory Timing

System	Clock Speed (MHz)	Wait States	Memory Access Time (ns)
PC Family:			
PC	4.77	1	200
XT	4.77	1	200
AT	6	1	150
AT	8	1	150
XT Model 286	6	0	150
PS/2 Family:			
Model 30	8	1	150
Model 30 286	10	1	120
Model 50	10	1	120
Model 50Z	10	0	85
Model 60	10	1	120
Model 70	16	0—2 (paged)	85

Table 12.1
IBM Motherboard Memory Timing

Model 70	20	0—2 (paged)	85
Model 70	25	0 (cache)	80
Model 80	16	1	80
Model 80	20	0—2 (paged)	80

information indicating minimum access time for motherboard memory is found in the technical reference manual for your particular system. For compatible systems, you can use table 12.1 as a guide. Because of the wide variety of system designs on the market today, however, you should acquire the proper information from the manufacturer.

For many systems with proprietary memory expansion busses like COMPAQ, you often have to purchase all memory expansion from that company. For other industry standard systems that allow non-proprietary memory expansion like the IBM PC, XT, AT, and PS/2 systems, you can purchase boards from hundreds of vendors. Be wary of purchasing nonstandard systems like the COMPAQ and AST because you may experience problems when adding or servicing memory.

Before installing memory, be sure that the system power is off. Remove the PC cover and any installed cards. SIMMs snap into place, but chips can be more difficult to install. A chip installation tool is not required, but the tool can make inserting the chips into sockets much easier. For removing chips, a chip extractor or small screwdriver is highly recommended. Never try removing a RAM chip with your fingers because you can bend the chip's pins or poke a hole in your finger with one of the pins. SIMMs are removed by unplugging them.

The three main problems encountered when installing or removing memory are Electro Static Discharge (ESD), broken or bent leads, and incorrect switch and jumper settings.

When installing sensitive memory chips or boards, do not wear synthetic clothes or leather-soled shoes. Discharge yourself to a system chassis ground before beginning or wear a commercial grounding strap on your wrist. This strap is grounded by a wire with an alligator clip on one end and is wrapped around your wrist on the other end. Be sure to use a well-made unit; *do not* make one yourself! Commercial units have a high value resistor in the unit that acts as a fuse if you touch live power. The resistor makes sure that you are not the path of least resistance to the ground. An improperly designed unit may cause you to conduct the power to the ground, possibly killing you.

Sometimes the pins on new chips are spread apart in a V shape, making them difficult to align with the socket holes. Place the chip on its side and press gently to bend the pins resting on the table inward. Install the chips into the sockets one at a time. Chip-insertion and pin-straightening devices are available that make sure the pins are straight and aligned with the socket holes. Using one of these inexpensive tools can save you a great deal of time.

Each chip has a U-shaped notch that matches a similar mark on the socket. If the socket is not marked, you should use other chips as a guide. The orientation of the notch indicates the location of pin number one on the chip. Aligning this notch correctly with the others on the board ensures that you do not install the chip backwards. Gently set each chip into a socket and push the chip firmly in with both thumbs until the chip is fully seated.

After adding memory chips, you may need to reset the motherboard switches or jumpers. For AT and PS/2 systems, no switches or jumpers exist, and you must run a setup program to inform the system of the total amount of memory installed. Two switch units are on the PC; the XT has one, and the AT has none. Positions 1 through 4 of a PC's second switch reflect the total installed memory. The single switch unit on the XT reflects only the total memory on the system board and does not deal with expansion card memory. The Appendix details the PC and XT switch settings.

Most memory expansion cards have switches or jumpers that you need to set. You often have to set a memory starting address for the card equal to the amount of memory on the system board. You also may have to set the total memory on the card. Because of the PS/2 influence, many memory and other boards are being made that do not have switches. Instead, these boards come with a configuration program that can be used to set up the card. The Intel AboveBoard 286 and Plus versions, for example, have this switchless operation.

After putting the system back together, run any memory diagnostics programs you have, note the total memory reported, and test for any definite failures.

You always have at least two or three memory diagnostics programs at your disposal. In order of accuracy, these programs are the POST (power-on self test), Diagnostics disk, and Advanced Diagnostics disk. The PS/2 systems include the Diagnostics and Advanced Diagnostics on a single Reference Disk. This disk is included with the system, ensuring that PS/2 owners have all three memory test programs. You use the POST every time the system is powered up, and Advanced diagnostics are accessed on the Reference Disk by pressing Ctrl-A at the opening menu.

Standard PC owners receive a Diagnostics disk with the system (in the guide to operations manual) that has a fairly good memory test. PC owners should purchase the Advanced Diagnostics disk as part of the hardware maintenance service manual package. If you have purchased this package, the Advanced Diagnostics is the recommended program to use.

Many additional diagnostics programs are available for purchase and in the public domain.

Installing 640K on the XT Motherboard

This section describes how to install 640K of RAM on the system board in the IBM XT and the IBM portable. IBM offers this upgrade in the form of a new Type 2 XT motherboard. IBM invented this upgrade much earlier, but they held the upgrade back for several years after the system was introduced. Many users who purchased the technical reference manual and looked at the schematic diagram did not wait for IBM. They figured out that the modification is performed by installing two banks of 256K chips and two banks of 64K chips directly on the motherboard and installing one additional multiplexer chip and a jumper wire. The jumper wire enables a decoder PAL chip (U44) to modify the chip selects and addressing as required. These modifications are easy to perform.

A memory chip is addressed by two signals called Row Address Select (RAS) and Column Address Select (CAS). These signals dictate where a value is located in a chip. These signals are modified by installing the jumper as indicated in the instructions so that the first two banks can be addressed four times deeper than originally.

Obtain the following parts from any chip house or electronics supply store:

- 18 256K-by-1-bit 200 nanosecond (or faster) memory chips
- 1 74LS158 multiplexer/decoder chip
- Small length of thin gauge jumper wire

After obtaining the parts, proceed as follows:

1. Remove the motherboard. (Instructions for removing the motherboard are provided in Chapter 6.)

2. Plug the 74LS158 chip into the socket labeled U84.

Note that all the components on the motherboard can be identified by a value, consisting of a letter and number combination. The letter usually indicates the type of component, and the number indicates the particular component of that type. This coding sometimes differs among manufacturers. Most manufacturers use a letter scheme that follows these conventions:

U = Integrated Circuit
Q = Transistor
C = Capacitor

R = Resistor
T = Transformer
L = Coil
Y = Crystal
D = Diode

The numbering of the components usually follows a pattern in which the numbers increase as you move from left to right along the first row of components and then start at the left side again, one row lower. You should be able to locate all of the IC chips, starting with U1 in the upper left corner of the board and ending with U90 in the lower right corner.

The next step involves inserting a jumper wire that modifies the memory chip select and addressing signals. The following method is the simplest way to accomplish this procedure.

3. Remove the IC installed in the socket labeled U44.

4. Install a jumper wire from pin 1 to pin 8 on U44. To avoid making any changes that cannot be removed later, the jumper can be wrapped directly onto the pins of the IC. Run this wire on the underside of the IC so that the wire is held in place. Reinstall the chip with the jumper in place. The IC may sit slightly higher in the socket, but make sure that it is seated properly.

Be careful with the U44 because this chip is a unique IBM Programmable Array Logic (PAL) chip that cannot be purchased separately. A PAL chip is burned with a unique pattern, much like a ROM chip. The only legal way to obtain this chip from IBM is to purchase a new motherboard. Some chip houses have copied this chip and offer a duplicate for sale. Some also have duplicated the PAL chip with the equivalent of the jumper modification internally programmed, so that you may purchase one of these duplicates and store your original PAL chip.

You also can solder two jumper pins into the plated holes numbered 1 and 2 in the jumper pad labeled E2. Using a standard plug-on jumper, install the jumper across these two pins. All XT Type 2 motherboards already have this modification performed, courtesy of IBM.

5. Remove the 18 64K-by-1-bit chips from banks 0 and 1. Reinstall them in banks 2 and 3 if 64K chips are not already in these banks or store them as spare chips.

6. Install the 18 256K-by-1-bit chips in banks 0 and 1.

7. Be sure that switches 3 and 4 of switch block SW1 are set off.

8. Replace the motherboard and restore all other system components, with the exception of any memory cards.

   Remember that you have 640K on the motherboard and no other boards must address that space.

9. Power-up the system and test the installed memory for 640K without other memory adapter cards.

You now have an inexpensive memory upgrade that matches the Type 2 XT motherboard from IBM.

Upgrading the Disk Subsystem

This section discusses adding floppy disk drives and hard disk drives to any system. The interfacing of the different types of floppy drives to a system can sometimes be a problem because of the differences in controllers and support software.

Adding Floppy Disk Drives

If you want to add floppy drives to an existing system, you need to connect them to a controller board. Virtually every PC, XT, or AT comes equipped with at least one floppy disk controller. These controllers and system BIOS routines support different drives.

You have four types of drives to consider when adding to any system: high- and double-density 5 1/4-inch and high- and double-density 3 1/2-inch. In the case of the 5 1/4-inch drives, you may be concerned about the track width differences between 40 and 80 track drives. All 3 1/2-inch drives, however, are 80 track drives and do not share these compatibility problems. Because high-density drives can read and write at the lower density as well, a system with as few as two high-density drives, one 5 1/4-inch and one 3 1/2-inch, can read and write any disk format. When upgrading, therefore, add the high-density drives whenever possible.

A high-density drive uses a higher data rate (500 KHz) than a double-density drive (250 KHz). To properly use these higher density drives, you need a controller and software capable of supporting the higher data rate. At least DOS 3.3 is required to support all of the disk formats, including the 1.44M high-density 3 1/2-inch drives. DOS 3.2 supports only the 720K double-density 3 1/2-inch format and cannot be used.

The standard controllers in PC and XT systems support only lower density drives. To save money, consider adding only the lower density versions of the 5 1/4-inch and 3 1/2-inch drives. Adding these drives requires no special controllers, cables, or software. DOS 3.3 has everything you need in a driver file called DRIVER.SYS. This driver is used to support the 3 1/2-inch 720K drive in systems without built-in ROM support. If you want to use the 1.2M or 1.44M drives in these systems, you need to purchase a controller and software that handle high-density formats. The AT floppy controllers support the higher data rate required by the 1.2M or 1.44M high-capacity drives, so that no additional controller is needed. You still need a driver program to support the 3 1/2-inch drives if your system does not support these drives directly in the motherboard ROM. The best alternative is to upgrade the ROM to a later version that supports these drives directly. Upgrading eliminates the need for special driver programs.

The PC and XT versions can connect to two drives internally through the supplied cable and two drives externally through a cable you purchase. The AT controller supports two floppy drives and two hard disks. If you are adding any large capacity floppy drives to a PC or XT system, you need a new controller card and driver programs that operate with the card to support the high-density drives. MicroSolutions and Manzana offer these high-density controllers and software drivers.

Both of these companies offer complete kits for installing the 720K and 1.44M drives in any PC, XT, or AT system.

Adding Hard Disks to a System

When adding hard disks to a system, purchase the entire package from one company unless you are very familiar with disk drive interfacing. Because IBM has stuck with industry standard interfaces, you can take a "plug and play" approach to hard disk interfacing. Be sure to follow the information given in Chapter 9 on hard disks for the nuances of various installations. If you are going to install an ESDI or SCSI system, use a single supplier until you are familiar with the ins and outs of these installations. Differences between these and the more common ST-506/412 interface can complicate the installation process.

Speeding Up a System

In this section the various ways to speed up a system are examined. You see advertisements for ''turbo'' this and ''turbo'' that, referring to products that make your system run faster. One of the most common and simplest ways to increase the calculating performance of a system is to add a math coprocessor. These devices are explained in this section, and the relative performance gains are examined.

Another type of performance improvement involves the main processor, increasing the clock rate, changing the processor for another type, or both. The idea of replacing the processor for a faster one can be extended to replacing the entire motherboard. In fact, you are not really upgrading your system, but are entirely changing the system. That sort of extreme upgrade is not always recommended.

This section also examines the processor speed upgrades from a cost-benefit point of view.

Adding Math Coprocessors

Adding a math coprocessor is an easy way to upgrade the performance of a system with a minimum of effort. Be sure that the software you use supports these chips, because they only lighten your wallet unless they are specifically recognized and supported with software. Depending on how your motherboard is designed and what type of main processor you have, you should add an 8087, 80287, or 80387 chip.

These chips are available to withstand different speeds of operation. Be sure that the chip you purchase is designed to operate at the clock rate at which the system runs the math chip. Be careful with static discharges when handling these chips; they are delicate and quite expensive. A 25 MHz 80387 chip costs more than $1,000.

Using 1-2-3 Release 2.01, a sample spreadsheet consisting of 10,000 cells of floating point multiplication, division, addition, and subtraction, shows *no improvement in speed* in a system with the math coprocessor compared to a system without one. The overhead to have these math operations transferred to the coprocessor, executed and returned, is not worth the additional speed gained. Because of this overhead, Lotus software does not use the math coprocessor for simple mathematical operations. Instead, Lotus software calculates these instructions on the main processor. High-level math like exponentiation, trigonometry functions, and logarithms are executed on the math coprocessor for about a 10-fold increase in speed. As an upgrade, a math coprocessor is a *selective* speed improvement. A math coprocessor works with software specifically written to recognize the coprocessor and only in limited areas within that program. A spreadsheet does not increase speed in all operations throughout a system.

To install a math coprocessor, execute the following steps:

1. Turn off the system power.

2. Remove the system unit cover assembly.

3. Touch the power supply to ensure that you are at the same electrical potential as the system unit.

4. Remove all plug-in adapter cards necessary to adequately access the coprocessor socket.

5. Locate the coprocessor socket on the motherboard. In almost all systems the math coprocessor socket is next to the main processor.

6. Remove the math coprocessor from the protective holder, place the coprocessor on the socket, and align pin 1 on the processor with pin 1 in the socket. To align the pins, look for a notch in the chip and make sure that the notch faces the same direction as the notches on other chips.

7. Carefully press the chip straight down, taking care that all of the pins are seated in the socket. Be careful not to bend pins.

8. If you are using a PC or XT, locate the DIP switch block of the PC on the system board and flip switch position 2 to off. On the AT or PS/2, run the SETUP program so that the computer becomes aware of the addition of the coprocessor.

9. Reinstall all adapter boards that were removed.

10. Replace the system unit cover.

11. Verify the operation of the math coprocessor by using the Diagnostics or Advanced Diagnostics disk.

Speeding Up PC Types of Systems

This section examines increasing the calculating speed of a PC type of system, including the IBM PC, XT, and all PC or XT compatibles. You have several methods for increasing the calculating speed of a PC, including replacing the processor with a more efficient unit, increasing the clock rate, replacing the processor with a device called an In Circuit Emulator, and replacing the entire motherboard with an adapter board or a complete physical motherboard.

Replacing the Processor with NEC V20 or V30 Chips

One of the simplest ways to increase the performance of any 8088- or 8086-based system is to use the more efficient NEC-produced alternatives. These replacement processors are plugged into the system as direct physical replacements for the original processors. The NEC unit selected varies according to the original processor and must run at the clock rate at which the system runs the new processor. The processors are swapped as follows:

Original Processor	Replacement Processor
Intel 8088	NEC V20
Intel 8086	NEC V30

If the system is an IBM XT, the original processor is a 4.77 MHz 8088, and the replacement processor is an NEC V20 rated for at least 4.77 MHz. Usually, the available V20 chips are rated to run at 8 MHz. This speed is fine because the actual speed of 4.77 MHz is less than 8 MHz. The rating of the chip has nothing to do with the actual speed at which the chip runs; the speed is controlled by the motherboard clock circuitry.

To install this type of upgrade, gain access to the 8088 or 8086 processor on the motherboard, remove the processor, and plug the NEC device into its place. NEC chips are available for about $15 to $25 depending upon the chip, the speed rating, and the retailer.

Although this upgrade is inexpensive and easy to install, the actual speed increase is so small that it is difficult to see or feel. You need to test run applications and time various operations with a stopwatch to actually determine any time benefits to be had with the new chip. The normal increase in performance is about 5 to 10 percent of the former speed. If an operation originally takes 10 seconds to complete, the same operation takes 9 to 9.5 seconds with the new NEC chip. A 5 percent average increase is not bad, however, for only $15.

The other problem with this upgrade is that the NEC chips are not 100 percent compatible with Intel units. The IBM PS/2 Model 25 and 30 systems cannot use the NEC chips at all. Some programs do not work when the NEC chips are installed, namely the special disk-duplicating programs that back up copy-protected disks.

Many people (especially Intel) believe that these chips were illegally designed directly from the Intel originals. Several years ago when Intel could not meet the demand for 8088 and 8086 production, they licensed other manufacturers to make these chips. NEC was one of those manufacturers, and at that time was given the complete mask specifications for these chips. Now, with complete access to the *source code* of the Intel processors, NEC has come out with a new processor that seems to mimic the Intel units, except the NEC processor is more efficient in several instructions. Intel has sued NEC and attempted to restrain NEC from manufacturing and importing these devices. At the time of this writing, an injunction has not been placed on the NEC chips.

With the problems that may be caused due to incompatibilities, the small performance gain realized, and the legal cloud hanging over these chips, business users might want to steer clear of the NEC chips. If you are thinking of this upgrade for your personal system and are somewhat of a hacker, you might want to try this upgrade anyway because of the low cost.

Increasing the Clock Rate of the PC

Another type of improvement is to increase the processor's clock rate. This type of upgrade is more difficult to implement for PC or XT types of systems, because the clock crystal cannot be directly altered or replaced. The crystal is soldered in place in these systems instead of being socketed, and the crystal is multiplexed—used for more than just the system clock.

The crystal in an IBM XT, for example, is a 14.31818 MHz unit whose frequency is divided by three by the timer circuits to generate the 4.77 MHz system clock. This 14.31818 MHz crystal frequency also is on the system bus (slot) connectors at pin B30. (This signal is one of the PC bus specifications.) Many cards depend on this oscillator signal to be present for their operation, such as some video boards. This oscillator signal is divided by four to obtain a 3.58 MHz signal used to drive circuits in the Color Graphics Adapter. Any upgrade that attempts to increase the clock rate of the main processor, therefore, must not interfere with the original crystal and its subset function of generating a 14.31818 MHz oscillator signal for the system bus.

All the devices that increase clock rate contain a complete clock circuit and require that the main processor be mounted on the motherboard for the upgrade to work. These devices also have to interface with the 8284 timer chip on the motherboard, because they will be taking over the function of that chip.

To install one of these upgrades, complete the following process:

1. Remove the main processor from the system and plug the processor into what looks like a small circuit board.

   Some of the better units already have installed a new 8088-2 processor rated to run at 8 MHz. In that case, you can store your processor for safekeeping.

2. Plug the small board with the processor attached directly into the processor socket on the motherboard. (The plug is located on the bottom of the board.)

3. Remove the 8284 timer chip and plug a connector directly into the timer chip socket.

   Because the removed timer chip has a faster version already installed on the small speedup board, your original timer chip can be stored.

The device now runs the processor clock at a faster rate of speed, dependent upon jumper or switch settings on the small board. You usually have settings for 6 MHz, 7 MHz, and 8 MHz. You need to test your system to determine the fastest speed that it can run without crashing.

To test the system, set the unit to run at the slowest speed to see whether the system works and run diagnostics programs or applications software. Be careful about writing to a disk drive during the testing; a crash at that time can be disastrous. If you are not completely backed up when performing an upgrade of this type, you are courting a major disaster.

If your system runs at the slowest setting, increase the speed to the next setting and retest. Continue this method until your system runs erratically, crashes, or locks up or until you reach the maximum speed setting the unit allows. The limiting factor in what speed your particular system reaches is often the speed of the memory chips on the motherboard. If these chips are the 200-nanosecond types, you probably will not get very far without crashing. You might attempt replacing all of your memory with faster 120- or 100-nanosecond chips that may enable your system to reach the maximum setting allowed by the speedup unit without crashing. Replacing all of the memory in the system is an expensive proposition, however, and is not recommended.

Replacing the timer chip costs about $100 and is cost-effective at that price. Replacing all 36 memory chips in an XT motherboard with faster versions costs between $120 and $260 depending on how much memory is installed on the motherboard (256K or 640K). Although you can get a much greater increase in speed for this additional cost, the PC motherboard has the first bank of memory soldered in place. Because these chips are soldered in, this upgrade becomes labor intensive as well as expensive.

Another glitch in this upgrade is that the 8284 timer chip also must be socketed for removal and to accept the plug from the speedup unit. In many motherboards, this timer chip is soldered in place. Nearly all the PC and about half of the XT motherboards have this chip socketed. If the timer chip is soldered in place, it has to be removed, and a socket must be installed in the chip's place, making this upgrade undesirable from a labor and cost point of view.

The speed increase may be estimated by the clock rate increase that your system achieves. If the system can run at 7 MHz after the upgrade, you have achieved an increase of about 47 percent over stock. This upgrade generally nets you an increase over stock between 30 and 50 percent before the system starts to become unreliable.

This upgrade also has several advantages. One of the nicest features is that no expansion slot is required, which may be important in a PC system with all of the slots filled. Most of the timer devices also have a switch that enables the clock to return to the original 4.77

MHz for testing and diagnostics purposes and to run finicky programs incompatible with the timing changes. Most of the units can be switched while the system is running, causing the computer to reboot when the switch is made.

Increasing the clock rate is another upgrade for the hacker or experimental user, because of the difficulties involved in installing the upgrade in a PC system with soldered memory or any system with a soldered timer chip or processor. Despite the gains in speed, no slot usage, and the switchability, other upgrades are more cost-effective.

In Circuit Emulator (ICE) Boards for the PC

You also can upgrade your system with an In Circuit Emulator (ICE) board. This board emulates the microprocessor chip by directly plugging into the processor chip socket.

An ICE board is an adapter board that plugs into one of the system's expansion slots. The board also simultaneously plugs into the microprocessor socket and takes over the system as the new processor. The better boards of this type have an 80286 or 80386 processor running at a high clock rate and high speed 16- or 32-bit memory onboard directly wired to the included processor. Another feature of some of the better boards enables your processor to be installed on the ICE board. Your processor can be switched back into the circuit for compatibility and reliability testing.

To install an ICE board, execute the following steps:

1. Remove the main processor from the motherboard.

   In some of these units, you install this processor onto the speedup board, and other units require that you store the original processor for safekeeping.

2. Plug the speedup board into an open slot, preferably next to the processor socket.

3. Run a cable from the board to the processor socket and plug in the cable.

The installation is complete. These units have their own onboard memory, a full complement of 640K or a small amount of cache memory. This high-speed memory is directly accessible by the 80286 or 80386 processor on the speedup board. Your system memory is still used on some of these units.

Some of the units run in synchronization with the motherboard clock circuits, and others do not. The units that run in sync handle input and output operations, such as dealing with disk drive controllers and other expansion boards in the slots, much faster. These synchronous units have a better overall "feel" because the speed increase they give the system applies to virtually all areas except the disk transfer rate between the controller and disk drives, which remains the same in all speedup operations.

The asynchronous units are much slower because of their design, even though the clock rates of the integral processor may be equal to or faster than a synchronous unit. For example, 12 MHz asynchronous units speed up the system overall by the same amount as a 7.2 MHz synchronous unit. Don't be fooled by a raw clock rate figure; these figures are often misleading, especially when used by an advertising department.

The asynchronous units have a distinct advantage: compatibility with more systems on the market. The synchronous units only work in systems with an 8088 processor running at 4.77 MHz. You cannot install synchronous units in any other systems, such as those with the 8086 processor. This restriction rules out many of the "turbo" XT compatibles on the market, unless the turbo mode can be disabled and the system can run at 4.77 MHz.

The typical speed increase with these units is about 350 to 450 percent for the units based on the 80286 processor, and the 80386-based units offer a 800 to 900 percent speed increase. The prices vary, but you should expect to pay $250 to $350 for the 80286 units, and $800 to $1,000 for the 80386-based units. For the increase in speed offered and the greater compatibility afforded by these units combined with the ability to switch the system back to the original speed for testing and compatibility purposes, ICE boards offer the greatest value in the speedup department. They give you the performance of an AT system (or far beyond) in your PC or XT system. Table 12.2 lists recommended boards and their speed increases.

Most of these boards do not convert your PC or XT into an AT with the capability to address 16M of memory and run OS/2 or perform other AT capabilities. These boards only give your system the *speed* of an AT type of system.

Table 12.2
Recommended ICE Boards

Type and Name of Board	Speed Increase
Asynchronous 80286 boards:	
Microway Fastcache 286-12	+350%
Synchronous 80286 boards:	
Orchid TinyTurbo 286	+350%
Orchid TwinTurbo 12	+450%
Synchronous 80386 boards:	
Intel Inboard 386/PC	+800%
Quadram Quad 386XT	+900%

Upgrading with Mothercards

The next level of upgrading is often hard to distinguish from the ICE boards. The real difference between ICE boards and *mothercards* is that mothercards do not emulate the microprocessor, nor do they plug into the processor socket. These boards are stand-alone computer systems that use your system as a host.

Mothercards are complete motherboards on a single card. This type of upgrade is the easiest to install of all of those considered. You just plug the mothercard into a slot. You do not remove or install any chips or plug in any connectors. The new board takes over your system when you run a special activation program. Your system acts as a host to the new board that uses your motherboard as an I/O processor and support device. Some of these mothercards have a complete ROM BIOS onboard, and others copy your system ROM BIOS into the mothercard memory for faster operation. The mothercards have a full complement of at least 640K of memory. The additional memory can be used by the card for special purposes, like caching the ROM or as expanded or extended memory.

These cards can give your system access to the 80286 or 80386 protected mode and may be capable of running a version of OS/2 developed especially for the card. Although this card may be the equivalent of an AT motherboard, you still do not have a *real* AT and may have many other things to change, like disk controllers, floppy disk drives, serial ports, and so on.

These systems usually offer the same levels of performance as the ICE boards and offer the ability to switch the card and software on and off. This switching capability enables you to test properly for compatibility problems if you suspect a problem in that area.

Mothercards take your system as far as you can go without replacing the entire motherboard, which may be intimidating and expensive. Mothercards are generally more expensive than ICE boards but also are easier to install.

Some of the recommended boards are the Sota Technology Mothercard 5.0 for 80286-based systems and the Applied Reasoning Corp. PC Elevator 386 for 80386-based systems.

Mothercards offer a high level of functionality and easy installation, and may have special versions of OS/2. These boards can take you far along the path of converting a PC system to an AT system. The only drawback to mothercards is the cost of around $1,000 for the 80286-based boards and $2,000 for the 80386-based boards.

Replacing the PC Motherboard

Another possible method for speeding up a system is to remove the original motherboard and replace it with another. Complete motherboard replacements consist of an AT type of motherboard in an 80286-based or 80386-based design. These replacements usually have 16-bit slots and the required AT architecture such as interrupts and DMA channels.

Installation of these boards is fairly difficult because the entire system must be disassembled down to the motherboard.

Problems with these boards occur in the reinstallation of the rest of your old system. Are you really going to use that XT hard disk controller in what is now an AT system? If so, you may encounter some of the following problems:

- You have to tell the SETUP program that no hard disks are installed so that your XT controller's built-in ROM BIOS can operate the card properly.

- The XT controller uses Interrupt 5, which conflicts with a second parallel port (LPT2:) in the AT.

- Your XT floppy controller does not support the high-density drives required to boot OS/2.

- For proper AT and OS/2 operation, you must change all of your serial ports.

- The memory you have in the XT system does not work properly in an AT.

These are only some of the problems you encounter with a "hybrid" system that is part AT and part XT.

The motherboard concept has several distinct disadvantages over the mothercard discussed earlier. One disadvantage is that the installation of a motherboard is more difficult than adding a plug-in card. You also are losing your original system completely, and if a compatibility problem is encountered, no "switch" can restore your original system to operation like in the mothercard design. Motherboards cost between $600 and $2,500 with 80286 or 80386 designs.

Replacing motherboards can convert a PC type of system into an AT design, but you must replace many other items to complete the process. By the time this conversion is complete and paid for, you could have bought an AT compatible system and left your poor PC or XT alone. You also can sell the PC type of system to create additional funds for options for the new AT. Remember that any investment in hard disk or floppy drives can be moved over to the new AT compatible system.

Because of the cost and complexity, this type of upgrade is recommended only in extreme cases where money is no object.

Speeding Up AT Types of Systems

The market for AT speedup devices is much simpler than the market for PC systems. Less alternatives are available, and those available are less complex.

For example, no drop-in processor replacements work like the NEC V20 and V30 chips do for the 8088 and 8086 processors. No replacements exist for the 80286 and 80386 systems to offer speed increases. Many thought that the new 80386SX chip (code named P9) was going to be a drop-in replacement for the 80286 that offered 80386 capabilities, but the SX chip is not pin- or plug-compatible with the 80286 and must have a motherboard designed around it. Some speedup boards for 80286-based AT systems may use this chip, but none were available at the time of this writing.

The most desirable and least expensive upgrade for the AT is to increase the clock rate. Another system speedup is installing the processor replacement In Circuit Emulator (ICE) boards available for the AT. These boards use an 80386 board to replace the 80286 processor in an AT system. The final alternative is to replace the entire motherboard with an 80386-based unit. For the AT, this upgrade does not have the same problems as the similar upgrade does for a PC system.

Each of these upgrades is explored in the next section.

Increasing the Clock Rate of the AT

IBM's decision to socket the clock crystal in the PC AT was greeted with much interest and speculation. The ability to easily remove the crystal is the key factor in speeding up the AT. The crystal is not multiplexed as in PC or XT systems. The oscillator signal required for pin B30 in the expansion bus connectors is independently generated by a 14.31818 MHz crystal also found on the motherboard. This oscillator crystal is under a large square piece of metal shielding to keep radio interference to a minimum. You are free, therefore, to replace the processor clock crystal with a faster one without interfering with the rest of the system. This upgrade can be inexpensive for an AT because no complex clock circuitry must be added to the system.

The main system clock crystal is contained in a 1/2-by-3/8-inch silver housing that plugs into the socket near the 80286 chip, behind the center opening for the hard disk. The crystal can be removed by inserting a small screwdriver between the crystal and socket, pushing the crystal out of the socket, and lifting it up and out of the retaining clip. A faster crystal can be inserted to increase the operating speed of the 80286 CPU chip driven at half the crystal's speed.

With the original AT Models 068 and 099, a trip to the local Radio Shack turns up a 16 MHz crystal for about 99 cents. This crystal can be plugged into the system in place of the original 12 MHz crystal. The system then can be powered up to run at 8 MHz. The total cost of this 30 percent improvement in processing speed is a whopping 99 cents. If the 16 MHz crystal works and your system runs fine at 8 MHz, why stop there? Go back to the store, pick up a 18 MHz crystal, and see whether your system runs at 9 MHz speed. If that works (it usually does), get a 20 MHz crystal and see whether your system runs at 10 MHz. Some systems take this speed, although the great majority do not. If yours did not, replace the last crystal that worked.

If you desire more speed than what your system allows, you can attempt to increase the maximum running speed by replacing the memory or processors. The memory can be replaced with faster access time chips. The standard speed chip in most AT systems is 150 nanoseconds. If you replace all of the memory with 120 or 100 nanosecond chips, you may be able to go that extra step to 10 MHz or more.

You also should replace the processor with one rated to run at the new speed. For example, replace the 80286-6 with an 80286-10 or 80286-12 if you want to use a crystal of greater frequency than your 80286-6 chip allows. Don't forget that the math coprocessor, if you have one, also may need to be replaced with a faster chip.

Memory chips and 80286 and 80287 chips are expensive. Replacing 512K of memory on a normal AT motherboard might cost $200, and the processor and math coprocessor run more than $150 each. With this cost, most people choose to replace only the crystal and see how far they get.

This simple crystal swap only works in the original AT models with 01/10/84 ROM BIOS. You cannot change the crystal speed of systems with 06/10/85 or 11/15/85 ROM BIOS dates, or the POST fails the motherboard test and issues the audio codes for motherboard failure—one long and one short beep. Fortunately, this failure is only temporary. When you reinstall the original crystal, the system works fine. This failed POST is the result of changes to the POST that IBM included in the latter ROM's. Some people say IBM made these changes to thwart this type of inexpensive speedup. IBM can't be blamed for trying, but where there is a will; there is a way. Several speedup devices can escape detection by POST routines.

The best way around the POST is to use a crystal replacement unit containing a timer and a Variable Frequency Oscillator (VFO). This unit can vary the output frequency continuously and does not have to live within the rigid step boundaries imposed by the fixed frequency crystals. This crystal replacement is a universally applicable way to increase the speed of any AT. Several companies make units that allow variable speed increases to the limits of what your system takes. These VFO units get around the POST speed check problem in a novel way; they use a timer circuit to delay the speedup action until the POST is completed. To the diagnostics, the system checks out OK, but you can still enjoy the speed increase.

The only problem with this speedup method is the cost. These units cost about $100, which is much more than 99 cents, but still a bargain for the speed increase achieved.

These units can be switched back to standard speed if you experience incompatibilities or problems. Some people like to slow down the system for games or recreational programs that run too fast. Because of the low cost, easy installation, and switchability, these units are recommended highly for an AT speed increase, especially the XCELX by Ariel.

The XCELX consists of a VFO with a rear-mounted potentiometer that acts as a throttle for your AT. This unit has the requisite timer circuits that fool the POST in the newer systems, allowing the motherboard to pass the diagnostics. A bonus is that the XCELX includes a reset switch wired to the Power Good line.

Installing In Circuit Emulator Boards for the AT

In Circuit Emulator (ICE) boards for ATs are not as diverse or complicated as those for PC types of systems. These boards follow a synchronous design and use 80386 chips as a base.

Install these boards like you did for PC types of systems. Place the ICE boards in a normal expansion slot, remove the 80286 processor, and replace the processor with a cable and plug from the ICE board. These boards have memory that can be accessed as 32-bit memory and is much faster than memory on the motherboard. In general, these boards are more expensive than boards for PC systems because they use 80386-based designs and come with 1M or more of memory.

Several of these ICE boards are on the market, but the one I recommend is the Intel Inboard 386. This board costs about $1,500 to $1,800 depending on whether memory is included. The Intel Inboard 386 does not affect the AT's capability to run OS/2, the board just runs the program faster than before. The speedup achieved with this type of board is typically double the original speed.

Replacing the AT Motherboard

You have many choices of motherboard replacements for AT systems, and like the ICE boards, these replacements use 80386-

based designs. These systems do not share the problems of upgrading an XT to this level, because you already have an AT type of system and the new board is an AT design. You do not have to change any expansion boards, including the hard disk controller, memory, serial ports, floppy controller, or floppy drives because they are already AT devices.

The only differences between these motherboards and the boards available for PC systems are the location of the mounting screw holes and the physical dimensions of the board. The AT chassis is much bigger than the PC, so these boards can be larger.

Adding Video Adapter Boards

Adding a high-resolution video display adapter and monitor is a great way to put some life into an early system. This type of upgrade, however, can be expensive. High resolution color graphic displays usually cost between $500 and $1,000. The adapters can cost from $200 to $500. Most upgrades of this nature are video adapter and display compatible with the IBM PS/2 VGA display system. This upgrade ensures software compatibility with the majority of programs. The earlier display adapters, including the Enhanced Graphics Adapter (EGA), are becoming obsolete and are not recommended for new system purchases, unless cost is the most important factor.

You can set up a monochrome VGA system for about $500, including an adapter and monitor, and upgrade to a full-color display when money becomes available. The VGA senses the type of display (mono or color) and adjusts the display to a mode in which 64 shades of gray are used instead of color. This adjustment is done with no changes in software configuration.

For example, I upgraded one of my systems to a VGA adapter and color display. I took 91M of software from a system with a Color Graphics Adapter and placed the software in this new system. I was able to run *every program* without reconfiguring any of them. None of the graphics programs could take full advantage of the VGA's higher resolution or additional colors, but the no-hassle upgrade was important. Now, I can take my time and upgrade or add new software that fully uses the VGA. I also can rest assured that no matter what system the program was written for, MDA, CGA, or

EGA, this new VGA system will handle the program without reconfiguration. The final bonus is that the same VGA software that runs on a system with a color display also runs on a system with a monochrome display without reconfiguration. If a monochrome display is sensed at boot time, the VGA adapter invokes a color-summing routine that converts all colors to 64 shades of gray.

Adding a Reset Switch

A switch that applies a full reset to your system keeps power going to the system and gets you out of a lock-up situation. A reset switch saves a lot of time and some of the wear and tear that your unit receives when you use the power switch as a reset button. Because IBM and most compatible vendors have built full reset circuitry into the motherboard, the hardest part of adding a reset switch to your system is figuring out where to mount the switch.

Adding a reset button is possible on any system with a power supply that provides a Power Good signal, including every IBM system.

On IBM computers, the Power Good signal is on the connector that plugs into the rear-most of the two power supply connectors. In PC and XT systems, this signal traces through the motherboard to the 8284a chip at pin 11. When this line is shorted to ground and returned to normal, the 8284a (82284 in an AT) generates a reset signal on pin 10. The reset signal is sent to the 8088 at pin 21, and the boot process begins. In other systems with different processors and timer chips, like AT or PS/2 systems, the Power Good signal also initiates a reset if the system is grounded and returns to normal.

In all systems, the CPU is reset, causing the CPU to execute code at memory location F000:FFF0, the power up reset vector. An immediate jump instruction at this location sends the CPU to the start location for the system ROM. The system begins the POST. The processor and DMA chips are tested, but before initiating a full bore system test, including all memory, the location 00472 is compared to the value 1234h. If they are equal, a *warm* start is indicated and the memory tests are skipped. If another value is there, a *cold* start causes all memory to be tested.

To add a reset switch, you need the following parts:

- 6 inches of thin gauge insulated wire

- 1 single pole, normally open momentary contact push-button switch

The idea behind installing a reset switch is to run a momentary contact switch parallel with the Power Good line and ground. To accomplish this, follow these steps:

1. Remove the power supply connector containing the Power Good signal from the motherboard.

   Look in your technical reference manual to make sure that you have the right connector and can identify the signal wire containing the Power Good signal. Sometimes this information also is found on a sticker attached to the power supply.

2. Poke the stripped end of a wire into the hole in the power supply connector in which the Power Good signal is carried.

3. Plug the connector back onto the motherboard with the wire inserted.

4. Run the other end of the wire under one of the screws that secures the motherboard. The screw serves as a ground.

5. Cut the wire in the middle, bare the ends, and attach the stripped wire ends to the normally open, single pole, momentary contact push-button switch.

6. Run the wire and the switch outside the case.

You now have a functioning reset button. You may want to mount the switch to an available place in the unit, such as an empty card bracket, in which you can drill a small hole to accept the switch.

Although a simple button and wire does the trick, you may want to place a 1/4-watt resistor with a value between 1K and 2.7K in-line with the wire from the Power Good line to the switch. When the switch is pressed, the boot sequence is initiated.

The actual boot process that occurs depends upon the status of memory location 00472. This location is 0000h when the system is first powered up and until a Ctrl-Alt-Del sequence is initiated. If the last boot operation was a cold boot due to an initial power on, every subsequent use of the reset button causes a cold boot to be performed. After a manual warm boot sequence, Ctrl-Alt-Del, is performed, every subsequent use of the reset button initiates a warm boot that skips the memory tests and saves time. To eliminate the need for a Ctrl-Alt-Del sequence, you can enter a program using DEBUG that produces WARMSET.COM to run in your AUTOEXEC.BAT file. This simple program quickly sets memory flags to indicate that a warm boot should be initiated when the switch is pressed.

The program listing for WARMSET.COM is as follows:

```
C:\UTIL›debug
-n warmset.com
-a 100
XXXX:0100 MOV     AX,0040
XXXX:0103 MOV     DS,AX
XXXX:0105 MOV     WORD PTR [0072],1234
XXXX:010B INT     20
XXXX:010D
-rbx
BX 0000
:0
-rcx
CX 0000
:D
-w
Writing 000D bytes
-q
```

Unlike the Ctrl-Alt-Del combination, the hardware reset cannot be ignored by your system no matter how locked up the system may be.

Upgrading to a New DOS Version

One upgrade overlooked by many users is an upgrade to a new version of the operating system. A DOS upgrade can be complicated by the use of different OEM versions of DOS, but normally you should not have to reformat your hard disk when upgrading from one version of IBM DOS to another. If you are using non-standard drivers or other non-DOS support programs, you may have to format the disk or use DEBUG or another low-level utility to modify the disk's boot sector and root directory. This modification enables the SYS command of the new version to operate properly. The following explanation of the procedure for moving a hard disk-equipped system from one version of DOS to a higher one, assumes that the source version of DOS is 2.0 or higher and the destination version is 3.21 or higher.

The easy way to perform this upgrade is done without reformatting the hard disk. The easy method can be accomplished in less than five minutes. The harder method involves a complete backup and restore operation of all data and program files on the disk. Depending upon what media and systems you have in place for backup, this operation takes at least an hour.

To perform a DOS version upgrade the easy way, use the following procedure:

1. Boot the new DOS version from drive A.

2. Transfer the system files to C: with this command:

   SYS C:

3. Place each disk in drive A and type *DIR REPLACE.EXE*. When you find the disk containing REPLACE.EXE, type *COPY REPLACE.EXE C:* and press Enter.

   The REPLACE.EXE program must be in an accessible place. REPLACE.EXE can be found on one of the following disks:

   IBM DOS 3.2 System Disk
   COMPAQ DOS 3.2 System Disk
   IBM DOS 3.3 Startup Disk
   COMPAQ 3.31 Operating Disk

4. Use the following command to replace all transient files on C: with new versions:

   C:\REPLACE A:*.* C: /S /R

5. Change the disk in drive A to the second DOS floppy disk and repeat the preceding step until all DOS floppy disks have been inserted.

6. Place the boot disk back in drive A.

7. Add any new transient files to the C:\DOS directory with this command:

   C:\REPLACE A:*.* C:\DOS /A

8. Replace the boot disk with the second DOS floppy disk and repeat the preceding step until all DOS floppy disks are inserted.

When you are done, the system boots from the hard disk. This method ensures that all previous DOS files are overwritten with new versions.

If you use a directory other than C:\DOS to store your DOS program files, replace *C:\DOS* in the preceding steps with that directory. If you have any problems with the SYS command, your installation probably has an abnormality. This abnormality can be caused by mixing different OEM versions of DOS or by using non-standard driver files to address limitations in DOS's partitioning capabilities. If you have problems, proceed with this upgrade by using the harder method.

You have to use the harder method if you want to take advantage of the newer DOS's disk-formatting capabilities. You can take any system and upgrade the hard disk to boot IBM DOS 4.01, but if you do not use DOS 4.01 to partition and format the disk, you cannot take advantage of the more than 32M volume sizes that DOS 4.01 is capable of.

To perform a DOS version upgrade by using the harder method, follow these steps:

1. Boot the system from the earlier version of DOS.

2. Execute a complete backup using the method of your choice.

3. Use the earlier DOS FDISK to remove the DOS partition(s).

4. Boot the new version of DOS.

5. Use the new DOS FDISK to create partitions.

6. Perform a high-level format and install the new DOS system files with this command:

   FORMAT C: /S

7. Restore the previous backup, but do not restore the system files (IBMBIO.COM and IBMDOS.COM).

8. Place each disk in drive A and type *DIR REPLACE.EXE*. When you find the disk containing REPLACE.EXE, type *COPY REPLACE.EXE C:* and press Enter.

9. Use the following command to replace all transient files on C: with new versions:

    REPLACE A:*.* C: /S /R

10. Place the second DOS floppy disk in drive A and repeat the preceding step until all DOS floppy disks are inserted.

11. Place the boot disk back in drive A.

12. Add any new transient files to the C:\DOS directory with this command:

    REPLACE A:*.* C:\DOS /A

13. Replace the boot disk with the second DOS floppy disk and repeat the preceding step until all DOS floppy disks are inserted.

When you are done, the system boots from the hard disk. If you use a directory other than C:\DOS to store program files, replace *C:\DOS* with that directory. This method ensures that all previous DOS files are overwritten with new versions.

Backup procedures make this method difficult, unless you have a proper tape backup system. You have to figure out how to prevent your backup system from restoring the system files.

If you are using the DOS 3.3 or higher BACKUP and RESTORE commands, preventing the overwriting of the system files has been greatly simplified. Because RESTORE can never restore the files IBMBIO.COM, IBMDOS.COM, and COMMAND.COM, the chances of overwriting them are eliminated.

The new version of DOS needs to use the FDISK for the newer partitioning capabilities to become available. The earlier version's FDISK also must be used to remove the partitions that it created, or you can redo the low-level format of the disk, wiping everything clean. An advantage to using the FDISK is that other non-DOS partitions survive. The low-level format, however, re-marks the sectors and tracks, which may be desirable if the hard disk is a stepper-motor-actuated type.

Chapter Summary

This chapter examines many types of system upgrades, including memory expansion, disk system expansion, speeding up a system, improving the video subsystem, adding a reset switch, and upgrading to a new DOS version. This chapter should give you some insight and useful recommendations so that you can avoid the pitfalls that have caused others to stumble. Upgrading a system can be a cost-effective way to keep up with the rest of the computing community and to extend the life of your system. By upgrading, however, you also can create a ''Frankenstein'' system with compatibility problems before realizing just how much money you have poured into the system. You have to learn when to say NO to more upgrades for a particular system and to recognize when it is time for a new system.

13

System Diagnostics

This chapter describes the three different levels of diagnostic software (POST, system, and advanced) and discusses how you can get the most out of them. IBM's audio codes, error codes, and their descriptions are listed also. This chapter also examines aftermarket diagnostics and public domain diagnostic software.

Diagnostic Software

The IBM PC, XT, AT, PS/2, and compatible computers have several types of diagnostic software procedures available to assist a user in identifying many of the problems that may occur with the computer's components. These programs can do most of the work in determining which PC component is defective. Three programs are available that can help you locate a problem; each program is more complex and powerful than the preceding one. These diagnostic programs include the following:

- A POST (power-on self test) that operates whenever a PC is powered up or turned on

- General diagnostics testing software that uses the diagnostics disk and accompanying problem determination procedures outlined in the guide to operations manual for each system

- Optional advanced diagnostics testing software and procedures that use the advanced diagnostics disk and procedures provided in the hardware maintenance service manual. The advanced diagnostics disk is provided free with the PS/2 systems.

Operators often use the first and last of these software systems to test and troubleshoot most systems.

The IBM advanced diagnostics disk is included with the hardware maintenance service manual, and it—along with the accompanying hardware maintenance reference and assorted updates to both manuals—costs more than $400. Although this price may seem expensive, any service technician uses the same manuals in diagnosing and repairing a system. Anyone supporting more than just a single PC system will quickly recoup the expense in saved labor costs and avoidance of the trouble of carry-in service.

Although the IBM service manuals are expensive, they are complete and represent the definitive word on the subject. Unlike many companies, IBM provides in-depth system documentation. Indeed, this documentation is one of the primary reasons for the success of the IBM systems in becoming an industry standard.

Power-On Self Test (POST)

When IBM first began shipping the IBM PC in 1981, it included "safety" features that had never been seen before in a personal computer. These features were the POST and parity-checked memory. The parity-checking feature is explained in Chapter 7. This section explains the POST. The POST is a series of program routines, buried in the motherboard ROM firmware, that tests all the main system components at power-on time. This program series is the cause for the delay after you turn on an IBM-compatible system; the program is executed before the system loads the operating system.

What Is Tested?

Whenever you start up your computer, the computer automatically performs a series of tests that check various components in your system. The components tested by this procedure are the primary ones. Items such as the CPU, ROM, motherboard support circuitry, memory, and major peripherals (such as the expansion chassis) are tested. These tests are brief and not very thorough compared with the other disk-based diagnostics that are available. This POST process provides error or warning messages whenever a faulty component is encountered. Two types of messages are provided: audio codes and display screen messages or codes.

Error Codes

POST error codes usually are audio codes consisting of variations of beeps that identify the faulty component. If your computer is functioning normally, you hear one short beep when the system is started up. If a problem is detected, a different series of audio codes is sounded. These audio codes and corresponding problem areas are listed in table 13.1.

Table 13.1
Audio Codes and Their Fault Domains

Audio Code	Probable Fault Domain
No beep	Power supply
Continuous beep	Power supply
Repeating short beeps	Power supply
1 long and 1 short beep	Motherboard
1 long and 2 short beeps	Video adapter card
1 short beep and bad/no display	Video cable and/or display
1 short beep and no boot	Disk cable, adapter, or drive

On the XT, AT, PS/2, and most compatibles, the POST also displays system memory as it is tested. The last number displayed (640KB OK, for example) is the amount of memory that tested properly. This number should agree with the total amount of memory actually installed in your system, including conventional and extended memory. Expanded memory is not tested by the POST and does not count in the numbers reported.

If an error is detected during the POST procedures, an error message is displayed. These messages usually are in the form of a numeric code several digits long. The information found in the hardware maintenance service manual identifies the malfunctioning component. This chapter includes an abbreviated list of the error codes, and an extended list is in the Appendix of this book.

System Diagnostics Disk

Every IBM computer comes with a Guide To Operations (GTO) manual; this manual is in the reddish purple binder. The GTO includes a diagnostics disk to assist you in identifying problems that your computer may be having. PS/2 computers now come with a much smaller quick-reference guide that includes a reference disk. This disk contains both the regular and advanced diagnostics, as well as the normal SETUP program.

The diagnostics disk and corresponding manual provide step-by-step instructions for you to test the various parts of your computer system, including the system unit and many installed options, such as the expansion unit, keyboard, display, and printer. Unfortunately, these diagnostics are at "customer level" and are lacking in many respects. The tests cannot be run individually; you always must run them all together, and many of the better tests have been deleted. These diagnostics really are a crippled version of the much more powerful advanced diagnostics that IBM sells. Many compatible system vendors do not segregate the diagnostics software like IBM does; many include an advanced type of diagnostics disk free with the system. AST, for example, includes its diagnostics program, called ASTute, free with every system. This program is similar to the IBM advanced diagnostics.

You must boot from the diagnostics disk to run this program because a special version of DOS resides on the diagnostics disk. This DOS suppresses the system parity checking during the boot process. Parity checking may allow a defective system to "limp" through the diagnostics, whereas normally the system would be constantly locking up with the parity-check message. After the disk is loaded, the main diagnostics menu is displayed. The opening menu looks something like this:

The IBM Personal Computer
DIAGNOSTICS
Version 2.06
(C)Copyright IBM Corp. 1981,1986

SELECT AN OPTION

0 - SYSTEM CHECKOUT
1 - FORMAT DISKETTE
2 - COPY DISKETTE

3 - PREPARE SYSTEM FOR MOVING
4 - SETUP
9 - END DIAGNOSTICS

SELECT THE ACTION DESIRED
?

Options 0, 1, and 2 are part of the diagnostics procedures. Option 3 is used to "park" or secure the heads on a hard disk so that the system unit can be moved safely without damaging the disk or its contents. Option 4 is seen only on the AT version of the diagnostics and is used with the AT to identify installed options when you first set up your system.

Option 1 is used to format a disk. This format is different from a normal DOS format, however, and this routine should not be used for formatting disks for use normally under DOS. This option really is designed to create a special "scratch disk" that is used by the diagnostics for testing purposes. Among other things, differences exists in the construction of the boot sector of this disk and a normal DOS disk.

Option 2 is used to copy a disk. This routine is exactly like the DISKCOPY command in normal DOS. Option 2 creates a mirror-image copy of a disk, exactly the same in every way. This routine really was designed to copy the diagnostics disk, because the original disk should not be used for testing purposes, and the entire disk was designed to be a stand alone usable system, without the presence of DOS. You normally use this option to make backups of your master diagnostics disk so that you can use the copies for actual testing purposes. The diagnostics disks can be copied by any other means as well because they are not copy protected. IBM never has protected any of the regular or advanced diagnostics, which allows you to make proper backups and keep the master disks safe.

For general testing, you select Option 0. When this option is selected, the diagnostics software loads various modules from the disk, which perform a "presence test" to see whether the device to which the module corresponds is in the system. A list of installed devices is presented, and you are asked whether the list is correct.

For several reasons, this list does not match the system configuration exactly. The only items that are listed are those that have modules on the disk. If you purchase a new type of expansion item, such as a VGA graphics card, the diagnostics may still identify this board as an EGA board instead. No modules are available for any of the expanded memory boards, so those never appear on the list. Nonstandard communications boards other than serial or parallel ports never are seen, either.

If, for example, you have an IBM Token Ring network adapter in your system, it is never incorporated on the list of installed devices because the diagnostics (or advanced diagnostics) disks do not incorporate the modules for these adapters. IBM has a separate diagnostics program on its own disk for this adapter. Most standard devices should show up on the list, even if the particular device has not been made by IBM. Your hard disk controller should show up, for example, as should your video board (although it may identify the type of video card incorrectly), serial and parallel ports, conventional and extended memory (not expanded), the floppy drives, and the motherboard.

If a device is installed that *should* show up but doesn't, the device is configured incorrectly or has a serious problem. Signify that the list is incorrect by answering no when asked whether the installed device list is correct. Then add the item to the list. If an item appears that you do not actually have installed, use the same procedure to remove the item from the list. This list represents all the tests that can be run. The only way you can test an item is to have it appear on this list.

After going through the installed devices list, you see another menu, which is similar to the following:

```
0 - RUN TESTS ONE TIME
1 - RUN TESTS MULTIPLE TIMES
2 - LOG UTILITIES
3 - END SYSTEM CHECKOUT
```

Option 0 normally is selected to test any one or all of the items in the system. Option 1 allows for any of these items (or all of them) to be tested repetitively as many times as you would like, or "forever." The forever option is handy because it enables you to run the diagnostics for an item continuously overnight or over a weekend to find particularly troublesome problems. This method can be an easy way to flesh out an intermittent problem. To record any errors that occur without your presence, you first select Option 2, which can be used to set up an error log. This log records the date, time, and actual error message to a floppy disk or a printer so that you can review them at a later time.

If an error does occur while these tests are running, a numerical error message appears along with the date and time. These numbers are listed in this chapter and in the Appendix. They follow the same conventions as the numbers displayed by the POST and are the same numbers in some cases. The diagnostic tests usually are much more powerful than the tests run in the POST.

Although the diagnostics do an excellent job of identifying specific problem areas or problem components, they provide limited assistance in telling you how to correct the source of the errors. Little documentation is provided with these diagnostics, and in fact, the information most often provided is, "Have your system unit [or problem device] serviced." These diagnostics are a crippled version of the real diagnostics, which are part of the hardware maintenance service manual. The advanced diagnostics are what you should be using, and the diagnostics to which the remainder of this book refers.

Advanced Diagnostics

For "technician level" diagnostics, IBM sells the hardware maintenance service manuals, which include the advanced diagnostics disks. These disks contain the "real" diagnostics programs and, combined with the hardware maintenance service manuals, represent the de facto standard diagnostics information and software for IBM and compatible systems. These programs produce error messages in the form of numbers. The number codes used are exactly the same as those used in the POST and general diagnostics software. The numbers are consistent in meaning across all diagnostic programs. This section will explore the advanced diagnostics and list most of the known error code meanings. IBM constantly adds to this error code list as it introduces new equipment.

Using Advanced Diagnostics

If you really want to service the system in-depth, you can purchase the IBM Hardware Maintenance Service manual (about $195). This one book covers all the earlier systems, including the PC, XT, and AT. Updates cover the XT-286 and PS/2 Models 25 and 30. The "real" PS/2 systems have their own separate version of this book called the PS/2 Hardware Maintenance and Service. This book costs $175 and includes spare copies of the standard reference disks.

You might be surprised at the inclusion of these disks, especially when you read in the book that you have had the advanced diagnostics for the PS/2 systems all along. The book says that in order to activate the hidden advanced diagnostics, you need to know the secret back door. When at the reference disk main menu, simply press Ctrl-A for Advanced, and the menu flips, leaving you in the world of advanced diagnostics.

Hiding access to advanced diagnostics from the average user is probably a good idea. An inexperienced person could do a lot of damage by low-level formatting of the hard disk, for instance. The rest of the contents of the PS/2 book are skimpy, because not too many parts are in a PS/2 system and they are easy to repair. This book often seems to end a troubleshooting session with this advice: "Replace the system board." If all you are looking for is the advanced diagnostics software, you have just saved $175.

Although the guide to operations manual is good only for identifying a problem component, the hardware maintenance service manual provides information for you to isolate and repair any failure of an FRU—any part or component with interchangeable replacement parts that are stocked by IBM or the Original Equipment Manufacturer (OEM).

The hardware maintenance service includes an advanced diagnostics disk and accompanying Maintenance Analysis Procedures (MAPs), which are instructions for you to isolate and identify problem components. To run the advanced diagnostic tests, follow the same procedures detailed in the section for general diagnostics testing.

After booting the advanced diagnostics disk for your particular system (PC or AT), you see a menu similar to the following:

The IBM Personal Computer
ADVANCED DIAGNOSTICS
Version 2.07
(C)Copyright IBM Corp. 1981,1986

ROS P/N: 78X7462
ROS DATE: 04/21/86

SELECT AN OPTION

0 - SYSTEM CHECKOUT
1 - FORMAT DISKETTE
2 - COPY DISKETTE
3 - PREPARE SYSTEM FOR MOVING
4 - SETUP
9 - END DIAGNOSTICS

SELECT THE ACTION DESIRED
?

Note again that the fourth option only appears on the AT type of diagnostics. If you are using the PC version, this item does not apply and does not appear.

The advanced diagnostics disks show the date of the ROM, as well as the IBM part number for the particular chips that are in your system. The screen shows this near the top as ROS (Read-Only Software). The 04/21/86 identifies the version of the ROM in this example. If you look up this date in the table in Chapter 7, which shows ROM identification information for IBM's systems, you see that this date indicates an IBM XT Model 286. The part number, which is read directly out of the ROM, is academic information, because IBM does not sell the ROM chips separately, but only with a complete motherboard swap.

After you select Option 0, which invokes the diagnostic routines, each module on the disk loads and executes a presence test to determine whether the applicable piece of hardware is truly in the system. In this example, the result looks like the following:

THE INSTALLED DEVICES ARE

1 - SYSTEM BOARD
2 - 2688KB MEMORY
3 - KEYBOARD
6 - 2 DISKETTE DRIVE(S) AND ADAPTER
7 - MATH COPROCESSOR
9 - SERIAL/PARALLEL ADAPTER
    - PARALLEL PORT
11 - SERIAL/PARALLEL ADAPTER
    - SERIAL PORT
17 - 1 FIXED DISK DRIVE(S) AND ADAPTER
74 - PERSONAL SYSTEM/2 DISPLAY ADAPTER

IS THE LIST CORRECT (Y/N)
?

You then answer yes or no depending on the accuracy of the list. Remember that not everything appears on this list. An IBM Token Ring network adapter does not appear, for example, and never will appear on this list because no software module designed for that particular option is present on the disk. The following list contains all the items that *could* appear on the list (as of Version 2.07 of these diagnostics). This list is different for other versions:

```
 1 SYSTEM BOARD
 2 MEMORY
 3 KEYBOARD
 4 MONOCHROME & PRINTER ADAPTER
 5 COLOR/GRAPHICS MONITOR ADAPTER
 6 DISKETTE DRIVE(S)
 7 MATH COPROCESSOR
 9 SERIAL/PARALLEL ADAPTER - PARALLEL PORT
10 ALTERNATE SERIAL/PARALLEL ADAPTER - PARALLEL PORT
11 SERIAL/PARALLEL ADAPTER - SERIAL PORT
12 ALTERNATE SERIAL/PARALLEL ADAPTER - SERIAL PORT
13 GAME CONTROL ADAPTER
14 MATRIX PRINTER
15 SDLC COMMUNICATIONS ADAPTER
17 FIXED DISK DRIVE(S) AND ADAPTER
20 BSC COMMUNICATIONS ADAPTER
21 ALT BSC COMMUNICATIONS ADAPTER
22 CLUSTER ADAPTER(S)
24 ENHANCED GRAPHICS ADAPTER
29 COLOR PRINTER
30 PC NETWORK ADAPTER
31 ALT. PC NETWORK ADAPTER
36 GPIB ADAPTER(S)
38 DATA ACQUISITION ADAPTER(S)
39 PROFESSIONAL GRAPHICS CONTROLLER
71 VOICE COMMUNICATIONS ADAPTER
73 3.5" EXTERNAL DISKETTE DRIVE AND ADAPTER
74 PERSONAL SYSTEM/2 DISPLAY ADAPTER
85 EXPANDED MEMORY ADAPTER --- 2 MB ---
89 MUSIC FEATURE CARD(S)
```

After certifying that the list is correct, or adding or deleting items as necessary to make it correct, you may begin testing each item listed.

The tests performed by the advanced diagnostics disk are far more detailed and precise than those of the general diagnostics disk in the GTO. In addition to identifying the problem component, the advanced diagnostics further attempt to identify the specific part of the device that is malfunctioning.

Once a problem is identified, the hardware maintenance service provides detailed instructions for performing adjustments, preventive maintenance, and removal and replacement of the affected part. To this end, comprehensive hardware and design information is available, including parts lists that specify replacement part numbers and internal design specifications.

Examining Error Codes

Nearly all the personal computer error codes for the POST, general diagnostics, and advanced diagnostics are represented by the device number followed by two digits other than 00. The device number plus 00 is used to indicate successful completion of a test. This listing is a compilation from various sources, including technical reference, hardware maintenance service, and hardware maintenance reference manuals.

If a designation such as *2xx* or *02x* is used, any error codes that begin with the first character(s) listed, and with any character in place of the *x*, indicate errors in the device listed. For example, *7xx* equals math coprocessor errors, which means that any 700 to 799 errors indicate that the math coprocessor is bad (or is having problems). Table 13.2 lists the error codes and their descriptions.

Table 13.2
Error Codes and Descriptions

Code	Description
01x	Undetermined problem errors
02x	Power supply errors
1xx	System board errors
2xx	Memory (RAM) errors
3xx	Keyboard errors
4xx	Monochrome Display Adapter (MDA) errors
4xx	PS/2 system board parallel port errors
5xx	Color Graphics Adapter (CGA) errors
6xx	Floppy drive/adapter errors
7xx	8087, 80287, or 80387 math coprocessor errors

Table 13.2—continued

Code	Description
9xx	Parallel printer adapter errors
10xx	Alternate parallel printer adapter errors
11xx	Asynchronous communications adapter errors
11xx	PS/2 system board async port errors
12xx	Alternate asynchronous communications adapter errors
12xx	PS/2 dual async adapter error
13xx	Game control adapter errors
14xx	Matrix printer errors
15xx	Synchronous Data Link Control (SDLC) communications adapter errors
16xx	Display emulation (327x, 5520, 525x) errors
17xx	Fixed disk errors
18xx	I/O expansion unit errors
19xx	3270 PC attachment card errors
20xx	Binary Synchronous Communications (BSC) adapter errors
21xx	Alternate binary synchronous communications adapter errors
22xx	Cluster adapter errors
24xx	Enhanced Graphics Adapter (EGA) errors
24xx	PS/2 system board Video Graphics Array (VGA) errors
26xx	XT/370 errors
27xx	AT/370 errors
28xx	3278/79 emulation adapter errors
29xx	Color/graphics printer errors
30xx	Primary PC network adapter errors
31xx	Secondary PC network adapter errors
33xx	Compact printer errors
36xx	General Purpose Interface Bus (GPIB) adapter errors
38xx	Data acquisition adapter errors
39xx	Professional graphics controller errors
71xx	Voice communications adapter errors
73xx	3 1/2-inch external disk drive errors
74xx	IBM PS/2 display adapter (VGA card) errors
85xx	IBM Expanded Memory Adapter (XMA) errors
86xx	PS/2 pointing device errors
89xx	Music feature card errors
100xx	PS/2 multiprotocol adapter errors
104xx	PS/2 ESDI fixed disk errors

Aftermarket Diagnostics

Besides those from IBM, many more diagnostics programs are available for IBM and compatible systems. Specific programs are available to test memory, floppy drives, hard disks, video boards, and most other areas of the system as well. The following section describes some of the best non-IBM diagnostics that are available, some of which should be considered essential in any toolkit.

Replacements for IBM Advanced Diagnostics

An IBM-compatible system should be able to run the IBM advanced diagnostics. Some manufacturers offer their own diagnostics. AT&T, Zenith, and Tandy, for example, offer their own versions of service manuals and diagnostics programs for their systems. Other systems that are without this type of manufacturer support can simply use the IBM diagnostics and repair manuals.

Several alternatives are available for those of you who do not want IBM's diagnostics but do want a good, comprehensive diagnostics program for your systems. At least one advanced diagnostics program for IBM and non-IBM systems can be recommended: Service Diagnostics by SuperSoft.

This program offers several advantages over the IBM diagnostics. The program is better at determining where a problem lies within the system. In particular, the memory tests are comprehensive and have identified problems that the IBM diagnostics sometimes have missed. Here are the main advantages to this program:

- All serial and parallel port "wrap plugs" are included. These plugs are required to properly diagnose and test serial and parallel ports. (IBM charges extra for these.)

- Floppy disk tests can properly determine drive alignment due to the use of specially created reference standard disks. Other software tests drives with any disk formatted by any drive and has no set of precisely placed recordings by which to judge the alignment of a drive.

- Special versions are available for IBM-compatible systems with different microprocessors, such as the 80386. Most other diagnostics programs simply treat any 80386 type of system as a regular AT, which misses special 80386 features such as advanced memory mapping capabilities. Also, the early versions of the 80386 have contained one or more bugs, which the special 80386 version of this program can locate.

And here are the disadvantages to the SuperSoft Service Diagnostics:

- The program is copy protected, but SuperSoft will make available an unprotected version on request.

- The manual is not as good as IBM's manual.

The costs start at around $195 per module, depending on what versions and how many modules are needed.

Other general-purpose advanced diagnostics programs are available, but all except IBM's are copy protected. Especially in a diagnostics program, some technicians find such copy protection unacceptable. Note that none of IBM's diagnostics or advanced diagnostics are protected in any way; as a matter of fact, they are designed to copy themselves, and the manual strongly recommends that you never use the original disk for actual work. The original is to be used for making backups only. This approach to the use of the software, along with the excellent manual that IBM provides, is the reason that many technicians recommend the IBM program over all others.

A simple method exists for copying copy-protected disks. You can use several programs legally to make copies of these protected disks. Two of these programs are CopyWrite by Quaid Software Ltd. and Copy II PC by Central Point Software. Each program makes backups of almost any program.

Disk Diagnostics

The advanced diagnostics from IBM and other manufacturers do a good job of covering most of the components in a system with a reasonable level of diagnostic capabilities. But these programs sometimes fall short in the area of testing disk drives. The disk drives are some of the most trouble-prone and complicated components in computer systems, and it is no wonder that a diagnostics program designed to cover everything may be a little weak in this area. IBM's own advanced diagnostics for the PC are extremely poor in the area of testing hard disks. The IBM PC version of this program (not the AT version) does not even allow for the entry of the manufacturer's defect list during a hard disk low-level format. This program also formats a hard disk at a fixed interleave value of 5 to 1, no matter what type of controller you have.

For the best floppy and hard disk diagnostics, you must use specialized software programs designed solely for these types of hardware. Several excellent programs are available specifically for testing floppy drives as well as hard disks. These programs are a welcome addition to anyone's toolkit and are an excellent supplement to the advanced diagnostics types of programs that do it all.

The next section of this chapter discusses some of the best disk diagnostic and testing programs on the market today and what they can do for you.

Htest/Hformat (Paul Mace Software)

For specific troubleshooting and low-level formatting of hard disks, the Htest/Hformat program from Paul Mace Software is the best on the market. At $89, this program belongs in every technician's toolkit. This program does not have the "hype" surrounding it that many remotely similar products on the market have today. This program is not flashy and overly friendly, but it is one of the most powerful hard disk utilities available.

Interrogator (Dysan)

Many programs on today's market evaluate the condition of floppy disk drives by using a disk created or formatted on the same drive. Any program that uses this technique simply cannot make a proper evaluation of a disk drive's alignment. What is required is a specially created disk that is produced by a tested and calibrated machine. This type of disk can be used as a reference standard by which to judge a drive. Dysan is a manufacturer of such disks, which are called Digital Diagnostics Diskettes, or DDDs. These disks can be read by a program designed to read them and evaluate the capabilities of a drive against the disk. These disks contain certain known errors, such as sectors that are progressively further and further from the precise track center. Just how many of these intentionally off-center sectors a disk can read is used to gauge the drive's alignment.

In the Dysan DDD, for example, one of the tracks has sectors recorded as shown in figure 13.1.

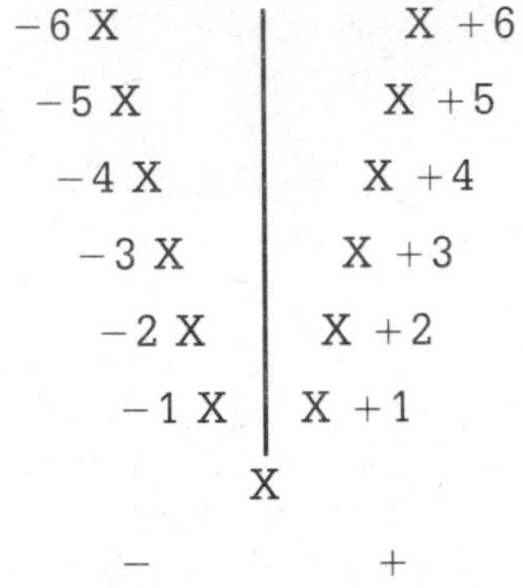

Fig. 13.1.

Special Digital Diagnostics Disk (DDD) track with off-center sectors used to measure disk alignment.

```
            -6 X    |    X +6
            -5 X    |    X +5
            -4 X    |    X +4
            -3 X    |    X +3
            -2 X    |    X +2
            -1 X    |  X +1
                  X
             -          +
```

Each X represents a sector, and the $+1$, $+2$, -1, -2, etc., indicate how far from the center of the track the sector is located. When another drive reads this specially formatted track, it identifies how many sectors outside $(+)$ or how many sectors inside $(-)$ the track can be read. A perfect score is $+12$, -12. This score indicates that the drive can read a span of 12 sectors out in each direction, which implies that the heads are centered over the track. Suppose that the score is reported as $+7$, -15. This score indicates that the drive is misaligned toward the center of the disk. A score of $+8$, -8 indicates that a drive may be aligned perfectly but it is not very forgiving of misaligned sectors on a disk. This last drive may experience problems reading disks written by other drives that are not perfectly aligned. These types of tests can be a valuable measure of what is going on with a particular drive.

The program designed to work with these specially created disks is called the Dysan Interrogator. This easy-to-use program has many useful tests that can report a drive's condition accurately.

Public Domain Diagnostics

Many excellent diagnostic programs are available in the public domain. Numerous programs are available for diagnosing problems with memory, hard disks, floppy disks, displays and adapters, and virtually any other part of the system, and these programs can be excellent substitutes for any of the other "official" diagnostics programs. Many of these programs really are commercial-quality programs that are simply distributed under a "try now, pay later" concept. This user-supported software is designed to use the typical public domain software channels for distribution but is supported by honest users' payments for use. Some programs are "user supported" by contributions and donations from satisfied users nationwide.

Although you can find many sources for public domain and user-supported software, including many distribution companies and electronic bulletin boards, one source stands out: the Public Software Library.

This organization started as an outgrowth of a Houston computer users group but has gone on to have the best single collection of public domain and user-supported software. What makes this company extraordinary is that all the software is tested before entering the library. Bugged programs usually don't make it in the front door, which also eliminates the so called "virus" or Trojan horse programs that damage a system. All the programs are the latest versions available, and earlier versions are purged from the library. Many other companies don't think twice about selling you a disk full of old programs. The programs in this library are not sold but simply distributed. The authors are aware of how these programs are being distributed, and no excessive fees are charged for the disk and copying services. This is truly a legitimate company that has a program author's approval to distribute the software in this fashion. All disks are $5 and are guaranteed, unlike many comparable organizations that seem bent on making as much money as they can.

Chapter Summary

This chapter examined the diagnostic software that can be used as a valuable aid in diagnosing and troubleshooting a system. The chapter explained IBM error codes and included a reference chart showing the meanings of these codes. Advanced diagnostics were discussed also, as were some of the better aftermarket replacements. This chapter also covered some of the specialized diagnostics for particular areas of the system, such as disk drives. The chapter ended with a discussion of public domain and user-supported software, which is a rich source of fantastic utilities that are relatively inexpensive and very good.

Part V

Troubleshooting Guides

Includes

Hardware Troubleshooting Guide

Software Troubleshooting Guide

A Final Word

14

Hardware Troubleshooting Guide

This chapter lists specific procedures for troubleshooting various system components. By now, you have a good understanding of how things work and should be installed. This information is the information you need for troubleshooting. To be a good troubleshooter, you need to understand a system better than the average person.

The procedures listed here are not meant to be a replacement for the hardware maintenance service manuals that your system manufacturer provides but are designed to augment that information. These procedures are simple and concise, and they can be applied to most any IBM or compatible system.

This chapter also lists the items that fail most often in a system and recommends the items you should carry in inventory as spare parts.

Getting Started with Troubleshooting

When you troubleshoot a system, you should approach the task with a clear mind and a relaxed attitude. If you get overexcited or panic, you will make figuring out the problem much more difficult.

Don't start taking apart the system unit right away. First, sit back and think about the problem. Make notes and record any observations. These notes can be valuable, especially for difficult problems. Don't throw away the notes once the problem is solved. These notes can be valuable for a recurring problem. You should develop a systematic approach to determining what the problem is.

Here are some basic troubleshooting rules of thumb:

1. Check the installation and configuration. Often, if I have just put together a system and it doesn't work properly, it's my own fault. I didn't set a jumper correctly, plugged a cable in backward or left it unplugged, or some other small detail.

2. Check the installation and configuration again! Even when I am sure it's correct, I still have made mistakes. Double check everything.

3. If you still have a problem, work your way through the system item by item, from those most likely to cause a problem to those least likely to cause a problem. Power supplies often cause problems, for example, so you should check the power supply before many other devices. An improper low-level format can cause hard disk problems, so check that possibility before you assume that the disk is bad.

4. A variation on the preceding rule is to work your way through the system from the simplest, least expensive, and easiest-to-replace item to the most complex, most expensive, and hardest-to-replace item. This is just common sense. Check cables before adapter cards, for example, and check adapter cards before disk drives.

5. Check the environment, including incoming power, ambient temperature fluctuations, humidity, static electricity, and airborne contaminants. Environmental influences can cause many problems, and these problems can be the most difficult to track down. (How can you see temperature or humidity variations?)

6. Keep the documentation and manuals close by. Write your own documentation for your systems and include anything you put into your system. Document the interrupt and DMA channel settings, port usage, memory usage, what slots the adapter cards are installed in, what kinds of memory chips you used in the system, and so forth. This documentation can save you from much unnecessary labor.

Keep these simple rules in mind, and your troubleshooting sessions can be enjoyable challenges.

Diagnosing Intermittent Problems

The bane of any troubleshooter is the intermittent problem. Often, you have to rely on a report from a user who cannot describe the symptom in an accurate, precise fashion. You have to interpret the user's description and guess what really happened. You may think you have fixed the problem only to find that the problem occurs again.

If you can, get the system user to write down when the problem occurs and what the exact symptoms are. Before you begin disassembling the system, try to re-create the problem. Once you have witnessed the intermittent problem yourself, run the diagnostics software.

One of the best resources in the case of an intermittent failure is the advanced diagnostics software. This software can execute a test in an endless loop mode, which can be set to run all night or over a weekend. Another weapon commonly used to track down these problems is heat. You can use a hair dryer to warm up the motherboard and other electronics to help the failure along. You must be careful not to do any real damage, and I almost hesitate to mention it. Only experience and practice can give you a feel for just how hot you should make a board and when enough is enough.

Sometimes the opposite approach can work too. When a system is exhibiting the problem, you can spray some "component cooler" or Freon onto the suspected component, which chills it. If the component's failure is heat related, this chilling often restores its operation.

Static electricity and other external environmental influences often can cause what appears to be an intermittent problem. Noting the state of the surrounding environment when the problems are occurring is important. Pay attention to time too. Sometimes strange time patterns can help you discover that a problem is related to an external influence, such as turning on any large motors at the same time each day.

Keep these tips in mind the next time you have an intermittent problem, and you may find it easier to handle.

Using a Troubleshooting Flowchart

Attempting to find a city in an unfamiliar state is made easy by the use of a road map. In the same vain, a map or flowchart can help you find a problem with a computer system. Knowing the appropriate path can get you to your destination for repairing the system with the least amount of detours. This section gives you the paths to follow to solve problems most successfully.

The Power Supply

If you suspect a power supply problem, the simple measurements outlined in this section can help you determine whether the power supply is at fault. These measurements will not detect many intermittent or overload failures, so you may have to use a spare power supply for long-term evaluation. If the symptoms and problems disappear with the replacement unit, you have found the source of your problem.

To test a power supply for proper output, check the voltage between pins 1 and 5 (ground) for 2.4 to 5.4 vdc on the system board connectors. If the measurement is not within that range, the supply is bad.

Continue by measuring for the following voltage ranges on the pins on the motherboard and drive power connectors:

Motherboard Connector Measurements

Voltages		Pins	
Minimum	Maximum	−Leads	+Leads
+4.8	+5.2	P8-5	P9-4
+4.5	+5.4	P9-3	P8-6
+11.5	+12.6	P9-1	P8-3
+10.8	+12.9	P8-4	P9-2

Disk Drive Connector Measurements

Voltages		Pins	
Minimum	Maximum	− Leads	+ Leads
+ 4.8	+ 5.2	2	4
+ 11.5	+ 12.6	3	1

Replace the power supply if these voltages are incorrect. Note that all these measurements must be made with the power supply installed in a system, and the system must be running.

The types of power supplies used in these systems are called "switching" power supplies. These supplies must always have a proper load to function correctly. If you take the supply out of the system unit, set it on a workbench, plug it in, and power it on, the supply will immediately shut itself down. It will not run unless it's plugged into a motherboard and at least one disk drive.

The original AT systems came with a huge load resistor mounted in place of the hard disk, which allowed the supply to operate properly even without a hard disk installed. If you are setting up a "diskless" system, make sure that you use a similar type of power load or you will have problems with the supply, and you may even burn it out.

The System Board

A motherboard failure can be difficult to detect. In many cases, the system is simply nonfunctional. If the system is nonfunctional or partially functional and you suspect a motherboard failure, the following troubleshooting procedures can be helpful:

- Check all connectors to ensure that they are plugged in correctly.

- Confirm that the wall outlet is a working outlet.

- Look for foreign objects such as screws that you may have dropped on the motherboard and make sure that the board itself is clean.

- Confirm that all system board switch settings are correct.

- Run the advanced diagnostics system board test.

Error codes are displayed as follows:

Code	Description
1xx	System Board Errors
101	System Board Error; Interrupt failure.
102	System Board Error; Timer failure.
103	System Board Error; Timer interrupt failure.
104	System Board Error; Protected mode failure.
105	System Board Error; Last 8042 command not accepted.
106	System Board Error; Converting logic test.
107	System Board Error; Hot Non Maskable Interrupt test.
108	System Board Error; Timer bus test.
109	System Board Error; Memory select error.
110	PS/2 System Board Error; Parity check error.
111	PS/2 Memory adapter error.
112	PS/2 MicroChannel arbitration error.
113	PS/2 MicroChannel arbitration error.
121	Unexpected hardware interrupts occurred.
131	PC system board cassette port wrap test failure.
161	System Options Not Set-(Run SETUP); Dead battery.
162	System Options Not Set-(Run SETUP); CMOS checksum/configuration error.
163	Time & Date Not Set-(Run SETUP); Clock not updating.
164	Memory Size Error-(Run SETUP); CMOS setting does not match memory.
165	PS/2 System options not set.
166	PS/2 MicroChannel adapter time-out error.
199	User indicated INSTALLED DEVICES list is not correct.

The Appendix contains an extensive listing of POST (power-on self test) and diagnostics error codes.

Next, check the supply voltage for 2.4 to 5.2 vdc between pins 1 and 5 (ground) at the system board. Turn off the power and remove all options adapters from the system board. Check for the following resistance values at the motherboard power connectors:

		Pin Minimums
− Lead	+ Lead	Resistance
5	3	17 Ohms
6	4	17 Ohms
7	9	17 Ohms
8	10	0.8 Ohms
8	11	0.8 Ohms
8	12	0.8 Ohms

Improper resistance readings may indicate that the motherboard is defective, particularly if the resistance is below the minimums indicated. If the voltage measurements aren't within the parameters specified, the power supply may be defective.

The Battery

A defective battery is usually indicated during the POST with a 161 error. The simplest way to determine whether the battery is defective is to replace it. Otherwise, first rerun the SETUP program; if this doesn't correct the problem, disconnect the battery from the system board. The battery voltage between pins 1 and 4 on the battery connector should be at least 6.0 vdc. Replace the battery if it doesn't meet the correct voltage specifications.

The Keyboard

Keyboard errors sometimes can be difficult to detect. To troubleshoot the keyboard and cable assembly, power on and observe the POST. Write down the 3xx error if you received one. Turn off the power and disconnect the keyboard. Then, turn on the power and check the voltage at the system board keyboard connector for the following specifications:

Keyboard Connector Specifications	
Pin	Voltage
1	+2.0 TO +5.5
2	+4.8 TO +5.5
3	+2.0 TO +5.5
4	GROUND
5	+2.0 TO +5.5

If your measurements don't match these voltages, the motherboard may be defective. Otherwise, the keyboard cable or keyboard itself may be defective. Replace the keyboard cable and run the advanced diagnostics keyboard test. The error codes are displayed as follows:

Code	Description
3xx	Keyboard errors
301	Keyboard did not respond to software reset or a stuck key failure was detected. If a stuck key was detected, the scan code for the key is displayed in hexadecimal.
302	System Unit Keylock is Locked.
303	Keyboard Or System Unit Error.
304	Keyboard Or System Unit Error; Keyboard clock high.
305	PS/2 Keyboard fuse (on system board) error.

The Video Adapter

If you suspect problems with the video board, make sure that the switch settings on the motherboard and video card are correct and turn on the power. Listen for audio response during the POST (one long and two short beeps indicate a video failure).

If the adapter is supported, run the advanced diagnostics video adapter test for the particular adapter you want to test. Adapters that aren't supported always fail the tests even though they may be good. Error codes are displayed as follows:

Code	Description
4xx	Monochrome Display Adapter (MDA) errors
4xx	PS/2 System board parallel port errors
401	Monochrome memory test, horizontal sync frequency test, or video test failure.
401	PS/2 System board parallel port failure.
408	User indicated display attributes failure.
416	User indicated character set failure.
424	User indicated 80x25 mode failure.
432	Parallel port test failure; monochrome display adapter.
5xx	Color Graphics Adapter (CGA) errors
501	CGA memory test, horizontal sync frequency test, or video test failure.

Code	Description
508	User indicated display attribute failure.
516	User indicated character set failure.
524	User indicated 80x25 mode failure.
532	User indicated 40x25 mode failure.
540	User indicated 320x200 graphics mode failure.
548	User indicated 640x200 graphics mode failure.
24xx	Enhanced Graphics Adapter (EGA) errors
24xx	PS/2 System board Video Graphics Array (VGA) errors
39xx	Professional graphics controller errors
74xx	IBM PS/2 Display adapter (VGA card) errors

The Hard Disk Drive

Problems with the hard disk are indicated by 17xx errors. If you suspect any problems with the drive, controller, or cable, you can substitute equipment that you know works properly for these items.

Check for proper configuration of drives (drive-select jumpers and terminating resistors). Turn off the power. Power on and boot the advanced diagnostics (or a similar program). Run the fixed disk drive and adapter tests. Error codes indicating various problems are displayed as follows:

Code	Description
17xx	Fixed disk errors
1701	Fixed disk POST error.
1702	Fixed disk adapter error.
1703	Fixed disk drive error.
1704	Fixed disk adapter or drive error.
1780	Fixed disk 0 failure.
1781	Fixed disk 1 failure.
1782	Fixed disk controller failure.
1790	Fixed disk 0 error.
1791	Fixed disk 1 error.
104xx	PS/2 ESDI Fixed disk errors
10480	PS/2 ESDI Fixed disk 0 failure.

Code	Description
10481	PS/2 ESDI Fixed disk 1 failure.
10482	PS/2 ESDI Fixed disk controller failure.
10483	PS/2 ESDI Fixed disk controller failure.
10490	PS/2 ESDI Fixed disk 0 error.
10491	PS/2 ESDI Fixed disk 1 error.

Check the cables to make sure that they aren't defective and measure voltages at the drive power connector as follows:

Hard Disk Response

+Lead Power 4	+4.8 to 5.2 Vdc
−Lead Power 5	
+Lead Power 1	+11.5 to 12.6 Vdc
−Lead Power 3	

If any of your voltages' measurements are outside of these boundaries, the power supply is defective. Error codes can indicate a variety of problems (see the Appendix for an extensive list of error codes).

The Floppy Disk Drive

If you suspect that the floppy drives are defective, make sure that the problem isn't with the disk being used. If the drive receives power separately from the computer, make sure that nothing is wrong with the outlet. Be sure that all cables and connectors are plugged in correctly. Check to see that all drives are configured properly (drive-select jumpers, terminating resistors, pin 34, and media sensor) and then run the advanced diagnostics disk drive and adapter tests. Error codes are displayed as follows:

Code	Description
6xx	Floppy drive/adapter errors
601	Floppy drive/adapter Power On Self Test failure.
602	Drive test failure; disk boot record is not valid.
606	Disk change line function failure; drive error.
607	Disk is write protected; drive error.
608	Bad command; drive error.
610	Disk initialization failure; track 0 bad.

Code	Description
611	Time-out; drive error.
612	Bad Controller chip.
613	Bad Direct Memory Access; drive error.
614	Bad Direct Memory Access; boundary overrun.
615	Bad index timing; drive error.
616	Drive speed error.
621	Bad seek; drive error.
622	Bad Cyclic Redundancy Check; drive error.
623	Record not found; drive error.
624	Bad address mark; drive error.
625	Bad Controller chip; seek error.
626	Disk data compare error.
73xx	3.5″ external diskette drive errors
7306	Disk change line function failure; drive error.
7307	Disk is write protected; drive error.
7308	Bad command; drive error.
7310	Disk initialization failure; track 0 bad.
7311	Time-out; drive error.
7312	Bad Controller chip.
7313	Bad Direct Memory Access; drive error.
7314	Bad Direct Memory Access; boundary overrun.
7315	Bad index timing; drive error.
7316	Drive speed error.
7321	Bad seek; drive error.
7322	Bad Cyclic Redundancy Check; drive error.
7323	Record not found; drive error.
7324	Bad address mark; drive error.
7325	Bad Controller chip; seek error.

Check the voltages at the power connector on drive A as follows:

Drive A Power Connector

Voltages		Pins	
Minimum	Maximum	− Lead	+ Lead
+ 4.8	+ 5.2	2	4
+ 11.5	+ 12.6	3	1

Test the drive for correct rotational speed and adjust the speed if the drive allows a speed adjustment. Make sure that the cable and connectors are good and check the cable for continuity. If the power connector voltages don't measure as they should, the power supply may be bad.

The Serial and Parallel Ports

To test any serial or parallel port cards, run the advanced diagnostics communications adapter tests. Error codes are displayed as follows:

Code	Description
9xx	Parallel printer adapter errors
901	Parallel printer adapter test failure.
10xx	Alternate parallel printer adapter errors
1001	Alternate parallel printer adapter test failure.
11xx	Asynchronous communications adapter errors
11xx	PS/2 System board async port errors
1101	Asynchronous communications adapter test failure.
1102	PS/2 System board async port or serial device error.
1106	PS/2 System board async port or serial device error.
1107	PS/2 System board async port or serial cable error.
1108	PS/2 System board async port or serial device error.
1109	PS/2 System board async port or serial device error.
1112	PS/2 System board async port error.
1118	PS/2 System board async port error.
1119	PS/2 System board async port error.
12xx	Alternate asynchronous communications adapter errors
12xx	PS/2 Dual async adapter error
1201	Alternate asynchronous communications adapter test failure.
1202	PS/2 Dual async adapter or serial device error.
1206	PS/2 Dual async adapter or serial device error.
1207	PS/2 Dual async adapter or serial cable error.
1208	PS/2 Dual async adapter or serial device error.
1209	PS/2 Dual async adapter or serial device error.
1212	PS/2 Dual async adapter or system board error.
1218	PS/2 Dual async adapter or system board error.
1219	PS/2 Dual async adapter or system board error.
1227	PS/2 Dual async adapter or system board error.
1233	PS/2 Dual async adapter or system board error.
1234	PS/2 Dual async adapter or system board error.

For serial ports only, check for a voltage reading of -10.8 to -12.9 vdc between pins 4 and 8 (ground) and the system board power connector. If the voltage measurement isn't within the range specified, the power supply may be defective.

The Speaker

To verify the operation of the speaker in the system unit, turn off the power. Set your meter to Ohms X1 Scale. Disconnect the speaker from the system board. Check the continuity of the speaker. If the speaker doesn't have continuity, it is defective and should be replaced.

Examining Some Common Failures

Of all possible problems that can occur with a computer, some are more common than others. This section reviews some of the computer's most common failures.

High Failure Rate Items

The most common failures in a PC are mechanical—disk drives (floppy and hard disk) and power supplies. These items can and do fail, sometimes with no warning. Memory devices also fail periodically.

The power supply is an extremely failure-prone item, especially in the IBM PC in which an underrated unit was used. I usually replace the PC power supply when I upgrade a PC because most upgrades (such as hard disks) use much power—more than is available in the original supply. Having too much power supply is better than not enough.

These are the system components most likely to fail:

- Power supply
- Hard disk low-level format

- Floppy drive
- Hard disk controller
- Hard disk
- Memory chips

Disk Drive Failure

Only two disk problems can be fixed quickly: the drive speed and dirty drives.

If you have other problems with a disk drive, you probably will have to replace the drive with a new or rebuilt unit. Because disk drives are relatively inexpensive, spending much time trying to fix them doesn't make sense.

Adjusting the speed of a disk drive is easy. You usually can do this with one of the many floppy disk testing programs available.

If you have many drives to be repaired or aligned, you should locate a service company that specializes in disk drive service and alignments. Most service companies will align a floppy drive for $25 to $50. This cost must be weighed against the replacement cost. I have purchased new half-height 360K drives for as low as $39 each, so I'm not sure that I would spend $50 to align an old drive. If you want to have your drives aligned, see the Appendix for a list of companies that perform this service.

Cleaning disk drives is normally part of a preventive-maintenance program, but it may have been neglected. Always remember to clean a problem drive. Some of the disk-based cleaners are abrasive to the drive heads, so always use the ''wet'' types of cleaners because they are gentler on the heads.

Spare Parts

I recommend carrying spares of the following items:

- Cables of all types
- Power supplies
- Memory chips

- Disk drives

- Floppy drive controllers

If the system is very important and must be up all the time, you should add a few more items to the spares list:

- Hard disk drives and controllers

- Keyboards

With these items on hand, you are prepared for 90 percent of all system failures and problems.

Using Last-Ditch Fixes

When all else fails when you are troubleshooting a particular problem, a fool-proof method exists for diagnosing the problem.

Locate a system identical to the failing one. The closer the match, the better. The duplicate system should be the same type from the same manufacturer. And, if possible, it should have the same adapter boards installed and be configured exactly the same way.

Verify that the duplicate system runs correctly and does not exhibit the symptoms of the failing unit. Begin placing items from the spare unit into the malfunctioning unit one by one and test after replacing each item. First replace each cable, for example, using the spare system's cables. Progress to each adapter card, disk drive, power supply, motherboard, and so on.

You will know when you have found the problem part when the malfunctioning unit begins to work.

Fortunately, this drastic measure is rarely required, but in a pinch, it does work. This method requires little thought, and it's a method that anyone can use. Keep it in mind when you are under pressure to fix a system.

Chapter Summary

This chapter has covered hardware troubleshooting techniques in detail. You received some basic tips for good troubleshooting. The body of this chapter covered specific component troubleshooting in detail, giving you the procedures, measurements, and observations to make to determine the location of a system fault. The last part of this chapter focused on failure-prone items and how to handle some troublesome situations.

15

Software
Troubleshooting
Guide

The focus of this chapter is the range of problems that occur because of faulty or incompatible software. First, you will learn about DOS, both its structure and how it works with hardware to result in a functioning system. Of particular interest is the discussion of the DOS file structure and how DOS organizes information on a disk. Programs that DOS offers for data and disk recovery also are covered. These programs present both capabilities and dangers. Finally, the chapter examines resident software and the problems it can cause, and shows you how to distinguish a software problem from a hardware problem.

Understanding the Disk
Operating System (DOS)

Information about DOS may seem out of place in a book on hardware upgrade and repair, but if you totally ignore DOS and other software when you troubleshoot a system, you miss a number of problems. The best system troubleshooters and diagnosticians are those who know the entire system, including both hardware and software.

Because this book cannot go into depth concerning DOS, you should read more about it. Que Corporation publishes some good books on the subject (*Using PC DOS* and *MS-DOS User's Guide*).

This section of the chapter covers some of the basics of what DOS is, where it fits into the system architecture, and what components comprise it. A discussion of what happens in a system when it "boots" or starts up is also included. An understanding of booting can be helpful when you're diagnosing start-up problems. This section also explains DOS configuration, a place where many people experience problems, and covers the file formats DOS uses, as well as how DOS manages information on a disk.

Operating System Basics

One of the first things to understand about DOS is where and how it fits into the total system architecture. In PC systems, a distinct hierarchy of software exists that controls the system at all times. Even when you are operating within an applications program such as 1-2-3 or another high-level applications program, several other layers of program always are executing underneath. Generally, the layers can be defined distinctly, but at times the boundaries are more vague. Also, communication between separate adjoining layers usually is occurring, but this is not a rule and many programs may ignore the services provided by the layer directly beneath it. These programs instead choose to "eliminate the middleman" and skip one or more layers to get the job done directly.

At the very lowest level exists the machine itself. If you examine the system at this level, you find that by placing various bytes of information at certain ports or locations within the memory structure of the machine, you can control virtually anything that is connected to the CPU. Control at this level is difficult to maintain, and it requires a complete and accurate knowledge of the actual system architecture. The fullest level of detailed knowledge of the software that operates at this level is required for this kind of control. Commands to the machine here are in *machine language* (basically binary groups of information applied directly to the microprocessor itself). These instructions are quite limited in their function, and many of them may be required to perform even the smallest amount of useful work. The large number of instructions required is not really a problem, however, because these instructions are executed extremely rapidly, and there is little wasted overhead.

Although programmers can write these instructions directly, they generally use a tool known as an *assembler* to ease the process. An *editor* is used to actually type the program into a file, which is then converted to pure machine language by the assembler. Assembler commands still are low level and require a great deal of knowledge on the part of the programmer for effective use. Because few programmers, if any, write in machine code directly anymore, assembly language is the lowest level of programming environment typically used today. But even assembly language is losing favor among programmers because of the amount of knowledge and work required and the programs' lack of portability between different systems.

When PC systems are started, a series of machine code programs assume control; they are the ROM BIOS. These programs are always present in the system and communicate (in machine code) with the hardware. The BIOS accepts or interprets commands supplied by programs above it and translates these commands to machine code commands that are then passed on to the microprocessor. These commands typically are called *services*. A programmer generally can use almost any language to supply these instructions to the BIOS. A complete list of these services is supplied by IBM in the technical reference manuals that are offered separately for each of the PC systems.

DOS is made up of several components. DOS attaches itself to the BIOS, and part of DOS actually becomes an extension of the BIOS itself, providing more interrupts and services for other programs to use. DOS provides for communications with the ROM BIOS in the PC, as well as for communications with higher level software, such as the applications software with which computer users are familiar. DOS gives the programmer a nice toolbox of services to use in programs. These DOS services prevent "reinventing of the wheel" as far as programming routines are concerned. DOS provides a rich set of file handling functions that can, for example, open, close, find, delete, create, and rename files on a drive. A programmer who wants to include some of these functions in his program can rely on DOS to do most of the work. Also, one of the primary functions of DOS is actually to load and run other programs. DOS provides the functions and environment required for running other software. *DOS Programmer's Reference*, published by Que, provides details for anyone interested in further information.

DOS Components

DOS consists of two main components: the input/output (I/O) system and the shell. The I/O system consists of the underlying programs that reside in memory while the system is running and are loaded first when DOS boots. The I/O system is stored in two files that are hidden on the disk. The files are called IBMBIO.COM and IBMDOS.COM on an IBM DOS disk. MS-DOS generic versions have IO.SYS and BIO.SYS files.

The shell is stored in the file COMMAND.COM, which also is loaded during a normal DOS boot-up. The shell is the portion of DOS that gives you the DOS prompt and that normally communicates with the user of the system.

This section examines these portions of DOS in more detail so that you will be able to properly identify and handle problems with DOS rather than blame the hardware.

The I/O System

This section briefly describes the two files that make up the I/O system: IBMBIO.COM and IBMDOS.COM.

IBMBIO.COM

The file IBMBIO.COM is one of the hidden files that the CHKDSK command reports on any DOS system (or bootable) disk. This file contains the low-level programs that interact directly with hardware devices on the system and the motherboard ROM BIOS. This file is loaded into memory at boot-up and remains there during system operation.

IBMDOS.COM

The file IBMDOS.COM is the core of the DOS file and disk handling system. This file is hidden and is found only on system disks. IBMDOS.COM is loaded at system start-up and remains in memory during normal system operation.

The Shell (Command Processor)

The DOS command processor is called COMMAND.COM. This program is the portion of DOS with which the user interacts. The function of COMMAND.COM is to be the user interface as well as a program loader. COMMAND.COM manages two types of commands (programs): resident programs and transient programs.

Resident programs are built into COMMAND.COM and are available at any time during system operation while you're at the DOS prompt. These commands usually are the simpler ones that are frequently used, such as CLS, DIR, and COPY, to name a few. These commands execute rapidly because the instructions for them are already loaded into memory. They are said to be memory resident. When looking up the definition of a particular command in the DOS manual, you see an indication of whether the particular command is resident or transient (normally indicated as internal or external, respectively). This information allows you to determine what is required for executing the particular command. A simple rule is that at a DOS prompt, all resident commands are instantly available for execution.

Transient programs often are also called utilities. These commands are not resident in memory and the instructions to execute the command must be located on a disk. The instructions are loaded into memory only for execution and then are overwritten after use, which is the reason that they are called transient commands. Examples of transient commands are FORMAT, DISKCOPY, and CHKDSK. The majority of DOS commands are transient; otherwise the memory requirements for DOS would be astronomical. Transient commands are less frequently used than the resident commands and take longer to execute because they must be found and loaded before they can be run.

DOS Start-Up Sequence

The term *boot* comes from the expression "pulling himself up by his bootstraps" and describes the method by which PCs become operational. What it really means is that a chain of events begins with the application of power and finally results in an operating computer. Each event is called up by the event before it and initiates the event after it. If you have a problem with your system during start-up and you can determine where in this sequence of events your system has stalled, then you know which events have occurred and you can probably eliminate them as a cause of the problem. The following are the steps in a system start-up:

1. You apply power to the system by turning on the switch.

2. The power supply performs a self-test, and when all voltages and current levels are acceptable, it sends the power good signal to the motherboard, which indicates stable power.

3. The 8284 timer chip receives the power good signal, which causes the timer chip to stop generating a reset signal for the processor.

4. The processor begins executing the instructions found at memory location FFFF:0000. This location contains a jump instruction to the actual BIOS start location.

5. The ROM BIOS is started and checks a flag at the locations 0000:0472 and 0000:0473 to see if this is a cold or warm start. Values of 34h and 12h, respectively, in these locations indicate a warm start, which causes most of the POST (power-on self test) to be skipped. Any other values in these locations indicate a cold start and full POST.

6. The POST is begun, which tests all major system components and memory. Audio and displayed error messages indicate various problems. This step is skipped if this was a warm start.

7. BIOS performs a ROM scan, looking for ROM programs contained on adapter cards in the slots. The locations for the scan vary among different systems. Locations C000:0000 through C780:0000 are scanned for a video adapter ROM BIOS. If a ROM is found, it is tested and initialized. The locations C800:0000 through DF80:0000 are scanned for any other ROMs. If others are found, they are tested and initialized. These adapter ROMs can alter existing BIOS routines and establish new ones.

8. The BIOS then searches for a boot record on track 0 sector 1 on drive A. If found, this sector is loaded and the program is executed. If the sector cannot be read, the BIOS continues to the next step.

9. The BIOS then looks for a master boot record on track 0 sector 1 of the first fixed disk. If found, this sector is loaded and the program is executed. This master boot record loads the boot record from the active partition and executes it. Problems here cause various error messages to be displayed, or the BIOS transfers control to Cassette BASIC and the boot process ends.

10. The Boot Record (now in control) loads IBMBIO.COM and IBMDOS.COM. Control is then given to IBMBIO.COM.

11. IBMBIO.COM (now in control) uses IBMDOS.COM to read CONFIG.SYS. The statements in CONFIG.SYS are used to establish a configuration, then any listed device drivers are loaded, and finally, any listed installable programs are loaded.

12. IBMBIO.COM uses IBMDOS.COM to load COMMAND.COM and passes control to COMMAND.COM.

13. COMMAND.COM loads and runs AUTOEXEC.BAT.

14. After AUTOEXEC.BAT finishes, the DOS prompt appears.

Some minor variations on this scenario are possible, such as those introduced by other ROM programs found in the various adapters that may be plugged into a slot. Generally, however, the computer follows this chain of events in coming to life.

Configuring DOS with Configuration File Commands

Right out of the box, DOS is configured with system defaults. In order to allow you to get the most out of it, however, DOS contains commands that allow you to reconfigure the system defaults for your specific computer setup. The following paragraphs explain these commands.

When you start DOS, either by pressing Ctrl-Alt-Del or by turning on the computer's power, DOS searches the root directory of the drive from which it was started for a file named CONFIG.SYS. If this file is found, DOS reads the statements it contains. The CONFIG.SYS file is an ASCII file that contains special configuration statements that help tailor the way DOS is configured. If you don't have a CONFIG.SYS file, or a particular configuration statement is not included, then DOS uses predetermined default values for the configurable items.

The DOS internal configuration commands available are the following:

BREAK = ON|OFF

The BREAK command controls the status of DOS Ctrl-Break checking. The default value is OFF, which causes DOS to check for entry of Ctrl-Break only when an I/O operation is being performed. The value ON causes DOS to check for Ctrl-Break whenever any DOS operation is performed. Leaving this value OFF is probably better because it adds to system overhead, and may allow DOS to be interrupted at inopportune moments.

BUFFERS = xx

By definition, xx is a number from 1 to 99 that specifies the number of disk buffers DOS allocates in memory at start-up time. The default is 2; but for the Personal Computer AT, the default is 3. This value should be increased to increase the efficiency of applications that perform random-access disk I/O. Such a change uses 528 bytes of memory for each buffer over the default of 2 or 3.

In any computer, read/write requests to disks can occur randomly, especially in a network server (the location of a network's large hard disk). Disk buffering improves overall performance for any computer in which random access occurs. Recommended minimum values for this parameter are the following:

10 PC with floppy disks only
20 PC XT (or any PCs with hard disks)
30 PC AT

These values are only recommendations, and they are conservative because disk buffering requires memory. If you have memory available, you can specify larger numbers for greater performance, but little performance improvement occurs above about 50 or so. Experiment with the number of buffers used on your system to find out what amount gives you the greatest benefit and least memory usage.

COUNTRY = xxx

By definition, xxx is a 3-digit international country code that defines the date and time formats used by the system, in addition to the currency symbol and the decimal separator. The default is 001 for the United States.

DEVICE = [d:][path]filename[.ext]

This command specifies the name of an installable device driver to be loaded into memory at system start-up. These drivers are DOS-resident programs that emulate hardware devices. The DOS device driver ANSI.SYS provides Enhanced Keyboard and display capabilities, and VDISK.SYS creates an electronic disk of variable size.

FCBS = m,n

The FCBS command is used to specify the number of file control blocks (FCBs) that can be open concurrently. The parameter m is the total number of files that can be open at one time. The default value is 4 (16 when the PC LAN program is started); the range is 1 to 255. The parameter n is the number of files opened by FCBS that cannot be closed automatically by DOS if a program tries to have more than m files opened by FCBs at any one time. The first n open files are protected from being closed. The default value is 0 (8 when the PC LAN program is started); the range is 0 to 255. The value of m must be greater than the value of n.

The FCBS command is valid only when file sharing is loaded. Some applications programs use file control blocks to create, open, delete, read, and write to files. DOS keeps track of the least recently used FCB. If the program tries to open more than m files, the action DOS takes depends on whether file sharing is loaded.

On a server configuration (file sharing), when a program tries to open more than m files, DOS closes the least recently used FCB and opens the new file. Note that the first n files are not included in the list of files that DOS tracks for the least recently used FCB. This prevents the closing of the first n files. If a program tries to read or write to a file that has been closed because it is the least recently used FCB, DOS issues the message FCB not available.

FILES = xxx

The FILES command is used to indicate the maximum number of files and handles on your disks or directories that can be open at one time. The parameter xxx indicates the number of files and handles that can be opened, from 8 to 255 (default is 8). If you exceed the value of xxx, you receive an error. The size of DOS increases by 48 bytes for each additional file specified over the default of 8.

This value is the maximum number of handles allowed for the entire system. This number includes handles in use by currently running foreground tasks and background tasks such as DOS PRINT and the network. The maximum number of file handles that a process can have open is 20. This number includes 5 used by DOS for standard input, standard output, standard error, auxiliary, and standard printer. The limit for the entire system is specified by FILES, although each process can only use 20. For this reason, on a single-user system, usually setting the value higher that 20 is of little or no benefit because COMMAND.COM itself is a process.

On a network server computer (multiuser), you should increase the value for FILES. The value specified for FILES must be large enough to provide for the programs run on the server as well as for the programs on the network using the server.

    LASTDRIVE = d

The LASTDRIVE command is used to indicate the maximum number of virtual and real drives that you can use at one time. The parameter d is any alphabetic character from A to Z that represents the last valid drive letter that DOS may accept. The default is E, or five total drives.

You can use a drive specifier (A:) to refer to physical drives that you have on your computer and also to refer to virtual drives that you do not have on your computer. You may refer to an electronic drive as your drive D, for example, even though you don't have a real drive D on your computer. The electronic drive is called a virtual drive. Network drives and directories also are referenced by a drive letter that is a virtual drive.

    SHELL = [d:][path]filename[.ext] [d:[path]] [/P][/D][/F][/E:**xxxxx**]

This command specifies the name and location of the initial copy of the top-level command processor that DOS loads in place of COMMAND.COM, and the drive and path from which it is to be reloaded. /P indicates that the substitution is to be permanent. This is required to prevent the top-level executing COMMAND.COM from being terminated with the EXIT command. /D indicates that AUTOEXEC.BAT is not to be executed upon system initialization. /F causes DOS to skip the response to the Abort, Retry, Ignore question in the system default INT 24h handler. /E:**xxxxx** is a decimal number that sets the size of the DOS environment area to **xxxxx** bytes. The default size is 160, and it may range from 160 to 32,768. The size is automatically rounded up to the nearest paragraph boundary (1 paragraph = 160 bytes).

DOS Disk Formats

Since DOS 1.0 debuted, the number of floppy disk formats supported by DOS has been on the increase. Fortunately, a newer version of DOS can always read and write the earlier versions' disks. The following is a list of all the formats currently supported (floppies are in order by capacity):

160K, 5 1/4-inch, single-sided, 40 tracks, 8 sectors per track.
This format was used by the original DOS 1.0 and 1.1 only.

180K, 5 1/4-inch, single-sided, 40 tracks, 9 sectors per track.
This format is used by DOS 2.0 or later.

320K, 5 1/4-inch, double-sided, 40 tracks, 8 sectors per track.
This format was used by DOS 1.1 only.

360K, 5 1/4-inch, double-sided, 40 tracks, 9 sectors per track.
This format is the standard used by DOS 2.0 and later.

720K, 3 1/2-inch, double-sided, 80 tracks, 9 sectors per track.
This format is used by the 3 1/2-inch drive found in the PC Convertible and the PS/2 Models 25 and 30.

1.2M, 5 1/4-inch, double-sided, 80 tracks, 15 sectors per track.
This format is used by the AT high-density floppy drive.

1.44M, 3 1/2-inch, double-sided, 80 tracks, 18 sectors per track.
This format is used by the 3 1/2-inch drive found in the PS/2 Models 30-286, 50, 60, 70, and 80.

DOS File Management

Disk file management is carried out by DOS with a combination of facilities. These facilities differ slightly between floppies and hard disks, and also between disks of different sizes.

To manage the disk *physically*, DOS uses the following several components:

Tracks. Tracks are concentric rings which data can be written. Disks usually have 40 or 80 tracks on each side, whereas hard disks can have from a hundred to several thousand tracks.

Cylinders. Cylinders are the tracks in a line through all the sides or platters of a disk. Double-sided floppies have cylinders that are made up of two tracks (one on each side), whereas hard disks can have up to 15 tracks for each cylinder (one track on each side of a platter times the number of platters in the hard disk). A cylinder represents the maximum amount of data that can be read without moving the heads. To maximize performance, DOS uses each track of a cylinder consecutively before moving the heads to a new cylinder.

Sectors. Sectors are slices of a track. Floppy formats use between 8 and 18 sectors per track, whereas hard disks usually use 17 or 26 sectors per track. Sectors created by standard DOS have always been 512 bytes, but this may change in the future. Sectors on a track are usually numbered sequentially on floppies, but on hard disks they often are *interleaved* at some preset value. This interleave is required because the disk spins so fast that the machine is not ready to read the very next physical sector, and instead the desired sector is spaced several sectors away. The number of sectors between logically ordered sectors is the interleave value. The interleave also represents the number of revolutions the disk must make for a complete track read. This is true unless the interleave is too low for the hardware to handle; then the revolution count is exactly the same as the number of sectors on each track.

To manage the files and data on a disk, DOS uses the following several items:

Boot Sector. The boot sector is the first sector on the disk (also called the boot record). This special sector contains a program that is loaded by the machine's ROM BIOS. This program is given control and attempts to load the first DOS system file (IBMBIO.COM). This sector is transparent to a running DOS system; it cannot be seen or accessed in any normal fashion. It is created by the FORMAT command. Hard disks have a master boot sector with a partition table instead of the standard boot sector, and the first sector of each partition is the equivalent of the standard boot sector.

Partition Table. The partition table is found on hard disks only and allows a single hard disk to be shared by several (up to four) operating systems at one time. This capability is accomplished with the use of the FDISK program to partition the disk, which creates the partition table. This table is also called the master boot sector because it is the first boot sector for a hard disk. The first sector of each partition is the boot sector.

File Allocation Table. The file allocation table is a table of entries describing how each cluster is allocated on the disk. Each cluster on the disk has an entry. The entries in a 16-bit file allocation table may be any of the following:

0000	Cluster is unused and available
FFF0 - FFF6	Reserved cluster (not available)
FFF7	Bad cluster (not available)
FFF8 - FFFF	Last cluster in a particular file
xxxx	Any other value indicates that this cluster is in use by a file; the actual value indicates the next sector occupied by this file.

On disks with greater than 20,740 sectors, DOS FORMAT creates a 16-bit file allocation table; otherwise DOS creates a 12-bit file allocation table. DOS keeps two copies of the file allocation table; however, DOS does not use the second copy. The usefulness of the second copy of the file allocation table is limited to manual repair.

Cluster. A cluster is equal to one or more sectors. Some floppies do maintain a "one sector equals one cluster" format, but with larger disks, such as hard disks, this would present a management overhead problem for DOS. Hard disks with greater than 20,740 total sectors get four sectors per cluster (2K clusters), whereas others generally get eight sectors per cluster (4K clusters). With nonstandard driver software, changing these values is possible.

Root Directory. The root directory is stored on the disk immediately after the file allocation tables. The root directory varies in size depending on the type of disk and its capacity. The root directory is a fixed length and cannot be changed. A 32M DOS partition has a root directory of 512 entries. Subdirectories are stored as files, and they have no such length limits. A directory entry is 32 bytes long, and the bytes contain specific information, such as the following:

Bytes	Contains
0-7	File name
8-10	Extension
11	Attribute
12-21	Reserved
22-23	Time of creation
24-25	Date of creation
26-27	Starting cluster
28-31	Size in bytes

Data Area. These clusters are the ones that store file data on the disk. This area is managed by the directories and file allocation table.

Known Bugs in DOS

Few things are more frustrating than finding out that software you depend on every day has some bugs and problems. But this is the case even with DOS. Every version of DOS ever produced has had bugs and problems, and you must simply expect them as a fact of life. Some of the problems are never actually resolved; you must live with them.

Sometimes the problems are severe enough, however, that IBM (and Microsoft) issues a patch disk that corrects the problems. You should keep in touch with your dealer to find out about these patches. Neither IBM nor your dealer will call to tell you about the patch disk. You should check in periodically to see whether any patch disks are available. Part of the job of being an IBM dealer is to distribute these patch disks and fixes to customers at the customer's request. Also, these patches are to be provided free of charge. You do not need to go back to the dealer where you purchased your DOS; any dealer must provide the patches for free. If a dealer does not know about these patches or does not provide the patches for any reason, whether or not you have ever bought anything there, you should contact another dealer for the patch disk. DOS is a warranted product and these patches are part of that warranty service.

The following information is provided by IBM in the patches for DOS 3.3 and 4.0. Both versions have official patch disks produced by IBM that are available at no cost from your nearest IBM dealer.

DOS 3.3 Patches and Fixes

The official patches and fixes from IBM for DOS 3.3 were issued from IBM's National Support Center on October 9, 1987. This disk fixes a number of problems with DOS 3.3. PS/2 systems and DOS 3.3 particularly had some problems. A special driver was provided to fix these problems. All these problems have been corrected in DOS 4.0, and the driver is not needed when you're using that version. The following problems were noted:

- Backup would not work properly when backing up a large number of subdirectories in a given directory. A new program called I17.COM resolves problems with slow serial printers that have small input buffers. Under some conditions, DOS displays a false "Out of paper" error when attempting to print.

Special problems occurred in the interaction of DOS 3.3 and the ROM BIOS of IBM PS/2 Models 50, 60, and 80. A special device driver called DASDDRVR.SYS is provided to fix these problems. DASDDRVR.SYS (Version 1.2) is a 698-byte file. This file fixes several problems with DOS 3.3 and the following PS/2 models:

```
8550-021
8560-041
8560-071
8580-041
8580-071
```

The problems are as follows:

- Intermittent read failures on 720K original applications software floppy disks on Models 50, 60, and 80 PS/2 systems. You may see Not Ready Error Reading Drive A when attempting to install an application. Attempts to perform DIR or COPY commands from the disk also produce the error message.

- Highly intermittent problems with either a floppy drive Not Ready Error Reading Drive A or a hard disk General Failure message. This problem may be aggravated by certain programming practices that mask off interrupts for long periods of time. This update ensures that interrupts are unmasked on each hard disk or floppy disk request.

- FORMAT fails on multiple 3 1/2-inch disks. The failure appears as a Track 0 bad or invalid media message when a user replies yes to the prompt Format another (Y/N)? after the first format is complete. The failure message appears when you're attempting to format the second disk. If the system is booted from disk, the format problem does not occur.

- 301 (keyboard) and 8602 (mouse) POST error messages. When power is interrupted or switched on and off quickly on a PS/2, a 301 and 8602 error may be posted.

- 162 (CMOS checksum/configuration) or 163 (Clock not updating) errors, and various other time-of-day problems. One example of a time-of-day problem is turning on the system in the morning and finding the time set at when the system was turned off the day before.

DOS 4.0 Patches and Fixes

A set of patches also is available for DOS 4.0. These patches are automatically included on disks marked "DOS 4.01." You need to look at the small print on the original disk to find out whether your DOS is the 4.01 version. If you use the DOS VER command, it always reports 4.00 instead and gives you no indication of whether you have the patches or not. The patch disk is known officially as Program Temporary Fix (PTF) UR22624 at IBM, and you may use this number when contacting your dealer or IBM for your free patch disk. This patch was made available on August 15, 1988.

These patches comprise two 3 1/2-inch disks or three 5 1/4-inch disks. Be sure to get the patches on the type of disk that your machine can boot from, because you install the patches by booting from the first disk.

The following is a list of some of the new files and a description of the problems they fix. These files are provided with either the PTF patch disk or the DOS 4.01 version.

New File	Fix
IBMBIO	Using INT 2FH for INT 67H causes the system to hang up (stop).
IBMDOS	Using "BUFFERS = XX /X" in CONFIG.SYS would not work correctly.
IBMDOS	Copying large files across a network would not work correctly.

New File	Fix
APPEND	The "/PATH:OFF" parameter was not working properly.
MODE	The MODE command would overwrite the user's application.
MODE	The MODE command would incorrectly allow a 19,200 baud rate on PS/2 Models 25 and 30.
PRINT	You would get a "nonexisting" file message the first time the PRINT command was invoked.
SELECT	Using CTRL/BREAK with the shell could hang up the system.
SELECT	The listing of printers should be reordered.
XMA2EMS	This program would sometimes hang up the system if you had a Token Ring network adapter.
XMA2EMS	There were problems in using DMA transfers to EMS.
XMA2EMS	The PS/2 Model 50Z cannot use DOS 4.00 EMS.
SHELL	Numerous problems with the shell.
SHELLC	Numerous problems with the shell.

Using the DOS Disk and Data Recovery Team

The CHKDSK, RECOVER, and DEBUG commands are the DOS damaged disk recovery team. They are crude and sometimes drastic in the actions they take, but at times they are all that is available or needed. RECOVER usually is known for its purpose as a data recovery program, and CHKDSK usually is used for innocent inspection of the file structure. Many users are unaware that

CHKDSK actually can implement repairs to a damaged file structure. DEBUG is a crude, manually controlled program that can be used to help in the case of a disk disaster, provided that you know exactly what you are doing.

The CHKDSK Command

CHKDSK.COM is a useful and straightforward program designed primarily to provide a memory statistics report for the PC's memory. CHKDSK.COM also has a minimum amount of file management capabilities for the magnetic media in the chosen disk drive.

Primarily, you use CHKDSK to answer questions like the following:

How much usable disk space is left?
How much usable RAM is left?
How fragmented are the disk files?
Is the file management system intact?

Files that are loaded into contiguous tracks and sectors of the disk are naturally more efficient. If they are spread over wide areas of the disk, access operations take longer. DOS always knows the location of all a file's fragments by using the pointer numbers in the file allocation table. These pointers are data that direct DOS to the next segment of the file. Sometimes, for various reasons, these pointers may be lost or corrupted and DOS is no longer able to locate some portion of a file. CHKDSK can alert you to this condition and even reclaim this unused file space for use by another file.

First, try the most basic of the program's commands and examine the results. Make sure that the program CHKDSK.COM is available and then type the following at the DOS prompt:

CHKDSK

Note that the drive light is activated for a time, and then a message similar to the following appears:

```
Volume MBS        created Dec 29, 1985 1:11p

 33280000 bytes total disk space
  2138112 bytes in 4 hidden files
   163840 bytes in 68 directories
```

```
27009024 bytes in 1991 user files
   81920 bytes in bad sectors
 3887104 bytes available on disk

  655360 bytes total memory    296096 bytes free
```

The line reporting the volume label only occurs if the selected disk previously has been given a volume name. If there are any problems with the integrity of the DOS file system, you also see a message similar to the following:

```
Errors found, F parameter not specified. Corrections will not be
written to disk.
```

Further messages indicate the actual problem. Usually these problems are either "lost clusters" or files that are "cross-linked." The messages reporting each of these problems look like the following:

```
X lost clusters found in Y chains. Convert lost chains to files
(Y/N)?

AAAA.XYZ is cross linked on cluster XXX
BBBB.XYZ is cross linked on cluster XXX
```

A lost cluster is a unit of storage with a pointer that says the cluster is in use by a file, but no directory entry claims ownership of that cluster. Basically, you can think of a chain of these lost clusters as a file fragment with no name. These fragments usually are created by programs that are terminated before they can finish an operation. A program usually writes to clusters on the disk as it saves information and then finishes the operation by closing the file, which allows DOS to create the directory entry for the file. If the program is terminated before any open files are closed, the lost clusters are the likely result.

If you answer yes to the `Convert lost chains to files` question, then CHKDSK gives the fragment a directory entry or name. The name it uses is FILE0000.CHK, and if there are any more fragments, they are given the name FILE0001.CHK, and so on. You may then examine these files to see whether they contain any necessary information. If not, simply delete the files. If you answer no, the lost cluster pointers are simply zeroed to indicate that these clusters are now available for other files to use.

By the way, because you did not specify the /F parameter when you ran CHKDSK, the program is actually prevented from making any corrections to the disk. Instead, all repairs are conducted in a mock fashion. This is a safety feature, because sometimes you do not want CHKDSK to take action before you first examine and think about the problem at hand. After deciding on the correct course of action, the CHKDSK command can be repeated with the /F parameter (which stands for "fix").

Cross-linked files are a more serious problem. This message indicates that two or more files claim ownership of the same cluster. Basically, this error is in the file allocation table pointer structure, which has several file fragments pointing to the same individual cluster on the disk. Only one file can actually own the cluster. To recover from this problem, make a copy of each of the files listed as cross-linked and then delete the original cross-linked versions from the disk. The delete action cleans up the file allocation table entries for these files by zeroing them out, and the cross-linking problem is now corrected. Now, examine each of the files you just copied. At best, only one of all the files linked together is intact and correct. The others contain garbage at the point where the cross-linking had taken place and probably need to be restored from a backup or re-created.

CHKDSK also can check a file or group of files for fragmentation; it can report just how many fragments a file has been split into on the disk. If you want to check all the files in a single directory for fragmentation, you type the following at the DOS prompt:

CHKDSK *.*

If the file FOO.BAR was not saved as one complete block, you see the following message on-screen:

```
\FOO.BAR Contains XX non-contiguous blocks.
```

This message tells you that when DOS originally saved this file to disk, it was not able to place the entire file in one area of the disk. Instead, the system was forced to break up the file and place it in more than one area of the disk and then set up pointers to help it find the entire file later. Fragmentation is not a problem unless you have many files in this condition, or the number of fragments is excessive (more than 50 or so). If this is the case, you may be wise to format a new disk; then use the COPY *.* command to copy your files to the newly formatted floppy. This method saves your files in contiguous locations on the new floppy, thus returning them to a more efficient format. This method works for floppy disks, but for hard disks, a complete backup, reformat, and restore operation is required. To make this easier, many companies have released "defragmenting" programs that can work "in place" on the disk and do not require the reformat and restore that the DOS method requires. Notice that the backup is still required no matter how you do the defragmenting. Imagine what would happen if the power were to go out while the unfragment program was descrambling your disk. Make a backup for safety.

The CHKDSK program has two parameters that may be used when the program is activated. These are the /F and /V parameters. The /F (fix) parameter allows CHKDSK to recover lost allocation units on the disk. The /V (verbose) parameter causes CHKDSK to display the name of each file name as it processes the DOS file structure.

To run the program using the /F command you type the following at the DOS prompt:

    CHKDSK /F

If any lost clusters were noted, you are now given the opportunity to recover these units. Assume that you see the following message:

    2 lost clusters found in 1 chains. Convert lost chains to files
    (Y/N)?

You reply with yes. Then you see the same messages as noted in our first use of the program. Now, after looking more closely, you find a new line displayed:

    XXXXX bytes in 1 recovered file

If you now check the directory, you find that a new file has been added. Because there was only one bad chain, you find FILE0000.CHK. If more chains were noted in the error message, you would have seen a correspondingly larger number of these new files, listed in sequence. Now that DOS has stored this data for you, you may check the file to see what data it contains. If you want to retain this data, rename the file as necessary and go on to other tasks. If not, erase this file, thus reclaiming the disk space for later use.

Remember, problems reported by CHKDSK usually are problems with software and not hardware. Although it is certainly possible, I have never seen a case where "lost clusters" or "cross-linked" files were caused directly by a hardware fault. The cause is a defective program or a program that is stopped before it can close files. A hardware fault certainly can stop a program before it can close files, and many people believe that these error messages signify some fault with the disk hardware. However, this is almost never the case.

A good practice is to run CHKDSK at least once a day on any hard disk system. Finding out about file structure errors as soon as possible is important. Whenever a program terminates abnormally, or the system crashes for some reason, run CHKDSK to see whether any file system damage has occurred.

The RECOVER Command

The DOS RECOVER command is designed to mark clusters as "bad" in the file allocation table when these clusters cannot be read properly. When a file cannot be read due to a problem with a sector on the disk going bad, the RECOVER command can mark the file allocation table so that those particular clusters are not used by another file. Essentially, they are barricaded off so that another file will never occupy those clusters. When used improperly, this program is highly dangerous to your data.

Users have a misunderstanding of how this program operates. Many believe that this program is used to recover the file or the data within the file in question. What really happens is that only the portion of the file before the defect is recovered or otherwise remains after the RECOVER command operates on it. The defective portion is marked off as bad in the file allocation table, and all data after the defect is returned to available status. You should always make a copy of the file to be recovered, because the COPY command will be able to get all of the information, including that after the location of the defect. The defective portion of the information, however, is gibberish.

An example might help explain how to use this command. Suppose that you are using a word processing program and tell it to load a file called DOCUMENT.TXT. The hard disk has developed a defect in a sector that is used by this file, and in the middle of loading it, you see the following message appear on the screen:

```
Sector not found error reading drive C
Abort, Retry, Ignore, Fail?
```

Normally, attempt to retry by typing *r*. You may be able to read the file on a retry, so attempt this several times. If you can load the file by retrying, then simply save the loaded version to a file with a different name, and you have preserved the data in the file. You still need to repair the structure of the disk so that this space is not going to be used again. If, after 10 retries or so, you still cannot read the file, the data will be more difficult to recover.

This recovery operation has two phases. The first phase is to preserve as much of the data in the file as possible. The second phase is to mark the file allocation table so that these bad sectors or clusters of the disk are not used again.

For the first phase, recovering the data in the file, use the DOS COPY command to make a copy of the file, giving it a different name. For example, type the following at the C prompt:

    copy document.txt document.new

Of course, in the middle of the copy, you see the Sector not found error message as before. The key to this operation is to answer with the Ignore option so that the bad sectors are simply ignored and the copy operation can continue to the end of the file. This procedure produces an intact copy of the file with all the file up to the error location as well as after the error location. The bad sectors themselves appear as gibberish in the new copied file, but at least the entire copy is completely readable. You probably need to use your word processor to load this new copy and remove or retype the garbled sectors, because they are permanently lost. Of course, if this file was a binary file, such as part of a program, you probably have to consider the whole thing a total loss, because you really do not have the option of "retyping" the bytes that make up a program file. Your only hope in this case is to have a backup of the file, which you should have anyway. This completes the first phase, which has now recovered as much of the data as is possible. Now you go on to the second phase, which is to mark the disk so that these areas cannot be used again.

Marking the disk is accomplished by the RECOVER command itself. After making the attempted recovery of the data (the first phase), you can mark the bad sectors in the file allocation table by using the RECOVER command and typing the following at the C prompt:

    recover document.txt

You see the following message:

    Press any key to begin recovery of the
    file(s) on drive C:

    XXXXX of YYYYY bytes recovered

The file DOCUMENT.TXT still is on the disk after this operation, but it has been truncated at the location of the error. Any sectors that the RECOVER command could not read are marked as "bad sectors" in the file allocation table. These show up the next time that a CHKDSK command is run. You might want to run CHKDSK before and after running the RECOVER command to see the effect of the additional bad sectors.

You then should delete the DOCUMENT.TXT file, because you have already created a copy of it with as much good data as is possible. This completes the second phase and, thus, the entire operation.

You now have a new file with as much of the original file as is possible, and the disk file allocation table is marked so that the defective location will not be a bother to you again.

As a final word, remember to be careful when using the RECOVER program, because when it is used improperly, it can do a great deal of damage to your files and the file allocation table. If you enter the RECOVER command without a file name for it to work on, the program assumes that you want *every file on the disk* recovered. The program then proceeds to operate on each and every file and subdirectory on the disk. All subdirectories are converted to actual files, and all file names are placed in the root directory and given the names FILE0000.REC, FILE0001.REC, and so on. This process essentially wipes out the file system on the entire disk. ***Warning:*** Do not use the RECOVER command without providing a file name for it to work on. This program is so dangerous to data when misused that you should immediately delete it from the hard disk, to prevent accidentally invoking this program.

The DEBUG Command

The DEBUG program included with DOS versions prior to 4.0 is a powerful debugging tool for technicians and programmers. For DOS 4.0 and later, DEBUG is included with the DOS Technical Reference Manual. It is a crude tool and is not very "friendly." The greatest thing about DEBUG is that everybody already has it, and it was basically free. Some of the things you can do with the DEBUG command are the following:

- Display data from any memory location
- Move blocks of data between memory locations

- Enter data directly into any memory location
- Read disk sectors into memory
- Write disk sectors from memory
- Write short assembly language programs
- Display the assembly source code of programs
- Trace the execution of a program
- Display or alter the contents of the CPU registers
- Input from a port
- Output to a port
- Perform hexadecimal addition and subtraction

To use the DEBUG program, make sure that DEBUG.COM is in the current directory or in the current DOS PATH and type the following at the C prompt:

DEBUG [file]

When the DEBUG prompt is displayed (-), you can enter a DEBUG command.

DEBUG is limited in how it is normally used. With more powerful programs available in the marketplace for debugging and assembling code, the most common use for DEBUG these days is patching assembly language programs to correct problems or to change an existing program feature.

DEBUG also can be used to read and write to a disk sector directly, but you must be careful with this feature. You must know precisely what you are doing when writing to a disk, or you can really mess it up. A backup of the hard disk or floppy disk you are using should be made before you try this area of the DEBUG program. You also may want to experiment on a floppy disk that has no important data on it, but be careful because DEBUG can read and write to or from any drive on the system.

Recognizing Memory-Resident Software Conflicts

One area where many users get into trouble is with memory-resident software. This software loads itself into memory and stays there, waiting for some activation key (usually a keystroke combination). The programs that can be activated by a key combination are sometimes called pop-up utilities or programs.

The problem with resident programs is that they often can conflict with each other as well as with applications programs or even DOS itself. Many types of problems can be experienced; sometimes these problems appear consistently, but other times the problems are intermittent. Some computer users do not like to use this type of software as a general rule, unless absolutely necessary.

If you are experiencing problems that you have traced to a memory-resident program conflict, the common way to correct the problem is to eliminate one of the programs that are conflicting. Another fix is to change the load order of the programs. Sometimes certain programs like to be "first," and others need to be "last." This order preference often can be discovered only by pure trial and error.

Finally, remember that device drivers also are a form of memory-resident software, and loading these drivers in CONFIG.SYS can be the cause of many problems. Again, eliminating the driver programs that cause the problem, as well as changing the load order, may solve the problems.

Unfortunately, these resident program conflicts and problems are likely to be around as long as DOS is used. But the light at the end of the tunnel is OS/2. The problem with DOS is that no real rules are established as to how resident programs should interact with each other as well as with the rest of the system. OS/2 is built on the concept of many programs resident in memory at once, all multitasking as well. This operating system will put an end to the problem of resident programs conflicting with each other.

Distinguishing between Hardware and Software Problems

One of the most aggravating situations in computer repair is opening up a system and troubleshooting all the hardware only to find later that the cause of the problem was a program, not the hardware itself. Many people have spent large sums of money on replacement hardware such as motherboards, disk drives, adapter boards, cables, and so on, all on the premise that the hardware was the cause of the problem when software actually was the culprit. To eliminate these aggravating, sometimes embarrassing, and often expensive situations, you must be able to distinguish a hardware problem from a software problem.

Fortunately, making this distinction is fairly simple. Often, software problems are caused by the custom configurations that many systems carry (the extensive CONFIG.SYS and AUTOEXEC.BAT files that load all kinds of resident programs and specify different configuration parameters). One of the first things to do when you suspect a software problem is to boot off of a "virgin" DOS disk that has no CONFIG.SYS or AUTOEXEC.BAT configuration files on board. Test for the problem that had been occurring, and if it has disappeared, the cause was likely something in these two files. At this point, begin restoring the files, one command line at a time, and retest each time to see where the actual problem lies. As indicated in the preceding section, you may have to change the order of command lines in these files or eliminate entirely the offending program or configuration item.

DOS can cause other problems, such as bugs or incompatibilities with certain hardware items. DOS 3.2 does not support the 1.44M floppy drive format, for example, so using this DOS version in a system equipped with one of those drives may lead you to believe (incorrectly) that the drive is bad. Be sure that you are using the correct version of DOS and that support is provided for the hardware you have. Find out whether your version of DOS has any official patches available; sometimes a problem you are experiencing may be one that many others have had, and IBM or Microsoft has released a fix disk that takes care of the problem. A perfect example of this is the floppy formatting problem that many PS/2 users have had under DOS 3.3. They would get a track 0 bad message after answering yes to the Format another message. This problem was solved by a special driver file found on the DOS 3.3 patch disk.

If you are having a problem related to a piece of applications software, you always should contact the company that produces the software and explain the problem to them. They may have a patched or fixed version if there really is a bug, or maybe you are operating the software in some strange or incorrect way.

Chapter Summary

In this chapter you examined the software side of your system. Often, a problem can exist in the software and not be hardware related. The chapter examined DOS and showed how DOS organizes information on a disk. You learned about the CHKDSK, RECOVER, and DEBUG commands to see how DOS can help you with data and disk recovery. Finally, the chapter examined resident software and the problems it can cause and gave you an idea of how to distinguish a software problem from a hardware problem.

16

A Final Word

The content of this book covers most of the components of an IBM or IBM-compatible personal computer system. In this book, you discovered how all the components operate and interact and how these components should be set up and installed. You looked at ways components fail and learned the symptoms of these failures. And, finally, you reviewed the steps in diagnosing and troubleshooting all the major components in the system so that you can locate and replace the failing component.

The information that I have collected and presented in this book represents years of practical experience with IBM and compatible systems. A great deal of research and investigation also have gone into each section. This information has saved companies many thousands of dollars.

Bringing microcomputer service and support in-house is one of the best ways to save a great deal of money today. The elimination of service contracts for most systems and the reduction of downtime are just two of the benefits to be realized through the application of the information presented here. As I have also indicated, you can save a great deal of money on component purchases by eliminating the middleman and purchasing the components directly from distributors or manufacturers. Most people cannot take advantage of direct purchasing, however, because it requires a whole new level of understanding of the component. This deeper level of knowledge and understanding is what I hope I have been able to give you in this book.

You can go many places today to gather information such as that presented in this book. I have personally taught several thousands of individuals this information through a seminar series presented for the American Institute. In presenting this information, I am often asked where more of this type of information can be obtained and whether I have any "secrets" for acquiring this knowledge. Well, there are no secrets, but I do know of several key sources of information that can make you a verifiable expert in PC upgrade and repair.

I have four key sources for the type of information that helps me (and can help you) solve upgrading, repairing, and general troubleshooting problems. These sources are the four M's:

> Manuals
> Machines
> Modems
> Magazines

Manuals—let me say it again—*manuals* are the single most important source of information you have. Unfortunately, manuals happen to be one of the most frequently overlooked sources of information. I owe much of my knowledge to pouring over the various technical reference manuals and other Original Equipment Manufacturers (OEM) manuals. I will not even consider purchasing a system that does not have a detailed technical reference manual available.

Let me use a simple analogy to explain the importance of manuals and documentation, as well as other issues concerning repair and maintenance of a system. Compare your business use of computers to a taxicab company. The company needs to purchase automobiles to use as cabs. The owners purchase not one car, but an entire fleet of cars. Do you think that they would purchase a fleet of automobiles based solely on performance or gas mileage statistics? Would they neglect to consider ongoing maintenance and service of these automobiles? Would they purchase a fleet of cars that could be serviced only by the original manufacturer and for which parts could not be purchased at all? Do you think that they would buy a car that did not have available a detailed service and repair manual? Would they buy some foreign-produced automobile for which parts were scarce and long waits for parts were inevitable? The answer (of course) to all these questions is No, No, No!

Doesn't your business (especially a larger one) use what amounts to a "fleet" of computers? If so, then why don't you think of this fleet as cars of the cab company, which would go out of business rapidly if these cars could not be kept running smoothly and inexpensively.

Now you know why the Checker Marathon automobile was so popular with cab companies. That car hardly changed at all over the span of its availability. In many ways, the standard PC and AT systems are like the venerable Checker Marathon. You can get technical information by the shelfful for these systems. You can get parts from so many sources that anything you need is immediately available—and at a discounted price.

But I still find people specifying for their companies computers that have no technical documentation, have no spare parts program or sell parts only to dealers, use nonstandard shaped and designed components available only from the company that made them, and so on. The upgrade, repair, and maintenance of the company's computer systems always seem to take a back seat to performance and style.

In addition to manuals, many good reference and tutorial books are available on the market today. Que specializes in computer books of this type, and my shelf is full of books from Que and the other major publishers.

The second item on the list, *machines*, refers to the systems themselves. The actual systems are one of my best sources of information. Suppose that I need to answer the question "Will this board work with that board?" The answer is as simple as plugging in both boards and pressing the switch. Experiments and observations of running systems are two of the best learning tools at your disposal. I recommend trying everything; rarely does anything you do really harm the equipment. Data is another thing, however, so keep regular backups as insurance! I know that people are much more reluctant to experiment with a system that cost them a great deal of money, but much can be learned through these systems directly.

The third item, *modems*, refers to the use of public information utilities, which are a modem and a phone call away. You can tie into electronic bulletin boards and information exchanges all over the country. These resources include computer enthusiasts and technical support people from various organizations, as well as experts in virtually all areas of these systems. This method can be a great way to have questions answered and to collect useful utility and help programs that can make your job much easier. The world of public-domain and user-supported software awaits, as well as more technical information and related experiences than you could ever imagine.

One of my favorite sources of information is the public access utility CompuServe. This source is a cluster of mainframe systems, based in Ohio, which you can log into from virtually anywhere in the country through a local telephone call. Among CompuServe's resources are special interest groups (SIGs), sponsored by most of the major software and hardware companies. Some interesting discussions take place in the SIGs. CompuServe, combined with a local electronic bulletin board or two, can greatly supplement the information you gather from other sources.

The last source of information, *magazines*, is one of the best sources of up-to-date reviews and technical data. Also featured are "bug fixes," problem alerts, and general industry news. Keeping a printed book up-to-date with the latest events in this industry is difficult. Things move so fast that the magazines themselves can hardly keep pace. I subscribe to most of the major magazines available and am hard pressed to pick any as the best. They are all important to me, and each one gives me different information—or the same information with a different angle or twist.

In the Appendix of this book, you will find a list of the vendors whose products have been named in this book and another list of the part numbers and prices for all of IBM's technical documentation and manuals.

I hope that this book has been beneficial to you and your business, and I hope that you have enjoyed reading it as much as I have enjoyed writing it!

Appendix

In this Appendix, you will find a great deal of useful information. This is mainly reference information, not designed to be "read" but instead to be "looked up." This information can be useful in your troubleshooting or upgrading sessions and is usually spread out among too many sources.

You will find information in the form of many reference charts and tables. In particular, you will find information as to the default interrupt, DMA channel, I/O port, and memory usage of the primary system and most standard options. This information is invaluable for those of you who are installing new boards or upgrading your system in any way. This information can prove important when you're troubleshooting a conflict between any two devices.

Some charts indicate the physical to logical organization of memory on the standard IBM types of motherboards. This information is useful for memory troubleshooting sessions, when you must take a logical address value and determine which physical chips or components are involved.

I have included charts indicating the hard disk drive tables found in the two versions of the IBM XT hard disk controller, as well as all versions of IBM AT system ROM BIOS to date. This information is necessary when you're adding a hard disk to any systems using these components. Note that most AT types of compatibles have a table whose values differ from IBM's, especially for any entries over 15. Users of these systems must resort to their system's technical reference manual.

One of the most useful tables in the Appendix is a concise listing of the IBM diagnostics error codes. These are the codes that can be generated by the POST (power-on self test) as well as the disk-based diagnostics programs. The codes are not documented by IBM in tabular form anywhere, and this compilation comes from the various hardware maintenance service, technical reference, and other manuals produced by IBM. I found some of the codes from directly reading the commented ROM listings in the technical reference manuals. You will find this information useful in deciphering the codes that are produced, without having to look through a stack of books.

Also included is a listing of all the available IBM technical manuals and a description of all the documentation available. The listing includes part numbers and pricing information as well as information useful in ordering this documentation.

The next section of the Appendix is a vendor list. Here, you will find a list of the various product vendors whose products—both hardware and software—have been mentioned throughout the book. This information is provided so that you can inquire further about the products mentioned, as well as locate a place to purchase the products. Of particular interest are the listings for the IBM service parts locations, which are the depots for parts distribution and purchase within IBM.

Although all this information has come from a wide variety of sources, most of it comes from the technical reference manuals and hardware maintenance service manuals available for various systems from IBM and other manufacturers. These documents are invaluable for those of you who really want to pursue this topic more extensively.

Charts

This section lists a variety of charts and tables describing the usage and allocation of various system resources. This information covers interrupts, DMA channels, I/O ports, memory usage, hard disk tables, and more. You also will find a listing of the meanings of the IBM error code numbers, which should be very useful for most people.

Standard ASCII Character Codes

Dec	Hex	Char		Control Code	Dec	Hex	Char	Dec	Hex	Char	Dec	Hex	Char
0	0	Ctrl-@	NULL	Null	32	20	SP	64	40	@	96	60	`
1	1	Ctrl-A	SOH	Start of Heading	33	21	!	65	41	A	97	61	a
2	2	Ctrl-B	STX	Start of Text	34	22	"	66	42	B	98	62	b
3	3	Ctrl-C	ETX	End of Text	35	23	#	67	43	C	99	63	c
4	4	Ctrl-D	EOT	End of Transmit	36	24	$	68	44	D	100	64	d
5	5	Ctrl-E	ENQ	Enquiry	37	25	%	69	45	E	101	65	e
6	6	Ctrl-F	ACK	Acknowledge	38	26	&	70	46	F	102	66	f
7	7	Ctrl-G	BEL	Bell	39	27	'	71	47	G	103	67	g
8	8	Ctrl-H	BS	Backspace	40	28	(	72	48	H	104	68	h
9	9	Ctrl-I	HT	Horizontal Tab	41	29	)	73	49	I	105	69	i
10	0A	Ctrl-J	LF	Line Feed	42	2A	*	74	4A	J	106	6A	j
11	0B	Ctrl-K	VT	Vertical Tab	43	2B	+	75	4B	K	107	6B	k
12	0C	Ctrl-L	FF	Form Feed	44	2C	,	76	4C	L	108	6C	l
13	0D	Ctrl-M	CR	Carriage Return	45	2D	-	77	4D	M	109	6D	m
14	0E	Ctrl-N	SO	Shift Out	46	2E	.	78	4E	N	110	6E	n
15	0F	Ctrl-O	SI	Shift In	47	2F	/	79	4F	O	111	6F	o
16	10	Ctrl-P	DLE	Data Line Escape	48	30	0	80	50	P	112	70	p
17	11	Ctrl-Q	DC1	Device Control 1	49	31	1	81	51	Q	113	71	q
18	12	Ctrl-R	DC2	Device Control 2	50	32	2	82	52	R	114	72	r
19	13	Ctrl-S	DC3	Device Control 3	51	33	3	83	53	S	115	73	s
20	14	Ctrl-T	DC4	Device Control 4	52	34	4	84	54	T	116	74	t
21	15	Ctrl-U	NAK	Negative Acknowledge	53	35	5	85	55	U	117	75	u
22	16	Ctrl-V	SYN	Synchronous Idle	54	36	6	86	56	V	118	76	v
23	17	Ctrl-W	ETB	End of Transmit Block	55	37	7	87	57	W	119	77	w
24	18	Ctrl-X	CAN	Cancel	56	38	8	88	58	X	120	78	x
25	19	Ctrl-Y	EM	End of Medium	57	39	9	89	59	Y	121	79	y
26	1A	Ctrl-Z	SUB	Substitute	58	3A	:	90	5A	Z	122	7A	z
27	1B	Ctrl-[	ESC	Escape	59	3B	;	91	5B	[	123	7B	{
28	1C	Ctrl-\	FS	File Separator	60	3C	<	92	5C	\	124	7C	|
29	1D	Ctrl-]	GS	Group Separator	61	3D	=	93	5D	]	125	7D	}
30	1E	Ctrl-^	RS	Record Separator	62	3E	>	94	5E	^	126	7E	~
31	1F	Ctrl-_	US	Unit Separator	63	3F	?	95	5F	_	127	7F	DEL

ASCII Character Code Chart

The preceding chart lists all the standard 7-bit ASCII codes and their decimal value, hexadecimal value, the actual character, and for the control codes (the first 32 codes), the mnemonic and full-length names for the code.

Interrupt Channels

Interrupt Request Channels (IRQ) are used by various hardware devices to signal the motherboard that a request must be fulfilled. These channels are represented by wires on the motherboard and in the slot connectors. Each interrupt is usually designated for a single hardware device, and most of the time cannot be "shared."

A device can be designed to share interrupts, and a few devices will allow this, but most cannot because of the way that interrupts are signaled. The PS/2 systems have revamped this signaling scheme, and now several boards easily can share an interrupt in these systems. Because they cannot usually be shared in the earlier systems, you often will run out of interrupts when adding boards to a system. If two boards use the same interrupt level to signal the system, a conflict will cause neither board to operate properly. These charts will allow you to see what interrupt channels that any standard devices use and what may be free in your system. Note that the AT systems have twice the number of interrupts and usually can be expanded much more easily.

PC and XT System Interrupts

The PC and XT have eight standard prioritized levels of interrupt, with the lower priority six (numbered 2 through 7) being bussed to the system expansion slots. Also, a special Non-Maskable Interrupt (NMI) exists, which has the highest priority of all. They are used as follows in order of priority:

IRQ	Use
NMI	Parity check, 8087
0	Channel 0 of the timer/counter for time of day clock
1	Keyboard
2	Most network adapters
3	Secondary asynchronous communications (COM2:)
4	Primary asynchronous communications (COM1: or AUX:)
5	Fixed disk controller
6	Floppy disk controller
7	Parallel printer port (PRN: or LPT1:)

AT System Interrupts

The AT supports 16 standard levels of interrupt, with 11 channels bussed to the expansion slots. Also, a special Non-Maskable Interrupt (NMI) exists, which has the highest priority. Two Intel 8259A controllers are used, with 8 channels per chip. The interrupts from the second chip are cascaded through IRQ 2 on the first chip. Interrupts 0, 1, 2, 8, and 13 are *not* on the bus connectors and are not accessible to expansion adapters. Note that the interrupts 8, 10, 11, 12, 13, 14, and 15 are from the second interrupt controller and are accessible only by boards that use the 16-bit extension connector. Also note that any board set to IRQ 2 will automatically be redirected as IRQ 9 even if it is an 8-bit board.

The interrupts are used as follows:

IRQ	Use
NMI	Parity check
0	Timer
1	Keyboard
2	Cascaded interrupts from second 8259 (IRQ 8-15)

	IRQ	Use
	8	Real time clock
	9	Redirected from IRQ 2 (appears as IRQ 2)
	10	Reserved
	11	Reserved
	12	Reserved
	13	80287 coprocessor
	14	Fixed disk controller
	15	Reserved

IRQ	Use
3	Serial port 2 (COM2:)
4	Serial port 1 (COM1:)
5	Parallel port 2 (LPT2:)
6	Diskette controller
7	Parallel port 1 (LPT1:)

Direct Memory Access (DMA) Channels

DMA channels are used by any high-speed communications devices that must send and receive information at high speed with the motherboard. A hard disk controller will use DMA, for example, but a floppy controller will not. A serial or parallel port will not use a DMA channel, but a network adapter often will. DMA channels sometimes can be shared if the devices are not of the type that would need them simultaneously. I could have a network adapter and a tape backup adapter both sharing DMA channel 1, for example, but I could not back up while the network was running. To back up during network operation, I would have to ensure that each adapter used a unique DMA channel. Note that twice as many DMA channels are available in an AT type of system.

PC and XT DMA Channels

Four Direct Memory Access (DMA) channels support high-speed data transfers between I/O devices and memory. Three of the channels are bussed to the expansion slots. These PC and XT DMA channels are used as follows:

0	Refresh system dynamic RAM
1	Reserved
2	Reserved
3	Hard disk controller

AT DMA Channels

The AT system supports seven Direct Memory Access (DMA) channels, with six bussed to the expansion slots.

DMA channel 4 is used to cascade channels 0 through 3 to the microprocessor. Channels 0 through 3 are for 8-bit transfers, and channels 5 through 7 are for 16-bit transfers. The AT DMA channels are used as follows:

0	Reserved
1	Reserved
2	Disk
3	Reserved
4	Cascade for DMA 0-3
5	Reserved
6	Reserved
7	Reserved

Port Usage

Input/output ports are addresses used by the processor to communicate with devices directly. These addresses are like memory addresses but are not for storage. There are 1,024 I/O ports available in the IBM system design for both XT and AT types of systems. These I/O ports must be uniquely assigned to only a single board or device, so the potential for conflicts does exist. Generally, more than enough are available to go around, but many boards do not allow the default port addresses to be changed. The charts that follow list the default port usage in PC and AT types of systems.

PC and XT

This chart lists all the default port addresses for any PC type of system. Note that the I/O addresses hex 000 to 0FF are reserved for the system board. Ports hex 100 to 3FF are available on the I/O channel.

PC and XT Type
I/O Port Address Map

Hex Range	Device
200-20F	Game control
201	Game I/O
20C-20D	Reserved
210-217	Expansion unit
21F	Reserved
278-27F	Parallel printer port 2
2B0-2DF	Alternate enhanced graphics adapter
2E1	GPIB (Adapter 0)
2E2 and 2E3	Data acquisition (Adapter 0)
2F8-2FF	Serial port 2
300-31F	Prototype card
320-32F	Fixed disk
348-357	DCA 3278
360-367	PC network (low address)
368-36F	PC network (high address)
378-37F	Parallel printer port 1
380-38F	SDLC, bisynchronous 2
390-393	Cluster
3A0-3AF	Bisynchronous 1
3B0-3BF	Monochrome display and printer adapter
3C0-3CF	Enhanced graphics adapter
3D0-3DF	Color/graphics monitor adapter
3F0-3F7	Disk controller
3F8-3FF	Serial port 1
6E2 and 6E3	Data acquisition (Adapter 1)
790-793	Cluster (Adapter 1)
AE2 and AE3	Data acquisition (Adapter 2)
B90-B93	Cluster (Adapter 2)
EE2 and EE3	Data acquisition (Adapter 3)
1390-1393	Cluster (Adapter 3)
22E1	GPIB (Adapter 1)
2390-2393	Cluster (Adapter 4)
42E1	GPIB (Adapter 2)
62E1	GPIB (Adapter 3)
82E1	GPIB (Adapter 4)
A2E1	GPIB (Adapter 5)
C2E1	GPIB (Adapter 6)
E2E1	GPIB (Adapter 7)

AT

This chart lists all the default port addresses for any AT type of system. Note that the I/O addresses hex 000 to 0FF are reserved for the system board. Ports hex 100 to 3FF are available on the I/O channel.

AT Type
I/O Port Address Map

Hex Range	Device
000-91F	DMA controller 1, 8237A-5
020-03F	Interrupt controller 1, 8259A, master
040-05F	Timer, 8254-2
060	8042 (keyboard)
061	System board I/O port
064	8042 (keyboard)
070-07F	Real time clock, NMI (Non-Maskable Interrupt) Mask
080-09F	DMA page register, 74LS612
0A0-0BF	Interrupt controller 2, 8237A-5
0F0	Clear math coprocessor busy
0F1	Reset math coprocessor
0F8-0FF	Math coprocessor
1F0-1F8	Fixed disk
20C-20D	Reserved
21F	Voice communications adapter
278-27F	Parallel printer port 2
2B0-2DF	Alternate enhanced graphics adapter
2E1	GPIB (Adapter 0)
2E2 and 2E3	Data acquisition (Adapter 0)
2F8-2FF	Serial port 2
300-31F	Prototype adapter
360-363	PC network (low address)
364-367	Reserved
368-36B	PC network (high address)
36C-36F	Reserved
378-37F	Parallel printer port 1
380-38F	SDLC, bisynchronous 2
3A0-3AF	Bisynchronous 1
3B0-3BF	Monochrome display and printer adapter
3C0-3CF	Enhanced graphics adapter
3D0-3DF	Color/graphics monitor adapter

AT Type
I/O Port Address Map—*continued*

Hex Range	Device
3F0-3F7	Disk controller
3F8-3FF	Serial port 1
6E2 and 6E3	Data acquisition (Adapter 1)
AE2 and AE3	Data acquisition (Adapter 2)
EE2 and EE3	Data acquisition (Adapter 3)
22E1	GPIB (Adapter 1)
42E1	GPIB (Adapter 2)
62E1	GPIB (Adapter 3)
82E1	GPIB (Adapter 4)
A2E1	GPIB (Adapter 5)
C2E1	GPIB (Adapter 6)
E2E1	GPIB (Adapter 7)

System Memory Maps

The following maps show where memory is located logically within a system. Two basic maps are provided: one showing the processor-addressable memory in real mode and the other showing processor-addressable memory in protected mode. A third map also is provided; it shows how expanded memory fits into the reserved space between 640K and 1M, and how it is actually not addressable by the processor directly. Expanded memory can only be addressed a small piece (page) at a time through a small window of memory. These maps can be useful for mapping out the logical locations of any of the adapters in your system. All memory locations must be uniquely supplied by a single device, and the potential for conflicts does exist if two devices are mapped into the same logical locations.

1 Megabyte (Real Mode)

The following map shows the logical address locations for an Intel processor running in real mode. Under this mode, the processor can see only 1 megabyte of memory, which is mapped in the following way:

- . = Program-Accessible Memory
- v = Video RAM
- a = Adapter Board ROM and RAM
- r = Motherboard ROM BIOS
- b = IBM Cassette BASIC

```
              IBM 1M Memory Map with 64K/Line

       : 0---1---2---3---4---5---6---7---8---9---A---B---C---D---E---F---
00000: ................................................................
10000: ................................................................
20000: ................................................................
30000: ................................................................
40000: ................................................................
50000: ................................................................
60000: ................................................................
70000: ................................................................
80000: ................................................................
90000: ................................................................
A0000: vvvvvvvvvvvvvvvvvvvvvvvvvvvvvvvvvvvvvvvvvvvvvvvvvvvvvvvvvvvvvvvvvv
B0000: vvvvvvvvvvvvvvvvvvvvvvvvvvvvvvvvvvvvvvvvvvvvvvvvvvvvvvvvvvvvvvvvvv
C0000: aaaaaaaaaaaaaaaaaaaaaaaaaaaaaaaaaaaaaaaaaaaaaaaaaaaaaaaaaaaaaaaaa
D0000: aaaaaaaaaaaaaaaaaaaaaaaaaaaaaaaaaaaaaaaaaaaaaaaaaaaaaaaaaaaaaaaaa
E0000: rrrrrrrrrrrrrrrrrrrrrrrrrrrrrrrrrrrrrrrrrrrrrrrrrrrrrrrrrrrrrrrrr
F0000: rrrrrrrrrrrrrrrrrrrrrrrrrrrbbbbbbbbbbbbbbbbbbbbbbbbbbbbbbrrrrrrrrr
```

16 Megabyte (Protected Mode)

The following map shows the logical address locations for an Intel processor running in protected mode. Under this mode, the processor can see a full 16 megabytes of memory, mapped in the following way:

```
. = Program-Accessible Memory
v = Video RAM
a = Adapter Board ROM and RAM
r = Motherboard ROM BIOS
b = IBM Cassette BASIC
```

IBM 16M Memory Map with 64K/Line

```
        : 0---1---2---3---4---5---6---7---8---9---A---B---C---D---E---F---
000000: ................................................................
010000: ................................................................
020000: ................................................................
030000: ................................................................
040000: ................................................................
050000: ................................................................
060000: ................................................................
070000: ................................................................
080000: ................................................................
090000: ................................................................
0A0000: vvvvvvvvvvvvvvvvvvvvvvvvvvvvvvvvvvvvvvvvvvvvvvvvvvvvvvvvvvvvvvvvvv
0B0000: vvvvvvvvvvvvvvvvvvvvvvvvvvvvvvvvvvvvvvvvvvvvvvvvvvvvvvvvvvvvvvvvvv
0C0000: aaaaaaaaaaaaaaaaaaaaaaaaaaaaaaaaaaaaaaaaaaaaaaaaaaaaaaaaaaaaaaaaa
0D0000: aaaaaaaaaaaaaaaaaaaaaaaaaaaaaaaaaaaaaaaaaaaaaaaaaaaaaaaaaaaaaaaaa
0E0000: rrrrrrrrrrrrrrrrrrrrrrrrrrrrrrrrrrrrrrrrrrrrrrrrrrrrrrrrrrrrrrrrr
0F0000: rrrrrrrrrrrrrrrrrrrrrrrrrrrbbbbbbbbbbbbbbbbbbbbbbbbbbbbbbbbrrrrrrrr
```

Intel real-mode memory ends here. Memory beyond this point is accessible only in protected mode. Only the Intel 80286 and 80386 currently have a protected mode. The 8086 and 8088 do not have a protected mode and therefore cannot access memory beyond the 1M barrier.

```
        : 0---1---2---3---4---5---6---7---8---9---A---B---C---D---E---F---
100000: ................................................................
110000: ................................................................
120000: ................................................................
130000: ................................................................
140000: ................................................................
150000: ................................................................
160000: ................................................................
170000: ................................................................
180000: ................................................................
190000: ................................................................
1A0000: ................................................................
1B0000: ................................................................
1C0000: ................................................................
1D0000: ................................................................
1E0000: ................................................................
1F0000: ................................................................
        : 0---1---2---3---4---5---6---7---8---9---A---B---C---D---E---F---
200000: ................................................................
210000: ................................................................
220000: ................................................................
230000: ................................................................
240000: ................................................................
250000: ................................................................
260000: ................................................................
270000: ................................................................
280000: ................................................................
290000: ................................................................
2A0000: ................................................................
2B0000: ................................................................
2C0000: ................................................................
2D0000: ................................................................
2E0000: ................................................................
2F0000: ................................................................
```

```
       : 0---1---2---3---4---5---6---7---8---9---A---B---C---D---E---F---
300000: ................................................................
310000: ................................................................
320000: ................................................................
330000: ................................................................
340000: ................................................................
350000: ................................................................
360000: ................................................................
370000: ................................................................
380000: ................................................................
390000: ................................................................
3A0000: ................................................................
3B0000: ................................................................
3C0000: ................................................................
3D0000: ................................................................
3E0000: ................................................................
3F0000: ................................................................
       : 0---1---2---3---4---5---6---7---8---9---A---B---C---D---E---F---
400000: ................................................................
410000: ................................................................
420000: ................................................................
430000: ................................................................
440000: ................................................................
450000: ................................................................
460000: ................................................................
470000: ................................................................
480000: ................................................................
490000: ................................................................
4A0000: ................................................................
4B0000: ................................................................
4C0000: ................................................................
4D0000: ................................................................
4E0000: ................................................................
4F0000: ................................................................
       : 0---1---2---3---4---5---6---7---8---9---A---B---C---D---E---F---
500000: ................................................................
510000: ................................................................
520000: ................................................................
530000: ................................................................
540000: ................................................................
550000: ................................................................
560000: ................................................................
570000: ................................................................
580000: ................................................................
590000: ................................................................
5A0000: ................................................................
5B0000: ................................................................
5C0000: ................................................................
5D0000: ................................................................
5E0000: ................................................................
5F0000: ................................................................
```

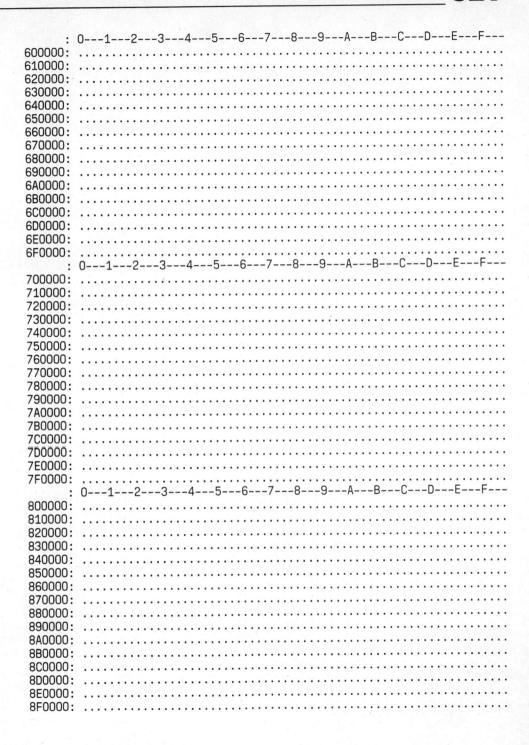

```
        : 0---1---2---3---4---5---6---7---8---9---A---B---C---D---E---F---
900000: ................................................................
910000: ................................................................
920000: ................................................................
930000: ................................................................
940000: ................................................................
950000: ................................................................
960000: ................................................................
970000: ................................................................
980000: ................................................................
990000: ................................................................
9A0000: ................................................................
9B0000: ................................................................
9C0000: ................................................................
9D0000: ................................................................
9E0000: ................................................................
9F0000: ................................................................
        : 0---1---2---3---4---5---6---7---8---9---A---B---C---D---E---F---
A00000: ................................................................
A10000: ................................................................
A20000: ................................................................
A30000: ................................................................
A40000: ................................................................
A50000: ................................................................
A60000: ................................................................
A70000: ................................................................
A80000: ................................................................
A90000: ................................................................
AA0000: ................................................................
AB0000: ................................................................
AC0000: ................................................................
AD0000: ................................................................
AE0000: ................................................................
AF0000: ................................................................
        : 0---1---2---3---4---5---6---7---8---9---A---B---C---D---E---F---
B00000: ................................................................
B10000: ................................................................
B20000: ................................................................
B30000: ................................................................
B40000: ................................................................
B50000: ................................................................
B60000: ................................................................
B70000: ................................................................
B80000: ................................................................
B90000: ................................................................
BA0000: ................................................................
BB0000: ................................................................
BC0000: ................................................................
BD0000: ................................................................
BE0000: ................................................................
BF0000: ................................................................
```

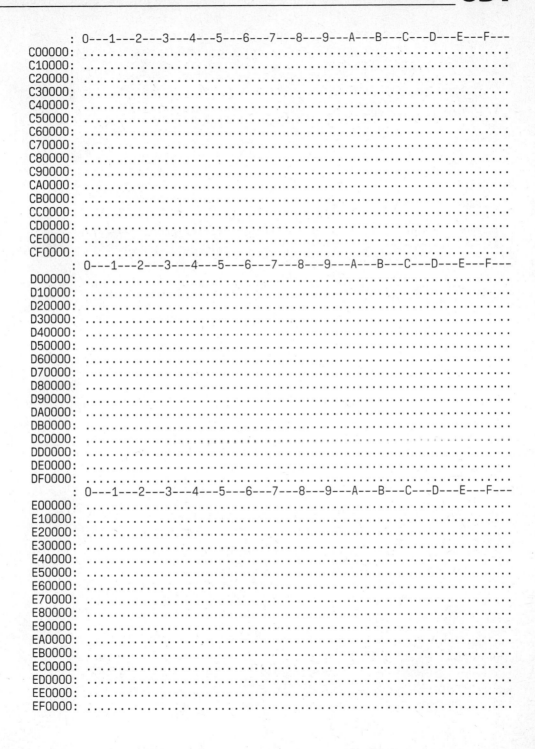

```
          : 0---1---2---3---4---5---6---7---8---9---A---B---C---D---E---F---
F00000: ................................................................
F10000: ................................................................
F20000: ................................................................
F30000: ................................................................
F40000: ................................................................
F50000: ................................................................
F60000: ................................................................
F70000: ................................................................
F80000: ................................................................
F90000: ................................................................
FA0000: ................................................................
FB0000: ................................................................
FC0000: ...........................................,...................
FD0000: ................................................................
FE0000: rrrrrrrrrrrrrrrrrrrrrrrrrrrrrrrrrrrrrrrrrrrrrrrrrrrrrrrrrrrrrrrr
FF0000: rrrrrrrrrrrrrrrrrrrrrrrbbbbbbbbbbbbbbbbbbbbbbbbbbbbbbrrrrrrrrr
```

Note that the motherboard ROM BIOS has a duplicated address space that causes it to "appear" both at the end of the 1M real-mode space and at the end of the 16M protected-mode space.

The addresses from 0E0000 to 0FFFFF are equal to FE0000 to FFFFFF, which is necessary because of differences in the memory addressing during the shift between real and protected modes.

Expanded Memory

Figure A.1 shows a map of expanded memory, where expanded memory fits with conventional and extended memory.

Motherboard Memory

The following error-code and memory-location information covers the original IBM PC. This system has a ROM BIOS that offers less information than the later XT systems concerning memory errors. Most compatible vendors have duplicated the XT error messages for their PC types of systems.

When a memory failure is detected during the POST, a 201 error message preceded by a four-character error code may be displayed. This error message lasts about one second before being replaced by a PARITY CHECK message. If a PARITY CHECK occurs during either POST or normal operation, single digit location code may follow the parity

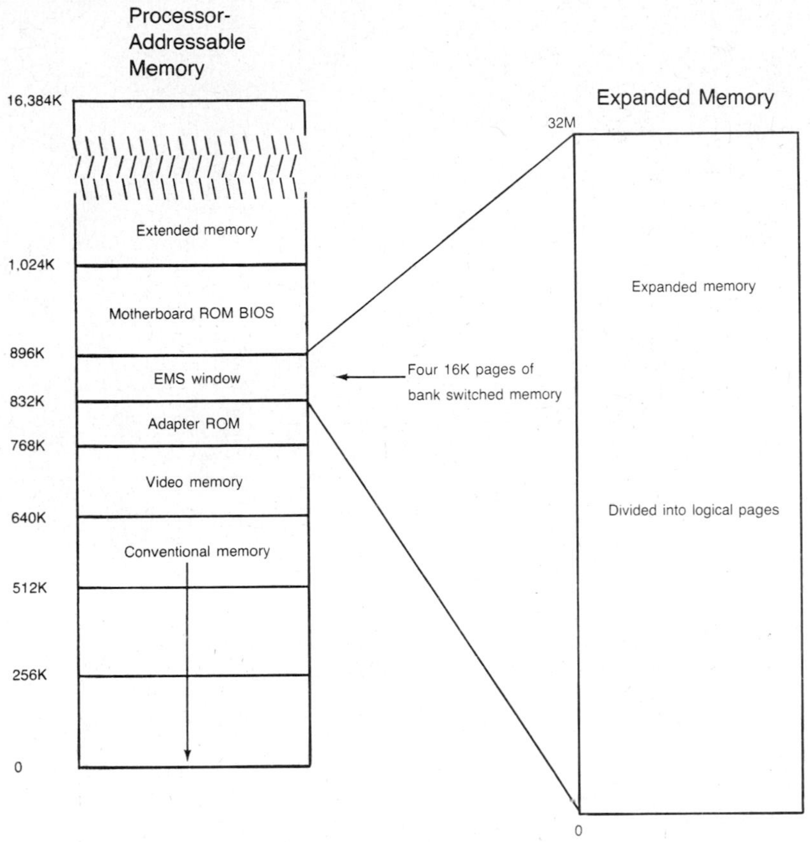

Processor-
Addressable
Memory

Fig. A.1.

*Map of expanded
memory.*

Expanded Memory

16,384K

Extended memory

1,024K

Motherboard ROM BIOS

896K

EMS window

832K

Adapter ROM

768K

Video memory

640K

Conventional memory

512K

256K

0

32M

Four 16K pages of
bank switched memory

Expanded memory

Divided into logical pages

0

check message. These messages appear in the form shown in
figure A.2.

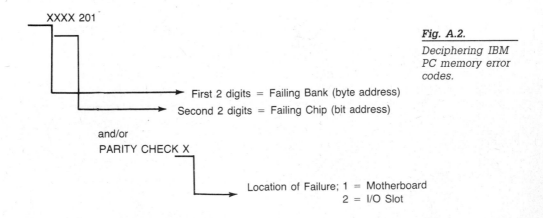

XXXX 201

First 2 digits = Failing Bank (byte address)
Second 2 digits = Failing Chip (bit address)

and/or
PARITY CHECK X

Location of Failure; 1 = Motherboard
2 = I/O Slot

Fig. A.2.

*Deciphering IBM
PC memory error
codes.*

The failing bank of memory is indicated by the first two digits of the error code, which are really the two most significant digits in the address of the failing byte. The failing chip is indicated by the last two digits of the error code, which is really the address of the failing bit.

The codes can be interpreted as follows:

16/64K Motherboard (Type 1)

Byte Address	Bank #	Bit Address								
		00	01	02	04	08	10	20	40	80
00xxx to 03xxx =	Bank 0	[]	[]	[]	[]	[]	[]	[]	[]	[]
04xxx to 07xxx =	Bank 1	[]	[]	[]	[]	[]	[]	[]	[]	[]
08xxx to 0Bxxx =	Bank 2	[]	[]	[]	[]	[]	[]	[]	[]	[]
0Cxxx to 0Fxxx =	Bank 3	[]	[]	[]	[]	[]	[]	[]	[]	[]

Chip locations

64/256K Motherboard (Type 2)

Byte Address	Bank #	Bit Address								
		00	01	02	04	08	10	20	40	80
00xxx to 0Fxxx =	Bank 0	[]	[]	[]	[]	[]	[]	[]	[]	[]
10xxx to 1Fxxx =	Bank 1	[]	[]	[]	[]	[]	[]	[]	[]	[]
20xxx to 2Fxxx =	Bank 2	[]	[]	[]	[]	[]	[]	[]	[]	[]
30xxx to 3Fxxx =	Bank 3	[]	[]	[]	[]	[]	[]	[]	[]	[]

Chip locations

All other reported byte addresses are not on the motherboard but, instead, must be on a memory expansion adapter plugged into a slot.

The following error-code and memory-location information covers the IBM XT and most compatible PC types of systems.

When a memory failure is detected during the POST or advanced diagnostics, a 201 error message preceded by a seven-character error code may be displayed. If a parity error occurs during normal operation, single digit location code may follow the PARITY CHECK message and a five-digit error code below the PARITY CHECK message.

These messages appear in the form shown in figure A.3.

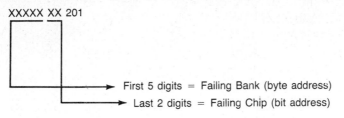

XXXXX XX 201

First 5 digits = Failing Bank (byte address)

Last 2 digits = Failing Chip (bit address)

Fig. A.3.

Deciphering IBM XT- and PC-compatible memory error codes.

or

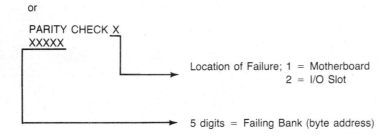

PARITY CHECK X
XXXXX

Location of Failure; 1 = Motherboard
2 = I/O Slot

5 digits = Failing Bank (byte address)

The failing bank of memory is indicated by the five-digit error code, which is really the address of the failing byte. The failing chip is indicated by the last two digits of the error code, which is really the address of the failing bit.

The address codes can be interpreted as follows:

64/256K Motherboard (Type 1)

		Bit Address								
Byte Address	Bank #	00	01	02	04	08	10	20	40	80
00000 to 0FFFF =	Bank 0	[]	[]	[]	[]	[]	[]	[]	[]	[]
10000 to 1FFFF =	Bank 1	[]	[]	[]	[]	[]	[]	[]	[]	[]
20000 to 2FFFF =	Bank 2	[]	[]	[]	[]	[]	[]	[]	[]	[]
30000 to 3FFFF =	Bank 3	[]	[]	[]	[]	[]	[]	[]	[]	[]

Chip locations

256/640k Motherboard (Type 2)

Byte Address	Bank #	00	01	02	04	08	10	20	40	80
					Bit Address					
00000 to 3FFFF =	Bank 0	[]	[]	[]	[]	[]	[]	[]	[]	[]
40000 to 7FFFF =	Bank 1	[]	[]	[]	[]	[]	[]	[]	[]	[]
80000 to 8FFFF =	Bank 2	[]	[]	[]	[]	[]	[]	[]	[]	[]
90000 to 9FFFF =	Bank 3	[]	[]	[]	[]	[]	[]	[]	[]	[]

Chip locations

The following error-code and memory-location information covers the IBM AT and most compatible AT types of systems.

When a memory failure is detected during the POST, a 201 error message preceded by a 10-character error code may be displayed. If a parity error occurs during normal operation, single digit location code may follow the PARITY CHECK message and a 5-digit error code below the PARITY CHECK message.

These messages appear in the form shown in figure A.4.

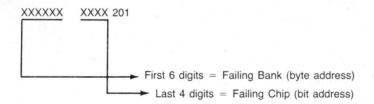

XXXXXX   XXXX 201

→ First 6 digits = Failing Bank (byte address)
→ Last 4 digits = Failing Chip (bit address)

Fig. A.4.

Deciphering IBM AT and AT-compatible memory error codes.

or

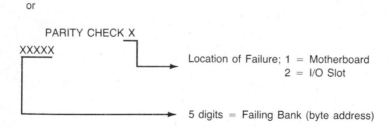

PARITY CHECK X

XXXXX

→ Location of Failure; 1 = Motherboard
    2 = I/O Slot

→ 5 digits = Failing Bank (byte address)

The failing bank of memory is indicated by the six-digit error code (or five-digit error code in the case of a PARITY CHECK message), which is really the address of the failing byte. The failing chip is indicated by the last four digits of the error code, which is really the address of the failing bit.

The address codes can be interpreted as follows:

Type 1 AT Motherboard

Byte Address	Bank #	Bit Address
040000 to 07FFFF =	Bank 1	[8] [9] [10] [11] [12] [13] [14] [15] [P]
		[0] [1] [2] [3] [4] [5] [6] [7] [P]
000000 to 03FFFF =	Bank 0	[8] [9] [10] [11] [12] [13] [14] [15] [P]
		[0] [1] [2] [3] [4] [5] [6] [7] [P]

The four-digit number corresponds to the bit address:

```
0000 = P (replace both parity modules in the bank)
0001 = 0
0002 = 1          0400 = 10
0004 = 2          0800 = 11
0008 = 3          1000 = 12
0010 = 4          2000 = 13
0020 = 5          4000 = 14
0040 = 6          8000 = 15
0080 = 7
0100 = 8
0200 = 9
```

Type 2 AT Motherboard

Only one bank vertically aligned (Bank 0)

```
[ 7] [15]
[ 6] [14]
[ 5] [13]
[ 4] [12]
[ 3] [11]
[ 2] [10]
[ 1] [ 9]
[ 0] [ 8]
[ P] [ P]
```

Byte Address	Bank #
000000 to 07FFFF =	Bank 0

All other memory is on a memory adapter card in one or more of the slots.

Fixed Disk Parameter Tables

When you're adding a hard disk to any system, the physical installation is the easiest part of the job. In fact, installing a hard disk is much easier than installing a floppy disk drive. But in order for the physical installation to work for you, you need to ensure that the system "knows" what type of drive you have installed. The several ways of knowing are discussed in Chapter 9. Here, you can examine lists of the preexisting hard disk drive tables found in all IBM systems to date. These tables are found in the controller card for the XT and in the motherboard ROM BIOS for any other system. The following charts list the XT controller tables and the motherboard ROM BIOS tables for IBM systems. If your system is a compatible of some type, this information may or may not match that given here. You will need to look up this type of information in your system's technical reference manual to be sure.

PC and XT

During the years that IBM sold the XT system, the company used two different ROM programs in the controllers. The two controllers are considered different due to the different ROM, even though physically they are the same thing. The controller IBM used was a Xebec Corporation Model 1210 hard disk controller, which IBM called the 10M Fixed Disk controller, or the 20M Fixed Disk controller, depending on the ROM used. Although different in other ways, the two ROMs are functionally identical except for the built-in drive parameter tables. These tables are four entries long, which limits the number of different types of drives that you can install on these controllers without resorting to modifying the ROM to change the tables.

IBM supplied the first version (labeled 10M Fixed Disk controller) with any XT systems that used the XT Type 1 (64/256K) motherboard, including IBM XT Models 5160 -068, -078, -086, and -087. The second version (labeled 20M Fixed Disk controller) was supplied with XT systems that used the XT Type 2 (256/640K) motherboard, including IBM XT Models 5160 -267, -268, -277, -278, -088, and -089. The tables found in these controllers follow:

IBM 10M Fixed Disk Controller (Xebec 1210)

Table Entry	Disk Type	Cyl	Heads	Write Precomp	Landing Zone	Capacity Megabytes
0	-	306	2	0	-	5
1	-	375	8	0	-	26
2	-	306	6	256	-	15
3	-	306	4	0	-	10

IBM 20M Fixed Disk Controller (Xebec 1210)

Table Entry	Disk Type	Cyl	Heads	Write Precomp	Landing Zone	Capacity Megabytes
0	1	306	4	0	305	10
1	16	612	4	0	663	21
2	2	615	4	300	615	21
3	13	306	8	128	319	21

AT

The IBM AT type of fixed disk parameter table is found in the ROM BIOS chips on the motherboard. These tables were only 15 entries long in the first AT version IBM released but were extended in later versions. IBM extended the possible number of entries to 47 (15 + 32) in the later model AT and any AT types of systems introduced so far. Provisions are built-in for extending the table to 255 entries, but IBM has not yet used up 47. I note this because some compatible vendors may take advantage of this "extra room."

As IBM has introduced more systems, the newer systems often have added to the existing table entries but never have changed the values of any previous ones. Thus, a Type 9 drive has the same meaning in the original AT as it does in the Model 80. The legend indicates what each column of data represents. In the table that follows, the information to the left of the vertical line is that which is actually stored in the table, and I have calculated the size information to the right of the line. Also note that this table includes all systems with ROM BIOS dates up to 04/18/88 (PS/2 Model 50Z).

Explanations of the column headings for this table follow:

Type: The drive type by number for table selection

Cyl: Total number of cylinders (or vertically aligned tracks)

Hd: Total number of heads (or tracks per cylinder)

WPC: Write precompensation starting cylinder

Ctrl: Control byte. Has values according to this table:

Bit 0 Not used
Bit 1 Not used
Bit 2 Not used
Bit 3 More than 8 heads
Bit 4 Not used
Bit 5 OEM defect map present at max. cyl. + 1
Bit 6 Disable retries
Bit 7 Disable retries

LZ: Landing zone cylinder for head parking

S/T: Number of sectors per track

Meg: Capacity in *megabytes*

Mb: Actual drive capacity in *millions of bytes*

IBM PC AT Fixed Disk Parameter Table

Type	Cyl	Hd	WPC	Ctrl	LZ	S/T	Meg	Mb	Notes
1	306	4	128	00h	305	17	10.16	10.65	
2	615	4	300	00h	615	17	20.42	21.41	
3	615	6	300	00h	615	17	30.63	32.12	
4	940	8	512	00h	940	17	62.42	65.45	
5	940	6	512	00h	940	17	46.82	49.09	
6	615	4	65535	00h	615	17	20.42	21.41	
7	462	8	256	00h	511	17	30.68	32.17	
8	733	5	65535	00h	733	17	30.42	31.90	
9	900	15	65535	08h	901	17	112.06	117.50	More than 8 heads
10	820	3	65535	00h	820	17	20.42	21.41	
11	855	5	65535	00h	855	17	35.49	37.21	
12	855	7	65535	00h	855	17	49.68	52.09	
13	306	8	128	00h	319	17	20.32	21.31	
14	733	7	65535	00h	733	17	42.59	44.66	
15	0	0	0	00h	0	0	0	0	Reserved (Do Not Use)

End Table 01/10/84 AT

IBM PC AT Fixed Disk Parameter Table—*continued*

Type	Cyl	Hd	WPC	Ctrl	LZ	S/T	Meg	Mb	Notes
16	612	4	0	00h	663	17	20.32	21.31	
17	977	5	300	00h	977	17	40.55	42.52	
18	977	7	65535	00h	977	17	56.77	59.53	
19	1024	7	512	00h	1023	17	59.50	62.39	
20	733	5	300	00h	732	17	30.42	31.90	
21	733	7	300	00h	732	17	42.59	44.66	
22	733	5	300	00h	733	17	30.42	31.90	
									End Table 06/10/85 AT
23	306	4	0	00h	336	17	10.16	10.65	
									End Table 11/15/85 AT
24	612	4	305	00h	663	17	20.32	21.31	
									End Table 04/21/86 XT 286
25	306	4	65535	00h	340	17	10.16	10.65	
26	612	4	65535	00h	670	17	20.32	21.31	
									End Table 12/12/86 PS/2 30
27	698	7	300	20h	732	17	40.56	42.53	Defect map (Cyl + 1)
28	976	5	488	20h	977	17	40.51	42.48	Defect map (Cyl + 1)
29	306	4	0	00h	340	17	10.16	10.65	
30	611	4	306	20h	663	17	20.29	21.27	Defect map (Cyl + 1)
31	732	7	300	20h	732	17	42.53	44.60	Defect map (Cyl + 1)
32	1023	5	65535	20h	1023	17	42.46	44.52	Defect map (Cyl + 1)
									End Table 10/07/87 PS/2 80
33	614	4	65535	20h	663	25	29.98	31.44	Defect map (Cyl + 1)
									End Table 04/18/88 PS/2 50Z
34	0	0	0	00h	0	0	0	0	Unused (Reserved)
35	0	0	0	00h	0	0	0	0	Unused (Reserved)
36	0	0	0	00h	0	0	0	0	Unused (Reserved)
37	0	0	0	00h	0	0	0	0	Unused (Reserved)
38	0	0	0	00h	0	0	0	0	Unused (Reserved)
39	0	0	0	00h	0	0	0	0	Unused (Reserved)
40	0	0	0	00h	0	0	0	0	Unused (Reserved)
41	0	0	0	00h	0	0	0	0	Unused (Reserved)
42	0	0	0	00h	0	0	0	0	Unused (Reserved)
43	0	0	0	00h	0	0	0	0	Unused (Reserved)
44	0	0	0	00h	0	0	0	0	Unused (Reserved)
45	0	0	0	00h	0	0	0	0	Unused (Reserved)
46	0	0	0	00h	0	0	0	0	Unused (Reserved)
47	0	0	0	00h	0	0	0	0	Unused (Reserved)

POST and Diagnostics Error Codes

The personal computer error codes for the POST, general
diagnostics, and advanced diagnostics are represented with the
device number followed by two digits other than 00. The device
number plus 00 indicates successful completion of the test. This

listing is a compilation from various sources including IBM technical reference manuals and IBM hardware maintenance service manuals. The messages are listed verbatim, according to the way they will be displayed.

Code	Description
01x	Undetermined problem errors.
02x	Power supply errors.
1xx	System Board Errors.
101	System Board Error; Interrupt failure.
102	System Board Error; Timer failure.
103	System Board Error; Timer interrupt failure.
104	System Board Error; Protected mode failure.
105	System Board Error; Last 8042 command not accepted.
106	System Board Error; Converting logic test.
107	System Board Error; Hot Non Maskable Interrupt test.
108	System Board Error; Timer bus test.
109	System Board Error; Memory select error.
110	PS/2 System Board Error; Parity check error.
111	PS/2 Memory adapter error.
112	PS/2 MicroChannel arbitration error.
113	PS/2 MicroChannel arbitration error.
121	Unexpected hardware interrupts occurred.
131	PC system board cassette port wrap test failure.
161	System Options Not Set-(Run SETUP); Dead battery.
162	System Options Not Set-(Run SETUP); CMOS checksum/ configuration error.
163	Time & Date Not Set-(Run SETUP); Clock not updating.
164	Memory Size Error-(Run SETUP); CMOS setting does not match memory.
165	PS/2 System options not set.
166	PS/2 Micro Channel adapter time-out error.
199	User indicated INSTALLED DEVICES list is not correct.
2xx	Memory (RAM) errors.
201	Memory test failure, error location will be displayed in hexadecimal.
202	Memory address error, address lines 00-15.
203	Memory address error, address lines 16-23.
215	PS/2 Motherboard memory failure.
216	PS/2 Motherboard memory failure.
3xx	Keyboard errors.

Code	Description
301	Keyboard did not respond to software reset or a stuck key failure was detected. If a stuck key was detected, the scan code for the key is displayed in hexadecimal.
302	System Unit Keylock is Locked.
303	Keyboard Or System Unit Error.
304	Keyboard Or System Unit Error; Keyboard clock high.
305	PS/2 Keyboard fuse (on system board) error.
4xx	Monochrome Display Adapter (MDA) errors.
4xx	PS/2 System board parallel port errors.
401	Monochrome memory test, horizontal sync frequency test, or video test failure.
401	PS/2 System board parallel port failure.
408	User indicated display attributes failure.
416	User indicated character set failure.
424	User indicated 80x25 mode failure.
432	Parallel port test failure; monochrome display adapter.
5xx	Color Graphics Adapter (CGA) errors.
501	CGA memory test, horizontal sync frequency test, or video test failure.
508	User indicated display attribute failure.
516	User indicated character set failure.
524	User indicated 80x25 mode failure.
532	User indicated 40x25 mode failure.
540	User indicated 320x200 graphics mode failure.
548	User indicated 640x200 graphics mode failure.
6xx	Floppy drive/adapter errors.
601	Floppy drive/adapter Power On Self Test failure.
602	Drive test failure; disk boot record is not valid.
606	Disk changeline function failure; drive error.
607	Disk is write protected; drive error.
608	Bad command; drive error.
610	Disk initialization failure; track 0 bad.
611	Time-out; drive error.
612	Bad Controller chip.
613	Bad Direct Memory Access; drive error.
614	Bad Direct Memory Access; boundary overrun.
615	Bad index timing; drive error.
616	Drive speed error.
621	Bad seek; drive error.

Code	Description
622	Bad Cyclic Redundancy Check; drive error.
623	Record not found; drive error.
624	Bad address mark; drive error.
625	Bad Controller chip; seek error.
626	Disk data compare error.
7xx	8087, 80287, or 80387 math coprocessor errors.
9xx	Parallel printer adapter errors.
901	Parallel printer adapter test failure.
10xx	Alternate parallel printer adapter errors.
1001	Alternate parallel printer adapter test failure.
11xx	Asynchronous communications adapter errors.
11xx	PS/2 System board async port errors.
1101	Asynchronous communications adapter test failure.
1102	PS/2 System board async port or serial device error.
1106	PS/2 System board async port or serial device error.
1107	PS/2 System board async port or serial cable error.
1108	PS/2 System board async port or serial device error.
1109	PS/2 System board async port or serial device error.
1112	PS/2 System board async port error.
1118	PS/2 System board async port error.
1119	PS/2 System board async port error.
12xx	Alternate asynchronous communications adapter errors.
12xx	PS/2 Dual async adapter error.
1201	Alternate asynchronous communications adapter test failure.
1202	PS/2 Dual async adapter or serial device error.
1206	PS/2 Dual async adapter or serial device error.
1207	PS/2 Dual async adapter or serial cable error.
1208	PS/2 Dual async adapter or serial device error.
1209	PS/2 Dual async adapter or serial device error.
1212	PS/2 Dual async adapter or system board error.
1218	PS/2 Dual async adapter or system board error.
1219	PS/2 Dual async adapter or system board error.
1227	PS/2 Dual async adapter or system board error.
1233	PS/2 Dual async adapter or system board error.
1234	PS/2 Dual async adapter or system board error.

Code	Description
13xx	Game control adapter errors.
1301	Game control adapter test failure.
1302	Joy-stick test failure.
14xx	Matrix Printer errors.
15xx	Synchronous data link control (SDLC) communications adapter errors.
1510	8255 port B failure.
1511	8255 port A failure.
1512	8255 port C failure.
1513	8253 timer 1 did not reach terminal count.
1514	8253 timer 1 stuck on.
1515	8253 timer 0 did not reach terminal count.
1516	8253 timer 0 stuck on.
1517	8253 timer 2 did not reach terminal count.
1518	8253 timer 2 stuck on.
1519	8273 port B error.
1520	8273 port A error.
1521	8273 command/read time-out.
1522	Interrupt level 4 failure.
1523	Ring Indicate stuck on.
1524	Receive clock stuck on.
1525	Transmit clock stuck on.
1526	Test indicate stuck on.
1527	Ring indicate not on.
1528	Receive clock not on.
1529	Transmit clock not on.
1530	Test indicate not on.
1531	Data set ready not on.
1532	Carrier detect not on.
1533	Clear to send not on.
1534	Data set ready stuck on.
1536	Clear to send stuck on.
1537	Level 3 interrupt failure.
1538	Receive interrupt results error.
1539	Wrap data compare error.
1540	Direct Memory Access channel 1 error.
1541	Direct Memory Access channel 1 error.
1542	Error in 8273 error checking or status reporting.
1547	Stray interrupt level 4.

Code	Description
1548	Stray interrupt level 3.
1549	Interrupt presentation sequence time-out.
16xx	Display emulation errors (327x, 5520, 525x).
17xx	Fixed disk errors.
1701	Fixed disk POST error.
1702	Fixed disk adapter error.
1703	Fixed disk drive error.
1704	Fixed disk adapter or drive error.
1780	Fixed disk 0 failure.
1781	Fixed disk 1 failure.
1782	Fixed disk controller failure.
1790	Fixed disk 0 error.
1791	Fixed disk 1 error.
18xx	I/O expansion unit errors.
1801	I/O expansion unit POST error.
1810	Enable/Disable failure.
1811	Extender card wrap test failure; disabled.
1812	High order address lines failure; disabled.
1813	Wait state failure; disabled.
1814	Enable/Disable could not be set on.
1815	Wait state failure; disabled.
1816	Extender card wrap test failure; enabled.
1817	High order address lines failure; enabled.
1818	Disable not functioning.
1819	Wait request switch not set correctly.
1820	Receiver card wrap test failure.
1821	Receiver high order address lines failure.
19xx	3270 PC attachment card errors.
20xx	Binary synchronous communications (BSC) adapter errors.
2010	8255 port A failure.
2011	8255 port B failure.
2012	8255 port C failure.
2013	8253 timer 1 did not reach terminal count.
2014	8253 timer 1 stuck on.
2015	8253 timer 2 did not reach terminal count or timer 2 stuck on.
2017	8251 Data set ready failed to come on.
2018	8251 Clear to send not sensed.

Code	Description
2019	8251 Data set ready stuck on.
2020	8251 Clear to send stuck on.
2021	8251 hardware reset failure.
2022	8251 software reset failure.
2023	8251 software "error reset" failure.
2024	8251 transmit ready did not come on.
2025	8251 receive ready did not come on.
2026	8251 could not force "overrun" error status.
2027	Interrupt failure; no timer interrupt.
2028	Interrupt failure; transmit, replace card or planar.
2029	Interrupt failure; transmit, replace card.
2030	Interrupt failure; receive, replace card or planar.
2031	Interrupt failure; receive, replace card.
2033	Ring indicate stuck on.
2034	Receive clock stuck on.
2035	Transmit clock stuck on.
2036	Test indicate stuck on.
2037	Ring indicate stuck on.
2038	Receive clock not on.
2039	Transmit clock not on.
2040	Test indicate not on.
2041	Data set ready not on.
2042	Carrier detect not on.
2043	Clear to send not on.
2044	Data set ready stuck on.
2045	Carrier detect stuck on.
2046	Clear to send stuck on.
2047	Unexpected transmit interrupt.
2048	Unexpected receive interrupt.
2049	Transmit data did not equal receive data.
2050	8251 detected overrun error.
2051	Lost data set ready during data wrap.
2052	Receive time-out during data wrap.
21xx	Alternate binary synchronous communications adapter errors.
2110	8255 port A failure.
2111	8255 port B failure.
2112	8255 port C failure.
2113	8253 timer 1 did not reach terminal count.
2114	8253 timer 1 stuck on.

Code	Description
2115	8253 timer 2 did not reach terminal count or timer 2 stuck on.
2117	8251 Data set ready failed to come on.
2118	8251 Clear to send not sensed.
2119	8251 Data set ready stuck on.
2120	8251 Clear to send stuck on.
2121	8251 hardware reset failure.
2122	8251 software reset failure.
2123	8251 software "error reset" failure.
2124	8251 transmit ready did not come on.
2125	8251 receive ready did not come on.
2126	8251 could not force "overrun" error status.
2127	Interrupt failure; no timer interrupt.
2128	Interrupt failure; transmit, replace card or planar.
2129	Interrupt failure; transmit, replace card.
2130	Interrupt failure; receive, replace card or planar.
2131	Interrupt failure; receive, replace card.
2133	Ring indicate stuck on.
2134	Receive clock stuck on.
2135	Transmit clock stuck on.
2136	Test indicate stuck on.
2137	Ring indicate stuck on.
2138	Receive clock not on.
2139	Transmit clock not on.
2140	Test indicate not on.
2141	Data set ready not on.
2142	Carrier detect not on.
2143	Clear to send not on.
2144	Data set ready stuck on.
2145	Carrier detect stuck on.
2146	Clear to send stuck on.
2147	Unexpected transmit interrupt.
2148	Unexpected receive interrupt.
2149	Transmit Data did not equal receive data.
2150	8251 detected overrun error.
2151	Lost data set ready during data wrap.
2152	Receive time-out during data wrap.
22xx	Cluster adapter errors.
24xx	Enhanced Graphics Adapter (EGA) errors.

Code	Description
24xx	PS/2 System board Video Graphics Array (VGA) errors.
26xx	XT/370 errors.
27xx	AT/370 errors.
28xx	3278/79 emulation adapter errors.
29xx	Color/graphics printer errors.
30xx	Primary PC Network adapter errors.
3001	Processor test failure.
3002	ROM checksum test failure.
3003	Unit ID PROM test failure.
3004	RAM test failure.
3005	Host Interface Controller test failure.
3006	+/− 12v test failure.
3007	Digital loopback test failure.
3008	Host detected Host Interface Controller failure.
3009	Sync failure and no Go bit.
3010	Host Interface Controller test OK and no Go bit.
3011	Go bit and no Command 41.
3012	Card not present.
3013	Digital failure; fall through.
3015	Analog failure.
3041	Hot carrier; not this card.
3042	Hot carrier; this card!
31xx	Secondary PC Network adapter errors.
3101	Processor test failure.
3102	ROM checksum test failure.
3103	Unit ID PROM test failure.
3104	RAM test failure.
3105	Host Interface Controller test failure.
3106	+/− 12v test failure.
3107	Digital loopback test failure.
3108	Host detected Host Interface Controller failure.
3109	Sync failure and no Go bit.
3110	Host Interface Controller test OK and no Go bit.
3111	Go bit and no Command 41.
3112	Card not present.
3113	Digital failure; fall through.
3115	Analog failure.

Code	Description
3141	Hot carrier; not this card.
3142	Hot carrier; this card!
33xx	Compact printer errors.
36xx	General Purpose Interface Bus (GPIB) adapter errors.
38xx	Data acquisition adapter errors.
39xx	Professional graphics controller errors.
71xx	Voice communications adapter errors.
73xx	3.5″ external diskette drive errors.
7306	Disk changeline function failure; drive error.
7307	Disk is write protected; drive error.
7308	Bad command; drive error.
7310	Disk initialization failure; track 0 bad.
7311	Time-out; drive error.
7312	Bad Controller chip.
7313	Bad Direct Memory Access; drive error.
7314	Bad Direct Memory Access; boundary overrun.
7315	Bad index timing; drive error.
7316	Drive speed error.
7321	Bad seek; drive error.
7322	Bad Cyclic Redundancy Check; drive error.
7323	Record not found; drive error.
7324	Bad address mark; drive error.
7325	Bad Controller chip; seek error.
74xx	IBM PS/2 Display adapter (VGA card) errors.
85xx	IBM Expanded Memory Adapter (XMA) errors.
86xx	PS/2 Pointing device errors.
8601	PS/2 Pointing device error.
8602	PS/2 Pointing device error.
8603	PS/2 Pointing device error or System board failure.
89xx	Music feature card errors.
100xx	PS/2 Multiprotocol adapter errors.
10002	PS/2 Multiprotocol adapter or serial device error.
10006	PS/2 Multiprotocol adapter or serial device error.
10007	PS/2 Multiprotocol adapter or communications cable error.
10008	PS/2 Multiprotocol adapter or serial device error.

Code	Description
10009	PS/2 Multiprotocol adapter or serial device error.
10012	PS/2 Multiprotocol adapter or system board error.
10018	PS/2 Multiprotocol adapter or system board error.
10019	PS/2 Multiprotocol adapter or system board error.
10042	PS/2 Multiprotocol adapter or system board error.
10056	PS/2 Multiprotocol adapter or system board error.
104xx	PS/2 ESDI Fixed disk errors.
10480	PS/2 ESDI Fixed disk 0 failure.
10481	PS/2 ESDI Fixed disk 1 failure.
10482	PS/2 ESDI Fixed disk controller failure.
10483	PS/2 ESDI Fixed disk controller failure.
10490	PS/2 ESDI Fixed disk 0 error.
10491	PS/2 ESDI Fixed disk 1 error.

IBM Technical Manuals and Updates

IBM provides extensive documentation to help troubleshooters and people responsible for upgrading and repairing any system. These manuals are grouped mainly in two categories: technical reference manuals and hardware maintenance service manuals. You purchase these manuals in a basic form and then update them to reflect changes in the newer systems as they are introduced.

All the manuals together with the updates present a bewildering array of documentation—not to mention expensive. If you are interested in obtaining any of this documentation, this section will be extremely useful. All the available manuals and updates are listed, with part numbers and prices included. Each manual type is also explained, and the information you need to order this documentation is given.

Software Reference Manuals

The following chart provides information on IBM software reference manuals:

Description	Part Number	Price
BASIC Reference Version 3.30	6280189	45.00
DOS Technical Reference Version 3.30	6280059	85.00
IBM OS/2 Technical Reference Version 1.0	6280201	200.00

The BASIC Reference Version 3.30 manual explains how to use the BASIC Interpreter for the IBM PC and contains the syntax and semantics of every command, statement, and function in the three versions of BASIC: Cassette, Disk, and Advanced.

In addition to the reference material, chapters are included on BASIC programming concepts and the BASIC program editor. Other chapters describe data representation, file names, and input and output features. Updated with each version of DOS, this manual also contains a chapter that describes the most recent enhancements.

The DOS Technical Reference Version 3.30 manual is the reference for the IBM PC Disk Operating System (DOS) and is intended for experienced DOS users, system programmers, and application developers. Included is information about the structure, facilities, and program interfaces of DOS.

Chapter information includes control blocks, memory management, disk allocation, interrupts and function calls, and file structure and loading. This package contains DOS utilities on a 3 1/2-inch and a 5 1/4-inch disk and a quick-reference card.

The IBM OS/2 Technical Reference Version 1.0 manual is the reference for the IBM OS/2 and is intended for experienced users, system programmers, and application developers. This manual describes the OS/2 interfaces and the architecture, control structures, data structures, and I/O formats necessary to understand and use them.

Guide to Operations and Quick-Reference Manuals

The following chart provides information on the guide to operations and quick-reference manuals:

Description	Part Number	Form Number	Price
Personal System/2			
Model 25	75X1051	S75X-1051	24.00
Model 30	68X2230	S68X-2230	45.00
Model 50	68X2247	S68X-2247	45.00
Model 60	68X2213	S68X-2213	45.00
Model 80	68X2284	S68X-2284	45.00
Personal Computer			
AT	6280066		49.50
AT Model 339	6280102		80.00
PC	6322510		50.00
PC Convertible	6280629		65.00
PCjr	1502292		21.25
Portable PC	6936571		66.75
XT	6322511		50.00
XT Models 089, 268, 278	6280085		80.00
XT Model 286	6280147		65.00

The guide to operations and quick-reference manuals contain instructions for system operation, testing, relocation, and option installation. A diagnostic disk is included.

The PS/2 Hardware Maintenance Library (Excluding the Models 25 and 30)

The following chart provides information on the hardware maintenance manuals:

Description	Part Number	Form Number	Price
PS/2 Hardware Maintenance Service			
Models 50 and 60	68X2222	S68X-2222	175.00
Supplements to 68X2222:			
Display Adapter 8514/A	68X2250	S68X-2250	6.00
Model 80	68X2255	S68X-2255	75.00
Model 80-111, -311	68X2286	S68X-2286	75.00
300/1200 Internal Modem/A	68X2274	S68X-2274	12.00
5.25-Inch External Diskette Drive	68X2273	S68X-2273	10.00
80286 Expanded Memory Adapter/A	75X1107	SA23-1032	22.75
PS/2 Hardware Maintenance Reference			
Models 50 and 60	68X2221	S68X-2221	125.00
Supplements to 68X2221:			
Color Display 8514	68X2218	S68X-2218	6.00
Display Adapter 8514/A	68X2249	S68X-2249	6.00
Model 80	68X2254	S68X-2254	50.00
Model 80-111, -311	68X2287	S68X-2287	50.00
300/1200 Internal Modem/A	(Included in 68X2274)		
5.25-Inch External Diskette Drive	(Included in 68X2273)		
80286 Expanded Memory Adapter/A	(Included in 75X1107)		

The PS/2 (except Models 25 and 30) hardware maintenance library consists of a two-part set of manuals. The library is intended for trained service representatives.

The PS/2 Hardware Maintenance Service contains all the information necessary for you to diagnose a failure. Maintenance Analysis Procedures (MAPs), the parts catalog, and reference disks containing the advanced diagnostics tests are in this manual.

The PS/2 Hardware Maintenance Reference contains product descriptions, Field Replaceable Unit (FRU) locations and removal procedures, and information about the diagnostic programs.

To maintain an accurate library, you should add all available supplements. (The PS/2 Model 25 and Model 30 supplements update the PC maintenance library.)

The Personal Computer Hardware Maintenance Library (Including the PS/2 Models 25 and 30)

The following chart provides information on the personal computer (including the PS/2 Models 25 and 30):

Description	Part Number	Form Number	Price
PC Hardware Maintenance Service			
PC, XT, AT, and Portable	6280087	S229-9603	195.00
Supplements to 6280087:			
AT Model 339	6280139	SS34-0001	9.95
Display Adapter	68X2216	S68X-2216	30.00
PC Music Feature	75X1049	SA23-1029	41.50
Personal System/2 Model 25	75X1054	SA23-1201	33.00
Personal System/2 Model 30	68X2202	S68X-2202	30.00
XT Model 286	68X2211	SS34-0021	9.95
XT Models 089, 268, 278	6280109	SN32-8202	9.95
2M Expanded Memory Adapter	74X9923	SA23-1031	53.75
3.5-Inch External Diskette Drive	6280111	SS34-0005	10.00
3.5-Inch Internal Diskette Drive	6280159	SS34-003	5.95
5.25-Inch External Diskette Drive	68X2273	S68X-2273	10.00

Description	Part Number	Form Number	Price
PC Hardware Maintenance Reference			
PC, XT, AT, and Portable	6280088	S229-9604	150.00
Supplements to 6280088:			
AT Model 339	6280138	SS34-0002	5.95
Color Display 8514	68X2218	S68X-2218	6.00
Display Adapter	68X2238	S68X-2238	6.00
Personal System/2 Model 25	75X1059	SA23-1200	9.00
Personal System/2 Model 30	68X2203	S68X-2203	10.00
XT Model 286	68X2212	SS34-0022	9.95
XT Models 089, 268, 278	6280108	SN32-8203	5.95
3.5-Inch External Diskette Drive	(Included in 68X2203)		
3.5-Inch Internal Diskette Drive	6280160	SS34-0004	5.95
5.25-Inch External Diskette Drive	(Included in 68X2273)		

This hardware maintenance library consists of a two-part set of manuals. It is intended for trained service representatives.

The PC Hardware Maintenance Service contains all the information necessary for you to diagnose a failing system. Maintenance Analysis Procedures (MAPs), jumper positions switch settings, a parts catalog, and diskettes containing the advanced diagnostics are in this manual.

The PC Hardware Maintenance Reference contains general information about the systems. This manual also describes the diagnostic procedures and Field Replaceable Unit (FRU) location, adjustment, and removal.

To maintain an accurate library, you should add all available supplements.

Hardware Maintenance Service Manuals

The following chart provides information on the hardware maintenance service manuals:

Description	Part Number	Form Number	Price
Color Printer	68X2237	S68X-2237	23.24
Graphics and Compact Printer	6280079	S229-9600	23.25
PC Convertible	6280641	SA23-1046	150.00
Supplement to 6280641:			
Speech Adapter	59X9964	SN20-9817	23.00
PC*jr*	1502294	ZR28-0498	88.00

These single-volume manuals provide the information needed for you to isolate and replace any Field Replaceable Unit (FRU). The Color Printer manual and the Graphics and Compact Printer manual are designed to be used with the system maintenance manuals.

You can use the following empty binders to store the hardware maintenance supplements.

Description	Part Number	Form Number	Price
Empty HMS (Service) Binder	1502561	S229-9605	7.25
Empty HMR (Reference) Binder	01F0200	S01F-0200	17.00

Hardware Technical Reference Library

The several listings that follow provide system-specific hardware and software interface information for the IBM PC and PS/2 products. These manuals are intended for developers who provide hardware and software products to operate with these systems. The library is divided into system, options and adapters, and BIOS interface publications.

System Technical Reference Manuals

The following chart provides information on the system technical reference manuals:

Description	Part Number	Form Number	Price
PC Convertible	6280648	SA23-1047	75.00
Supplements to 6280648:			
Speech Adapter	59X9965		23.00
256K Memory and Enhanced			
Modem	75X1035		5.20
PC*jr*	1502293	S229-9609	35.00
Personal Computer	6322507	S229-9610	30.00
Personal Computer AT	6280070	S229-9611	105.00
Supplements to 6280070:			
Personal Computer AT Model 339	6280099	S229-9608	49.75
Personal Computer XT			
and Portable	6280089	S229-9607	49.75
Personal Computer XT Model 286	68X2210	S229-9615	50.00
Personal System/2 Model 25	75X1055	SA23-1202	28.75
Personal System/2 Model 30	68X2210	S68X-2201	75.00
Personal System/2 Models			
50 and 60	68X2224	S68X-2224	125.00
Personal System/2 Model 80	68X2256	S68X-2256	125.00
Supplements to 68X2256:			
Model 80-111, -311	68X2285	S68X-2285	6.00

These publications provide interface and design information for the system units. Information is included for the system board, math coprocessor, power supply, video subsystem, keyboard, instruction sets, and other features of the system.

Options and Adapters Technical Reference Manuals

The following charts provide information on the options and adapters technical reference manuals:

Description	Part Number	Form Number	Price
Options and Adapters Technical Reference	6322509	S229-9612	125.00

Includes

Asynchronous Communications
   Adapter
Bisynchronous Communications
   Adapter
Cluster Adapter
Color Display
Color/Graphics Monitor Adapter
Color Printer
Expansion Unit
Fixed Disk Drive Adapter
Game Control Adapter
Graphics Printer
Monochrome Display
Monochrome/Printer Adapter
Printer Adapter
SDLC Adapter
Slimline Diskette Drive
10M Fixed Disk Drive
5.25-Inch Diskette Drive
5.25-Inch Diskette Drive Adapter
64/256K Memory Option

Description	Part Number	Form Number	Price
Engineering/Scientific	6280133	SS34-009	27.95

Includes

Data Acquisition and Control
   (DAC) Adapter
DAC Distribution Panel
General Purpose Interface
   Bus Adapter
Professional Graphics Controller
Professional Graphics Display

Description	Part Number	Form Number	Price
Personal Computer AT	6280134	SS34-0010	9.95

Includes

Double-Sided Diskette Drive
Fixed Disk and Diskette
  Drive Adapter
High-Capacity Diskette Drive
Serial/Parallel Adapter
128K Memory Expansion Option
20M Fixed Disk Drive
512K Memory Expansion Option

Description	Part Number	Form Number	Price
Communications			
Dual Async Adapter/A (Second Edition)	68X2315	S68X-2315	6.00
Multiprotocol Adapter/A (Second Edition)	68X2316	S68X-2316	12.00
300/1200 Internal Modem/A	68X2275	S68X-2275	6.00

Description	Part Number	Form Number	Price
Diskette and Fixed Disk			
Double-Sided Diskette Drive (Half-Height)	6280093	SS34-0016	5.95
Fixed Disk Drive Adapter/A	68X2226	S68X-2226	12.00
Fixed Disk Drive Adapter/A, ESDI	68X2234	S68X-2234	12.00
Fixed Disk and Diskette Drive (XT 286)	68X2215	SS34-031	6.00
20M Fixed Disk (XT Models 089, 268, 278, 286)	68X2208	SS34-0019	7.00
Fixed Disk Adapter (XT Models 089, 268, 278)	6280092	SS34-0015	5.95
3.5-Inch External Diskette Drive	59X9945		5.95
3.5-Inch External Diskette Drive Adapter	59X9946		5.95

Description	Part Number	Form Number	Price
Diskette and Fixed Disk—continued			
3.5-Inch 20M Fixed Disk Drive (Model 30)	68X2205	S68X-2205	6.00
3.5-Inch 20M Fixed Disk Drive (Model 50)	68X2219	S68X-2219	10.00
3.5-Inch 720K/1.44M Diskette Drives	68X2225	S68X-2225	6.00
30M Fixed Disk Drive	68X2310	S68X-2310	5.95
44M Fixed Disk Drive (Second Edition)	68X2317	S68X-2317	6.00
5.25-Inch External Diskette Drive	68X2272	S68X-2272	10.00
70/115/314M Fixed Disk Drives	68X2236	S68X-2236	6.00

Description	Part Number	Form Number	Price
Displays			
Personal System/2 Color Display 8514	68X2214	S68X-2214	6.00
Personal System/2 Display Adapter	68X2251	S68X-2251	10.00
Personal System/2 Display Adapter 8514/A	68X2248	S68X-2248	10.00
Personal System/2 Displays	68X2206	S68X-2206	6.00

Includes

Color 8512
Color 8513
Monochrome 8503

	Part Number	Form Number	Price
Enhanced Graphics Adapter	6280131	SS34-0007	9.95

Includes

Enhanced Color Display
Graphics Memory Expansion Card

Description	Part Number	Form Number	Price
Memory			
128/640K Memory Adapter	1502554	SS34-0017	5.95
2M Expanded Memory Adapter	75X1086	SA23-1033	8.75
265K Memory Expansion	6280132	SS34-0008	9.95
512K/2M Memory Adapter	6183075	SS34-0018	5.95
80286 Expanded Memory Adapter/A	75X1109	SA23-1043	5.75
80286 Memory Expansion Option	68X2227	S68X-2227	6.00
80386 Memory Expansion Option	68X2257	S68X-2257	10.00

Description	Part Number	Form Number	Price
Other			
Binder, Options, and Adapter (empty)	6280115	S2229-960	7.25
Mouse	68X2229	S68X-2229	6.00
PC Music Feature	75X1048	SA23-1035	17.75
Personal System/2 Speech Adapter	68X2207	S68X-2207	13.00
Voice Communications Adapter	55X8864	SS34-0011	5.95

These publications provide interface and design information for the options and adapters available for the various systems. This information includes a hardware description, programming considerations, interface specifications, and BIOS information (where applicable).

BIOS Interface

The following chart provides information on the BIOS interface publications:

Description	Part Number	Form Number	Price
PS/2 and PC BIOS Interface	68X22680	S68X-2260	75.00
Supplement to 68X2260:			
Advanced BIOS Interface	68X2288	S68X-2288	50.00

This publication provides Basic Input/Output System (BIOS) interface information. It is intended for developers of hardware or software products that operate with the IBM PC and PS/2 products.

Hardware Application Developer's Guide

The following chart provides information on the hardware application developer's guide:

Description	Part Number	Form Number	Price
8514/A Adapter Application Developer's Guide	68X2279	S68X-2279	25.00

Ordering Information

To obtain publications listed in the Technical Directory, you can contact an IBM authorized dealer or an IBM sales representative. When placing an order through an IBM sales representative, use form numbers only.

You can order publications by calling toll-free 1-800-IBM-PCTB (1-800-426-7282), Monday through Friday, from 8 a.m. to 8 p.m. Eastern time. When ordering by telephone, you can use VISA, MasterCard, American Express, or IBM credit cards. Please have the part numbers, quantities, and credit card information available when you call.

Purchase orders will be accepted when you place orders through an IBM sales representative or an IBM branch office.

In Canada, call toll-free 1-800-465-1234, Monday through Friday, from 8:30 a.m. to 4:30 p.m. Eastern time. In British Columbia, call toll-free 112-800-465-1234. In Alaska, call 1-414-633-8108.

You also may call to request additional copies of the Technical Directory or to inquire about the availability of IBM PC or IBM PS/2 technical information on newly announced products that may not be listed in this directory.

When ordering by mail, list the product names, part numbers, quantities, and total price for the manuals you want. Enclose your check, money order, or credit card information with the order. VISA, MasterCard, American Express, and IBM credit cards are accepted. Make your check or money order payable to IBM Corporation. Cash, CODs, or purchase orders are not accepted. Please add your applicable state and local sales/use tax, plus $5 for postage and handling. Be sure to include shipping information.

In the United States, Puerto Rico, and the U.S. Virgin Islands, mail to the following address:

IBM Technical Directory
P.O. Box 2009
Racine, WI 53404-3336

IBM reserves the right to substitute the most recent version of any manual listed in this directory, which may affect the price of the manual.

Please allow one to two weeks for delivery of telephone orders; allow two to four weeks for delivery of mail orders.

All prices are subject to change without notice. Orders received with incorrect payments or other errors will be returned. The products and prices quoted are for the United States, Puerto Rico, and the U.S. Virgin Islands only. Orders must include applicable state and local sales/use tax, plus $5 for postage and handling.

Vendors and Suppliers

This section lists the vendors and suppliers whose names are used in this book. Following each vendor's address is a brief explanation of the products the vendor offers.

3M Magnetic Media Division
Building 223, 5N-01 3M Center
St. Paul, MN 55144
(612)733-0623

The 3M Magnetic Media Division manufactures magnetic disk and tape media. This company's DC-600 and DC-2000 media are standards for tape backup data cartridges.

A.Q.A., Inc.
12891 Western Avenue, Suite A
Garden Grove, CA 92641
(714)897-3655

A.Q.A., Inc., is a service organization that handles component-level board repair and service.

AST Research
2121 Alton Avenue
Irvine, CA 92714
(714)863-1333

AST Research manufactures an extensive line of adapter boards and components for IBM and compatible computers. AST Research also manufactures a line of AT-compatible systems.

AT&T
55 Corporate Drive
Bridgewater, NJ 08807
(404)446-4734

AT&T manufactures a line of IBM-compatible computer systems.

Alps America
3553 N. First Avenue, Suite A
San Jose, CA 95134
(408)432-6000

Alps America is a supplier of 5 1/4-inch and 3 1/2-inch floppy drives to IBM for use in the original XT and AT and now the PS/2 systems. Alps America also manufactures a line of printers.

Ariel Corporation
P.O. Box 866
Flemington, NJ 08822
(201)788-9002

Ariel Corporation manufactures a line of AT speedup components and is also a vendor of high-speed mil-spec crystals, processors, and memory chips.

Award Software, Inc.
130 Knowles Drive
Los Gatos, CA 95030
(408)370-7979

Award Software, Inc., manufactures a line of IBM-compatible ROM BIOS software.

Boston Computer Exchange
P.O. Box 1177
Boston, MA 02103
(617)542-4414

Boston Computer Exchange is a broker for used IBM and compatible computers.

Byte Magazine
One Phoenix Mill Lane
Peterborough, NH 03458
(603)924-9281

Byte Magazine is a monthly magazine covering all lines of microcomputers.

C. Itoh Electronics
19300 S. Hamilton Avenue
Torrence, CA 90508
(231)327-9100

C. Itoh Electronics is a supplier of 5 1/4-inch floppy drives to IBM for use in the XT and AT systems. The company also manufactures a line of printers.

California Software Products, Inc.
525 North Cabrillo Park Drive
Santa Ana, CA 92701
(714)973-0440

California Software Products, Inc., manufactures the California 10 pak and other utility programs for IBM and compatible systems.

Central Point Software, Inc.
15220 NW Greenbrier Parkway, #200
Beaverton, OR 97006
(503)690-8090

Central Point Software manufactures the PC Tools and Copy II PC utility programs.

Cherry Corporation
3600 Sunset Avenue
Waukegan, IL 60087
(312)662-9200

Cherry Corporation manufactures a line of keyboards for IBM-compatible systems.

Chicago Case Company
4446 S. Ashland Avenue
Chicago, IL 60609
(312)927-1600

Chicago Case Company manufactures equipment shipping and travel cases.

Chips and Technologies, Inc.
521 Cottonwood Drive
Milpitas, CA 95035
(408)436-0600

Chips and Technologies, Inc., manufactures specialized chip sets for compatible motherboard manufacturers.

Cipher Data Products Inc.
10101 Old Grove Road
San Diego, CA 92138
(800)4-CIPHER

Cipher Data Products Inc. manufactures a line of tape backup products. The company is also a supplier of DC-600 media-based tape backup systems to IBM.

COMPAQ Computer Corporation
20555 FM 149
Houston, TX 77070
(713)370-0670

COMPAQ Computer Corporation manufactures IBM-compatible computer systems.

Computer Repair Corporation
21751 Melrose
Southfield, MI 48075
(313)350-1520

Computer Repair Corporation is a service company that handles component-level circuit-board repair and hard disk remanufacturing.

Computer Shopper Magazine
5211 S. Washington Avenue
Titusville, FL 32780
(305)269-3211

Computer Shopper Magazine is a monthly magazine for experimenters and bargain hunters. It features a large number of advertisements.

Conner Peripherals Inc.
2221 Old Oakland Road
San Jose, CA 95131
(408)433-3340

Conner Peripherals Inc. manufactures 3 1/2-inch hard disk drives. The company is partly owned by COMPAQ and supplies most of COMPAQ's smaller hard drives.

Curtis Manufacturing
305 Union Street
Peterborough, NH 03458
(800)548-4900

Curtis Manufacturing makes a line of computer accessories, cables, and toolkits.

Data Spec
20120 Plummer Street
Chatsworth, CA 91311
(818)993-1202

Data Spec manufactures a complete line of switch boxes for parallel, serial, video, and other connections.

Dell Computer Corporation
9505 Arboretum Blvd.
Austin, TX 78759
(800)426-5150

Dell Computer Corporation manufactures a line of low-cost, high-performance IBM-compatible computer systems.

Design Software Inc.
1275 W. Roosevelt Rd. Suite 104
West Chicago, IL 60185
(312)231-4540

Design Software Inc. manufactures a line of help, backup, and other utility software.

Disk Drive Repair Inc.
8220 SW Nimbus
Beaverton, OR 97005
(503)626-7104

Disk Drive Repair Inc. is a service company specializing in hard disk and floppy drive component-level repair and alignment.

Dynatech Computer Power Inc.
5800 Butler Lane
Scotts Valley, CA 95066
(408)438-5760

Dynatech Computer Power Inc. manufactures a line of computer power-protection devices.

Emerson Computer Power
P.O. Box 1679
Santa Ana, CA 92702
(714)545-5581

Emerson Computer Power manufactures a line of computer power-protection devices.

Fifth Generation Systems
11200 Industriplex Blvd.
Baton Rouge, LA 70809
(504)291-7221

Fifth Generation Systems manufactures the Fastback floppy disk backup program.

Fujitsu America
3055 Orchard Drive
San Jose, CA 95134
(408)432-1300

Fujitsu America manufactures a line of hard disk drives.

Geneva Enterprises
0804 Waterloo Geneva Road
Waterloo, NY 13165
(315)539-5083

Geneva Enterprises manufactures the Second Nature AT ROM BIOS kit that extends the hard disk drive tables in an AT type of system.

Golden Bow
2870 Fifth Avenue, Suite 201
San Diego, CA 92103
(619)298-9349

Golden Bow manufactures the VOPT program for defragmenting
hard disks, the DUB-14 AT ROM BIOS kit for extending the hard disk
tables, and other utility software.

IBM Corporation, National Distribution Dept.
101 Paragon Drive
Montvale, NJ 07645
(201)930-3000

The IBM Corporation National Distribution Department manufactures
a line of IBM-compatible computer systems.

IBM Parts Order Center, Department E54
P.O. Box 9022
Boulder, CO 80301
(303)924-4100

This department is IBM's nationwide service parts ordering center.

IBM Service Parts Distribution Center, California
2946 West Seventh Street
Los Angeles, CA 90005
(213)385-4618

IBM Service Parts Distribution Center, California
411 Borel Avenue
San Mateo, CA 94402
(415)573-3110

IBM Service Parts Distribution Center, Colorado
4700 South Syracuse Parkway
Denver, CO 80237
(303)773-5931

IBM Service Parts Distribution Center, Connecticut
One Commercial Plaza
Hartford, CT 06103
(203)727-6133

IBM Service Parts Distribution Center, DC
1801 K Street NW, 4th Floor
Washington, DC 20006
(202)778-5636

IBM Service Parts Distribution Center, Georgia
1440 Spring Street NW
Atlanta, GA 30309
(404)888-4300

IBM Service Parts Distribution Center, Illinois
525 West Monroe Street
Chicago, IL 60606
(312)559-4502

IBM Service Parts Distribution Center, Massachusetts
One Gateway Center
Newton, MA 02158
(617)243-9588

IBM Service Parts Distribution Center, Michigan
27800 Northwestern Highway
Southfield, MI 48086
(313)262-3017

IBM Service Parts Distribution Center, Minnesota
7900 Xerxec Avenue, Suite 100
Bloomington, MN 55431
(612)893-2490

IBM Service Parts Distribution Center, Missouri
2345 Grand Avenue
Kansas City, MO 64108
(816)556-6950

IBM Service Parts Distribution Center, Missouri
One Centerre Plaza
St. Louis, MO 63101
(314)554-9564

IBM Service Parts Distribution Center, New Jersey
No. 5 Executive Campus
Cherry Hill, NJ 08002
(609)488-7751

IBM Service Parts Distribution Center, New Jersey
317 Route 17
Paramus, NJ 07653
(201)967-9430

IBM Service Parts Distribution Center, New York
200 South State Street, 2nd Floor
Syracuse, NY 13202
(315)424-2444

IBM Service Parts Distribution Center, North Carolina
706 Green Valley Road
Greensboro, NC 27408
(919)333-7150

IBM Service Parts Distribution Center, Ohio
250 East Fifth Street
Cincinnati, OH 45202
(513)762-2992

IBM Service Parts Distribution Center, Ohio
1300 East Ninth Street, Lobby Level
Cleveland, OH 44114
(216)664-7668

IBM Service Parts Distribution Center, Texas
1607 LBJ Freeway
Dallas, TX 75234
(214)888-4715

IBM Service Parts Distribution Center, Texas
Two Riverway Plaza
Houston, TX 77056
(713) 940-137

IBM Service Parts Distribution Center, Washington
4800 South 188th Street
Seattle, WA 98188
(206)433-8384

The preceding listings are regional IBM parts distribution centers.

Imprimis/Control Data Corporation
P.O. Box 0 (HQN08H)
Minneapolis, MN 55440
(800)828-8001

The Imprimis division of CDC manufactures the highest quality, largest capacity 5 1/4-inch and 3 1/2-inch hard disk drives in the industry today.

Intel Corporation
5200 NE Elam Young Parkway C03
Hillsboro, OR 97124
(800)538-3373

Intel Corporation manufactures the microprocessors used in IBM and compatible systems. Intel also makes a line of memory and accelerator boards.

Iomega Corp.
1821 West 4000 South
Roy, UT 84067
(801)778-1000

Iomega Corporation manufactures the Bernoulli Box high-capacity cartridge floppy disk drive.

Irwin Magnetics Systems Inc.
2101 Commonwealth Blvd.
Ann Arbor, MI 48105
(313)996-3300

Irwin Magnetics Systems Inc. manufactures a line of tape backup products based on the DC-2000 media. The company is also a supplier of IBM tape backup systems using DC-2000 media.

Jameco Eletronics
1355 Shoreway Road
Belmont, CA 94002
(415) 592-8097

Jameco Electronics stocks and distributes over 5,000 items ranging from computer peripherals and enhancements to integrated circuits and passive components.

JB Technologies, Inc.
21011 Itasca Street #F
Chatsworth, CA 67893
(818)709-6400

JB Technologies, Inc., is a service company that performs hard disk and tape backup component-level repair and remanufacturing.

JDR Microdevices
110 Knowles Drive
Los Gatos, CA 95030
(403)866-6200

JDR Microdevices is a vendor for chips, disk drives, and various computer and electronic parts and components.

Kaypro Corporation
533 Stevens Avenue
Solana Beach, CA 92075
(619)481-4300

Kaypro Corporation manufactures a line of IBM-compatible computer systems.

Manzana Microsystems, Inc.
P.O. Box 2117
Goleta, CA 93118
(805)968-1387

Manzana Microsystems, Inc., manufactures 3 1/2-inch floppy drive subsystems for IBM and compatible systems.

Maxtor Corporation
211 River Oaks Parkway
San Jose, CA 95134
(408)432-1700

Maxtor Corporation manufactures a line of large-capacity, high-quality hard disk drives. Maxtor also has introduced a revolutionary line of high-capacity, high-speed, Optical drives with full read and write capabilities.

Media Software & Systems
600 N. Commons Drive
Aurora, IL 60504
(312)898-2228

Media Software & Systems is a distributor for the Dysan Interrogator and Dysan digital diagnostics test disks.

Megahertz Corporation
2681 Parleys Way
Salt Lake City, UT 84109
(801)485-8857

Megahertz Corporation manufactures a line of AT speedup products.

Mentor Electronics, Inc.
7560 Tylor Blvd. #E
Mentor, OH 44060
(216)951-1884

Mentor Electronics, Inc., is a supplier of surplus IBM PC (10/27/82) ROM BIOS update chips.

Micro Solutions, Inc.
132 W. Lincoln Highway
DeKalb, IL 60115
(312)756-7411

Micro Solutions, Inc., manufactures a complete line of internal and external 3 1/2-inch floppy drive systems. The company also manufactures the Compaticard high-density floppy controller for IBM and compatible systems.

MicroWay Inc.
P.O. Box 79
Kingston, MA 02364
(617)746-7341

MicroWay Inc. manufactures a line of accelerator products for IBM and compatible systems. The company also specializes in math coprocessor chips, math chip accelerators, and language products.

Micropolis Corp.
2123 Nordhoff Street
Chatsworth, CA 91311
(818)709-3300

Micropolis manufactures a line of 5 1/4-inch and 3 1/2-inch hard disk drives.

Microsoft
16011 NE 36th Way
Redmond, WA 90852
(206)882-8080

Microsoft manufactures many software and some hardware products.
Under a joint agreement with IBM, Microsoft produces OS/2
and DOS.

Miniscribe Corp.
1861 Lefthand Circle
Longmont, CO 80501
(303)651-6000

Miniscribe manufactures a line of 5 1/4-inch and 3 1/2-inch hard disk
drives. Miniscribe also was a supplier to IBM for XT hard disks.

Mountain Computer Inc.
360 El Pueblo Road
Scott Valley, CA 95066
(408)438-6650

Mountain Computer Inc. manufactures a complete line of tape
backup products.

Mueller Business Systems
227 South Hale Street
Palatine, IL 60067
(312)358-5524

Mueller Business Systems is a service company specializing in
computer training and consulting.

Newbury Data
6 New England Executive Plaza
Burlington, MA 01803
(617)723-9513

Newbury Data manufactures a line of hard disk drives under a
license from Maxtor.

Ontrack Computer Systems
6266 Bury Drive
Eden Prairie, MN 55344
(612)937-1107

Ontrack Computer Systems manufactures the Diskmanager hard disk utility program that circumvents the many limitations of DOS versions 2.x through 4.01.

Orchid Technology
45365 Northport Loop West
Fremont, CA 94538
(415)683-0300

Orchid Technology manufactures a line of accelerator products for IBM and compatible systems.

PC Cooling Systems
P.O. Box 518
Bonsall, CA 92003
(619)723-9513

PC Cooling Systems manufactures a line of high-quality, high-output power supplies for IBM and compatible systems.

PTI Industries
269 Mount Hermon Road
Scott Valley, CA 95066
(408)438-3900

PTI Industries manufactures a line of computer power-protection devices.

Paul Mace Inc.
123 N. 1st Street
Ashland, OR 97520
(503)488-0224

Paul Mace Inc. manufactures the Htest/Hformat hard disk low-level format and repair utility package. The company also manufactures the Mace Utilities program.

Peter Norton Computing
2210 Wilshire Blvd.
Santa Monica, CA 90403
(213)453-2361

Peter Norton Computing manufactures the Norton Utilities program and many other useful utilities.

Priam Corp.
20 W. Montague Expressway
San Jose, CA 95134
(408)434-9300

Priam manufactures a line of 5 1/4-inch and 3 1/2-inch hard disk drives.

Proto PC, Inc.
2424 Territorial Road
St. Paul, MN 55114
(612)644-4660

Proto PC, Inc., manufactures the HD-Test hard disk diagnostic program. The company also manufactures a floppy disk testing machine and is a vendor for various computer parts and accessories.

Quadram Corporation
265 Mitchell Road
Norcross, GA 30071
(404)923-6666

Quadram Corporation manufactures a line of memory and other types of adapter boards for IBM and compatible systems.

Quaid Software Limited
45 Charles Street East, 3rd Floor
Toronto, ON, M4Y1S2
(416)961-8243

Quaid Software Limited manufactures the CopyWrite disk duplication utility, as well as the Disk Explorer utility.

Que Corporation
11711 N. College Avenue
Carmel, IN 46032
(317)573-2500

Que is a publisher of high-quality computer software and hardware books.

Rodime Inc.
901 Broken Sound Parkway NW
Boca Raton, FL 33431
(305)994-6200

Rodime Inc. manufactures a line of 5 1/4-inch and 3 1/2-inch hard disk drives.

Rotating Memory Service
473 Sapena Court, Suite 26
Santa Clara, CA 95954
(408)988-2334

Rotating Memory Service is a service company that specializes in hard disk drive component-level repair and data recovery.

Scientific Micro Systems
339 N. Bernardo Ave.
Mountain View, CA 94043
(515)964-5700

Scientific Micro Systems manufactures the OMTI line of hard disk controllers for IBM and compatible systems.

Seagate Technologies
920 Disc Drive
Scotts Valley, CA 95066
(408)439-2277

Seagate Technologies is the largest hard disk manufacturer in the industry. Seagate manufactures some of the lowest cost drives available.

Sola Electric
1717 Busse Road
Elk Grove, IL 60007
(312)439-2800

Sola Electric manufactures a line of computer power-protection devices.

Sony Corporation of America
Sony Drive
Park Ridge, NJ 07656
(201)930-1000

Sony Corporation of America manufactures all types of high-quality electronic and computer equipment.

Storage Dimensions Inc.
981 University Avenue
Los Gatos, CA 95030
(408)395-2688

Storage Dimensions Inc. is a division of Maxtor. The company
manufactures the Speedstor partitioning software that was used
with DOS 3.2 or earlier to overcome the limitations of FDISK. This is
not required for DOS 3.3 or later. Storage Dimensions is a vendor of
Maxtor drives.

SuperSoft
P.O. Box 1628
Champaign, IL 61820
(217)359-2112

SuperSoft manufactures a complete line of high-quality advanced
hardware diagnostics programs for IBM and compatible systems.

Sytron Corp.
117 Flanders Road
Westboro, MA 01581
(508)898-0100

Sytron manufactures the SyTOS tape backup utility software. The
company is a supplier of this software to IBM and other companies.

Tandon Corporation
405 Science Drive
Moorpark, CA 93021
(805)523-0340

Tandon Corporation manufactures IBM-compatible computer systems
and disk drives. Tandon supplied IBM with most of the full-height
floppy drives used in the PC and XT systems.

Tandy Corporation
1800 One Tandy Center
Fort Worth, TX 76102
(817)360-3011

Tandy Corporation manufactures a line of IBM-compatible systems.

Teac Corporation of America
7733 Telegraph Road
Montebello, CA 90640
(213)726-0303

Teac Corporation of America manufactures a complete line of 5 1/4-inch and 3 1/2-inch floppy disk drives.

Tecmar Inc.
6225 Cochran Road
Solon, OH 44139
(216)349-0600

Tecmar Inc. manufactures a wide variety of adapter boards for IBM and compatible systems.

Toshiba America Inc.
9740 Irvine Blvd
Irvine, VA 92718
(714)583-3000

Toshiba America Inc. manufactures a complete line of 5 1/4-inch and 3 1/2-inch floppy and hard disk drives. The company also manufactures a line of portable IBM-compatible systems.

Tripp Lite
500 North Orleans
Chicago, IL 60610
(312)329-1777

Tripp Lite manufactures a line of computer power-protection devices.

Verbatim/Cybernetics
323 Soquel Way
Sunnyvale, CA 94086
(408)245-4400

Verbatim/Cybernetics manufactures the Datalife DDA floppy drive diagnostics program.

Wave Mate Inc.
2341 205th Street, Suite 110
Torrance, CA 90501
(213)533-8190

Wave Mate Inc. manufactures a line of high-speed replacement motherboards for IBM and compatible systems.

Western Digital Corporation
2445 McCabe Way
Irvine, CA 92714
(714)863-0102

Western Digital Corporation manufactures a complete line of disk drive controller boards for IBM and compatible systems. Western Digital also manufactures the Paradise line of high-resolution EGA/VGA video adapters.

Windsor Technologies
66 Bovet Road, Suite 380
San Mateo, CA 94402
(415)345-5700

Windsor Technologies manufactures a line of advanced hardware diagnostics programs. The company also offers a ROM-based diagnostics product.

Xidex/Dysan CE Division
1244 Ramwood Avenue
Sunnyvale, CA 94089
(408)988-3472

Xidex/Dysan CE Division manufactures the Interrogator floppy disk drive diagnostics program and digital diagnostics disks.

Zenith Data Systems
1000 Milwaukee Avenue
Glenview, IL 60025
(312)699-4800

Zenith Data Systems manufactures a line of IBM-compatible systems.

Manufacturers' Logos

This section provides you with a listing of various manufacturers' logos, supplied by JAMECO Electronics.

MANUFACTURER'S LOGO DIRECTORY

LOGO	MANUFACTURER/ADDRESS
ADVANCED ANALOG A Division of Intech AM	**Advanced Analog** 2270 Martin Avenue Santa Clara, CA 95050 (408) 988-4930
	Advanced Micro Devices P.O. Box 3453 Sunnyvale, CA 94088 (408) 732-2400
TFK	**AEG-Telefunken Corp.** P.O. Box 3800 Somerville, NJ 08876 (201) 722-9800
ANALOG DEVICES	**Analog Devices** One Technology Way Norwood, MA 02062-9106 (617) 329-4700
ANALOGIC	**Analogic Corporation** 8 Centennial Drive Peabody, MA 01961 (617) 246-0300
BECKMAN	**Beckman Instruments** 2500 Harbor Boulevard Fullerton, CA 92634 (714) 773-8603
BURR-BROWN BB	**Burr-Brown** P.O. Box 11400 Tucson, AZ 85734 (602) 746-1111
CALIFORNIA MICRO DEVICES MICROCIRCUITS DIVISION	**California Micro Devices** 2000 W. 14th Street Tempe, AZ 85281 (602) 968-4431
CHERRY SEMICONDUCTOR	**Cherry Semiconductor Corp.** 2000 South County Trail East Greenwich, RI 02818-0031 (401) 885-3600
C	**Commodore Semiconductor Group** 950 Rittenhouse Road Norristown, PA 19403 (215) 666-7950
	Cybernetic Micro Systems P.O. Box 3000 San Gregorio, CA 94074 (415) 726-3000
CYPRESS SEMICONDUCTOR	**Cypress Semiconductor** 3901 N. First Street San Jose, CA 95134 (408) 943-2600
	Data General Corp. 4400 Computer Drive Westborough, MA 01580 (617) 366-8911

LOGO	MANUFACTURER/ADDRESS
HYUNDAI ELEXS AMERICA	**Hyundai Elexs America** 166 Baypointe Parkway San Jose, CA 95134 (408) 286-9800
inmos	**INMOS Corp.** 1110 Bayfield Road Colorado Springs, CO 80906 (303) 630-4000
intel i	**Intel** 3065 Bowers Avenue Santa Clara, CA 95051 (408) 987-8080
INTERSIL	**Intersil** 2450 Walsh Avenue Santa Clara, CA 95051 (408) 996-5000
ITT semiconductors	**ITT Semiconductors** 470 Broadway Lawrence, MA 01841 (617) 688-1881
Jameco ELECTRONICS	**JAMECO ELECTRONICS** 1355 SHOREWAY ROAD BELMONT, CALIFORNIA 94002 (415) 592-8097 FAX 415-592-2503
	Lambda Semiconductor 121 International Drive Corpus Christi, TX 78410 (512) 289-0403
LINEAR	**Linear Technology** 1630 McCarthy Boulevard Milpitas, CA 95035-7487 (408) 432-1900
3M	**3M/Electronic Products Division** P.O. Box 2963 Austin, TX 78769-2963 (512) 834-1800
MICRON TECHNOLOGY, INC.	**Micron Technology Inc.** 2805 E. Columbia Road Boise, ID 83706 (208) 383-4000
MN	**Micro Networks** 324 Clark Street Worcester, MA 01606 (617) 852-5400
M	**Micro Power Systems** 3151 Jay Street, Box 54965 Santa Clara, CA 95054-0965 (408) 727-5350
	Mitel Corporation 350 Lagget Drive, P.O. Box 13089 Ontario, Canada K2K 1X3 (613) 592-5630

LOGO	MANUFACTURER/ADDRESS
SANYO	**Sanyo Semiconductor Corp.** 7 Pearl Court Allendale, NJ 07401 (201) 825-8080
seeq	**SEEQ Technology Inc.** 1849 Fortune Drive San Jose, CA 95131 (408) 432-7400
	SGS Semiconductor 1000 E. Bell Road Phoenix, AZ 85022 (602) 867-6100
SIEMENS	**Siemens Components** 1900 Homestead Road Cupertino, CA 95014 (408) 725-3531
Signetics	**Signetics** 811 E. Arques Avenue Sunnyvale, CA 94088-3409 (408) 991-2000
Silicon General	**Silicon General** 11861 Western Avenue Garden Grove, CA 92641 (714) 898-8121
	Silicon Systems 14351 Myford Road Tustin, CA 92680 (714) 731-7110
B	**Siliconix** 2201 Laurelwood Road Santa Clara, CA 95054 (408) 988-8000
S-MOS SYSTEMS	**S-MOS** 2460 North First Street San Jose, CA 95131 (408) 922-0200
S	**Solitron Devices, Inc.** 1177 Blue Heron Boulevard Riviera Beach, FL 33404 (407) 848-4311
SPRAGUE	**Sprague Electric** 115 N.E. Cutoff Worcester, MA 01613-2036 (617) 853-5000
SPRAGUE SOLID STATE	**Sprague Solid State** 3900 Welsh Road Willow Grove, PA 19090 (215) 657-8400
	Standard Microsystems 35 Marcus Boulevard Hauppauge, NY 11788 (516) 273-3100

Datel
11 Cabot Boulevard
Mansfield, MA 02048
(617) 339-3000

EG&G Reticon Corp.
345 Potrero Avenue
Sunnyvale, CA 94086
(408) 738-4266

EXAR Integrated Systems
2222 Qume Drive
San Jose, CA 95161
(408) 732-7970

Ferranti
87 Modular Avenue
Commack, NY 11725
(516) 543-0200

Fujitsu Microelectronics, Inc.
3545 North First Street
San Jose, CA 95134
(408) 922-9000

General Electric Solid State
724 Route 202, P.O. Box 591
Somerville, NJ 08876-0591
(201) 685-6000

General Instrument
600 W. John Street
Hicksville, NY 11802
(516) 933-9000

Goldstar Semiconductor Ltd.
1130 E. Arquez Avenue
Sunnyvale, CA 94086
(408) 737-8576

Gould Semiconductors
2300 Buckskin Road
Pocatello, ID 83201
(208) 233-4690

Harris Semiconductor
P.O. Box 883
Melbourne, FL 32901
(305) 724-7000

Hitachi America, Ltd.
2210 O'Toole Avenue
San Jose, CA 95131
(408) 435-8300

Honeywell
1150 E. Cheyenne Mountain Blvd.
Colorado Springs, CO 80906-4599
(303) 576-3300

Hughes Aircraft
500 Superior Avenue, P.O. Box H
Newport Beach, CA 92658-8903
(714) 759-2349

Hybrid Systems
22 Linnell Circle
Billerica, MA 01821
(617) 667-8700

Mitsubishi Electronics America
1050 E. Arques Avenue
Sunnyvale, CA 94086
(408) 730-5900

Monolithic Memories
P.O. Box 3453
Sunnyvale, CA 94088
(408) 970-9700

Motorola
5005 E. McDowell Road
Phoenix, AZ 85008
(602) 244-7100

National Semiconductor
2900 Semiconductor Drive
Santa Clara, CA 95051
(408) 721-5000

NCR
8181 Byers Road
Miamisburg, OH 45342
(513) 866-7217

NEC Electronics, Inc.
401 Ellis Street
Mountain View, CA 94039-7241
(415) 960-6000

OKI Semiconductor, Inc.
650 N. Mary Avenue
Sunnyvale, CA 94086
(408) 720-1900

Panasonic (Matsushita)
1 Panasonic Way
Secaucus, NJ 07094
(201) 348-7000

Plessey Semiconductor
1500 Green Hills Road
Scotts Valley, CA 95066
(408) 438-2900

Precision Monolithics, Inc.
1500 Space Park Drive
Santa Clara, CA 95052-8020
(408) 727-9222

Raytheon Semiconductor
350 Ellis Street
Mountain View, CA 94039-7016
(415) 968-9211

Rockwell International
4311 Jamboree Road, P.O. Box C
Newport Beach, CA 92658-8902
(714) 833-4700

Samsung Semiconductor, Inc.
3725 North First Street
San Jose, CA 95134
(408) 434-5400

STS Thomson Micro Electronics
1310 Electronics Drive
Carrollton, TX 75006
(214) 466-6000

Supertex
1350 Bordeaux Drive
Sunnyvale, CA 94089
(408) 744-0100

Teledyne Philbrick
40 Allied Drive
Dedham, MA 02026-9103
(617) 329-1600

Teledyne Semiconductor
1300 Terra Bella Ave., Box 7267
Mountain View, CA 94039-7267
(415) 968-9241

Texas Instruments
P.O. Box 655474
Dallas, TX 75265
(214) 995-2011

TRW Semiconductors
P.O. Box 2472
La Jolla, CA 92038
(619) 457-1000

Thomson-CSF Components Corp.
6203 Variel Avenue, Unit A
Woodland Hills, CA 91365
(818) 887-1010

Toshiba America, Inc.
9775 Toldeo Way
Irvine, CA 92718
(714) 455-2000

United Microelectronics Corp.
3350 Scott Boulevard #57
Santa Clara, CA 95054
(408) 727-9239

Vitelic Corp.
3910 North First Street
San Jose, CA 95135-1501
(408) 433-6000

Western Digital
2445 McCabe Way
Irvine, CA 92714
(714) 863-0102

Xicor
851 Buckeye Court
Milpitas, CA 95035
(408) 432-8888

Zilog, Inc.
210 Hacienda Avenue
Campbell, CA 95008
(408) 370-8000

Glossary

8086. An Intel microprocessor with 16-bit registers, a 16-bit data bus, and a 20-bit address bus. It can operate only in real mode.

8088. An Intel microprocessor with 16-bit registers, an 8-bit data bus, and a 20-bit address bus. It can operate only in real mode. This processor was designed as a low-cost version of the **8086**.

80286. An Intel microprocessor with 16-bit registers, a 16-bit data bus, and a 24-bit address bus. It can operate in real and protected modes.

80386. An Intel microprocessor with 32-bit registers, a 32-bit data bus, and a 32-bit address bus. It can operate in real, protected, and virtual real modes.

80386SX. An Intel microprocessor with 32-bit registers, a 16-bit data bus, and a 24-bit address bus. It can operate in real, protected, and virtual real modes. This processor was designed as a low-cost version of the **80386**.

AC. Alternating Current. The frequency is measured in cycles per seconds (cps) or Hertz (Hz). The standard value coming through the wall outlet is 120 volts at 60 Hz, through a fuse or circuit breaker that can usually handle about 20 amps.

Accelerator board. An add-in board that replaces the computer's **CPU** with circuitry that enables the system to run faster.

Access time. The time taken from the instant information is called for to the point delivery is completed. Usually described in **nanoseconds** for memory chips. The IBM PC requires memory chips with an access time of 200 nanoseconds, and the AT requires 150 nanosecond chips. For hard disk drives, access time is described in **milliseconds**. Most manufacturers rate average access time on a hard disk as the time required for a seek across one-third of the total number of cylinders plus one-half of the time for a single revolution of the disk platters (latency).

Accumulator. A register in which the result of an operation is formed.

Active high. Designates a digital signal that has to go to a high value (binary 1) to produce an effect. Synonymous with positive true.

Active low. Designates a digital signal that has to go to a low value (binary 0) to produce an effect. Synonymous with negative true.

Actuator. The device that moves a disk drive's read/write heads across the platter surfaces.

Adapter. This term is used by IBM to be synonymous with **circuit board**, circuit card, or **card**. It is the device that serves as an interface between the system unit and the devices attached to it.

Address. Where a particular piece of data or other information is found in the computer. Can also refer to the location of a set of instructions.

Address bus. One or more electrical conductors used to carry the binary-coded **address** from the microprocessor throughout the rest of the system.

Alphanumeric. A character set that contains both letters (A-Z) and digits (0-9). Other characters, such as punctuation marks, also may be allowed.

Ampere. One ampere (amp) is the basic unit for measuring electrical current.

Analog. Pertaining to data in the form of continuously variable physical quantities. This is in contrast with digital.

AND. A logic operator having the property that if P is a statement, Q is a statement, R is a statement, . . . , then the AND of P,Q,R, . . . is true if all statements are true, false if any statement is false.

AND gate. A logic gate in which the output is 1 only if all inputs are 1.

ANSI. American National Standards Institute. One of several organizations that develop standards for the electronics and computer industries.

APA. All Points Addressable. A mode in which all points of a displayable image can be controlled by the user or a program.

Archive bit. The bit in a file's attribute byte that sets the archive attribute. This tells whether the file has been changed since it was last backed up.

Archive medium. A storage medium (floppy disk, tape cartridge, removable cartridge) that holds files which need not be instantly accessible.

ASCII. American Standard Code for Information Interchange. One of the few genuine standards in the microcomputer world. This code assigns binary (on/off) values to the 7-bit capability of the computer (plus the extra 8th bit to signal the end of the character or to be used as a parity bit to check for errors). IBM Extended ASCII is a similar code set that uses the 8th bit for an additional 128 characters rather than as a parity bit. ASCII is used in sending data and other binary information, such as through a telephone modem.

ASCII character. A 1-byte character from the ASCII character set, including alphabetic and numeric characters, punctuation symbols, and various graphic characters.

Assemble. To translate a program expressed in an **assembler language** into a computer machine language.

Assembly language. A computer-oriented language whose instructions are usually in one-to-one correspondence with machine language instructions.

Asynch. An abbreviation for "asynchronous," generally applied to communications and the way in which a character is transmitted and checked. Each character is segmented individually, such as with a stop bit.

Asynchronous communication. Data transfer, the timing of which is dependent on the actual time for the transfer to take place, as opposed to synchronous communication, which is rigidly timed by an external clock signal.

Attribute byte. A byte of information, held in the directory entry of any file, that describes various attributes of the file, such as whether it is a read-only file or has been backed up since it was last changed. These attributes can be set by the DOS ATTRIB command.

Audio. A signal that can be heard, such as through the speaker of the PC. Diagnostics use both visual codes (on the screen) and audio signals.

Audio frequencies. Frequencies that can be heard by the human ear (approximately 20 Hz to 20,000 Hz).

AUTOEXEC.BAT. A special batch file that **DOS** will execute upon starting. It contains any number of **DOS** commands, which are automatically executed.

Automatic head parking. Disk drive head parking performed automatically whenever the drive is powered off. This feature is found in all hard disk drives with a voice coil actuator.

Auxiliary storage. A storage device that is not main storage.

Average latency. The average time required for any byte of data stored on a disk to rotate under the disk drive's **read/write head**. This is equal to one-half of the time for a single rotation of a platter.

Average seek time. The average time required for a disk drive's **read/write heads** to move from one track to another. Usually expressed as the time for a seek across one-third of the total number of tracks.

Backup. The process of duplicating a **file** or library onto a separate piece of media. Good insurance against loss of an original.

Backup disk. Contains information copied from another disk. Used to make sure that original information is not destroyed or altered.

Bad sector. A disk sector that cannot reliably hold data because of a media flaw or damaged format markings.

Bad track table. A label affixed to the casing of a hard disk drive that tells which tracks are flawed and cannot hold **data**. The listing is entered into the low-level formatting program.

Bank. The collection of memory chips that make up a block of memory that is readable by the processor in a single bus cycle. This block must therefore be as large as the data bus of the particular **microprocessor**. In IBM systems, the processor data bus is usually 8, 16, or 32 **bits**, plus a **parity** bit for each 8 bits, resulting in a total of 9, 18, or 36 bits for each bank.

BASIC. Beginner's All-Purpose Symbolic Instruction Code. One of the most common computer languages. The IBM PC has three versions: Cassette, Disk, and Advanced. Cassette BASIC resides in **read-only memory** (ROM) and is loaded automatically if no **DOS** is found when the system is started. Disk BASIC and Advanced BASIC (BASICA) are on the **DOS** diskette.

Batch file. A file that contains a series of commands that **DOS** executes when the file is called. Batch files have a BAT extension.

Baud. A measure of the rate of data transmission. The transmitting signal is split into a certain number of parts (usually frequency or signal changes) per second. A rate of 300 baud means that 300 frequency or signal changes per second are being sent. This is usually roughly equivalent to an equal number of **bits** per second.

Bay. An opening in a computer cabinet, that holds disk drives.

Bezel. A cosmetic panel that covers the face of a drive or some other device.

Bisynchronous. A method of communication between a mainframe computer and a minicomputer.

Bidirectional. Refers to lines over which data can move in two directions, like a data bus or a telephone line. It also refers to the capability of a printer to print alternately from right to left and from left to right.

Binary. Refers to the computer numbering system consisting of two numerals, 0 and 1. Also called Base-2.

BIOS. Basic Input/Output System. The part of an operating system that handles the communications between the computer and its **peripherals**. These programs are often burned into **read-only memory** (ROM) chips.

Bit. *Binary digit*. A bit is represented logically by 0 or 1 and electrically by 0 volts (low condition) and (typically) 5 volts (high condition). Other ways are available to physically represent binary digits (tones, different voltages, lights, etc.), but the logic is always the same.

Block. A string of records, a string of words, or a character string formed for technical or logic reasons, to be treated as an entity.

Block diagram. The logical structure or layout of a system in graphic form. Does not necessarily match the actual physical layout and does not specify all the components and their interconnections.

Boolean operation. Any operation in which each of the operands and the result take one of two values.

Boot. To load a program into the computer. The term comes from "bootstrap," which in turn comes from "pulling a boot on by the bootstrap." In simple terms, it means the computer is loading and starting an operating system.

Boot record. A one-sector record that tells the computer's built-in operating system (BIOS) the most fundamental facts about a disk and **DOS**. The information it supplies instructs the computer how to load the operating system files into memory, thus booting the machine.

Boot strap. A technique or device designed to bring itself into a desired state by means of its own action.

Buffer. A segment of memory used to store **data** temporarily while the data is being transferred from one device to another. A common example is a printer buffer. This device stores the incoming data at full computer speed and sends it to the printer at a speed the printer can handle.

Bug. An error or defect in a program.

Bus. An electrical pathway over which power, **data**, and other signals travel.

Byte. A collection of **bits** that makes up a character or other designation. Generally a byte is 8 data bits.

Capacitor. A device consisting of two plates separated by insulating material and designed to store an electrical charge.

Card. A printed **circuit board** that contains electronic components that form the entire circuit. Also called an adapter.

Carrier. The reference signal used for the transmission or reception of data. The most common use of this signal with computers involves **modem** communications over phone lines. The carrier is used as a signal on which the information is superimposed.

Cathode ray tube. A device that contains electrodes surrounded by a glass sphere/cylinder and that will display information by creating a beam of electrons that strike a phosphor coating inside the display unit.

Channel. A path along which signals can be sent.

Checksum. Short for summation check, a technique for determining whether a package of data is valid. The package, a string of binary digits, is added up and compared with the expected number.

Chip. Another name for an IC, or integrated circuit. Derived from the "chip" of silicon contained within the IC. Chips are either housed in a plastic or ceramic carrier device with pins for making electrical connections.

Circuit. A complete electronic path.

Circuit board. The collection of circuits gathered together on a sheet of plastic, usually with all contacts made through a strip of pins. The circuit board is usually made by chemically etching metal-coated plastic.

Clean room. A dust-free room in which certain electronic components must be manufactured to prevent contamination. Required for servicing these components (such as hard disk drives) as well. These rooms are rated by a "Class" number. A Class 100 clean room must have fewer than 100 particles larger than 0.5 microns per cubic foot of space.

Clock. The source of a computer's timing signals. Every operation of the **CPU** is synchronized by the clock.

Cluster. A group of one or more sectors, that is the basic unit in which **DOS** allocated disk space. The number of sectors in a cluster varies by disk type and DOS version.

CMOS. Complementary Metal Oxide Semiconductor. A type of chip design that requires very little power to operate. In an AT type of system, a battery-powered CMOS memory and clock chip is used to store and maintain the clock setting and system configuration information.

Coprocessor. Additional computer processing unit designed to handle specific tasks in conjunction with the main or central processing unit.

Coated media. Hard disk platters coated with a reddish iron-oxide medium on which data is recorded.

Command. An instruction that tells the computer to start, stop, or continue an operation.

COMMAND.COM. An operating system **file**, which is loaded last when the computer is booted. The command interpreter or user interface and program loader portion of **DOS**.

Common. The ground or return path for an electrical signal. If this is a wire, it is usually colored black.

Composite Video. Television picture information and sync pulses combined. The IBM Color Graphics Adapter (CGA) will output a composite video signal.

Computer. Device capable of accepting **data**, applying prescribed processes to this data, and displaying the results or information produced.

CONFIG.SYS. A **file** that may be created to tell **DOS** how to configure itself when the machine starts up. CONFIG.SYS can load device drivers, set the number of DOS buffers, and so on.

Configuration file. A file kept by application software to record various aspects of the software's configuration, such as the printer it uses. CONFIG.SYS is the DOS configuration file.

Console. The unit in your system from which you communicate to the computer, such as a terminal or a keyboard.

Contiguous. Touching or joined together at the edge or boundary, in one piece.

Continuity. In electronics, an unbroken pathway. Testing for continuity normally means testing to find out whether a wire or other conductor is complete and unbroken (by measuring 0 ohms). A broken wire will show infinite resistance (or infinite ohms).

Control cable. The wider of two cables that connects a hard disk drive to a controller card.

Controller. The electronics that control a device, such as a hard disk drive, and intermediate the passage of **data** between the device and the computer.

Controller card. An adapter holding the control electronics for one or more devices such as hard disks. Ordinarily, this adapter takes up one of the computer's slots.

Core. An "old-fashioned" term for your computer's memory.

CP/M. Control Program for Microcomputers. One of the first and, until the advent of the IBM PC, most widely used microcomputer operating systems. It survives in the PC world primarily under the name CP/M-86 (for the **8088/8086 microprocessors**).

CPS. Cycles Per Second. Usually expressed as "Hertz" (Hz). For printers, this also can mean Characters Per Second, which is used to benchmark the speed of a printer.

CPU. Central Processing Unit. The computer's microprocessor chip, the brains of the outfit. Typically, this is an IC using VLSI (very large scale integration) technology to pack several different functions into a small area. The most common electronic device in the CPU is the transistor, of which there are usually 30,000 to 1,000,000 or more.

Crash. A malfunction that brings work to a halt. A system crash is usually caused by a software malfunction, and you ordinarily can restart the system by rebooting the machine. However, a head crash entails physical damage to a disk and probable data loss.

CRC. Cyclic Redundancy Check. A technique for checking transmitted data for errors. It is commonly used to verify data written to disk.

CRT. Cathode Ray Tube. A term used to describe a television or monitor screen tube.

Current. The flow of electrons through a conductor of electricity. Electrical current energy is measured in amperes.

Cursor. The small flashing mark that appears on the monitor screen to indicate the point at which any input from the keyboard will be placed.

Cycle time. The period of time between the beginning and end of any type of cycle.

Cylinder. A number of **tracks** on a disk that are on each side of all of the disk platters in a stack and that are the same distance from the center of the disk. A cylinder is the total number of tracks that can be read without moving the heads. A floppy drive with two heads may be capable of reading 160 tracks, which are accessible as 80 cylinders (80 tracks by 2 sides). A typical 20-megabyte hard disk will have 2 platters with 4 heads and 615 cylinders, where each cylinder is 4 tracks.

Daisy chain. Stringing up components in such a manner that the signals move in serial fashion from one to the other. Most microcomputer multiple disk drive systems are daisy chained. The SCSI bus system is a daisy-chain arrangement, wherein the signals move from computer to disk drives to tape units, etc.

Data. Groups of facts that are processed into information. Data is a graphic or textual representation of facts, concepts, numbers, letters, symbols, or instructions used for communication or processing.

Data cable. The narrower of two cables that connect a hard disk drive to a controller card.

Data transfer rate. The maximum rate at which data can be transferred from one device to another.

DC. Direct current, such as that provided by a power supply or batteries.

DC-600. Data Cartridge 600, a media, invented by 3M in 1971, that uses 1/4-inch wide tape that is 600 feet in length.

DCE. Data Communications Equipment. Hardware that does the actual communication. Data Terminal Equipment (DTE) is the source and destination of data. A computer or terminal is usually configured as DTE, and a modem is configured as DCE.

Deallocated cluster. A cluster of disk space marked in the file allocation table as "available" after the file that used it has been erased.

DEBUG. The name of a utility program included with **DOS** that is used for specialized purposes such as altering memory locations, tracing the execution of programs, patching programs and disk sectors, and other low-level tasks. Also a term used to find problems in hardware or software, with the intent of eliminating the problem.

Dedicated servo surface. In voice-coil-actuated hard disk drives, a dedicated servo surface is one side of one platter given over to servo data that is used to guide and position the **read/write heads**.

Default. An assumption the computer makes when no other parameters are specified. When you type *dir*, for example, without specifying the drive to search, the computer automatically searches the default drive and assumes that this is what you want. The term is used in software to describe any action the computer or program takes on its own with embedded values.

Density. The amount of data that can be packed into a given area on a floppy disk.

Device driver. A memory-resident program, loaded by **CONFIG.SYS**, that controls an unusual device, such as an expanded memory board.

Diagnostics. Programs used to check the operation of a computer system. These programs allow the operator to check the entire system for any problems and to indicate in what area the problem lies.

DIP. Dual Inline Package. The plastic or ceramic carrier device that houses a chip or other electrical device.

DIP switch. A tiny switch (or group of switches) found on a **circuit board**. Named for the form factor of the carrier device in which the switch is housed.

Direct memory access. A process by which **data** moves directly between a disk drive (or other device) and system memory without direct control of the central processing unit, thus freeing it up for other tasks.

Directory. An area of a disk that stores the titles given to the **files** saved on the disk. The directory serves as a "table of contents" for the files saved on the disk. The directory contains **data** that identifies the name of a file, the size, the attributes (system, hidden, read-only, etc.), the date and time of creation, and a pointer to the location of the file.

Directory entry. The 32-**byte** record, held in a directory, that tells a **file's** name, size, time and **data**, starting cluster, and other pertinent information.

Disk Operating System. DOS. A collection of programs stored on the DOS disk. These programs contain **routines** that allow the system and user to manage information and the hardware resources of the computer. A DOS must be loaded into the computer before you start other programs.

Diskette. A floppy disk. The disk is made of a flexible material that is coated with magnetic substance. The disk spins inside its protective jacket, and the **read/write head** comes in contact with the recording surface to read or write **data**.

DMA. Direct Memory Access. This is a circuit by which a high-speed transfer of information may be facilitated between a device and the memory of a system. This transfer is managed by a specialized processor that relieves the burden of managing the transfer from the main **CPU**. DMA channels may work simultaneously.

Downtime. Operating time lost due to a computer malfunction.

Drive. A mechanical device that manipulates data storage media.

DTE. Data Terminal Equipment. The source of data and the destination of data. Data Communication Equipment (DCE) is the hardware that does the actual communication. A computer or terminal is usually configured as DTE, and a **modem** is configured as **DCE**.

Edit. The process of rearranging data or information.

Electronic mail. A method of transferring messages from one computer to another.

Embedded servo data. Magnetic markings embedded between or inside of **tracks** on disk drives that use **voice coil actuators**. These markings allow the actuator to fine tune the position of the **read/write heads**.

Encoding. The protocol by which **data** is carried or stored by a **medium**.

Encryption. The translation of **data** into unreadable codes to maintain security.

EPROM. Erasable Programmable Read-Only Memory. A type of read-only memory (ROM) where the data pattern may be erased to allow a new pattern. EPROMs are usually erased by ultraviolet light and recorded by a higher than normal voltage programming signal.

Error message. A word or combination of words to indicate to the user that an error occurred while the program was operating.

Extended partition. Starting with DOS 3.3, a hard disk may have two partitions that serve **DOS**—an ordinary, bootable partition (called the primary partition) and an extended partition, which may contain any number of volumes of up to 32 **megabytes** each.

File. A collection of information that is kept somewhere other than in the **random-access memory**.

File allocation table. A table held near the outer edge of a disk that tells which **sectors** are allocated to each file and in what order.

File attribute. Information held in the attribute **byte** of a file's directory entry.

File defragmentation. The process of rearranging disk **sectors** so that **files** are compacted onto consecutive or *contiguous* **sectors** in adjacent **tracks**.

File recovery. Techniques for repairing and reassembling **files** that have incurred one or more bad **sectors**.

File name. The name given to the disk **file**. Must be one to eight characters long and may be followed by a file name extension, which can be one to three characters long. A file name can be made up of any combination of letters and numbers but should be descriptive of the information contained on the **file**.

Fixed disk. Referred to also as a hard disk. A disk that cannot be removed from its controlling hardware or housing. Made of rigid material with a magnetic coating and used for the mass storage and retrieval of **data**.

Floppy tape. A tape standard using drives that connect to an ordinary floppy disk controller.

FM encoding. Frequency Modulation encoding. An outdated method of encoding data on the disk surface that uses up half the disk space with timing signals.

Form factor. The physical dimensions of a device. Two devices with the same form factor are physically interchangeable. The IBM PC, XT, and XT Model 286, for example, all use power supplies that are internally different but have exactly the same form factor.

FORMAT.COM. The **DOS** format program that performs both low- and high-level formatting on floppy disks but only high-level formatting on hard disks.

Formatted capacity. The total number of **bytes** of **data** that can fit onto a disk after it has been formatted. The unformatted capacity is higher because space is lost defining the boundaries between **sectors** after the disk has been formatted.

Formatting. Preparing a disk so that the computer can read or write to it. Formatting checks the disk for defects and constructs an organizational system to manage information on the disk.

Function Keys. Special-purpose keys that can be programmed to perform various operations. These keys serve many different functions depending on the program being used.

Giga. A multiplier indicating one billion (1,000,000,000) of something. Abbreviated as ''g'' or ''G.'' When used to indicate a number of **bytes** of memory storage, the multiplier definition changes to 1,073,741,824. One gigabit, for example, equals 1,000,000,000 bits, and one **gigabyte** equals 1,073,741,824 bytes.

Gigabyte. A unit of information storage. One gigabyte equals 1,073,741,824 **bytes**.

Global backup. A **backup** of all information on a hard disk, including the directory tree structure.

Hard error. An error in reading or writing data, caused by damaged hardware.

Hardware. Physical components that make up a microcomputer, monitor, printer, etc.

Head. A small electromagnetic device inside a drive, that reads, records, and erases data on the media.

Head actuator. The device that moves **read/write heads** across a disk drive's platters. Most drives use a **stepper motor actuator** or a **voice coil actuator**.

Head crash. A rare occurrence in which a **read/write head** strikes a platter surface, gouging the magnetic medium.

Head parking. A procedure in which a disk drive **read/write heads** are moved to an unused **track** so that they will not damage **data** in the event of a **head crash** or other failure.

Head seek. The movement of a drive's **read/write heads** to a particular **track**.

Hexadecimal number. A number encoded in base-16, such that digits include the letters A through F as well as the numerals 0 to 9 (for example, 8BF3, which equals 35,827 in base-10).

Hidden file. A file that is not displayed in DOS directory listings because its attribute byte holds a special setting.

High-level formatting. Formatting performed by the DOS FORMAT program. Among other things, it creates the **root directory** and the **file allocation tables**.

History file. A file created by utility software to keep track of earlier use of the software. Many backup programs, for example, keep history files describing earlier backup sessions.

I/O. Input/Output. A circuit path that allows independent communications between the processor and external devices.

IBMBIO.COM. One of the DOS system files required to **boot** the system. This is the first **file** loaded from disk during boot, and it contains extensions to the **ROM BIOS**.

IBMDOS.COM. One of the DOS system files required to **boot** the machine. This **file** contains the primary DOS **routines**. Loaded by IBMBIO.COM, it in turns loads **COMMAND.COM**.

Incremental backup. A backup of all **files** that have changed since the last backup.

Input. **Data** sent to the computer from the keyboard, the telephone, the video camera, another computer, paddles, joysticks, etc.

Instruction. Program step that tells the computer what to do for a single operation.

Interface. A communications device or protocol that allows one device to communicate with another. The interface matches the output of one device to the input of the other device.

Interleave. The numbering of **sectors** on a **track** so that the "next" sector arrives at the **read/write heads** just as the computer is ready to access it.

Interleave factor. The number of **sectors** that pass beneath the **read/write heads** before the "next" numbered sector arrives. When the interleave factor is 3 to 1, for example, a sector is read, two pass by, and then the next is read.

Internal command. In **DOS**, an internal command is one contained in **COMMAND.COM** so that no other **file** must be loaded to perform the command. DIR and COPY are two examples of internal commands.

Internal drive. A disk or tape drive mounted inside one of a computer's disk drive **bays** (or a hard disk card, which is installed in one of the computer's slots).

Interrupt. A suspension of a process, such as the execution of a computer program, caused by an event external to that process and performed in such a way that the process can be resumed.

Interrupt vector. A pointer in a table that gives the location of a set of instructions that the computer should execute when a particular interrupt occurs.

Jumper. A tiny connector that slips over two pins that protrude from a **circuit board**. When in place, the jumper connects the pins electrically. By doing so, it connects the two terminals of a switch, turning it "on."

Key disk. In software copy protection, a key disk is a distribution disk that must be present in a floppy disk drive for an application program to run.

Keyboard macro. A series of keystrokes automatically input when a single key is pressed.

Kilo. A multiplier indicating one thousand (1,000) of something. Abbreviated as "k" or "K." When used to indicate a number of **bytes** of memory storage, the multiplier definition changes to 1,024. One kilobit, for example, equals 1,000 bits, and one **kilobyte** equals 1,024 **bytes**.

Kilobyte. A unit of information storage. One kilobyte equals 1,024 **bytes**.

Landing zone. An unused **track** on a disk surface that the **read/write heads** can land on when power is shut off. This is the place that a parking program or a drive with an autopark mechanism will park the heads.

Logical drive. A drive as named by a DOS drive specifier, such as C: or D:. Under DOS 3.3 or later, a single physical drive may act as several logical drives, each with its own specifier.

Lost clusters. Clusters that have accidentally been marked as "unavailable" in the **file allocation table** even though they belong to no **file** listed in a **directory**.

Low-level formatting. Formatting that divides **tracks** into **sectors** on the platter surfaces. This type of format will place sector identifying information before and after each sector and fill each sector with null data (usually hex F6). In this format, the sector interleave is specified and defective tracks are marked. A defective track is marked when invalid **checksum** figures are placed in each sector on a defective track.

Magnetic domain. A tiny segment of a **track** just large enough to hold one of the magnetic flux reversals that encode **data** on a disk surface.

Magneto-optical recording. An erasable optical disk recording technique that uses a laser beam to heat pits on the disk surface to the point that a magnet can make flux changes.

Master boot record. On hard disks, a one-sector record that gives essential information about the disk and tells the starting locations of the various **partitions**. This is always the first physical **sector** of the disk.

Mean time between failure. A statistically derived measure of the probable time a device will operate before a hardware failure occurs. Usually abbreviated as MTBF.

Medium. The magnetic coating or plating that covers a disk or tape.

Mega. A multiplier indicating one million (1,000,000) of something. Abbreviated as "m" or "M." When used to indicate a number of **bytes** of memory storage, the multiplier definition changes to 1,048,576. One megabit, for example, equals 1,000,000 bits, and one **megabyte** equals 1,048,576 bytes.

Megabyte. A unit of information storage. One megabyte equals 1,048,576 **bytes**.

Memory. Any component in a computer system that stores information for future use.

Memory caching. A service provided by extremely fast memory chips that keeps copies of the most recent memory accesses. When the **CPU** makes a subsequent access, the value is supplied by the fast memory rather than from relatively slow system memory.

Memory-resident program. A program that remains in **memory** once it has been loaded, consuming memory that might otherwise be used by application software. Once loaded in memory, the program may be activated at any time, even during another program.

Menu software. Utility software that makes a computer easier to use by replacing DOS commands with a series of menu selections.

MFM. Modified Frequency Modulation encoding.

MHz. Megahertz. A measurement of millions of cycles per second.

Micro. A prefix indicating one millionth (1/1,000,000 or 0.000001) of some unit. Abbreviated as μ.

Microprocessor. A solid state central processing unit that is much like a computer on a chip. It is an integrated circuit that accepts coded instructions for execution.

Microsecond. A unit of time equal to one millionth (1/1,000,000 or 0.000001) of a second. Abbreviated as μs.

Milli. A prefix indicating one thousandth (1/1,000 or 0.001) of some unit. Abbreviated as "m."

Millisecond. A unit of time equal to one thousandth (1/1,000 or 0.001) of a second. Abbreviated as "ms."

Modem. Modulator/demodulator. A device that converts electrical signals from a computer into an audio form transmittable over telephone lines, or vice versa.

Modified frequency modulation encoding. A method of encoding **data** on the surface of a disk. The coding of a **bit** of data varies by the coding of the preceding bit to preserve clocking information.

Module. An assembly that contains a complete circuit or subcircuit.

Motherboard. The main **circuit board** in the computer. Also called Planar, System Board, or Backplane.

MTBF. Mean Time Between Failure. A statistical figure giving the average time before an electrical component or device should fail.

Multitasking. The act of running several programs simultaneously.

Multiuser system. A system in which several computer terminals share the same **CPU**.

Nano. A prefix indicating one billionth (1/1,000,000,000 or 0.000000001) of some unit. Abbreviated as "n."

Nanosecond. A unit of time equal to one billionth (1/1,000,000,000 or 0.000000001) of a second. Abbreviated as "ns."

Network. A system in which a number of independent computers are linked together to share **data** and **peripherals**, such as hard disks and printers.

Nonvolatile RAM disk. A **RAM** disk powered by a battery supply so that it continues to hold its **data** during a power outage.

Operating System. Collection of programs for operating the computer. Operating systems perform housekeeping tasks such as input/output between the computer and **peripherals** and accepting and interpreting information from the keyboard.

Optical disk. A disk that encodes **data** as a series of reflective pits that are read (and sometimes written) by a laser beam.

OS/2. IBM and Microsoft's new generation multitasking operating system for ATs and most PS/2 systems.

Output. Information or the act of sending the information processed by the computer to a mass storage device such as a video display, a printer, or a **modem**.

Overlay. Part of a program that is loaded into memory only at the times it is required.

Overrun. A situation in which **data** moves from one device faster than a second device can accept it.

Overwrite. To write data on top of existing data, erasing the original data.

Parallel. A method of transferring **data** in which the **bits** travel down a number of wires simultaneously.

Parity. Method of error checking in which an extra **bit** is sent to the receiving device to indicate whether an even or odd number of binary 1 bits were transmitted. The receiving unit compares the information received against this bit and can obtain a reasonable judgment about the validity of the character.

Park program. A program that executes a seek to the highest cylinder, or just past the highest cylinder of a drive. This is so that the potential of data loss is minimized if the drive is moved.

Partition. A section of a hard disk devoted to a particular operating system. Most hard disks have only one partition, devoted to **DOS**. A hard disk can have up to four partitions, each occupied by a different operating system. DOS 3.3 or higher can occupy two of these four partitions.

Peripheral. Any piece of equipment used in computer systems that is an attachment to the computer itself. Disk drives, terminals, and printers are all examples of peripherals.

Physical drive. A single disk drive. **DOS** defines logical drives, which are given a specifier, such as C: or D:. A single physical drive may be divided in multiple logical drives. Conversely, special software can span a single logical drive across two physical drives.

Plated media. Hard disk platters that have a form of thin film media in which the platters are plated with a metal film on which **data** is recorded.

Platter. A disk contained in a hard disk drive. Most drives have two or more platters, each with data recorded on both sides.

Port. Plug or socket that allows an external device such as a printer to be attached to the adapter card in the computer. Also a logical **address** used by a **microprocessor** for communications between itself and various devices.

Port address. On a system of addresses used by the computer to access devices such as disk **drives** or printer ports. You may need to specify an unused port address when installing any adapter boards in a system unit.

POST. Power-on self test. A series of tests run by the computer at power on.

Power-on self test. When power is initially applied, the computer will automatically scan and test many of its circuits and sound a beep from the internal speaker if this initial test indicates proper system performance.

Power supply. Electrical/electronic circuit that supplies all operating voltage and current to the computer system.

Presentation Manager. The graphical icon- and window-based software interface offered with OS/2.

Primary partition. Starting with DOS 3.3, a hard disk may have two partitions that serve DOS—a primary partition, which is an ordinary, single-volume bootable partition, and an extended partition, which may contain any number of volumes up 23 total. Using both partitions, a single disk can be divided into 24 volumes.

Processor speed. The clock rate at which a **microprocessor** processes **data**. A standard IBM PC, for example, operates at 4.77 **MHz** (4.77 million cycles per second).

Program. Set of instructions or steps telling the computer how to handle a problem or task.

PROM. Programmable Read-Only Memory. A type of memory chip that can be permanently programmed to store information. This information cannot be erased.

Proprietary. Anything that is invented by a company and not used by any other company. This especially applies to cases where the inventing company goes to lengths to hide the specifications of the new invention. Proprietary is the opposite of Standard.

QIC. Quarter Inch Committee. An industry association that sets hardware and software standards for tape backup units that use 1/4-inch wide tapes.

Rails. Plastic strips attached to the sides of disk drives mounted in IBM ATs and compatibles so that they may slide into place. These rails fit into channels in the side of each disk drive **bay** position.

RAM disk. A "phantom disk drive" by which a section of system memory (RAM) is set aside to hold data, just as if it were a number of disk sectors. To **DOS**, a RAM disk looks like and functions like any other drive. Synonymous with **virtual disk**.

Random-access file. A **file** in which all data elements (or records) are of equal length. They are written in the file end to end, without delimiting characters between. You can find any element (or record) in the file directly by calculating its offset in the file.

Random-access memory. All memory accessible at any instant (randomly) by the **microprocessor**.

Read-only file. A **file** in which a setting has been made in the attribute **byte** of its directory listing so that **DOS** will not allow software to write into or over the file.

Read-Only Memory (ROM). A type of memory that has values permanently burned in. These locations are used to hold important programs or **data** that must be available to the computer when the power is first turned on.

Read/write head. A tiny electromagnetic device that reads and writes **data** on a disk **track**.

Real time. When something is recorded or processed as it is happening in the outside world.

Refresh cycle. A cycle in which the computer accesses all memory locations stored by dynamic RAM chips so that the information will remain intact. Dynamic RAM chips need to be accessed several times a second, or the information will fade.

Register. Storage area in memory having a specified storage capacity, such as a **bit**, a **byte**, or a computer word, and intended for a special purpose.

Resolution. A reference to the size of the pixels used in graphics. In medium-resolution graphics, pixels are large. In high-resolution graphics, pixels are small.

RLL. Run Length Limited encoding. An encoding scheme used to encode binary data for storage on a disk **medium**. Variations of this encoding scheme are efficient and can store more information than the **MFM** scheme.

RMA number. Return Merchandise Authorization or Return Material Authorization number. A number given to you by a vendor when you arrange to return an item for repairs. This number is used to track the item and the repair.

ROM BIOS. Read-Only Memory Basic Input/Output System. A BIOS that is encoded in a form of read-only memory for protection. This is often applied to important start-up programs that must be present in a system for it to operate.

Root directory. The main directory of any hard disk or floppy disk created upon formatting the disk. It has a fixed size and location for a particular disk volume and cannot be dynamically resized like subdirectories.

Routine. Set of instructions that are used frequently. May be considered as a subdivision of a program with two or more instructions that are functionally related.

Run Length Limited encoding. A data encoding method in which patterns in the **data** are translated into codes. The techniques can increase data densities by 50 to 100 percent over conventional **MFM encoding** methods.

Scratch disk. A disk that contains no useful information and can be used as a test disk. IBM has a routine on the advanced diagnostics disks that creates a specially formatted scratch disk used for testing floppy drives.

Sector. A section of one **track**, defined with identification markings and an identification number. Most sectors hold 512 **bytes** of **data**.

Security software. Utility software that uses a system of passwords and other devices to restrict an individual's access to subdirectories and **files**.

Sequential file. A file in which varying-length data elements are recorded end to end, with delimiting characters placed between elements. To find a particular element, you must read the whole file up to that element.

Servo data. Magnetic markings written on disk platters, that guide the **read/write heads** in drives that use **voice coil actuators**.

Settling time. The time required for **read/write heads** to stop vibrating once they have been moved to a new **track**.

Shell. The generic name of any user interface software. **COMMAND.COM** is the standard shell for **DOS**. **OS/2** comes with three shells: a DOS command shell, an OS/2 command shell, and the OS/2 presentation manager. The presentation manager is a graphical shell.

Shock rating. A rating (usually expressed in G force units) of how much shock a disk drive can sustain without damage. You usually will find two different specifications for a drive: powered on or off.

Soft error. An error in reading or writing **data**, that occurs sporadically, usually because of a transient problem, such as a power fluctuation.

Software. A series of instructions loaded into the computer that tells the computer how to accomplish a problem or task.

Source Disk. A disk that contains information that is to be copied onto another disk.

Spindle. The post on which a disk drive's platters are mounted.

ST-506/412. The standard interface used by most hard disk drives in IBM microcomputers. This interface was invented by Seagate Technologies and introduced in 1980 with the ST-506 drive.

Standby power supply. A backup power supply that will quickly switch into operation during a power outage.

Starting cluster. The number of the first **cluster** occupied by a **file**. A starting cluster is listed in the directory entry of every file.

Stepper motor actuator. An assembly that moves disk drive **read/write heads** across platters by a sequence of small partial turns of a stepper motor.

Storage. Device or medium onto or into which **data** can be entered, held, and retrieved at a later time. Synonymous with **memory**.

Streaming. In tape backup, a condition in which **data** is transferred from the hard disk as quickly as the tape drive can record it so that the drive does not start and stop or waste tape.

String. A sequence of characters.

Subdirectory. A **directory** listed in another directory. Subdirectories themselves exist as **files**.

Subroutine. Segment of a program that can be executed by a single call. A program module.

Surge protector. A device that provides minimal protection against voltage spikes and other transients in the power line that feeds the computer.

System crash. A situation in which the computer seizes up and refuses to proceed without rebooting. System crashes are usually caused by faulty software. Unlike a hard disk crash, no permanent physical damage occurs.

System files. The two DOS files **IBMBIO.COM** and **IBMDOS.COM** are the system files. A third file, **COMMAND.COM**, is the shell. The system files are hidden on a disk.

System integrator. A computer consultant or vendor who tests available products and combines them into highly optimized systems.

Temporary backup. A second copy of a work file, usually named with extension BAK. Often, application software creates these files so that you easily can return to a previous version of your work.

Temporary file. A **file** temporarily (and usually invisibly) created by a program for its own use.

Tera. A multiplier indicating one trillion (1,000,000,000,000) of something. Abbreviated as "t" or "T." When used to indicate a number of **bytes** of memory storage, the multiplier definition changes to 1,099,511,627,776. One terabit, for example, equals 1,000,000,000,000 bits, and one **terabyte** equals 1,099,511,627,776 bytes.

Terabyte. A unit of information storage. One terabyte equals 1,099,511,627,776 **bytes**.

Thin film media. Hard disk platters that have a very thin film of **medium** deposited on the aluminum substrate through a sputtering or plating process. A type of disk media where the thickness of the **medium** is about 3 millionths of an inch thick.

TPI. Tracks Per Inch. Used as a measurement of magnetic track density. Standard 5 1/4-inch 360K floppy disks have a 48 TPI density, and the 1.2M disks have a 96 TPI density. All 3 1/2-inch disks have a 135 TPI density, and hard disks can have densities greater than 1,000 TPI.

Track. One of the many concentric circles that hold **data** on a disk surface. A track consists of a single line of magnetic flux changes. A number of tracks are on a disk, and information is written onto the tracks. Each track is divided into some number of **sectors**, each of which is 512 **bytes** long.

Track density. The number of **tracks** that can be fit on a platter side, as measured by the total number of tracks on a side, or in Tracks Per Inch (TPI).

Track-to-track seek time. The time required for **read/write heads** to move between adjacent tracks.

TSR. Terminate and Stay Resident. A program that remains in **memory** after it loads. Also called a memory-resident program.

Unformatted capacity. The total number of **bytes** of **data** that could be fit onto a disk. The **formatted capacity** is lower because space is lost defining the boundaries between **sectors**.

Uninterruptible power supply. Also known as a UPS. A device that supplies power to the computer from batteries so that power will not stop, even momentarily, during a power outage. The batteries are constantly recharged from a wall socket.

Update. To modify information already contained in a **file** or program with current information.

Utility. Programs that carry out routine procedures to make computer use easier.

Virtual disk. A "phantom disk drive" by which a section of system memory (usually RAM) is set aside to hold **data**, just as if it were a number of disk **sectors**. To **DOS**, a virtual disk looks like and functions like any other "real" drive. Synonymous with **RAM disk**.

Virtual memory. A technique by which operating systems (including OS/2) load more programs and **data** into memory than there actually is system memory to hold them. Parts of the programs and data are kept on disk and constantly swapped back and forth into system memory. The applications software is oblivious to this; all applications software programs think that a large amount of **memory** is available to them.

Voice coil actuator. A device that moves **read/write heads** across hard disk platters by magnetic interaction between coils of wire and a magnet. This action is similar to that of an audio speaker, from where the name originated.

Voltage regulator. A device that smoothes out voltage irregularities in the power fed to the computer.

Volume. A volume is a portion of a disk signified by a single drive specifier. Under DOS 3.3 and later, a single hard disk may be partitioned into several volumes, each with its own logical drive specifier (C:, D:, E:, and so on).

Volume label. An identifier or name of up to 11 characters that names a disk.

Winchester drive. Any ordinary, nonremovable (or fixed) hard disk drive. The name originates from a particular IBM drive in the 1960s that had 30 megabytes of fixed and 30 **megabytes** of removable storage. This 30-30 drive matched the caliber figure for a popular series of rifles made by Winchester, so the slang term Winchester was applied to any fixed platter hard disk.

WORM drive. A Write Once Read Mostly optical disk drive. It uses cartridge disks on which any sector may be written on only once but that can be read back any number of times after that.

Write precompensation. The varying of the timing of the head current from the outer tracks to the inner tracks of a disk to compensate for the **bit** shifting that occurs on the inner cylinders.

Y-adapter. A Y-shaped splitter cable that divides a source input into two output signals.

N-O

More Computer Knowledge from Que

Lotus Software Titles

1-2-3 Database Techniques	24.95
1-2-3 Release 2.2 Business Applications	39.95
1-2-3 Release 2.2 Quick Reference	7.95
1-2-3 Release 2.2 QuickStart	19.95
1-2-3 Release 2.2 Workbook and Disk	29.95
1-2-3 Release 3 Business Applications	39.95
1-2-3 Release 3 Quick Reference	7.95
1-2-3 Release 3 QuickStart	19.95
1-2-3 Release 3 Workbook and Disk	29.95
1-2-3 Tips, Tricks, and Traps, 3rd Edition	22.95
Upgrading to 1-2-3 Release 3	14.95
Using 1-2-3, Special Edition	24.95
Using 1-2-3 Release 2.2, Special Edition	24.95
Using 1-2-3 Release 3	24.95
Using Lotus Magellan	21.95
Using Symphony, 2nd Edition	26.95

Database Titles

dBASE III Plus Applications Library	24.95
dBASE III Plus Handbook, 2nd Edition	24.95
dBASE III Plus Tips, Tricks, and Traps	21.95
dBASE III Plus Workbook and Disk	29.95
dBASE IV Applications Library, 2nd Edition	39.95
dBASE IV Handbook, 3rd Edition	23.95
dBASE IV Programming Techniques	24.95
dBASE IV QueCards	21.95
dBASE IV Quick Reference	7.95
dBASE IV QuickStart	19.95
dBASE IV Tips, Tricks, and Traps, 2nd Edition	21.95
dBASE IV Workbook and Disk	29.95
dBXL and Quicksilver Programming: Beyond dBASE	24.95
R:BASE User's Guide, 3rd Edition	22.95
Using Clipper	24.95
Using DataEase	22.95
Using Reflex	19.95
Using Paradox 3	24.95

Applications Software Titles

AutoCAD Advanced Techniques	34.95
AutoCAD Quick Reference	7.95
AutoCAD Sourcebook	24.95
Excel Business Applications: IBM Version	39.95
Introduction to Business Software	14.95
PC Tools Quick Reference	7.95
Smart Tips, Tricks, and Traps	24.95
Using AutoCAD, 2nd Edition	29.95
Using Computers in Business	24.95
Using DacEasy	21.95

Using Dollars and Sense: IBM Version, 2nd Edition	19.95
Using Enable/OA	23.95
Using Excel: IBM Version	24.95
Using Generic CADD	24.95
Using Harvard Project Manager	24.95
Using Managing Your Money, 2nd Edition	19.95
Using Microsoft Works: IBM Version	21.95
Using PROCOMM PLUS	19.95
Using Q&A, 2nd Edition	21.95
Using Quattro	21.95
Using Quicken	19.95
Using Smart	22.95
Using SmartWare II	24.95
Using SuperCalc5, 2nd Edition	22.95

Word Processing and Desktop Publishing Titles

DisplayWrite QuickStart	19.95
Harvard Graphics Quick Reference	7.95
Microsoft Word 5 Quick Reference	7.95
Microsoft Word 5 Tips, Tricks, and Traps: IBM Version	19.95
Using DisplayWrite 4, 2nd Edition	19.95
Using Freelance Plus	24.95
Using Harvard Graphics	24.95
Using Microsoft Word 5: IBM Version	21.95
Using MultiMate Advantage, 2nd Edition	19.95
Using PageMaker: IBM Version, 2nd Edition	24.95
Using PFS: First Choice	22.95
Using PFS: First Publisher	22.95
Using Professional Write	19.95
Using Sprint	21.95
Using Ventura Publisher, 2nd Edition	24.95
Using WordPerfect, 3rd Edition	21.95
Using WordPerfect 5	24.95
Using WordStar, 2nd Edition	21.95
Ventura Publisher Techniques and Applications	22.95
Ventura Publisher Tips, Tricks, and Traps	24.95
WordPerfect Macro Library	21.95
WordPerfect Power Techniques	21.95
WordPerfect QueCards	21.95
WordPerfect Quick Reference	7.95
WordPerfect QuickStart	21.95
WordPerfect Tips, Tricks, and Traps, 2nd Edition	21.95
WordPerfect 5 Workbook and Disk	29.95

Macintosh/Apple II Titles

The Big Mac Book	27.95
Excel QuickStart	19.95
Excel Tips, Tricks, and Traps	22.95
Using AppleWorks, 3rd Edition	21.95
Using AppleWorks GS	21.95
Using dBASE Mac	19.95
Using Dollars and Sense: Macintosh Version	19.95
Using Excel: Macintosh Verson	22.95
Using FullWrite Professional	21.95

Using HyperCard:	24.95
Using Microsoft Word 4: Macintosh Version	21.95
Using Microsoft Works: Macintosh Version, 2nd Edition	21.95
Using PageMaker: Macintosh Version	24.95
Using WordPerfect: Macintosh Version	19.95

Hardware and Systems Titles

DOS Tips, Tricks, and Traps	22.95
DOS Workbook and Disk	29.95
Hard Disk Quick Reference	7.95
IBM PS/2 Handbook	21.95
Managing Your Hard Disk, 2nd Edition	22.95
MS-DOS Quick Reference	7.95
MS-DOS QuickStart	21.95
MS-DOS User's Guide, Special Edition	29.95
Networking Personal Computers, 3rd Edition	22.95
Norton Utilities Quick Reference	7.95
The Printer Bible	24.95
Understanding UNIX: A Conceptual Guide, 2nd Edition	21.95
Upgrading and Repairing PCs	27.95
Using DOS	22.95
Using Microsoft Windows	19.95
Using Novell NetWare	24.95
Using OS/2	23.95
Using PC DOS, 3rd Edition	22.95

Programming and Technical Titles

Assembly Language Quick Reference	7.95
C Programmer's Toolkit	39.95
C Programming Guide, 3rd Edition	24.95
C Quick Reference	7.95
DOS and BIOS Functions Quick Reference	7.95
DOS Programmer's Reference, 2nd Edition	27.95
Power Graphics Programming	24.95
QuickBASIC Advanced Techniques	21.95
QuickBASIC Programmer's Toolkit	39.95
QuickBASIC Quick Reference	7.95
SQL Programmer's Guide	29.95
Turbo C Programming	22.95
Turbo Pascal Advanced Techniques	22.95
Turbo Pascal Programmer's Toolkit	39.95
Turbo Pascal Quick Reference	7.95
Using Assembly Language	24.95
Using QuickBASIC 4	19.95
Using Turbo Pascal	21.95

For more information, call

1-800-428-5331

All prices subject to change without notice. Prices and charges are for domestic orders only. Non-U.S. prices might be higher.

MS-DOS User's Guide, Special Edition
Developed by Que Corporation

A special edition of Que's best-selling book on MS-DOS, updated to provide the most comprehensive DOS coverage available. Includes expanded EDLIN coverage, plus **Quick Start** tutorials and a complete **Command Reference** for DOS Versions 3 and 4. A **must** for MS-DOS users at all levels!

Order #1048
$29.95 USA
0-88022-505-X, 900 pp.

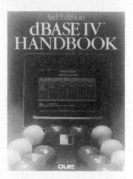

dBASE IV Handbook, 3rd Edition
by George T. Chou, Ph.D.

A complete introduction to dBASE IV functions! Beginning users will progress systematically from basic database concepts to advanced dBASE features, and experienced dBASE users will appreciate the information on the new features of dBASE IV. Includes Quick Start tutorials.

$23.95 USA
Order #852
0-88022-380-4, 785 pp.

Using 1-2-3 Release 2.2, Special Edition
Developed by Que Corporation

Learn professional spreadsheet techniques from the world's leading 1-2-3 books! This comprehensive text leads you from worksheet basics to advanced 1-2-3 operations. Includes Allways coverage, a Troubleshooting section, a Command Reference, and a tear-out 1-2-3 Menu Map. The most complete resource available for Release 2.01 and Release 2.2!

$26.95 USA
Order #1040
0-88022-501-7, 850 pp.

Using WordPerfect 5.1, Special Edition
Developed by Que Corporation

The #1 best-selling word processing book, updated for new WordPerfect 5.1! This Special Edition leads readers from WordPerfect basics to sophisticated techniques. The text covers the latest software enhancements—including tables, pull-down menus, mouse support, "hot linking" to spreadsheets, and the new Equations Editor.

Order #1100
$24.95 USA
0-88022-554-8, 900 pp.

Free Catalog!

Mail us this registration form today, and we'll send you a free catalog featuring Que's complete line of best-selling books.

Name of Book _____

Name _____

Title _____

Phone (_____) _____

Company _____

Address _____

City _____

State _____ ZIP _____

Please check the appropriate answers:

1. Where did you buy your Que book?
   - ☐ Bookstore (name: _____)
   - ☐ Computer store (name: _____)
   - ☐ Catalog (name: _____)
   - ☐ Direct from Que
   - ☐ Other: _____

2. How many computer books do you buy a year?
   - ☐ 1 or less
   - ☐ 2-5
   - ☐ 6-10
   - ☐ More than 10

3. How many Que books do you own?
   - ☐ 1
   - ☐ 2-5
   - ☐ 6-10
   - ☐ More than 10

4. How long have you been using this software?
   - ☐ Less than 6 months
   - ☐ 6 months to 1 year
   - ☐ 1-3 years
   - ☐ More than 3 years

5. What influenced your purchase of this Que book?
   - ☐ Personal recommendation
   - ☐ Advertisement
   - ☐ In-store display
   - ☐ Price
   - ☐ Que catalog
   - ☐ Que mailing
   - ☐ Que's reputation
   - ☐ Other: _____

6. How would you rate the overall content of the book?
   - ☐ Very good
   - ☐ Good
   - ☐ Satisfactory
   - ☐ Poor

7. What do you like *best* about this Que book?
   _____
   _____

8. What do you like *least* about this Que book?
   _____
   _____

9. Did you buy this book with your personal funds?
   - ☐ Yes   ☐ No

10. Please feel free to list any other comments you may have about this Que book.
    _____
    _____
    _____

que

Order Your Que Books Today!

Name _____

Title _____

Company _____

City _____

State _____ ZIP _____

Phone No. (_____) _____

Method of Payment:

Check ☐   (Please enclose in envelope.)

Charge My: VISA ☐   MasterCard ☐

American Express ☐

Charge # _____

Expiration Date _____

Order No.	Title	Qty.	Price	Total

You can **FAX** your order to **1-317-573-2583**. Or call **1-800-428-5331, ext. ORDR** to order direct. Please add $2.50 per title for shipping and handling.

Subtotal _____

Shipping & Handling _____

Total _____

que

BUSINESS REPLY MAIL
First Class Permit No. 9918   Indianapolis, IN

Postage will be paid by addressee

11711 N. College
Carmel, IN 46032

NO POSTAGE
NECESSARY
IF MAILED
IN THE
UNITED STATES

BUSINESS REPLY MAIL
First Class Permit No. 9918   Indianapolis, IN

Postage will be paid by addressee

11711 N. College
Carmel, IN 46032